Glossographia Anglicana Nova

Blunt, Thomas

Gloſſographia Anglicana Nova:

OR, A

DICTIONARY,

INTERPRETING

Such HARD WORDS of whatever Language, as are at preſent uſed in the Engliſh Tongue, with their *Etymologies, Definitions, &c.*

ALSO,

The Terms of Divinity, Law, Phyſick, Mathematicks, Hiſtory, Agriculture, Logick, Metaphyſicks, Grammar, Poetry, Muſick, Heraldry, Architecture, Painting, War, and all other Arts and Sciences are herein explain'd, from the beſt Modern Authors, as, Sir *Iſaac Newton*, Dr. *Harris*, Dr. *Gregory*, Mr. *Lock*, Mr. *Evelyn*, Mr. *Dryden*, Mr. *Blunt*, &c.

Very uſeful to all thoſe that deſire to underſtand what they read.

LONDON,

Printed for *Dan. Brown, Tim. Goodwin,* *John Walthoe*, *M. Newborough, John Nicholſon, Benj. Took, D. Midwinter,* and *Fran. Coggan.* 1707.

THE
PREFACE.

IT may not be amiss to let the Reader
know the Author's aim in this small
Work; purposely small, that if it shou'd
not wholly answer the Design with which it
was wrote, the mischief and inconvenience
of it might not be great. I have observ'd,
that Blunt, Philips, Cole, and others, have
been favourably receiv'd, I may add, have
been, in some measure, useful to that rank
of Readers to which they address'd themselves. It is true, Blunt offer'd his Service to the Learned World, and generously
submitted to the Labour and Drudgery of
gleaning the scatter'd Sciences, and rang-
ing the Definitions and Terms of Art each
Alphabetically; the misfortune was, he went

A 2   a simpa simpling in a Field Twenty Years, as himself confesses, without discovering many new Plants; which had been pardonable in him, had he given us the true Names, and not been mistaken in the Description, Vertues and Qualities of several of the old. Philips, to whose laudable Industry we owe a much more bulky Performance, was no better qualified for paving the Way to any one of the Sciences, having neither Skill, Tools nor Materials : So that Cole, after all, with his few Pretences, has as much real Worth as either of the former, and may make good the part of a Guide to Tradesmen and illiterate Readers, who are suppos'd to seek for the Etymology of every word that Custom has not familiarly acquainted 'em with.

I confess this Performance to be begun and carry'd on with the same view of instructing the Ignorant, and calculated (some part of it) for the use of such as are not able to read a good Historian, or any Polite English Writer without an Interpreter. If this be all, it may be ask'd, what need is there of the Publication of such a Dictionary as this is; since I propose no other End, and answer it no better than Philips, Cole, and the rest, who are known to deal chiefly

in

in words not of English Growth, in delivering their significations, and by some Characteristick directing to the Languages whence they were deriv'd? In reply to such Objections as this, I think fit to say, that tho' I have taken care that it shou'd be useful even to the lowest sort of illiterate, yet I have chiefly consulted the advantage of such as are gently advancing to Science; and for want of opportunities of Learned Helps have the misfortune to be their own Conductors, or have not Money sufficient to lay in the necessary Furniture of Learning. These I have chiefly respected, and for the sake of these it is to be wish'd, that they whose Abilities are greatest, wou'd employ 'em in making Knowledge as easie as may be. Whilst I was compiling this, the ingenious Dr. Harris's Lexicon Technicum laid before me, to which I am indebted for a considerable part of this Book. I had likewise recourse to the Lexicographers of less note, from whom I borrow'd what I thought for my purpose, and follow'd 'em where I safely might; for I did not think my self oblig'd to stumble after them because I follow'd them: Tho' I frankly own, that abating for that part of the Book which defines

The PREFACE.

fines Terms of Art in Natural Philosophy, Astronomy, and other Mathematical Sciences, the rest of it may come in for a share of that inacuracy they have been censur'd for. I did not make it my business so much to mark their Errors in other things as to avoid 'em in these. 'Tis to be hop'd that the Reader will candidly accept of this little Book; and since neither the Nature of an Abridgment allows it to be compleat, nor can the most successful Attempts of this kind be altogether free from Imperfections, the Author flatters himself that he shall easily be pardon'd for the deficiencies to which the Fate of small things subjects them; and the more because by this very fault he has avoided that other of tediousness, which sometimes against a great Volume, whether good or bad in other respects, is a most important Article of Complaint.

AD-

Advertisement.

PROPOSALS

For Re-printing the First, and for Printing a Second Volume *of* Dr. Harris's *Universal English Dictionary of Arts and Sciences, Explaining not only all the Terms of Arts, but the Arts-themselves, and Entituled,* Lexicon Technicum.

The PROPOSALS *are,*

I. EACH Volume will contain about Two Hundred Sheets of Paper; which, with many Hundreds of Cutts, will make the Charge equal to Three Hundred Sheets.

II. Both Volumes shall be Printed on the same Paper with these Proposals, and the same Character that the Account of the Work is on the following Page.

III. The Price to Subscribers is Twenty five Shillings each Volume *per* Book in Quires; Ten Shillings for each Volume to be paid down, and the rest on the Delivery: Those that procure Subscriptions for Six Books shall have a Seventh *Gratis.* Not to be Sold under Thirty Shillings each Volume to any but Subscribers. Any Subscriber to the former Edition of the First Volume may have the Second Volume alone to compleat his Book, at the Price aforesaid.

IV. There

IV. There will be a small Number Printed on a Larger Paper for those that desire it; of which there will be no more Printed than are Subscrib'd for: The Price of the Large Paper will be two Guineas each Volume, one of which to be paid down, and the other at the Delivery, with no Allowance.

V. The Expence in this Work being very great, and the Design universally Useful, we hope it will meet with proportionable Encouragement; and those Persons that Subscribe shall have their Name, Title, Seat, &c. Printed before the Work as Encouragers thereof.

VI. Subscriptions will be taken in by the Author at his House in *Ormond-street*, by *Red-Lyon-Square*, by the Undertakers, and most other Booksellers till the First of *July* next; the Book being design'd to be finish'd by *Easter Term* then next following.

The Undertakers are,

Daniel Brown at the *Black-Swan* without *Temple-Bar.*

Tim. Goodwin at the *Queen's-Head* against *St. Dunstan's Church, Fleet-street.*

John Walthoe in the *Middle-Temple Cloysters.*

M. Newborough at the *Golden-Ball* in St. *Paul's-Church Yard.*

John Nicholson at the *King's-Arms* in *Little-Britain.*

Benj. Took at the *Middle-Temple-Gate.*

D. Midwinter at the *Rose* and *Crown* in St. *Paul's-Church-Yard.*

Fran. Coggan in the *Inner-Temple-Lane*, Booksellers.

ABACOT, a Royal Cap of State, wrought up in the shape of two Crowns, and anciently used by the Kings of *England*.

Abaction, (Lat.) is Stealing of Cattle by Herds or Flocks.

Abactors, (Lat.) the same with *Abigei,* are such as Steal or drive away Cattle by Herds or Flocks.

Abacus, sometimes signifies the A, B, C; sometimes the Multiplication Table, commonly call'd *Pythagoras*'s Table; sometimes the Numeral Figures.

Abacus, in *Architecture,* is the four Square Table, that makes the Capital on the top of a Column, especially those of the *Corinthian* Order, and is a Drip or *Corona* to the Capital.

Abaft or *Aft,* a Sea Term, signifying always those parts which are towards the Stern, or hinder part of the Ship.

Abaisance, (Fr.) is a low bending of the Body, in token of Submission and Respect.

Abalienation, a Term in the old *Roman* Law, signifying a simple Sale of the Goods of one Citizen to another.

Abandon, (Spa.) to Banish; to cast off or forsake.

Abannition, (Lat.) a Banishing for a Year, properly a-

mong the *Greeks,* for Manslaughter.

Abaptiston or *Anabaptiston,* a Surgeon's Instrument; see *Modiolus.*

Abese, (Fr.) to *Abase,* to bring down the Pride, or humble any one; at Sea it signifies to lower or take in.

Abashed, made Ashamed.

Abassi, a Coyn, current in the *Eastern* Countries, worth about one Shilling and two Pence Sterling.

Abate, (Fr.) signifies to break down or destroy, and in the vulgar Sence, to diminish or take away: to *Abate* a Writ, signifies to destroy it for a time thro' want of good ground or other Defect.

Abatement in Law, is the taking possession of Land by a Person that hath no Right to it, after the Death of the Ancestor, and before the Entry of the right Heir.

Abatement, in Heraldry is an accidental Mark annexed to a Coat of Arms, whereby its Dignity is abased, by Reason of some dishonourable Quality or Stain in the Bearer; and 'tis either by adding a Mark of *Diminution,* or by *Reversion* of the whole *Escutcheon.*

The Marks of Diminution are First a *Delf,* which is a

B   Square.

Square born in the Middle of the Field, thus; and belongs to one that revokes his Challenge.

II. *A Point Dexter parted Tenn*, due to one that boasts of more than he can do.

III. *A Point in Point Sanguine*, thus; due to one that is Lazy in the Wars.

IV. *A Point Champain Ten*, due to one that kills his Prisoner after Quarter demanded, and Leave given from his Commander to give it.

V. *A plain Point Sanguine*, due to one that is a Lyer; and is born thus.

VI. *A Goar Sinister Tenn*, due to one that is a Coward; and is born thus.

VII. *A Gusset Sanguine*, is an Abatement proper for an Effeminate, Lascivious Man; and is then born on the Right Side; but if a Drunkard, it is born on the Left; if both, he bears two, as in this Figure.

Abawed, Abashed, Daunted. *Chaucer.*

Abbord, (Ital.) to go near the Shore.

Abbrevoir, (Fr) in Masonry, signifies the Spaces between the Stones, where the Mortar is put.

Abbrochment, in Law, is the Engrossing or Buying up of Wares before they are brought to a Market or Fair, and selling them again by Retail. The forestalling of a Market.

Abbuttals, are the Buttings or Boundings of Lands any way, showing how they ly in respect to other places.

Abdication, (Lat.) is the voluntary renouncing an Office, Employment, or a disobedient Child.

Abdicere, (Lat.) signifies to debar a Man from his Demands, or not to allow them.

Abdomen, (Lat.) the lowermost of the three Venters in an human Body, properly the *lower Belly*, that contains the Guts.

To

To Abduce, (Lat.) to lead away by Force or Flattery, to Entice.

Abducent Muscles, are universally those Muscles which serve to open or pull back divers Parts of the Body, as the Arms, Legs, Eyes, Nostrils, Lips, &c.

Abduction, (Lat.) a leading or taking away.

Abductores, (Lat.) in the General signifies the same with *Abducent Muscles*.

Abductor Indicis, a Muscle of the Fore Finger, which draws it to the Thumb, or from the rest of the Fingers.

Abductor Oculi, a Muscle of the Eye, so called from its drawing off the Eye from the Nose.

Abductor Pollicis, a Muscle of the Thumb, which draws it from the rest of the Fingers.

Abelins, a sort of Christian Hereticks in *Africa*, who adopted Sons and Daughters to inherit their Estates, believing their Children by their Wives to be Illegitimate.

Aberration, (Lat.) is a going or wandring out of the way.

Abessed, (Fr.) debased, dejected, or brought down.

To Abet, in our common Law signifies to encourage or set on to some Evil; also to maintain or Patronize.

Abettors, in common Law, are such as procure others to sue out false Appeals of Murder or Felony against Men, for no other Reason than to make them Infamous.

Abettors, in Murder, are those which advise or procure a Murder to be committed.

Abeyance, in Law, signifies a Thing's being in *posse* only, and not in *Actu*.

Abgregate, (Lat.) to lead out from the Flock, to separate.

Abhorrency, (Lat.) an Aversion; a Hating, or Detesting.

Abie, Suffer, Abide. *Spencer*.

Abject, (Lat.) cast away, vile, base.

Ability, Power, and very often it signifies Skill, and Learning; for Instance, when we say such a Man is a Man of great Abilities in the Art of Physick, or any other Art or Science; we mean, such a Man is a very able, learned and skilful Physician, or the like.

Abisherising, in the common Law, is being acquitted of *Amerceaments* before whomsoever of Transgression prov'd.

Abjudicate, (Lat.) to give away by Judgment.

Abjuration, (Lat.) a Forswearing or Denying upon Oath. In our common Law it is an Oath taken to forsake the Kingdom for ever.

Ablactation, (Lat.) a Weaning; also a kind of Grafting, so called.

Ablation, (Lat.) a taking away from, a bearing away by Stealth.

Ablegation, (Lat.) a sending forth or out of the way.

Ablepsy, (Lat.) Blindness of Mind, Unadvisedness.

Ablo-

Ablocate, (Lat.) to let, to hire; to take from one, and let to another.

Abluent Medicines, the same with Abstergent, which see.

Ablution (Lat.) the Preparation of a Medicine in any Liquor, to cleanse it from its Impurities; also, a washing used by Popish Priests.

Abnegation, (Lat.) an earnest denying or refusing.

Abnodation, (Lat.) in Agriculture, signifies the Pruning of Trees.

Aboard, a Sea Word; to go *aboard* is to enter a Ship.

Abolition, (Lat.) is a perfect Disannulling, or Destroying utterly.

Abomasus, is one of the Stomachs of ruminant Animals, or such as chew the Cud.

Abominate, (Lat.) to detest or abhor.

Aborigines, are such Nations as pretend to have been without Original.

Abortion, (Lat.) is the bringing forth a Child (or *Fœtus*) before its due time.

Abortive, (Lat.) is any thing brought forth before its due time.

Abreding, a Word used by *Chaucer*, signifying Upbraiding.

Abrenunciation, (Lat.) is a forsaking or renouncing any thing utterly.

Abreviate, (Lat.) to abridge or make short.

Abreviation, (Lat.) an Abridgment or Contraction of a Writing into a narrower Compass, or expressing it in fewer Terms.

Abreviator, is one that Abridges or Contracts any Writing.

Abrevoirs, see *Abbrevoirs*.

Abric, with some Chymists the same with *Sulphur*.

Abridgment, commonly signifies the same thing with *Abreviation*, which see.

Abridgment of a Plaint in Law, is when one Part of the Plaintiff's Demand is left out, and it is pray'd that the Defendant may answer to the other.

Abrogate, (Lat.) signifies to disannul or repeal.

Abrogation of a Law, is the repealing it, or taking it quite away.

Abrupt, (Lat.) broken off, rash, out of order.

Abscesse, An Exulceration arising in any Part of the Body after a *Crisis*.

Abscissa, (Lat.) a Term in Mathematicks, signifying that Part of the Axis or Diameter of a Curve, that lies between any Ordinate and the Vertex of the Axis, or of the respective Diameter.

Abscission, (Lat.) is a cutting off, or away.

Abscond, (Lat.) signifies to hide or conceal.

Absis, see *Apsis*.

Absolute: This Word is variously used; sometimes the Terms of a Proposition are said to be taken absolutely, that is, without Relation to any thing else. A Prince is said to be absolute when he
makes

makes his Will his Law. Abfolute is fometimes taken in
Oppofition to Terms or Conditions; thus, God doth not
forgive Men their Sins abfo-
lutely, but on Condition of
their Repentance.

Abfolute Number, in Algebra, is that Side of the Æquation which is entirely known.

Abfolute Equation, in Aftronomy, is the Sum of the Eccentrick and OptickEquations.

Abfolute Space, fee *Space*.

Abfolution, (Lat.) is a forgiving or difcharging.

Abfonant (Lat.) is untunable, jarring.

Abforb, (Lat.) fignifies to
fup up, or devour.

Abforbents, are Medicines
that temper and qualify the
acid Juices in the Body, by
imbibing and drinking them up.

Abftemious, (Lat.) Temperate, Sober.

Abftenfion, in Law, is with-
holding an Heir from taking
Poffeffion of his Land.

Abftergent, or *Abfterfive Medicines*, are fuch as clear the
Skin from any Filth.

Abfterfion, (Lat.) a cleanfing
or wiping away.

Abftinence, is a Moderation
in the Ufe of Diet, according
to the Dictates of Reafon.

Abftraction, (Lat.) a drawing
away or from; alfo a Power of
the Mind of Man, whereby he
can make his Idea's, arifing
from particular Objects, become general Reprefentatives
of all of the fame kind.

Abftract, (Lat) is frequent-

ly ufed for an Epitome or fmall
Draught of a large Work.

Abftrufe, fecret, dark, difficult to be underftood.

Abfurd, (Lat.) Foolifh, without Senfe or Wit.

Abyfs, any vaft deep Gulph
or Pit which cannot be founded, and fo is fuppofed to have
no Bottom.

Academicks, the followers
of *Plato*; but now applyed to
Gentlemen belonging to an U-
niverfity.

Academy, properly the Place
where *Plato* taught his Schollars; now generally ufed for
a kind of higher School or U-
niverfity, where young Men
are inftructed in the liberal
Arts and Sciences.

Acaid, a Book that contains
the Principles and chief Articles of the Mahometan Religion.

Acantabolus, an Inftrument
like a Pair of Pincers, which
Surgeons ufe to take any prickly Subftance out of the Gufler.

Acantha, the moft back-
ward Protuberance of the
Vertebres of the Back; alfo
the Thorn of Trees or Plants.

Acarnar, the fame with *A-
cherner*, which fee.

Acatalectick Verfe, is one exactly perfect, where not fo
much as one Syllable is either
redundant or deficient.

Acatalepfy, (Gr.) Incompre-
henfiblenefs.

Accedas ad Curiam, a Writ
commanding the Sheriff to
make Record of fuch or fuch
a Suit.

     Acce-

Accedas ad Vicecomitem, in Law, is a Writ, commanding the *Coroner* to deliver a Writ to the Sheriff.

Accelerated Motion, is the Motion of Bodies whofe Velocity continually encreafes the farther they move.

Acceleration, (Lat) is a haftening the doing any thing.

Acceleratrix vis, is a Force, which by its inceffant Action, produces an accelerated Motion.

Acceleratores Urinæ, are a pair of Mufcles belonging to the *Penis,* whofe Ufe is to expedite the Urine and the *Genitura.*

Acconfion (Lat.) is the Enkindling or fetting any Body on Fire.

Accent in Grammar, is a Mark placed over a Syllable in Grammar, to fhow that it is to be pronounced either with a ftronger or a weaker Voice.

Accent in *Mufick,* is a Modulation of the Voice, to exprefs the Paffions either Naturally or Artificially.

Acceptance, a Receiving; alfo an Agreement to fome Act done by another, which, without fuch an Agreement, might have been left undone.

Acceptation, (Lat.) the received Meaning of a Word, or the Senfe in which it is ufually taken.

Acceptilation,(Lat.) in the *Civil Law,* is the fame with *Acquittance* in the Common Law; *viz.* a verbal Difcharge from the Creditor to the Debtor.

Accefs,(Lat.) an approaching or coming to; a Paffage or Way to a Place; alfo the Fit or *Paroxyfm* of a Difeafe.

Acceffible, (Lat.) that may be come to; *Acceffible Height,* a Height whofe Bafe or Foot may be come to, neither Rivers nor Rocks hindring the Approach.

Acceffory or *Acceffary,* (Lat.) a Common Law Term, fignifying a Perfon advifing or procuring before the Fact, or aiding and affifting, receiving or protecting after the Fact, one that hath committed Felony. In general, 'tis ufed for Aiding and Affifting.

Accident, (Lat.) that which happeneth by Chance, a Cafualty.

Accident, the Logicians ufe this Word to denote what does not effentially belong to any Subftance; and thefe Accidents are fometimes Subftances, as the Cloaths a Man has on; fometimes Qualities, as Red, Blew, &c. And in Oppofition to Subftance, it is ufed for a Thing whofe Effence and Nature it is to fubfift in fome Subftance, and cannot be alone; in this Senfe the nine laft Predicaments in Logick are Accidents.

Accidental Point in Perfpective, is a Point in the *Horizontal Line,* where the reprefentation of Lines Parallel amongft themfelves, tho' not Perpendicular to the Picture, do meet.

Acclamation, (Lat.) a loud Expreffion of Joy; the Applaufe

plaufe given to Perfons and Things.

Acclivity, (Lat.) is a Steepnefs reckoned upwards on a floping Line.

Accloyeth, Overchargeth. *Spencer*.

Accomodate, (Lat.) to fit or furnifh; alfo to compofe a Difference.

Accomplice, a Partaker in the Guilt of a Crime,

Accomplifh, to fulfil, to bring to Perfection.

Accompt, a Writ fo called, lying againft a Bayliff or Receiver, who will not bring in his Accounts of what he has received.

Accord, to agree, confent to.

Accoft, (Fr.) to joyn Side to Side, to approach or draw near to, to fet upon in Difcourfe, to affront.

Account of Sca'es, in Traffick fignifies an Account wherein the Sale of Goods is exprefled.

Accountable, liable to give Account, anfwerable.

Accountant, a Perfon well skill'd in cafting up of Accounts, an able Arithmetician.

Accoutred, (Fr.) Arrayed, Dreffed.

Aceoyed, pluck'd down. *Spencer*.

Accretion, (Lat.) is properly an addition of Matter to any Body *Externally*; an Increafing or Growing.

Accrew, to encreafe, to be added unto.

Accumulate, (Lat.) to heap up, or together.

Accurate, Exact, Curious.

Accufation, (Lat.) a charging a Man with a Crime; alfo the Articles containing the Crime.

Acephali, (Gr.) a Sect of Chriftian Hereticks that acknowledged no Head or Supream; they appeared firft about the Year 500; they afferted but one Subftance in *Chrift*, and therefore but one Nature.

Acerbity, is a Taft between four and bitter, fuch as moft Fruits have before they're ripe.

Acervate, (Lat) to heap together.

Acetabulum, is that Cavity in the Huckle Bone, which receives the Thigh Bone within it.

Acetabulum, a Roman Meafure of Capacity for things Liquid, containing ¼ Pint, and 704½ decimal Parts of a Solid Inch Wine Meafure; alfo a Meafure of Capacity for things dry, containing ¼ Pint, and 06 decimal Parts of a folid Inch, Corn Meafure.

Acetars, Sallets of fmall Herbs and Roots, with Vinegar put amongft them.

Achamech, with fome Chymifts fignifies the Drofs of Silver.

Acherner, a bright Star of the firft Magnitude in *Eridanus*.

Achievements, warlike deeds, noble Exploits.

Achlis, Darknefs in the Eyes, or Dimnefs of Sight.

Acholite, an inferior Church Ser-

Servant, which formerly waited on the Priests and Deacons, performing the Offices of lighting the Candles, carrying the Bread and Wine, and paying other servile Attendance. b

Achor, is a sort of hard Sca which causes an Itching and Stink on the Surface of the Head.

Achronical rising or setting of a Star : In Astronomy a Star is said to rise *Achronically* ; when it rises at the same time that the Sun sets ; and a Star is said to set *Achronically*, when it sets at the same time that the Sun does. But to rise or set *Achronically*, according to *Kepler*, is to rise or set in that Point which is opposite to the Sun, so that with him to rise *Achronically*, is to rise when the Sun sets, but to set *Achronically*, is to set when the Sun rises, which is the same as to set *Cosmically* in the common Acceptation.

Acidity, Sharpness, Sourness.

Acids, are those Bodies which produce the Taft of Sharpness or Sourness, caus'd from the Particles of those Bodies being sharp pointed and piercing.

Acidulæ, any Medicinal Waters that are not hot.

Aciniformis Tunica, the same with the *Tunica Uvea* of the Eye.

Acinus, a sort of Fruit resembling a Grape.

Acloy'd, a Word used in *Chaucer* for overcharged.

Acme, (Gr.) a Term used by Physicians signifying the Height of a Disease ; some Diseases have four Periods. 1. the *Arche* or Beginning, 2. the *Anabasis, i. e.* the Growth or Encrease, 3. the *Acme* when the Matter of the Distemper is fully ripe, 4. the *Paracme* or the declining of it.

Acontias, is a kind of Comet like a Javelin.

Acosmy, an ill State of Health, accompanied with the Loss of the naturally florid Colour in the Face.

Acousticks, (Gr.) are Medicines or Instruments which help the Hearing.

Acquests, (Lat.) Purchases made, or things bought.

Acquiesce, (Lat.) to rest satisfied, or to be at quiet.

Acquietandis Plegijs, a Writ for the getting an Acquittance after the Debt is paid.

Acquire, (Lat.) to Purchase, or attain to.

Acquisition, a getting or Purchasing.

Acquittal, in Law, signifies the Discharge of a Tenant from any Entries or Molestations, for any Manner of Service issuing out of the Land to any Lord ; also a Deliverance or setting free from the Suspicion or Guilt of an Offence.

Acquittance, signifies a Discharge in Writing of a Sum of Money, or other Duty which ought to be paid or done.

Acrasy, a Predominancy of one Quality above another in an humane Body.

Acre,

Acre, a Piece of Land 40 Poles or Perches in Length, and 4 in Breadth.

Acrimonious Bodies are such, whose Particles do eat, fret or dissolve what comes in their way.

Acrimony, sharpness of Humours.

Acrisy, is such a State of Disease, that no right Judgment can be made whether the Patient will recover or not.

Acromion, is the upper Process of the Shoulder Blade, or the top of the Shoulder.

Acromphalum, the Middle of the Navel.

Acros, (Gr.) the Height or Top of any thing.

Acrosticks, are a determinate Number of Verses, whose initial Letters make up some Name, Word, Title, &c.

Acrospire, the same with *Plume*, which see.

Acroteria, signify those sharp and spiry Battlements or Pinacles, that stand in Ranges about flat Buildings with Rails and Balasters.

Actinobolism, a Diffusion or Diradiation of Light every way from its Center.

Action, when any thing is done, or any Change or Alteration produced by any Person or Body, that thing which is done, or that Change or Alteration produc'd with regard to the Cause is called an Action.

Action, in Law, is the Process or Form of a Suit given by the Law, to recover a Right, and of this there are several sorts, *viz.*

Action mixed, is when it is part *Real* and part *Personal*; also a Suit given by the Law to recover the thing detained, and Damages for the Wrong done, as an Action for Tythes, &c.

Action Penal, is an Action which aims at some Penalty or Punishment on the Party sued, either on his Body, or by way of Fine on his Estate.

Action Personal, is an Action which one may have against another, upon account of any Bargain for Money or Goods, or for any Wrong done to his Person by him or any other for whose Fact he is answerable.

Action Popular, an Action given upon the Breach of some Penal Statute, which any Man that will may sue for himself and the King, by Information or otherwise.

Action Real, an Action whereby one claims Title to Lands, Tenements, Rents or Commons, in Fee-simple, Fee-tail or for Term of Life.

Action of a Writ, a Phrase used when one pleads some Matter whereby he shews, that the Plaintiff had no Cause to have the Writ which he brought, and yet it may be he may have another Writ or Action for the same thing.

Action upon the Case, is a Writ brought for an Offence done to any Man without Force, as for Non-performance of Promise, for Defamation, &c.

Acti

Action upon the Statute, is a Writ founded upon any Statute, whereby an Action is given to one where no Action was before.

Actionable, that will bear an Action at Law.

Active Principles, in Chymiftry, are Spirit, Oil and Salt, becaufe their Parts being in a brisk Motion, do caufe Action in other Bodies.

Active, Nimble, Brisk or Stirring.

Actor, one who acts a Part, and reprefents fome Perfon in a Tragedy or Comedy; alfo one who has an *Action* againft another; he who profecutes another in the Court of Judicature.

Actual, Real, in oppofition to Chymerical or Potential.

Actuary, the Clerk that Regifters the Acts and Conftitutions of a Convocation.

Actuate, to bring into Act, to move, to ftir up, to quicken.

Actus major, a Square Meafure among the *Romans* containing 14400 Square Feet, or 1 *Englifh* Rod, 1 Square Pole, and 68 Square Feet.

Actus minimus, a Square Meafure among the *Romans* containing 4800 Square Feet, or 8 Square Poles, and 68 Square Feet, *Englifh*.

Acuminate, (Lat.) to fharpen.

Acute, (Lat.) fharp Pointed, alfo fharp Witted.

Acute Angle, an Angle lefs than a Right one.

Acute Difeafe, is that which is quickly over, but not without imminent Danger to the tient.

Acute Accent, in Grammar, fhows when the Voice is to be raifed, and is thus exprefſed (').

Acute Angular Section of a Cone, with the ancient Geometricians fignify'd an *Ellipfis*.

Adage, (Lat.) a Proverb, or common Saying.

Adagial, Proverbial, or full of *Adages*.

Adamantine, (Lat.) belonging to, or as hard as Adamant or Diamond; alfo Invincible.

Adamites, a fort of Hereticks, who, by the Death of Chrift, pretending to be reftored to *Adam's* Innocence, went naked in their Affemblies, afferting, if *Adam* had not finned, there had been no Marriages. They rejected Prayer, and held it not neceffary to confefs *Chrift*.

Adapt, to fit, or apply.

Adarige, a Chymical Term, fignifying Sal Armoniack.

Adawed, Daunted. *Spencer.*

Addict, to give ones felf up wholly to any thing, to follow it clofe.

Addicted, (Lat.) given up to, naturally enclined.

Additaments, things added anew to the ordinary Ingredients of any Compofition; a Supplement.

Addition, (Lat.) is the putting of two or more Things or Quantities together.

Addition, in Law, is that which

which is given to a Man besides his Proper Name and Sirname, to show of what Estate, Degree or Mystery he is, the Place of his Birth or Habitation.

Addition Simple, in Arithmetick, is the gathering together of several Numbers that express things of the same kind into one Sum, as Pounds, Miles, Yards, &c.

Addition Compound, is the gathering together of several Numbers that express things of different kinds into one Sum, as Pounds, Shillings and Pence, &c.

Addition Simple, in *Algebra,* is the collecting Algebraick Quantities of the same Name into one Sum, as 2*b* and 3*b* makes 5*b*, &c.

Addition Compound, in *Algebra,* is the collecting of Algebraick Quantities of different Denominations into one Sum, which is performed by putting the Sign of Addition + between them, as 2*a* and 3*b* are thus to be added 2*a* + 3*b*, and so of others.

Address, (Fr.) A dexterous Carriage in the managing of Business; also an Application to any Person. A short Remonstrance made by the Parliament to the King.

Adducent Muscles, are those that bring forward, or close, or draw together the Parts of the Body whereunto they are annexed.

Adductor Occuli, a Muscle of the Eye, which enclines the Pupil towards the Nose,

Adductor Pollicis, a Muscle of the Thumb, which brings the Thumb nearer to the Fore-finger.

Adductores, the same with *Adducent Muscles.*

Adeption, an obtaining or getting any thing.

Adeptists, are such Alchymists as pretend to have gained the Secret of the Transmutation of Mettals, or of making the Philosophers Stone.

Adequate, (Lat.) perfectly agreeing with, or equal to.

Adequate Idea's, are those Idea's which perfectly represent the Archytypes or Images which the Mind supposes them to be taken from; which it intends them to stand for; and to which it refers them.

Adfected Æquation, is an Æquation, which, besides the highest Power of the unknown Root, hath on the unknown Side of the Æquation, some intermediate Power or Powers of the unknown Root multiplyed into known Quantities.

Adhere, (Lat.) to stick or cleave to a Thing, Party, Opinion, &c.

Adhesion, a sticking or cleaving to.

Adjacent, lying by, bordering upon.

Adiaphonous, (Gr.) Opaque, not transparent, which cannot be seen through.

Adiaphorous, Indifferent.

Adjectives in *Grammar,* are Words which describe the manner only of the Being of a Thing, and have no Subsistence of their own, but do subsist by Noun Substantives.

Adieu, (Fr.) God be with you, Farewell.

Ad inquirendum, a Writ in Law, commanding an Enquiry to be made about the Merits of a Cause depending in the King's Court.

Adjourn, to put off to another Day.

Adjournment, the putting off of any Court or Meeting, and appointing it to be kept at another time.

Adjoyning Angles, See *Adjacent Angles*.

Adiposa Vena, a Vein arising from the Trunk of the *Cava*, and spreading it self on the Coat and Fat that covers the Kidneys.

Adiposi ductus, are Veffels which convey the Adeps or Fat into the Interstices of the Muscles, or the Parts between the Flesh and the Skin.

Adit, is the *Shaft* or Entrance into a Mine.

Adjudge, (Lat.) to give by Sentence, Judgment or Decree.

Adjudication, (Lat.) a giving by Judgment, Sentence or Decree.

Adjunct, (Lat.) is whatever comes to any Being from without, and does not naturally and effentially belong to it, but is fuperadded and adjoyned to it.

Adjuration, (Lat.) a Requiring an Oath of another; also an earnest Charging another to say or do somewhat.

Adjure, (Lat.) to Swear earneftly; also to put another to his Oath; to command a thing by Interpofing the Name of God or Chrift.

Adjuft, (Fr.) to place Juftly, joyn Handfomly, difpofe Orderly feveral things together.

Adjutant, (Lat.) Helping or Aiding, properly in that which is Good; also a Military Officer that affifts the General.

Admeasurement of Pafture, is a Writ which lies againft those, who having Common of Pafture Appendant to their Freehold, do furcharge it with more Cattle than they ought to do.

Admeasurement in Common Law, is a Writ that lies for the bringing of those to Reason, that ufurp more than their Part or Share.

Admeasurement of Power, is a Writ that lies againft the Widow of one deceafed, who holds from the Heir or his Guardian, more, under Colour of her Dower, than she has a juft Title to.

Administration (in Law) is the difpofing of a Man's Goods or Eftate that died Inteftate or without any Will, with an Intent to give an Account thereof.

Administrator, a Man who hath the Goods or Eftate of one who dy'd Inteftate committed to his Charge by the Ordinary, and is accountable for the fame. If the Perfon be be a Woman, she is called an *Administratrix*.

Admiral, or Lord High Admiral of England, a Principal Officer of the Crown, who has the Chief Government of the Royal Navy, and the determining of all Causes Maritime as well Civil as Criminal. Also a Title given to the Chief Commander of any distinct Squadron or Number of Ships.

Admiration, (Lat.) a Passion of the Soul occasioned by some unwonted Object; a Wondring at.

Admit, (Lat) to let in, to allow of, to permit, or suffer.

Admittendo Clerico, a Writ granted to him that hath recovered his Right of Representation against the Bishop in the common Bench.

Admittendo in Socium, a Writ for the Association of certain Persons to Justices of Assize before appointed.

Admonition (Lat.) a Giving, Warning, Advising.

Adnata Tunica, is the common Membrane of the Eye, commonly called *Conjunctiva,* and *Albuginea.*

Adnihilation, a bringing or reducing to nothing.

Ad octo, a Term us'd by some of the old Philosophers, signifying the Superlative or highest Degree whereby Qualities or Accidents are distinguished.

Adolescency, (Lat.) Youth.

Adonick Verse, a sort of Verse consisting of a *Dactile* and a *Spondee,* as *Rara juventus,*

seldom used but at the end of each *Stanza* of *Saphick* Verses.

Adopt, (Lat.) to take a Stranger into one's Family, chusing him for a Son or Heir; to make one not a-Kin capable to inherit.

Adoption, a chusing one for his Child out of the Course of Inheritance.

Adoration, (Lat.) Worship, profound Respect and Submission.

Adorer, one that renders a profound Respect and Submission, or worships any thing.

Adoulce, (Fr.) to sweeten.

Ad quod damnum, a Writ to enquire what hurt it would be to grant a Fair, Market, &c.

Adscititious or *Ascititious,* (Lat.) falsly taking to one's self; Counterfeit.

Ad terminum qui preteriit, a Writ of Entry for the *Lessor,* who is kept from the Possession of Leased Lands or Tenements, either by the Tenant or a Stranger.

Advance Ditch, in Fortification, is a Ditch dug all along the *Glacis* beyond the *Counterscarp,* usually filled with Water.

Advanced Guard, is the first Line or Division of an Army ranged or marching in Battel Array.

Advancement, (Fr.) a Raising or Promoting.

Advantageous, (Fr.) conducing to any one's Good or Profit.

Adventitious, (Lat.) which is

is brought or carried from another Place ; Foreign.

Advent, (Lat.) is the time from the Sunday that falls either upon St. *Andrews,* or next to it till *Christmas* ; the Word properly signifies a coming unto, or approaching.

Adventaile, a Word used by *Chaucer* signifying a Coat of Armour or Defence.

Adventitia bona, were anciently such Goods as came to a Man unexpectedly ; *Windfalls* as we now call them.

Adventitious, that comes by Chance, Casual, Accidental.

Adventure, Chance, an Encounter by Accident.

Adverb, is a Part of Speech undeclined ; and is commonly joyned with a Verb to expres the manner of Action.

Adverse, contrary, opposite.

Advertency, Heed, Carefulness, Attention.

Advertise, to Warn or give Intelligence.

Advertisement, Advice, Warning, Intelligence.

Adulation, (Lat.) Flattery.

Adulatory, apt to Flatter, or full of Flattery.

Adult, grown up, of full Age.

Adulteration of any thing, as Wine, Medicinal Drugs, Chymical Preparations, &c. is a mixing some baser Matter with it, which hinders it from being truly good and Genuin in its kind.

Adultery, is a Violation of the Marriage Bed.

Adumbration, a Shadowing ;

Amongst Painters a Sketch or rude Draught of a Picture : In Heraldry, an absolute taking away the Substance of the Charge or Thing born, so that there remains nothing of it besides the out Lines ; it is also called Transparency.

Aduncous, crooked downwards.

Advocate, a Gentleman of the Civil Law, that Pleads, Assists, or Sollicits another Man's Cause.

Advowson, the Reversion of a Spiritual *Benefice* ; it signifies in Law a Right to present is Clergy-man to a *Benefice,* it a as much as *jus Patronatus* in the Canon Law.

Adust, burnt, parch'd.

Ægrimony or *Ægritude,* (Lat.) Sickness.

Ægylops, Angilops, or *Anchilops,* a Tumour or Swelling in that Corner of the Eye next the Nose, either with or without an Inflammation.

Ægyptiacum Unguentum, is a kind of detersive Ointment, so called from its black Colour.

Ænigma, (Gr.) a dark and obscure Proposition, often Contradictory in appearance.

Ænigmatical, (Gr.) hidden, obscure.

Æolipile, a kind of Engine called the *Hermetical* or Wind Bellows, useful for Smiths and Chymists.

Æquanimity, (Lat.) an Evenness of Temper in all States and Conditions.

Æquator, (Lat.) See *Equator.*

Æquie

Æquilateral, See *Equilateral*.

Æquilibrium, See *Equilibrium*.

Æquipollence, Se *Equipollence*.

Æquiponderancy, an Equality of Weight; the same with *Equilibrium*, which see.

Æquivalent, See *Equivalent*.

Æquivocal, See *Equivocal*.

Æra, a Chronological Term signifying some remarkable Event, from which People begin their Computations, as the Jews from *Abraham*'s Journey out of *Chaldea*; the Christians from the Birth of *Christ*, &c.

Aerial, (Lat.) belonging to the Air.

Aeromancy, a sort of Divination by some certain Signs in the Air.

Æschinomenous Plants, the same with *Sensitive*, which see.

Æs ustum, (Lat.) calcined Copper.

Æstimation, a Term of the Roman Law, used in Buying and Selling; and is taken not only for an Appraisement, Value or Price, but also for the things Appraised.

Æstival Solstice, See *Solstice*.

Æstuate, (Lat.) to burn, boyl or rage like the Sea.

Ætate probanda, is a Writ of Office directed to the Sheriff, to enquire whether the Heir of a Tenant holding of the King in Chief, can prove himself of full Age.

Æternity, (Lat.) an unlimited or infinite Duration.

Æther, (Lat.) sometimes signifies that Medium in which all other Bodies do as it were swim and move; sometimes in a more limited Sense, it signifies that finer Fluid which is extended round our Atmosphere, above it and beyond it, up to the Planets, or to an indefinite Distance.

Ætherial, belonging to the *Æther*; also Heavenly.

Æthiops Mineral, a Medicine usually made of running Mercury and Flower of Sulphur.

Ætiology, (Gr.) in Physick signifies an Account of the Causes and Reasons of Diseases, and their various Symptoms, in order to their Cure.

Affability, Courtesy in Speaking to, and Hearing others.

Affectation, is the assuming of an Air in Language, Manners or Deportment, out of a fond Desire of appearing more accomplish'd than a Man really is.

Affection, (Lat.) a Passion of the Soul, whereby we bear a good Will or good liking to Persons or Things.

Affectionate, Kind, Loving.

Affiance, Trust, Confidence; also in Law, the plighting of Troth between a Man and a Woman, upon an Agreement of Marriage to be had between them.

Affidavit, in Law, signifies a De-a Depofition, or the Witnef-fing a thing upon Oath.

Affinage, (Fr.) a Refining of Mettals.

Affinity, (Lat.) Kindred or Alliance by Marriage ; alfo Likenefs and Agreement.

Affirmation, (Lat.) an af-ferting any thing to be true.

Affix, (Lat.) to faften to.

Affliction, (Lat.) Pain or Trouble of Mind or Body.

Affluence, (Lat.) Plenty.

Afforeft, in the *Foreft Law,* is to lay Waft a Piece of Ground, and turn it into *Fo-reft.*

Affranchife, a freeing or fet-ting at Liberty from Slavery, or Duty.

Affray, in Common Law, is a Fright put upon one or more Perfons ; as if a Man fhould fhow himfelf in Ar-mour, or furnifhed with Wea-pons not ufually worn, it may ftrike a Fear into others that are Unarm'd ; which there-fore is a common Wrong, and inquirable into in a *Court leet.*

Affrettamentum, in old La-tin Records the Fraight of a Ship ; from the French Word *Fret* of the fame Signification.

Affrication, (Lat.) a rubbing againft.

Affufion, (Lat.) a pouring upon, a fprinkling Liquor up-on a thing.

Aft, See *Abaft.*

After-Sails, in a Ship, are the Sails that belong to the Main and Miffen Mafts, and keep the Ship to the Wind.

Agai, in Merchandife, is the Difference in *Holland* or *Venice* of the Value of current Money and Bank Notes, which in *Holland* is often 3 or 4 *per Cent.* in Favour of the Notes.

Agaft, an old Word, figni-fying Difmay'd with Fear.

Agent, a Factor, or one that acts and deals for another ; in Logick, any acting Body is called the Agent.

Ageprier, in Common Law, is a Petition of one in Mino-rity to ftop the Suit till he come of Age.

Agglomerate, to fold or foul up together.

Agglutinate, to faften or glue together.

Aggrandize, to make Great, to Enlarge, or Advance.

Aggrandized, made Great in Honour or Eftate.

Aggravate, (Lat.) to Load, to make Heavy or Grievous, to make a thing worfe by Words.

Aggregate, the whole which arifes from the joyning or ga-thering together of feveral Quantities.

Aggreffes, a Term in He-raldry. See *Balls.*

Aggreffor, (Lat.) the firft Beginner of an Affault, Quar-rel or Difference.

Agild, in Law, fignifies free from Penalty.

Agifter, (Fr.) one that re-ceives in Cattle to be Paftur-ed or *Gifted,* keeps them with-in their Bounds, and delivers them to the Owners upon the Payment of fuch Terms for their Feeding.

Agi-

Agitation, (Lat.) in general, signifies Motion or Action; but it is commonly used in a Philosophical Sense, for the brisk intestin Motion of the Corpuscles of natural Bodies.

Agnation, (Lat.) in the Civil Law, that Line of Consanguinity or Kindred by Blood, which is between Males descended from the same Father.

Agnition, (Lat.) an Acknowledgment or Recognisance; an Owning.

Agnoites, a sort of Hereticks about the Year 370. Followers of *Theophronius* and *Cappadocian*; they call'd in Question the Omniscience of God; also another sort, who appear'd about the Year 535. asserting, that Christ knew not when the Day of Judgment should happen.

Agony, Horrour or Trembling. Torment of Body or Mind.

Agrarian Laws, Laws amongst the Romans made by the Tribunes of the Commons; as well for Division of Lands (conquer'd from the Enemies) among the Commons, as to restrain the Possessions of the Nobles within a certain *Limit*.

Agriculture, is the Art of Tilling of Land, in order to make it Fruitful.

Agroted, swelled, or made big. *Chaucer*.

Agrutched, Abridged. *Chaucer*.

Agrypnia, a watching of dreaming Slumber proceeding

from a Disorder of the Brain.

Agynnii, a sort of Christian Hereticks who began about 694. they said that God forbad eating of Flesh, and Marriage.

Aide de Camp, in an Army, is an Officer always following one of the Generals, to receive or carry their Orders as Occasion requires.

Aide Major, is an Officer whose Business it is to ease the *Major* of part of his Duty, and to perform it all in his Absence.

Aile, in Law, is a Writ which lies where Land descends from the Grandfather to the Son or Daughter of his Son, the Father being Dead before the Entry by him, and one abateth; the Heir shall have this Writ against the Abator.

Air, is a diaphanous, compressible and elastick Fluid, surrounding the Earth and Seas to a great Height above the highest Mountain.

Airy Meteors, See *Meteors*.

Aistheterium, (Gr.) is the common *Sensory*, or that Place in the Brain where all Sensation is produced.

Ajutage, (Fr.) is the Spout for a *jet d'eau* in any Fountain.

Ala, in Botany, signifies the Angle that either the Leaves, or the Foot-Stalks of the Leaves, make with the Stalk of the Plant.

Alabastra, in a Plant, are those little green Leaves which

which compass in the Bottom of the Plant.

Alacrity, (Lat.) Chearfulness, Liveliness.

Alamire, the lowest Note but one in each of the three Septenaries of the *Gamut* or Scale of Musick.

Alarm or *Alarum*, a sudden Outcry to Arms; Also any sudden Fear or Apprehension.

Alba Firma, in Land, is an annual Rent in Money, payable to the chief Lord of any Hundred.

Alba Pituita, the same with *Leucophlegmatia*, which see.

Albanou, a Sect of Christian Hereticks that appeared in the Eight Century. They held two Principles or Beginnings of Things, the one Good, the Father of Jesus Christ, and the Author of the New Testament; and the other Bad, the Author of the Old Testament which they rejected. They held, that the World was from all Eternity, that the Son of God brought a Body from Heaven, &c.

Albuginea Oculi, a very thin white Coat or Tunick of the Eye.

Albuginea Tunica, the Second of the Proper Integuments, which immediately covers the *Testicles*, so called from its white Colour.

Albugineous, belonging to the White of the Eye.

Albugo, is a white Speck in the Horny Tunick of the Eye, which hinders the Sight.

Alcaicks, a sort of Verses

consisting of 4 Feet, 2 Dactyles and 2 Trochees; or according to *Fabricius*, of 5 Feet; 1. a Spondee or Iambick; 2. an Iambick; 3. a long Syllable; 4. a Dactyl; 5. a Dactyl or *Amphimacer*.

Alchymist, one that Studies Alchymy.

Alchymy, the Sublimer Part of Chymistry, which teaches the Transmutation of Metals, and the Philosopher's Stone according to their Cant.

Alcohol, in Chymistry, signifies a very Fine and Impalpable Powder; and is also a very pure Spirit well Rectified or Dephlegmated.

Alcoholization, is a reducing Bodies to a Fine and Impalpable Powder; also a Freeing of Spirits from Phlegm and Waterish Parts.

Alcoran, (Arab.) the Book of the Mahometan Laws, or the Turk's Religion.

Alcove, (Span.) is Part of a Chamber separated by a Partition; in which is placed a Bed or Seats to entertain Company.

Aldebaran, (Arab.) a Star of the first Magnitude in the Head of the Bull.

Alegge, to lessen or asswage. *Spencer*.

Alembick, (Arab.) a Still.

Alcophanginæ, (Pillulæ) are Purging Pills made out of Aloes, and several Spices.

Alersans jour, in Law, signifies to be finally dismiss'd from the Court, because there is no further Day appointed for Appearance.   *Alc-*

Ale-Taster, an Officer appointed to look to the Goodness of Bread and Beer.

Aleuromancy, (Gr.) a kind of Divination by Bread or Cake Paste.

Alexipharmicks, are Medicines or Antidotes against Poison, or infectious Diseases.

Alexiterical, See *Alexipharmick*.

Algarot, in Chymistry, is a strong Emetick and Cathartick Powder.

Algebra, the Art of Resolution and Æquation. 'Tis a Science of Quantity in general, and is chiefly Conversant in finding Æquations, by comparing unknown and known Quantities together; and is distinguish'd into *Numerical*, which serves for the Solution of Arithmetical Problems; and Specious which is conversant about Quantity denoted by General or Universal Symbols, which are commonly the Letters of the Alphabet, and serves indifferently for the Solution of all Mathematical Problems, whether *Arithmetical* or *Geometrical*.

Algenib, a Star of the Second Magnitude in the right Side of *Perseus*.

Algol, a fixed Star of the third Magnitude in the Constellation *Perseus*.

Algorism, is the Practical Operation in the several Parts of *Algebra*.

Algorithm, is the Sum of the Principal Rules of Numeral Computation; viz. *Nume-*

ration, *Addition*, *Substraction*, *Multiplication*, and *Division*.

Alidada, (Arab.) the Label or Ruler that moves on the Center of an Astrolabe, Quadrant, or other Mathematical Instrument, and carries the Sight.

Alien, (Lat.) a Foreigner.

Alienate, to transfer the Property of a thing to another, to Sell.

Alienation, (in Law) is the making a thing another Man's, or putting the Possession of any thing from one Man to another; Selling.

Aliformes Musculi, are Muscles arising from the *Pterygoid* Bones and Ending in the Neck of the lower Jaw.

Aliformes Processus, in Anatomy, are the Prominences of the *Os Cuneiforme* from the Fore Part.

Aliment, is whatever Nourishes or Supplies the Decays of an Animal or Vegetable Body.

Alimony, in Law, that Allowance which a Married Woman sues for, upon a Separation from her Husband, wherein she is not charged with Adultery.

Aliquant Part of a Number, is such a Part as is not contain'd in the Number precisely so many times, but that some Remainder will be left.

Aliquot Part of a Number, is such a Part as is contained in the Number precisely so many times.

Alkahest, used by Chymists

C 2   for

for an universal Disolvent, or a Menstrum that will dissolve all manner of Bodies.

Alkali, in Chymistry, signifies the fixt Salt of any Plant.

Alkermes, is a Confection made of Red or Scarlet Grains.

Allaborate, (Lat.) to Labour vehemently.

Allanton or *Allantoides*, in Anatomy, is one of the Coats that belong to a Child in the Womb ; which being placed between the *Amnion* and the *Chorion*, receives the Urine that comes out of the Bladder.

Allay, to Mitigate or Asswage ; also to mix Mettals with a baser Sort.

Allbee, although, albeit. *Spencer*.

Allegation, is a Citation of any Book or Author, to make good any Point or Assertion.

Allegiance, is the Oath of Legal Obedience which every Subject takes to perform to his Prince.

Allegiare, is to justifie and clear himself by Course of Law, of the Crimes objected to him.

Allegory, a Figure in Rhetorick consisting of one continued Metaphor running thro' the whole Discourse.

Alleluia, (Hebr.) Praise ye our Lord.

Allemande, is a kind of grave solid Musick, where the Measure is good and the Movement Slow.

Alleviate or *Allevate*, (Lat.) to lift up, to Ease, or Comfort, to Asswage.

Alliance, properly is a Connexion of two Persons or Families together by Marriage ; but often used for Leagues and Treaties between Princes.

Alligation, (Lat.) in Arithmetick, a Rule by which such Questions are resolved, as relate to the mixing of divers Merchandizes, Metals, Simples, Druggs, &c. of unequal Price with one another, so as to find how much of each must be taken, according to the Tenour of the particular Question. It is of two Sorts, viz. *Alligation Medial* and *Alligation Alternate*.

Alligation Medial, is when having the several Quantities and Rates of divers Simples proposed, we discover the mean Rate of a Mixture compounded out of these Simples.

Alligation Alternate, is when having the several Rates of divers Simples given, we find out such Quantities of them, as are necessary to make a Mixture which may bear a certain Rate proposed.

Allioth, a Star in the Tail of the great Bear.

Allision, (Lat.) a dashing against.

Alliteration, (a Figure in Rhetorick) a Repeating and Playing on the same Letter.

Allocation, (Lat.) placing or adding unto; also in Law, an Allowance made upon an Account.   *Al-*

Allocatione facienda, a Writ for an Accountant to receive such Sums from the Treasurer or Barons of the Exchequer, as he by the Vertue of his Office hath Lawfully and Reasonably Expended.

Allocution, a Talking unto, a Speech of a General to his Soldiers to animate them to Fight, or to appease Sedition.

Allodial Lands, are those for which no Rents, Fines nor Services are due.

Allodium, in Law, signifies a Man's own Land, &c. which he possesses merely in his own Right, without Acknowledgment of any Services, or Payment of any Rent to another.

Allogotrophy, with some Physicians, is a disproportionate Nutrition of the Body; when one Part of it is Nourished more than another.

Alloy, is a certain Quantity of a baser Mettal mix'd with a Finer, in order to make it of a due Temper.

Allude, (Lat.) to speak in Reference to some other Thing or Matter.

Allusion, a likening or applying one thing to another.

Almacanters, (Arab.) on the Globe, are Parallels of Altitude, or Circles Parallel to the Horizon either above or below.

Almonds of the Throat, a Glandulous Substance representing two Kernels, placed on each Side the *Uvula*, at the Root of the Tongue.

Almoner, ... Officer belonging to a King or Prince, whose Business is to take Care of the Distribution of Alms.

Aloeticks, Medicines consisting chiefly of Aloes.

Alogians, a sort of Christian Hereticks, who deny'd that part of Scripture where the Son of God is said to be the Word of the Father.

Alopecy, a shedding of the Hair occasioned by the Pox, or otherwise.

Alphabet, the whole Order of Letters in any Language; the Word being derived from *Alpha* and *Beta*, the Names of the two first Letters of the Greek Tongue.

Alphabetical, belonging to, or agreeing to the Order of the Alphabet.

Alphus, a Cutaneous Distemper, in which the Skin is rough, and looks as if there were Drops of white Colour upon it.

Alramech, (Arab.) the same with *Arcturus*.

Als, Alas. *Spencer*.

Altarage, the Offerings made upon the Altar; also the Profit that arises to the Priest from the People's Offering at the Altar.

Alteration, Change; in a Physical Sense it is the Acquisition or Loss of such Qualities in any Body, as are not Essential to the Form of the Body.

Altercation, a Contentious Dispute,

Altering Medicines, are such Medicines as purifie and restore the due Mixture of the Blood, and other circulating Humours.

Alternate or *Alternative*, done by turns.

Alternate Angles, in Geometry, are two equal Angles, which a Line cutting two Parallels makes with those Parallels, One on one Side of the cutting Line, and the Other on the other.

Alternate Proportion, in Geometry, is when in any Set of Proportionals, the Antecedents are compared together, and the Consequents together.

Altimetry, the Art of taking or measuring of Heights, whether *Accessible* or *Inaccessible*.

Altitonant, Thundring from on High.

Altitude, (Lat.) Height.

Altitude of a Figure, in Geometry, is the nearest Distance between the *Vertex* or Top of that Figure and its Base.

Altitude of the Sun, or a Star, is the Height of the Sun or a Star above the *Horizon*, or the Ark of an Azimuth intercepted between the Sun or Star and the *Horizon*.

Altivolant, (Lat.) flying or soaring aloft.

Alvearium, (Lat.) a Beehive; also the Cavity of the inward Ear, where that bitter and excrementitious Stuff is bred, called *Ear-wax*.

Amain, is a Word sometimes used by a Ship to his Enemy by way of Defiance,

or Commanding him to strike his *Top-sails*, that is, to Yield; *Strike amain*, i. e. lower your Top-sails.

Amalgamate, in Chymistry, is to mix Quick-Silver with some melted Metal, either to make it into a sort of Past to be extended on some Works, as in Guilding; or to reduce it into a very fine Powder.

Amalgame, any Mettal that is Amalgamated, or reduced to a fine Powder.

Amand, to send away, or remove.

Amanses, with some Chymists, signifies Gems and precious Stones.

Amanuensis, a Clerk or Secretary; one that writes what is indited by another.

Amaurosis, a Disease in the Eyes.

Ambages, an idle Circumlocution, or a connecting of Words far from the Purpose.

Ambassador, a Commissioner sent by one Prince to another, to treat about State-Affairs.

Ambe, a superficial Jutting out of the Bones.

Ambidexter, one that useth both Hands alike; in Law, a Juror who takes Money of both Parties for giving his Verdict.

Ambient, Encompassing round about.

Ambiguous, (Lat.) Doubtful, Uncertain.

Ambiguous Word, is one that has two or more Significations.

Ambit.

Ambit, is the Bounds, Perimeter or Circumference of any Figure.

Ambition, a Thirst after Honour.

Ambligonial, (Gr.) Obtuse-Angular.

Ambliopia, is a Dulness or Dimness of Sight; the Object being seen but Obscurely at what Distance soever placed.

Amblosis, (Gr.) Abortion or Miscarriage.

Ambulatory, walking up and down.

Ambuscade, a Place where Souldiers hide themselves, to suprize the Enemy.

Amebean Verse, a Song or Verse sung Alternately, or by Turns.

Amenable, (Fr.) easy to be led or ruled; in our Law, it is apply'd to a Woman that may be Governed by her Husband.

Amendment, Reformation, Correction; in Law it is the Correction of an Errour committed in Process, and espy'd before Judgment, which may also be amended by the Judges after Judgment.

Amerciament, a pecuniary Punishment imposed upon Offenders *a la Mercie*, at the Mercy of the Court; and therefore in our Law Cases, is frequently called *Miserecordia*; and therefore there is this Difference between *Fines* and *Amerciaments*; *Fines* are Punishments Certain, and determined by some Statute; *Amerciaments* are Arbitrary

Impositions, proportioned to the Fault at the Discretion of the Court.

Amethyst, (Gr.) in Heraldry, is the Purple Colour in the Coat of a Nobleman; also a precious Stone.

Amiable, Lovely, Charming.

Amicable, Friendly, like a Friend.

Amission, (Lat.) Loss.

Amittere legem terræ, in Law, is to lose the Liberty of Swearing in any Court; to become Infamous.

Ammunition, all sort of Warlike Stores and Provisions, more especially Powder and Ball.

Amnion or *Amnios*, is the innermost Membrane with which the *Fœtus* in the Womb is immediately covered.

Amort, (Fr.) Extinguished, Dead.

Amortize, a Word used by *Chaucer*, to kill; in Law, to make over Lands and Tenements to a Corporation or Fraternity, and their Successors.

Amouses, in Chymistry, counterfeit Gems, or precious Stones.

Ampelite, in Agriculture, a kind of black and bituminous Earth, used about Vines to make them Thrive.

Amphibious, (Gr.) used for an Animal that lives both in Land and Water.

Amphibleſtraides, (Gr.) in Anatomy, is the some with *Tunica Retina* of the Eye, so called, because being thrown

C 4   into

into Water it refembles a Net.

Amphibology, (Gr.) a Figure in Grammar, when our Expreffions feem to look one way, and are intended another ; a dark Speech, having a double Meaning.

Amphibrachys, (Gr.) is the Foot of a Latin Verfe confifting of three Syllables, where the two Extreams are fhort, and the Middle long.

Amphibranchia, in Anatomy, certain Places about the Glandules or Kernels in the Jaws, that ferve to moiften the Throat, Stomach, &c.

Amphidæum, in Anatomy, is the Top of the Womb.

Amphimacer, (Gr.) the Foot of a Latin Verfe confifting of three Syllables , where the two Extreams are long, and the Middle fhort.

Amphiproftyle, in Architecture, a kind of Temple among the Ancients, which had four Columns in the Front, and as many in the Face behind.

Amphifcii, the Inhabitants of the Torrid Zone, fo called becaufe their Shadows fall both ways at different times of the Year.

Amphifmela, an Anatomical Inftrument ufed in the Diffection of Bones.

Amphitheatre, a Place built by the old Romans of a round or oval Figure, and containing a great Number of Seats one above another, where the People faw divers Shows and Sports.

Amphora, (Lat.) a Roman Meafure of Capacity for liquid things, containing, according to our Wine Meafure, 7 Gallons, 1 Pint, 10 Solid Inches, and 66 Decimal Parts.

Ample, (Lat.) Large, Wide, Spacious, Abundant.

Ampliation (Lat.) an Enlargement ; in Law, a deferring of Judgment till the Caufe be better certified.

Amplification, (Lat.) an Enlarging or Dilating.

Amplify, to Enlarge or Dilate.

Amplitude, Largenefs of Extent.

Amplitude, of the Sun or Stars, is an Ark of the Horizon intercepted between the Eaft or Weft Point, and that Point where they Rife or Set ; and is either Northern or Southern.

Amputation, (Lat.) a Surgeon's Term for the cutting off any Member of the Body.

Amulet, any thing that is hung about the Neck or any Part of the Body againft Witchcraft or Difeafes.

Amufe, to ftop a Man with a trifling Story ; to make a Man lofe his time ; to Feed with vain Expectations.

Amufement, an idle Employment to fpin away the time ; a Divertifement.

Ana, a barbarous Word amongft the Phyficians, fignifying an equal Quantity of Ingredients.

Ana-

Anabaptists, a Sect of Christians, so called, because they
deny the Lawfulness of Infant
Baptism. They appeared first in
Germany about the Year 1521,

Anabasis, in Physick, the
Growth or Encrease of a Disease.

Anabibaxon, The Dragon's
Head, or the Northern Node
of the Moon.

Anabrochismus, is a Way
of drawing out the inverted
pricking Hairs of the Eye-lid.

Anabrosis, is a Consumption
of the Body by sharp Hu-
mours.

Anacamptick, (Gr.) signifies Reflecting.

Anacathartick Medicines, are
such as cause Vomiting.

Anacephalæosis, (Gr.) a Summary of the Heads of any
Speech or Writing.

Anaclaticks, a Part of Opticks which treats of all Sorts
of Refractions; the same
with *Dioptricks*.

Anacreontick Verses, is a
kind of Verses consisting of
seven Syllables, without being ty'd to any Law or Quantity; so called from *Anacreon*,
the Author of that Sort of
Verse.

Anacronism, (Gr.) an Errour in the Computation of
time, or an undue Connexion
of it.

Anadiplosis, (Gr.) a Figure
in Rhetorick, when one Verse
begins with the same Word
the last ended with.

Anadosis, (Gr.) in Physick

the Distribution of the Chyle
thro' its proper Vessels; also
whatever tends upwards, as
a Vomit.

Anaglyphick Art, the Art
of Carving and Engraving.

Anagogical, Mysterious, or
which hath an elevated, raised and uncommon Significa-
cation.

Anagram, (Gr.) a short
Sentence made by transposing
the Letters of one's Name, in
order to make out something
to the Honour of the Person;
thus *Galen* by Transposition is
Angel.

Analemma, is an Orthographick Projection of the Sphere
upon the Plain of the Meridian. See *Orthographick*.

Analeptick, Restorative.

Analize, (Fr.) to resolve a-
ny thing into its component
Principles or Parts.

Analogism, (Gr.) in Logick,
a forcible Argument from the
Cause to the Effect.

Analogous, bearing the same
Relation or Respect to another thing.

Analogy, (Gr.) in Mathe-
maticks, an Equalitiy of Ra-
tio's, Proportion; as in four
Terms; the First where-
of is contained or contains the
Second, as oft as the Third
contains or is contained in the
Fourth; the Equality of the
Ratio's of the two Pair of
Terms is called an *Analogy*.

Analysis, (Gr.) *Resolution*;
the Art of discovering the
Truth or Falshood, Possibility

or

or Impoffibility of a Propofi-tion, and proceeds in a Re-trograde Way to *Synthefis* or *Compofition* ; *viz.* by fuppofing the Queftion to be already done, and then examining the Confequences that follow from it, till you arrive to fome known, clear and evident Truth, or Impoffibility of the Propofition in Hand. This Term is very often ufed for *Algebra* it felf.

Analytick, is a Part of Lo-gick that teaches to decline and conftrue Reafon, as Grammar does Words.

Anamnefis, (Gr.) a Rheto-rical Figure, whereby we call to Mind things that are paft.

Anapæft, (Gr.) a Latin Verfe, whofe Feet confift of three Syllables, the two firft fhort, and the laft long.

Anaphora, in Rhetorick, a Repetition of the fame Word in the Beginning of feveral Sentences or Verfes.

Anaplerotick Medicines, are fuch as fill up Ulcers with Flefh.

Anarchy, (Gr.) is want of all Government in a Nation, where there is no fupream Authority lodged in either Prince or Rulers, but the Peo-ple live without any Govern-ment at all.

Anaftomatique (Gr.) Medi-cines, are fuch as open the Orifices of the Veffels, and procure a free Circulation of the Blood.

Anaftomofis, (Gr.) an Efflux-ion of the Blood or Chyle, at the meeting of the Veffels that clofe not narrowly.

Anaftrophe, (Gr.) a Figure in Grammar ; a prepofterous placing of Words, when that is placed firft which fhould naturally follow.

Anathema, (Gr.) a Solemn Curfe or Sentence of Excom-munication ; alfo the Thing accurfed, or Perfon cut off from the Communion of the Church.

Anathematize, (Gr.) to Excommunicate.

Anatocifm, (Gr.) is the an-nual Encreafe or Intereft of Money, whether Simple or Compound.

Anatomize, (Gr.) to cut up the Body of Man or Beaft.

Anatomy, (Gr) is the Dif-fection or cutting up of the Body of Man or Beaft, as Surgeons do, to difcover the Subftance, Actions and Ufe of the feveral Parts of it.

Anatripfis. (Gr.) in Surge-ry, the bruifing or breaking of a Bone, or of a Stone in the Kidneys.

Anchile, in Anatomy, is the back Part of the Knee.

Anchor, of a Ship, is an In-ftrument ufed to ftop the Courfe of a Ship on the Sea or in a River ; there are feve-ral forts of *Anchors*, differing only in Weight, according to the Burden of the Ship.

Anchor, in Architecture, is a fort of Carving fomewhat refembling an *Anchor* or an Arrow-head. With this fort of Work are commonly En-rich'd rich'd the Boultins of Capitals of the Tuscan, Dorick and Ionick Orders; as also of the Boultins of Bed Mouldings of the Dorick, Ionick and Corinthian Cornishes.

Anchorage, is Ground fitting to hold a Ship's Anchor, so that she may ride it out Safely.

Anchorage, in Law, is a Duty taken of Ships for the *Pool* of the *Haven* where they cast Anchor.

Ancient, the Flag or Streamer in the Stern of a Ship.

Ancon, is the Top or Point of the Elbow.

Aconæus, a Muscle of the Cubit which helps to extend it.

Ancyroides, the Shooting forth of the Shoulder Bones in the Form of a Beak.

Andratomy, (Gr.) a cutting up, or Dissection of human Bodies.

Androgynus, (Gr.) an Hermaphrodite, or one that is both Male and Female.

Andromeda, a Northern Constellation.

Anemius Furnus, (among Chymists) a Wind Furnace, used to make strong Fires for Distilling or Melting.

Anemoscope, (Gr.) an Instrument Invented to foreshew the Change of the Air or Wind.

Aneurism, (Gr.) a Disease consisting in a Dilatation or Bursting of the Arteries.

Anfractuous, (Lat.) full of Turnings and Windings, Intricate.

Anfractuosity, (Lat.) a Winding or Turning, Intricacy.

Angaria, in Law, signifies any troublesome or vexatious Duty or Service paid by the Tenant to his Lord.

Angelici, a Sort of Christian Hereticks, suppos'd to have their Rise in the Apostle's time; they Worshipped Angels, from whence they had their Name.

Angiglossus, (Gr.) one that stuttereth.

Angina, (Lat.) an Inflammation of the Jaws and Throat, attended with a continual Feaver, and a Difficulty of Breathing and Swallowing. The Quinsy.

Angiology, (Gr.) a Discourse or Treatise of the Vessels of a humane Body, as the Veins, Arteries, Nerves, &c.

Angle Plain, is the Inclination or Aperture of two Lines meeting in a Point.

Angle Rectilineal, is when the two Lines which form the Angle are right Lines.

Angle Curvilineal, is when the two Lines that Form the Angle are curved or crooked.

Angle mixt, is when one of the forming Lines is Right, and the other Curved.

Angle of Incidence, is the Angle which the incident Line makes with the Perpendicular.

Angle of Reflection, is the Angle which the reflected Line makes with the Perpendicular.

Angle of Refraction, is the Angle which the Refracted

Ray

Ray makes with the Incident Ray, continued without any Refraction.

Angle Flanking, is that which is made by the meeting of two *Rafant* Lines of Defence, *viz.* the two Faces of the Baftion prolonged.

Angle Re-entring, is what points towards the Body of the Place; fuch is the Angle of the Counterfcarp before the Center of the Curtin.

Angle Salliant, in Fortification, is what Advances with its Point towards the Country; as the Angle of the Counterfcarp before the Point of a Baftion.

Angle Refracted, is the Angle made by the Refracted Ray and the Perpendicular.

Angle Spherical, is an Inclination or Aperture of the Peripheries of two great Circles of the Sphere meeting in a Point.

Angle Solid, is an Angle made by the meeting of three or more plain Angles joyning in a Point.

Anglicifm, is the Englifh Idiom, or Manner of Speech peculiar to *England*.

Anhelation, (Lat.) a Difficulty in fetching one's Breath.

Anhelote, in Law, fignifies that every one fhould pay his refpective Part and Share, according to the Cuftom of the Countrey.

Animadverfion, (Lat.) fometimes fignifies Correction, fometimes Remarks and Obfervations made upon a Book; and fometimes ferious Confideration upon a Subject.

Animadverfive, that Confiders or Reflects.

Animadvert, to bend or turn the Mind to a thing, to take Notice of; to Remark or Obferve.

Animate, (Lat.) to Enliven or Quicken, to Hearten or Encourage.

Animated Needle, is one touched with a Load-ftone.

Animation, (Lat.) is the informing an Animal Body with a Soul.

Anima Hepatis, Vitriol or Salt of Steel, according to fome Chymifts.

Anima Saturni, is (in Chymiftry) the Extract of Lead.

Animal, (Lat.) a living Creature; alfo Living, that has Life.

Animalcula, very fmall Animals, fuch as by the Help of Microfcopes, have been difcovered in feveral Fluids; as in Pepperwater, in human Seed, &c.

Animodar, a Method of rectifying Nativities in Aftrology.

Animofity, (Lat.) Stoutnefs, Stomachfulnefs; *Animofities*, Quarrels, Contentions.

 Ankred, fo the Heralds call one of their Croffes in a Coat of Arms of this Figure.

Anlace, a Falchion or Sword, fhaped like a Scithe.

Annalift, a Writer of Annals.

An

Annals, are a yearly Chronological Account of the remarkable Events of a State; as the Annals of *Tacitus*.

Annates, (Lat.) firſt Fruits paid out of ſpiritual Benefices.

Anneal, a Commodity brought from *Barbary*, uſed by Painters and Dyers.

Annealing, a Staining and Baking of Glaſs, ſo that the Colour may go quite through it.

Annex, (Lat.) to unite or joyn one thing to another.

Annexation, uniting of Lands or Renrs to the Crown.

Annihilation, (Lat.) is a deſtroying or turning any created Being into nothing.

Anni nubiles, (Lat.) the Age in which a Maid becomes fit for Marriage, which is at twelve Years.

Anniverſary, that comes every Year at a certain time; Yearly. Alſo the yearly Return of the Day of Death of any Perſon, which the Religious regiſtered in their Obitual or Martyrology, and Annually obſerved in Gratitude to their Founders and Benefactors.

Anno Dom. (Lat.) ſignifies the Year of our Lord.

Annomeans, the Name of the thorough paced *Arians* in the 4th Century, becauſe they held the Eſſence of the Son of God unlike that of the Father.

Annotation, (Lat.) a Noting or Marking; alſo a Remark, Note, or Obſervation.

Annoyance, (Fr.) Prejudice, Damage, Injury.

Annual, (Lat.) of or belonging to the Year, yearly.

Annuates Muſculi, a Pair of Muſcles at the Root of the Tranſverſe *Vertebra* of the Back; called alſo *Recti interni minores*; ſerving to nod the Head directly forward.

Annuity, a yearly Rent to be paid for Term of Life or Years.

Annular Cartilage, the Second Griſtle of the *Larynx*.

Annular Protuberance, part of the human Brain lying between the *Cerebellum* and the bakward Prominences.

Annu'et, a little Ring, which, in Heraldry, is a Mark of Diſtinction which the fifth Brother of any Family ought to bear in his Coat of Arms. Alſo in Architecture, a narrow flat Moulding, uſed in the Baſes, Capitals, &c. of Columns.

Annull, (Lat.) to make void.

Annumerate, to put into the Number.

Annunciation, Delivery of a Meſſage: Alſo *Lady-Day* March 25. ſo call'd from the Angel's Meſſage to *Mary*.

Anodynes, (Gr.) are ſuch Remedies as alleviate or quite take away the Pain.

Anomalous, Unequal, Uneven, Irregular.

Anomaly, (in Grammar) an Irregularity in the Conjugations of Verbs or Declenſions of Nouns, when they do not follow the common Rule.

Ano

Anomaly mean or equable, in the new Astronomy, is the Area comprehended under the *linea Apsidum*, a Line drawn from the Sun to the Planets, and that Ark of the Elliptical Orbit which is comprehended between these two Lines, and computed from the *Linea Apsidum*, according to the natural Order of the Signs.

Anomaly coequated or *true*, in the new Astronomy, is the Angle comprehended under the *Linea Apsidum*, and a Line drawn from the Sun to the Planet.

Anon, by and by. *Milton*.

Anonymous, Nameless, or without a Name.

Anopsy, (Gr.) want of Sight, Blindness.

Anorexy, (Gr.) want of Appetite, arising from an ill Disposition of the Stomach.

Ansae, (Lat.) Handles.

Ansae Saturni, the Ring of Saturn, which sometimes appears like Handles to the Body of the Planet.

Antaces, a Star of the first Magnitude in *Scorpio*, called the Scorpion's Heart.

Antagonist, (Gr.) he that in Disputation opposes another; also an Adversary.

Antanaclasis, (Gr.) is a Figure where the same Word in Appearance, is used in a different Signification.

Antaphroditick Medicines, are such as are used for the French Pox.

Antarctick Pole, the Southern Pole either of the Earth or

Heavens; so called from its being Diametrically opposite to the Northern or Arctick Pole

Antarctick Circle, a lesse Circle of the Earth or Heavens, described at 23 Degrees and a Half from the Antarctick Pole.

Antarthritick Medicines, are such as are used against the Gout.

Antecedence in, or *in Antecedentia*, in Astronomy, is when a Planet appears to move contrary to the natural Order of the Signs of the Zodiack.

Antecedent, in Mathematicks, is that Term of Quantity which the Mind considers first in comparing it with another.

Antecessor, one that goes before: The Predecessor in an Office or Estate.

Antedate, (Lat.) to date a Letter before hand.

Antediluvian, is whatever was before the Flood.

Antemeridien, before Noon.

Antemieticks, Medicines against Vomiting.

Antepast, (Lat.) a Foretaste.

Anterides, (Gr. in Architecture) Buttresses set against the Walls to uphold or bear up the Building.

Anterior, (Lat.) that is before, the former.

Antes, in Architecture, are square Pilasters which the Antients plac'd at the Corners of their Temples.

Anthelix, in Anatomy, is the

the inward Brink of the outward Ear, being a Semi-circle within the *Helix*, and almost Parallel to it.

Anthelminticks, are such Medicines as destroy Worms.

Anthem, a Divine Song sung Alternately by two opposite Quires and Chorus's.

Anthology, (Gr.) a Discourse or Treatise of Flowers.

Anthonians, an Order of Monks founded by St. *Anthony*, about the Year 324.

St. *Anthony's Fire*, is a very painful and burning Inflammation, of a fiery red Colour.

Anthropology, a Discourse or Description of Man, or of a Man's Body.

Anthropomorphites, (Gr.) a Sect of Hereticks that appeared in *Ægypt A. D.* 395. they were so called from the chief of their Tenets, *viz.* that God had a Bodily Shape.

Anthropophagi, (Gr.) Men Eaters.

Anthropophagy, (Gr.) a Feeding on Man's Flesh.

Antiaphroditicks, are Medicines that lay Lust.

Antiarthriticks, (Gr.) are Medicines against the Gout.

Antiasthmaticks, (Gr.) are Medicines against Shortness of Breath.

Anticachecticks, Remedies that correct the ill Disposition of the Blood.

Anticardium, in Anatomy, the same with *Scrobiculus cordis*, which see.

Antichamber, (Fr.) any outward Chamber which is next

or near the Bed Chamber.

Antichrist, (Gr.) an Adversary to Christ; a Seducer that puts himself in Christ's Room and Stead.

Anticipate, (Lat.) to do a thing before the proper time come; to prevent.

Antick, Ancient; a Piece of Antiquity. Also a Buffoon or Juggler.

Antichthones, (Gr.) the same with *Antipodes*, which see.

Antidicomarians, Hereticks that were against the Virgin *Mary*.

Antidote, a Medicine against deadly Poison.

Antiœci, are such Inhabitants of the Earth who live on contrary Sides of the Equinoctial, but at equal Distances from it, and under the same Meridian.

Antiemeticks, Medicines against Vomiting.

Antiepileptick, (Gr.) Medicines against the falling Sickness.

Antihecticks, Remedies against the Hectick Feaver or Consumption.

Antihypocondriacks, are Medicines against Melancholly.

Antihypnoticks, (Gr.) Medicines against Sleeping.

Antilogy, (Gr.) a Contradiction between any Words or Passages in an Author.

Antimonarchial, that is against Kingly Government.

Antimony, is a Mineral consisting of a Sulphur like unto common Sulphur; and of a
Sub-

Substance near opproaching to Metallick.

Antinomasy, (Gr.) a Figure in Grammar, whereby an Appellative is used instead of a Proper Name.

Antinomians, a sort of Christian Hereticks, so called, because they rejected the Law, as a thing of no Use under the Gospel Dispensation; they said, that good Works do not further, nor evil Works hinder Salvation; that the Child of God cannot Sin; that Murder, Adultery, Drunkenness, &c. are Sins in the Wicked, but not in them; with many more such like Heretical Doctrines.

Antinomy, (Gr.) a Contrariety between two Laws.

Antipagments (in Architecture) are the Garnishing of Posts and Pillars.

Antipasis, the same with the Revulsion of a Disease.

Antipathy, (Gr.) a Contrariety of natural Qualities betwixt some Creatures and Things; a natural Aversion.

Antiperistasis. according to the Peripateticks, is a certain Invigoration of any Quality, by its being environed and kept in by its contrary.

Antiperistaltick Motion, is the wormlike or wavelike Motion of the Guts inverted.

Antipharmacum, see *Antidote.*

Antiphon, (Gr.) the Answer made by one Choir to another, when a Psalm or Anthem is sung between two. Eccl.

Antiphrasis, (Gr.) is a Figure whereby we mean contrary to what we speak.

Antipodes, (Gr.) are such Inhabitants of the Earth as live Feet to Feet, or Diametrically opposite to one another.

Antiphthisical Medicines, such as withstand Consumption or Phthisick.

Antipope, a false Pope, chosen by a particular Faction against one duely Elected.

Antiprdicaments, are Notions previously necessary to understand the Doctrine of the *Prdicaments.*

Antiptosis, (Gr.) a Grammatical Figure, whereby one Case is put for another.

Antiquary, one that is well vers'd in Antiquities, or the Customs and Learning of the Ancients.

Antiquated, grown out of Date.

Antique, (Lat.) Ancient. Antique Work, in Sculpture or Painting, is a confus'd Mixture or Composition of Figures, as of Beasts, Birds, Flowers, Fishes, &c. without any Order and Regularity.

Antisabbatarians, such as deny the Sabbath.

Antiscii, (Gr.) are such People as inhabit the Torrid Zone, so called, because when the Sun is on the North Side of them, their Shadow at Noon falls towards the South; and when he is on the South Side of them, their Meridian Shadow falls Norward.

Antiscor

Antiscorbutick Medicines, are Medicines against the Scurvy.

Antispasmodieks, (Gr.) are Remedies against Convulsions.

Antitactes, a fort of Christian Hereticks, who taught that Sin deserved rather Reward than Punishment.

Antithesis, (a Rhetorical Figure) is a setting together of Opposites, so that they may shew one another the better.

Antitragus, a little Prominence in the lower end of the *Antihelix*.

Antitrinitarians, the Name of all those who deny the Holy Trinity.

Antitype, (Gr.) that which answers to, or is prefigured by a Type; as the Paschal Lamb was a Type, to which our Saviour, *that Lamb of God*, was the Antitype.

Antivenereal, (Lat.) that is good against the *French* Pox.

Antler, a Branch of a Stag's Horn.

Antocow, a swelling in the Breast of a Horse, about half as big as one's Fist.

Antæci, See *Antiœci*.

Antonomasia, (a Trope) is an applying one proper Name to several things; or on the contrary.

Anus, the Extremity of the *Intestinum Rectum*, or the Orifice of the Fundament.

Anxiety, (Lat.) Vexation, Trouble of Mind.

Aonian Mount, the Muses Hill, *Parnassus* in *Bæotia*.

Aorist, (Gr.) indefinite, two Tenses in the *Greek*, that may signifie a thing, either a doing, done lately or long ago, or likewise to be done.

Aorta, the great or greatest Artery of a Human Body, proceeding from the left Ventricle of the Heart.

Apagogical Demonstrations, are such as do not prove the thing directly, but show the Absurdity which arises from denying it.

Apathy, (Gr.) a freeness from all Passion, Insensibility of Pain, Indolence.

Apepsie, (Gr.) a bad Digestion.

Aperiens Palpebram, a Muscle of the upper Eye-lid, which pulls it upwards.

Aperient, (Lat.) opening.

Aperitive, (Lat.) opening, as *aperitive* Medicines are such as open the obstructed passages in the small Vessels.

Aperture, in Geometry, is the Inclination of Lines which meet in a Point.

Aperture in Opticks, is the Hole next to the Object Glass of a Telescope, thro' which the Light and Image of the Object comes into the Tube, and thence it is carried to the Eye.

Apex, Top, Point, or uppermost part of a thing.

Aphelium, is that point of a Planet's Elliptical Orbit which is the farthest from the Sun.

Apheresis, a Figure, whereby a Letter or Syllable is taken

D   ken

ken from the beginning of a Word.

Aphorism, (Gr.) a short select Sentence briefly expressing the Properties of a thing, and experimented for a certain Truth.

Aphrodisical, (Gr.) belonging to *Venus* or Love.

Aphtha, an Exulceration in the Mouth.

Apiary, a place where Bees are kept, a Bee-hive.

Apices, (Lat) of a Flower are those little Knobs that grow on the Top of the Stamina in the middle of the Flower.

Apnœa, (Gr.) want of Breath; an entire Suppression of Breathing; at least as to Sense, as it happens to People in a Swoon.

Apocalyptical, (Gr.) belonging to a Vision or Revelation.

Apocope, (Gr.) a Grammatical Figure, wherein the last Letter or Syllable, of a Word is cut off.

Apocryphal, (Gr.) hidden, unknown, doubtful.

Apodictical Argument or *Syllogism*; is a plain proof of a thing.

Apodioxis, (Gr.) a Figure in Rhetorick, whereby any Argument is with Indgnation rejected as absurd.

Apodosis, a Recompencing, or giving again: Also a Figure in Rhetorick, call'd *Reddition*, which is the Application, or latter part of a Similitude.

Apogee or *Apogæum*, is that point of the Orbit either of

the Sun or of any of the Planets which is farthest from the Earth.

Apollyon, (Gr.) a Destroyer, a Name in Scripture given to the Devil.

Apologetical, (Gr.) belonging to an Apology or Excuse.

Apologue, (Gr.) a Tale or Moral Fable, such as those of *Æsop*.

Apology, (Gr.) a Defence or Excuse.

Apomecometry, (Gr.) the Art of Measuring things at a distance.

Aponeurosis, in Anatomy, is the spreading or Extension of a Nerve or Tendon out in Breadth, in the manner of a Membrane.

Apophlegmatisms, (Gr.) Medicins that by the Mouth or by the Nose Purge the Head of cold phlegmatick Humours.

Apophthegm, a short, pretty, and instructive Sentence, chiefly of a grave and eminent Person.

Apophyge, in Architecture, is that part of a Column where it seems to fly out of its Base like the Process of a Bone in a Man's Leg, and begins to shoot upwards.

Apophysis, in Anatomy, a Protuberance most commonly at the end of a Bone, made by the Fibres of that Bone jutting out above its Surface.

Apoplexy, (Gr.) a Disease that suddenly surprizes the Brain, and takes away all manner of Sense and Motion.

Aporia, (Gr.) Doubting, Perplexity; a Figure in Rhetorick, when one is at a stand what to do.

Aporime, (Gr.) is a Problem very difficult to be resolved, and which has not yet ever been resolved, although to be done, as the Quadrature of the Circle.

Aporrbea, in Physick, Vapours exhaling through the Pores of the Body.

Aposiopesis, (Gr.) a Figure in Rhetorick, whereby a Person suddenly breaks of his Discourse; yet so as that it may be understood what he meant.

Apostacy, (Gr.) Revolting, Falling away from the true Religion.

Apostata capiendo, a Writ for the taking up of one, who after having professed some Religion, forsakes it, leaves his House and wanders about the Country.

Apostate, (Gr.) one that Renounces the true Religion.

Apostatize, (Gr.) is to Renounce the true Religion.

Apostem, (Gr.) a Swelling, called commonly an *Abscess* or *Impostume*.

Apostle, (Gr.) in General, signifies a Messenger, a Person sent upon some especial Errand, for the discharge of some peculiar Affair of him that sent him, as the *Apostles* of our *Saviour*.

Apostrophe, (Gr.) a Digression; a Figure in Oratory or Poetry, in which things animate or inanimate Persons present or absent are address'd or appealed to as if they were sensible or present.

Apothecary, (Gr.) one that keeps a Shop for selling all manner of Medicins and Druggs prepar'd by himself.

Apotheosis, an Enrolling of great Men deceas'd in the Number of the Gods, anciently practis'd by the Heathens; a Canonization.

Apotome, (Gr.) is an irrational Remainder or residual, when from a rational Line as a, another is cut off as b, that is only Commensurable in Power than $a - \sqrt{b}$, that is an *Apotome*.

Apozeme, (Gr.) a Medicinal Decoction of Roots, Herbs, Flowers, Barks, &c.

Appall, to Daunt, Astonish, Discourage. *Spencer*.

Apparatus Major and *Minor*, the greater and lesser Preparation, being two particular Methods us'd by *Lithotomists* in cutting for the Stone.

Apparel, Rayment; Also Furniture for Dressing in Surgery; Also, the Tackle, Sails and Rigging of a Ship.

Apparent, (Lat.) Visible, Certain, Evident.

Apparitour, One that Summons Offenders, and serves the Process in a spiritual Court.

Appartment, a separate Lodging in a House.

Appeach, to impeach; or accuse of any Crime.

D 2   *Appeal*,

Appeal, in Law, a remoʒving a Cauſe from an Inferiour to a Superiour Judge.

Appellation, (Lat.) a Calling or Pronouncing ; alſo an Appeal from ſome Sentence or Juriſdiction to a preſumedly higher Judicature, which Appeals were frequent both from the Civil Magiſtrates to Eccleſiaſtical Powers, and again from the Courts Chriſtian to the Common Law.

Appellative, in Grammer, is a Word in Grammer which belongs to the whole Species or Kind, as Man.

Appendant, in Law, things are ſaid to be Appendant, that by Line of Preſcription have belonged, appertained and are joyned to another principal Thing, by which they paſs and go as acceſſary to the ſame ſpecial thing, as Lands, Commons, &c. to a Mannor, &c.

Appendage, any thing which being conſidered as leſs principal, is added to another.

Appendix, (Lat.) a Supplement to a Treatiſe by way of Addition or Illuſtration.

Appetency, earneſt Deſire, great Inclination.

Appetite, (Lat.) Deſire, Luſt, a Stomach to Victuals.

Applauſe, a clapping of Hands in token of Joy or Congratulatior.

Applicate Ordinate, See Ordinate.

Application, (Lat.) the ſame as Appeal ; Alſo Addreſs, in Geometry it is us'd for Diviſion of Lines.

Applicable, that may be Apply'd to a thing.

Apply to, to Addreſs, or Appeal to, to Divide by.

Apportionment, in Law, is a Dividing into Parts a Rent, which is Dividable, and not entire and whole.

Apportum, in Law, is Revenue, Gain, or Profit accruing from any thing to the Owner.

Appoſale of Sheriffs, is the charging them with Money received upon their Account in the *Exchequer*.

Apportion, in Law, is to Proportion or Divide into convenient Parts.

Appoſite, Added ; Alſo fit, pat, to the purpoſe

Appoſition, is a putting or laying one thing by the ſide of another; Alſo the putting two or more Subſtantives together in the ſame Caſe.

Appraiſe, to Rate or ſet a Price on Goods, to Value.

Apprehenſion, (Lat.) a catching hold off ; in Logick it ſignifies the ſimple Contemplation of things which preſent themſelves to the Mind, without pronouncing any thing about them.

Apprendre, in Law, is a Fee or Profit to be taken or received.

Apprentice, (Fr.) a Learner, one Bound by Indenture to learn an Art or Myſtery.

Appretiate, to ſet an high Eſteem upon any thing.

Approach, to draw near, or come to.

Approaches,

Approaches, in Fortification are all the Works whereby the Besiegers approach to the Besieged.

Approbation, A liking, or approving of.

Appropriate, is to set aside any thing for the Use of any One.

Appropriation, when the Profits of a Church Living are made over to a Lay-man or a Body Corporate ; only maintaining a Vicar.

Appropriare ad Honorem, to bring a Mannor within the Extent and Liberty of such an Honour.

Appropriare Communam, to separate and enclose an open Common, or part of it.

Approve, to like, or allow of ; to render one's self Commendable.

Approvement, in Law, is where a Man hath Common within the Lord's Waste for himself, having nevertheless sufficient Common, with Egress and Regress for the Commoners. This Enclosing is called *Approvement*.

Approver, in Law, is one who being guilty of Felony, to save himself, accuses his Accomplices.

Approximation, in Arithmetick or Algebra, is a continual approaching still nearer and nearer to the *Root* or *Quantity* sought, without ever expecting to have it exactly.

Appurtinences, signifies in Common Law, things both Corporeal belonging to ano-

thet thing as the more Principal ; as Hamlets to a Chief Mannor, Common of Pasture, Turbary, Piscary, &c. Courts, Yard, Drains to a House ; and Incorporeal, as Liberties and Services of Tenants.

Apsides, are those two Points in the Orbit of a Planet, one of which the farthest from and the other the nearest to the Sun.

Apsychy, (Gr.) a fainting away; or Swooning ; want of Courage.

Aptitude, (Lat.) Fitness.

Aptote, (Gr.) in Grammer, a Noun without any Case.

Apyrexy, (Gr.) is an Intermission or abating of a *Fever*.

Apyrotos, (Gr.) the best sort of Carbuncle, a precious Stone that will endure the Fire.

Aquarii, a sort of Hereticks so call'd, because they used only Water at the Lords-Supper.

Aquarius, one of the 12 Signs of the Zodiack, which is the eleventh reckoning from *Aries*.

Aquatick } that belongs to,
Aquatical } or lives mostly
Aquatile } in the Water.

Aqueduct, (Lat.) is a Conduit or Pipe, to convey Water from one place to another.

Aqueous humour, one of the Humours of the Eye so call'd ; it fills the Space between the *Cornea Tunica* and the Chrystalline Humour.

Aquila, a Conſtellation in the Northern Hemiſphere conſiſting of 32 Stars.

Aquiline, of or belonging to an Eagle.

Aquoſe, (Lat.) Wateriſh.

Aquoſity, Wateriſhneſs.

Appulſe, in Aſtronomy is the approach of any Planet to a Conjunction.

Ara, a Southern Conſtellation, conſiſting of eight Stars.

Arabian Pole, a Scripture Meaſure of Length, of 14 Engliſh Feet, 7 Inches and 104 Decimal Parts.

Arable, (Lat.) Ploughable.

Areoſtyle, a Term in Architecture, ſignifying a ſort of Edifice where the Pillars are ſet at a great diſtance from one another.

Araignee, (Fr.) a Spider; Alſo the Branch, Return or Gallery of a Mine in Fortification.

Aranea Tunica, that Tunicle of the Eye, which ſurrounds the *Chriſtalline Humour*; it is alſo called *Arachnoides*, ſo called from the Reſemblance it bears to a Spider's Web.

Araneous, (Lat.) full of Spider's Webs.

Arbiter, an Uimpire, one choſen by mutual Conſent to decide a Controverſy between Parties.

Arbitrary, (Lat.) that which is voluntary or left to our Will.

Arbitrator, a Perſon choſe by two or more contending Parties, to decide the Controverſy between them.

Arbitrement, is the Power with which an *Arbitrator* is inveſted, and by which he determines between two or more contending Parties.

Arboreous, (Lat.) of, belonging, or like unto a Tree.

Arboriſt, (Lat.) a Perſon skilful in Trees.

Arbour, a Bower in a Garden, a ſhady Place made by Art to ſit and take Pleaſure in.

Arcaiſms, are obſolete Expreſſions, now out of uſe to be met with only in ancient Authors.

Arcanum, (Lat.) is a Name given to ſeveral, eſpecially Chymical, Preparations, at firſt kept ſecret by their Authors, as *Arcanum Corallinum*, &c.

Arch, prefix'd to any Word, adds Prince or chief to its Signification; as *Archangel*, *Archduke*, *Archbiſhop*.

Arch, a Part or Portion of a Curve Line; alſo Arrant or Notorious.

Arch Deacons, Dignitaries of the Church; they were at firſt employ'd by the Biſhops in more ſervile Duties, and alway in Subſervience to the Urban or Rural Deans of Chriſtianity, to whom they were as much Inferiour, as their Order of Deacon was to that of Prieſt, till by the Advantages of a Perſonal Attendance on a Biſhop, and a Delegation to examine and report ſome Cauſes, and a Commiſſion to viſit ſome remoter Parts of a Dioceſe, their Power and Dignity was advanced

vanced beyond that of Deans.

Archer, one Skill'd in shooting with the long Bow.

Archery, the Art of shooting with the long Bow.

Arches, a Court of the Archbishop of *Canterbury*, so called from the Arches that were formerly in the Steeple of *Bow-Church* where it was held.

Archetype, (Gr.) The Original from whence any Figure, Picture or Copy is drawn.

Archeus, is the Principle of Life, Health and Vigour, according to the *Paracelsians*.

Archiatre,(Gr.) a chief Physician, a Physician to a Prince.

Archipelago, in Geography, is a part of the Sea containing several small Islands, and consequently several little Seas denominated from those Isles, as the *Ægean Sea*.

Architect, a Person skilful in Architecture.

Architectonick Spirit, the same with Plastick Nature, which see.

Architecture, a Mathematical Science, giving Rules for designing and raising all sort of Structures, according to Geometry and Proportion.

Architecture Civil, is the Art of Building private Houses, Churches, &c.

Architecture Military, the same with Fortification, which see.

Architrave, in Architecture, signifies th: Mouding next above the Capital of a Co-

lumn; also the principal Beam in a Building.

Archives, a Place where ancient Records, Charters and Evidences are kept, as the Office of the Master of the Rolls, &c.

Archontiques, Christian Hereticks, so called because they held that Archangels created the World; they denied the Resurrection, and said that the God of Sabbaoth exercised a cruel Tyranny in the 7th Heaven; that he Engendered the Devil, who begat *Abel* and *Cain* upon *Eve*.

Arctation, (Lat.) streightning or crouding.

Arctick Circle, a lesser Circle in the Earth or Heaven, 23°. 30'. distant from the Arctick Pole.

Arctick Pole, the Northern Pole of the Earth or Heavens, so called from *Arctos* a Constellation very near it.

Arctos, (Gr. *the Bear*) is a Constellation in the Northern Part of the Heavens.

Arctos minor, the same with *Ursa minor*, which see.

Arcturus, a fixed Star of the first Magnitude in the Skirt of *Arctophylax* or *Bootes*.

Ardency, (Lat.) See Ardour.

Ardor Ventriculi, a kind of Pain in the Stomach commonly called *Heart burning*.

Ardor Urinæ, the same with *Dysuria*.

Ardour, (Lat.) Heat, Vehemency, Love or fervent Desire.

Area, in Geometry, signifies

Res the superficial Content of any Figure measured in Inches, Feet, Yards, &c.

Areed, Judge, Pronounce. *Spencer*.

Arefaction, (Lat.) a drying.

Areometer, (Gr.) an Instrument to measure the Gravity of Liquors.

Areostyle, in Architecture, is a Building where the Columns stand a little too thick; or, as some will have it, at a convenient Distance.

Areotectonicks, is that part of Fortification which teaches to attack an Enemy safely, and fight Advantagiously.

Argent, (Lat.) Silver or Coin; in Heraldry it stands for the white Colour.

Argentum vivum, (Lat.) Quicksilver, Mercury.

Argo Navis, a Constellation in the Southern Hemisphere, consisting of 24 Stars.

Argument, a Proof of the Truth or Falshood of any Proposition.

Argument, of *the Moon's Latitude*, is her Distance from the *Dragon's Head* or *Tail*, which are her 2 Nodes.

Argute, (Lat.) Subtle, Wirty, Shrill.

Arians, a sort of Christian Hereticks, so called from *Arius* their first Founder. They denyed the three Persons in the Holy Trinity to be of the same Essence; and affirmed the Word to be a Creature; and that there was a time when he was not.

Aries, (Lat.) a Ram. With Astronomers 'tis the first Sign of the *Zodiack*, into which the Sun enters in the beginning of *March*; it consists of 19 Stars, and is denoted by this Character (♈).

Arista, in Botany, is that long slender Beard which grows out of the Husk of Corn or Grass.

Aristocracy, (Gr.) a Form of Government where the supream Power is lodged in the Nobles or Peers.

Aristocratical, belonging to Aristocracy, or that Form of Government.

Arithmetick, a Science which teaches the Art of Accompting, and all the Powers and Properties of Numbers.

Arithmetical Proportion, See *Proportion*.

Ark, the same with *Arch*, which see.

Arles-penny, Earnest Money.

Armada, (Span.) a great Navy.

Armiger, (Lat.) one that bears a Coat of Arms; also an Esquire.

Armillary Sphere, is an Instrument composed of 6 greater and 4 lesser Circles of the Sphere, put together in their natural Order and due Distances from one another.

Arminianism, is the Doctrine of the *Arminians*, so called from *Jacobus Arminius*, who held free Grace and universal Redemption.

Armiſtice, (Lat.) a Ceſſation from Arms for a time; a ſhort Truce.

Armory, a Place to keep Arms in; alſo *Heraldry*.

Aromatick, Odoriferous, of a ſweet Smell.

Aromatization, a mingling any Medicine with a due Proportion of Aromatick Spices.

Arquebuſe, (Fr.) an Handgun, ſomewhat bigger than a Muſquet.

Arraign, is to put a thing in order, or in its due Place; alſo to Indict and put a Priſoner to his Trial.

Arrant, mere, downright.

Array, a ranking of Soldiers in Battel; alſo in Law, a ranking or ordering of a Jury.

Arrearage, a Debt remaining on an old Account.

Arrears, the Remains of a Debt or Reckoning.

Arreed, Award. *Milton*.

Arrentation, in Law, is the Licencing an Owner of Lands in the Foreſt, to encloſe them with a Hedge and a little Ditch, under a yearly Rent.

Arreſt, is when one is legally taken, and reſtrained from his Liberty.

Arreſtandis bonis ne diſſipentur, a Writ for him whoſe Cattel or Goods being taken, during the Controverſy are like to be waſted and conſumed.

Arreſtando ipſum qui pecuniam recepit ad proficiſcendum in obſequium Regis, &c. a Writ for the Apprehenſion of him that has taken Preſt-money towards the King's Wars, and hides himſelf when he ſhould go.

Arreſto facto ſuper bonis mercatorum alienigenorum, a Writ for a *Denizon* againſt the Goods of Strangers of another Country found within the Kingdom, in recompence of Goods taken from him in that foreign Country, after denial of Reſtitution.

Arride, to ſmile or look pleaſantly upon.

Arrive, to come to ſhore; alſo to come to a Place, to attain to, or compaſs a thing.

Arrogate, to aſſume too much to one's ſelf, to boaſt.

Arſenick, is a mineral Body conſiſting of much Sulphur and ſome cauſtick Salts.

Arſinal, (Fr.) a royal or publick Storehouſe of Arms, or warlike Ammunition.

Art, (Lat.) Skill or Cunning; a Collection of Rules, Inventions and Experiments, that facilitate Undertakings.

Arteriotomy, (Gr.) the cutting or opening of an Artery.

Artery, is a ſanguiferous Veſſel, and generally holds the ſame Courſe with a Vein, but lies deeper; it can no where be ſeen in the Surface of the Body, but may be felt to beat in ſeveral Parts at the ſame time with the Heart, and its Pulſe is chiefly Indicative of the Temper of the Blood, but partly alſo of the
Vigour

Vigour or Defect of Spirits. It conveys Blood and vital Spirits from the Heart into all the Parts for their Nourishment, and the Conservation of their innate Heat.

Arthritical, (Gr.) belonging to the Joynts, or Gout, Gouty.

Arthrodia, is the Articulation of one Bone into the shallow *Sinus* of another.

Arthrosis, (Gr.) the same as *Articulation.*

Article, (Lat.) a Joynt; also a Point, Clause or Member of a Covenant, Discourse, Treaty, Account, &c. in Grammar 'tis a small Word for distinguishing the Genders.

Articulately, a Man that pronounces his Words clearly and distinctly, is said to speak *Articulately.*

Articulation, in Anatomy, is a joining together of the Bones of an Animal Body.

Artifice, (Lat.) a cunning Trick, Subtlety.

Artificer, a Handicraftsman or Workman; an Artist.

Artificial Day, is the time between the Sun's Rising and Setting in any Position of the Hemisphere.

Artificial Lines, on a Sector or Scale, are Lines placed thereon, divided from the Logarithms, and the Logarithms of the Sines, Tangents and Secants.

Artificial Numbers, are Logarithms or logarithmetick *Sines, Tangents* and *Secants.*

Artillery, is all sort of great fire Arms, with their Appurtenances.

Artisan, an Artificer or Tradesman.

Artist, a Master of an Art, an ingenious Workman.

Arval, (Brothers) twelve Roman Priests, Judges of *Landmarks.*

Arvil, a Burial or Funeral Solemnity.

Arundiferous, (Lat.) bearing Reeds.

Aruspicy, (Lat.) a Divination by looking into the Intrals of Animals.

Arytænoides, the Name of the third and fourth Cartilage of the Larinx; they reach from the middle of the concave side of the *Thyroides,* to the upper and back part of the *Annularis,* and make that Chink which is the Mouth of the *Larinx* called *Glottis.*

As, a Weight among the *Romans* of 12 Ounces; also one of their Square Measures containing two *English* Rods and 19 Poles; also one of their Coins worth $3\frac{1}{8}$ Farthings of our Money.

Asa fætida, a stinking Gum brought from *Persia,* good against Fits in Women.

Asaphy, is a lowness of the Voice, proceeding from an ill Constitution.

Asbestine Paper or *Cloth,* is such as will burn in the Fire, be purify'd by it, and yet not consume.

Ascarides, small Worms that

that breed in the ſtraight Gut.

Aſcaunſe, athwart or acroſs.

Aſcendant, (Lat.) that Degree of the Ecliptique which riſes at one's Nativity; alſo a Power or Influence over one.

Aſcenſion Right, of the Sun or of a Star, is an Ark of the Æquator, reckoning towards the Eaſt, intercepted between the beginning of Aries, and that Point of the Æquator which riſes at the ſame time with the Sun or Star in a Right Sphere.

Aſcenſion Oblique, of the Sun, or a Star, or any Point of the Heavens, is an Ark of the Æquator, reckoning towards the Eaſt, intercepted between the firſt Degree of *Aries*, and that Point in the Æquator which riſes with the given Star or Point in a given Oblique Sphere.

Aſcenſional Difference of the Sun or Star, is the Difference between its right Aſcenſion and its oblique Aſcenſion, in any given Poſition of the Sphere.

Aſcent, (Lat.) ſteepneſs accounted upwards, or the Motion upwards of any Body.

Aſcertain, to aſſert for certain, to aſſure.

to *Aſcetick*, (Gr.) belonging Religious Exerciſes; Monaſtick, Monkiſh.

Aſcii, (Gr.) are ſuch Inhabitants of the Earth as have no Shadows at 12 a Clock; ſuch are all the Inhabitants of the Torrid Zone; for twice every Year the Sun is in their Zenith at 12 a Clock, and conſequently at that time they have no Shadows.

Aſcites, (Gr.) is a Dropſy, or ſwelling of the *Abdomen*.

Aſcitick, affected with a Dropſy.

Aſclepiad, a ſort of Verſe conſiſting of four Syllables, a Spondee, a *Choriambus*, and two Dactyles.

Aſcodrogiles, a ſort of Chriſtian Hereticks that appeared about the Year 173. who pretended they were repleniſh'd with *Montanus*'s Paraclet; and introduced the *Bacchanals* into the Churches, where they had a Buck Skin full of Wine, and went in Proceſſion round it, ſaying, This was the Veſſel of new Wine ſpoken of in the Goſpel.

Aſcribe, (Lat.) to attribute, to impute.

Aſcriptitious, (Lat.) regiſtred, enrol'd.

Aſhtaroth, a Goddeſs of the *Sidonians*, Siſter to *Dagon*, and worſhipt by the *Philiſtines*.

Aſh-wedneſday, ſo called from the Cuſtom that prevailed in the ancient Church for Penitents at this time to expreſs their Humiliation, by lying in *Sackcloth* and *Aſhes*.

Aſia, one of the four Parts of the World.

Aſiaticks, People or Inhabitants of *Aſia*.

Aſtin·

Asinine, (Lat.) belonging to an Ass.

Askaunce, asquint. *Spencer*.

Aspect, (Lat.) Sight, a Look, an Appearance; in *Astronomy* it signifies the Situation of the Stars and Planets, in respect one of another.

Asper, (Lat.) a *Turkish* Coin about five Farthings *English*.

Asperity, (Lat.) Roughness, Harshness.

Aspersion, a sprinkling or bespattering; also a Blemish in any Person's Reputation; a Slandering.

Asphaltites, the dead Sea, where *Sodom* and *Gomorrha* stood.

Aspiration, (Lat.) Breathing; also Influencing; also a Note over a Greek Letter, which hath the Force of an *h*.

Aspire, to breath; also to pretend to, or to seek after any Dignity or Honour.

Asportation, (Lat.) carrying away.

Aspyxia, (Gr.) is the highest Degree of Swooning.

Assail, to attack or set upon.

Assasine, one that robs or murthers another for Gain.

Assation, (Lat.) a Roasting.

Assault, is a violent kind of Injury offered to a Man's Person.

Assay, (Fr.) to prove or try.

Assay'd, endeavoured. *Milton*.

Assemblage, a joining or uniting things together.

Assemble, (Fr.) to call, gather, or come together.

Assent, (Lat.) Approbation, Consent.

Assent, is an Act of the Mind, by which it receiveth, acknowledgeth or embraceth any thing as a Truth; it being the Nature of the Mind to embrace whatsoever appeareth to be true.

Assentation, (Lat.) Flattery, a flattering Compliance.

Assert, (Lat.) to affirm or maintain.

Assertion, an Affirmation, or a Maintaining.

Assess, to Rate or Tax.

Assessor, one joined in Authority to another; also one that appoints what Proportion every one shall pay of a publick Tax.

Assets, (in Law) signifies Goods enough to discharge that Burden which lies upon the Executor or Heir, in satisfying the Testator's or Ancestor's Debts or Legacies.

Asseveration, an earnest Affirmation.

Assewiare, (a Law Term) to drain Water from Marshy Ground.

Assiduity, (Lat.) a constant or unintermitted Diligence.

Assiduous, continual, diligent.

Assign, to appoint or depute another to do any thing.

Assignation, an Appointment.

Assign;

Assignment, the making a thing over to another.

Assimilation, a making like; in Physick it signifies the Change that is made either of Chyle into Blood, or of the nutritious Juice into the Substance of an animal Body.

Assimulate, to feign or counterfeit a thing.

Assisa, (Lat.) Originally a Court wherein the Judges or *Assessors* did hear and determine any Cause. We now apply the Word to another Court of Judicature, besides the County Courts held by the Itinerant Judges, which Courts are called the *Assises*.

Assisors, the same in *Scotland* as Jurors here.

Assistance, Help, Aid.

Association, an entering into Society with others.

Assoil, to acquit or pardon; to answer; a Word used by *Chaucer*.

Assuefaction, an accustoming one's self to any thing.

Assumption, a taking to or upon; also the minor Proposition of a Categorical Syllogism.

Asswage, to allay or appease; to abate or grow calm.

Asterisk, a little Star, in Writing being placed before or over any Word or Sentence, it denotes some Defect, or somewhat to be noted.

Asterism, a Constellation of fixed Stars.

Astert, startle. *Spencer.*

Asthma or *Phthisick*, is a difficulty in Breathing, pro-

ceeding from an ill Affection of the Lungs.

Astipulation, (Lat.) an Agreement, Assent, or Affirmation of a thing.

Astismus, (Gr.) a Figure in Rhetorick, expressing some pleasant Jest.

Astonishment, an extream Surprize, Amazement.

Astounded, astonisht. *Milt.*

Astragal, in Architecture, is by the *French* called *Talon*, and by the *Italians Tondino*; and is a kind of half *Tore*, sometimes wrought like an overcast Edge or Hem of a larger *Tore*.

Astragal, in Gunnery, is the Cornice Ring of a Piece of Ordnance.

Astriction, a binding or fastening together.

Astringent, (Lat.) binding.

Astrolabe, a Mathematical Instrument to take the Altitude of the Sun with.

Astrologer, a Person skill'd in the Art of *Astrology*.

Astrological, belonging to *Astrology*.

Astrology, is an Art which pretends to foretell things from the Motions of the Heavenly Bodies, and their Aspects to one another; as also that there are I do not know what Qualities in the Stars, which are the Causes of all sublunary Effects.

Astronomer, a Person skill'd in the Science of Astronomy.

Astronomical, belonging to Astronomy.

Astronomi-

Astronomical Place of a Planet, is its Longitude or Place in the *Ecliptick*, reckoned from the beginning of *Aries*, in *consequentia* or according to the natural Order of the Signs.

Astronomy, a Science which teaches the Knowledge of the Heavenly Bodies, their Magnitudes, Distances, Eclipses, Order and Motions.

Asylum, a Sanctuary or Place of Refuge for Offenders.

Asymmetry, the same with *Incommensurability*, which see.

Asymphony, a Disorder in Descant, a Disagreement.

Asymptote, is a Right Line so drawn, that a Curve shall continually approach to it, but yet shall never meet, tho' produced *ad infinitum*; such are the Assymptote or Assymptotes, to the common *Hyperbola*, Conchoid, &c.

Asyndeton, (Gr.) a Figure in Grammar, implying a Defect or want of Conjunctions.

Atchievement, the Performance of any noble Exploit; also in *Heraldry* it signifies the Coat of *Arms* of any Gentleman. set out fully with all that belongs to it.

Athanor, (in Chymistry) a kind of large digesting Furnace, made with a Tower, and contrived so as to keep a constant Heat for a Fortnight, Month, &c.

Atheism, a denying or not believing the Being of a God.

Atheist, a Person which denies or disbelieves the Being of a God.

Atheling, a Title given to the King's Eldest Son in the *Saxon's* time.

Athenian, belonging to the City of *Athens* in *Greece*; also curious of Novelties.

Atheroma, (Gr.) a sort of Tumour or Swelling, consisting of a thick and tough Humour like Pap, contained in a Bag or Membrane.

Athletick, belonging to the Art of Wrestling.

Athymia, (Gr.) is a Dejection or Anxiety of the Mind.

Atlas, in Anatomy, is the first *Vertebra* of the Neck under the Head; so called because it seems to uphold the Head.

Atmosphere, is that Sphere of gross Air (in opposition to the Æther) which surrounds the Earth, or any of the other Planets.

Atome, according to *Epicurus*, is one of the component Particles of Bodies, all which he supposed so small, that they were perfectly indivisible.

Atonement, a Reconcilement, or appeasing of Anger.

Atony, a Faintness, Infirmity, or want of Strength.

Atra bilis, black Choler, Melancholy.

Atreus, one whose Fundament or privy Parts are not perforated.

Atrocity, Cruelty, Outragiousness. Heinousness.

Atrophy, (Gr.) a kind of Consumption of the Body, caused

caused by Meat not turning into Nourishment.

Attachiamenta bonorum, a Distress taken upon the Goods or Chatels of any, sued for Personal Estate or Debt, by the legal *Attachiaters*, or Bayliffs, as a Security to answer the Action.

Attachiamenta de Spinis & Bosco, a Privilege granted to the Officers of a Forest, to take to their own Use Thorns, Brush, and Windfall, within their own Precincts or Liberties.

Attachment, (Fr.) a laying Hands on, a seasing upon, a distress of Goods, or an Arrest of a Person.

Attachment foreign, is the Process which is used to Attach a Foreigner's Goods found within the Liberty or City.

Attachment of the Forest, is a Court held there every 40 Days throughout the Year.

Attack, an Assault; also to assault, to endeavour to carry a Place by Force.

Attain, (Lat.) to obtain, get, or compass a thing; to come to.

Attainder, (Fr.) is when a Man hath committed Felony or Treason, and Judgment is passed upon him; for then his Blood is said to be *attainted*, *i.e.* corrupted; and if he were Noble and Genteel before, his Posterity are degraded and made Base.

Attaint, (Fr.) a Writ against a Jury that has given a

false Verdict in any Court of Record, if the Debt or Damages amount to above forty Shillings; the Punishment of such Offenders is, That their Meadows shall be ploughed, their Houses pulled down, all their Lands forfeited to the King, and their Persons imprisoned.

Attemper, (Lat.) to allay, qualify, or moderate.

Attemperate, (Lat.) to make fit, to mix in due Proportion.

Attempt, to endeavour, to undertake, or try.

Attendance, Waiting, Service; a Retinue.

Attention, an Application of the Ears and Mind to any Discourse, and of the Eyes and Mind to any piece of Work.

Attentive, diligently hearkening to.

Attenuating Medicines, are such as opening the Pores with their sharp Particles, cut the thick and vicious Humours in the Body, so as that they may easily be circulated through the Vessels.

Attenuation, in Physick, is a lessening the Power or Quantity of the morbifick Matter.

Attestation, a Witnessing or Affirming.

Attick, Neat, Elegant.

Attiguous, a joyning or touching; lying by or near unto.

Attinge, to touch lightly, or softly.

Atting.

Attire, Drefs, Apparel; in Heraldry, the Horns of a Stag or Buck.

Attracting, a drawing unto.

Attraction, is the drawing of one thing to another; in natural Philofophy it fignifies that univerfal Tendency which all Bodies have towards one another, from which a great many of the furprizing Phenomena of Nature may be eafily accounted for.

Attribute, is a Property belonging to any Subftance or Being; alfo to impute.

Attrition, a rubbing or wearing; alfo in Divinity, Attrition is a Slight and Imperfect, as Contrition is a more deep and ferious Sorrow for Sin.

Attturney, (Fr.) is fuch a Perfon as by Confent, Command, or Requeft, takes care of another Man's Bufinefs in his Abfence.

Avail, bring down. *Spencer.*

Avant foffe, a Moat or wet Ditch encompaffing the Counterfcarp on the outfide.

Avant-ward, the Avant Guard or Front of any Army.

Avarice, (Lat.) Covetoufnefs.

Avaft, make haft, difpatch; alfo ftop, hold, or ftay.

Avaunt, begon, away. *Milton.*

Auburn, dark Brown, or Chefnut Colour.

Auction, an open Sale; where he that bids moft is the Buyer.

Audacious; (Lat.) Confident, overbold, daring.

Audience, hearing; alfo an Affembly of People hearkening to fomething fpoken.

Audit, hearing and examining an Account.

Auditor, a Hearer.

Auditory, the Place where Men hear Lectures, Orations, Sermons, &c. alfo the Affembly of thofe that hear.

Avenage, Oats payed to a Landlord inftead of other Duties.

Aventure, a mortal or deadly Mifchance.

Avenue, a Paffage lying open to a Place.

Aver, (Fr.) to affirm or juftify.

Aver, a labouring Beaft.

Average, a certain Allowance out of the Freight to a Mafter of a Ship: The Contribution paid by Infurers to make Satisfaction for infured Goods caft overboard: A Service in Horfe or Carriage a Tenant owes his Lord: Alfo Pafturage.

Averiis captu in Withernam, a Writ for the feifing of Cattle to his ufe, that has his Cattel wrongfully taken away by another, and driven out of the Country that they can't be replevy'd.

Averment, is when the Defendant offers to juftify an Exception pleaded in Bar, of the Plaintiff's Action.

Aver

Avenue, a Paffage lying open to a Place.

Averruncation, a fcraping or cutting off, as Men do Vines.

Averfion, a turning or driving away; alfo a Hatred or Diflike.

Auff, a Fool, or filly Fellow.

Auger, a Wimble, a Tool for boring.

Aught, any thing. *Milton.*

Augment, to encreafe, enlarge or improve any thing.

Augmentation, (Lat.) an increafing.

Augur, a Soothfayer or Diviner.

Augury, Divination by the Singing, Flight or Feeding of Birds.

Auguft, Royal, Majeftical, Sacred.

Auguftinians, Hereticks, called alfo *Sacramentarians*, holding that the Gates of Heaven are fhut till the Refurrection.

Aviary, a great Cage or Place to put Birds in.

Avidity, (Lat.) Greedinefs, eager Defire.

Aumone, a Law Term for Alms.

Avocation, (Lat.) a calling away, a let or hindrance to Bufinefs.

Avoidance, is when a Benefice becomes void of an Incumbent.

Avoir-du-pois, (Fr.) to have over-weight; a Weight of fixteen Ounces in the Pound, by which all fuch things as

have a Refufe or Wafte are weigh'd.

Avouch, to maintain or juftify.

Avow, (Fr.) to own, confefs or acknowledge; in Law to juftify.

Avowee, one that has the Right of Advowfon, or prefenting to a Benefice in his own Name.

Auricle, (Lat.) an Ear.

Auricular, (Lat.) belonging to, or fpoken in the Ear, as Auricular Confeffion.

Auriga, (Lat.) a Northern Conftellation.

Aurora, the Morning, Dawn, or break of Day.

Aufcultation, (Lat.) a hearkening, or liftening to.

Aufpicious, (Lat.) Lucky, Happy.

Auftere, (Lat.) Sour, Crabbed, Stern.

Auftral, (Lat.) belonging to the South.

Authentick, of juft or good Authority.

Author, (Lat.) the Inventor, Contriver, or Maker of a thing; the Writer of a Book; the Head of a Party or Faction.

Authority, (Lat.) Power, Rule, Credit, Intereft; alfo a Paffage of a Book quoted.

Autograph, (Gr.) of the Author's own Writing; One's peculiar Hand-writing.

Automa, (Gr.) a felf moving Inftrument or Engine, as Clock, Watch, &c.

Autopfy, an ocular Infpection,

E

on, or seeing a thing with a Man's own Eyes.

Avulsion, (Lat.) a pulling away from.

Awkward, untoward, unhandy.

Awmbry, a Cupboard for Victuals.

Aux, the same with *Apsis*, which see.

Auxiliary, helpful, that comes to aid or assist.

Axioms, are common self evident Principles; which are so clear in themselves, that they are not capable of being made clearer by any kind of Proof; but which all will easily admit of, as soon as they understand the Terms of such Principles or Propositions.

Axis of the *World*, is an imaginary Line drawn from one Pole to the other.

Axis of a *Figure*, is a streight Line conceived to pass from the Vertex or Top to the Base. In a Circle or Sphere from one Side to the other through the Center; and is the same with *Diameter*.

Aye, always. *Spencer*.

Azimuths, are great Circles of the Heavens intersecting one another in the Zenith and Nadir; and consequently are at Right-angles to the Horizon.

Azure, in Heraldry, signifies a blew Colour in the Coats of all Persons under the Degree of a Baron; but in Noblemen 'tis called *Saphir*, and in those of Soverign Princes, Jupiter: in Engraving, 'tis expressed by Horizontal Lines thus.

B.

Baalim, the Plural Number of *Baal* or *Bel*, a God of the *Phœnicians*, and *Samaritans*.

Baanites, Christian Hereticks, the Followers of one *Baanes*, who taught the Errors of the *Manicheans* in the ninth Century.

Bacchanals, drunken Feasts, or Revels of *Bacchus*.

Bacchius, is a Foot in Latin Verse consisting of 3 Syllables, the first short, and the 2 last long.

Bacciferous, are such Plants or Trees as bear Berries.

Baccivorous Animals, are such as live upon Berries.

Back-board, Sea Term, behind the Ship.

Back Staff, a Sea Instrument to take the Sun's Altitude with.

Baculometry, is the Art of measuring Distances by two or more Staves.

Badger, one that buys Victuals in one Place, in order to sell it at another for Gain; also an Animal.

Baga-

Bagatel, a Toy or Trifle.

Bagnio, an Hot-house for Bathing and Sweating.

Bagnolenses, a sort of Christian Hereticks who followed the Errors of the *Manicheans*; they rejected the Old Testament and Part of the New; they maintained that God foresaw nothing of himself, and that the World had no Beginning.

Bail, (Fr.) in Law, is the freeing or setting at Liberty one Arrested or Imprisoned upon Action either Civil or Criminal, under Surety taken for his Appearance at a Day and Place assigned. The Word Baily, from the (Fr.) Bailler to deliver or commit, originally signifyed the Person to whom an Authority and Trust was committed within such a District.

Bails, Hoops to bear up the Tilt of a Boat.

Bailiffs Errant, are Persons appointed by the Sheriff to go about the Country to execute Writs, to summon to the Country Sessions; Assises, &c.

Bailiwick, was the whole District, within which the Trust of a Bailiwick was to be executed. A whole County was so called in respect of the Sheriff; a whole Barony in respect of the Lord or Baron; a Hundred in respect of the chief Constable; a Manor in respect of the Steward, &c.

Balcony, (Fr.) A Frame before the Window of a House.

Balderdash, a Mingle-mangle, a confus'd Discourse.

Bale, Grief, Misery. *Spencer*.

Bale, a Pack, as of Cloth, Silk, Books.

Ballance, a Pair of Scales; also a Term in Merchant's Accounts, when the Reckoning between the Debtor and Creditor is even; also one of the 12 Signs of the *Zodiack* in *Latin Libra*.

Ballast, Sand or Gravel laid in the Ship's Hold, to make her Sail upright.

Ballista, a Warlike Engine the Ancients used to fling Stones with.

Balloting, a kind of casting Lots, or electing by Balls.

Balluster, is the lateral Part of the Scrol in the *Capital* of the *Ionisk* Column; also a little Pillar.

Ballustrade, a Row of Ballusters.

Balneary, a Bathing Place.

Balneator, one that keeps a Bath or Stew.

Balneum, a Word frequently used in Chymistry; it properly signifies a Vessel of Water, in which the *Body* or *Cucurbit*, containing any Matter to be distilled, is placed; so that the Water heating, may heat the Cucurbit gently and by degrees; and this way of Distillation they call *Balneum Mariæ*.

Balneum vaporosum, in Chymistry, is when the Vessel

E 2   con-

containing the Matter to be distilled, is heated by the Vapour or Steam of hot boiling Water.

Balsamick, having the Quality of Balsam.

Balsame, (Lat.) the Juice of the Balm Tree; 'tis us'd also to signify sundry Compositions.

Bandage, (Fr.) a binding up; also Linnen Cloath fitted for binding up Wounds, Sores, &c.

Banded, Confederated. *Milton.*

Banditti, Outlaw'd, Persons turn'd Robbers, Highway-men.

Bandy, to tofs; also to debate or canvafs; also to gather in a Faction.

Bank, in Law, the Bench or Seat of Judgment; also a Place where there is a great Sum of Money let out to Use, returned by Exchange, or otherwise difpofed by Profit.

Banker, a Trader in Money, or one that gives Bills to receive Money from Place to Place.

Bankrupt, one that hath confumed his Eftate, or is run out in his Trade.

Bann, a Publick Proclamation.

Bannians, *Indian* Merchants; they have a peculiar Religion, and are of three forts.

Banner, (Fr.) a Standard or Enfign.

Baptifm, (Gr.) fignifies Wafhing; also a Sacrament of Divine Appoint.

Barb, a *Barbary* Horfe.

Barbara, a technical Word, each of whofe Syllables are prefix'd before the Propofitions of a Categorical Syllogifm in the firft Mood and firft Figure; denoting the Univerfality and Affirmation of the Propofitions.

Barbarifm, (Gr.) a Fault in Pronunciation, a Rudenefs of Behaviour.

Barbarous, Rude, Cruel, Savage.

Barbed, bearded like a Fifh Hook.

Bardefanifts, Chriftian Hereticks, the Followers of *Bardefanes*, who followed the Errors of the *Valentinians*, and held that the Doctrine of the Refurrection was falfe.

Bards, Poets among the ancient *Britains* and *Gauls.*

Barm, Yeft, the Head of Beer or Ale.

Barnacle, a fort of Curb for a Horfe; also a foland Goofe.

Baroco, a technical Word, expreffing a Syllogiftick Mood in Logick; wherein the firft Propofition is an univerfal Affirmative, and the other 2 particular Negatives.

Barometer, is an Inftrument for eftimating the Minute Variations of the Weight and Preffure of the Air.

Baron, a Degree of Nobility next to a Vifcount.

Baron and *Femme*, Law Term for a Man and his Wife. *Baronet*,

Baronet, the lowest Degree of Honour Hereditary, founded by King *James* I.

Baroscope, the same with Barometer, which see.

Barrack, a Hut for Souldiers to lodge in, to shelter themselves from bad Weather.

Barrel, an *English* Measure of Capacity for Wine, containing 31½ Gallons, or 7276½ Solid Inches.

Barretor, (Fr.) in Law, is a Wrangler, a Stirrer up, or Maintainer of Quarrels.

Barricado, (Sp.) an hasty Defence of empty Barrels, and such like Vessels fill'd with Earth, against an Enemy's Shot or Assault.

Barrier, (Fr) a Boundary or Defence.

Barrister, a Pleader at the Bar, a Lawyer.

Barrow, a little Hill or Mount of Earth.

Barules, Christian Hereticks, who said that the Son of God had onely a Phantom of a Body.

Barry, a Term in Heraldry, when an Escutcheon is divided *Barr-ways* into an even Number of Partitions; 'tis expressed by this Word *Barry*, and the Number of Pieces is to be specified.

Barry-Bendy, is when an Escutcheon is divided evenly both *Bar* and Bendways, as thus, *Barry, Bendy, Argent* and *Sable*.

Barry-Pily, is when a Coat is thus divided, it is to be blazon'd *Barry-Pily* of Eight Pieces.

Barter, to truck, to change one Commodity for another.

Barton, a Coop or Place for Poultry.

Baryotony, a Difficulty in Speaking.

Base, the Bottom of any Figure.

Bass, (Fr.) Low, Shallow Mean.

Basselred, a Dagger or Woodknife.

Bastion, in Fortification, is a Mass of Earth raised on the Angles of the Polygon, and consists of two Faces, two Flanks and a *Gorge*.

Battalion, is a Body of Infantry of 7 or 800 Men, whereof ⅓ are commonly Musqueteers, posted on the Wings, and the rest Pike Men, posted in the Middle; but now there are few or no Pikes.

Battery, in Fortification, is a Place raised on purpose to

E 3   place

place Cannon upon, thence to fire upon the Enemy.

Bafilick, (Gr.) Kingly, Royal ; Alfo a Magnificent Church.

Bafilisk, a Serpent called a Cockatrice.

Battlements, the Turrets of Houfes built flat.

Battology, is a vain and foolifh Repetition of the fame Words over and over again in any Difcourfe ; the Word comes from one *Battus*, who was very Guilty of this Fault.

Battoon, in Heraldry, fignifies a fourth Part of a *Bend Sinifter* ; it is the ufual Mark of Illegitimacy, and is always born *Couped* or cut off after this Manner.

Baulk, to crofs, to difappoint.

Bay, an Arm of the Sea coming up into the Land.

Beacons, are Fires maintain'd on Sea Coafts to prevent Shipwracks, and give Notice of Invafions, &c.

Beadle, in Law, fignifies a Meffenger or an Aparitor of a Court, that cites Men to the Court to appear and anfwer ; alfo an Officer belonging to the Univerfity.

Bearing, in Navigation, is the Point of the Compafs that one Place bears or ftands off from another.

Beatitude, (Lat.) Bleffednefs, Happinefs, Profperity.

Becalm'd, is when the Water is fo very fmooth, that the Ship has fcarce any Motion, or moves but flowly.

Bechicks, are Medicines good againft a Cough.

Bedell, (Sax.) a Cryer, or one that Publifhes a thing.

Begirt, encompaffed. *Milton.*

Beguards, and *Beguines*, a fort of Hereticks who appeared in *Germany* in the 13th Age of Chriftianity. They believed that Man might be as perfect in this Life as he fhall be in Heaven ; That every Intellectual Nature is of its felf Happy, without the Succour of Grace ; And that he who is in the State of Perfection, ought to perform no good Works.

Behefts, Orders, Commands, Meffages.

Behight, called. *Spencer.*

Bekah, a Jewifh Coin worth 1 s. 1 *Far.* and $\frac{11}{16}$ Decimal Parts, being reduced to our Money.

Belage, to faften any running Rope.

Belated, benighted. *Milton.*

Belay, to way-lay, or lay wait for ; alfo at Sea, to make faft the Ropes in their proper Places.

Belial, (Heb.) Wicked, Unprofitable ; alfo the Devil.

Bellive

Belive; quickly. *Spencer.*

Bellibone, or *Bonnibel*, a fair Maid. *Spencer.*

Bellicofe, (Lat.) Warlike, Valiant in Arms.

Bellipotent, Mighty or Powerful in Wars.

Bellona, a falfe Divinity among the Pagans, being reputed to be the Goddefs of War.

Belluine, (Lat.) of or belonging to Beafts.

Belte, a Girdle. *Spencer.*

Belvidere, (Ital.) Pleafant to behold; alfo the Name of the *Pope's Palace* in *Rome.*

Bend, one of the eight Honourable Ordinaries in Heraldry, containing ⅕ when Uncharged, but when Charged ⅓ Part of the Efcutcheon.

To *Bend*, at Sea, is to make faft, as to *bend* the Cable, is to make it faft to the Ring of the Anchor.

Bendlet, is ⅙ of the Shield.

Bends, the outmoft Timbers of a Ship's Side, on which Men fet their Feet in climbing up.

Beneaped, a Ship is *beneaped*, when the Water does not flow high enough to bring the Ship off the Ground.

Benediction, Praifing of God; alfo the Blefling given by a Parent to his Children.

Benefactor, (Lat.) a Doer of Good Offices, a Patron.

Benefice, originally fignify'd Funds given to Souldiers for a Reward of their Services; but it afterwards paffed into the Church, wherein the like Funds were given for the Subfiftence of the Clergy; an Ecclefiaftical Living.

Beneficence, a Virtue whereby Men delight to do Good to others, and to confer Benefits upon them.

Beneficial, Profitable, Advantagious.

Benempt, named. *Spencer.*

Benevolence, (Lat.) Good Will; that fort of Love which difpofes one Man to confer a Kindnefs upon another.

Benevolent, bearing good Will, wifhing well.

Benign, Favourable, ufually apply'd to the Influences of the Stars.

Bent, inclined. *Milton.*

Bequeath, to leave by laft Will.

Bequeft, a Legacy.

Bereave, to deprive.

Bereft, for bereav'd, taken away, depriv'd.

Berme, in Fortification, is a Space of Ground left at the Foot of the *Rampart*, on the Side next the Country, defigned to receive the Ruins of the *Rampart*, to prevent its filling up the *Fofs.*

Bernardins, Monks of the Order of *Bernard* a *Cafterci-an.*

Bes, a Weight or Coin among the *Romans*, containing ⅔ of the *As*, or 8 Ounces; alfo one of their fquare Mea-

E 4   fure

sures of one *English* Rod and 26 Square Poles.

Beseech, to entreat, humbly to pray.

Besestein, an Exchange for Merchants with the *Turks* and *Persians*.

Bespatter, to dash with Dirt, to Defame.

Bespren, besprinkled. *Spencer*.

Bestad, disposed, ordered. *Spencer*.

Bestail, (Fr.) Law-Term, all sort of Beasts or Cattel.

Bestial, Beastly, Brutish.

Betight, happened. *Spencer*.

Betroth, (Dutch) to give or receive a Promise of Marriage.

Bett, to lay Wagers on either Side in Gaming.

Bett, better. *Spencer*.

Bettee, an Instrument to break open Doors.

Beverage, (Fr.) a mingled Drink.

Bevile, in Heraldry, signifies broken, or opening like a Carpenter's Rule; thus he beareth *Argent* a chief *Bevile* *Vert*.

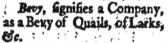

Bevy, signifies a Company, as a Bevy of Quails, of Larks, &c.

Bewildred, Scared or Frighted; also that has lost his Way.

Bewray, to befoul or daub with Ordure; also to reveal or discover a Secret.

Bezants, a Term in Heraldry for round Plates of Gold without any Stamp, frequently born in Coats of Arms.

Bezel or *Bezil*, the upper Part of the Collet of a Ring, that fastens and encompasses the Stone.

Bezoardick Remedies, cordial Medicines against Poison or infectious Diseases.

Bias, (Fr.) a Weight fix'd on one Side of a Bowl, turning the Course of the Bowl that way towards which the Bias looks.

Bible, (Gr.) i. e. Book, the Holy Scriptures are so called by way of Excellency.

Bibliographer, (Gr.) a Writer of Books.

Bibliopolist, (Gr.) a Bookseller.

Bibliotheque, (Gr.) a Library, a Place where Books are kept, also the Books themselves.

Bicipitan, that hath two Heads or Tops.

Bickering, Tilting, or Skirmishing; Quarrel, Dispute.

Bicornous, that hath two Horns, Forked.

Bidental, (Lat.) a Place where they used to Sacrifice Sheep, for its having been blasted with Lightening; whatsoever is struck with Lightening: Also any Instrument with two Teeth, a Fork.

Biennial, (Lat.) of two Years continuance, 2 Years old.

Bisa-

Bifarious, two Fold, or that may be taken two Ways.

Biformed, having two Shapes.

Bigamy, (Gr.) the Marriage of two Wives.

Biggin, a sort of Linnen Cap for a young Child.

Bigot, (Fr.) an Hypocrite; also one that obstinately adheres to his own Opinions and Humour.

Bigottery, Hypocrisy; also a stiff Adherence to a Man's own Opinions and Humours.

Bilancis deferendis, a Writ directed to a Corporation for carrying of Weights to a particular Haven.

Bilboes, a sort of Punishment at Sea.

Bildged, so a Ship is said to be, when she has struck off some of her Timber on a Rock or Anchor, and thereby leaks.

Bile, is a Liquor partly Sulphureous, partly Saline, separated from the Blood of Animals in the Liver; in *English* it is called Gall.

Bilinguis, (Lat.) double-tongued. A Jury made up of partly *English,* partly Foreigners.

Bilious, full of Bile or Choler, Cholerick.

Bilk, to disappoint, to deceive, to bubble.

Bill, an Edge-tool of Husbandmen. It hath many other Significations.

Billet, a Log of Wood cut for Fewel; also a Letter or Note folded up; also a Ticket for quartering Souldiers.

In Hraldry 'tis a common Bearing of this Form, *Argent Billette,* a Cross engrailed *Gules.*

Billet-doux, (Fr.) a short Love Letter.

Billow, a Surge of the Sea, a great rolling Wave.

Binocle, (Fr.) a double Telescope, to see Objects with both Eyes together.

Binomial, a Term in *Algebra,* expressing a Quantity divided into two Parts, as $a + b.$

Biolychnium, the vital Flame, natural Heat, or Life of Animals.

Biovac, a Night Guard performed by the whole Army, when there is any Apprehension of Danger.

Bipartient, that divides into two Parts: A Number is so call'd, when it divides another into two, without a Remainder.

Bipartition, a Division of any thing into two Parts.

Bipatent, open on both Sides.

Biquadrate, the fourth Power in *Algebra,* arising from the Multiplication of a Square Number or Quantity by it self.

Biquintile, a new Aspect invented by *Kepler,* consisting of $\frac{2}{5}$ of the whole Circle, or $144°.$

Birth

Birth, Sea Term, convenient Sea Room for Ships at Anchor or under Sail; Also a convenient Place to moor a Ship in; Also a Place Aboard for a Mess to put their Chests.

Bishop, from the *Saxon Bi-scop*, and this from the *Greek*, an Overseer.

Bismuth, Tin-glass, is a Mettallick Matter, White, Smooth, Sulphureous like to Tin, but hard, sharp, brittle, disposed into Facets or shining Scales, as Pieces of Glass, whence its Name.

Bissect, (Lat.) to cut or divide any thing, as a Line or Angle, into two equal Parts.

Bissection, a Division of any thing into two equal Parts.

Bissegment, one of the Parts of a Line divided into two equal Halves.

Bissextile, Leap-Year, which happens every fourth Year; for once in every four Years, a whole Day is added, to make up the odd 6 Hours, whereby the Course of the Sun yearly exceeds 365 Days, being inserted next after the 24th of *February*.

Bittacle, a Timber Frame where the Compass stands before the Steer's-Man.

Bitumen, (Lat.) Brimstone; also a kind of Clay or Slime, naturally clammy like Pitch.

Bituminous, full of Brimstone or unctuous Clay.

Bitts, two main Pieces of Timber, to which the Cable is fastened when she rides at Anchor.

Bivalve, a Term used in natural History for such shell Fishes as have two Shels; also for the Seed Pods of such Plants, as open all their whole Length to discharge their Seeds, as Beans.

Biventral, with two Bellies.

Black-rod, the Usher of the Order of the Garter, so called from his Black Rod with a Golden Lyon at Top. He also attends the Queen's Chamber, and the House of Lords in Parliament.

Blanch, (Fr.) to Whiten, to take the Skins off Almonds, Beans, &c.

Blandiloquence, (Lat.) fair and flattering Speech, courteous Language, Complement.

Blandishment, a Complement, a Cajole, a thing pleasantly done or spoken.

Blank, Pale, Wan, out of Countenance.

Blank Verse, is Verse without Rime.

Blasphemy, (Gr.) Cursing and Swearing, vile reproachful Language, tending to the Dishonour of God, or to the Hurt of any Man's Name or Credit.

Blaze, to publish, divulge, or spread abroad.

Blazon, to express or display the Parts of a Coat of Arms in proper Colours and Metals. Also to set forth one's good or ill Qualities.

Blemish

B'emiſh, a Stain in a Man's Reputation and Honour.

Blend, to mix or mingle together.

Blinkard, one that winks or twinkles with his Eyes.

Blith, (Brit.) that is, yielding Milk; ſignifies Pleaſant, Jocund, Merry.

Bloccade, is the encompaſſing a Town or Place with armed Troops, ſo as 'tis impoſſible to relieve it; ſo that it muſt either be Starved, or Surrender.

Blood-wit, a Fine paid for ſhedding Blood, granted in ſome Charters.

Bluff-headed, ſo a Ship is ſaid to be that hath a ſmall Rake forward on, and her Stern too ſtraight up.

Board and Board, a Term uſed when two Ships come ſo near as to touch one another.

Boat-ſwain, is an Officer aboard a Ship, who hath Charge of all her Rigging, Ropes, Cables, Anchors, Colours, Pendants.

Bocardo, the fifth Mood of the third Figure in Logick, in which the Middlemoſt Propoſition is an univerſal Affirmatives, the Firſt and Laſt particular Negatives.

Body, in Geometry, is that which hath three Dimenſions, as Length, Breadth and Thickneſs; and it is oppoſed to Body as it is a Term in natural Philoſophy, in as much as the Firſt is Penetrable, and the Second Impenetrable.

Boggle, to waver, or be uncertain, to ſcruple.

Bolt-rope, is that Rope into which the Sail of a Ship is fix'd or faſtened.

Bolt-ſprit, or *Bow-ſprit*, the Maſt in the Head of a Ship that ſtoops forwards, of the ſame Length and Thickneſs with the Fore-maſt.

Bombs, are hollow Balls of Iron, which are charged with Powder, and ſometimes with Nails and Pieces of Iron, to be ſhot into beſieged Towns.

Bombard, is to ſhoot Bombs out of Mortars into Towns, &c.

Bonaſians, certain Hereticks that appeared in the fourth Age of Chriſtianity, who held that *Jeſus Chriſt* is the Son of God only by Adoption.

Bongomiles, or *Bogomiles*, certain Hereticks, ſo called from *Bogomilus* a Monk; they called the Churches the Devil's Temples, and made no Account of the Holy Sacrament; they believed that God had a Human Form; and that they could conceive and bring forth the Word as, well as the bleſſed Virgin, &c

Bongrace, to Mariners, is a Frame of old Ropes or Juncks of Cables, laid out at the Bows, Stems and Sides of Ships ſailing in cold Latitudes, to preſerve them from Damage of great Flakes of Ice.

Bonket, Liveries, Gray Coats. *Spencer*.

Bonne-

Bonne mine, (Fr.) a good Aspect or Countenance.

Bonnets, small Sails set upon the Courses, or Main-Sail and Fore-Sail.

Boom, a long Pole used on Ship-board, to spread out the Clew of the Studding Sail; also a Cable stretched athwart the Mouth of a River or Harbour, with Yards, Top-masts, Batling, or Spars of Wood, &c. lash'd to it, to prevent an Enemy's entring in.

Boon, (old Word) a Request, a Favour.

Boot, Advantage, Profit.

Bootes, a Northern Constellation in the Heavens.

Borborites, a Sect of Gnosticks, who, besides the Errors of that Heresy, deny'd the last Judgment.

Borborygm, a rumbling Noise in the Guts.

Bordel, (Sax.) a small Cottage; but now it signifies a Stews or Bawdy-house.

Bordure, a Term in Heraldry for an ancient Difference, whereby several Families of the same Name, or Persons, are distinguished from one another; 'tis a

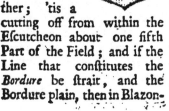

cutting off from within the Escutcheon about one fifth Part of the Field; and if the Line that constitutes the *Bordure* be strait, and the Bordure plain, then in Blazon-

ing you only name the Colour of the Bordure, as here he beareth *Gules a Bordure or,* without saying a plain Bordure.

Bordures, are sometimes *Engrailed, Gobonated, Invected, Indented, Counter Compony, Vairy, Checky.*

Boreal, belonging to the North, Northern.

Borough, a Corporate Town that is not a City.

Borrell, a plain rude Fellow, a Boor. *Spencer.*

Boscage, a Grove, a Thicket; in Painting, a Picture representing much Wood and Trees.

Bosen, see *Boat-swain.*

Bosphorous, (in Geography) is a long narrow Sea running in between two Lands, by which two Continents are separated.

Botqnick or *Botanical,* (Gr.) belonging to Herbs or Plants.

Botanist, an Herbarist, or one Skilful in Plants and Herbs.

Botany, is that part of *Natural History* which teaches rightly to distinguish the several kinds and subordinate Species of *Plants, Trees, Shrubs,* &c.

Bottomry, borrowing Money on a Ship, and lending Money on Bottomry, is to lend Money to the Master of a Ship, to be pay'd with Interest at 40 or 50 *per Cent.* at the Ship's safe Return, otherways the Money is all lost.

Bottony,

Bottony, the Herald's Term for a Cross of this Figure. *Argent a Cross Bottony* Sable.

Boundary, that which sets out the Limits or Bounds of a Country.

Bourgeon, (Fr.) to bud, or shoot.

Boutefeu, a wilful Firer of Houses; an Incendiary, or Sower of Dissension.

Bow of a Ship, is the broadest Part of a Ship before.

Bower, any Anchor carried at the Bow of a Ship, is called her *Bower*.

Bowge, a Rope fastened to the Middle of the Sail, to make it stand closer by the Wind.

Bowse, a Sea Term, signifying as much as hale or pull.

Bow-sprit, vid. *Bolt-sprit*.

Bowyer, a Maker or Seller of Bows and Arrows.

Box and Needle, is a small Compass apply'd to a *Theodolite*, and used in Surveying.

Braced, the Herald's Term for the intermingling of 3 *Chevronells* thus, *Azure a Chief or*, and three *Chevronells* braced in the Base of the *Escutcheon*.

Braces, are Ropes belonging to all the Yards of a Ship except the Missen, two to each Yard.

Brachial, (Lat.) belonging to the Arm.

Brachiolum, (Lat.) a little Arm; also a kind of Index or Label put upon Astrolabes, and other Projections of the Sphere.

Brachygraphy, (Gr.) is the Art of short Hand.

Brachylogy, (Gr.) a shortness of Speech.

Brackets, in a Ship, are small Knees serving to support the Galleries; also the Timbers that support the Gratings in the Head.

Brade, broad. *Spencer*.

Bragadocio, a coined Word with us for a Coward or bragging Fellow.

Brails, are small Ropes belonging to the two Courses and the Mizen, whose use is, when the Sail is furled across, to hale up its Bunt, that it may the more readily be taken up or let fall.

Brait, a rough Diamond.

Bramines, Philosophers in *India* that live on Herbs and Fruits, skilful in Astrology.

Brancher, a young Hawk or other Bird, that begins to fly from Branch to Branch.

Brandish, (Fr.) to make shine with gently shaking or moving.

Bravado, (Fr. Sp.) a shew of Challenge, or of Daring.

Breach, (in Fortification) is the Ruins made in any Part of the Works of a Town.

Break Bulk, to take Part of a Ship's Cargo out.

Break Ground, to open the Trenches.

Breast-fast, is a Rope fastened to some Part of a Ship forward on, to keep her Head fast to a Wharf, or the like.

Breast-Hooks, in a Ship, are the compassing Timbers before.

Breast-Ropes, in a Ship, are those which fasten the Parrels to the Yards.

Breast-Work, the same with Parapet, which see.

Breechings, Ropes by which the Guns are lash'd fast, or fastened to the Ship's Sides.

Breme, Chill, Bitter, Rageing. *Spencer*.

Breve, a Writ directed to the Chancellour or Judges, &c. so call'd from its shortness; Also a Musical Note containing two *Semibreves*, four *Minims*, and eight *Crotchets*, &c.

Breviary, an Abridgment or compendious Draught; a short Collection.

Breviate, a short Extract, or Copy of a Process, Deed, or Writing.

Brevier, a Printing Letter, one Degree smaller than *Long-Primmer*.

Breviloquence, (Lat.) a short way of speaking.

Brevity, (Lat.) Shortness, Conciseness.

Brigade, an Army is divided into *Brigades* of Horse, and *Brigades* of Foot; a *Brigade* of Horse is a Body of eight or ten Squadrons; a *Brigade* of Foot consists of four, five, or six Battalions.

Brigandine, an ancient kind of Armour, with many Plates and Joints, like a Coat of Mail.

Brigantine, (Fr.) a small light Vessel for Sea.

Brigue, Quarrel, Dispute.

Brilliant, Glittering, giving a sparkling Light.

Broker, a Buyer or Seller of Goods for others.

Brokerage, or *Brokage*, the Wages of a Broker.

Bronchotomy, (Gr.) is the Section of the Wine-pipe in a membranous Part betwixt two of the Rings.

Brooming of a Ship, is the washing or burning off all the Filth she has contracted on her Sides.

Brownists, an Heretick Sect broached in *England* by one *Robert Brown* in 1583.

Brumal,

Brumal, belonging to Winter.

Brutal, or *Brutish*, Irrational, Senseless.

Buccaneers, the ungoverned Rabble in *Jemaica* are so called ; Also a Pirate.

Buccellation, (Lat.) in Chymistry, is a dividing into Gobbets.

Buccinate, (Lat.) to blow a Trumpet.

Bucolicks, (Gr.) are Pastoral Songs, or Poems.

Buffoon, (Fr.) a Jester, or one that lives by making others Merry.

Buffoonery, Jesting.

Buggery, is a Copulation of Man or Woman with Brute Beasts ; or of one Man with another.

Bulbus, a Term in Botany, is any Root that is round, and wrapped with many Skins or Coats, as Onions.

Bulimy, (Gr.) an Ox-like Appetite.

Bulk-Heads, in a Ship, are Partitions made athwart a Ship with Boards, whereby one Part is divided from another.

Bull, properly signifies a Golden Ornament or Jewel for Children, hollow within, made like a Heart, and used to be hung about their Necks ; and hence the Briefs or Mandates of the Pope are called Bulls, from the Lead, and sometimes Golden Seal affixed thereto.

Bullion, Gold or Silver in the Mass, before it is Coined

Bulwark, an old Term for Rampart, which see.

Bunt of a Sail, is the Middle Part of it, which is purposely formed into a kind of Bag or Cavity, that the Sails may receive the more Wind ; it is mostly used in Topsails.

Bunt Lines, are small Ropes in a Ship, made fast to the Bottom of the Sails.

Burglary, is a Felonious entering into another Man's House, with an Intent to steal something.

Burlesque, (Ital.) Merry ; Pleasant ; also a Merry or Drollish sort of Poetry, or a mock Poetry.

Burnish, to make bright, to polish.

Burse, an Exchange for Merchants to meet in.

Burton, in a Ship, is a small Tackle to be fastened any where at Pleasure, consisting of two single Pullies.

Bushel, a dry Measure of 4 Pecks Land, and 5 Water Measure.

Bushet, little Bush. *Spencer.*

Buskins, a sort of Pumps worn by Tragedians.

Bust, a Statue representing only Head, Breast and Shoulders of a human Body.

Butt, is the End of any Plank which joyns to another

on

on the Outside of the Ship under Water.

Buttock, of a Ship, is that Part of her which is her Breadth right aftern from her Tack upwards.

Buttress, an Arch, or Mass of Stone, to bear up a Wall.

Buxome, Flexible; also Merry, Wanton, Jolly.

Buzzar, or *Bazar*, a Market Place among the *Persians*.

By, or *Bye*, (Danish) an Habitation or Place of Abode. 'Tis yet retain'd in the End of Names of Places, as *Appleby*, *Danby*, &c.

Bylander, a small swift sailing Vessel, so called from its coasting as it were by Land.

C.

Cab, a Jewish Measure of Capacity for things Liquid, containing 3 Pints and 10 solid Inches Wine Measure.

Cab, a Jewish Measure of Capacity for things dry, containing 2½ Pints, and 120 Decimal Parts of a solid Inch of our *English* Corn Measure.

Cabal, (Fr.) a secret Science which the Hebrew Rabbins pretend to, by which they unfold all the Mysteries in Divinity, and expound the Scripture ; it is also used for a Society of Men united by the same Interest, taken oftner in a bad Sense than a good one.

Caballine, (Lat.) belonging to Horses.

Caballine Aloes, is that Aloes which Farriers use.

Cable of a Ship, is a great Rope, which being fastened to the Anchor, holds the Ship when she rides.

Cabossed, (Span.) in *Heraldry*, is when a Beast's Head is cut off by a Section parallel to the Face.

Caburns in a Ship, are Lines used to bind Cables withal.

Cacatoria Febris, is an intermittent Fever, accompanied with a violent Purging.

Cachexy, (Gr.) an ill Habit of the Body, proceeding from a bad Disposition of the Fluids and Humours.

Cachinnation, (Lat.) loud or immoderate Laughter.

Cacochymy, (Gr.) ill Juice, or ill Blood.

Cadaverous, of a dead Body, or Carcass.

Cadelesher, a chief Magistrate or Governour in *Turkey*, whereof there are only two, viz. those of *Natolia* and *Greece*.

Cadence, (Lat.) a just fall of the Tone or Voice in a Sentence.

Cadent, i. e. Falling, so a Planet is said to be, when 'tis in a Sign opposite to that of its Exaltation.

Cadet, or *Cadee*, (Fr.) a younger Brother, or a Volunteer in the Army, on his own Charge.

Cainites, Christian Hereticks, a Sect of the *Gnosticks*,

fo called from *Cain*, who, according to them, was formed by a Celeftial and Almighty Power, and *Abel* was made but by a weak one.

Cæcity, (Lat.) Blindneſs.

Cæfarian Section, is by cutting to take a Child out of the Mother's Womb.

Caimacan, an Officer of great Dignity among the *Turks*.

Cajole, to footh up, inveigle, or beguile.

Caiſſon, in Fortification, is a Cheft of Wood holding four or fix Bombs, fometimes filled only with Powder, and buried by the Befieged under Ground, to blow up a Work which the Befiegers are like to be Mafters of.

Caitiff, a miferable Wretch, a forry Fellow.

Calamina, a Mineral, or Earth digg'd out of the Ground, and mixed with Copper to make it Yellow.

Calamity, (Lat.) Mifery, Trouble, Misfortune.

Calufticks, purging Medicines.

Calcation, (Lat.) a treading or ftamping.

Calcination, is the Solution of a mixed Body into Powder by Fire, or any other corrofive things.

Calcin'd, reduced to Powder by Fire or Corrofives.

Calculation, is cafting of Accounts, Reckoning; and is either Algebraick or Numerical.

Calefaction, (Lat.) a Heating or Warming.

Calends, (Gr.) the *Romans* called the firft Day of each Month by this Name.

Calender or *Almanack*, is a Political Diftribution of Time, accomodated to Ufe, and taken from the Motions of the Heavenly Bodies.

Calenture, a burning Fever.

Caliber, a Term in Gunnery, fignifying the Diameter or Wideneſs of the Bore of a Piece of Ordnance.

Calidity, (Lat.) Warmneſs or Heat.

Caligation, (Lat.) Dimneſs of Sight, Blindneſs.

Callid, (Lat.) Crafty, Cunning.

Calliope, the firft of the nine Mufes, that prefides over Harmony, Heroick Poetry, and Divine Hymns.

Callipers, Compaſſes with crooked Legs, to meafure the Diameters of things round.

Callous, hard, brawny.

Callow, unfledg'd, bare, without Feathers.

Calvinifts, the Followers of *Calvin*.

Calumniate, to accufe falfly, to detract.

Calumny, (Lat.) falfe Accufation, Detraction.

Calx, is that Powder which any Body is reduc'd to by Calcination; alfo a Bone in the Foot.

Camail, (Fr.) a Bifhop's purple Ornament worn over the Rochet.

Campaign, (Fr.) a plain Field; alfo that time of the Year

Year during which the Armies are in the Field, or in Service.

Campatou, a sort of Christian Hereticks, who followed the Doctrine of the *Donatists* and *Circumcellians* ; this Sect arose in the fourth Century.

Canal, a Chanel for Water or other Fluids to run in or through.

Cancel, (Lat.) to rase, to blot out.

Cancer, a Constellation, or one of the 12 Signs of the *Zodiack* so called.

Candid, (Lat.) White ; also Innocent, Sincere.

Candidates, (Lat.) are those who stand for any Place or Preferment. They were so called by the *Romans*, from the white Garment they were obliged to wear, during the two Years of their solliciting for the Place.

Candisation, the Candying or Crystallizing of Sugar, after it has been dissolv'd in Water, and purify'd.

Candlemass-Day, the Festival of the Purification of the blessed Virgin, *Feb.* 2. so called from the Consecrating of Candles that Day.

Candour, Whiteness ; also Innocency, Sincerity.

Canibals, a People of the *West-Indies* that feed on human Flesh.

Canicular, belonging to the Dog-Star.

Canine, belonging to, or like a Dog.

Canis Major, the greater Dog, is a Constellation drawn upon the Globe in that Form.

Canis minor, the lesser Dog, is a Constellation drawn upon the Globe in that Form.

Can-hooks, Iron Hooks made fast to the End of a Rope, whereby things weighty are help'd in and out of Ships.

Canon, (Gr.) properly a Rule or Line to make any thing streight, or try the Streightness of it by ; hence Laws or Decrees for Church Government are called Canons, and certain times of Prayer are called *Canonical* Hours.

Canonical, according to Rule, or Order, Authentick.

Canonical Hours, time appointed for Divine Service by Church-Canons.

Canonist, a Doctor or Professor of the Canon Law.

Canonize, to examine by Rule ; also to declare and pronounce one for a Saint.

Canopy, a Piece of Furniture of State, being a Coverture of Cloth of Gold or rich Stuff, fix'd over the Thrones of Princes.

Canorous, (Lat.) Loud, Shrill.

Canthus, the Angle or Corner of the Eye.

Canting, is a peculiar affected kind of Speech used by Beggars, Rogues, Gypsies, &c.

Canto, (Ital.) a Song ; also a Division in any Heroick Poem,

Poem, as Chapter and Section in Prose.

Canton, a Division or Part of a Country, in Form of a Province. In Heraldry 'tis an Ordinary consisting of two Lines, one drawn perpendicularly from the Chief, and the other so from the Side of the Escutcheon, and is always less than the Quarter of the Field. *Verbally*, it signifies to retire into a Quarter, to Fortify one's self in a Place.

Cantonize, to divide into Cantons or Quarters.

Canvass, to sift or examin a Business.

Capable, (Fr.) able, or fit to do any thing.

Capacitate, (Lat.) to make capable, or fit to do any thing.

Capacity, an aptness to contain or receive.

Cap-a-pe, from Head to Foot.

Caparison, a kind of Trappings or Furniture for a Horse. *Shakesp.*

Cape, is a Mountain or other high Place which runs out into the Sea farther than the rest of the Continent.

Capella, a Star of the first Magnitude in the left Shoulder of *Auriga*.

Caph, a Jewish Measure of Capacity for things Liquid, containing ½ of a Pint, and 15 Decimal Parts of a solid Inch, of our *English* Wine Measure.

Capillaments, are those small Threads or Hairs which grow upon the Top of a Flower and are adorned with little Knobs at the Top; also the little Fibres which compose the Nerves are called Capillaments.

Capillary, (Lat.) belonging to, or like Hair.

Capital, belonging to the Head; also worthy of Death; also the Ornament on the Top of a Column; also, in Fortification, the Line drawn from the Angle of the Gorge to the Flanked Angle.

Capitation, a Tax or Tribute paid by the Head.

Capitol, an ancient Citadel of *Rome*, so call'd, as some say, from the Head of one *Tolus*, that was there dug up.

Capitulate, to treat upon Terms, or make Articles.

Caponiere, in Fortification, is a Work sunk on the Glacis of a Place about 4 or 5 Foot deep.

Capouche, (Fr.) a Coul, Hood, or Cover for the Head.

Capouchines, a Religious Order of Friers, so called from their *Capouche*.

Caprichio, (Sp.) a Whimsy, or fantastical Humour.

Capricious, Humoursome, Fantastical, full of Whimsies.

Capricorn, one of the 12 Signs of the Zodiack, in the Form of a Goat, the 10th from *Aries*.

Capriole, (Fr.) a Caper in Dancing; also the Goat-leap in Horsemanship.

F 2   *Capstan*,

Capſtan, Main Capſtan is a great Piece of Timber in the Nature of a Windlaſs placed next behind the Main-maſt; its uſe is to weigh the Anchors, to hoiſe up or ſtrike down Top-maſts, to heave any weighty thing, or to ſtrain any Rope that requireth a mighty Force.

Capſtan Bars, are the Bars or Pieces of Wood that are put into the Capſtan-holes, to heave up any thing of Weight into the Ship, by the help of as many Men as can well ſtand at them.

Capſula Seminalis, in Botany, is the Caſe or Husk that holds any Plant.

Caption, (Lat.) a taking.

Captious, (Lat.) full of Craft, catching or taking hold of every little Occaſion to wrangle or ſquabble.

Captive, a Priſoner in War.

Captivity, Slavery, Bondage.

Capture, a Prize, a Booty; alſo a Taking, an Arreſt, a Siezure.

Capuchins, Friers of the Order of St. *Francis,* having their Name from the Cowl they wear.

Caput mortum, one of the Chymical Principles, and denotes that thick dry Matter which remains after Diſtillation of any thing.

Crack, a great *Portugueſe* Ship.

Carat, of Gold, is properly the Weight of one Scruple or four and twenty Grains; of Pearls, Diamonds, and other precious Stones, 'tis but four Grains.

Caravan, properly ſignifies a Body of Travellers or Merchants, that unite together in order to travel for their greater Safety into foreign Countries; but this Name is chiefly given to the *Mahometan* Pilgrims of *Mecca.*

Caravanſera, an Inn amongſt the *Turks* and *Perſians.*

Caravel, a light round Ship with a ſquare Poop, Rigg'd like a Galley, that ſails well, of about 120 or 140 Tuns Burthen.

Carbine, a Gun, of Size between a Piſtol and a Muſket; alſo a Horſeman with ſuch Arms.

Carbonado, a Steak broil'd on the Coals.

Carcaſs, a dead Body; alſo a ſort of Caſe, ſometimes all of Iron, with two or three Holes; ſometimes of Iron Hoops, cover'd over with pitch'd Canvas, fill'd with Granadoes, charg'd Barrels of Piſtolets, wrap'd in Tow, dipt in Oyl, and other Materials for firing Houſes. They are ſhot out of Mortar Pieces.

Carcellage, Priſon Fees.

Carceral, bolonging to Priſon.

Cardiacal, good for, or belonging to the Heart.

Cardinal, (Lat.) belonging to a Hinge; alſo a high Dignity in the Church of *Rome,* whereof there are 70 in Number.   *Cardinal*

Cardinal Points, are the East, West, North, or South.

Cardiognoſtick, (Gr.) a Knower of Hearts.

Careen, to refit, or trim, or mend a Ship upon the Water, which is done by bringing her down as much as poſſible on one Side, and ſupporting her by a lower Veſſel, whilſt the other Side is mended.

Careſs, to treat obligingly, or make much of.

Careſſes, (Fr.) Cheriſhings, great Expreſſions of Friend-ſhip and Endearment.

Cariere, the Ring or Cir-cle where they run with Hor-ſes; alſo their Courſe or full Speed.

Carking, Diſtracting, Per-plexing.

Carmelites, an Order of Monks founded by *Almericus* Biſhop of *Antioch*, A. D. 1122, at Mount *Carmel* in *Syria*.

Carnage, (Lat.) a Maſſacre, or great Slaughter.

Carnal, (Lat.) belonging to the Fleſh, Fleſhly, Senſu-al.

Carnality, (Lat.) Fleſhlyneſs.

Carnation, a Fleſh Colour; alſo a kind of Gilliflower. In *Painting*, the Parts of a Body that are drawn naked.

Carnaval, Shrove-tide, a Time of Mirth and Feaſting among Papiſts, continuing from *Twelfth-Day* till *Lent*.

Carnivorous, (Lat.) Fleſh-devouring, or feeding upon Fleſh.

Carnoſity, (Lat.) Fleſhineſs;

alſo a Piece of Fleſh growing in, and obſtructing any Paſ-ſage in the Body.

Carnous, Fleſhly, approach-ing the Nature of Fleſh.

Carouſe, (Fr.) hard Drink-ing; *Verbally*, to quaff, to drink large Draughts.

Carpocratians, the Follow-ers of *Carprocrates*, Hereticks that are ſaid to have denied the Divinity of Chriſt, and the Creation of the World by the ſupreme God, about A. C. 120.

Cartel, a Challenge to Duel; alſo an Agreement betwixt Parties at War, for Exchanging and Redeeming Priſoners.

Carteſian, a Follower of the deſervedly admir'd *Des Cartes*, the *French* Philoſopher.

Carthuſians, an Order of Monks founded by *Bruno* Canon of *Rheims*, in the Year 1100, who retired to a Place called *La Chartreuſe*, in *Dauphine*.

Cartiloge, (Lat.) a Griſtle, which is a middle Subſtance betwixt a Ligament and a Bone.

Cartilaginous, Griſtly.

Cartouche, (Fr.) is a Charge of Powder put into a Paper Caſe exactly fitted to the Muzzle of the Gun. It is u-ſually, tho' corruptly, called Cartrage.

Carucate, from the French, *Carrue* a Plough, or as much Arable Ground as in one Year could be tilled with one Plough.

Caruncle, a little Piece of Flesh, a Flesh Kernel.

Caryatides, an Order of Pillars in Architecture, in the Form of the Bodies of Women with their Arms cut off, and cloathed down to their Feet.

Cascabel, the Pummel, or hindermost round Knob at the Breech of a great Gun.

Cascade, (Ital.) a Fall of Waters, whether Natural or Artificial.

Case-mate, a Loop-hole in a Wall to shoot through; also a Vault of Mason's Work in the Flank of a Bastion next the Curtin, to fire on the Enemy; also a Well with its several Branches under Ground, in the Passage of the Bastion.

Casern, (Fr.) a little Building between the Rampart and Houses of a Fortified Town, for lodging the Soldiers of the Garrison.

Case-shot, small Bullets, Nails, Pieces of old Iron, &c. put into Cases, to be shot out of Murdering Pieces.

Cash, among the Merchants signifies ready Money.

Cashier, a Cash-keeper.

Caskets, small Strings of Sinnet, that in Furling make fast the Sails to the Yards.

Cassation, a making null or void.

Cassiopæa, a Nothern Constellation.

Castalian Spring, the Fountain *Hippocrene* where the Muses haunt.

Castellany, the Manour belonging to a Castle, the Extent of its Land and Jurisdiction.

Castigate, to Punish or Chastize.

Castrametation, (Lat.) the Art of Encamping an Army.

Castrate, (Lat.) to Geld, or cut out the Stones of an Animal; also to publish only a Part of an Author's Work.

Castration, (Lat.) Gelding.

Casual, (Lat.) happening by Chance.

Casualty, an unforeseen Accident.

Casuist, one that writes upon Cases of Conscience, or is well skill'd therein.

Catabaptist, one averse from, or that Abuses Baptism.

Catacatharticks, (Gr.) are those Medicines that purge downwards.

Catacausticks, the Science of reflected Sounds; also Curves form'd by Reflexion; thus, If an indefinite Number of Rays, issuing from any one Point, fall upon all the Points of a Curve, the Intersections of those reflex Rays, which are infinitely near one another, will form a Curve, which is called the *Catacaustick* of the former Curve.

Catachrestical, (Gr.) Abusive.

Catacresis, is a Trope in Rhetorick, whereby Liberty is

is given to the Writer or Speaker, upon the Account of his wanting a proper Word, to borrow the next or the likeft to the thing, to exprefs his Meaning by.

Cataclyfm, (Gr.) a Deluge or overflowing with Water; an Innundation.

Catacombs, are Grottoes about 3 Leagues from *Rome*, where the primitive Chriftians hid themfelves in time of Perfecution, and buried the Martyrs.

Catagmaticks, (Gr.) Medicines for knitting of broken Bones.

Catalepfis, a Difeafe, confifting in an Abolition of all the Animal Functions, Refpiration remaining entire.

Catalogue, (Gr.) a Lift of Names, either of Perfons or of things, as of Books.

Catamite, a Boy kept for Sodomy.

Cataphryges, Chriftian Hereticks, fo call'd becaufe the chief Promoters of this Sect came out of *Phrygia*; they followed the Errours of *Montanus*; they Chriftened the Dead, and made up the Communion Bread or *Eucharift* with young Children's Blood.

Cataplafm, (Gr.) an external Medicine made of Herbs, Roots, Seeds, &c. of the Confiftence of a Poultifs.

Catapulta, a Warlike Engine, with which the Anci-

ents ufed to throw Javelins twelve or fifteen Foot long.

Cataract, a great Fall of Waters from a high Place; alfo a Difeafe in the Eyes.

Catarrh, (Gr.) a falling down of Humours from the Head toward the lower Parts.

Cataftafis, (Gr.) is the third Part of a Comedy, and is the full Height and Vigour of the Plot.

Cataftrophe, the laft Part of a Comedy, and is the unraveling of the Plot; alfo the Conclufion or fhutting up of the Matter.

Catechifm, (Gr.) a fhort Syftem of Inftructions of what is to be believed and done.

Catechize, (Gr.) to inftruct or teach by Word of Mouth; to inftruct Youth in the Principles of Religion.

Catechumens, in the Primitive times, were Perfons who were for fome confiderable time inftructed in the Principles of Chriftianity, in order to qualify them for Baptifm.

Categorem, that Part of a Propofition which is prædicated of the other.

Categorematical, belonging to a *Catagorem*.

Categorical, Affirmative, Pofitive.

Category, (Gr.) an Accufation; alfo a Term in Logick, being the fame with Prædicament.

Catenaria, in Mathematicks, is a Curve Line which

a Rope, hanging freely between two Points of Suspension, forms it self into.

Catharpings, are small Ropes in a Ship, running in little Blocks from one Side of the Ship to the other.

Catharticks, (Gr.) purging Medicines.

Cathedra, a Chair.

Cathedral Church, the Episcopal Church of any Place; so called from the Bishop's Chair in every such Church.

Catheti, (Gr.) in a Right-angled Triangle, are the two Legs including the Right Angle.

Cathetus, a Perpendicular.

Catholick, (Gr.) universal, general.

Catling, in Surgery, a dismembring Knife.

Catopsis, see *Myopia*.

Catoptricks, is a Science which teaches how Objects may be seen by Reflexion, and explains the Reasons of it.

Catereticks, vid. *Catharticks*.

Cavalcade, (Fr.) a Show or Troop of Horsemen; a pompous March of Persons of Quality on Horseback, upon some solemn Occasion, to accompany and Honour their Prince.

Cavalier, a Knight or Gentleman serving on Horseback, or any Souldier that is mounted on Horseback. In Fortification, it is a Heap or Mass of Earth raised in a Fortress, to lodge the Cannon for scour-

ing the Field, or opposing a commanding Work.

Cavalry, (Sp.) Horsmen in an Army.

Caveat, a Caution, Warning or Admonition.

Cavern, a Cave, Den, or Hole under Ground.

Cavernous, full of great Holes or Caverns.

Cavefon, a false Rein to lead or hold a Horse.

Cavil, (Lat.) a Quirk, Shift, or captious Argument; Verbally, to Wrangle, to find Fault.

Cavillation, Wrangling, a School Term, signifying a false sophistical Argument.

Cavity, (Lat.) Hollowness.

Cauliferous, (Lat.) that hath a Stalk, as *Cauliferous Plants*.

Causality, (Lat.) is the Action or Power of a Cause in producing its Effect.

Causidick, a Lawyer or Pleader of Causes.

Caustick, burning or corroding.

Caustick Curves, see *Catacaustick* and *Diacaustick*.

Cautelous, (Lat.) Wary, Heedful.

Cauterize, to apply a *Cautery*.

Cautery, (Gr.) with Surgeons, is that which they use for searing or burning the Flesh; and 'tis either actual by Fire or an hot Iron, or potential by burning Medicines.

Caution

Caution, (Lat.) Heedful-
nefs, Warinefs, alfo Warning.

Cautionary, given in Pledge.

Cautious, Heedful, well
Advifed.

Cecity, Blindnefs.

Cecutient, waxing or
growing Blind.

Celature, the Art of Engraving.

Celebrate, to Honour any
Perfon with Praifes, Monuments, Infcriptions or Tro-
phies.

Celebrious, Famous, Noted,
Eminent.

Celebrity; Famoufnefs;
Magnificence.

Celerity, is the Swiftnefs
of a Body in Motion ; and it
is defin'd to be an Affection
of Motion, by which any
Moveable runs through a
given Space in a given time.

Celestial, Heavenly, belonging to the Heavens.

Celibacy, the State of unmarried Perfons ; fingle Life.

Cellarage, Cellar Room ;
alfo Rent for Ufe of a Cellar.

Celfitude, Tallnefs, Heighth.

Cement, a ftrong cleaving
Mortar.

Cenfer, a Veffel for burning Incenfe, a perfuming
Pan.

Cenfor, (Lat.) a Mafter of
Difcipline, a Judge or Re-
former of Manners ; one that
Valueth or Taxeth Men's
Eftates, in which Senfe it was
ufed by the ancient *Romans*.

Cenforious, belonging to a
Cenfor, fevere ; apt to find
Fault with or reprove others ;
Impertinently Critical.

Cenfural, belonging to Valuation or Affeffments.

Cenfure, Reflexion or Reproof.

To *Cenfure*, to Condemn,
to Criticize.

Centaur, half a Man, and
half a Horfe.

Centenary, belonging to an
Hundred.

Center of a Circle and
Sphere, is the middle Point,
from whence all Lines drawn
to the Citcumference are
equal.

Center, of a *Regular Polygon*, is the fame with the
Center of either an Infcribed
or Circumfcribed Circle.

Center, of an *Ellipfis* and
Hyperbola, is a Point in the
Middle of the Tranfverfe
Axis.

Center of Magnitude of a
Body, is a Point which is as
equally remote as is poffible
from its Extremities.

Center of *Gravity*, is a
Point upon which, if a Body
were fufpended, all its Parts
would be in *Equilibrio*.

Center of heavy Bodies here
on the Earth, is the Center
of the Earth, whither all
heavy Bodies tend.

Center of Motion of a Bo-
dy, is a Point about which, a
Body being faftened to it,
may or does move, as the
Middle of a Ballance is the
Center upon which it moves.

Centefm, the hundreth Part
of any Integer or thing.

Central,

Central, (Lat.) belonging to, or placed in the Center or Middle.

Centrifugal Force, is that Force by which any Body in Motion, revolving about an immovable Point, endeavours to receed from that Centre.

Centripetal Force, a Force whereby Bodies tend toward the Center much the same with Gravity.

Centuple, a hundred Fold.

Centuriators, four Protestant Divines of *Magdeburg*, that divided into Centuries the universal Church History.

Century, (Lat.) a Band of 100 Footmen, an Age containing 100 Years.

Centuriate, to divide into Bands or Hundreds.

Centurion, a Captain over 100 Footmen.

Cephalick, (Gr.) belonging to the Head.

Cerate, an external Medicine of a middle Confiftence betwixt an Oyntment and a Plaifter, a Cere-cloth.

Ceremonial, full of Ceremony.

Cerdonifts, a Sect of Hereticks, so called from *Cerdo* their firft Father, who taught two contrary Principles to be in the Caufe of every thing, a good Good, and a Bad.

Ceremonious, Formal, Complimental.

Ceremonys, the Rights and Coftoms of the Church; alfo among private Perfons, Ceremonies are Acts of Civi-

lity and Decency, in Token of Refpect and Kindnefs, as to give the Wall, the upper End of the Table, &c.

Cerinthians, a fort of Hereticks, who held that Chrift at his fecond coming fhould give to his People all carnal Pleafures and Delights; they are fo called from their Author *Cerinthus*.

Certificate, a Teftimony given in Writing of the Truth of any thing.

Certitude, (Lat.) Certainty, Affurance.

Cervical, (Lat.) belonging to the Neck.

Cerufs, is white Lead, or Lead made white by the Smoak of boiling Vinegar.

Ceffation, (Lat.) a leaving off, a ceafing.

Cetaceous, of the Whale kind, belonging to a Whale.

Chace, a Place for wild Beafts larger than a Park, which yet may be poffeffed by a Subject, as a Foreft cannot.

Chaconne, (Fr.) a fort of Dance, whofe Meafure is ever Tripla-time.

Chafe, to make hot with rubbing; to be ruffled, or in a Paffion.

Chaffred, fold. *Spencer*.

Chagrin, (Fr.) Melancholy, Anxiety, Heavinefs of Mind.

Chain-fhot, are two Bullets or half Bullets fixt or link'd together with a Chain.

Chalaftick Medicines, are fuch as by their temperate and moderate Heat do Comfort and Strengthen the Parts to which they are apply'd.

Chalcographer, (Fr.) an Engraver in Brass.

Chalibeat, is that which partakes of the Nature of Steel, as Chalibeat Medicines.

Chalice, (Lat.) a Communion Cup.

Chamade, (Fr.) a Signal by Drum or Trumpet, made by the Enemy for a Parley.

Chamber, is that part of the Concave Cylinder of a great Gun, where her Charge lies.

Chamfred, Chapt, Wrinkled. *Spencer.*

Champain Lands, fine even plain Country Downs.

Chance-medly, is the casual Slaughter of a Man, not altogether without the Fault of the Slayer.

Chancery, the Court of Equity and Conscience, moderating the Severity of other Courts that are more strictly ty'd to the Rigour of the Law.

Chandry, an Apartment in a Prince's House, where Candles and other Lights are kept.

Channel, the middle or deepest Part of any Sea, River, &c.

Chantry, a Chappel endow'd for the maintaining a Priest or Priests to sing Mass for the Souls of their Founders.

Chaos, a confused Mixture of all sorts of Particles together; a disorderly Heap of things.

Chapeau, (Fr.) in Heraldry, is a Cap of Dignity used to be worn by Dukes.

Chapiters, in Architecture, is the Crown or upper Part of a Pillar.

Chaplet, a Wreath or Garland for the Head.

Chappe, the Herald's Term for the Partition of an *Escutcheon* of this Figure; and it is thus Blazoned, *Chappe or,* and *Vert.*

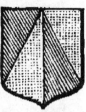

Characters, (Gr.) are Marks, Signs, or Symbols of things invented by Artists, and peculiar to several Sciences, as Geometry, Algebra, Printing, &c.

Characteristick, belonging to a Character; also a Mark or Sign.

Characteristick, of a *Logarithm,* the same with *Index* or *Exponent,* which see.

Charge, in Heraldry, signifies whatever thing is born in the Field of a Coat of Arms; also an Accusation; as also an Employment of Trust.

Charlatan, (Fr.) a Mountebank, a Quack, a coaksing Cheat.

Charles wain, a Northern Constellation, the same with *Ursa major.*

Charm, (Fr.) Inchantment, Spell.

Charnel-house, a Place where the Sculls and Bones of the Dead are laid.

Chart, is a Draught projected for the Use of Seamen, containing a View of the Sea-

Sea-coasts, Sands, Rocks, &c.

Charter, (Fr.) written Evidences of things done between Party and Party; also Letters Pattents, wherein Privileges are granted by the King to Towns and Corporations.

Chartulary, a Keeper of a Register, Roll, or reckoning Book.

Chase, when one Ship pursues another, she is said to give her Chase.

Chasm, a Gap or Opening in the Earth or Firmament.

Chasmatical, pertaining to a Chasm.

Chastity, is an abstaining from the unlawful Pleasures of the Flesh, and using those which are Lawful with Moderation.

Chastizment, Correction, Punishment inflicted upon Offenders.

Check-roll, a Book containing the Names of all the Houshold Servants of the Queen, or other great Personage.

Checky, a Bordure or Ordinary in *Heraldry* that has no more than two Checkers, is so called.

Chemin des Rondes, vid. Fausse Bray.

Cherfonese, (Gr.) a Tract of Land encompass'd every where by the Sea, save at one small Neck where it joyns to the Continent.

Cherubims, Angels of the second Rank of the first Hierarchy.

Chest, the Breast.

Chevaux de Frise, (Fr.) large Joists, or Pieces of Wood stuck full of Wooden Pins, arm'd with Iron, us'd to stop up Breaches, or to secure the Passages of a Camp.

Chevils, are small Pieces of Timber nailed to the Inside of a Ship, to belay or fasten the Sheets and Tacks.

Chevisance, a Contract or Bargain.

Chevron, is one of the Honourable Ordinaries in Heraldry; it represents 2 Rafters of an House set up as they ought to stand; it

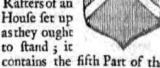

contains the fifth Part of the Field, and is thus exprest.

Chevronel, half of a Chevron.

Chicanry, (Fr.) is Wrangling, crafty Pleading, or Perplexing a Cause with Tricks and impertinent Words.

Chief, one of the 8 Honourable Ordinaries, containing a third of the Field; and determined by a Line straight or crooked drawn through the Chief Point. Thus the Field is *Gules*, a *Chief Argent*.

He beareth *Gules* a *Chief Crenelle*.

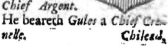

Chilead,

Chiliad, the Number of a Thousand; also the Tables of Logarithms are frequently called Chiliads.

Chiliarch, (Gr.) Commander of a Thousand, a Colonel.

Chiliasts, a Party of Christians who believe, that after the general or last Judgment, the Saints shall live a thousand Years upon Earth, and enjoy all manner of innocent Satisfaction.

Chiliogon, (Gr.) is a plain Figure of 1000 Sides and Angles.

Chimæra, a strange Fancy, a Castle in the Air, an idle Conceit.

Chimærical, Imaginary, Whimsical, that never was, nor will be.

Chinch, a Bug, a Wallloufe.

Chiragra, (Gr.) the Gout in the Hands only.

Chirology, (Gr.) is a talking or speaking with the Hand, and Signs made thereby.

Chiromancy, is a ridiculous Divination or Foretelling, by the Wrinkles and Lines in the Hand.

Chirurgery, (Gr.) that is manual Operation. See *Surgriy*.

Chivalry, (Fr.) Horsemanship, Valour.

Choinix, (Gr.) an Attick Measure of Capacity for things dry, containing ⅞ Pint and 72 Decimal Parts of a Solid Inch of our Corn Measure.

Cholerick, subject to Anger, Passionate.

Chomer, see *Coron.*

Choral, belonging to a Choir.

Chord, is a Right Line in any Curvilineal Figure, connecting the two Ends of any Ark.

Choriambick, (Gr.) is a Foot of a Verse consisting of four Syllables, two long ones at each End, and two short ones in the Middle.

Chorion, is the outer Membrane which involves the *Fœtus* in the Womb.

Chorographer, (Gr.) is a particular Description of some Countries, Provinces or Shires.

Chorography, (Gr.) is a particular Description of some Country, or of any Shire or Province in it.

Choroides, is the fourth Coat of the Eye which lies under the *Sclerotica*; in this Coat is a Hole before for the Passage of the Rays of Light, called *Pupilla*.

Chorus, the Singing or Musick in a Stage Play; also a Company of *Choristers* in a Church.

Chous, an Attick Measure of Capacity for things Liquid, containing 7 Pints, 4 solid Inches, and 942 Decimal Parts.

Chowse, to deceive or impose on.

Chrism, (Gr.) a Mixture of Oil and Balsam, Consecrated by a Popish Bishop to be be us'd in Baptism, Confirmation, extreme Unction, Coronation of Kings, &c.

Chrisom, or Chrisom-cloth, the Face-Cloth of a Child newly baptiz'd.

Chrisoms, Infants that die within the Month of Birth, or at the time of their wearing the *Chrisom-cloth*.

CHRIST, (Gr.) signifies Anointed, and is the Name of the Saviour of the World.

Chromatick, that never blushes, whose Colour never changeth; also Pleasant, or Delightful.

Chronical, (Gr.) temporal, or returning at certain times; as Chronical Diseases are such as come at certain times by Fits.

Chronicle, a History according to the Order of time.

Chronological, belonging to Chronology.

Chronology, (Gr.) a Science which teaches how to compute the time from the Creation of the World for the Use of History; and rightly dating of all such Events as have come to our Knowledge.

Chrystalline Heavens, in the Ptolemaick System were two; one serv'd them to explain the slow Motion of the fixed Stars by, the other helped them out in solving the Motion of *Libration* or *Trepidation*.

Chrystallization, is an Operation in Chymistry, by which the Salts, dissolved in any Liquor, are made to shoot into little prettily Figur'd

Lumps or Fragments, which they call Chrystals, from their being pellucid and clear like Chrystal.

Church, a voluntary Society of Men joyning themselves together of their own Accord, in order to the publick Worshipping of God in such a Manner, as they judge Acceptable to him, and effectual to the Salvation of their Souls.

Chyle, the white Juice of digested Meat, the Matter whereof the Blood is made.

Chyliferous, that carries or conveys the Chyle.

Chylification, is the Action of the Stomach and Guts in making the Chyle.

Chymere, a kind of Jacket; also a Herald's Coat of Arms.

Chymical, of, or belonging to Chymistry.

Chymist, a Person skilful in the Art of Chymistry.

Chymistry, is the Anatomy of natural Bodies by Fire, or a reducing them to their component Parts or Elements by the help of Fire.

Chymosis, is a Distortion of the Eye-lids by an Inflammation.

Chyronia, is a great Ulcer, and of difficult Cure.

Cicatrice, (Lat.) a Skar which remains after the Wound or Ulcer is healed.

Cicatrize, (Lat.) to close up a Wound, or to bring it to a Scar.

Cicatrizing Medicines, are such things as by drying, binding,

binding, and contracting, fill up Ulcers with Flesh, and cover them with a Skin.

Ciceronian, Pure, Eloquent, Oratorical.

Cilicious, belonging to Hair-cloth.

Cimeliarch, (Gr.) the chief Keeper of Plate, Vestments, &c. belonging to the Church; a Church Warden.

Cimeter, (Fr.) a crooked Sword.

Cimmerian, that sees no Sun, obscure, dark, from *Cimmerii*, a People in *Italy* so environed with Hills, that the Sun never comes at them.

Cincture, (Lat.) a girding; in *Architecture*, the Middle of a Pillar.

Cinefaction, a reducing into, or burning to Ashes.

Cinnabar, Vermillion or red Lead.

Cipher, in Arithmetick is exprest thus (o) and is of no Value, except when it is joyned with other Figures, and then it encreases their Value; it also expresses the Letters of a Person's Name, curiously interwoven together, as in a Seal; also certain odd Marks and Characters, wherein Letters are written, that they may not be understood in case they should be intercepted.

Circensian, belonging to the *Circus* at *Rome*, as the *Circensian Games*.

Circle, is a plain Figure bounded with one only Line, and to which all the Right Lines that can be drawn from a Point in the Middle of it, are equal to one another.

Circles of Altitude, see *Almicanters*.

Circles of Declination, are the same with the *Hour Circles*, or Circles of the Sphere passing through the Poles of the World, on which are accounted the Declination of a Planet or Star.

Circles of Longitude, of the Sun or Stars, are great Circles of the Globe passing thro' the Poles of the Ecliptick, on which are accounted the Latitude of the Stars or Planets, and whose Intersections, with the Ecliptick, determine their Longitude.

Circlet, a Ring of Pewter or other Metal, to set and turn a Dish on at Table.

Circuition, a compassing, or going about.

Circular, round, pertaining to a Circle.

Circulation, properly an incircling or environing; also the Motion of any thing round or Circle-wise, is called Circulation.

Circumaggeration, (Lat.) a heaping round.

Circumambient, (Lat.) encompassing or flowing about, an Epithet mostly apply'd to Air and other Fluids.

Circumambulation, (Lat.) a walking about.

Circumcision, (Lat.) a cutting about; more properly it is a cutting away a Part of the Prepuce or double Skin which

which covers the Penis, a Ceremony us'd by the Jews and Turks.

Circumduction, (Lat.) a leading about; also deceiving.

Circumference, (Lat.) is that Line which bounds the Circle; it is also us'd, tho' improperly, for the Bound or Bounds of any plain Figure.

Circumferenter, an Instrument used in Surveying, being the same with *Theodolite*, which see.

Circumflex, an Accent, which being placed over a Syllable, makes it long; it is marked thus (⁀).

Circumfluous-fluent, flowing about.

Circumforaneous, carried about a Market or Court.

Circumfusion, (Lat.) a pouring about.

Circumgyration, (Lat.) a turning or wheeling about.

Circumjacent, (Lat.) lying round about.

Circumligation, a binding or tying about.

Circumlocution, (Lat) an uttering that in many Words which might be said in few.

Circumplication, a folding, winding, or rolling about.

Circumposition, (Lat.) a putting about.

Circumrotation, (Lat.) a wheeling or turning about.

Circumscribe, to limit or stint; in *Geometry*, to draw a Figure round another.

Circumspection, (Lat) is a looking about, Heed, Wari-

ness, a marking and considering diligently.

Circumstances, are the Particulars that accompany any Action, as Time, Place, &c.

Circumvallation, a Line or Moat made round a Town by the Besiegers, to prevent its being succoured by the Enemy.

Circumvent, (Lat.) to come about; also to over-reach, to deceive.

Circumvolution, (Lat.) a rolling, or turning about.

Cisalpine, (Lat.) on this side the *Alps*.

Cissoid, a curvineal Figure invented by *Diocles*.

Cistercian Monks, an Order founded *A.* 1098, by *Robert* Abbot of *Citeaux* in *France*.

Citadel, is a Fort of 4, 5 or 6 Bastions, built somewhere near a City, that it may command it in case of Rebellion.

Citation, (Lat.) a citing or quoting; also summoning to appear before an Ecclesiastical Judge.

Citrine, or *Citron Colour*, a golden Colour.

Civilian, a Student in the Civil Law, or a Doctor of the Civil Law.

Civil Law, is properly the peculiar Law of each State, Country or City; but what we usually mean by the Civil Law, is a Body of Laws composed out of the best of the *Roman* and *Grecian* Laws.

Civil

Civil-Year, is the legal Year, or annual Account of time which every Government appoints to be uſed within its own Dominions.

Civilize, to make Courteous and Tractable.

Clamor, (Lat.) a Noiſe, an Outcry, a Shriek, a Bauling.

Clamorous, Noiſy, full of Clamour.

Clancular, privy, ſecret.

Clandeſtine, done in ſecret, privately, contrary to the Law, by ſtealth.

Clangor, (Lat.) a ſhrill Noiſe, a Shriek.

Clarencieux, the ſecond King at Arms, appointed by *Edw.* IV. on the Death of his Brother the D. of *Clarence*, who is to exerciſe his Office on the South of the River *Trent*.

Clarify, (Lat.) is to make Juices or Decoctions become clearer and finer.

Clarion, a Bearing in Heraldry of the following Figure, *Ruby* 3 *Clarions Topaz*.

Claſs, a Diſtribution of Perſons and Things according to their ſeveral Degrees and Natures.

Claſſical, belonging to a Degree or Claſs.

Claſſicks, are thoſe Authors which are generally read in Schools.

Claudent, (Lat.) ſhutting or cloſing.

Clavicles, the two Channel Bones.

Claudicate, (Lat.) to be Lame, or Halt.

Clauſe, an Article or Concluſion.

Clauſtral, belonging to a Cloiſter.

Cleat, is a Piece of Wood faſtened on the Yard Arm of a Ship, to keep the Ropes from ſlipping off the Yards.

Cleche, the Herald's Term for any Ordinary, pierced through with the ſame Figure, as here; He beareth *Gules*, a *Saltier Cleche*; that is, one pierced through with another.

Clemency, (Lat.) Meekneſs, Gentleneſs, Courteſy.

Clementines, a Part of the Canon Law, being Decretals or Conſtitutions of Pope *Clement* V. and enacted in the Council of *Vienna*.

Clepſydra, an Inſtrument anciently uſed by the *Egyptians*, to meaſure time by the running of Water out of one Veſſel into another; alſo an Hour-glaſs.

Clerk, a Clergy-man; alſo one that writes in any Office or Court.

Clergy, (Gr.) that Order of Men that are peculiarly appropriated to the Service of God, and devoted to wait at

G   the

Altar, as God's *Lot* and *Inheritance* are called by this Name.

Clerical, belonging to a Clergy-man, *&c.*

Cleromancy, (Gr.) a Divination by Lots.

Clever, Skilful, Ingenious, Neat-handed, well Shap'd.

Clew of a Sail, is the lower Corner of it, which reaches down to where the Tackles and Sheet-ropes are fastened.

Clew-Garnet, a Rope made fast to the Clew of a Sail, and thence running in a Pulley fastened to the Middle of the Main and Fore-yard, to hale up the Clew of the Sail close to the Middle of the Yard.

Clew-Line, is the same to the Top-Gallant and Spritsails, that the Clew-garnet is to the Main and Fore-sail.

Client, among rhe *Romans*, was a Citizen who put himself under the Protection of some great Man, who, in respect of that Relation, was called Patron. This Patron affisted his Client with his Protection, Interest and Goods; and the *Client* gave his Vote for his Patron, when he fought any Office for himself or his Friends. Amongst us it is commonly used for one who retains a Lawyer to plead his Cause.

Cliff, in *Musick*, a Character plac'd on one of the Lines, by which the Places of all the other Notes are known and prov'd.

Climacterical Years, are certain observable Years which are supposed to be attended with some grand mutation of Life or Fortune, as the 7th Year; the 21ft (made up of 3 times 7;) the 49th (made up of 7 times 7;) the 63d (made up of 9 times 7;) and the 81ft (made up of 9 times 9.

Climate, is a Part or Portion of the Earth between two Circles parallel to the Equator; and where there is half an Hour's Difference in the longest Day of the Summer.

Clinch, a smart and witty Expression.

Clinch of a Cable, that Part which is made fast to the Ring of an Anchor.

Clinke, Key-hole. *Spencer.*

Clitoris, is a Part in the *Pudendum muliebre*, and is of a long round Figure, naturally about the Bigness of the *Uvula.*

Cloister, a Place in a Monastry with Piazza's, or the Monastry it self.

Clomb, climbed, got up. *Milton.*

Closet, in *Heraldry*, the half of a Bar; the Bar ought to contain the fifth Part of the Escutcheon.

Closetting, private Consultations, or Intrigues of the Cabinet Council of a Prince.

Clouds, are a Congeries of (chiefly) watery Particles, drawn out of the Earth in Vapour; which, when these Particles

Particles are placed very near one another, appear dense and thick; but when they are more remote, are clear and bright, and almost transparent.

Cluniac Monks, an Order of Monks founded in the Year 900, by *Berno* Abbot of *Cluny* in *Burgundy*.

Clypei-formis, in form like a Shield; also a fort of Comet of that Form.

Coacervation, (Lat.) a heaping together.

Coaction, (Lat.) a forcing, or compelling.

Coadjutor, (Lat.) a Fellow-labourer, an Affiftant, a Helper.

Coadjuvate, (Lat.) to help or affift together.

Coadunation, (Lat.) a gathering or uniting together.

Coagmentation, a joyning or glewing together.

Coagulate, to give a Confiftence to Liquors; to make what was thin thick.

Coalition, or *Coalefcency*, is a Reunion or growing together of Parts before feparated.

Coanguftation, (Lat.) a making one thing ftrait by another.

Coarctation, (Lat.) a ftraitning, a preffing together.

Cob, a rich and covetous Wretch; also a foreign Coin.

Coccinean, (Lat.) of a Crimfon or Scarlet Dye.

Cock-a-hoop, all upon the Spur; also ftanding upon high Terms.

Cock-fwain, or *Cockfon*, of a Ship, an Officer who takes care of the Cock-boat, Barge, or Shallop, with all its Furniture; and is at Readinefs, with his Crew, to Man the Boat upon all Occafions.

Cockatrice, a Serpent, called otherwife a *Bafilisk*; bred, as fome fay, of a Cock's Egg.

Coction, (Lat.) a boiling; also Digeftion.

Code, from Codex, which comes from Caudex, the Trunk of a Tree; becaufe antiently their Books were made of Wood. Alfo a Volume of the Civil Law, which the Emperor *Juftinian* collected from all the Pleas and Anfwers of the antient Lawyers (which, in thofe Days, were in loofe Scrols, or Sheets of Parchments, or Paper) and compil'd them into a Book which he called Codex.

Codicil, (Lat.) a Supplement to a Will, or other Writing.

Coefficient, is the known Quantity that is multiply'd into any of the unknown Terms of the *Equation*.

Cæliack, or *Cæliacal*, (Gr.) belonging to the Belly.

Coemption, (Lat.) a buying together.

Coercion, (Lat.) a keeping in, or reftraining.

Coercive, keeping in, reftraing.

Coeffential, of the fame Effence.

Coetaneous, (Lat.) of the fame Age, living together at the fame time.

Coeternal, (Lat.) that is eternal to another.

Coexiftent, having an Exiftence

G 2

ftence or Being together, or at the fame time.

Cogent, preffing, ftrong, enforcing.

Cogitation, is the Action of Thinking; under which are comprehended various Modes or Ways of Thinking, as *Willing, Reasoning, &c.*

Cogitative, Thoughtful.

Cognation, Kindred or Alliance.

Cognisance, Knowledge; alfo in *Heraldry*, 'tis the fame with *Creft*; alfo a hearing a thing judicially.

Cognosee, or *Connusee*, the Person to whom a Fine is acknowledg'd.

Cognisor, or *Connusor*, he that acknowledges or paffes a Fine of Lands or Tenements to another.

Cognition, a knowing or judging of a thing.

Cognoscitive, belonging to Knowledge.

Cohæsion, a fticking or cleaving together; alfo in natural Philofophy, 'tis that Principle, whatever it be, which makes the Parts of Bodies cohere and ftick to one another.

Coherence, a fticking or hanging together; alfo Difcourfes are faid to be *coherent*, when there is fome Connection and Agreement between their Parts.

Cohibition, (Lat) a keeping back, or reftraining.

Cohobation, a Chymical Term, fignifying a repeated Diftillation of the fame Liquor, having poured it again

on its Fæces, or the Matter which remains in the Veffel.

Cohort, amongft the *Romans*, was ordinarily a Band of 500 Soldiers, or the 10th Part of a Legion.

Cohortation, (Lat.) an Exhortation or Perfuafion.

Coincident, a happening together, a falling in with; thus, in Geometry, Figures which being placed one upon another, do exactly agree or cover one another, are faid to be Coincident Figures.

Coindications, in Phyfick, are Signs which do not indicate by themfelves alone, but together with other things, Circumftances, &c.

Coition, (Lat.) a mutual Tendency of Bodies towards one another, an Affmbly, or meeting together; alfo carnal Copulation.

Colation, (Lat.) paffing any thing through a Sieve or Strainer.

Colature, is that which after boiling is percolated or ftrained through a Sieve or Cloth.

Colcothar, is the dry Subftance which remains after Diftillation of Vitriol, commonly called *Caput mortuum*.

Colick, a violent Pain in the *Abdomen*, taking its Name from the Gut *Colon*, the principal Part affected.

Collapfed, fallen to decay, ruined.

Collar of a Ship, is a Rope faftened about her Beak-head, unto which the Dead-man's-eye is feized, that holds her

main

main Stay ; also one about the Main-Mast-Head.

Collateral, not direct, on one side ; thus, Collateral Pressure is a Pressure side-ways ; and Collateral Relations are Brothers and Sisters, and their Children.

Collateral Assurance, is a Bond that is made, over and beside the Deed it self, for the Performance of Covenants between Man and Man.

Collation, (Lat.) a comparing together; also a handsom *Treat* or *Entertainment*.

Colleague, a Fellow, or Copartner in any Office; a Fellow Collegian.

Collect, (Lat.) a short Prayer appropriated to any particular Day or Occasion. *Eccl.*

Collectaneous, (Lat.) gathered out of several things or Places.

Collection, a gathering together, or picking up; also things gathered together or picked up, are very usually called a Collection ; as a Collection of Books, &c.

Collectitious, gathered up and down.

Collective, that is gathered together into one.

College, (Lat.) a Company or Society of Persons of the same Profession ; also the Buildings where they live.

Collegiate Church, is built and indowed for a Body corporate of a Dean and Prebendaries.

Collid., to beat, knock, or

bruise together ; to dash one against another.

Collimation, an aiming at.

Colliquation, (Lat.) a melting or dissolving.

Colliridians, a Sect of Hereticks, that worshipped the Holy Virgin *Mary* as a Goddess, and offered Sacrifice to her.

Collision, (Lat.) a dashing or striking of a Body against another.

Collocation, (Lat.) a placing or setting in order.

Colloquy, a talking together, a Conference.

Colluctation, a struggling together.

Collusion, Deceit or Cousenage, a fraudulent Contrivance or Compact between two or more Parties, to bring an Action one against the other for some deceitful End; or to prejudice the Right of a third Person.

Collutio, (Lat.) a washing of the Mouth.

Collyrium, any liquid Medicine designed to cure Diseases in the Eyes.

Colobona, a preternatural growing together of the Lips, Eyelids, &c.

Colon, is the second of the great Guts ; also a Point in Grammer marked thus (:) and shews a Sentence to be perfect or entire, but yet the Sense depending or continuing on.

Colonel, the chief Commander of a Regiment of Horse, Dragoons or Foot.

G 3   *Colony*,

Colony, a Plantation; a Company of People transplanted from one Place to another.

Coloration, (Lat.) a Colouring; also brightning of Gold or Silver.

Coloſs, a large Statue, as that of the Sun at *Rhodes* 70 Cubits high, between whoſe Feet the Ships ſailed.

Colour, ſignifies either that Senſation which we perceive when we look upon any coloured Body; or that Quality in any Body, which is the Occaſion of ſuch a Senſation.

Colourable, Plauſible, Fair.

Columbary, a Dove or Pigeon-houſe.

Column, in the Art Military, is the long File or Row of Troops, or of Baggage, of an Army in its March.

Column, in Architecture, is properly that round long Cylinder or Part of a Pillar which is called the *Shaft*, Trunk, *&c.* and reaches from the Aſtragal of the Baſe to the Capital.

Columna naſi, the fleſhy Part of the Noſe, prominent in the Middle near the upper Lip.

Colures, are two great Circles which interſect one another at Right Angles in the Poles of the World; one of which paſſes thro' the 2 Equinoctial Points, the other through the two Solſticial Points.

Comb, in a Ship, is a ſmall Piece of Timber ſet under the lower Part of the Beak-

head near the Middle; its uſe is to help to bring the Tacks aboard.

Combatant, a Champion; alſo in Heraldry, two Lions are ſaid to be *combatant*, when in a Coat of Arms they are born in a fighting Poſture Rampant, and their Faces towards each other.

Combination, (Lat.) a joyning together, a Conſpiracy; alſo in Mathematicks, it is an Art of finding how many different Ways a certain given Number of things may be varied and taken, by one and one, two and two, three and three, *&c.*

Combuſtible, (Lat.) apt to take fire, or burn.

Combuſtion, a burning, or hurly burly.

Comeſſation, (Lat.) Riotous Banqueting and Revelling.

Comedy, a Play compoſed with Art either in Proſe or Verſes, to repreſent ſome humane Action agreeable, and not cruel.

Comedian, either a Writer or an Actor of a Comedy.

Comet, a blazing Star.

Comical, (Lat.) Merry, Facetious, Pleaſant.

Comitatu & caſtro commiſſo, is a Writ whereby the Charge of a County, together with the keeping of a Caſtle, is committed to the Sheriff.

Comitialis morbus, ſee *Epilepſy.*

Comitial, belonging to a Meeting

Meeting, or an Assembly of People.

Comma, is one of the Points or Stops used in Writing, and is marked thus (,) implying only a small rest, or little Pause.

Commemorate, to mention or remember.

Commemoration, a mentioning or remembring.

Commence, (Fr.) to begin; also to proceed in a Suit; also to take a Degree in an University.

Commendam, a void Benefice commended to an able Clerk, till it be otherwise disposed of.

Commendation, a Praising, or setting one forth.

Commensurable Quantities, are such as will either measure one another precisely; or if some other third Quantity may be found, that will measure them both.

Commensurable in Power; Right Lines are said to be commensurable in Power, when their Squares are measured by one and the same Space or Superficies.

Comment, an Exposition or Gloss.

Commentary, an Interpretation of an obscure and difficult Author; also a brief Abstract, or historical Abridgment of things.

Commentator, a Writer of Commentaries.

Commentitious, forged, counterfeit.

Commerce, a Trafficking, or Exchanging of Wares.

Commigration, a going from one Place to dwell in another.

Commination, (Lat.) a vehement Threatning.

Comminution, is a dividing a thing into very small Parts or Particles.

Commiseration, (Lat) a taking Pity.

Commissary, a Church Officer that supplies the Bishop's Place in the remote Parts of his Diocess; also one that has the Distribution of Provisions in an Army.

Commission, a Power given from one Person to another of doing any thing, or exercising a Jurisdiction, confirm'd by *Letters Patents*, the publick Seal, or any other way.

Commissure, (Lat.) a Joint of any thing; a joyning close, or couching things together.

Committee, he or they to whom the ordering of any Matter is referred.

Commixture, (Lat) a mingling things together.

Commodious, fit, convenient.

Commodity, (Lat.) Conveniency, Profit; also any Goods or Merchandize.

Commonalty, the common People.

Common-Law, is either simply the Law of the Land, without any other Addition; or more generally taken for the Law, before any Statute was made to alter the same.

Common,

Common-Pleas, is the King's Court now held in *Westminster Hall*.

Common Sensory, that Place in the Brain where all Sensation is supposed to be performed; where the Soul takes Cognizance of all Objects that present themselves to the Senses.

Commoration, (Lat.) a tarrying or dwelling in a Place for a time.

Commotion, (Lat.) a Disturbance, Disquiet; an Uproar.

Communicable, (Lat.) that may be imparted.

Communicate, (Lat.) to impart, or shew; also to partake of the Lord's Supper, or Communion.

Communi Placita non tenenda, &c. a Writ forbidding the *Treasurer* and *Barons* of the Exchequer, to hold Plea between two common Persons in that Court where neither of them belong to it.

Communication, there is said to be a Communication between Men, Countries, &c. when they freely impart their Thoughts or Goods, &c. one to another; Lines of Communication, are Trenches made to preserve a safe Correspondence betwixt two Forts or Posts, or at a Siege betwixt two Approaches.

Communicative, a Man is said to be Communicative, when he freely imparts his Thoughts to another.

Communion, (Lat.) Fellowship, Union in Faith; also

the Sacrament of the Lord's Supper.

Community, a Society of Men inhabiting the same Place.

Commutation, (Lat.) a changing one thing for another.

Commutative, belonging to Exchange, or Commutation.

Comœdy, a Dramatick Poem, or a Representation of the common Actions of human Life, digested into some formal Story, and acted upon a Stage by several Persons talking to one another.

Compact, (Lat.) close, well joyned; also brief, and pithy; *verbally*, to join.

Compact, a Bargain, or Agreement.

Companion, (Fr.) Fellow, Mate, Partner.

Comparable, (Lat.) that may be compared.

Comparative, (Lat.) capable of being compared with.

Comparison, is a setting 2 things together, to see wherein they agree or disagree.

Compartiment, a proportional Division in Building, &c. also a regular Disposition of agreeable Figures, all round any Picture, Map, Draught, &c.

Compass, in Navigation, is a Circle divided into four Quadrants, representing the four Cardinal Winds, or Principal Points, East, West, South, and North; and each Quarter subdivided into eight other equal Parts, making in all

all 32 Parts, which are called Rhumbs or Points.

Compaſſion, a Senſe of the Miſery or Misfortunes of others, as it were a Fellow-ſuffering in their Calamities.

Compatible, (Fr.) that agrees or ſuits with another thing.

Compatriot, (Lat.) one that is of the ſame Country.

Compeer, (Lat.) a Fellow, an Equal, a Conſort.

Compel, (Lat) to force, or conſtrain.

Compellation, (Lat.) a calling by Name, a friendly Saluration.

Compendious, very conciſe, brief, or ſhort.

Compendium, (Lat.) an Abridgment.

Compenſation, (Lat.) a Recompence, or making amends for a good Turn.

Comperendination, a delaying, deferring, or adjourning.

Compertorium, a judicial Inqueſt in the Civil Law, made by Delegates or Commiſſioners, to find out or relate the Truth of a Cauſe.

Competency, (Lat.) Conveniency, Meetneſs; but moſt uſually it is taken for a Sufficiency.

Competent, convenient, meet; but uſually it ſignifies ſufficient.

Competible, (Lat.) ſuitable, or agreeable to.

Competitour, (Lat.) a Candidate, or one that ſtands for any Place or Preferment, together with one or more.

Compile, (Lat.) to place one upon another; alſo to compoſe; as to compile Dictionary, is the ſame as to compoſe it.

Complacency, (Lat.) a taking Delight in a thing.

Complainant, a Plaintiff at Law, one that prefers a Complaint.

Complaiſance, (Fr.) an obliging Carriage, or an aptneſs to comply with the Sentiments and Will of other Perſons.

Complement, (Lat.) a filling up.

Complement of an Ark of a Circle, is what that Ark wants of 90°.

Complement of the Courſe, in Navigation, is what the Angle of the Courſe wants of 90 Degrees.

Complete, (Lat.) perfect, full; alſo near, fine.

Completion, (Lat.) a fulfilling, performance.

Complex, compound, or conſiſting of ſeveral Simples.

Complex Ideas, in Logick, are Ideas compounded, or conſiſting of ſeveral ſimple Ideas.

Complexion, (Lat.) an Embracing; alſo the State and Conſtitution of the Body; and very frequently it ſignifies the Appearance of the Face.

Complexus, a Muſcle of the Head, ſerving to move it backwards.

Complice, or *Accomplice,* a Partner in an ill Action.

Complicated, wrapt up together.   *Compli-*

Complication of Diseases, is when divers Diftempers feize on the Body at the fame time, efpecially if they depend one upon another.

Complot, to plot together, to combine or confpire.

Comportment, (Fr.) Carriage, Behaviour.

Compofe, is to affemble feveral Parts together, for the making up of one Body ; to compofe a Difference, is to make it up ; to compofe one's Actions, Words, or Manners, is to regulate them.

Compofite, (Lat.) compounded.

Compofite Order, in Architecture, is the fifth Order compounded of the other four, call'd alfo the *Italick,* or *Roman.*

Compofition, (Lat.) a fetting or joyning together ; alfo any Treatife, or Piece of Mufick is called a *Compofition.*

Compofition, in Mathematicks, is the Reverfe of the *Analytical* Method or *Refolution* ; it proceeds upon Principles in themfelves felf-evident, on *Definitions,Poftulatums,*and *Axioms,* and a previoufly demonftrated Series of Propofitions, ftep by ftep, until it give you a clear Knowledge of the thing to be demonftrated ; this is what they call the *Synthetical* Method ; and is ufed by moft of the old *Geometricians.*

Compofition of Motion, is a compounding two or more Motions together , whether they be uniform or accelerated.

Compofition of Proportion, is a comparing the Sum of the Antecedent and Confequent, with the Confequent in two equal *Ratio's.*

Compofitor, in Printing, he that compofes the Characters, and makes up the Forms, to be in readinefs for the Prefs.

Compaft, Dung or Soil for improving Land.

Compofure, any thing compofed ; alfo Calmnefs of Mind.

Compotation, (Lat.) a drinking together.

Compound, made up together. *Verbally,* to make up of feveral Ingredients ; alfo to come to an Agreement, efpecially with Creditors for Debt.

Compound Quantities in Algebra, are fuch Quantities as confift of fimple ones connected by the Signs $+$ or $-$.

Comprehenfible, (Lat.) that may be underftood, contained, or laid hold off.

Comprehenfion, (Lat.) a laying hold on, an underftanding of a thing, *&c.*

Compreffible , (Lat.) that may be compreft or fqueafed into a narrower compafs, as may the Air, and moft other Fluids more or lefs.

Compreffion, (Lat.) a fqueazing or preffing together.

Comprint, (Law-Term) is to print by ftealth a Copy or Book belonging to another, to his Prejudice.

Comprife,

Comprife, (Fr.) to contain or comprehend.

Compromife, in Law, is a Promife of two or more Parties at Difference, to refer the Deciding their Controverfies to the Arbitrement of one or more Arbitratours.

Compt, (Lat.) Fine, Neat, Polite.

Comptroll, fee *Controll*.

Compulfion, (Lat.) a conftraining or forcing.

Compunction, (Lat.) a pricking; alfo Remorfe of Confcience.

Compurgation, (Lat.) is a Term in Law, fignifying a clearing or juftifying by Oath.

Computation, (Lat.) a Reckoning or cafting up of Accounts.

Computift, an Accountant.

Con, can, know. *Spencer*.

Conarium, or the *Glandula Pinealū*, is a part of the Brain hanging in a fmall Cavity called the *Anus*, in the hinder Part of the third Ventricle of the Brain, and leading into the fourth; it is fo called from the Shape of a Pine Cone. *Defcartes* fuppos'd this Glandule to be the Seat of the Soul.

Concamerate, (Lat.) a Word in Architecture fignifying to Vault or Arch.

Concatenate, (Lat.) to chain or link together.

Concatenation, (Lat.) a chaining or linking together.

Concave, (Lat.) hollow, bending.

Concave Speculums, are hollow reflecting Glaffes, or Glaffes which reflect on their hollow Side.

Concavity, (Lat.) Hollownefs.

Conceal, to keep clofe or fecret.

Concede, (Lat.) to grant, or yield, or condefcend unto.

Conceive, to imagin or apprehend, to form an Idea of; alfo to breed a Child.

Concenter, to meet in the fame Center.

Concention, (Lat.) a Confort of many Voices or Inftruments in one.

Concentration, (Lat.) a driving towards the Middle or Center.

Concentrick, (Lat.) that Hath one and the fame Center.

Conceptacle, (Lat.) any hollow thing which is fit to receive or contain.

Conception, a Breeding or Conceiving a Child; alfo a comprehending; and in Logick it is the fimple Apprehenfion, Perception or Idea that we have of any thing, without proceeding to affirm or deny any thing of it.

Concert, (Fr.) to ftate or debate Matters; to contrive or lay a Defign.

Conceffion, a granting or yielding.

Concha, is the Winding of the Cavity of the inner Part of the Ear.

Conche, an attick Meafure of Capacity for things Liquid, containing $\frac{1}{12}$ of a Pint, and $234\frac{1}{2}$ Decimal Parts of a folid Inch

Inch, of our *English* Wine Measure.

Conchoid, in Mathematicks, is the Name of a Curve Line, invented by *Nichomedes*.

Conciliate, to reconcile, make agree, or unite.

Conciliation, (Lat.) a Reconcilement, Agreement, or Union.

Concinnity, Properness, Aptness, Handsomness, Decency.

Concional, (Lat.) pertaining to a Sermon, Oration, or an Assembly.

Concise, short, brief.

Conclamation, (Lat.) a shout or noise of many together.

Conclave, (Lat.) a Closet or inner Room; also the Assembly of the Cardinals for the Election of the Pope, or for the Decision of any important Affair in the Church; also the Place it self where the Pope is Elected.

Conclude, to resolve upon, to determine; also to draw a Consequence from something said before.

Conclusion, an End; in Logick, it is the last of the three Propositions in a Syllogism.

Conclusive, an Argument is said to be Conclusive, when the Consequences are rightly and truly drawn.

Concoction, (Lat.) is a boiling; also a Digestion of the Meat in the Stomach.

Concomitant, (Lat.) accompanying; also a Companion.

Concord, Agreement.

Concords, in Musick, are certain Intervals between Sounds; which delight the Ear when heard at the same time.

Concordance, an Agreement; also a general Index of all the Words in the Bible.

Concordant, (Lat.) agreeing together.

Concorporation, (Lat.) a mixing or tempering into one Body, an Incorporation.

Concourse, (Lat.) a Multitude of People assembling together upon some particular Occasion.

Concrete, in Natural Philosophy and Chimistry, is a Body made up of different Principles, and signifies much the same with *mixed*.

Concrete, in Logick, is when we consider any Quality, as Whiteness, inhering in any Subject; thus when we say *Snow is white*, we speak of Whiteness in the Concrete, or as it is an inherent Quality: But Whiteness considered by it self, without regard to any Subject in which it inheres, is said to be taken in the Abstract.

Concrete Numbers, are Numbers which express or denote some particular Subjects, as 2 Men, 3 Stones, &c.

Concretion, (Lat.) is the uniting together of several small Particles of a Natural Body into sensible Masses or Concretes.

Concubinage, keeping of a Miss or Concubine. In a Law Sense, 'tis an Exception against a Woman that sues for

for her Dower, whereby 'tis alledg'd she is not his lawful Wife, but a Concubine.

Conculcate, to stamp upon, or tread under Foot.

Concupiscence, (Lat.) a vehement Desire of enjoying any thing; but more particularly a venereal Desire.

Concupiscible Faculty, is the Unreasonable or Sensual Part of the Soul, which only seeks after the Pleasures of Sense.

Concurrence, (Lat.) a running together; also an Agreement in Judgment or Opinion.

Concurrent, a Rival, or Competitor.

Concussion, a shaking or jumbling together.

Cond, or *Conn*, in the Sea Phrase, is to guide or conduct the Ship in her right Course; he that Conns stands aloft with a Compass before him, and gives the Word of Direction to the Man at the Helm how to Steer.

Condemnation, (Lat.) a Blaming or Disapproving; also a Sentencing to Death.

Condensation, is a making any natural Body take up less Space, or confining it within less Dimensions than it had before.

Condescendency, Complaisance, a Compliance.

Condescension, a yielding unto, or complying with.

Condign, (Lat.) Worthy, according to Merit.

Condisciple, (Lat.) a School Fellow, or Fellow Student.

Condited, (Lat.) Seasoned.

Condition, (Lat.) Nature, Disposition; the Quality of a thing that renders it Good or Bad, Perfect or Imperfect; also Estate or Fortune; likewise a Bargain or Agreement, or a Clause and Term of it.

Conditional, (Lat.) implying Conditions or Terms.

Conditional Propositions, are Propositions consisting of two Parts, connected by the conditional Particle (*if*.)

Conditioned, indued with certain Humours or Qualities.

Condole, to Grieve, or express Grief for another's Misfortunes.

Condolence, (Lat.) a Sympathy in Grief, a Fellow-feeling of another's Sorrows and Misfortunes.

Condonation, (Lat.) a Pardoning or Forgiving.

Conducible, (Lat.) Profitable, Good; also which may be hired.

Conduct, to Guide; also a Guiding; likewise the Management of any Affair, or one's self; as when we say such a one is a Man of good Conduct; we mean, he manageth himself or his Business with a great deal of Prudence.

Conductor, (Lat.) a Leader or Guider.

Conduit, (Fr.) a Pipe for conveying Water.

Condyli, are the Joynts and Knuckles of the Fingers.

Condylomia, is the knitting
or

or joynting of the Joynts of an Animal Body.

Cone, is a Geometrical Solid in the Form of a Sugar Loaf; which may be conceived to be formed by the Revolution of a Right-angled Triangle round rhe Perpendicular.

Cone Right, is when its *Axis* is Normal to its Bafe; and then its Sides are equal.

Cone Scalene, is when its *Axis* is inclined to its Bafe, and then its Sides are unequal.

Cone of Rays, are a Parcel of Rays in the Form of a Cone, iffuing from any Radiating Point.

Confabulation, (Lat.) a familiar Difcourfing or talking together.

Confalon, a Confraternity of Seculars in the Church of *Rome* called Penitents; eftablifhed firft of all by fome *Roman* Citizens.

Confectioner, a Maker or Seller of Comfits or Sweetmeats.

Confections, a Compofition of Powders, Sugar, Honey, Syrups, &c. made up into one Subftance.

Confederacy, is an Union of two or more Perfons together, to do any Hurt or Damage to another. Alfo an Alliance between Princes and States, for their Defence againft a common Enemy.

Confederates, are Princes or States entered into an Alliance for their common Society.

Confer, to give or beftow; to compare; alfo to Difcourfe and talk together.

Conferences, are Difcourfes held either between Minifters of State, or private Perfons, about particular Affairs:

Confefs, to acknowledge, or own.

Confeffionary, the Chair wherein a Prieft firs to hear Confeffion.

Confeffor, (Lat.) a Perfon that has adher'd to the Faith, notwithftanding cruel Perfecutions and Sufferings upon that Account; alfo a *Father Confeffour* or Prieft, to hear Confeffions, and give Abfolution.

Confide in, is to truft in, or rely upon.

Confident, an intimate Friend employ'd in Matters of Secrecy and Truft; alfo Adjectively it fignifies Pofitive, Sure.

Configuration, (Lat.) a Fafhioning or making of a like Figure; a Likenefs or Refemblance of Figures.

Confine, to reftrain, or to imprifon; alfo to border upon.

Confinement, Imprifonment, Slavery.

Confines, the Limits or Borders of a Field, County, or Country.

Confirm, to give new Affurance of the Truth or Certainty of any thing.

Confirmation, is a giving new Affurance or Evidence of the

the Truth and Certainty of any thing.

Confiscation, in Law, is a Forfeiting a Man's Goods to the publick Treasury.

Conflagration, a general burning or consuming with Fire.

Conflict, a Skirmish, or Combat.

Confluence, a flowing together, as of Waters, People, &c.

Conflux, (Lat.) a flowing together, as of Humours.

Conform, agreeably, suitably.

Conform, to comply, to make like to.

Conformable, agreeable, of the like Nature.

Conformation, (Lat.) Fashioning or Framing of a thing. In *Anatomy*, it denotes the Figure and Disposition of the Parts of the Body of Man.

Conformist, one that conforms to any Establishment.

Conformity, (Lat.) a Compliance.

Confound, (Lat.) to mix together ; to mistake one thing for another.

Confraternity, (Lat.) a Brotherhood or Society, united together chiefly on a religious Account.

Confront, to oppose, or compare ; to bring Face to Face.

Confusion, (Lat.) Disorder, a Jumble, or Mishmash.

Confute, to disprove or overthrow the Reasonings and Arguments of one's Adversary.

Conge, (Fr.) Leave, Permission. In *Architecture*, Rings about the Ends of Wooden Pillars, to preserve them from splitting, and after imitated in Stone Work.

Conge d'eslier, the King's Permission to a Dean and Chapter, to choose a Bishop.

Congeable, Lawful, or lawfully done.

Congeal, to Freeze ; or, in Chymistry, to grow into a Consistency.

Congee, a low Bow, or Reverence.

Congelation, a freezing, or growing into a Consistency.

Congenerous, (Lat.) of the same sort or kind.

Congenial, of the same Stock or kind.

Congeniality, a Likeness of Genius, or kind with another.

Congeon, one of low Stature, or a Dwarf.

Congestion, (Lat.) a heaping or gathering together.

Congius, a *Roman* Measure of Capacity for things Liquid, containg 7 Pints, four solid Inches, 942 Decimal Parts of our Wine Measure.

Conglobate Glands, are such Glands in an Animal Body, as are smooth in their Surface, and seem to be made up of one continued Substance.

Conglobation, a gathering together in a Mass or Lump.

Conglomerate Glands, are such in an animal Body, as are

are made up as it were of lesser Glands.

Conglomeration, a rolling up into a Heap, or winding upon a Bottom.

Conglutination, a fastening together of Bodies with Glue, or any other Glutinous and Tenacious Substance.

Congratulate, to rejoyce with one for some good Fortune that has befaln him.

Congregation, (Lat.) an Assembly, Society, or Company of People; also an Assembly or gathering together.

Congress or *Congre*, a Society of Booksellers, who have a Joynt Stock for Trading.

Congress, (Lat.) a meeting or coming of People together; also an Engagement or Fight.

Congruent, agreeable, suitable.

Congruity, (Lat.) Agreeableness, Conformity.

Congruous, agreeable; as such a thing is congruous to Reason, *i. e.* it agrees with Reason.

Congeries, (Lat.) a Collection of many Bodies or Particles in one Mass; a Heap, a Hoard.

Conical, of, or belonging to a Cone.

Conick, belonging to a Cone.

Conick Sections, are the *Parabola*, *Hyperbola*, and *Ellipsis*, which are form'd or produc'd by cutting a Cone with a Plain according to such and such Conditions.

Coniferous Plants, are such Shrubs, Trees, or Herbs, as bear a Wooden Sort of a Fruit in the Shape of a Cone.

Conjectural, (Lat.) that which is only grounded upon Supposition or Probability.

Conjecture, a Guessing or Judging without Certainty.

Conjoyn, (Lat.) to join or put together.

Conjugal, belonging to a Married Couple.

Conjugation, (Lat.) a coupling or yoking together in Pairs; also a Grammatical Term.

Conjunction, (Lat.) a joyning together; in *Astronomy*, 2 Planets are said to be in Conjunction, when one passes under the other, so as to make one Right Line in respect of any Part of the Earth; and is either *True* or *Apparent*.

Conjunction True, is when a right Line passing thro' the Center of the two Planets, and being produced, passes also thro' the Center of the Earth.

Conjunction Apparent, is when a right Line drawn thro' the Centers of the two Planets, does not pass thro' the Center of the Earth.

Conjuration, (Lat.) a Plot, or Conspiracy; also a Personal Dealing with the Devil or evil Spirits.

Conjure, to demand upon Oath, to adjure, or earnestly intreat.

Connascency, a being born or growing up together with.

Connate, or *Connatural*, born

born together with.

Connatural, that is, natural to one or more things with others.

Conne, learn. *Spencer*.

Connexion, (Lat.) a joyning things together, a Dependency of one thing upon another.

Connivance, a winking at, or passing by the Faults of others without Punishment.

Connive, (Lat.) to wink, or to take no Notice of.

Conniventes Glandulæ, are those Wrinkles which are found in the Inside of the *Intestinum Ileum*, and *Jejunum*.

Connubial, (Lat.) belonging to Wedlock or Marriage, mutual, or between Man and Wife.

Conoid, is a Solid produced by the circumvolution of any Section of a Cone about its Ax; and is either *Parabolical*, *Elliptical*, or *Hyperbolical*, according as the Solid produced is form'd from a *Parabola*, *Ellipsis*, or *Hyperbola*.

Conquassation, (Lat.) a Shaking, as in an Earthquake. In *Pharmacy*, the beating Herbs with a Pestle in a Mortar.

Consanguinity, (Lat.) is the Relation between two or more Persons descended from the same Family.

Conscience, is the Opinion or Judgment which the rational Soul passes upon all her Actions.

Conscientious, that has a good Conscience, Just, Upright in Dealing.

Conscionable, see *Conscientious*; also Equitable, Reasonable.

Conscious, (Lat.) inwardly Guilty, privy to ones self of any Fault or Error.

Conscription, (Lat.) an Enrolling or Registring

Consecrate, (Lat.) to Dedicate, to Devote, to Hallow; also to Canonize.

Consecration, a Consecrating or Hallowing.

Consectary, (Lat.) a Consequence or Deduction from a foregoing Proposition or Argument.

Consecutive, Following or Succeeding; It is always said of Things, not Persons.

Consent, to yield to the Truth, or to the doing of a thing.

Consent, an Agreement to the truth of a Thing, or to the doing of it.

Consentaneous, Agreeable, Suitable.

Consentient, (Lat.) Willing, Agreeing.

Consequence, when one thing follows from another it is call'd a Consequence of that other thing.

Consequent, Following; in Mathematicks it is the latter of the two Terms, which are immediately compared with one another in any sett of Proportionals.

Conservation, (Lat.) a Keeping or Preserving.

Conservatory, a Place to keep or lay things up in.

Conserve, a Composition of

H   Flowers

Flowers or Herbs beat toge-ther; to which, if dry, is ad-ded three, if moister, two Pounds of Sugar.

Considerate, Wise, Advised, Discreet.

Consideration, a weighing Things well, or a due atten-tion to the nature of a Thing or Action.

Consignation, (Lat.) a Seal-ing; a Writing sealed.

Consign, to Appoint, to De-liver, to Make over.

Consimilar, Alike or Agree-ing.

Consistence, when any Li-quor is boiled until it become thick, it is said to be boiled to a Consistency.

Consistent Bodies, are solid or firm Bodies, in opposition to such Bodies as are fluid.

Consistory, the Court Chri-stian, or Spiritual Court, held formerly in the Nave of the Cathedral Church, or in some Chappel, Isle or Portico be-longing to it, in which the Bishop presided, and had some of his Clergy for Asses-sors and Assistants.

Consociate, to joyn in mu-tual Society.

Consolation, (Lat.) Com-forting; also a Discourse tending to comfort or allevi-ate the Sorrows of others.

Console, in Building is a kind of Bracket or Shoulder-ing-piece, which hath a Pro-jecture, and serves to support a Cornice, bear up Figures, &c.

Consolidation, (Lat.) a So-dering or making Solid: In *Physick* it is the uniting strongly together of the Fra-ctures of broken Bones, or the Lips of a Wound.

Consonance, in Musick, is an agreement of two Sounds, the one Grave, and the other Acute; compounded by such a Proportion of each, as shall prove agreeable to the Ear.

Consonant, (Lat.) i. a Sounding together, Conform-able. Agreeable.

Consort, a Fellow or Com-panion: Also a piece of Mu-sick consisting of three or more Parts.

Conspersion, (Lat.) a Strew-ing or Sprinkling about.

Conspicuous, (Lat.) Clear, Manifest.

Conspiracy, (Lat.) a secret Consultation, a Plot.

Conspiratione, a Writ a-gainst Conspirators.

Constable, (a Lat. *Comes Stabuli*) the Master of the Horse, or Prefect of the Im-perial Stables, in the decline of the *Roman* Empire: Af-terwards apply'd to any Of-ficer who had the Guard or Custody of any Place or Per-sons.

Constancy, an immovable-ness of Mind in all Condi-tions.

Constat, (Lat.) a Certificate given out of the Court of all that is on Record, touching such and such a thing.

Constellation, a Parcel of fix'd Stars, imagined to re-present

present some Animal or Thing which it is suppos'd to represent.

Consternation, (Lat.) a great Fear or Astonishment; also a Mutiny or Rising of the People.

Constipation, (Lat.) is when the Parts of any natural Body are more closely united than they were before.

Constituent, that Constitutes, or Makes up.

Constitute, to Appoint.

Constitution, (Lat.) an Ordinance or Decree; also the State of the Body; also the Form of Government used in any Place: Likewise the Laws of a Kingdom are called its *Constitutions*.

Constraint, Force or Compulsion.

Constriction, (Lat.) is the crowding the Parts of any Body close together, in order to *Condensation*.

Constrictor Labiorum, & orbicularis Labiorum, a Muscle of the Lips, which purses them up, and is by some call'd *Osculatorius*.

Constrictores Alarum nasi ac depressores Labii superioris, are Muscles which draw the Upper-Lip and *Ale* downwards.

Construction, a Building, or Making.

Construction of *Equations* in *A'gebra*, is the contriving such Lines and Figures as shall demonstrate the *Equation, Canon*, or *Theorem* to be true Geometrically.

Construction, in *Geometry*, is the drawing of such Lines as are previously necessary for the Demonstration of any Proposition.

Construction, in *Grammar*, is the natural, just, and regular placing and disposing of Words in a Discourse, so as to make proper and intelligible Sense.

Construe, or *Conster*, to Interpret or Expound.

Constupration, (Lat.) a Debauching or Deflow'ring of Maids or Women.

Consubstantial, (Lat.) of the same Substance.

Consubstantiation, is the Doctrine of the Substantial Presence of the Body and Blood of Christ in the Lord's Supper, together with the substance of Bread and Wine maintain'd by the *Lutherans*.

Consul, (Lat.) was the Name of a sovereign Magistrate among the *Romans*, whereof there were two in number. It is now given to Chief Governours of several Cities, but especially to the principal Managers of Trade or Residents for Merchants in foreign Places.

Consular, belonging to a Consul.

Consult, to Advise with or ask Advice of any one: To consult an *Author*, is the same as to see what is his Opinion of the Matter.

Consultation, (Lat.) an asking or taking Counsel or Advice:

vice : Also an Examination of a Question, Affair or Disease ; also a Writ removing a Cause from the King's to the Ecclesiastical Court.

Consume, (Lat.) to Destroy or Waste ; to Spend, to Pine away, Wear out, or Decay.

Consummate, (Lat.) to Fulfil, Finish or make Perfect. An End.

Consummation, (Lat.) a fulfilling, finishing or perfecting. An End.

Consumption, is a defect of Nourishment, or the consuming, wasting or decaying of the Body, and particularly of the muscular Flesh.

Contabulation, a fastning of Boards or Planks together, a Flooring.

Contact, a Touch ; so Places or Points of Contact, are those Places or Points in which one Line or Body touches another.

Contagion, (Lat.) the same with *Infection*, is the communicating or transferring of a Disease from one Body to another, by some certain Effluvia or Steams.

Contagious, (Lat.) Infectious, apt to Infect.

Contain, to Comprehend or Enclose.

Contamination, (Lat.) a Polluting or Defiling.

Contecke, Contest, Strife. *Spencer*.

Contemn, to Despise or Slight ; to set at Nought.

Contemplation, (Lat.) is the preserving of the Idea,

which is brought into the Mind for some time in view, in order to meditate upon it, or look upon it attentively.

Contemplative, given to Contemplation.

Contemplatives, Friers of the Order of *Mary Magdalen*, who wore black upper Garments, and white underneath.

Contemporary, (Lat.) of the same Time or Standing.

Contemptible, (Lat.) worthy to be Despised and Scorned.

Contemptuous, Scornful, Slighting.

Content, in *Geometry*, is the Area or Solidity of any Surface or Body, estimated or measured in square or solid Inches, Feet, Yards, &c.

Contentation, Satisfaction of Mind.

Contention, (Lat.) Strife, Dispute, Quarrel.

Contentious, Litigious, Quarrelsom.

Conterminate, (Lat.) to lie near or border upon.

Conterminous, lying near or bordering upon.

Contest, to Quarrel, or Wrangle.

Context, the Scripture that lies about the Text before or after it.

Contexture, the joyning together or framing of a Discourse, or other Thing.

Contignation, (Lat.) a laying of Rafters together in Architecture, it signifies Flooring.

Conti-

Contiguity, is the touch of two distinct Bodies.

Contiguous Things or Bodies, are such as touch one another.

ontinence, (Lat.) is the abstaining from unlawful Pleasures.

Continent, Abstaining from unlawful Pleasures: In *Geography*, it signifies a great extent of Land, which comprehends several Regions and Kingdoms, which are not interrupted and separated by Seas.

Contingence, a Casualty or Event that happens by chance, or which may or may not happen to come to pass.

Contingent, Casual.

Contingent Line in Dialing, is a Line arising from the Intersection of the Plane of the Dial, with the Plane of the Equinoctial; and consequently in this Line the Hour Lines of the Dial, and Hour Circles intersect one another.

Continual Claim, is a Claim made from time to time within every Year and Day, to Land or other Thing, which in some respect we cannot attain without danger.

Continual Fever, is that which sometimes remits or abates, but never perfectly intermits.

Continuando, In Law, is when the Plantiff would reA cover Damages for several Trespasses in the same Action.

Continuation, (Lat.) the lasting of any thing without interruption

Continued Quantity, or *Continuum*, is that whose Parts are so joyn'd and united together, that you cannot tell where one begins and another ends.

Contorsion, (Lat) a pulling awry, a wresting.

Contour, (Fr.) Circumference or Compass. In *Graving* or *Painting*, *Contours* are the Out-lines of a Figure or Picture.

Contrabanded Goods, are such as are forbidden to be exported.

Contract, (Lat.) a Covenant, Agreement or Bargain.

Contraction, (Lat.) a Drawing together; also a making short.

Contradiction, (Lat.) a contrariety of Words and Sentiments.

Contradictory Propositions in Logick, are such as consist of an Universal and Particular; of which one affirms, and the other denies; as *all Men are endued with a rational Soul; Some Man is not endued with a rational Soul*.

Contradistinction, (Lat.) a Distinguishing on the other side.

Contra formam feoffamenti, is a Writ for a Tenant that is infeoffed by the Lord's Charter, to make certain Suit and Service to his Court, and is afterwards distrain'd for more than is contained therein.

Contra Fissure, is a Fissure

on one fide of the Head, occafion'd by a Blow or Fall on the other.

Contra fermam collationii, a Writ againft the Governour of any Religious Houfe, Hofpital, &c. that has alienated the Lands given thereunto, contrary to the intent of the Donor.

Contra-Queue d'yronde, in Fortification, is the fame with *Counter* Swallow's Tail.

Contraindications, are divers Confiderations in a Difeafe, that diffwade a Phyfician from ufing fuch a Remedy, when other things induce him to it.

Contra-mure in Fortification, is a little Wall built before another Partition-Wall to ftrengthen it, fo that it may receive no damage from the adjacent Buildings.

Contrapofition, a putting againft. Logical Term.

Contrariety, (Lat.) Oppofition, Difagreement.

Contrary Propofitions, in Logick, fuch as confift of two Univerfals; one affirming and the other denying.

Contraft, (Fr.) a fmall Difpute or Difference.

Contravallation, or the Line of Contravallation in Fortification, is a Trench guarded with a Parapet, and ufually cut round a Place by the Befiegers, to fecure themfelves and ftop the Sallies of the Garifon, it is without Musket-fhot of the Town.

Contravene, to infringe or break a Law or Agreement.

Contrafltation, (Lat.) a Touching or Handling.

Contribute, to affift towards the doing any thing.

Contributione facienda, a Writ for thofe that are put to the burden of a thing, which others are equally obliged to.

Contribution, (Lat.) a joynt giving of Money towards any Bufinefs of importance; as towards the building of Churches, &c.

Contrite, worn, bruifed; but it is moft commonly ufed for forrowful, penitent.

Contrition (Lat.) a Sorrow for Sin, proceeding from love to God, not fear of Punifhment.

Contrive, to Invent, Devife or imagine.

Control, to Difprove, call to an Account, or Overlook.

Controller, is an Officer who keeps a Roll of all other Officers Accompts.

Controverfy, a Difpute about a thing that is uncertain.

Controverted, Undetermin'd, not agreed upon, that may be difputed on pro and con.

Contumacy, Stubbornnefs, Wilfulnefs.

Contumelious, one that gives reproachful Language, or an Affront.

Contumely, (Lat.) Reproach, Abufe, fcurrilous Language.

Contufion, (Lat.) a Beating or Bruifing; alfo a Blunting.

Convalescence, (Lat.) a Recovery of Health.

Convene, to Meet or come together, to warn into an Assembly.

Conveniency, (Lat.) Agreeableness, Ease, Advantage.

Convent, a Monastery or Religious House.

Conventicle, (Lat.) a private Assembly, most commonly an Assembly of Dissenters.

Convention, (Lat.) a Covenant; also an Assembly of the States.

Conventual, belonging to a Convent.

Converging Lines or *Rays*, are such which incline towards one another, till at last they meet and cross, and then become *Diverging*.

Conversant, well vers'd, or keeping company with.

Converse, to Discourse or Talk familiarly with.

Conversation, (Lat.) Discourse amongst Persons; Intercourse, Behaviour.

Converse, in Mathematicks, one Proposition is call'd the Converse of another, when after a Conclusion is drawn from something supposed in the first Proposition; in the second Proposition, the Conclusion of the first is made a Supposition; and what was supposed in the first, is thence concluded.

Conversion, a changing from one State to another; especially from Bad to Good.

Conversion of Propositions, in Logick, is the changing of

the Subject into the Place of the Predicate; and the Predicate into the Place of the Subject, still retaining the *Quality* of the Proposition.

Convertible, Changeable, that may be turn'd.

Convexity, (Lat.) signifies any Protuberancy or Swelling out of any thing. Concavity differs from Convexity thus; in any globulous Body, which is hollow within, the outside of it is called *Convex*, and the inside *Concave*.

Conveyance, in Law, a Deed wherein Land is convey'd from one to another.

Conviction (Lat.) is in Law, the proving of a Man guilty of an Offence by the Verdict of a Jury; or when a Man that is Outlaw'd appeareth and confesseth.

Convince, to perswade a Man of the Truth of any thing by Reason and Argument.

Convocation, (Lat.) a Meeting together, most commonly of the Clergy for Church Affairs: Also, the Persons so met together are call'd a *Convocation*.

Convolution, (Lat.) a Wrapping, Rolling, or Winding about.

Convoy, (Fr.) a Guide or Conductor; also a Man or Men of War that go along with Merchant Ships, to defend them from their Enemies.

Conus fusorius, a sort of Crucible to melt Iron, or any   other

other Mettal in.

Conusant, in Law, signifies Knowing or Understanding.

Convulsion, (Lat.) is a Motion whereby the Nerves, Muscles and Members are contracted or pull'd together, against, or without the Will; as in the *Cramp, Epilepsy,* &c.

Coo, to make a Noise like Turtles or Pigeons.

Co-operation, (Lat.) a Working together with.

Co-ordinate (Lat.) of equal Order, Degree, or Rank.

Coparceners, or *Parceners,* in Common-Law, are such as have equal Shares in the Inheritance of their Ancestors.

Cope, to Jut out as a Wall; also to oppose or make head against.

Cope, (from the *Saxon Coppe,* the Height or Top of a thing) the upper Garment; as the outer Vest of a Priest, or the Cloak or Surtout of any other Person: The Top of an Hill or any other Thing.

Copernican System, an old System revived by *Copernicus,* in which the Sun is supposed to be placed in the Center, next to him *Mercury,* then *Venus,* then our Earth with her Satellit the Moon, then *Mars,* next to him *Jupiter,* and lastly *Saturn.*

Cophosis, (Gr.) is the Deafness in the Ears.

Copious, Plentiful, Abounding.

Copos, a Weariness of the Body, proceeding some vicious Humours, loading and obstructing the Fibres, and rendring them unfit for Motion.

Coppel, (Fr.) the Pot in which Goldsmiths Melt or Fine their Metal: Also, a sort of Crucible used by Chymists in purifying Gold or Silver.

Copulation, (Lat.) is the Conjunction of Male and Female.

Copy-hold, in Law, is a Tenure for which the Tenant has nothing to show, but the Copy of the Rolls, made by the Steward of the Lord's Court.

Coquet, an amourous Courtier; one that by his affected Carriage and silly Tattle endeavours to gain the Love of the Ladies.

Coquetry, an affected Carriage to win the Love of Men or Women; Tattle in Men, and Gossopry in Women tending for the most part to amourous Intreague.

Coracle, a small Boat used by Fishermen on the *Severn.*

Coracobrachialis, is a Muscle of the Arm, which moves it upwards, and turns it somewhat obliquely outwards.

Coracoides, is the Process of the Shoulder Blade in form of a Beek.

Coram non judice, in the Common Law, is when a Cause is brought into a Court out of the Judges Jurisdiction.

Coral, a petrified Plant, or rather, a certain Shoot from a Rock that hath received the Form of a Plant.

Cor

Corban (Heb.) an Offering on the Altar, or a Gift dedicated to God.

Corbeils, in Fortication, are little Baskets fill'd with Earth, and placed upon the Parapet to secure the Besieged from being seen by the Enemy.

Cordage, at Sea, signifies all the Ropes belonging to the Rigging of a Ship.

Cordelier, a Grey-Frier of the Franciscan Order, that wears a Cord full of Knots about his Middle.

Cordial, Comfortable; also Sincere, Hearty.

Cords, in Musick, properly signifie the Strings of an Harp, Violin, Lute or any other Musical Instrument. Also it denotes the Sounds which proceed from such Instruments, even those which have no Strings.

Cordon, in Fortification, is a Stone jutting out between the Rampart and the Basis of the Parapet : It goes quite round the Fortification.

Cor Hydræ, a Star of the first magnitude in the Constellation *Hydra*.

Corinthian Order, is one of the Five Orders of Architecture, so call'd from *Corinth* the Place of its invention.

Cornea Oculi Tunica, the second or horny Coat of the Eye, which contains the aqueous Humour.

Cornelian, a kind of Precious Stone of a Red colour.

Cornish in Architecture, is the third and highest part of the *Entablature*, and commonly signifies the upermost Ornament of any Wainscot, &c. in reference to the Pillar, it is different, according to the several Orders of Architecture.

Corniculate Plants, are such as after each Flower produce many distinct and horned Seed Pods, call'd *Siliqua*.

Cornigerous, wearing Horns.

Cornish Ring of a Gun, is that Ring near the Muzzle.

Cornute, (Lat.) Horned, having Horns; a Cuckold.

Corporate, united into one Body.

Corollary, a Consequence drawn from something already proved or demonstrated.

Coron, a Jewish Measure of Capacity for things liquid, containing 75 Gallons, 7 Pints, 7 solid Inches of our *English* Wine Measure.

Corona, commonly called *Halo*, a Circle appearing about the Sun; in Architecture it signifies the flat and most advanced part of the Cornish, called by us the *Drip*, because it defends the rest from Wind and Weather.

Coronall, Garland. *Spencer.*

Coronal Suture, is a Cleft in the Head made like a Comb, and joyns as if the Teeth of two Combs were closely compacted into one another.

Coronaria vasa, the Veins and Arteries which surround the Heart to nourish it.

Corone, an Acute Process of the lower Jaw, in the form of a Beek. Co-

Coroner, an Officer, who with the affiftance of a Jury of 12 Men, enquires on behalf of the Crown, into all untimely Deaths.

Coronet, a little Crown or Chaplet.

Corporal, belonging to the Body.

Corporation, a political Body or Company eftablifhed by a Royal Charter.

Corpora Striata, two Prominences in the Brain; the Tips of the *Crura Medullæ oblongatæ*.

Corpora Pyramidalia, are 2 Prominences in the *Cerebellum*, in length about an Inch.

Corpora Olivaria, are two Prominences, one on each fide the *Corpora Pyramidalia*.

Corporature, the Form, Bulk, or Conftitution of the Body.

Corporeal, that is of a bodily Subftance, or pertaineth to Body.

Corporeity, the School Term for the Nature of a Body.

Corporification, a making a Body. In *Chymiftry*, 'tis the giving to a Spirit the fame, or a like Body to that it had before.

Corps de garde, are Souldiers entrufted with the Guard of a Poft, under the command of one or more Officers.

Corpulent, (Lat.) Grofs, Fat, Bulky.

Corpufcle, in Natural Philofophy, fignifies the minute Parts or Particles, or Phyfical Atoms of a Body.

Corpus cum causâ, in Law, is a Writ iffuing out of the Chancery, to remove both the Body and the Record into the King's-Bench.

Corpus callofum, in Anatomy, which lies immediately under the *Dura Mater*, is the covering of two lateral Ventricles, form'd by the union of the Medullary Fibres on each fide.

Corpufcular Philofophy, is that which explains natural *Phænomena*, by the Motions and Affections of the minute Particles of Matter.

Corr, a Meafure containing two Quarts.

Corrade, (Lat.) to Scrape together.

Correct, to Chaftife; alfo it fignifies without Faults: As a correct Writer is one with whom no fault can be found.

Correction, a Chaftening; alfo an Amending.

Corrective, that Corrects, Tempers, or Allays.

Correctives, Medicines that adminiftred with others, correct fome bad Quality or Malignity in them.

Correlatives, are Things which bear fuch a relation to one another, that their very Nature confifts in that Relation, as Father, Son, &c. for the very Nature of a Father, confifts in his having a Son; and the very Nature of a Son confifts in his having a Father.

Correption, (Lat.) a Correction in Words; a Snatching away.   *Cor-*

Correfpond, to Anfwer, Fit, or Agree with ; to hold a mutual Commerce and Familiarity.

Correfpondence, an Anfwering, Fitting, or Agreeing of one thing with another ; a holding a mutual Commerce and Familiarity.

Correfpondent, one that holds Correfpondence, or one with whom it is kept, which is either perfonal, or at a diftance by Letters.

Corridor, (Fr.) in Fortification, is the *Covert-way*, lying round about the whole compafs of the Fortification of a Place, between the outfide of the Moat and the Pallifadoes.

Corrigible, that may be Corrected or Amended.

Corrival, a Competitor, either in Love or Bufinefs.

Corroberate, (Lat.) to Strengthen, to Confirm.

Corrode, to Gnaw or Fret.

Corrofion, (Lat.) a Gnawing or Fretting ; in Chymiftry, it is a diffolution of mix'd Bodies by *Corrofive Menftruums*.

Corrofive, that hath a gnawing or fretting Quality.

Corrofivenefs, is the Quality that fome Liquors, which are called *Menftruums*, have of diffolving Bodies.

Corrugata, in Anatomy, is a Mufcle of the Eye-brows, helping to knit them when we Frown.

Corrugation, (Lat.) a contracting or drawing into Wrinkles.

Corruption, is the Deftruction of the Form of any Body ; for when ever any Body lofes its Form, or that peculiar Modification which was neceffary to conftitute it fuch a Body, then it is faid to Corrupt, or be in a ftate of Corruption.

Corrufcant, (Lat.) Gliftering, Shining or Lightening.

Corrufcation, (Lat.) a flafh of Lightning, or a kind of feeming fparkling Fire, which appears oftenr by Night. A Glittering.

Corfair, (Fr.) a Pirate or Robber.

Cortex, (viz. *Peruvianus*) is the Jefuits Bark, famous for curing of intermitting Fevers.

Cortical Part of the Brain, is the external Part of it ; and is foft, glandulous, and of the colour of Afhes.

Cortin, in Fortification, is the Wall or Diftance between the Flanks of two Baftions.

Corvus, a Southern Conftellation in the Heavens, confifting of Seven Stars ; alfo a warlike Engine to pull down Walls.

Coryza, (Gr.) a Defluxion of a fharp Humour into the Mouth and Lungs, from the Brain by the Olfactory Nerves.

Cofcinomancy, Divination by a Sieve.

Co-fecant, the Secant of an Ark, which is the Complement of another to 90°.

Cofenage, in Law, is a Writ for

for the right Heir againſt an Intruder.

Co-ſine, is the Sine of the Complemental Ark. Thus if an Ark of 40°. be the Ark you conſider, then is an Ark of 50°. the Complement of the former, and the right Sine of 50°. is the Co-ſine of 40°.

Coſmeticks, are Medicines which whiten and ſoften the Skin, or in general, any thing which tends to promote the Beauty of the Perſon that uſeth them.

Coſmical, (Gr.) belonging to the World ; alſo a Term in Aſtronomy, expreſſing one of the poetical Riſings or Settings of a Star ; for a Star riſes *coſmically*, when it riſes together with the Sun, and a Star ſets *coſmically*, when it ſets at the ſame time that the Sun riſes: But to riſe or ſet *coſmically*, according to *Kepler*, is to aſcend above the *Horizon*, or deſcend below it.

Coſmographer, one skill'd in Coſmography.

Coſmography, (Gr.) is a Deſcription of the ſeveral Parts of the viſible World, delineating them according to their Number, Poſitions, Motions, Magnitude, Figures, &c. the two Parts of which are, *Aſtronomy* and *Geography*.

Coſſacks, a Militia or Body of Souldiers in *Poland*, ſet up by King *Stephen Bathorī*.

Coſſe and *Coſſick*, the old Word for Algebra, which the

Italian ſword. *Coſa* ſignifies

Coſſet, a Lamb brought up by Hand. *Spencer*.

Coſt, in Heraldry, is the fourth part of a Bend.

Coſtard, an Apple : hence *Coſtard-monger*, a Seller of Apples : A Fruiterer.

Coſtæ, the Ribs are 24 in Number, 12 on each ſide the *Vertebræ* of the Back.

Coſtæ veræ, are the ſeven uppermoſt Ribs, ſo called becauſe their cartilaginous Ends are received into the *Sinus* of the *Sternum*.

Coſtæ falſæ, are the five lowermoſt, ſo called, becauſe they are ſhorter and ſofter, and not joyn'd to the Extremity of the *Sternum*.

Coſtive, Bound in the Belly.

Cotage, (Sax.) a little Houſe or Hutt.

Co-tangent, is the Tangent of any Complemental Ark ; or what any Ark wants of a Quadrant, or 90°.

Cotyle, an Attick Meaſure of Capacity, for Things liquid or Things dry : For Things liquid, it contains $\frac{1}{12}$ of a Pint, two ſolid Inches, and 818 decimal Parts of our Wine Meaſure : For Things dry, it contains $\frac{1}{12}$ of a Pint, and 24 decimal Parts of a ſolid Inch, of our Corn Meaſure.

Couchant, lying or ſquatting cloſe to the Ground : It is uſed in Heraldry to expreſs that Poſture, as a Lion Couchant.

Covenant,

Covenant, an Agreement, or the mutual Consent of two or more to one thing; to do, or give somewhat, &c. In Law, Covenant is that which the Law intendeth to be made, tho' in words not to be expres'd,

Covent or *Convent*, a Monastery.

Covert, an Umbrage or shady Place.

Coverture, in Law, is the State and Condition of a married Woman, who by the Laws is dissabled from making any Bargains without her Husband's Content.

Covert-way, see *Corridor*.

Covine, (in Law) is a deceitful Assent or Agreement between two or more, to the prejudice of another.

Council, in respect of Ecclesiastical Matters, signifies an Assembly of Church-men or Prelates, that confer and decide what belongs to Religion and Ecclesiastical Discipline. Also an Assembly of the chief Persons of a Nation met together to confer about Affairs of State; also Advice.

Countenance, the Face or Visage: Also it is frequently used for Encouragement; as to countenance any one, is as much as to encourage him.

Counter-approaches, in Fortification, are Works made by the Besieged, to hinder the approach of the Enemy, when they design to attack them in form.

Counter-Battery, is a Battery raised to play upon another.

Counter-Ballance, to weigh one thing against another.

Counter-changed, in Heraldry, is when there is a mutual changing of the Colours of the Field and Charge in an Escutcheon, by reason of one or more Lines of Partition, as in the Figure, he beareth *Party per pale Argent* and *Gules* a *Bend counterchanged*.

Counter-componed, in Heraldry, is a *Bordure*, or any Ordinary, which hath 2 Rows only of *Checkers* of two different colours.

Counterfoil or *Counterstock*, that part of a Tally struck in the Exchequer, which is kept by an Officer of that Court.

Counter-Fugues, in Musick, is when the Fugues proceed contrary to one another.

Counter-Guards, in Fortification, are large heaps of Earth, in form of a Parapet, raised above the Moat, before the Faces and Points of the Bastions to preserve them.

Countermand, is revoking a former Command.

Counter-march, in the Art of War, signifies the changing of the Face or Wings of a Battallion.

Countermine, is a subterraneous Passage, or Mine made

by

by the Besieged, in search of the Enemies Mine, in order to hinder the mischievous Effects of it.

Counter-part, a Term in Musick, only denoting one part to be opposite to another, as the Base is the Counter-part of the Treble.

Counter-Passant, in Heraldry, two Beasts are said to be *Counter-passant*, which are born walking contrary ways.

Counter-point, in Musick, is the old manner of composing Parts before Notes of different Measure were invented, which was to set Pricks or Points one against another, to denote the several Concords, the Length or Measure of which Points were sung, or play'd according to the Length or Quantity of the Words or Syllables whereunto they were apply'd.

Counter-poise, to weigh one thing against another.

Counter-salient, Leaping contrariwise, the posture of two Beasts in a Coat of Arms.

Counter-scarp, in Fortification, is that side of the Ditch which is next the Camp.

Counter-Swallows-Tail, is an Out-work in Fortification, in the form of a single Tenliale, wider at the Gorge than at the Head.

Counter-tenor, one of the middle Parts of Musick; so call'd, because it is as it were opposed to the *Tenor*.

County-Court, a Court held every Month by the Sheriff or his Deputy.

Couped, cut off; in Heraldry, it is any thing in an Escutcheon, which is cut clear and evenly off.

Couple-close, in Heraldry, is the fourth part of a Cheveron.

Course, in Navigation, is the Angle made by the *Rhomb Line* and the Meridian.

Court, in Law, is a Place where Justice is judicially administred, of which there are various kinds.

Courtesan, a Lady or Gentlewoman belonging to the Court; also a professed Strumpet or Whore.

Courtesie, the same with Civility, is a kind and obliging Behaviour and Management of one's self.

Couth, Could, Knew, *Spencer*.

Couthentlaugh, one that receiveth and hideth an Out-law.

Coward, a Term in Heraldry, for a Lion born in an Escutcheon, with his Tail doubled or turn'd in between his Legs.

Coxendix, or *Os Ischium*, is the inferior part of the *Ossa innominata*, having a large Cavity which receives the Head of the Thigh Bone.

Cozen, to Bubble, Cheat, Chouse, or Gull.

Cozenage, a Cheating.

Crabbed, Sour as Unripe Fruit; Rough, Uneven, Surly.

Cradle,

Cradle, in Navigation, is a Frame of Timber raised along the outside of a Ship by the *Bilge*, serving the more securely and commodiously to Launch a Ship.

Craft, a Sea Word, signifying all manner of Lines, Nets, Hooks, &c. for Fishing.

Cragg, Nock, *Spencer*.

Cramp, a Disease which is caused by a violent distortion of the Nerves.

Cranage, in Law, is the Duty paid for the use of a Crane to draw out Wares out of a Ship, &c.

Crane-Lines, are Lines in a Ship, going from the upper-end of the Sprit-sail Top-mast to the middle of the Fore-Stays.

Cranes-Bill, an Instrument used by Surgeons; it is a sort of *Forceps* or *Pincers*.

Cranium, the Skull, or the whole Compages of the Bones of the Head, which like an Helmet defends the Brain from external Injuries.

Crank, at Sea, when a Ship cannot bear her Sails, or can bear but a small part for fear of over-setting, they say she is *Crank*.

Crasis, (Gr.) is a convenient Mixture of Qualities in an Animal Body.

Crass, (Lat.) Fat, Gross.

Crassitude, Thickness.

Crayon, (Fr.) a small Pencil of any sort of Coulouring Stuff, made up unto Paste and dry'd; to be used for Drawing in dry Colours, upon Paper or Parchment.

Creation, is a forming Something out of Nothing, or no pre-existing Materials, and is proper to God. It differs from all other sorts of Formations, whereas they all suppose something to work, but this does not suppose any thing at all.

Credentials, Letters of Credit.

Credibility, that may be believed. See *Credible*.

Credible, that is properly Credible, which is not apparent in its self, nor certainly to be collected, either antecedently from its Cause, or reversly by its Effect; and yet, tho' by none of these ways, hath the Attestation of Truth.

Credit, Trust, Belief; also that Esteem which a Man acquires by his Virtue, his Probity, his Honesty, and his Merit.

Credulous, (Lat.) Easy or rash of Belief.

Creek, a Part of a Haven where any thing is landed.

Cremaster, a Muscle in the Testicles of Men; the use whereof, is to draw them up in the Act of Generation.

Crenated Leaves, Leaves of Plants that are jagged or notched.

Crencles, in a Ship, are small Ropes, spliced into the Bolt Ropes of the Sails of the *Main-Mast* and *Fore-mast*.

Cre-

Crenelle, a Term in Heraldry, signifying the same as *Embattled*; which see.

Crepitation, a crackling or creaking Noise.

Crepuscle, Twilight, or that dubious half Light which we perceive in the Morning before the Sun's Rising, and at Night after the Sun's Setting.

Cressent, in Heraldry, signifies a Half-moon, which is usually drawn of this Figure.

Crest, any imagery or carv'd Work to adorn the Head or Top of any thing, like our Modern Cornish; this Word is now adapted by the Heralds, and apply'd to the Device set over a Coat of Arms.

Crevice, a Chink or Cleft between the Boards of a Floor, Ceiling, Door, &c.

Cribration, (Lat.) is the Chymists word for Sifting any Powder, or passing it thro' a Fine Sieve.

Cricothyroides, the first pair of proper Muscles of the *Larinx*; by moving a little obliquely; its use is to pull up the *Annularis*.

Crico-Arytænoides Lateralis, the second pair of proper Muscles of the *Larinx*; the Use whereof is to dilate the *Arytænoides*.

Crico-Arytænoides Posticus, the third pair of the Muscles of the *Larinx*.

Crimnoides, is Urine, with thick Sediment at the Bottom like Bran.

Criminal, guilty of any Crime or Fault.

Crisis, (Gr.) a Judgment pass'd upon a thing: Also in *Physick*, it signifies a sudden Change in a Disease, towards a Recovery or Death.

Crista Galli, in Anatomy, is a small Process in the middle of the *Os Ethmoides*, not much unlike the Comb of a Cock.

Cristæ, Excrescencies of Flesh growing about the Fundament.

Criterium, a Judgment made of the Truth or Falshood of a Proposition; also a Mark whereby to judge of the Truth of a thing.

Critical, of a Nice Judgment, Censorious.

Criticism, is the Art of Judging or Censuring Men's Words, Writings or Actions.

Criticize, to Judge and Censure a Man's Works, and Correct the Defects of it; it commonly signifies, to find Fault with.

Critick, a Person skill'd in the Art of Criticism.

Cronie, an intimate Friend, a contemporary Disciple.

Crosiers, are four Stars in the form of a Cross, by the help of which, those that sail in the Southern Hemisphere find the Antarctick Pole.

Cross,

Cross, one of the honourable Ordinaries in Heraldry; containing one fifth of the Field: There is great variety in its Form, according to the lines that compose

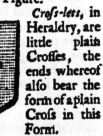

it. A plain Cross is of this Figure, *Argent*, a *Cross sable*.

Cross-voided, in Heraldry, is when a Line is drawn parallel to the Out-lines of the Cross, & then the Field is supposed to appear thro';
as in this Figure.

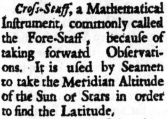

Cross-lets, in Heraldry, are little plain Crosses, the ends whereof also bear the form of a plain Cross in this Form.

Cross-Staff, a Mathematical Instrument, commonly called the Fore-Staff, because of taking forward Observations. It is used by Seamen to take the Meridian Altitude of the Sun or Stars in order to find the Latitude.

Cross-Jack, in a Ship, is a small Yard, flung at the upper end of the Mizen-mast under the Top.

Cross-piece, is a great piece of Timber, going a cross the Bitts of a Ship; and unto it is the *Cable* belay'd when she rides at Anchor.

Cross-Trees, in a Ship, are four pieces of Timber, bolted and let into one another across at the Head of the Mast.

Crotchet, a Measure in Musick, being half a Minum.

Crown, in Geometry, is a *Ring*, comprehended between two Concentrick Peripheries.

Crown Works, in Fortification, are certain Bulwarks advanced towards the Field to gain some Hill or rising Ground; being composed of a spacious *Gorge*, and two Wings that fall on the *Counterscarp* near the Faces of the *Bastion*.

Crucial, of the form of a Cross.

Cruciate, (Lat.) to torment.

Crucible, is a Chymical Vessel made of Earth, so temper'd and baked as to endure the greatest degrees of Fire.

Crucifers, (Lat. *i. e.* Cross-bearers, the same as Crouched Friers.

Crucifix, an Image or Figure of our Saviour on the Cross.

Crucifixion, (Lat.) a Crucifying.

Crucify, to nail or fasten to a Cross; also, to Kill or Mortify.

Crudity, Rawness, ill Digestion of the Stomach; as when the Aliment or Meat are not duly fermented, and
regularly

regularly turn'd into Chyle.

Cruife, (Fr.) the Courfe of a Ship. *Verbally*, to fail up and down for Guard of the Seas.

Crumnal, Purfe : *Spencer*.

Crura Medullæ Oblongatæ, the internal Subftance of the two Sides of the *Cerebrum*, gathered as it were into two Bundles.

Crural, (Lat.) belonging to the Thighs.

Crureus, a Mufcle of the Leg, fo call'd from its fitua-tion on the Bone on the Thigh: It helps to extend the Tibia.

Crufade or *Croifade*, the Expedition of Chriftian Princes for Conqueft of the Holy Land ; fo call'd from wearing of the Crofs.

Cruftaceous Fifhes, are Shell Fifhes, fuch as Crabs, Lob-fters, &c.

Cruftula, a Difeafe in the Eye, being a falling of Blood from the Arteries into the *Tunica conjunctiva*, occafion'd by a Wound, Stroak, &c.

Crymodes, a cold fhivering Feaver, but often accompa-nied with an Inflammation of the inner Parts.

Cryptography, (Gr.) the Art of Secret Writing.

Cryptology, a fpeaking or difcourfing in fecret.

Cryforchis, is an abfcond-ing of the Tefticles in the Belly.

Cryftalline, of Chryftal, clear as Chryftal.

Cryftalline Humour, is one of the Humours of the Eye,

feated in the middle, in the form of of a Protuberant dou-ble *Convex lens* ; and which is commonly, tho' falfly thought, to be the principal Caule of our feeing Objects diftinctly at various Di-ftances.

Cryftallization, (in *Chymi-ftry*) is the reducing of Salts into fmall figured Particles clear as Chryftal.

Cubature, in *Geometry* is finding exactly the folid Con-tent of any propofed Body in folid Inches, Feet, Yards, &c.

Cubbridge-Heads in a Ship, are the Bulk-Heads of the *Fore-caftle* and the *Half Decks*.

Cube, is a folid Body, ter-minated by fix equal Squares, as a Dye truly made.

Cube, in *Algebra*, is the fecond Power from the Root, and is form'd by mul-tiplying the Root continually into its felf twice.

Cubical Paraboloid, is a fort of Parabola, the Cubes of whofe Ordinates are as their refpective Abfciffa's, and confequently the Ordinates themfelves are in a fubtripli-cate Ratio of their Abfciffa's : This fort of Parabola differs from the femicubical Parabo-loid thus ; in this the Cubes of the Ordinates are as the Squares of their Abfciffa's, and confequently the Ordinates themfelves are in the Ratio of the Cube of the Squares of their Abfciffa's, or in the

eft

subtriplicate Duplicate Ratio of their Abscissæ.

Cubick Equations in *Algebra*, are such, where the highest Power of the unknown Quantity is a Cube.

Cubicular, (Lat.) belonging to a Bed-chamber.

Cubit, (Lat.) the length of the Arm from the Elbow to the end of the Middle Finger, which is usually about a Foot and a half.

Cubit, a Scripture Measure of Length, containing 1 *English* Foot, 9 Inches, and 888 decimal Parts.

Cubitæus Internus & Externus; are two Muscles of the Wrist, the first of which serves to bend it, and the latter to extend it.

Cubiture, (Lat.) a Lying down.

Cubo-cube, is the sixth Power of any Number or Quantity; and is form'd by multiplying the Root continually into its self five times.

Cucupha, a Medicine for the Head.

Cucurbite, (Lat.) a Chymical Vessel, made of Glass, Earth, Copper, in the form of a Gourd: This Vessel is most commonly used in Distillations and Rectifications.

Cucurbitula or *Cucurbita*, a Cupping-glass.

Cudden or *Cuddy*, a Changeling, Nizey, or silly Fellow.

Cuddy, in a first Rate Man of War, is a Place lying between the Captain and Lieutenant's Cabbin, under the Poop; and divided into Partitions for the Master and Secretary's Officers.

Cue, an Item to Stage-Players, what or when to Speak: Also a Mood or Humour.

Cuerpo, (Spanish) a Body. *To walk in Cuerpo*, is to go without a Cloak.

Cui ante Divortium; a Writ, impowering a divorc'd Woman to recover her Lands from him to whom her Husband did alienate them, during the Marriage, because she could not gainsay it.

Cui in vitâ, a Writ of Entry, for a Widow, upon her Lands, alienated by her Husband.

Cuirass, (Fr.) an Armour of Steel or Iron that covers the Body from Neck to Waste; as well behind as before.

Cuirassier (Fr.) one arm'd with a *Cuirass*; most commonly spoken of Horsemen.

Culeus, a Roman Measure of Capacity for things liquid, containing 243 Gallons, 3 Pints, 11 solid Inches, 075 decimal Parts of our Wine Measure.

Culinary, (Lat.) belonging to the Kitchin.

Cullions, the Stones or Testicles: Among Gardiners, they are round Roots of Herbs whether single, double or treble.

Cully, (Ital.) a Fool, a silly soft Headed Fellow.

Culmiferous, (Lat.) Stalk-bearing, or that bears a Stalk.

I 2   *Culminate,*

Culminate, (Lat.) to come to the Meridian; thus any Star is said to Culminate, when it is in the highest Point in the Heavens that it is possible for it to be; that is, when it is upon the Meridian.

Culpable, that may be Blamed or found Fault with.

Cultellation, (Lat.) a measuring of Heights or Distances by Piece-meal, that is by Instruments, which give us such Heights or Distances by Parts, and not all at one Operation.

Cultivate, (Lat.) to Plow, Till or Manure Land.

Cultivation, (Lat.) a Manuring or Tilling.

Culture, Husbandry, Tillage, Improvement, Good Education.

Culverin, a piece of Ordnance, about 5 Inches and a Quarter Diameter in Bore, carrying a Ball of 18 Pound.

Culvertaile, is the fastening of a Ships Carlings into the Beams.

Cumber, to Trouble, to Stop or Crowd.

Cumulate,(Lat.) to heap up.

Cumulation, a heaping up.

Cun, a Sea Term; to Cun a Ship, is to direct the Person at the Helm how to steer her.

Cunctation, (Lat.) a Delaying, Lingring or Deferring.

Cunette, in Fortification, is a deep Trench about three or four Fathom wide, sunk along the middle of a dry Moat to make the Passage more difficult to the Enemy.

Cuneiformia Ossa, are three Bones of the *Tarsus*, which is a part of the Foot.

Cupidity, (Lat.) Covetousness or Desire.

Cupola, (Ital.) an arched Tower in a Building, in form of the Bell of a Watch; or a Cup turn'd upside down.

Cuppel, in Chymistry, is an Instrument, the use whereof is to try and purify Gold and Silver.

Curable,that may be cured.

Cure, is a restoring the Sick or Wounded to a State of Health; also a Charge of Souls committed to the Minister.

Curious, one that is inquisitive to see and know every Thing: A Person that is nice in his Cloaths, Books, &c. is so called.

Curiosity, sometimes signifies the same with *Rarity*; and sometimes it denotes Inquisitiveness.

Curmudgeon, a covetous Hunks, a pityful close-fisted Fellow.

Current, (Lat.) that goes, or is established or received. *Substantively*, a Stream, or the Course of Water.

Cursory, Slight or Hasty.

Curtail, to cut off a Horse's Tail; to Dismember, to Diminish.

Curtain, in Fortification, is the Front of the Wall of a fortify'd Place between two Bastions.

Curtana or *Curteyn*, King *Edward* the Confessor's Sword without

without a Point; which as an Emblem of Mercy, is carried before the Kings and Queens of *England* at their Coronation.

Curtation of a *Planet*, in *Aftronomy*, according to fome, is a little part of a Line cut off from his Diftance from the Sun.

Curtilage, (Law-word) a Piece of Ground, Yard , or Garden-Plot, belonging to, or lying near a Houfe.

Curvature, fignifies Crookednefs.

Curve, Crooked.

Curve Lines, are crooked Lines, as the *Periphery* of a Circle, Ellipfis, &c.

Curvet, a Gate, or Prancing of a Managed Horfe.

Curvilineal Figures, are Spaces bounded by Curve Lines ; as the Circle, Ellipfis, Spherick Triangles, &c.

Curules, (Lat.) were thofe of the *Roman* Senators which were carried to Court in Chariots , and were feated upon Chairs of State made of Ivory.

Cufp, (Lat.) the firft Point of the Houfes in a Scheme or Figure of the Heavens.

Cuftodo admittendo aut removendo, a Writs for the admitting or removing of Guardians.

Cuftody, (Lat.) Ward, or Keeping, fafe Hold or Prifon.

Cuftom, is a Law or Right, which, not being committed in Writing, but eftablifh'd by long Ufe, and the Confent of our Anceftors, hath been, and is daily practifed.

Cuftomary Tenants, are fuch as hold by the Cuftom of the Mannor.

Cutaneous, (Lat.) belonging to the Skin.

Cutaneous Diftempers, are fuch as affect the Skin, as the Itch or Scab.

Cuticle, *Scarff-Skin*, is a Membrane or thin Skin which covers the thicker Skin all over the Body.

Cutis, is the Skin of a living Man, or the outermoft of a Human Body: It is a pretty thick Membrane wrought of feveral Filaments of the Veins and Arteries, Nerves and Nervous Fibres, complicated and interwoven with one another, full of Glandules and Lympheducts or Veffels that convey or carry off Vapours and Sweat.

Cut-water, the Sharpnefs of the Head of a Ship below the Water ; fo call'd, becaufe it cuts or divides the Water before it comes to the Bow.

Cuvette, in Fortification, is a deeper Trench, about four Fathom broad ; which is ufually funk in the middle of the great dry Ditch, till you meet with Water that ferves both to prevent the Befiegers Mining, and alfo the better to keep off the Enemy.

Cycle, is a continual Revolution of certain Numbers, which fucceffively go on without any interruption, from the firft to the laft, and then

return

return again to the firſt, and
ſo circulate perpetually. There
are 3 principal Cycles in the
Calendar.

Cycle of the Sun, is a Revolution of 28 Years, for finding out the Dominical Letters, which then return all
in the ſame Order as before.

Cycle of the Moon, or Golden Number, is a Period or
Revolution of 19 Years;
after the Expiration of which,
all the Lunations return to
their former Place in the Calendar, that is, the New
Moons happen in the ſame
Months and Days of the
Month.

Cycle of Indiction, is a Revolution of 3 *Luſtrums* or 15
Years; after which, thoſe
who uſed it began it again.
This is more ancient than the
two former ones, and has
nothing to do with the Heavenly Motions, being eſtabliſhed by *Conſtantine*, who ſub-
ſtituted them in the room of
the *Olympiads*; they were ſo
called by ſome Authors, becauſe they denoted the Year
that Tribute was to be paid
to the Republick.

Cycloid, is a Figure in Geometry, thus form'd: Suppoſe a
Circle moving upon a ſtreight
Line, make one entire Revolution: The Track deſcribed
by that Point of the Generating Circle, which touch'd
the Right Line at its firſt
ſetting out, is call'd the *Cy-
cloidal Curve*; and the Space
which is comprehended be-
tween the Curve and the
Right Line, is what we call
the *Cycloid*.

Cyclopædy, (Gr.) the whole
Circle of Arts and Sciences.

Cylinder, is a Solid in Geometry, form'd by the Revolution of a *Rectangle*, round
one of its Sides.

Cylinder (in *Gardening*) a
round Stone or piece of Wood
to break Clods, or to make
Garden Walks ſmooth: A
Roller.

Cylindrical, belonging to,
in form of, or like unto a
Cylinder.

Cylindroid, is a ſolid Figure
with Elliptical Baſes, parallel
and alike ſituated.

Cyllum, ſignifies a Leg put
out of Joynt outwardly; alſo
one Lame and Crooked.

Cyma, in Botany, is the
Top of any Plant or Herb.

Cymatium, a Member of
Architecture, whereof one
half is Convex, and the other
Concave.

Cynick, (Greek) Dogged,
Crabbed: There was in
Greece an old Sect of Philoſophers, call'd Cynicks, firſt
inſtituted by *Antiſthenes*, and
were ſo call'd, becauſe they
did ever bark at, and rebuke
Men's Vices, and were not
ſo reſpectful in Behaviour as
Civility required.

Cynorexy, a greedy Appe-
rite.

Cynoſura or *Cynoſure*, the
Conſtellation of the *Leſſer
Bear*, or the Polar Star in the
Tail of it.

Cypher:

Cypher : See *Cipher.*

Cystis, (Gr.) a Bladder, especially that of the Urine and Gall : Also a Skin containing the Matter of an Impostume.

Cystotomy, (Gr.) an opening of the Bladder to take out the Stone.

Czar, (a Corruption of *Cæsar*) is the Title of the Emperour of *Muscovy.*

D

Dabuze, a kind of Weapon carried before the Grand Signior.

Dactyle, a Foot or Measure in a Latin Verse, consisting of one long Syllable & two short.

Dactylogy, (Gr.) a Discoursing by Signs made with the Fingers.

Dactylonomy, (Gr.) is the Art of Numbring on the Fingers.

Dactylus, a Grecian Measure of Length, which reduced to the English Measure, contains 7554 $\frac{11}{18}$ Decimal Parts of an Inch.

Daddock, the Heart or Body of a Tree that's throughly rotten.

Dado, in Architecture, is used by some Writers for the Dye, which is the Part in the middle of the Pedestal of a Column between its Base and Cornice.

Daff, a Dastard or Coward.

Dag, a Leather Latchet; also a Hand Gun.

Dagon, an Idol of the Philistines, 1 *King.* 5,

Daily Motion of a Planet : See *Diurnal Motion.*

Dam, a Flood-gate or Stoppage in a River or Pond. *Verbally,* to Stop or Shut up.

Damage, is generally taken to signify any Hurt or Hindrance that a Man taketh or suffereth in his Estate ; but in Common Law, it is a part of that the Jurors be to enquire of, passing for the Plaintiff or Defendant in a Civil Action, be it Personal or Real.

Damage Feasant, in Common Law, is when a Stranger's Beasts feed and spoil in other Men's Ground without leave.

Damnata Terra, is the same with the *Caput Mortuum* of the Chymists, being only the Earth or Mass which remains in the Retort, after the other Principles are forced out by the Fire.

Damnation, (Lat.) a condemning or passing Sentence upon a Person : Also, the Tortures and Pains of Hell.

Dancette, in Heraldry, is when the out Line of any Bordure is largely indented.

There is a Bearing of a Bend, call'd double *Dancette* thus ; he beareth *Azure,* a Bend

Double *Dancette Argent.*

Dank, somewhat Wet or Moist.

Dapper, Fine, Neat, Spruce.

Darapti, an Artificial Word, expressing the first Mood of the

the third Figure in Logick; wherein the two firſt Propoſitions are univerſal Affirmatives, and the laſt a particular Affirmative.

Darrein, Law-Term ſignifying Laſt.

Darſis, is an Exulceration of the Skin.

Dartus, is the Coat which immediately covers the Teſticles.

Daſtard, a Coward or faint hearted Fellow.

Data, in Mathematicks, are ſuch Things or Quantities as are ſuppoſed to be given or known; in order thereby to find out Quantities or Things that are unknown and ſought for.

Datary, the chief Officer in the *Chancery* of *Rome*, thro' whoſe Hands moſt vacant Benefices paſs: Alſo the Charge or Juriſdiction of that Officer.

Dative, (Lat.) of, or belonging to giving, or that may be given.

Davis's Quadrant, is the common Back Quadrant uſed at Sea, to take the San's Meridian Altitude.

Davit, a Piece of Timber in a Ship, having a Notch at one end, in which, by a Strap, hangs a Block, called the *Fiſh-Block*; and the uſe of this Block is to Hale up the Fluke of the Anchor, and to faſten it to the Ships Bow or Loof.

Day, is either *Natural* or *Artificial*; the firſt is an entire Revolution of the Sun, perform'd in 24 Hours; the 2d. is the time between the Sun's Riſing and Setting, or his Stay above the Horizon.

A Days Journey in Scripture, is 33 Engliſh Miles, 172 Paces and 4 Feet.

Deacon, one whoſe Office it is in the Church where he ſhall be appointed, to aſſiſt the Prieſt in Divine Service, to help him in the diſtribution of the Holy Sacrament, to inſtruct the Youth in the Catechiſm.

Dead Men's Eyes, Little Blocks or Pullies in a Ship, with many Holes, but no Shivers, wherein run the *Lanniers*.

Dead Reckoning at Sea, is that Eſtimation, Judgment, or Conjecture which the Seamen make of the Place where the Ship is, by keeping an account of her Way by the Log, and by knowing the Courſe they have Steer'd by the Compaſs.

Dead-Riſing, a Term at Sea for that Part of a Ship which lies *Aft*, between the Keel and her Floor Timbers.

Dead-water, is the Eddy Water juſt behind the Stern of a Ship.

Debauchery, (Fr.) Riot, Diſorder, Incontinency, Revelling.

Debentur, a Bill drawn upon the Publick for the payment of any Seaman's or Land Souldier's Arrears to the Creditor.

Debet

Debet & solet, a Writ of Right, as if a Man sue for any thing that is now deny'd, and which hath been enjoy'd by himself and his *Ancestors* before him; as for a Mill, Common of Pasture, *&c.*

Debilitate, (Lat.) to Weaken or make Feeble.

Debilitation, a Weakening.

Debito, in Law, is a Writ for Money due by Obligation or Bargain.

Debonaire, (Fr.) Sweet, Affable, Courteous.

Deboshee, (Fr.) a dissolute Fellow, a lewd Wretch.

Debruised, a Term in Heraldry, when a *Pale*, &c. is born upon any Beast in an *Escutcheon*, for then they say *The Beast is Debruised of the Pale.*

Decad, signifies the Number Ten.

Decadency, a Falling down, Decay, Ruin.

Decagon, (Gr.) a ten sided Figure; or a Figure encompass'd by Ten Sides.

Decalogue, (Gr.) the Ten Commandments, imparted to the *Jews* from God by *Moses.*

Decamp, signifies to leave the present Place of Encampment in order to Camp in another Place.

Decant, (Lat.) to Pour off from the Dregs.

Decantation, (Lat.) in Chymistry, is a Pouring off the clear Part of any Liquor by *Inclination*, as the Chymists speak, so that it may be without any Sediment or Dregs.

Decapitate, to Behead.

December, (Lat.) the Name of a Month, so called, because 'tis the Tenth from *March.*

Decempedal, (Lat.) Ten Foot long.

Decemvirate, the Office of the *Decemviri*, who were Ten Noblemen amongst the *Romans*, chosen to govern the Common-wealth instead of the two Consuls.

Decency, Seemliness, Comliness, Beseemingness.

Decennial, of ten Years continuance, ten Years old.

Decent, (Lat.) Handsome, Becoming.

Deception, Deceit, Fallacy, Cousenage; also a false Judgment of the Mind concerning any thing.

Decerption, (Lat.) a Plucking or Cropping off.

Decertation, (Lat.) a Contending or Striving for.

Deciduous, is that which is apt or ready to fall; and is frequently used in reference to the Flowers and Seeds of Plants.

Decies tantum, ten times as much, which in Common Law is recoverable from a Juror that is brib'd to give his Verdict.

Decile, a New Aspect invented by *Kepler*, *Viz.* when two Planets are distant 36°.

Decimal Arithmetick, or the Arithmetick of *Decimal Fractions*, is an Art which treats of Fractions, whose Denominators are in a Decuple continued Geometrick Progression,

Progreſſion, as 10, 100, 1000, 10000, &c.

Decimal Chain, a Chain for meaſuring of Lands, divided Decimally, or into a 100 equal Parts, Marks being placed at every 10.

Decimation, (Lat.) a gathering Tyths; alſo a Puniſhing every Tenth Souldier by Lot, was term'd *Decimatio Legionis* by the old Romans.

Decipher, to find out the Alphabet of a Cypher, or the Meaning of a Letter or Book written in Cyphers or difficult Characters; alſo to penetrate into, or ſee to the Bottom of a difficult Affair.

Deciſion, a Determining or Deciding any thing in debate.

Deciſive, Deciding, Determining, fit or able to Determine a Controverſy or any thing in debate.

Declamation, (Lat.) an Oration made upon ſome feigned Subject; for the Exerciſe of ſome young Scholar or Student; alſo a crying out aloud.

Declaration, a ſetting forth. In Common Law, it is a ſhewing in Writing the Grief and Complaint of the Demandant or Plaintiff, againſt the Defendant or Tenant; wherein he is ſuppoſed to have received ſome Wrong; and this ought to be plain and certain, becauſe it both impeaches the Defendant and compels him to anſwer thereto.

Declare, to make known; to publiſh.

Declenſion, an Abating; alſo a Grammatical Term, being a variation of Nouns through the Caſes.

Declination, a Bowing down.

Declination of the *Sun* or *Planet*, is an Ark of a Meridian, paſſing thro' the Sun or Planet, intercepted between the Equinoctial and that Point where the aforeſaid Meridian cuts the Sun or Planet; or in other words, it is the Diſtance of the Sun or any Planet or Star from the Equinoctial, either North or South.

Declination of the Mariners Compaſs, is its Variation from the true Meridian of any Place.

Declination of a Wall or Plane for a Dial, is an Ark of the Horizon, comprehended either between the Plane and the Prime vertical Circle, if you account it from *Eaſt* and *Weſt*, or elſe between the Meridian and the Plane, if you account it from the North or South.

Declinatories, are Boxes fitted with a Compaſs and Needle, to take the Declination of Walls for Dialling.

Decline, to Bow down, to Diminiſh, Decay; alſo, to Avoid, to Refuſe.

Declining Dials, are Dials drawn upon Declining Planes: See *Declination*.

Declivity, (Lat.) a Steepneſs reckon'd

reckon'd downwards on a Sloping Line.

Decoction, (Lat.) a Boiling or Seething : In Phyſick it ſignifies any Liquor in which Medicinal Roots, Herbs, Flowers, &c. have been boiled.

Decollation, (Lat.) a Beheading.

Decompoſit, compounded of more than two.

Decoration, (Lat.) an Adorning or Beautifying.

Decortication, (Lat.) a pulling off the Bark of any thing.

Decorum, (Lat.) that Comlineſs, Order, Decency, which it becomes every Man to obſerve in all his Actions.

Decoy, a Place fitted for catching of Wild Fowl ; a Lure, a Wheedle. *Verbally*, to Allure or Entice.

Decreaſe, (Lat.) to grow leſs, decay, or wear away.

Decrees or *Decretals*, a Volume of the Canon Law, ſo call'd, compoſed by *Gratian* a Monk, of the Order of St. *Benedict*.

Decrement, a Decreaſing.

Decrepit, very Old, which has one Foot in the Grave.

Decrepitation, in Chymiſtry, is uſed for the cracking noiſe which ariſes from Salt being thrown into an unglazed Earthen Pot, heated red hot over the Fire.

Decreſſant, (Lat.) the Moon decreaſing, or in the Laſt Quarter.

Decretals, the Name given to the Letters of Popes.

Decretory, a definitive Sentence.

Decruſtation, an Uncruſting or taking away the uppermoſt Cruſt or Rind of any thing.

Decry, to cry down ; to forbid the uſe of Money, Goods, or any other thing.

Decumbiture, (Lat.) a Lying down : In *Phyſick*, 'tis when one through Sickneſs is obliged to take his Bed. In *Aſtrology*, a Scheme of the Heavens erected for the Moment a Diſeaſe invades, or confines one to Bed.

Decupelation, the ſame with *Decantation* ; which ſee.

Decuple, Ten-fold.

Decurion, a Captain over Ten Horſe.

Decurſion, (Lat.) a haſty Running, a running down or unto.

Decury, a Band of Ten Souldiers.

Decuſſation, a cutting a Croſs ; in Opticks, it is the croſſing of any two Rays, &c. when they meet in a Point, and then go on, parting from one another.

Decuſſorium, is a Surgeon's Inſtrument, wherewith the *Dura Mater* being highly preſs'd is accurately joyn'd to the Skull, that the Purulent Matter gather'd betwixt the Skull and the Skin call'd *Dura Mater*, may be evacuated by a Hole made with a Surgeon's Inſtrument, call'd a *Trepanum*.

Decuſſion, a Shaking off, a Beating down.

Dedicate,

Dedicate, to set apart for sacred use ; to inscribe or address a Book to a Person of Distinction or Quality.

Dedication, (Lat.) the Act of Dedicating : Also a Consecrating.

Dedicatory, belonging to a Dedication.

Dedignation, (Lat.) a Disdaining or Contemning.

Dedimus Potestatem, a Writ whereby Commission is given to a Private Man, for the speeding of some Act appertaining to a Judge : By the Civilians it is called *Delegation*.

Deduce, (Lat.) to draw one thing from another, to infer.

Deducible, that may be inferred.

Deduct, to subtract, to take from, to lessen.

Deeds, in Common Law, signifies Writings that contain the Effect of a Contract between Man and Man. See *Fair*.

Deem, to Judge or Think.

Deep-Sea-line, is a small Line to found with, when the Ship is in deep Water at Sea; at the End of which is a piece of Lead, call'd the *Deep Sea Lead*, at the Bottom of which is a Coat of white Tallow, to bring up Stones, Gravel, Sand, Shells or the like, to know the difference of their Ground.

Deface, to Mar or Spoil; to Blot out.

De facto, (Lat.) *Law-Term*, actually, really, in very deed.

Defaillance, (Fr.) a Failing or Defect.

Defalcation, (Lat.) a Pruning or Cutting ; a Deducting or Abating in Accompts.

Defamation, (Lat.) is taking away a Person's Character and Reputation ; a speaking slanderous Words.

Defamatory, Slanderous, Abusive.

Defatigable, that may be wearied or made weary.

Defatigate, (Lat.) to make weary, to tire.

Default, (in Law) is a Non-appearance in Court, without sufficient Cause made out.

Defecate, (Lat.) to purge from Dregs, to Refine.

Defecation, (Lat.) a purging from Dregs, a Refining.

Defect, a Fault, an Imperfection, Want of.

Defection, a Failing ; also a Revolting or Falling off.

Defective, (Lat.) Faulty, Imperfect.

Defeisance, (Fr.) in Law, is the making void an Act, Obligation, &c by performing a Condition thereto annex'd.

Defence, is an upholding, maintaining, justifying, a keeping off any Act of Violence, a making a stout Resistance.

Defences, in Fortification, are all sorts of Works that cover and defend the opposite Posts, as *Flanks*, *Parapets*, *Casemates*, *Fausse-Brays*.

Defend, (Lat.) to protect, support, uphold, bear out, maintain,

maintain, assert or justify: Also to forbid. *Chaucer.*

Defendant, in Common Law, is he that is sued in an Action personal, as Tenant is he that is sued in an Action real.

Se Defendendo, (Lat.) Law Term, used when one kills another *in his own Defence* ; which justifies the Fact.

Defender of the Faith, a Title given by Pope *Leo* the Tenth, to King *Henry* VIII. of *England* ; and continued ever since as the proper Title of the Kings of *England* ; as *Most Christian* is the Title of the Kings of *France*, and *Catholick* of the Kings of *Spain*.

Defensatives, are Medicines which hinder or keep Humours from coming to a Sore or Place affected, and which prevent an Inflammation thereof.

Defensible, that may be defended.

Defensive or *Defensative*, that serves to defend.

Defer, (Lat.) to delay or put off.

Deference, Respect, Submission.

Deferent, an imaginary Circle or Orb in Astronomy (in the Ptolemaick System) that is supposed as it were to carry about the Body of the Planet.

Defiance, (Fr.) Challenge, Out-braving.

Deficiency, Defect, Want, Failing.

Deficient, full of Wants and Failings.

Defile, or *Defilee*, (Fr.) a straight narrow Lane or Passage, through which a Company of Horse or Foot can pass only in File, by making a small Front.

Defile, to Pollute or Corrupt, to Daub or Stain, Deflower or Ravish : Also to go off, or March File by File.

Define, (Lat.) to Explain, Determine, Decide, Appoint.

Definite, (Lat.) Certain, Limited or Bounded.

Definition, (Lat.) a short and plain Declaration or Description of the meaning of a Word, or of the essential Attributes of a Thing : Also a Decision, or Determining.

Definitive, serving to Decide, Decisive, Positive, Express.

Deflagration, a Burning or Inflammation. In Chymistry, it is the enkindling and burning off in a Crucible, a Mixture of a Salt, or some Mineral Body with a Sulphureous one, in order to make a Purification of the Salt, or a *Regulus* of the Mineral.

Deflexion, a bending down, a turning aside. In Navigation it is the turning of a Ship from her true Course, by reason of Currents.

Deflower, is the cropping the Flower of a Maids Virginity against her Will.

Defluxion, (Lat.) is a flowing downwards : In Physick, it is the flowing down
of

of Humours to any part of the Body.

Deforcement, the witholding Lands or Tenements from the right Owner.

Deformation, (Lat.) a making Ugly, a putting out of Form.

Deformed, Ugly, out of Form.

Deformity, Uglineſs, that which is unpleaſing to the Sight for want of due Proportion.

Defraud, (Lat.) to Cheat, Cozen, or Beguile, to Deprive by a Trick.

Defray, to pay the Charges of another Perſon.

Deftly, Nimbly, Neatly. *Spencer.*

Defunct, Dead.

Degenerate, to grow out of kind, to forſake the vertuous Steps of our Anceſtours.

Degenerous, Degenerated, Baſe, Vile, Infamous.

Deglutination, an Unglewing.

Deglutition, Swallowing.

Degrade, to put out of Office, Eſtate, Degree, Dignity.

Degradation, a Degrading: In *Painting*, 'tis the leſſening and rendring confuſed the Appearance of things diſtant in a Landskip.

Degree, a Step or Stair; alſo any flowing State or Condition, in which may be conſidered different Aſcents and Deſcents; or, as it were, a variety of Steps one above another.

Degree, in Mathematicks, is the 360th Part of a Circle: it is ſubdivided into 60 Parts,

call'd Minutes, and each of them again into 60 others call'd Seconds, and ſo into Thirds, &c.

Degrees of Fire in Chymiſtry are four; the firſt is made by two or three Coals, and is the moſt gentle of all; the ſecond is made with four or five Coals, of only juſt to warm the Veſſel, but ſo that you may endure your Hand upon it for ſome time. The third Degree, is when there is Heat enough to make a Pot boil that contains 5 or 6 Quarts of Water. The fourth is as great a Heat as can be made in the Furnace.

Dehors, (Fr.) the Outſide of a thing. In *Fortification*, 'tis all ſorts of ſeparate Outworks, for the better ſecurity of the Main Place.

Dehortation, a Diſſwading.

Deicides, (i. e. God-killers) ſo are the *Jews* term'd for Murdering our Saviour.

Dejection, (Lat.) a caſting down; alſo an Evacuation of the Excrements, or going to Stool.

Dejeration, (Lat.) a taking a ſolemn Oath.

Deify, to make a God of one; to Worſhip as a God.

Deipnoſophiſts, (Gr.) a Company of Wiſe Men diſcourſing at Supper.

Deiſm, is the Belief of thoſe who denying all Revealed Religion, acknowledge only the Natural; namely, the Exiſtence of One GOD, His Providence, Virtue and

             Vice;

Vice; the Immortality of the Soul, and Rewards and Punishments after Death.

Deist, one that adheres to Deism.

Deity, (Lat.) Godhead, the Nature or Essence of GOD.

Delapsion, a Sliding or Falling down.

Delator, an Informer or Accuser.

Deigne, Vouchsafe. *Shakespear.*

A Delay, a putting off the time set for the doing any thing.

Delay'd, Deferr'd, Put off; also, to be mingled with Water.

Delectable, (Lat.) Delightful, Pleasant.

Delectation, Delight, Pleasure.

Delegate, one to whom Authority is committed from another, to handle and determine Matters.

Deleterious Medicines, are such, whose Particles are of a poisonous Nature.

Deletery, deadly, destructive.

Deletion, (Lat.) a Blotting out.

Delibate, (Lat) to Taste, to Sacrifice.

Delibation, (Lat.) a Tasting; also a Sacrificing.

Deliberate, to examine the Pro and Con of an Affair or Proposition, and thereupon to judge and determine.

Deliberation, a Consulting or Debating; the Examination of any thing, in order to pass a true Judgment thereupon.

Deliberative, that carefully considers, weighs and examines what he says and does.

Delicate, Fine, Nice, Curious, Excellent.

Delicious, pleasant to the Taste; Sweet, Charming.

Deligation, Swathing, is a part of Surgery that concerns the binding up of Wounds, Ulcers, Broken Bones, &c.

Delineate, (Lat.) to draw the Form or Pourtaiture of a thing.

Delineation, (Lat.) a Drawing, a Draught or Form of a thing.

Delinquent, a Criminal, or Person guilty of a Fault or Crime.

Deliquation, in *Chymistry,* the preparing of things melted on the Fire.

Deliquium Animi, a Swooning.

Deliquium Chymicum, is either a Distillation by the force of Fire, or the melting of the *Calx* which is suspended in moist Cellars, and a Resolution of it into a Lixivious Humour.

Deliration, a Doting or being Besides one's self.

Delirium, (Lat.) Dotage; in Physick, it is the frantick or idle Talk of Persons in a Feaver; being a depravation of the Imagination and Judgment, occasion'd by a disorderly Motion of the Animal Spirits.

Dell, a Pit. *Spencer.*

Delphinus,

Delphinus, a Conſtellation in the Northern Hemiſphere, containing 10 Stars.

Deltoides, is a Triangular Muſcle in the form of the Greek Letter △ faſtened to the *Os Humeri*.

Deluge, is an Inundation or Overflowing of the Earth, either in part or in whole, by Water.

Deluſion, a Deceiving or Beguiling, a Cheat.

Demagogue, (Gr. *i. e.* Leader of the People) the Head of a Faction, a Ring-leader of the Rabble, a popular and factious Orator.

Demain, is commonly uſed to' diſtinguiſh thoſe Lands that a Lord of a Mannor hath in his own Hands or in the Hands of his *Leſſee*, from ſuch other Lands of the ſaid Mannor, which belong to Free or Copy-hold; howbeit the Copy-hold of any Mannor, is in the Opinion of many good Lawyers, accounted *Demain*.

Demand, is an asking any thing of another with a ſort of Authority.

Demi, (Lat.) a word which being joyn'd to another, always ſignifies half; as

Demi-Baſtion, a half Baſtion, or a kind of Fortification, which hath only one Face and one Flank,

Demi-Cannon, a Half Cannon, or the name of a Great Gun, about 10 or 11 Foot long, and 6 Inches in Bore: It carries a Ball of 30 Pound

Demi-Culverin, a half Culverin, or the Name of a piece of Ordnance, of about 10 Foot long, and 4½ Inches in Bore; it carries a Ball of about 12 Pound 11 Ounces.

Demi-Gorge, in Fortification, is half the Gorge or Entrance into the Baſtion, not taken directly from Angle to Angle, where the Baſtion joyns to the Curtin, but from the Angle of the Flank, to the Center of the Baſtion.

Demigrate, to Shift, Flit, or Remove.

Demi-quaver; a Note in Muſick, half a Semi-quaver.

Demiſe, (Law-word) a Letting or Making over of Lands, Tenements, &c. by Leaſe or Will; alſo Death when apply'd to the King.

To *Demiſe*, to Farm or Let.

Demiſſion, (Lat.) a Caſting down, an Abaſement.

Democracy, a Form of Government, where the Supreme or Legiſlative Power is lodged in the Common People, or Perſons choſe out of them.

Demoliſh, (Lat.) to pull or throw down any thing built, to ruin or raze a Building.

Demolition, a Razing or Throwing down.

Demon, (Gr.) an Intelligence or Spirit. In Scripture 'tis taken in a bad Senſe.

Demoniack, a Perſon poſſeſs'd with an Evil Spirit.

Demonology, a Treatiſe of Evil Spirits or Devils.

Demonſtra-

Demonstration, is a Chain of Arguments depending one on the other, and founded primarily on first and self evident Principles; ending in the invincible Proof of a thing to be demonstrated.

Demonstrative, convincing, evident, certain.

Demure, affectedly Grave, Reserv'd, or Bashful.

Dempt, Deemed. *Spencer.*

Demurrer, in Common-Law, signifies a Pause upon a Point of difficulty in any Action.

Denarius, (Lat.) a Roman Coin worth 7 Pence, 3 Farthings of our Money.

Denary, of, or containing Ten.

Denigrate, to make Black.

Denizen, a Foreigner Enfranchised by the King's Charter, and made capable of bearing any Office, purchasing and enjoying all Privileges, except inheriting Lands by Descent.

Denomination, (Lat.) a Naming or giving a Name unto a thing; also the Name it self.

Denominatives, in Logick, are such Terms as take their Original and Name from others.

Denominator of a Fraction, is that Part of the Fraction which stands below the Line of Separation, which always tells you into how many Parts the Integer is supposed to be divided.

Denote, (Lat.) to shew by a Mark, to Signify.

Denounce, (Lat.) to Proclaim, to Publish or Declare.

Dense, A Body is called dense or thick by Philosophers, when it hath more Matter in proportion to the Space or Room it takes up, than other Bodies have.

Density, is the Thickness of Bodies, or that whatever it be which makes them dense.

Dentifrice, a Medicine for the Whitening, Scouring and Cleansing the Teeth and Fastening the Gums.

Dentiloquent, One that speaks thro' the Teeth or Lips.

Dentils, in Architecture, is a Member of the Ionick Cornice, Square, and cut out at convenient Distances, which gives it the Form of a Set of Teeth, from whence its Name.

Dentition, is the Time that Children breed Teeth, which is about the 7th Month or later.

Denudation, (Lat.) a making bare or naked.

Denunciation, a Denouncing or giving Warning, a Proclaiming.

Deobstruent Medicines, are Medicines which open Obstructions.

Deodand, a thing devoted or consecrated to God for the Expiation of his Wrath.

Deoppilative Medicines, such as serve to remove Obstructions or Stoppages.

K   *Deoscu-*

Deosculation, (Lat.) a Kissing with eagerness.

Depaint, to make the Representation of any Story, Passage, or thing with a Pen; also figuratively to represent the noble Actions or Vices of any Person in Words.

Depart, is a certain Operation in Chymistry, whereby the Particles of Silver are made to *depart* from Gold, when they were before melted together in the same Mass, and cou'd be separated no other way.

Depauperation, a making Poor.

Depeculation, a publick Robbing, or a Robbing the Prince or Common-wealth.

Depend, to hang down; to stay or rely upon.

Dependance, a hanging down; also a resting, staying or relying upon.

Dephlegmated, a Chymical Term, and signifies cleared from Phlegm or Water.

Depilatory, an external Medicine that takes away the Hair from any Part of the Body.

Deplantation, a taking up Plants.

Deploration, a Mourning for or Bewailing.

Deplore, to Bewail or Lament any One's Misfortune.

Deplume, to pluck off the Feathers, to Unfeather.

Deponent, Laying down: In Grammar, a Verb deponent is one which hath a

Passive Termination, and an Active Signification; also, One that gives Information upon Oath before a Magistrate.

Depopulation, (Lat.) a Dispeopling, Spoiling, Wasting or Destroying a Country.

Deportation, (Lat.) a conveying or carrying away.

Deportment, Carriage, Behaviour.

Depose, to give Testimony in a Court of Justice of what a Man has seen and heard. Also to deprive a Person of his Dignity or Employment.

Deposite, to Lay down, or Trust a Thing with any One.

Deposition, what is laid down; a Testimony given in a Court of Justice, of what a Man has seen or heard.

Depositum, a Pledge left in the Hands of another; also, a Wager.

Depravation, (Lat.) a Spoiling, Corrupting, Wresting.

Deprecation, (Lat.) a praying against any Calamity.

Depredation, (Lat.) a Robbing, a making a Prey of, a Spoiling.

Deprehension, a Catching or Taking away unawares.

Depress, to Weigh down or make Lower.

Depress the Pole, so many Degrees as any One travels from the Pole towards the Equinoctial, he is said to *Depress the Pole*.

Depression of an *Equation*,

is

is a bringing it into lower and more simple Terms by *Division.*

Depression of a Star below the Horizon, is the distance of a Star from the Horizon below, and is measured by an Ark of a Vertical Circle or Azimuth passing through the Star, intercepted between the Star and the Horizon.

Depretiate, to Lessen the Price of any thing, to Vilify.

Deprivation; a Bereaving or Taking away; as when any Person is *Deprived* of or Deposed from his Preferment.

Depth of a *Squadron* or *Battalion,* is the Number of Men that are in File; which of a Squadron is Three, and of a Battalion, generally Six.

Depulsion, a Driving away, a Putting off.

Depuration, is the Cleansing any Body from its Excrementitious Dregs, more gross Parts, or Filth.

Depute, is to appoint any One to represent the Person, and act in the room of another.

Deputy, is a Person appointed to represent and act in the room of another.

Dereliction, an utter Forsaking or Leaving.

Deride, to Mock or Laugh at.

Derision, a Laughing, Mocking.

Derivation, a Drawing or Taking from.

Derivative, Drawn or Taken from another.

Derogate, to Lessen or take from the Worth of any Person or Thing; to Disparage.

Derogation, a Disparaging or Detracting from the Worth of another Person or Thing.

Derring, Daring. *Spencer.*

Dervises, an Order of Religious Persons among the *Turks,* that undergo very strict Penances.

Deruncination, a Cutting of Trees, Bushes, or any Thing encumbering the Ground.

Descant, in Musick, is to run Division or Variety with the Voice upon a Musical Ground in true Measure; and Metaphorically, it signifies to Paraphrase ingeniously upon any pleasing Subject.

Descention Right of a Sign, is an Ark of the Æquator, which descends with the Sign below the Horizon of a Right Sphere; or the time the Sign is setting in a Right Sphere.

Descension Oblique of a Sign, is an Ark of the Æquator, which descends with the Sign below the Horizon of an oblique Sphere.

Descent, signifies a Fall; as the *Descent* of heavy Bodies is the same as the Fall of heavy Bodies: Also to make a *Descent* into an Enemies Country, is the same as to Land a Hostile and Invading Force.

Descents, in Fortification, signifies the Holes, Vaults and hollow Places made by undermining the Ground.

K 2   *Descen-*

Defcenforium, a Chymical Furnace, in which Subftances are Diftill'd by defcent or downwards.

Defcribe, (Lat.) to Reprefent a Thing or Action in Speech or Writing ; to draw a Line or Circle.

Defcribent, in Geometry, expreffes fome Line or Surface, which by its Motion produces a Plain Figure or a Solid.

Defcription, a fetting forth the Nature and Properties of any thing, either by Figures or Words.

Defcry, to Difcover afar off.

Deferter, (Lat.) One that leaves his Religion, Prince, or Captain, and goes to another.

Defertion, a Leaving or Forfaking.

Deficcation, a Drying up.

Deficative, (Lat.) apt to Dry, of a Drying Quality.

Defignation or *Defign*, a Purpofe or Contrivance, a Project or Enterprize.

Defipience, (Lat.) Foolifhnefs, Indifcretion, Doting.

Defift, to Leave off, to Ceafe.

Deflaby, Leacherous, Beaftly. *Chaucer*.

Defolation, a Laying wafte, a Deftroying whole Countries by Fire and Sword.

Defpair, to be out of all Hopes of obtaining our Ends : Alfo a timerous Confternation of an abject Mind.

Defpection, a Looking down.

Defperado, a defperate, a mad hair-brain'd Fellow.

Defpicable, liable to Contempt, or to be Defpifed.

Defpoliation, a Robbing or Spoiling.

Defpond, to be quite dejected or Defpair.

Defpondency, a Dejection of Spirit, Defpairing.

Defponfation, a Betrothing, a giving in Marriage.

Defpot, (Gr.) a Lord or Ruler of a Country.

Defpotical, of or belonging to a Lord or Mafter.

Defpumation, in Pharmacy, is the clearing and cleanfing any Liquor, by letting it boil fo as to take off the Scum.

Deffert, (Fr.) the laft Courfe at a Feaft, confifting of Fruits, Sweet-meats, &c.

Deftillation, is an Extraction of the moift or unctuous Parts which are rarify'd into Vapour or Smoak, as it were by the force of Fire.

Deftination, an Ordaining, Purpofing or Defigning.

Deftiny, Fate ; the difpofal or enchainment of Second Caufes, ordained by Providence, which carries with it the Neceffity of the Event.

Deftitute, Left, Forfaken.

Deftitution, a Leaving or Forfaking.

Deftroy, to Ruin, Undo, Annihilate.

Deftruction, a Ruining, Undoing, Annihilating.

Defue-

Desuetude, a leaving or forsaking any Custom or Habit.

Desultory, Vaulting or Leaping; also Inconstant, Mutable.

Desumption, (Lat.) a choosing, or taking out.

Detail, (Fr.) the Particulars, or particular Circumstances of an Affair.

Detatchment, (Fr.) properly a loosening or untying; but it is commonly used for a Party of Souldiers sent from one Army to the strengthning of another.

Detection, (Lat.) a Discovering or Laying open.

Detention, a detaining or with-holding by Force or Violence.

Detents, in a Clock, are those Stops, which by being lifted up, or let fall down, do lock or unlock the Clock in striking.

Deterge, (Lat.) to wipe or rub off.

Deterioration, (Lat.) a making worse or spoiling.

Determination, a final Resolution upon the doing or not doing any Action; so any Matter is said to be brought to a determination, when it is resolved what shall be done in it.

Deterr, to Frighten or Discourage.

Deterration, is the removal of Earth, Sand, &c. from higher Grounds to the lower by Rains.

Detersion, a Cleansing or Wiping.

Detersive, of a cleansing Nature.

Detersive Medicines, such as cleanse the Body from Sluggish and Viscous Humours.

Detest, to Abhor or Loath.

Detestation, an Abhorring or Loathing.

Dethrone, to drive a Sovereign from his Throne.

Detinue, is a Writ that lyeth against him who refuseth to deliver back Goods or Chattels which are delivered to him to keep.

Detonation, in Chymistry, expresses the thundering Noise that is often made by a Mixture being enkindled in the containing Vessel; for the Volatile Parts do fly out with great vehemence and impetuosity.

Detorsion, (Lat.) a turning or bending aside.

Detraction, (Lat.) a pulling away; also Slandering, Back-sliding.

Detrectation, a Refusal or Denial to do, a Drawing back.

Detriment, (Lat.) Damage, Loss, Hurt.

Detrimental, Hurtful, Dangerous.

Detrition, (Lat.) a wearing or rubbing off Particles from any thing.

Detrude, to thrust down or out.

Detruncation, (Lat.) a Cutting short, a Lopping off.

Detrusion, (Lat.) a thrusting down.

K 3 De

Devaſtation, (Lat.) a laying waſte.

Devaſtaverunt bona Teſtatorū, is a Writ lying againſt Executors, for paying Legacies and Debts without Speciality, before the Debt upon the ſaid Specialities be due to the prejudice of Creditors.

Devection, a Carrying away or down.

Developed, (Fr.) unwrapped, unfolded, undone, opened.

Deveſt, (Lat.) to Strip or Uncloath.

Devexity, the Hollowneſs of a Valley, a Bending down.

Deviation, (Lat.) a going out of the Way, a going Aſtray.

Devious, (Lat.) out of the Way, Swerving from.

Deviſe, in Common-Law, is, when a Man in his Will bequeaths his Lands and Goods to another after his Deceaſe, and he to whom the Lands or Goods are bequeathed, is called the *Deviſee.*

Devoir, (Fr) Duty, that which every one ought to do, according to the Rules and Laws of Civility and Reaſon.

Devolve, to Roul or Tumble down; to Happen from one to another.

Devolution, a Rouling or Tumbling down; alſo Happening from one to another.

Devote, (Lat.) to Vow or Conſecrate to God.

Devotion, a Vowing or Conſecrating; alſo Piety, Religiouſneſs.

Devouring, when Fiſhes in an Eſcutcheon are born in a feeding Poſture, the Heralds term it *Devouring.*

Deuteronomy, (Gr.) a Second Law, ſo is the Fifth Book of *Moſes*, called by the *Greeks*, becauſe the Law is therein repeated.

Deuteropathia, (Gr.) is a Diſeaſe that proceeds from anotherDiſeaſe, to wit, If the Headach comes from the Diſtemper of another Part, the Morbifick Matter being tranſlated from its former Repoſitories.

Dew, is compoſed of the Steams and Vapours of the Earth, which being exhaled by the Heat of the Sun, and kept ſuſpended during his Preſence, do upon his Abſence convene into Drops, and then fall down to the Earth again.

Dexterity, (Lat.) Nimbleneſs, Aptneſs, Readineſs.

Dexter-Point, in Heraldry, is the Right Side or Point in an Eſcutcheon.

Diabetes, a Diſeaſe attended with a violent Thirſt; it conſiſts in too great a fuſion of the Blood, whereupon the *Serum* paſſes the Reins, and is voided in great Quantities by the Paſſages of the Urine.

Diabolical, Devilish.

Diabroſis, (Gr.) a Solution of the *Continuum* by Corroſion of the Parts.

Diacauſticks, is the Science of refracted Sounds; alſo a kind of Curves in Geometry, which are form'd by refracted Rays.   *Dia-*

Dialyſma, (Gr.) is a waſhing of the Mouth, to cleanſe it or to ſtrengthen the Teeth and Gums.

Diaconal, of, or belonging to a Deacon.

Diacriſis, (Gr.) a Diſtinction and Dijudication of Diſeaſes and Symptoms.

Diadem, an Imperial or Royal Crown; properly, a white Fillet or Linnen Wreath, with which Kings encircled their Fore-heads.

Diadrome, the ſame with the Vibration or Swing of a Pendulum.

Diæreſis, a dividing; alſo a Poetical Figure, wherein for the Verſe-ſake, one Syllable is divided into two, which are noted over head with two Points, as Evolüiſſe for Evolviſſe.

Diætetica, is a Part of Phyſick, that preſcribes the Uſe and Knowledge, of the Rules of Diet, & of the Uſe of ſuch Things as are not Natural.

Diagnoſtick, that Knows or Diſcerns throughly; *Diagnoſtick* Signs of a Diſeaſe are thoſe Signs which are apparent.

Diagonal, in Geometry, is a Line drawn from Angle to Angle in any Figure.

Diagram, is a Scheme drawn for the proving or demonſtrating of any Propoſition or Thing.

Diagraphick Art, is the Art of Painting or Graving.

Dial, is a Plane, upon which are drawn ſeveral Lines and Figures, and a Gnomon fix'd for the Indication of the Hour of the Day.

Dialect, is a Manner of Speech peculiar to ſome Part of a Country or People, and differing from the Manner uſed by other Parts or People, yet all uſing the ſame Radical Language for the main Subſtance of it.

Dialectick Art, the Art of Logick, which teaches to Reaſon and Diſcourſe in Mood and Figure.

Diallel-Lines, in *Geometry,* ſuch as run a-croſs or cut one another.

Dialogue, a Conference or Diſcourſe between two or more Parties; or a written Diſcourſe, wherein two or more Parties are brought in talking together.

Diameter, in Geometry, with regard to thoſe Figures that include Space, is a Right Line drawn thro' the Center of the Figure, and terminated at each ſide by the Periphery.

Diameter of the Parabola, is any Line drawn parallel to the *Axis,* and which may be ſuppoſed to meet it at any infinite Diſtance, or in the Center of the Figure.

Diameter of the Hyperbola, is any Line which paſſes thro' the middle of the Tranſverſe *Ax,* which is the Center of the Figure.

Diametrically Oppoſite, is when two things are oppoſed to one another right a-croſs, or directly contrary, as one

K 4   end

end of a Diameter is to the other.

Diamond, the Herald's word for a Black Colour in the Arms of Noblemen.

Diapason, (Gr.) a Term in Musick, is an *Octave;* the Terms whereof are as 2 to 1.

Diapedesis, is an Eruption of the Blood by reason of the thinness of the Vessels.

Diapente, (Gr.) a Term in Musick, its Terms are as 3 to 2.

Diaper, in Heraldry, signi-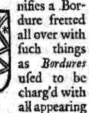nifies a Bordure fretted all over with such things as *Bordures* used to be charg'd with all appearing between the Frets.

Diaphaneity, Transparency, Clearness.

Diaphanous, (Gr.) Transparent like Glass, or which may be seen thro'.

Diaphoreticks, are Medicines which cause Sweat.

Diaphragm, (Gr.) the Midriff or a Muscle composed of two others, which separates the middle from the lower Cavity.

Diaphrattontes, (Gr.) are the Membranes commonly call'd the *Pleura,* which cover the inside of the *Thorax,* and leave a kind of Partition in the middle, commonly call'd *Mediastinum.*

Diaphthora, (Gr.) is a Corruption of any Part of the Body.

Diaplasma, is an Ointment or Fomentation.

Diapyetica, are Medicines which ripen and concoct purulent Matter.

Diarrhoetick, that hath a Lask or Looseness in the Belly without Inflammation.

Diarrhœa, (Gr.) is a Looseness in the Belly, which ejects several bilious, pituitous or other feculent Excrements.

Diarthrosis, a kind of loose Articulation of the Bones, whereby they move easily and strongly.

Diary, (Lat.) an Account of what passes every Day, a Journal or Day-Book.

Diastole, Extension; also a Figure of *Prosodia,* whereby a Syllable short by Nature becomes long; also, the Dilatation of the Heart when the Blood flows into it from the Lungs.

Diastyle, a sort of Edifice where the Pillars stand at a distance of three of their Diameters from one another.

Diasyrmus, (Gr.) a Figure in Rhetorick, whereby we elevate a Person or Thing by way of Dirision.

Diatessaron, a word used in Musick, to denote an Interval composed of a greater and a lesser Tone, the *Ratio* whereof is that of 4 to 3.

Diathesis, is the natural or preternatural Disposition of the Body, whereby we are disposed to perform all natural Actions ill or well.

Diatribe, a Place where Orations are spoke, or Disputations held,

Diato-

Diatonick, a Term which signifies the ordinary sort of Musick, proceeding by different Tones, either in ascending or descending.

Diatyposis, (Gr.) a Description; a Figure in Rhetorick, whereby things are so lively represented, that they seem, as it were, to be before our Eyes.

Dibble, a Tool wherewith Herbs are set in a Garden; also a kind of Hat-Brush.

Dicacity, (Lat) Talkativeness, Drollery, Buffoonry.

Dicæology, (Gr.) a Pleading of One's Cause.

Dichoræus, is the Foot of a Latin Verse; in which the first Syllable is long, the next short, the third long, and the last short.

Dichotomize, (Gr.) to cut or divide into two Parts.

Dichotomy, (Gr.) a cutting or dividing into two Parts.

Dictate, (Lat.) to tell another what and how he shall Write.

Dictator, (Lat.) he that tells another what he writes; also a chief Ruler among the *Romans*, from whom no Appeal was granted, who for Half a Year had a King's Power; never chosen but when the Common-wealth was in some eminent Danger or Trouble; and at the Half Years end, under pain of Treason, yielded up his Office.

Dictionary, a Collection of all the Words in a Language;

or in one or several Sciences, explaining the Signification of them.

Dictitate, to Speak or Tell often.

Didactick, Instructive.

Didder, to Shiver or Shake with Cold.

Diennial, of, or belonging to two Years.

Diesis, a Term in Musick.

Diet, in *Germany*, is the same thing as Parliament in *England*: A Convention of the States or Princes of a Kingdom or Empire.

Dietetical, belonging to Diet; especially such as is prescribed for Health.

Dieu & Mon Droit, (Fr.) the Motto of the Arms of *England*; and signifies, *God and my Right*.

Diffarreation, (Lat.) a Solemnity anciently used among the *Romans* in the Divorcement of Man and Wife.

Difference, in Logick, is that Attribute or Property, which essentially distinguishes one Species from another.

Difference, in Mathematicks, is the Excess of one Quantity above another; or the Remainder when one Quantity is taken out of another.

Difference of *Longitude* of two Places on the Earth, is an Ark of the Equator intercepted between the two Meridians of the two Places.

Difference Ascensional, of the Sun or Planet, is the Difference between the Right and Oblique Ascension of the

the Sun or Planet.

Differences in a Coat of Arms, the Heralds call such Things as distinguish one Family from another ; or Persons of the same Family from each other.

Difficult, Troublesome to perform or understand.

Difficulty, troublesomeness in performing or understanding any thing ; Hardness, Obscurity in the Writings of any Author.

Diffidence, Doubtfulness, Mistrustfulness.

Diffident, Doubtful, Mistrustful.

Difflation, (Lat.) a Blowing down, a Scattering with blowing.

Diffluence, (Lat.) a Flowing forth, Abroad or several Ways.

Difform, is a Word used in opposition to *Uniform*, and signifies no manner of Regularity in the Form or Appearance of a thing.

Diffuse, to spread here and there. *Adjectively*, Ample, Large, Extended.

Diffusion, (Lat.) a Scattering abroad ; in Philosophy, it signifies the dispersing of the subtle *Effluvia* of Bodies into a kind of Atmosphere all round them.

Diffusive, that spreads its self far, or is of a great extent.

Digastrick, (Gr.) that has a double Belly ; so is a Pair of Muscles belonging to the Lower Jaw, termed.

Digester, a Vessel so call'd by its Inventer Mr. *Papin*, and is a kind of *Balneum Mariæ Clausum*.

Digestion, the Decoction of the Aliments in the Stomach, or the Dissolution of them, by which they are turn'd into *Chyle*.

Digestion Chymical, is a Dissolution of Things by an Artificial Heat, or by Fire.

Digestive Medicines, are Medicines which procure Digestion.

Digests, the first Volume or Tome of the Civil Law is call'd the *Digest* ; because the Author hath digested all Things, every Book and Title in its proper and natural Place and Order.

Dight, to Deck, or Set off, or Adorn. *Spencer*.

Digit, in Astronomy, signifies the twelfth Part of the Diameter of the Sun or Moon ; and is used to denote the Quantity of an Eclipse : For when so many of those Parts are darkened, we say the Sun or Moon was Eclipsed so many *Digits*.

Digit, a Scripture Measure of Length of 912 Decimal Parts of an Inch ; also any of the Figures under Ten.

Digital, (Lat.) pertaining to a Finger.

Digitation, a Pointing with the Fingers ; also the Form of the Fingers of both Hands joyned together, or the Manner of their so joyning.

Digladiation,

Digladiation, a Fighting or Contesting the Matter with Swords.

Digne, Worthy, Neat, Genteel.

Dignify, to advance to a Dignity, especially an Ecclesiastical One.

Dignitary, an Ecclesiastical Officer that hath not a Cure of Souls, as *Dean*, *Prebend*, &c.

Dignity, Honour, Reputation, Advancement, some considerable Preferment or Employment.

Digression, a wandring out of the way, a going from the Matter in Hand, an Errour or Fault which a Writer is guilty of, when he leaves his Subject and treats of other Matters,

Dijudication, a deciding a Difference between two.

Dikins, a Corruption of *Devilkins*, i. e. little Devils.

Dilaceration, a tearing or rending in pieces.

Dilaneation, the same with Dilaceration, which see.

Dilapidation, to rid a Place of Stones; also to Consume or Waste.

Dilate, to make wide or lay open.

Dilatation, a making wide or enlarging, a taking up more space than before.

Dilatores alarum nasi, a Pair of Muscles of the Nose, they pull up the *Alæ* and dilate the Nostrils.

Dilatory, full of Delays;

also a Surgeon's Instrument, wherewith the Mouth is dilated or opened.

Dilemma, is an Argument compounded of two or more Propositions; and so disposed, that own or grant which you will of them, yet still the Argument shall press you, and hem you in with Difficulties not readily to be granted or surmounted.

Diligence, is that Care which every one ought to take in the Doing or Performance of his Business.

Dilucidate, to make clear or plain.

Dilucidation, a making clear or plain.

Dilute, a word used in Chymistry and Pharmacy, and signifies to dissolve the Parts of a dry Body, in a moist or liquid One. To *Dilute* Wine, is to allay it with Water.

Dimension, is the Measure or Compass of any Thing; in *Geometry* it signifies either *Length*, *Length* and *Breadth*, or *Length* *Breadth* and *Thickness*. And Dimension taken in the first Sense, agrees only to Mathematical Lines; in the second Sense it agrees to Mathematical Surfaces, and taken in the third, it agrees to all Bodies in Nature.

Dimication, a Fighting or Contending.

Dimidiation, a Halving, or Dividing into two Halves.

Diminution, a Diminishing, Lessening,

Leſſening or Abating.

Diminutive, Little, Small.

Dioceſan, a Biſhop who has the care of a Dioceſs committed to him.

Dioceſs, the Juriſdiction of a Biſhop.

Dioptra, a Surgeons Inſtrument to enlarge or open the Womb for the Extraction of a *Fœtus,* &c.

Dioptrical, belonging to *Dioptricks.*

Dioptricks, is a part of Opticks which treats of refracted Rays and their Unions with one another, according as they are received by Glaſſes of this or that Figure.

Diorthoſis, a Surgical Operation, by which crooked or diſtorted Members are made even, and reſtored to their right and due Shape.

Diplaſiaſmus, is a Reduplication of Diſeaſes.

Diploe, the lower thin Plate or Shell of the Skull; alſo a Chymical Veſſel.

Dipteron, in Architecture, is a Term which the Antients apply'd to thoſe Temples, that were ſurrounded with a double row of Pillars, making two Portico's which they called *Wings,* but we commonly *Iſles.*

Diptotes, are ſuch Words in Grammer as have but two Caſes.

Dire, Cruel, Terrible, Unmerciful.

Direct, in Aſtronomy, a Planet is ſaid to be Direct, when by its proper Motion it goes forward in the Zodiack, according to the natural Order and Succeſſion of the Signs, or when it appears to do ſo, the Obſerver's Eye being placed in the Earth.

Direction, a Term in Mechanicks, ſignifying ſuch or ſuch a way; as a Body moves in ſuch a Direction, is the ſame as a Body moves ſuch a way; and the Line of Direction is the ſame with the Line of Motion that any Body obſerves, according to the Force impreſt upon it.

Direption, a Robbing, Spoiling or Ranſacking of Places and Perſons for Riches, a Snatching or Taking by force.

Dirge, a Service for the Dead uſed by Roman Catholicks: Alſo a mournful Ditty, Song, or Lamentation at a Funeral.

Dirigent, in Geometry, ſignifies the Line of Motion, along which, the *Deſcribent* Line or Surface is carried in the *Geneſis* of any Plane or ſolid Figure.

Diruption, a burſting or breaking aſunder.

Diſability, a being unable or unfit.

Diſadvantage, Loſs, Damage, Prejudice.

Diſaffected, diſſatisfied with, diſcontented.

Diſagreeable, that which does not pleaſe, but is ſome way offenſive to the Sight or Mind.

Disannul, to repeal, abolish, or make void.

Disappear, to vanish, to go out of sight.

Disapprove, to condemn or disallow of.

Disarray'd, (Fr.) disorder'd, put into confusion.

Disastre, (Lat.) ill Luck, a very great Misfortune deriv'd from the evil Influence of the Stars.

Disavow, to disown or not acknowledge for a Man's own.

Disburse, to spend or lay out Money.

Disburthen, to ease one of a Weight that lies heavy upon him.

Discalceated, (Lat.) wearing no Shoes, unshod.

Discard, to lay out Cards; to discharge from Service.

Discent, in Common-Law, is an Order, whereby Lands are derived unto any Man from his Ancestors.

Disceptation, a Disputation, Debating or Arguing upon any Question to be discuss'd.

Discern, to perceive or know one thing from another.

Discernment, an exact Judgment pais'd upon Things.

Discerpible, that may be torn in pieces.

Discerption, a renting, or tearing in sunder.

Discession, (Lat.) a departing.

Discharge, to dismiss a Person from his Service; to shoot off a Gun.

Disciple, (Lat.) a Scholar or Learner.

Discipline, a teaching or instructing.

Discind, (Lat.) to cut off or in pieces.

Disclaim, utterly to refuse, renounce, or disown.

Disclose, to discover or make known a Secret.

Disclosed, discovered or made known.

Discolour, to alter or defile any Colour.

Discomfit, to defeat or overthrow in Battel.

Discomfiture, Rout, Overthrow.

Discompose, to put out of Humour or Ruffle.

Discomposed, out of Humour, Ruffled.

Disconsolate, Comfortless, Melancholy.

Discontinuance, an Interruption, or Breaking off.

Discords, in Musick, are certain Intervals of Sounds, which being heard at the same time, offend the Ear.

Discover, to bring some thing to light which was not known before.

Discount, a Term among Merchants, who in exchanging of Wares don't count how much they are to receive, but how much less they have to pay, they being before in the other Parties Debt; some call it Setting of.

Discourse, in Logick, is that rational act of the Mind, by which we deduce or infer one thing from another.

Dis-

Discourteous, unkind, uncivil.

Discrepant, differing, disagreeing.

Discrete, separate or distinguished one from another.

Discrete Proportion, is when the Proportion disjoyns in the middle; or when the *Ratio* of the first Term to the second, or of the third to the fourth, is not the same with that of the second Term to the third.

Discrete Quantity, is such whose Parts are not connected and joyn'd together; as *Number*.

Discretion, (Lat.) a discreet Management, Wisdom; also Will or Pleasure.

Discretive, that serves to separate.

Discrimination, (Lat.) a differencing one thing from another.

Discumbence, (Lat.) a sitting down upon a Bed, a lying down to Sleep.

Discure, to Discover. *Chaucer*.

Discursion, a running to and fro.

Discus, among the Romans signified a round Quoit of about a Foot in Diameter, which they threw in the Air to shew their Strength.

Discus or *Disk*, in Astronomy, is the round Phases of the Sun or Moon; which at their great distance appear plain or flat.

Discussion, an Examination of a Question, Affair, or any

difficult Matter to discover the Truth.

Discussive, that can dissolve or disperse Humours.

Disdain, Scorn proceeding from Pride or Aversion.

Disdiapason, (Gr.) Term in Musick, a double Eighth or Fifteenth.

Disembark, to go from on Shipboard to Land.

Disembogue, (Sp.) to cast out of the Mouth, to Vomit; to Discharge it self as a River does into the Sea.

Disfigure, to alter the Figure of any thing for the worse, or impair the Beauty of it.

Disforest, to Displant or Cut down the Trees of a Forest.

Disfranchize, to exclude out of the Number of free Denizens or Citizens.

Disgarnish, to take away the Garnish: Also to take away most part of a Garrison and Ammunition from a Place.

Disgorge, to throw up by Vomiting.

Disgregate, to Scatter, separate or disperse

Disgust, to Distaste; also, Substantively a Distaste or Disrelish.

Disheritor, one that Disinherits or puts another out of Possession.

Dishonour, Infamy, Disgrace; to Dishonour is to render infamous.

Disimbellish, to disfigure or impair the Beauty of any thing.

Disin-

Disinchant, to break off an Enchantment.

Disingenuity, want of Sincerity, Dissimulation.

Disintangle, to disengage, to free from, to unravel.

Disinteressed or *Disinterested*, void of Self-interest, Impartial.

Disjunction, a separating or disjoyning.

Disjunctive, separating or disjoyning.

Dislocate, to displace or put out of its right place. In Surgery it signifies to put a Bone out of joynt.

Dislodge, is to raise any thing out of its Lodging.

Disloyalty, (Fr.) Unfaithfulness, Perfidiousness; commonly used with regard to one's Prince.

Dismantle, to take off a Cloak or Mantle; also, to demolish the Fortifications of a Place.

Dismayed, Astonished, Terrified.

Dismes, Tithes, or the 10th Part of all Fruits due to God; and consequently to be paid to those who take upon them Holy Orders.

Dismission, a sending away.

Dismount, to unhorse; to *Dismount Cannon*, is to throw them off the Carriages.

Dispand, to stretch out or spread abroad.

Disparage, to Disgrace or Undervalue.

Disparagement, a Disgracing or Undervaluing.

Disparates, things separate;

in Logick, it is when something is opposed to many others in the same kind of Opposition.

Disparity, a Disagreement between two or more things compared together.

Dispart, in Gunnery, signifies a setting a Mark at, or near the Muzzle-Ring of a Piece, that a Sight-line taken upon the top of the Base Ring against the Touch-hole, may thereby be parallel to the Axis of the Concave Cylinder of the Piece.

Dispaupered, put out of Capacity of suing, *in forma Pauperis*.

Dispend, to spend or lay out Money.

Dispensation, (Lat.) a distributing or dealing; also a suffering or permitting a Man to do a thing contrary to Law.

Dispense, to distribute or dispose of; to administer, bestow, or manage; to *Dispense with*, to exempt or excuse; to free from the Obligation of a Law.

Dispeople, to unpeople, to lay waste.

Disperse, (Lat.) to spread abroad or scatter.

Dispersion, (Lat.) a scattering or spreading abroad.

Dispirit, to pull down one's Spirit, to discourage.

Displace, to put out of a Place, to remove, to turn out of an Office.

Displant, to pluck up that which was planted.

Display,

Display, a particular Explication or Unfolding.

Display'd, spread wide, unfolded, laid open : In Heraldry, it signifies an Eagle in an erect Posture, with her Wings spread abroad.

Displeasant, displeasing, unpleasant.

Displeasure, Affront, Shrewd Turn, Discontent, Anger.

Displosion, a breaking asunder with a great Noise or Sound ; also the letting off a Gun.

Dispoliation, a Spoiling or Robbing.

Dispone, (old Word) to dispose.

Disport, Pastime, Divertisement.

To *Disport one's self*, to divert one's self, to take his Pleasure.

Dispose, to set things in order ; to be in a condition or have an inclination to do a thing.

Disposition, a placing or disposing of things ; also, the natural inclination of the Inclination of the Mind, or the constitution of the Body : in Ethicks, it signifies an imperfect Habit, where the Person operates but with some difficulty, as in Learners.

Dispositor, a Disposer or Setter in order. In *Astrology* 'tis that Planet which is Lord of the Sign where another Planet chances to be.

Dispossess, to deprive any one of their Possessions.

Disposure, a Disposing, Disposal.

Dispraise, Censure, Blame, Reproach.

Disprofit, Damage, Loss, Prejudice.

Disproportion, an inequality of Ratio's, as in four Terms, when the Ratio of the first to the second is unequal to the Ratio of the third Term to the fourth : This inequality of the two Ratio's is call'd Disproportion.

Disproportionable, that bears no proper proportion to, unequal.

Disprove, to prove the contrary.

Disputable, (Lat.) that may be disputed.

Disputant, a Disputer.

Disputation, is an arguing *pro* and *con* upon any doubtful Subject.

Disputative, apt to dispute, contentious, quarrelsome.

Disquamation, is an unscaling a Fish or the like ; a taking off the Shell or Bark.

Disquiet, Unquietness, Trouble.

Disquisition, (Lat.) a diligent search or enquiry into.

Disrank, to put out of Rank or Order.

Disregard, to despise, to slight.

Disrelish, to disapprove or dislike.

Disreputation, ill Name, Discredit.

Disrespect, Incivility, Slight.

Dis-

Disrobe, to pull off one's Robe, to Strip.

Dissalted, cleared from Salt, or made fresh.

Dissatisfaction, Discontent, Disgust, Displeasure.

Dissect, to cut open a dead Body, to Anatomize.

Dissection, (Lat.) a cutting asunder or in pieces : It is frequently more limited, and signifies the cutting up or anatomizing the Bodies of Animals.

Disseise, (Fr. Law-word) to Dispossess or turn out of Possession.

Disseisee, a Person that is put out of his Lands.

Disseisin, in Law, signifies an unlawful dispossessing a Man of his Land, Tenement, or other immovable or incorporal Right.

Disseisor, he that puts another out of his Possession.

Dissemblable, unlike, having no resemblance.

Dissemble, to feign or pretend, to conceal, to counterfeit.

Dissemination, a sowing or scattering here and there.

Dissension, Disagreement, Strife, Quarreling.

Dissent, (Lat.) contrariety of Opinion.

Dissentaneous, disagreeing or not agreeing.

Dissenter, one of a different or contrary Opinion. 'Tis chiefly used to signify a Non-conformist, who complies not with the Church of *England* by Law establish'd.

Dissentery, (old Word) a kind of Still.

Dissertation, a Debate, Reasoning, or Discourse upon any Point, or Subject.

Disserve one, to do him a Prejudice.

Disservice, a Diskindness, an ill Turn, or bad Office ; as to do any one a piece of *Disservice*, is to do him a Diskindness or an ill Turn.

Dissevered, separated, divided, put asunder.

Dis-shevelled, (Fr.) that has the Hair hanging down loose.

Dissidence, Disagreeing or Falling out, Discord.

Dissilience, (Lat.) a leaping down off a Place ; a leaping from one Place to another ; also a bursting or leaping asunder.

Dissimilar, unlike : In Anatomy, those Parts are call'd *Dissimilar*, which consists of other Parts differing from one another as to their Nature ; as the Hand consist of Veins, Arteries, Muscles, Nerves, &c. all which differ from one another both in Name and Denomination.

Dissimilitude, Unlikeness.

Dissimulation, (Lat.) is a pretending one thing and designing quite the contrary ; an acting the Hypocrite.

Dissipate, to disperse or scatter ; to dissolve ; to consume, waste or spend.

Dissipation, (Lat.) a consuming, Wasting, Scattering.

L   *Dissoci-*

Diſſociation, a ſeparating of Company.

Diſſoluble, (Lat.) that may be diſſolved.

Diſſolvent, a Medicine fitted to diſperſe collected Humours: In Chymiſtry, 'tis a Liquor proper for diſſolving a mix'd Body, call'd uſually a *Menſtruum*.

Diſſolution, is that Action by which Fluids looſen the Texture of immerſed Bodies, and reduce them into very ſmall Particles; as Water diſſolves Sugar, Salt, &c. *Aqua Fortis*, Silver, Braſs, &c. alſo it ſometimes ſignifies Deſtruction.

Diſſonance, in Muſick, is a diſagreeable Interval between two Sounds, which being continued together offend the Ears.

Diſſonant, untunable, jarring, diſagreeing.

Diſſwade, to divert, to put one off from a Deſign, to adviſe to the contrary.

Diſſwaſion, a perſwading one contrary to a Reſolution taken.

Diſſwaſive, an Argument or Diſcourſe proper for diſſwading.

Diſtaff, an Inſtrument uſed in Spinning.

Diſtance, is the remoteneſs of one thing from another, whether in point of Time, Place or Quantity. In *Navigation*, it is the number of Degrees or Leagues that a Ship has ſailed from any given Point.

Diſtant, (Lat.) far aſunder, differing.

Diſtaſte, Diſlike.

Diſtemper, Sickneſs, Indiſpoſition, Diſorders in Kingdom or State. In *Painting*, when the Colours are mix'd with Size, Whites of Eggs, or ſuch proper glewy Subſtance, and not with Oil or Water, the Piece is ſaid to be done in *Diſtemper*.

Diſtend, to ſtretch out, to enlarge.

Diſtenſion, a ſtretching out, an enlarging.

Diſterminate, to bound Place from Place, or to ſeparate one Place from another.

Diſtich, (Gr.) a couple of Verſes in a Poem, making a compleat Senſe.

Diſtillation, a dropping down; it is defined by Chymiſts to be an Extraction of the humid Part of Things by vertue of Heat; which humid Part is firſt reſolv'd into Vapour, and then condenſed again by Cold: Alſo a flowing of Humours from the Brain.

Diſtinct, a Thing or Idea is ſaid to be *diſtinct*, wherein the Mind perceives a difference from all other.

Diſtinction, is an aſſigning or putting a difference betweeen one thing and another: Alſo, it often denotes the Difference it ſelf.

Diſtinctive, that makes a Diſtinction.

Diſtinguiſhable, that may be diſtinguiſhed.

Diſtort,

Distort, (Lat.) to wrest a-side, to pull awry.

Distortion, is when the Parts of an Animal Body are ill placed or ill figured.

Distract, (Lat.) to draw or pull asunder: Also to perplex or interrupt; to make one Mad; to rend or divide.

Distrain, to attach or seize upon one's Goods for the satisfaction of a Debt.

Distraction, (Lat.) a drawing several ways; also Perplexity, or a kind of Phrensy that takes off the Mind of Man from attending to what is said to him.

Distress, in Law, a Distraining; also, a Compulsion to appear in Court to pay a Debt or Duty denied; also a pressing Calamity.

Distribute, to divide or share; to dispose or set in order.

Distribution, is a dividing something amongst many.

Distributive, (Lat.) that serves to distribute.

District, (Lat.) a particular Territory, the Extent of a Jurisdiction.

Distringas, is a *Writ* directed to a Sheriff or any other Officer, commanding him to distrain One for Debt to the King, &c. or for his Appearance at a Day.

Distrust, Suspicion, Jealousy.

Disturb, (Lat.) to hinder, to vex, to disorder.

Disturbance, a Bustle, Trouble or Uneasiness.

Disunion, Division, Disagreement.

Disunited, disjoyn'd or separated from.

Disusage, a being out of Use.

Ditone, a double Tone, or the greater Third is an Interval in Musick, which comprehends two Tones. The Proportion of the Tones that make the *Ditones*, is as 4 to 5, and that of the *Semi-ditones* as 5 to 6.

Ditto, a Word used by Merchants, which signifies *the same*, as when some Commodity or Place hath been mention'd, and they have occasion to speak of it again, they say *Ditto*.

Dittology, a double Reading, as in several Scriptural Texts.

Ditty, a Song which is set to a Tune.

Divan, a great Council or Court of Justice amongst the *Turks* and *Persians*.

Divaporation, (Lat.) in *Chymistry*, the driving out of Vapours by Fire.

Divarication, a winnowing and tossing to and fro; a striding wide, a setting asunder, or at distance.

Diverberation, a striking or beating.

Divergent, going further and further asunder: Thus any two Lines forming an Angle, if they be continued will be divergent, that is, will go farther and farther asunder; also Rays issuing from one and the same Point are diverging. L 2 *Divert*,

Divers, fundry, feveral, many.

Diverfe, various, different, contrary, unlike in Circumftances.

Diverfify, (Lat.) to make diverfe, to alter.

Diverfity, different or diverfe.

Divert, (Lat.) to lead or turn afide ; to mifapply or embezzle ; alfo to delight or make chearful.

Divertifement, Recreation, Sport, Paftime.

Dives, (Lat.) Rich.

Divide, (Lat.) to part afunder, to diftinguifh ; to fet at variance ; to fhare.

Dividend, a Share of a yearly Salary, equally divided among Fellows of a College : Alfo an equal Share of the Profits of a Joint Stock : In *Arithmetick,* 'tis a Number given to be divided.

Dividers, a Mathematical Inftrument like Compaffes, ufually of Steel, and confined by a Screw for greater Steadinefs.

Dividual, that which may be fevered or divided.

Divination, a Prefage or foretelling of things to come.

Divine, belonging or like unto God, Godly ; Excellent. *Verbally,* to foretel, to difcover by guefs.

Diviner, a Soothfayer ; a Cunning Man or Conjurer.

Diviniftre, a Divine or Doctor of Divinity. *Chaucer.*

Divinity, (Lat.) the Divine Nature, the Godhead : Alfo

that Science which has for its Object God and Revelations.

Divifibility, is that Difpofition of a Body, whereby it is conceived to have Parts, into which it may be divided, either actually or mentally.

Divifion, (Lat.) a fevering of any thing into its Parts : A going into Parties ; Variance, Difcord. In *Arithmetick,* 'tis a Rule to know how often one Number is contained in another ; or how to divide a Number into what Parts you pleafe.

Divifor, the Number by which the Dividend is to be divided.

Divorce, a Diffolution of a Marriage, or a Separation of Man and Wife.

Diuretical, that caufes Urine.

Diureticks, are thofe Medicines, which by parting, diffolving & fufing the Blood, do precipitate the Serum by the *Reins* into the Bladder.

Diurnal, of or belonging to the Day ; the *Diurnal* Motion of a *Planet* is fo many Degrees, Minutes, &c. as any Planet moves in the Space of 24 Hours.

Diurnal-Arch, is the Arch or Number of Degrees defcribed by Sun, Moon or Stars, between Rifing and Setting.

Diurnal, a Book for writing down Things done every Day ; a Journal, a Day-Book,

Diutur-

Diuturnity, Lastingness or long Continuance.

Divulgation, a publishing or spreading abroad.

Divulge, to spread abroad, to make known.

Divulsion, a pulling away or asunder.

Dizzard, a silly, sottish Fellow.

Dizziness, Giddiness or Swimming of the Head.

Dobeler or *Doubler*, a great Dish or Platter.

Doced or *Douced*, (old Word) a Dulcimer.

Docible or *Docile*, (Lat.) apt to learn.

Dock, is a Pit, great Pond, or Creek by the Side of an Harbour, made convenient to work in, in order to build or repair Ships; and is of two sorts, either *dry* or *wet* : A *dry Dock*, is where the Water is kept out of the Dock by great Flood-gates, till the Ship is built or repaired, but after that, can easily be let in to Float or Launch her. A *wet Dock* is any Place in the Ouze, out of the Tides way, where a Ship may be haled in, and so dock her self or sink her self a Place to lie in.

Docket, a Bill with a Direction ty'd to Goods. In a Law sense, a small piece of Paper or Parchment with the Heads of a larger Writing : Also a Subscription at the Foot of Letters Patent by the *Clerk of the Dockets*.

Doctor; (Lat. that is a Teacher) one who has taken the highest Degree in any Art or Science at an University.

Doctoral, belonging to a Doctor.

Doctrinal, belonging to Doctrine, Instructive.

Doctrine, (Lat.) Learning, Maxims, Tenets.

Document, a Lesson or Admonition.

Documentize, to Instruct,

Dodecadactylum, is the first of the small Guts, beginning from the Pylorus of the Stomach, and ending where the Gut *Jejunum* begins.

Dodecahedron, (Gr.) in Geometry, is a solid Figure of 12 Sides or Faces that are regular Pentagons, it is one of the Platonick or Regular Bodies.

Dodecagon, in Mathematicks, is a Figure of 12 Sides and 12 Angles : In Fortification, 'tis a Place with 12 Bastions.

Dodecatemory, the Twelve Signs of the Zodiack, *Aries, Taurus*, &c. so call'd, because each of them is the twelfth Part of the Zodiack.

Dodkin, a small Piece of Money about the value of a Farthing.

Dodrans, a *Roman* Weight of 9 Ounces; also one of the *Roman* Square Measures, containing one *English* Rood, 34 Square Poles, and 68 Square Feet.

Dodrantal, of or belonging to the Weight of 9 Ounces.

L 3   Do

Dog-days, certain Days in *July* and *August*, so call'd from the Star *Canis* or Dog-Star, which then rises with the Sun and greatly encreaseth the Heat.

Dog One, to follow close in order to know where he goes.

Doge, is the Title or Dignity belonging to the supream Magistrate amongst the *Venetians*; who is call'd Duke, and is the Head of that Republick.

Dogged, Sullen, Surly, Crabbed.

Dogger, a small Vessel of about 80 Tun Burden, with a Well in the middle to bring Fish alive to Shore.

Doggrel Rhyme, pityful Poetry; Paltry Verses.

Dogma, (Gr.) a Decree, a Maxim, a Tenet.

Dogmatical, imposing a Man's own Opinions; also Prudent.

Dogmatist, One that is Opinionative or Bigotted to his own Opinions: Also One that is the Author of any new Sect or Opinion.

Dogmatize, to teach new Opinions.

Doit or *Doitkin*, a small Coin in the *Low Countries*, not amounting to a Farthing in value.

Dole, Sorrow. *Spencer.*

Dole, (Sax.) a Part or Portion. It signifies still a Share, a distributing of Alms; a Gift of a Nobleman to the People.

Dole-meadow, a Meadow wherein divers Persons have a Share.

Dolgbote, (Sax) a Recompence made for a Wound or Scar.

Dollar, a Dutch Coin worth about 4 s. 4 d. of our Money.

Dolorous, full of Grief, Sorrow or Pain.

Dolour, (Lat.) Pain, Grief, Torment, Anguish.

Dolphin or *Dauphin*, the Title of the *French* King's eldest Son, whose Coat of Arms is set out with *Dolphins* and *Flower-de-luces.*

Dolphins, (in Gunnery) are Handles made to some Pieces of Ordnance.

Dolt, a Sot or Blockhead.

Doltish, Dull, Stupid.

Dombot, (*i. e.* Book of Judgment) a Statute Book of the *English Saxons*; in which was contained the Laws of their Kings.

Dome, (Ital.) a Town-house. A Vaulted Roof or Tower of a Church, a Cupola. Among Chymists, an Arched Cover for a Reverberatory Furnace.

Domesday-Book; when K. *Alfred* divided his Kingdom into Counties, Hundreds and Tithings, he had an Inquisition taken of the several Districts, and digested into a Register called *Dom-boc,i.e.* the Judicial or Judgment-Book. The General Survey of *William* the Conqueror was after the Precedent of K. *Alfred*, and call'd by the Name of *Domesday-*

Domefday-Book, which is the same with *Dom-Boc* or *Doom-Book*; that is a Register from which Sentence and Judgment might be given in the Tenure of Estates.

Domestick, belonging to the Houshold.

Domicil, (Lat.) a Dwelling House, an Habitation or Abode.

Domination, Dominion, Rule or Authority over others.

Dominical Letter, one of the first seven Letters of the Alphabet, wherewith the *Sundays* are mark'd throughout the Year in the Almanack. It changes every Year; and after the Term of 28 Years, the same Letter is used again.

Dominicum, *Demain*, or *Demesne*, are Lands not rented to Tenants, but held in Demesne, or in the Lord's own Use and Occupation.

Diminicum Antiquum Regis, the King's ancient Demesne; or such Royal Mannors as were not disposed of to Barons or Knights, to be held by any Feudatory or Military Service, but were reserv'd to the Crown.

Dominion, (Lat.) Government, Authority, Rule, Jurisdiction; the Extent of a State or Kingdom.

Domo raparanda, a Writ lying against One, whose House going to decay, may endanger his Neighbour's House by falling.

Don, (Span.) Lord or Master.

Donary, a Thing that is given to a sacred or holy Use.

Donation, (Lat.) a giving or bestowing.

Donatists, a Sect of Hereticks, so call'd from *Donatus* Bishop of *Carthage*, the first Broacher of the Heresy: They were distinguished into two sorts; the more Rigid, which were called *Circumcellians*, and the more Moderate, which were called *Rogatists*, they all held, that the true Church was only in *Africk*; as also, that the Son in the Trinity was less than the Father, and the Holy Ghost less than the Son.

Donative, a Largess in Money, or Grain, bestow'd upon Souldiers by the Emperors, to obtain their Favour and Votes in time of need: 'Tis used now for a Dole, free Gift or Present, made by a Prince or Nobleman. In a Law-sense, 'tis a Benefice given and collated to a Clerk by the Patron, without Presentation to the Bishop, or Institution and Induction by his Order.

Donative, that is able or apt to give.

Donax, (Gr.) a kind of Reed or Cane, of which Arrows were made; also a kind of Sea-fish.

Donee, in Common-Law, is he to whom Lands are given, as *Donour* is he that giveth them.

Donjon, in Fortification, is generally taken for a large Tower or Redoubt of a Fortress, where the Garrison may retreat in case of necessity, and capitulate with greater Advantage.

Donour, (Lat.) a Giver, a Benefactor. In a Law-sense, one that gives Lands, &c. to another. See Feoffee.

Dorado, (Span.) a thing that is gilt.

Dorick Dialect, is one of the Five Dialects of the Greek Tongue.

Dorick Order, in Architecture, is One of the Five Orders, invented by the Dorians, a People of Greece. If its Columns are Simple without Pilasters, they ought, according to Palladio, to be Seven and a half, or Eight Modules in length; but if the Columns have Pilasters, they ought to be Seventeen and a half Modules in length.

Dorick Musick, so call'd from the Dorians, is a kind of grave and solemn Musick, consisting of a slow spondaick Time.

Dormant; Sleeping: In Heraldry, it signifies lying in a sleeping Posture.

Dormant Writing, a Deed that has a Blank to put in the Name of any Person.

Dormer or Dormer-Windows, is a kind of Window made in the Roof of a House.

Dormitory or Dorter, a Sleeping Place or Bed-chamber; chiefly in a Monastery.

Doron, a Grecian Measure of Length, containing of our English Measure 3 Inches, and 0218 ½ Decimal Parts of an Inch.

Dorsiparous Plants, are such as are of the Capillary kind without Stalk, and do bear their Seed on the backsides of their Leaves.

Dorsum, (Lat.) the Back, is the hinder Part of the Thorax.

Dose, is the Quantity of Physick which a Physician appoints his Patient to take at once.

Dosel or Dorsel, a rich Canopy, under which Princes sit; also the Curtain of a Chair of State.

Dossil, a sort of Tent to be put in Wounds.

Dotage, a Doting, Stupidness or Dulness.

Dotard, a doting Fellow.

Dotchien, is a hard Swelling or Push, as big as a Pigeon's Egg, accompanied with a grievous Pain.

Dote, to grow Dull, Foolish or Senseless.

Dote assignanda, in Law, is a Writ for the Escheator, to assign a Dowry to the Widow of a Tenant of the Kings, Swearing in Chancery not to Marry without the King's Leave: These are the King's Widows.

Dote unde nihil habet, in Law, is a Writ of Dower for a Widow of the Land sold by her Husband, whereof he was so seized, as the Issue of
them

them both might have inherited.

To *Dote upon*, to be very Fond of.

Double Horizontal Dial, is a Dial invented by our Country-man Mr. *Outred*.

Double Tenaille. See *Tenaille.*

Double Plea, in Law, is that wherein the Defendant alledgeth two several Matters in Bar of the Action, whereof either is sufficient to effect his Desire in debarring the Plaintiff.

Double Vessel, in Chymistry, is when the Neck of one Matrass is put and well luted into the Neck of another.

Doublets, with regard to Dice, are two Throws of the same sort, as 2 Fives, 2 Fours, &c.

Doubling, in a Military Sense, is putting two Files of Souldiers into One.

Doublings, (in *Heraldry*) the Linings of Robes, Mantles of State or other Garments.

Doubt, Uncertainty; when the Mind does not know on which Side to determine in any Matter, it is said to *Doubt.*

Doucine, in Architecture, is an Ornament of the highest Part of the Cornish.

Doughty, (old Word) Stout, Couragious.

Dowager, a Widow that enjoys her Dower: This Title is usually given to the Widows of Princes, Dukes and other Persons of Honour.

Downes, Hilly Plains; also the Sea lying near the Sand upon the Coast of *Kent* where our English Navy rides.

Dowry, in Common Law, signifies that which a Wife hath with her Husband after Marriage; it also signifies the Portion which she brings.

Dowtremere, Fair Weather. *Chaucer.*

Doxology. (Gr.) a Song of Praise, a giving of Praise.

Doxy, a She Beggar or Trull.

Drabler, a small Sail in a Ship, the same to a Bonnet, that a Bonnet is to a Course; and is only used when the Course and Bonnet are too shoal to Cloath the Mast.

Drachma, a Weight containing 3 Penny weight, 6 $\frac{9}{14}$ gr. Troy; also a Piece of Money among the *Grecians*, worth 7 Pence 3 Farthings of our Money.

Draco, a Dragon: Also, an Ensign in shape of a Dragon peculiar to the several Companies of *Roman* Souldiers, as the Eagle to the whole Regiment: Also, a Constellation in the Northern Hemisphere of that form, consisting of 33 Stars.

Draco volans, according to the Meteorologists, is a Meteor appearing in the form of a flying Dragon.

Draco's Laws, certain severe Laws made at *Athens* by one *Draco*; whence a severe Punishment for a slight Offence, is term'd *Draco's* Law.

Dra

Dracunculus, is an Ulcer, which even eats through a Nerve it self.

Drag, a Hook; also, amongst Hunters a Fox's Tail. *Verbally*, to draw by force, or to draw after one.

Dragoman or *Druggerman*, an Interpreter in the Eastern Countries, used for more easy managing of Commerce and Trade.

Dragon's Head and *Tail*, are those two Points in which the Orbit of the Moon intersects the Orbit of the Sun or the Ecliptick.

Dragoon or *Dragooner*, a Souldier that fights sometimes on Horseback and sometimes on Foot.

Drags, Pieces of Timber joyn'd together, so as floating upon the Water, they may bear a Boat Load of Wood, or other Wares, down a River.

Drain, in Fortification, a Trench cut to clear a Moat or Ditch of Water.

Drake, a Male Duck; also a sort of Gun.

Dram or *Drachm*, (Gr.) the weight of 60 Grains; among Apothecaries ⅛ of an Ounce: In *Averdupois* weight 1/16.

Dramatick, (Gr.) Active: *Dramatick Poetry*, is when the Persons are every one adorn'd and brought upon the Theatre to speak and act their own Parts.

Drap, (Fr.) Cloth, Woollen Cloth. Hence *Drap de Berry*, a sort of thick Cloth first made in *Berry* in *France*.

Drapery, in *Painting* or *Sculpture*, signifies the cloathing of any Humane Figures; and when the Folds of the Garments hang easy and natural and yet appear strong, we say the *Drapery* is good.

Drastick Remedies, are such Remedies as work briskly and effectually.

Draught, (in *Navigation*) the quantity of Water a Ship draws when afloat, or the Number of Feet under Water, when laden, whereby she is called of more or less Draught. In *Military* Affairs, 'tis a Detachment of Souldiers; and in Trade, an Allowance in weighing Commodities.

Draught Compasses, a kind of Compasses with several moveable Points, for fine Draughts of Maps, Charts, Architecture, Fortification, Dialling, &c.

Draw, a Ship is said to draw so much Water, according to the number of Feet she sinks into it.

Draw-Bridge, is a *Bridge* made after the manner of a Floor, to be drawn up or let down as occasion serves before the Gate of a Town or Castle.

Drawing, is the Representation of Things delineated with a Pen or Pencil.

Drawing amiss, with *Hunters*, is when Hounds or Beagles

gles hit the Scent of their Chace contrary; so as to hit it up the Wind, instead of down the Wind; in this case, the Expression is, *They Draw amiss.*

Drawing on the Slot, is when Hounds having touch'd the Scent, draw on till they hit on the same again.

Dredge or *Dreg,* (Country Word) is a Mixture of Oats and Barly.

Dredgers, Fishers for Oysters: 'Tis a Term in the Law of the Admiralty.

Dreery, (Old Word) Lamentable, Sorrowful, Dismal.

Drench, a Physical Potion for a Horse: *Verbally,* to give such a Drench; also to Bath or Soak.

Drent, Drowned. *Spencer.*

Drerement, Sadness. *Spencer.*

Dribblet, (Old Word) a small Portion; 'tis still used for a small Sum of Money paid or owing.

Drift, a Boat is said to go *Adrift* when it hath no Body to Row or Steer it; this Word is sometimes used for Policy, Aim or Intention.

Drift Sail in a Ship, is a Sail used under Water; its veered out right a Head upon the Sea in a Storm, having Sheets fasten'd to it as other Sails have.

Drill, a Baboon or overgrown Ape; also a sort of Boring Tool managed with a

Bow, and used by all sorts of Artificers that work in hard Materials: *Verbally,* to bore Holes with such an Instrument; also to draw or entice; to protract time.

Drinkham, or *Drinklean,* a certain Quantity of Drink, provided by Tenants for the Entertainment of the Lord or his Steward: 'Tis otherwise call'd *Scot-Ale.*

Drive, a Ship is said to drive, when an Anchor let fall will not hold her fast, but she sails away with Wind or Tide: Also, when a Ship is *a-hull* or *a-try,* with her Sails taken in, they say *She drives to the Leeward; or in with the Shore.*

Drive-bolts, (in a Ship) are long Iron Pins used for driving out other Bolts, Nails, Pins, &c.

Drizzle, to fall in small Drops like the Rain.

Droit, (Fr.) Right, Equity, Justice; 'tis of the same sense in Common Law; also a sort of Measure.

Droll, (Fr.) a good merry Fellow, a boon Companion, one that cares not how the World goes.

Drollery, a merry and facetious way of Writing or Speaking; full of merry and waggish Wit.

Dromo, a Caravel or swift Bark that scours the Seas; also a kind of Fish of great swiftness.

Drop.

Drop, in *Architecture*, an Ornament of the Pillars of the Dorick Order, representing Drops or little Bells, underneath the *Triglyphs*.

Dropsical, subject to the Dropsie, or troubled therewith.

Dropsy, a Disease, the settlement of a watry Humour, either through the whole Body, or else in some Part of it; as the Belly, Head, Breast, &c. whereby they are very much encreased in Bulk.

Drub, is a beating the Soles of the Feet with a Stick, a Punishment among the *Turks*: In *Barbary*, *Drubbing*, is beating on the Bum and Belly; but with us to Drub is to beat a Person.

Druggerman : See *Dragoman*.

Drugs, all kinds of Simples, for the most part dry, for the use of Physick; as also of Painters and other Artificers. The Word is also apply'd to sorry Commodities and of little value that stick on Hand.

Druids, were certain learned Pagan Priests among the ancient *Britains* and *Gauls* that lived naked in the Woods, giving themselves to the Study of Philosophy, and avoiding Company as much as possible.

Drum, a well known Instrument of Martial Musick: also a Membrane that runs athwart the Cavity of the Ear, and separates the outward

Passage from the inward Parts.

Drury, (old Word) Sobriety, Modesty.

Dry-Exchange, (in *Usury*) when something is pretended to be Exchanged on both sides, yet nothing really passes but on one side.

Dry-Stitch, (in *Surgery*) is when by means of a Piece of Linnen Cloth, with strong Glew, or other binding Composition, stuck on each side of a Wound, its Lips are drawn together.

Dryades,(Gr.) certain Wood Nymphs or Wood Fairies, having the Name from *Drys*, an Oak; because their Life was feigned to be included in Trees.

Dry-shave, to Chouse, Gull, or Cheat notoriously.

Dual, of or belonging to two.

Duarchy, (Gr.) a Form of Government where two govern conjoyntly.

Dub a Knight, to confer the Honour of Knighthood on one.

Dubing of a Cock, with Cock-masters, is the Cutting off a Cock's Comb and Wattles.

Dubious,(Lat.)Doubtful, Uncertain.

Ducal, belonging to a Duke.

Ducatoon, a certain piece of Money, much of the same value with a *Ducket*; which see.

Ducet

Duces tecum, is a Writ commanding one to appear at a Day in the Chancery, and to bring with him some Evidence or other Things which that Court would view.

Ducker or *Dourıker,* a kind of Cock that in Fighting runs about the Clod, almost at every Blow.

Ducket, a certain Gold Coin worth about Six Shillings and Eight Pence.

Ducking at the Main-yard, a Punishment used at Sea, when a Malefactor having a Rope fasten'd under his Arms, about his Waste, and under his Breech, is hoifed up to the End of the Yard, and thence violently let fall into the Sea two or three times. If the Offence be great, he is also drawn underneath the Ship's Keel; which is term'd Keel-raking.

Duckup, a Word used at Sea by the Steersman, or him that is at Helm, when either Main-fail, Fore-fail, or Spritfail hinder his Sight, so that he cannot fee to fail by a Land Mark or the like; for then his Word is *Duckup* the Clew-lines of those Sails.

Ductile, is a word moft ufually apply'd to Metals, and fignifies capable of being dilated or drawn out with a Hammer.

Ductility, is an eafy yielding and fpreading of the Parts of any Mettal under a Hammer.

Ductus Alimentalis; the Gullet Stomach and Bowels; fo call'd by Dr. *Tyfon,* becaufe they make but one continued Canal.

Ductus Bilarius : See *Porus Bilarius.*

Ductus Chyliferus, in Anatomy, is a Veffel in the lower Part whereof, call'd the *Receptaculum Chyli,* all the *Lacteal* Veins and many Lympheducts are terminated : It conveys the Chyle and the Lympha from the lower Parts to the Heart.

Ductus Cyfticus, a Pipe going from the Neck of the Gall Bladder, to that Part where the *Porus Bilarius* joyns it. It is of the bignefs of a Goofe's Quill.

Ductus Lachrymalis, a Paffage whereby the Water that moiftens the Eyes is convey'd to the Nofe.

Ductus Pancreaticus; is a little Channel arifing from the *Pancreas,* and running all along the middle of it, and is inferted into the *Duodenum,* into which it difcharges a Juice, to ferment and volatalize the Juice from the Acid Ferment of the Stomach and the Mixture of the Gall.

Ductus Roriferus, fo term'd by the Learned *Bilfius,* the fame with *Ductus Chiliferus.*

Ductus Salivares, are little Canals, which proceeding from the *Maxillary* Glands, go as far as the Jaws and Sides of the Tongue, where they emit

emit the Juice we call Spittle.

Ductus Thoracicus, the same as *Ductus Chyliferus*; which see.

Ductus Urinarius. See *Ureters*.

Ductus Umbilicalis, the Navel Passage in a Child in the Womb.

Ductus Wirtsungianus, so call'd from *Wirtsungus* the Inventer, the same with *Ductus Pancreaticus*.

Dudgeon, (old Word) Stomachfulness, Disdain, Wrath, Grudge.

Dudgeon-Dagger, a little Dagger.

Duel, (Lat.) a Fight between two at a Place and Hour appointed in pursuance of a Challenge.

Duella, a Weight containing of our *English* Troy 6 Penny Weight, and 1 ⅐ Grains.

Duellists, so are *Alcali*'s and *Acids* term'd by the incomparable Mr. *Boyle*, with respect to these Philosophers, who wou'd explain, by their Enmity, all Natural *Phenomena*.

Duke, the highest Title of Honour in *England*, next to Prince of *Wales*, from the Latin *Dux*, a Leader; they being either Generals in War, or in Peace Governours of Provinces. He is Created by Patent, Girding with a Sword, a Mantle of State, a Cap and Coronet of Gold on his Head, and a Rod of Gold in his Hand.

Dulcarnon, a certain Pro-

position found out by *Pythagoras*; upon which Account he sacrificed an Ox to the Gods; in token of Thankfulness, and call'd it *Dulcarnon*: Whence the Word by *Chaucer* and other old *English* Authors, is taken for any hard knotty Question or Point.

To *Beat Dulcarnon*, to be at One's Wits end.

Dulcification, (Lat.) a making sweet.

Dulcify, to make Sweet: In Chymistry, when equal Parts of Spirit of Wine and any acid Menstruum, such as Spirit of *Sa.t*, *Nitre*, *Vitriol*, &c. are digested together for 3 or 4 Days, they call it *dulcifying* acid Spirit.

Dulcinists, a sort of Hereticks, so call'd from one *Dulcin* the Head of them; he pretended to Preach the Reign of the Holy Ghost; asserting, That the Father had Reigned from the beginning of the World to the coming of Christ; and the Son's Reign began then, and continued till the Year 1300. when began the Reign of the Holy Ghost, of which he made himself the Head, having rejected the Authority of the Pope.

Dulcitude, Sweetness

Dulcisonant, sounding sweet.

Dulcoration, a making sweet.

Dulocracy, (Gr.) a kind of Government, where Servants and Slaves have so much Freedom and License that
they

they Domineer and Rule.

Dumal, pertaining to Bryers and Brambles.

Dum fuit intra ætatem, in Law, is a Writ to recover Land fold at under Age.

Dum non fuit compos mentis, in Law, is a Writ to recover Lands of Aliens by one not of found Memory.

Dumb-Signs : See *Mute-Signs*.

Dumose, full of Bryers and Brambles.

Dump, a fudden Aftonifhment, a Melancholy Fit.

Dun, is to demand or prefs a Man to pay his Debts.

Dunch, (old Word) Deaf.

Dungeon, the moft loathfome and darkeft Part of a Prifon, where Perfons Condemn'd are put a little time before Execution.

Dung-meers, Places or Pits where Soils, Dungs, Weeds, &c. are mix'd and lye and rot together, for the Improvement of Husbandry.

Dunum or *Duna*; a Word ufed in Domefday-Book for a Down or Hilly Plain. This Word a little altered is found in the Names of many Towns, as *Afhdown*, *Cleydon*, &c.

Duodecennial, of twelve Years.

Duodecimo, (Lat.) a Book is faid to be in *Duodecimo*, or in Twelves, when twelve Leaves are contain'd in a Sheet.

Duodenum, is the firft of the Inteftines or Guts, and is

about twelve Fingers breadth long.

Duple, Double.

Duplicate, a fecond Letter Patent granted by the Lord Chancellor, of the fame Contents with the former ; alfo, any Tranfcript or Copy of a Writing.

Duplicate Ratio, in *Geometry*, is the Product of the *Ratio* multiply'd by it felf, or the Square of that *Ratio*. In *Law*, 'tis an Allegation brought to weaken the Pleader's Reply : In *Rhetorick*, 'tis the fame with *Anadiplofis*.

Duplication, a Doubling or Multiplying by Two.

Durable, (Lat.) of long Continuance, Lafting.

Dura Mater, (Lat.) the outward Skin that encompaffes or enwraps the Brain.

Durance, Imprifonment, Confinement.

Duration, is the continuation of the Exiftence of any Thing ; and is the fame with *abfolute Time*.

Durden, a Copfe or Thicket of Wood in a Valley.

Durefs, (Lat.) *i. e.* Hardfhip : 'Tis a Plea in Law for one that being Imprifon'd, or otherwife hardly ufed, is forc'd to feal a Bond, during Reftraint.

Durgen, a little thick and fhort Perfon ; a Dwarf.

Dusky, (Greek) Obfcure, Dark.

Dutchy, the Territory of a Duke : In *England*, 'tis a Signiory,

Signiory or Lordship, established by the Sovereign under that Title, with several Priviledges, Honours, &c. as the *Dutchy* of *Cornwal*, *Lancaster*, &c.

Duty, any thing that one is obliged to : A Publick Tax ; in Trade, Money paid for Custom ; in War, the doing what pertains to the Function of a Souldier.

Duumvirate, the Office of the Duumviri at *Rome*, who were two Persons of equal Authority,

Dwarf, any Person that is very short and little.

Dwindle, to Decay or Waste ; to Shrink or Consume.

Dwining, (old Word) Confuming, Wasting away.

Dyalling, is the Art of describing Hour Lines truly on any given Plane, so as thereby to know the Hour of the Day when the Sun shines.

Dye, in Architecture, is the middle of the Pedestal, or that Part which lies between their Base and their Cornice.

Dynasty, (Gr.) supream Government or Authority ; Also a List of the Names of several Kings that have reign'd in a particular Kingdom successively.

Dypteron, or Dypterick Figure, or Order of Pillars, in Architecture, is where the Temple, Edifice, &c. is environ'd with a two-fold Range of Pillars in the Form of a double Portico.

Dysæsthesia, (Cr.) a Difficulty or Fault in Sensation.

Dyscrasy (Gr.) or Intemperature, is when some Humour and Quality abounds too much in the Body.

Dysentery, a Looseness accompanied with Gripings in the Belly.

Dysepulotica, are great Ulcers beyond cure.

Dysorexy, (Gr.) want of Appetite.

Dyspepsy, (Gr.) a difficulty of Digestion, or Fermentation in the Stomach and Guts.

Dyspathy, (Gr.) an Impatience or very great Uneasiness under some violent Distemper or Trouble.

Dysphony, (Gr.) a difficulty in Speaking.

Dyspnœa (Gr.) a difficulty in Breathing.

Dystichia, a double Row of Hairs on the Eye-lids.

Dysury, (Gr.) a difficulty of Urine, or making Water.

E A

E_Aring_, a board a Ship, is that part of the Bolt-rope, which at the four Corners of the Sail is left open in Form of a Ring: Also In-gathering, or Harvest.

Earl, a Title of Nobility, betwixt a Marquess and a Viscount.

Earned, longed earnestly. _Spencer_.

Earnest, Money given to bind a Bargain.

Earning, what Cheese is made with.

Earst, Before, formerly. _Milt_.

Earthquakes, are Trem-blings or Shakings of the Earth, which are sometimes particular, and felt only by one Country or Nation; and sometimes general, and felt by several Nations at the same time.

Ease a Ship, among the Sea-men signifies to slacken the Shrouds when they are too stiff.

Easement, in Common Law, is a Service that one Neighbour hath of another by Charter or Prescription without Profit; as a Way thro' his Grounds, a Sink, or such like.

Easter, the Time of the Ce-lebration of the Resurrection of our Saviour. So called from _Eoster_, an ancient God-dess of the _Saxons_, whose Feast they celebrated about the same time, _viz._ about _April_.

Easter-Offerings, an Offer-ing to the Priest at that time.

Easterlings, Eastern Mer-chants, who occasioned the Name of Sterling-Money.

Eastern Mile, a Scripture Measure of Length, contain-ing one _English_ Mile, 403 Paces, and 1 Foot.

Eaves-dropper, a lurking Listner.

Ebionites, were a certain sort of Hereticks, who de-nied the Divinity of our Sa-viour, and rejected all the Go-spels but St. _Matthew's_. They were so called from their Founder _Ebion_.

Ebraick, belonging to the Hebrew Tongue.

Ebriety, (Lat.) Drunken-ness.

Ebulliency, the same with Ebullition.

Ebullition, (Lat.) the boyl-ing, struggling, or Efferve-scence which arises from the mingling together of an Acid and Alkalizate Liquor; and hence any intestine violent Motion of the Parts of a Flu-id, occasioned by the strug-gling of Particles of different Natures, is called by this Name of _Ebullition_.

Eburnean, (Lat.) belonging to Ivory, or white like Ivory.

Ecbolica, are Medicines which help Delivery in hard Labour, also Medicines which cause Abortion.

Escentrick, that hath not the same Center; thus an

A a   _Eccen-_

Eccentrick Circle is a Circle which hath not the same Center with another. It is a Term used in the *Ptolemaick Astronomy.*

Eccentricity, is the distance of the Centers of the two Eccentrick Circles from one another; also the distance between the Center and the Focus of an Ellipsis.

Ecchymona, are Marks and Spots in the Skin, arising from the Extravasation of Blood.

Ecclesiastical, belonging to the Church.

Eccrimocritica, are Signs to judge of a Distemper from particular Excretions.

Eccrisis, is a Secretion of Excrements out of an Animal Body, or out of some part of it.

Eche, to encrease; to add or help out.

Echinus, in Botany, is the prickly Head, Cover of the Seed or Top of any Plant; so called from its Likeness to a Hedge-hog.

Echinus, in Architecture, is a Member or Ornament first placed on the Top of the Ionick Capital; so called from the Roughness of its carving, resembling the thorny Coat of a Hedge-hog.

Echo, or *Eccho,* is that Noise or Voice which is reflected from Woods, Rocks, Caves, hollow Places, and the like.

Eclegma, a Medicine designed to heal or ease the Lungs in Coughs, Peripneumonies, &c.

Eclipse, (Gr.) is a Defect of Light in one of the Luminaries, the Sun or Moon; the Sun is *eclipsed,* or we are deprived of its Light, when the Moon interposes between us or the Earth and the Sun; and the Moon is eclipsed or darkened to us, when the Earth happens to come between the Sun and it, and so deprives it of the Light of the Sun.

Ecliptick, is a great Circle of the Heavens, in which the Sun moves in his Annual Motion. It is supposed to be drawn thro' the middle of the Zodiack, and makes an Angle with the Equinoctial of $23^{\circ}\ 30'$.

Eclipsis, in Physick, is a Defect of the Spirits, fainting or swooning.

Eclogue, a Pastoral Poem, or a Discourse in Verse, between two Shepherds.

Eclysis, is when the Strength of the Patient is a little decayed, proceeding from a want of sufficient Warmth and Spirits in the Body.

Ecphonesis, (Gr.) an Exclamation; a Pathetical Figure or Sentence, whereby the Orator both expresses his own Passion and Affection, and stirs up that of his Auditors, &c.

Ecpiesma, a Juice squeezed out; also the Dregs which remain of any thing that is squeezed: Likewise a Fracture

œture of the Skull, wherein the broken Parts press upon the Meninges or Skins of the Brain.

Ecpiesmus, is a very great Protuberance of the Eyes.

Ecpuctica, are condensing Medicines.

Ecstacy, (Gr.) a Trance or Swooning; a Transportation of the Spirit by Passion.

Ecstastick, taken up with Ecstacy or Trance.

Ecthymata, are Pimples, or certain Breakings out in the Skin, as the Small-pox, &c.

Ecthymosis, is a Commotion and Intumescence of the Blood; also a Chearfulness of the Mind.

Ectype, (Gr.) a thing drawn after a Copy; also a Counterfeit.

Edacity, a greedy eating or devouring.

Eddy, is the running back of the Water at any Place, contrary to the Tide or Stream, and so falling back into the Tide again; occasioned by some Head-land or Point jutting out suddenly, and so hindering the Current of the Water, and throwing it back again.

Eddy Wind, is that Wind which is reflected from a Sail or any other thing, and so goes contrary to its Course before it struck the Sail, &c.

Edge, the Sharpness of a Weapon; also a Border, &c.

Edible, eatable, or that may be eaten.

Edict, a Commandment, Ordinance, or Decree.

Edification, Building; also Instruction, where he that is instructed profitteth by it.

Edifice, a House or Building.

Edifie, to profit by Instruction.

Edile, an Inferiour Officer among the *Romans*, whose Business it was to register Sanctions, look after the Buildings of Temples, private House, &c. They were something like our Church-Wardens, or Surveyors.

Edition, a publishing any thing; but most commonly it is used for an Impression of a Book: As when a Book has been printed once, twice, thrice, &c. We say it has had the first, second, third, &c. Edition.

Editor, a Publisher.

Educate, (Lat.) to bring up or nourish.

Education, is a bringing up of Children; a Person of a *good Education*, is a Person that has been brought up well, or instructed in the Knowledge of Wisdom, good Arts, or good Manners.

Edulcoration, Sweetening; in Chymistry it signifies the clearing any Matter from the Salts it may be impregnated with, by washing it thoroughly in common water.

Effable, that may be spoken, uttered, or expressed.

To *Effect*, any thing done or finished, considered as done or finished, is called an Effect; also Merchants when

A a 2   they

they leave off trading or corresponding in any place, and
remove what they have there,
they are said to carry off their
Effects, so that here *Effects*
signifie Goods.

Effectually, to do a thing
effectually, is as much as to
go thorow stitch with it, or
to do it thorowly.

Effections, in Geometry, is
sometimes used for *Geometrical Constructions*, and often for
Problems or *Practices*, so far
as they are deducible from
some general Proposition.

Effeminate, tender, delicate, voluptuous like a Woman.

Effervescence, a word used
in Philosophy and Chymi-
stry, signifying a greater degree of motion and struggling
of the small parts of any Liquor than we understand by
Fermentation, and denotes a
great ebullition or boyling up
with some degree of heat.

Efficacious, full of *Efficacy*,
Efficacy, Force, Strength,
Vertue, Ability.

Efficient Cause, is the Cause
which immediately produces
the Effect.

Effigies, an Image made after the likeness of a thing.

Efflagitate, (Lat.) to desire
earnestly.

Efflorescence, the outward
Face; the uppermost Rind
or Skin of any thing: In
Physick, the appearance of
spots is called an *Efflorescence*.

Effluence, (Lat.) a flowing
running out.

Effluvium, (Lat.) are such
small Particles as are continually flowing out of almost all mixt Bodies.

Efforts, (Fr.) violent Es-
says, or strivings for a matter, whole Force and Power.

Effractor, a House-breaker.

Effrenation, (Lat.) a headlong or unbridled rashness.

Effrontery, Impudence, Malapertness.

Effusion, a pouring out. In
Chymistry, it is a pouring
out the Water, when the
matter, by its weight, is sunk
to the bottom of the Vessel.

Eft, a venemous Creature
like a Lizard.

Eftsoons, immediately, often.

Egestion, an Evacuation of
the Excrements, or a going to
Stool.

Egg on, to provoke or stir
forward.

Egistments, Cattle taken to
feed for a time.

Eglantine, the wild Rose.

Egregious, excellent, singular, remarkable.

Egress, (Lat.) a Passage,
or going out.

Egression, the same with
Egres.

Egritude, Sickness, Grief.

Egurgitate, (Lat.) to empty or disgorge.

Ejaculation, a shooting, or
casting forth; a fervent Prayer; also the Phanatical Ra-
ptures of *Extempore* Enthusiasts.

Ejection, (Lat.) a casting
out.

Ejectione

Ejectione Custodiæ, is a Writ that lieth properly against him that casteth out the Guardian from any Land during the minority of the Heir.

Ejectione Firmæ, a Writ for casting out a Lessee for term of Years.

Eigne, the first-born.

Einecia, Eldership.

Eke, to add to.

Eirenarchy, (Gr.) the Government of Peace.

Ejulation, (Lat.) wailing or crying out in a pitiful manner.

Ejuration, (Lat.) a renouncing or resigning one's Place.

Elaborate, done with a great deal of pains and exactness.

Elaboratory., a place to work in, properly a place where Chymists work.

Elacerate, to tear in pieces.

Elapidate, to clear a place of Stones.

Elapidation, a clearing a place of Stones.

Elapsed, that is passed or slid away.

Elapsion, a passing or sliding away.

Elastick, springy, or that is endued with an

Elastick force, the force of a Spring when bent, and endeavouring to unbend it self again.

Elasticity, is a springiness, which most Bodies have more or less; the Air has it in a very remarkable manner, and being compressed, it endeavours with a very great force to restore it self to its former state.

Elate, puffed up, proud.

Elaterium, the same with *Elasticity*; also the juice of wild Cucumbers made up in a thick and hard consistence; and, according to some, any Medicine that purges the Belly.

Elaterists, Mr. *Boyle* uses this word to denote those who hold the Doctrine of an Elaterium, or Spring and Weight of the Air.

Elaxate, (Lat.) to unloose or make wider.

Eld, old Age. *Spencer*.

Elcesaeitæ and *Sampseans*, a Sect of Hereticks in the third Century, who rejected all St. *Paul*'s Epistles; they taught that there were two Christs, one in Heaven, and the other on Earth, and that the Holy Ghost was Christ's Sister.

Election, (Lat.) a choosing.

Elective, pertaining to Election or Choosing, or that may be chosen.

Electors, certain Princes of *Germany*, by whom, according to the institution of the Emperor *Charles* the IVth. each successive Roman Emperor was to be chosen.

Electricity, is the quality that *Amber*, *Jet*, *Sealing-wax*, &c. have of attracting very light Bodies to them, when the attracting Body is rubb'd or chafed.

A a 3   *Electuary*

Electuary, is a Medicine of a confiftence thicker than a Syrup, and compofed of hard things reduced to a Powder, and accurately mixed with Syrups, Honey, &c.

Eleemofynary, freely given by way of Alms.

Elegancy, neatnefs, beauty in Speech, Apparel, &c.

Elegiack Verfe, the fame with Pentameter a fort of Verfe, feldom ufed by it felf, but moft commonly joined alternately with Hexameter.

Elegy, a mournful Song or Verfe, commonly ufed at Funerals, or upon the death of any Perfon.

Elementary, belonging to Elements.

Elements, is ufed by natural Philofophers and Chymifts, to denote the firft Principles out of which all natural Bodies are compofed; as alfo it often fignifies the Principles of any Art or Science, or thofe *Definitions*, *Axioms* and *Poftulates*, upon which any Art or Science is built.

Elench, a fubtle Argumentary proof.

Elenchical, belonging to an *Elench*.

Elevate, to lift up, to exalt.

Elevation, a lifting up, an exalting. The Chymifts ufe it to denote the rifing up of any Matter in manner of Fume or Vapour.

Elevation, of the Pole, is the height of the Pole above the Horizon, or the number of Degrees the Pole is raifed above the Horizon.

Elfe, a Fairy, alfo a Dwarf.

Elibation, (Lat.) a tafting or offering of Sacrifices.

Elicitation, (Lat.) a drawing out or alluring.

Elide, (Lat.) to ftrike or knock out.

Eligible, (Lat.) to be elected, fit or worthy to be chofen.

Elimation, (Lat.) a cutting off with a File.

Elimination, (Lat.) a throwing over the Threfhold, a turning out of Doors.

Eliquament, (Lat.) a fat juice which is fqueezed out of Fifh or Flefh.

Elifion, (Lat.) a ftriking or dafhing out.

Elixation, a feething or boiling.

Elixir, in Chymiftry, is a very fine and ufeful Tincture, as *Elixir proprietatis*, *falutis*, &c.

Ellipfis, in Grammar, is a Figure whereby fome part of our Difcourfe is left out or retrench'd.

Ellipfis, (Gr.) in Mathematicks, is an oval Figure, or a Figure longer one way than the other, and the fquares of whofe Ordinates to any Diameter are in proportion to one another, as the refpective Rectangles under the fegments of that Diameter.

Elliptical, belonging to an *Ellipfis*.

Elocution,

Elocution, (Lat.) Utterance, Delivery; as a Man of a good *Elocution*, is a Man of a good and handsome Delivery.

Elogy, a Certificate, Report, or Testimonal of one's praise or difpraife.

Elongate, (Lat.) to remove a far off.

Elongation, (Lat.) in Aftronomy, fignifies the removal of a Planet from the Sun, as it appears to an Eye placed on the Earth.

Elopement, in Law, is when a married Woman departs from her Husband, and dwels with an Adulterer; for which, without voluntary Reconcilement to her Husband, fhe fhall lofe her *Dowry*, nor fhall her Husband in fuch a cafe be obliged to allow her any maintenance.

Eloquence, (Lat.) a good grace of fpeaking; a gift which *Cicero* had in a very peculiar manner; he truly underftood what Arguments to make ufe of, and what Flowers to beautifie his Speech with, to work upon the Paffions and Affections of his Auditors.

Elucidation, (Lat.) a making bright, or clear; alfo an explaining or clearing the difficulties in any crabbed Author, is called by this name.

Elucubration, a Watching, Writing, or Studying by Candle-light,

Elude, to efcape any impending trouble or danger.

Elyfium, a fort of Paradife, into which the Heathens believed the Souls of the Juft went after Death.

Elythroides. See *Vaginalis Tunica.*

Emaceration, (Lat.) a making lean or wafting.

Emaciation, (Lat.) a making lean, thin or flender.

Emanation, (Lat.) a flowing from; alfo what does flow from another is often called an *Emanation.* Thus the Effluviums of Bodies are called Emanations; as are the Rays of the Sun, &c.

Emancipation, a Term in the Roman Law, fignifying the fetting free of a Son from the fubjection of his Father; which was done thus, his natural Father fold him three times to another Man; and this Perfon the *Lawyers* called *Pater Fiduciarius*, a Father in truft; after which his Father bought him again, and then on his Manumiting him he became free. Now they call'd this imaginary Sale *Mancipation*; the Children thus alienated from their natural Father were called *Emancipati*, and this Form of fetting them free Emancipation.

Emargination, a Term in Surgery, which fignifies the taking away the Scurf from the brims of Wounds and Sores.

Emasculation, an unmanning, or making effeminate.

Embalming, is the seasoning of a dead Body with Gums and Spices to preserve it from Putrefaction.

Embarasment, (Fr.) a perplexing, entangling or hindering.

Embargo, (Sp.) a Stop or Arrest, properly of Ships.

Embassy, the Errant an Ambassador is sent upon; 'tis used also for the Ambassador's Train.

Embater, the hole you look through to take aim by in a Cross-bow.

Embatteled, put in Array; also a Term in Heraldry, when the Out-line of any Ordinary resembles the Battlements of a Wall.

Embellish, to adorn, beautifie, or set out to the Eye.

Embellishments, Ornaments.

Ember Days, are the *Wednesday*, *Fryday* and *Saturday* after the first *Sunday* in *Lent*, after *Whitsunday*, after the 14th of *September*, and after the 13th of *December*, antiently appointed by the Church for Prayer and Fasting, to implore God's Blessing upon the ordination of Priests and Deacons, usually celebrated on the *Sundays* following at those Seasons.

Embezel, (Ital.) to steal, or convert to one's own use what a Man has no right to.

Emblem, (Gr.) is properly any curious Work inlaid in Wood, as we see in Chess-Boards and Tables; also an expressing a moral Symbol by way of Picture.

Emblematical, belonging to an Emblem.

Emblements, in Law, are the Profits of Lands which have been sowed.

Embolism, (Gr.) an adding of a Day to a Year, which makes Leap Year; also an adding together the Lunations which happen every subsequent Year, eleven Days sooner than in the preceding, by which means the common Lunar Year becomes equal to the Solar.

Embossing, a kind of Sculpture or Engraving, where the Figure is protuberant or sticks out from the Plain on which it is engraven.

Embost, (Sp.) in Hunting, is foaming at the Mouth, or a Deer so hard chased that he foams at the Mouth.

Embowel, to take out the Bowels.

Embrace, to fold in one's Arms, or clasp one's Arms round any one in token of Love and Kindness.

Embraceur, in Law, is he, that when a matter is in Trial between Party and Party, comes to the Bar with one of the Parties, being bribed so to do, and speaks in the case, or privately labours the Jury; the penalty whereof is 20 *l.* and Imprisonment during the Justice's displeasure.

Embrasure,

Embrasure, in Architecture, is the enlargement made in the Walls, to give more light, or greater convenience to the Windows, Doors, &c.

Embrasures, in Fortification, are the holes in a Parapet, through which the Cannons are laid to fire into the Moat or Field.

Embraue, adorn. *Spencer.*

Embrocation, (Gr.) is a kind of fomentation, wherein the fomenting Liquor is let distil from aloft, drop by drop, very slowly upon the Part or Body to be fomented.

Embryo, is the Foetus in the Womb of the Mother after its Members come to be distinctly formed.

Embryothlastes, (Gr.) a Surgeon's Instrument wherewith they break the Bones of an Embrio, that it may be taken out of the Womb more conveniently.

Emendation, a correcting or mending.

Emergent, (Lat.) rising up above Water, also accidental, appearing on a sudden.

Emersion, in Astronomy, is when a Star that is so nigh the Sun that it cannot be seen, by reason of the Sun's light, begins to come out of that light and appear again. The word is sometimes used for the Sun or Moon's coming out of an *Eclipse* ; also when any Body, specifically lighter than Water, being thrust down violently into it, rises

again, it is said to *Emerge.*

Emetical, belonging to Vomiting.

Emetick Medicines, are Medicines which cause Vomiting.

Emication, (Lat.) a shining forth.

Emigration, (Lat.) a departing or going from one place to live at another.

Eminency, Excellency; also a Title of Honour given to *Cardinals,* and is held to be above *Excellency.*

Eminent, Excellent; also any Hill is said to be eminent.

Emissary, a Person sent out to observe the motions of an Enemy, or to sound the thoughts of another: A Spy, a Scout.

Emission, (Lat.) a sending forth, a casting out.

Emit, to send forth or cast out.

Emmet, an Ant or Pismire.

Emollient, making soft, pliant, loose; *Emollient Medicines,* are such as make the part to which they are apply'd soft and pliant.

Emolument, Advantage, Profit.

Emotion, a stirring or moving forth, also a violent motion of the Mind.

Empale, a Punishment us'd in *Nero's* time, and signifies to run a Stake through the Body of a Person.

Empannel,

Empannel, to enter the Names of the Jury into a Parchment or Roll, which are summon'd to appear for the publick Service.

Emparlance, in Common Law, is a Petition in Court of a Day to pause and consider what is best to be done.

Empasms, (Gr.) are Medicines composed of sweet Powders, to take away Sweat, and allay Inflammations; they are also applied to the *Scrobiculus Cordis* to strengthen the Stomach.

Emphasis, Earnestness, or an express Signification of one's Intention; a strong or vigorous Pronunciation of a Word.

Emphatical, spoken with Earnestness or Emotion of Mind.

Empirick, a Quack, or an unskilful Physician, that makes use of Receipts taken upon Trust, without knowing any thing of the Disease or Medicine he applies.

Emphraxis, (Gr.) is an Obstruction in any Part.

Emphysema, (Gr.) is an Inflammation, or a windy swelling of any part of the Body.

Emplasmagium, the Palsie, a Disease.

Emplasticks, are Medicines, which constipate and shut up the Pores of the Body that sulphureous Vapours cannot pass.

Emplastrum, a Plaster, is a Medicine applied outwardly to the Skin, spread upon Linen or Leather.

Empneumatosis, an opening of the Chest for breathing.

Emporetical, belonging to Markets or Fairs.

Empory, a Market-Town, a Place where a general Fair or Market is kept; also the common *Sensory* in the Brain.

Emprimed, a Huntsman's Term when a Deer has left the Herd.

Emprise, Enterprize. *Spencer*.

Emption, (Lat.) a buying.

Empyema, (Gr.) is a Collection of purulent Matter in the Cavity of the *Thorax*; but largely taken, signifies the same in the *Abdomen*.

Empyreal Substance, the fiery Element, which is above the Ethereal.

Empyreumata, Relicks of a Fever after the critical time of the Disease; also a Settlement in Distillations.

Emucid, mouldy.

Emulate, to strive to exceed or go beyond another in any thing; also to envy or disdain.

Emulation, (Lat.) a striving to excel or go beyond another in any thing; also envying or disdaining.

Emulgent (Lat.) stroaking. *Emulgent Vessels*, are the two large Arteries and Veins, the former from the descending Trunk of the *Aorta*, the latter from the *Vena Cava*.

Emulsion, (Lat.) is any liquid Medicine, to be taken inwardly of the Form and Colour of Milk.

Emunctories, are the Cavities

ties into which the Excrements of an Animal Body are emptied, as the Pituitous Humour of the Brain into the Nostrils, &c.

Enact, to make a Law.

Enamon, is a Medicine which stops the Blood.

Enareoma, a gathering in the middle of an Urinal, or in distill'd Waters.

Enallage, (Gr.) a Figure in Grammar, whereby there is a Change, either of a Pronoun, as of a Positive for a Relative, as *Suus* for *Ejus*; or of a Verb, as when one Mood and Tense is put for another.

Enaluron, a Term which the Heralds use for *Martlets*, or any other kind of Birds.

Enamel, to vary with little Spots, to paint with Mineral Colours.

Enantiosis, (Gr.) Contrariety.

Enarration, a Rehearsal.

Enarthrosis, (Gr.) the Anatomists use this Word to denote a kind of joynting; when the Cavity that receives it is deep, and the Bone that is inserted long.

Enaunter, least that. *Spencer*.

Encanthis, a fleshy Excrescence in the corner of the Eye.

Encardia, a precious Stone, bearing the Figure of a Heart.

Encarpa, Flower-work or Fruit-work on the Tops of Pillars.

Encathisma, a Bathing for the Belly.

Encauma, is a deep, hard and crusty Ulcer of the Eye.

Encaustick, enamell'd, varnished, wrought with Fire.

Enceint, an Inclosure in Fortification, *viz.* the whole Compass of Ground fortified.

Encephalos, is all that Substance which is contained within the Scull.

Enchace, is to set any thing in Gold, Silver, or any other Metal.

Enchant, to conjure, or bewitch.

Enchantment, Witchcraft, Conjuration.

Encharaxis, an Ingraving, also scarifying or lancing the Flesh.

Enchafed, engraven. *Spencer*.

Encheiresis Anatomica, is a Readiness or Dexterity at Dissections.

Encheson, is a Law *French* Word, signifying as much as Occasion, Cause, or Reason why any thing is done.

Enchiridion, a small Book that one may clasp or carry in one's hand.

Enchymona, is an Afflux of the Blood, whereby the external Parts become black and blue, as in the Scurvy, &c.

Enchyta, an Instrument for Infusion of Liquor into the Eyes, Ears or Nostrils.

Encircle, to compass about.

Enclitick, (Gr.) that enclines or gives back; in Grammar, it is a *Conjunction*, which being joyn'd to the end of a Word, enclines or turns

the

the Accent to the Syllable just going before.

Encomiastick, belonging to an Encomium, or Commendatory Speech.

Encomium, is a Speech made in Praise and Commendation of another.

Encompass, to surround or close in.

Encope, (Gr.) is an Incision of any Part of the Body.

Encranium, the *Cerebellum*, or hinder part of the Brain.

Encratitæ, Hereticks of the second Century of Christianity; they condemned Marriage, and forbad their Disciples the Use of Wine and Flesh.

Encroachment, in Common Law, is an unlawful gaining upon the Rights and Possessions, or a pressing too far upon the Grounds of one's Neighbour.

Encumbrance, a Hindrance, when we say such an one's Estate is very much encumbred; we mean such an one is mightily in Debt, or his Estate is deeply mortgaged to another.

Encyclopedy, that Learning which comprehends all Liberal Sciences.

End for *End*, at Sea when a Cable, Hawsar, or other Rope of a Ship is run clear off from the Block or Place it was wound about, they say, 'tis run out *End* for *End*.

Endanimage, to do hurt unto, or damnifie.

Endemical Disease, is a Dis-

ease which infects a great many in the same Country, proceeding from some Cause peculiar to the Country where it reigns.

Endictment, in Common Law, is a Bill of Accusation for some Offence, exhibited against any one, and by a Jury presented to an Officer or Court that hath Power to punish. In Civil Law it is called Accusation.

Endorse, in Heraldry, is an Eighth part of a Pale.

Endorsed. See *Indorsed*.

Endowment, is the giving or assuring of a Dower to a Woman, or the setting of a sufficient Portion for a Vicar for his perpetual Maintenance, when the Benefice is appropriated.

Endued, qualified with any Knowledge.

Energetical, forcible, efficacious; Energetical Bodies are Bodies which are eminently active, and very efficacious in producing their Operations.

Energy, (Gr.) Force, Efficacy.

Enervate, to weaken, or deprive of one's Strength.

Enervation, a weakening or enfeebling.

Enfranchise, to make free, to incorporate any Man into a Society or Body Politick.

Engagement, a Tie, or Obligation; also a Fight at Sea.

Engender, to beget; most commonly applied to Animals not Humane, yet which
             are

are produced by the ordinary Methods of Generation.

Engine, is any Mechanick Instrument composed of Wheels, Screws, &c. in order to raise, cast, or sustain any Weight.

Engiscope, the same with Microscope; which see.

Engisoma, a Fracture in the Scull, which sinks the Bone to the inner Skin of the Brain; also an Instrument used about such a Wound.

Engouted, a Term in Heraldry for black Spots in a Hawk's Feathers.

Engrailed, in Heraldry, is when a Bordure is formed by an arched Line, when the little Arches turn outward from the Center of the Escutcheon.

Engrave, to cut any Figure in Wood or Copper, &c.

Engross, in Law, is to write fair over a rude Draught of a thing.

Engrained, died in Grain. *Spencer.*

Enharmonical, a Musical Term, usually apply'd to the last of the three sorts of Musick, and abounds in Diesis's or Sharps.

Enhaunce, to encrease, or raise the Price of any thing.

Enigma, a Riddle, a dark or intricate Speech.

Enigmatical, hidden, obscure.

Enneagon, a Figure of nine Sides.

Enneatical Days, signifie every ninth Day of a Sick-ness; which, according to some, doth bring some great Alteration in the Disease.

Enneatical Years, are every ninth Year of a Man's Life, which some weak People suppose brings a great Mutation of Fortune along with it.

Enodation, an untying, a making any Difficulty plain and easie.

Enormity, Irregularity, Excess.

Enormous, prodigious, excessive.

Enquest, is the Enquiry of the Jury into Matter of Fact in all Causes, both Civil and Criminal, in order to give their Verdict.

Enrage, to put one in a Passion, or provoke one to Rage and Anger.

Ens, is whatever hath any kind of Being or Existence: If its Being or Existence be real or positive, then it is called *Ens Reale* or *Ens Positivum*; but if its Being be imaginary, then it is called *Ens Rationis.*

Ensconse, an old Word for Entrenching.

Ensign, Escutcheon; also a Military Banner, or he that bears it.

Ensiform, (Lat.) in the Form of a Sword, or like a Sword.

Enstal, to set upon a Throne, or endow with a Robe of Honour.

Entablature, is properly the flooring or lofting with Boards. In Architecture, it is is that Part which is composed of the *Architrave*, *Frise*, and *Cornish* of a Pillar; being in effect the Extremity of the Flooring, which is either supported by Pillars, or by a Wall, if there are not Pillars.

Entayle, in Common Law, signifies *Fee-Tail*, or Fee intayled or abridged.

Entelechia, (Gr.) an inward Soul or Power, to move or act.

Entendment, in Law, is the true Meaning of a Word or Sentence.

Enterocele, a bursting or falling of the Entrails into the Groin, or Skin that covers the *Scrotum*.

Enterology, a Treatise of the Entrails.

Enteromphalus, a Rupture at the Navel.

Enteropiplocele, another sort of Rupture, when the Guts fall together with the Call into the Cod.

Enterplead, in Common Law, is to discuss a Point incidently falling out before the principal Cause can have an end.

Enterprize, a bold Attempt or Design in War.

Entertainment, Pastime, Diversion; to meet with a kind *Entertainment* is to meet with a kind Reception. And such an one's Conversation is very entertaining, is as much as his Conversation is very diverting.

Enthusiasm, (Gr.) an Inspiration, whether real or imaginary; a Ravishment of the Spirit, a Poetical Fury.

Enthusiasts, are those People, who fancy themselves inspired with the Divine Spirit, and consequently to have a true Sight and Knowledge of things.

Enthymeme, is an imperfect Syllogism, where either the *major* or the *minor* Proposition is wanting, as being too clear and easily to be supply'd by those with whom we converse.

Entire Tenancy, is contrary to *Several Tenancy*, signifying the sole Possession in one Man; whereas the other signifies joynt or common in more.

Entity, is being in general, or being considered abstractedly, without being apply'd to any particular Being in Nature, and taken in this Sense, it is the Object of pure *Metaphysicks*.

Entoyre, in Heraldry, signifies encompassed.

Entrayled, wrought between. *Spencer.*

Entreat, to beseech, to court with fair Words.

Entreaty, a Beseeching, a Courting with fair Words.

Entriconiata, the Edges on which the Hair of the Eyelids grow.

Entrusion, in Common Law, is a violent Entrance into Lands or Tenements void of Possession, by him that hath no Right unto them.

Entry,

Entry, in Common Law, fignifies a taking Poffeffion of Lands or Tenements. Merchants are faid to make an Entry in the *Cuftom-houfe.*

Enucleation, (Lat.) is a taking out the Kernel, alfo an expounding or explaining any thing that is difficult.

Envelope, (Sp.) to enwrap, involve; alfo to pefter or incumber.

Envelope, in Fortification, is a Mount of Earth, fometimes raifed in the Ditch of a place, and fometimes beyond it, it being either in the form of a fimple Parapet, or of a fmall Rampart bordered with a Parapet.

Envenome, to infect with Poyfon.

Environ, to enclofe, encompafs, or befet.

Enunciation, (Lat.) Utterance or Pronounciation. In Logick, it is a Propofition which fimply affirms or denies any thing.

Envoy, a Perfon fent from one Prince to another for the tranfaction of Affairs.

Enure, to accuftom.

Enurny, in Heraldry, is a Border of a Coat of Arms being charged with any kind of Beafts.

Enumeration, a reckoning up, or numbering.

Envy, is an uneafie Paffion which Men feel on beholding the Profperity of others.

Eolian, pertaining to *Eolus* the God of the Winds.

Eolipile, an Inftrument in Hydraulicks, being a round Ball of Iron or Copper, with a Tail to it, and a hole to fill it.

Epact, is the difference between the common Solar and Lunar Year; thus as the common Solar Year confifts of 365 Days, and the common Lunar one of 354, it follows that the Epact is eleven Days, which added to the common Lunar Year, gives the common Solar one.

Epagoge, a Figure in Rhetorick, in which like things are compared.

Epanadiplofis, (Gr.) a Rhetorical Figure, wherein a Sentence begins and ends with the fame word.

Epanados, a Figure wherein the fame found or word is twice repeated in the fame Sentence in an inverted Orper, as *nec fine fole fuo lux nec fine luce fua fol.*

Epanalepfis, (Gr.) a Figure in which the fame word is for inforcemen fake reiterated.

Epanaphora, (Gr.) a Figure in which the fame word begins feveral Sentences.

Epanorthofis, (Gr.) is a pathetical form of Speech, in which the firft Expreffion appearing too weak, the Speaker ftill endeavours to correct and mend it by ufing ftronger ways of fpeaking.

Eparch, (Gr.) is the Prefident of a Province.

Epaule, in Fortification, is the fhoulder of a Baftion, or the

the Angle of the Face and Flank, which is often call'd the Angle of the *Epaule*.

Epaulment, in Fortification, is a Side-work, made either of Earth thrown up, of Bags of Earth, Gabions, or of Fascines and Earth : It sometimes signifies a Demi-bastion, and sometimes a square Orillon.

Epenthesis, (Gr.) is the addition of a Vowel or Consonant in the middle of a word.

Epha, a Jewish Measure of Capacity for things dry, containing 3 Pecks, 3 Pints, 12 solid Inches, and 11 decimal Parts, according to the English Corn Measure ; also a Measure for things Liquid, containing 7 Gallons, 4 Pints, and 15 solid Inches of our Wine Measure.

Ephemeris, (Gr.) is a *Diary*, or daily Register of the motions of the Planets, and other Circumstances relating thereto, commonly call'd an *Almanack*.

Ephialtes, or *Incubus*, the *Night Mare*, is a deprav'd Imagination, whereby People asleep fancy that their Wind-pipe is oppressed by some superincumbent Body, and that their Breath is stopped.

Ephidrosis, a discharge of Humour through the Skin by Sweat.

Ephod, a kind of Breast-plate, or Priestly Garment, worn by the Jewish Priests.

Epicarpium, a Plaister for the Wrist to drive away Agues.

Epicauma, is a crusty Ulcer that sometimes happens to the black of the Eye.

Epicheirema, a Complex Argumentation, consisting of four or five Propositions, proving one another, or some Point to be made out.

Epick-Poem, is a Poem written in Heroick Verse, whose Subject is always a Prince or some great Person.

Epicrasis, (Gr.) is a gradual evacuation of ill Humours in the Blood.

Epicurean Philosophy, the Philosophy of *Epicurus*. It is much the same with the Mechanical Philosophy.

Epicycle, (Gr.) a little Circle, whose Center is in the Circumference of a greater, or a small Orb, which being fastened in the *Deferent* of a Planet, is carried along with its motion, and yet with its own peculiar motion carries the Body of the Planet fixed to it, round about its proper Center, which the Ptolemaick Astronomers attribute to all the Planets for solving their appearances.

Epicyema, is a Superfœtation.

Epidemy, (Gr.) an universal Sickness, a general Infection, or contagious Disease.

Epidemical, Universal, Infectious, Contagious.

Epidermis, (Gr.) the outward
ward

ward Skin which covers the main Skin of a Man's Body.

Epididymida, a Term in Anatomy, signifying Vessels, making, with their various windings, that Body that is fixed on the back of the Testicles.

Epigæum, the part of the Circle of a Planet neatest the Earth.

Epigastrick, (Gr.) belonging to the *Epigastrium*, or fore part of the lowermost Belly.

Epiglottis, (Gr.) is the fifth Cartilage of the Larynx, the Cover of the opening of the Wind-pipe.

Epigonatis, the Pan of the Knee.

Epigram, (Gr.) an Inscription upon a Statue, or the like, whether in Verse or Prose: It is usually taken for a short witty Poem, which, under some feigned Name, does covertly praise or dispraise some particular Person or Thing.

Epigrammatist, a Writer, or maker of Epigrams.

Epigraph, (Gr.) an Inscription or Title.

Epilepsy, (Gr.) the falling Sickness, so called because the Person affected with it falls down on a sudden.

Epilogue, (Gr.) a Conclusion; also a Speech made at the end of a Play.

Epimythium, the Moral of a Fable.

Epinicion, a Triumphal Song.

Epinyctodes, Pimples painful in the Night; also sores, which make the corners of the Eye water.

Epiparoxysmus, a double fit in a Feaver.

Epiphany, (Gr.) an appearing of Light, or a manifestation; also the Feast celebrated on the twelfth day after *Christmas*, or our Saviour's Nativity, whereon he was manifested to the Gentiles by a miraculous Blazing Star, conducting the *Magi* to the place of his abode.

Epiphonema, (Gr.) is an Exclamation, an Applause of a thing approv'd, or a sententious Clause of a Discourse worthy of Credit and Observation.

Epiphora, a Figure in Rhetorick, in which one word is repeated at the end of several Sentences.

Epiphora, in Physick, is a defluxion of Humours into any part, but more especially a defluxion of a thin Rheum from the Eyes, which is commonly called involuntary Weeping, and flows continually from the corner of the Eyes.

Epiplexis, (Gr.) a Figure in Rhetorick, which, by an elegant kind of upbraiding, endeavours to convince.

Epiploce, (Gr.) a gradual rising of one Clause of a Sentence out of another.

Epiploon, the Cawl of the Belly.

B b   *Episcopal*,

Episcopal, belonging to a Bishop.

Episemasia, (Gr.) is the very time that a Disease seises a Person, and is properly called *significatio*.

Episode, is a separate Story or Action, which a Poet inserts and connects to the main Plot of his Poem, in order to give it a pleasing diversity; as the Story of *Dido* in *Virgil*.

Epispastick, the same with blistering Medicines.

Epistolary, belonging to a Letter or Epistle.

Epistomia, are the utmost gaping and meetings of Vessels.

Epistrophe, a turning to the same sound; a Figure wherein divers Sentences end alike.

Epistyle, in Architecture, is a mass of Stone, or piece of Timber laid upon the Capital of a Pillar. Among the ancient *Gracians Epistyle* signified the same with what we call *Architrave*.

Epitaph, (Gr.) an Inscription on a Tomb, in lamentation or praise of the Party there buried.

Epitasis, is the second and busiest part of a Comedy, wherein the Plot thickens, and is as it were brought to perfection.

Epithalamium, a Nuptial Song or Poem in praise of the parties married.

Epithet, (Gr.) a word expressing the Nature or Quality of another word to which it is joyned; as *formosa mulier*.

Epitome, (Gr.) an Abridgment, or short draught of any Book, Matter, &c.

Epitrope, (Gr.) Permission; a Figure wherein a thing is seriously or ironically permitted.

Epizeuxis, (Gr.) a repetition of the same word in the same Sentence or Verse.

Epoch, (Gr.) in Cronology, is some remarkable Occurrence, from whence some Nations date and measure their computations of Time; as *ab urbe condita*, among the *Romans*; *a Nativitate Christi* among us Christians, &c.

Epode, (Gr.) a Pindarique Ode.

Epomis, is the upper part of the Shoulder.

Epomphalium, (Gr.) is a Plaister, or any such thing apply'd to the Protuberances of the Navel.

Epulary, belonging to a Feast or Banquet.

Epuloticks, are Medicines that dry up Ulcers or other sores.

Equable Motion, is a motion performed always with the same swiftness, and is neither accelerated nor retarded.

Equable Acceleration, is when the velocity of any Body in motion encreases equally in equal time; as *Equable retardation*, is when the velocity of of any Body in motion is equally leffened in equal times.

Equably, equally fwift.

Equality, is the exact agreement of two things in refpect of Quantity.

Equanimity, is an even and calm frame of Mind and Temper under good and bad Fortune; whereby a Man appears to be neither difpirited, foured, nor rendered uneafie by Adverfity, nor puft up, nor overjoy'd with Profperity.

Equation, in Algebra, is the mutual comparing of two equal things of different Names and Denominations, as $2^o. == 12'o$; &c.

Equation of Time, is the difference between the Sun's true Longitude, and his right Afcenfion.

Equator. See *Equinoctial*.

Equiangular, of equal Angles.

Equicrural, of equal Legs or Sides; thus a Triangle which has two Legs equal to one another, is call'd *Equicrural*.

Equidiftant, equally diftant from another thing, as two parallel Lines are equally diftant from one another.

Equilateral, equal fided; as Equilateral Triangle, is a Triangle whofe three fides are all equal to one another.

Equilibrium, (Lat.) in Mechanicks, is when the two ends of a Ballance hang fo exactly even and level, that

neither can afcend or defcend, but do both keep in a Pofition parallel to the Horizon; which is occafioned by their being both charged with an equal weight.

Equimultiples, are Numbers that contain their Submultiples an equal number of times; as 16 and 8 are Equimultiples of their refpective Submultiples 4 and 2, becaufe each contains its Submultiple four times.

Equinoctial, is an imaginary Circle in the Heavens, equally diftant from the Poles of the World, interfected by the Ecliptick or Path of the Sun in the two Points *Aries* and *Libra*; it is fo call'd, becaufe when the Sun moves in this Line the Days and Nights are equal. It differs from the Equator; for tho' they be both Circles in the fame Plane, yet the Equator is a great Circle of the Earth equally diftant from the Poles of the Earth, and commonly by Sailors call'd the Line.

Equinoxes, are the precife times in which the Sun enters into the firft Points of *Aries* and *Libra*, for then moving exactly in the Equinoctial, he makes our Days and Nights equal.

Equip, to fet forth or accoutre.

Equipage, (Fr.) a fetting forth of a Man, Horfe, or Ship; Furniture; good Armor, fit attire; Attendance;

it is frequently used amongst us for a Coach and good number of Footmen.

Equipollence , a being of equal Force or Value.

Equiponderate , to weigh equally.

Equiponderous , of equal Weight.

Equitable, agreeable to Reason.

Equity, is the Virtue of treating all other Men, according to common Reason and Justice, as we would be treated our selves were we in their Circumstances.

Equity, in Law, usually signifies the *Court of Chancery*, where Controversies are supposed to be determined according to the exact Rules of Equity and Conscience, by mitigating the Rigour of the Common Law.

Equivalent, (Lat.) of equal Might, Value or Worth.

Equivotal, is that which hath a double or doubtful Signification.

Equivocation, is a double Signification of a Word or Speech; also a saying one thing and meaning another.

Equorean, (Lat.) belonging to the Sea.

Erd, a Modern Word, signifying the same as *Epoch*; which see.

Eradication, (Lat.) a destroying or pulling up by the Roots.

1. *Erased*, scraped, scratched, or torn out; in Heraldry, the Member of any Beast which

seems torn from the Body is called *Erased*.

Erastians, a sort of Hereticks, founded by one *Erastus* a Physician, who amongst other things, held that the Power of Excommunication in a Christian State principally resides in the secular Magistrate, &c.

Erect, standing upright, or at right Angles to the Horizon.

Erection, a raising, or making to standing upright.

Erectores, Lifters up; in a Physical Sense it signifies the Muscles which cause the Erection of the Yard.

Ereption, a taking away by Violence or Force.

Erewhile, lately, not long since, or not long hence.

Eridanus, a Southern Constellation consisting of twenty eight Stars; also the River *Po*.

Ermin, in Heraldry, signifies a Coat where the Field is Argent, and the Powdering is Sable: And on the contrary,

Ermines, is when the Field is Sable and the Powdering Argent.

Eroding Medicines, are such as prey upon the Flesh with their acute Particles.

Erogation, (Lat.) a bestowing or laying out; a profuse spending of Money.

Erosion, an eating up; a preying upon or consuming.

Errant, (Lat.) wandring or straying out of the Way: as

Knights

Knights Errant are those Fabulous Romantick Knights supposed to travel all the World over, and to do great Feats at Arms, with infinite Hazards to their Persons.

Errata, are commonly Faults, or Omissions, which escape Correction in Printing.

Erratick or *Erratical*, wandring or straying out of the Way.

Errhines, Purgers of the Nostrils, without making the Patient sneeze.

Erroneous, subject to, or full of Errors and Mistakes.

Error, a Mistake or false Opinion; in Law, it is a Fault in Pleading or in the Process.

Erubescency, a blushing for Shame; it is also that Uneasiness of the Mind, by which it is hindered from doing Ill for fear of Loss of Reputation.

Eructation, a belching forth.

Erudition, (Lat.) Learning, Knowledge, or Instruction.

Eruption, (Lat.) a breaking forth with Violence.

Erysipelas, (Gr.) a Disease called S. *Antony*'s Fire, which is a Swelling of a reddish Colour, possessing the Skin and going no deeper, attended with a pricking Pain, but not beating; if the Skin be pressed with the Finger, it yieldeth, and the Redness vanishes for a time.

Erythemata, are red Spots like Flea-bites, common in Pestilential Feavers.

Escalade, or *Scalade*, is a furious Attack upon a Wall or a Rampart, carried on with Ladders to mount up upon it, without going on in form, breaking Ground or carrying on of Works to secure the Men.

Escambio, a Licence granted for the making a Bill of Exchange to a Man over Sea.

Escape, to get away.

Escara, or *Eschara*, a Scar remaining after the healing of a Sore.

Escheat, in Common Law, signifies any Lands or Profits that fall to a Landlord within his Mannor by way of Forfeiture, or by the Death of his Tenant dying without Heir.

Escheator, is an Officer who takes notice of the King's *Escheats* in the County, and certifies them into the Exchequer.

Eschew, to shun.

Escroll, A Roll, Deed, or Inventory.

Escuage, a Tenure of Land, which obliges a Tenant to follow his Lord into the Wars at his own Charges.

Esculent, that may be eaten, or pertaining to eating.

Escurial, a famous Monastery in *Spain*, built by King *Philip* II. in the Shape of a Gridiron, to the Honour of St. *Lawrence*, has its Name from a Village near *Madrid*.

Escutcheon, is the Coat or

Bb 3   Field

Field on which any Arms are born in Heraldry.

Ejnecy, is a Right of chufing firft in a divided Inheritance, belonging to the eldeft Copartner.

Efpaul. See *Epaul.*

Efpaulment, in Fortification, the fame with *Epaulment*; which fee.

Efplees, in Law, fignifies the full Profits that the Ground or Land yieldeth.

Efplenade, a Term in Fortification, the fame with the Glacis of the Counterfcarp originally; but now it is ufually taken for the empty Space between the Glacis of a Cittadel and the firft Houfes of the Town.

Efpoufe, to marry; figuratively, to *efpoufe a Party* or *Opinion*, is to adhere clofely to a Party or Opinion.

Efpy, to difcover, fee, or behold.

Efquire, fignifies with us, that Degree of Gentry which is next below a Knight.

Effay, a Proof or Tryal, a Preamble.

Effence, is that which conftitutes the peculiar Nature of any thing, and makes it to be what it is. In Chymiftry it fignifies the Balfamick part of any thing feparated from the thicker Matter, by means of Extraction.

Effential Properties, are fuch as neceffarily depend on the Nature and Effence of any thing.

Effere, are little Pufhes or Wheals, fomething red and hard, which quickly infect the whole Body with a violent Itching, as if one were ftung with Bees, Wafps, Nettles, &c.

Effoine, (Fr.) in Law, is the alledging of an Excufe by him that is fummoned to appear at any Court, and cannot come for good Reafons.

Eftablifh, to fettle upon a Foundation, to make firm and fure.

Eftablifhment, a Settlement upon a Foundation, an Affurance.

Eftate, Condition, or a Man's Worth in Land or Money.

Efteem, reputation or value.

Eftimable, (Lat.) that is of Value, or worthy to be efteemed.

Eftimation, (Lat.) a Value or Efteem.

Eftival, belonging to the Summer.

Eftopel, in Law, is an Impediment or Bar of an Action growing from his own Fact, that hath or otherwife might have had this Action.

Eftovers, in Common Law, fignifieth the Suftenance that a Man accufed of Felony is to have out of his Lands or Goods during his Imprifonment.

Eftrange, to alienate or become ftrange.

Eftreat, (Lat.) in Law, is ufed for the true Copy of an Original Writing.

Eftreet,

Estrepe, in Law, is to make Spoil in Lands or Woods, by a Tenant for Life, to the Prejudice of him in Reversion.

Estrepment, is a Spoil made in Lands or Woods, by a Tenant for Life, to the Prejudice of him in Reversion.

Esurine Salts, are such as are of a fretting, corroding, and eating Nature.

Etate Probanda, in Law, is a Writ that lies for the Heir of the Tenant, that holds of the King in chief, to prove that he is of full Age.

Etching, is a way used in making Prints, by taking a Copper Plate and covering it over with a Ground of Wax, and blacking it well with the Smoak of a Link, that it may take off the drawing of the Figure or Print; which having its back-side tinctur'd with White-Lead, will by running over the stroaken-out Lines with a *Stift*, impress the exact Figure on the black or red Ground: Which Figure is afterwards drawn deeper with Needles quite through the Ground, and all the *Shadows* and *Hatchings* put in; and then a Wax Border being made all round the Plate, there is poured on a sufficient Quantity of well tempered *Aqua Fortis*, which insinuating into the Streaks made by the Needles in the Ground, eats the Figure of the Print, or Drawing, in the Copper Plate. There is

no certain time in which this is done, but usually the *Aqua Fortis* will eat deep enough in half an Hour.

Eternal, of an infinite Duration, or which neither had a Beginning nor will ever have an End.

Eternity, an infinite Duration, or a Duration which is infinite both *a parte ante* and *a parte post*, or without Beginning and End.

Ethe, easily. *Spencer.*

Etherial, belonging to the *Æther*; which see.

Ethicks, is that Art which teaches us to seek out those Rules and Measures of Humane Actions that lead to true Happiness; and which acquaints us with the means to practise them.

Ethnarchy, Principality or Rule.

Ethnick, Heathenish, or which is of or belongs to the Heathens.

Ethology, a Discourse of Manners.

Etiology, (Gr.) a rendring of a Cause, or giving the Reason of.

Etymological, belonging to Etymology.

Etymology, (Gr.) is that Part of Grammar, which teaches the Original of Words, in order the better to distinguish and settle their true Meaning and Signification; also the Derivation of Words from their first Originals.

Evacuate, (Lat.) to empty,

Evacuation, (Lat.) an emptying.

Evade, to escape, to pass without Danger.

Evagination, an unsheathing, or drawing out of a Sheath or Scabbard.

Evangelist, (Gr.) a Messenger of good Tidings; whence the four Pen-men of the Gospels are so called. Also an Ecclesiastical Officer in the Apostles times.

Evanid, (Lat.) soon decaying, frail.

Evaporate, to breath or steam out, to send out Vapours.

Evaporation, is a steaming or sending out Vapours by Chymistry, it is when any Liquor is set over a gentle Heat, that the Fire may carry off some of the Moisture, and yet not lessen the Quantity of Matter the Liquor is impregnated with.

Evasion, an escaping; a Shift.

Eucharist, a Thanksgiving, from whence the Holy Sacrament of our Lord's Body is so called.

Euchymy, (Gr.) is a good Temper of the Blood, other Juices or Fluids in an Animal Body.

Eucrasy, (Gr.) is a good Temperament of Body.

Eudoxians, certain Hereticks, so called from *Eudoxius* their Founder; they affirmed the Son to be differently affected in his Will from the Father, and made of nothing.

Evection, (Lat.) a lifting up; a praising, or extolling.

Even Number, is that which may be divided into two equal Parts, without any Fraction.

Evenly even, is a Number which an even Number may measure by an even Number, as 64 is evenly even, because 16 which is an even Number, measures it by 4, which is an even Number also.

Evenly odd, is that which an even Number may measure by an odd one, as 30; which 2 or 6 even Numbers do measure by 15 or 5 odd ones.

Event, the Issue or Success of things.

Eventilation, (Lat.) a winnowing or sifting.

Ever among, ever and anon. *Spencer.*

Eversion, (Lat.) an overthrowing or overturning.

Evestigation, a finding or seeking out.

Eugeny, (Gr.) Gentility, Nobleness of Blood.

Evibration, (Lat.) a shaking, brandishing or darting.

Eviction, (Lat.) a convincing by Law or Argument.

Evidence, Perspicuity, Plainness; in Law, it is used for any Proof either of Men or Instrument.

Evil, mischievous, hurtful, whence the King's Evil.

Evince, to vanquish or overcome;

come; to convict by Law or Argument.

Eviscerate, (Lat.) to unbowel, or draw out the Bowels.

Evitation, (Lat.) a shunning.

Eulogy, (Gr.) a praising, or speaking well of.

Eunomians, a sort of Hereticks who maintained that no Sin cou'd be hurtful to one having Faith.

Evocation, (Lat.) a calling out, forth or upon; a mustering, calling back, or withdrawing.

Evolution, in Mathematicks, is used for Extraction of Roots of any Powers; also a particular Method of forming one Curve from another.

Evolution, (Lat.) an unfolding, unrolling; also countermarching as Soldiers do.

Euphemism, (Gr.) a setting forth any one's good Name.

Euphony, (Gr.) a graceful Sound; a smooth running of Words.

Eupnæa, a good Faculty of breathing.

Eurithmy, (Gr.) in Architecture, signifies the exact Proportion between all the Parts of a Building.

Eustyle, in Architecture, is a kind of Building wherein the Pillars are placed at a most convenient Distance from one another.

Eutaxy, (Gr.) a handsom Disposition of things.

Euthanasy, (Gr.) a soft quiet Death, or an easy Passage out of this World.

Eutychians, a sort of Hereticks, instituted by one *Eutyches,* in the Year 443; they deny'd the Flesh of Christ to be like ours, but said he had a Celestial Body, which passed through the Virgin as through a Channel; that there were two Natures in Christ before the Hypostatical Union, but that after it there was but one compounded of both; and thence concluded that the Divinity of Christ both suffered and died.

Evulsion, (Lat.) a plucking or pulling out.

Exacerbation, a making sowr; in Rhetorick it is the same with *Sarcasmus.*

Exact, punctual, precise, nice.

Exaction, in Law, is a Wrong done by an Officer, or one pretending to have Authority in taking a Reward or Fee for that which the Law allows not; or in taking a Fee where none is due.

Exactness, Nicety, Care, Diligence.

Exæresis, (Gr.) is an Extraction out of the Body, things that are hurtful to it.

Exaggerate, (Lat.) to heap up together, to enlarge, to set a thing out, and make it more than it is.

Exaggeration, (Lat.) an heaping up together, an enlarging; also the same as *Aggravation.*

Exa

Exagitation, a ſtirring up.

Exagon, the ſame with *Hexagon*; which ſee.

Exaltation, a raiſing or lifting up; a praiſing.

Exalted, raiſed or lifted up, ſublime, excellent,

Examen, (Lat.) a Trial, a Proof, particularly of one to be admitted to any Employment.

Example, (Lat.) a Pattern or Copy, any thing propoſed to be imitated or avoided.

Exanaſtomoſis, an opening of the Mouths of Arteries, Veins, or other Veſſels.

Exanguis, Bloodleſs.

Exanimation, a depriving of Life, alſo a diſmaying.

Exanthema, is a certain Eiflorercence upon the Skin of the Head, like thoſe which appear in the Skin of the whole Body.

Exaration, (Lat.) a Plowing up.

Exarticulation, (Lat.) a diſjoynting or putting out of joynt.

Exaſperate, (Lat.) to make ſharp; to provoke to Anger.

Exauctoration, (Lat.) to put out of Office, Pay or Service.

Excambio, an Exchange.

Excandeſcency, (Lat.) great Heat, a violent Anger.

Excavation, (Lat.) a hollowing or making hollow.

Execcate, to make blind.

Excellent, (Lat.) commonly ſignifies extraordinary good or valuable; alſo a Title of Honour given particu-

cularly to Embaſſadors and other Perſons to whom the Title of Highneſs is not ſo proper.

Excentrick. See *Eccentrick*.

Exception, (Lat.) a Clauſe reſtraining in ſome Point a Generality; in Law it is a Bar or Stop to an Action, a Demur.

Excerption, (Lat.) a picking out or chuſing.

Exceſs, an exceeding or Superfluity.

Exchange, in Law, is as much as *Permutation* with the *Civilians*; it hath a peculiar Signification, and is uſed for that Compenſation which the *Warrantor* muſt make to the *Warrantee*, Value for Value, if the Land warranted be recovered from the Warrantee.

Exciſe, a Tax upon Liquors.

Exciſion, (Lat.) a cutting out, or cutting off any part of the Body.

Exxitation, (Lat.) a ſtirring up, or Provocation.

Exclamation, an Outcry, alſo an Admiration.

Excluſion, (Lat.) a ſhutting out, a debarring.

Ecluſive, that hath Power to exclude or ſhut out.

Excluſively, in a manner *excluſive of*, or not taking in.

Excogitate, (Lat.) to invent.

Excommunication, is a Puniſhment inflicted by the Church upon Offenders; being a ſecluding them from the Church or Communion of Saints.

Excommunicatum Capias, a Writ directed to the Sheriff ffom from the Court of Chancery, for the Apprehension of a Person who has stood obstinately excommunicate for forty Days.

Excoriation, (Lat.) a flaying or pulling off the Skin.

Excreation, a straining in spitting.

Excrements, of an Animal Body, are whatsoever is separated from the Aliments after Concoction, and is to be thrown out of the Body, as the Moisture of the Mouth, Spittle, Snot, Milk, Bile, Sweat, the Wax of the Ears, the Excrements of the Belly and Bladder.

Excrescence, (Lat.) any sort of Swelling, and more particularly a fleshy Tumour.

Excretion, the separating of Excrements or Excrementitious Humours from the Aliments and Blood.

Excruciation, a tormenting or putting to Pain.

Excursion, a Skirmish, an Invasion or Inrode, a Digression in Speech, a running out.

Excusation, an excusing.

Excussion, a shaking off; a diligent Inquisition or Examination.

Execration, (Lat.) a cursing or banning, a wishing Mischief to one.

Execution, in Common Law, signifies the last Performance of an Act, as of a Fine, or of a *Judgment.*

Executione facienda, in Law, is a Writ commanding the Execution of a Judgment.

Executor, (Lat.) one that executes or does a thing. But more particularly, it is he that is appointed by any Man's Will and Testament to have the disposing of all his Substance, according to the Contents of the said Will.

Executrix, a Woman executing the same Powers.

Exegesis, Numerosa aut Linealis, is the Numeral or Lineal Solution or Extraction of Roots out of adfected Equation in *Algebra.*

Exegetical, explanatory.

Exemplification, a giving of an Example; or a drawing out of an Example, or Draught out of an Original Record.

Exempted, privileged, free'd.

Exemption, a privileging, freeing from Duty, or taking out.

Exenterate, to draw out the Bowels.

Exequies, Funeral Rites or Solemnities.

Exercise, (Lat.) ordinary Labour.

Exercitation, a frequent exercising, also a critical Comment.

Exert, to thrust out or put forth, to *exert* ones self in any thing is to use his utmost Endeavours in it.

Exfoliation, the scaling of a Bone.

Exhalation, is whatever is raised up from the Surface of the Earth or Water, by means of the Heat of the Sun, Subterraneal Fire, &c.

Exhausted,

Exhausted, (Lat.) drawn out, emptied, wasted.

Exhaustions, a certain method which the antient Mathematicians made frequent use of; Dr. *Wallis* gives a good account of this Method of Exhaustions in his *Algebra*.

Exheredate, to disinherit or set aside the right Heir.

Exhibit, (Lat.) to hold forth, to show, to make, to appear, to represent.

Exhibition, (Lat.) a shewing, or representing; also an allowance for Meat orDrink, such as the Religious Appropriators to the poor depending Vicar.

Exhilaration, (Lat.) a making merry or refreshing.

Exhort, to incite or perfuade.

Exigency, ftraitness, narrowness, need, necessity.

Exigent, (Lat.) Needy, Poor, Necessitous.

Exigent, is a Writ that lieth where the Defendant in an Action Personal cannot be found, nor any thing within the County whereby he may be Attached or Diftrained; and is directed to the Sheriff to call and proclaim five County Days one after another, charging him to appear under pain of Outlawy.

Exiguity, (Lat.) littleness, scarceness, slenderness.

Exile, (Lat.) Banishment; also one that lives in Banishment; also verbally, to banish one, or send one into some remote Country under a penalty if he return.

Exility, (Lat.) slenderness, leanness, smallness.

Eximious, (Lat.) choice, singular, excellent, passing good.

Exinanition, (Lat.) an emptying, an evacuation, a bringing to nothing.

Exischios, a Term in Surgery, when the Ischium or Thigh-bone is disjointed.

Existence, is the being of any thing, and it is either imaginary or real ; thus any thing exists imaginarily, or has an imaginary Existence, when it exists only in Man's Imagination; as a *Centaur*, there being no such thing in Nature; but any thing which is in Nature, has a real Existence, as *Peter*, or any other individual Person or Thing.

Existimation, a thinking or judging.

Exit, is commonly used for Death, thus, a Man made his Exit, is as much as he died.

Exitial, dangerous or deadly.

Exomphalos, is a Protuberance of the Navel common to Infants.

Exonerate, (Lat.) to unload, unburthen.

Exophthalmia, (Gr.) is a Protuberance of the Eye, out of its natural Position.

Exorable, (Lat.) easie to be intreated.

Exorbitant, irregular, immoderate.

Exorcism, (Gr.) an Adjuration, Prayers used of old by

by the Church for the difpoffeffing of Devils.

Exordium, (Lat.) a begining, an entrance.

Exornation, an adorning, or fetting forth to advantage.

Exoftafis, is a Protuberance of the Bones out of their natural order.

Exotick, (Gr.) brought out of a ftrange Country, outlandifh.

Expanfion, in the common acceptation of the word, fignifies a difplaying, an opening, a fpreading forth. Mr. *Lock* ufes this word to denote fpace; whofe parts are permanent. Naturalifts often ufe this word for the fwelling or encreafe of the apparent bulk of Fluids, when agitated by heat.

Ex parte talis, is a Writ that lieth for a Bailiff or Receiver, that having Auditors affigned to hear his account, cannot obtain of them reafonable allowance, but is caft into Prifon.

Expatiate, to wander or ftray abroad; alfo to enlarge upon a Subject.

Expectation, (Lat.) a tarrying or looking for; hope or fear of things to come.

Expectoration, (Lat.) the raifing and cafting forth of Phlegm or other Matter out of the Lungs.

Expedient, fit, convenient; alfo a means found out to get rid of fome troublefome Bufinefs, or to manage it with more eafe.

Expedite, (Lat.) to difpatch, to difcharge, to prepare, to bring to pafs.

Expedition, (Lat.) a difpatch, or quicknefs in difpatch of Bufinefs; alfo a fetting forward to the War, a Voyage.

Expel, to drive out.

Expence, Coft or Charges.

Experience, long Proof or Trial upon Sight or Obfervation, Knowledge without inftruction happening by ufe.

Experiment, a Proof or Trial wherein the Senfes are judges of the truth of it.

Experimental, grounded upon Experiment.

Experimentum Crucis, is fuch an Experiment, as like a Crofs fet up where divers Ways meet does direct Travellers in their true Courfe, guides and directs Men into the true knowledge of the thing they enquire into.

Expert, cunning, skilfull, dextrous in his Art.

Expetible, defirable, worth feeking after.

Expiation, (Lat.) a fatisfaction or Atonement by Sacrifice.

Expiatory, that ferves to make a fatisfaction or amends for.

Expiration, (Lat.) is an alternate contraction of the Cheft, whereby the Air, together with fuliginous Vapours are expreft by the Wind-pipe; alfo a giving up the Ghoft.

Explana-

Explanation, a making plain or manifeft; an Expofition.

Expletive, filling up; alfo a Particle added to a Conjunction; is called an Expletive.

Explication, (Lat.) an unfolding or explaining of any thing that is obfcure or ambiguous.

Explicit, unfolded, declared, ended.

Explicta, in Law, the Rents or immediate Profits of an Eftate in truft.

Explode, to hifs or cry down.

Exploit, a great act performed by fome Captain or General of an Army.

Exploration, a viewing or fearching diligently, an endeavour to find out; a Trial.

Explore, to view or fearch diligently, an endeavour to find out.

Explofion, a difgracing publickly, a driving off the Stage by hiffing, or clapping of Hands; alfo it is ufed by Naturalifts to denote an Action of the Animal Spirits, whereby they are fuddenly contracted. The *reafon is*, that fome *Heterogenious* Particles are mixed with the Animal Spirits, by which they are violently expanded and driven into confufion, like the parts of fired *Gunpowder*. A violent Expanfion of the parts of Air, Gunpowder, or any Fluid, is called *Explofion*.

Exponent, is a number which being placed over any Power, fhows how many Multiplications are neceffary to produce that Power; thus in x^3, 3 being placed over x, is its exponent, and fhows that it is produced by three continued Multiplications of x from Unity, for $1 x x x x x = x x x = x^3$.

Export, to fend abroad or over Sea.

Expofe, to bring a thing into publick view; to *expofe one's felf*, is either to run into danger, or to make one's felf ridiculous, by laying his failings open to other Men.

Expofition, an interpretation of any Book or Paffage which has difficulty in it; an expofing of a thing to hazard and danger.

Expoftulation, a quarreling for a thing done; a reafoning the Cafe.

Expound, to conftrue or explain.

Exprefs, manifeft, apparent, lively fet forth, done to the Life; alfo an immediate account of any Action done by Sea or Land.

Expreffion, (Lat.) an uttering or pronouncing; alfo the thing expreffed or utter'd. In Chymiftry or Pharmacy it fignifies the action of preffing out the Juices or Oyls of Vegetables.

Exprobration, (Lat.) a Reproach, a Twitting, an Upbraiding.

Expugnation, a conquering by force, or taking of a Town by Storm.

Expulfion, (Lat.) an expelling,

pelling, banishing, or turning out.

Expunge, (Lat.) to put, cross, or blot out.

Expurgatory Medicines of a cleansing purging quality.

Exquisite, singular, curious, exact.

Extacy. See *Ecstacy*.

Extant, appearing above others; which is in being

Extatick. See *Ecstatick*.

Extempore, (Lat.) out of hand, on a sudden, without Premeditation.

Extend, (Lat.) to stretch out, enlarge, or prolong.

Extendi facias, is a Writ commonly called *a Writ of Extent*; a Writ whereby the value of the Land, &c. is commanded to be made and levy'd in divers cases.

Extension, (Lat.) in the common acceptation of the word, signifies a stretching out or enlarging; in a Philosophick sense it is used to denote the distances there is between the Extremities or Terms of any Body.

Extensive, large, or that may be stretched out or prolonged.

Extent, of great Extent, is the same with very large.

Extenta, in Law, the survey and valuation of an Estate made upon Inquisition, or the Oaths of a Jury, impannelled by the Sheriff by virtue of the King's Writ.

Extenuation, a diminution, lessening or undervaluing.

Exteriour, more outward,

in a lower place or degree.

Exterminate, (Lat.) to drive or cast out, to banish or destroy.

External, that which is without, or in open view.

Extersion, (Lat.) a wiping out.

Extimulation, (Lat.) a pricking forward, a stirring up or inciting.

Extinct, (Lat.) quenched, put out, dead.

Extinction, (Lat.) a quenching or putting out.

Extinguish, to put out any thing that burns.

Extinguishment, in common Law, is an effect of Consolidation, as if a Man hath a yearly Rent due to him out of any Lands, and afterwards purchase the same Lands, now both Property and Rent are consolidated or united in one Possessor, and therefore the Rent is said to be *extinguished*. Also where a Man hath a Lease for Years, and afterwards buyeth the Property; this is a Consolidation of the Property and the Fruits, and is an *extinguishment* of the Lease.

Extirpate, to pluck up by the Roots.

Extirpation, (Lat.) a plucking up by the Roots, a destroying.

Extol, to commend highly.

Extorsion, (Lat.) an Exaction, a wresting or wringing out of one; in Law, it signifies an unlawful or violent
lent

lent wringing of Money or Money worth from any Man; as also the exaction of unlawful Usury, winning by unlawful Games, and All taking more than his due.

Extract, to draw or pull out; also, is it that pure, unmixt, efficacious Substance, which, by the help of some Liquour, is separated from the duller and more unactive parts of Plants.

Extraction, (Lat.) a drawing out: An Abridgment; also a descending from such a Family; also a separation of the subtile part of a mixt Body from the more gross.

Extraction of Roots, in Mathematicks, is the finding a Number or Quantity, which being multiplied by it self once, twice, thrice, &c. gives the respective power, out of which the Root proposed was to be extracted.

Extrageneous, Alien, or of a foreign Kind.

Extrajudicial, done out of the ordinary Course of Law.

Extramundane Space, is the infinite empty Space, which is by some supposed to be extended beyond the Bounds of the Universe, and in which there is nothing at all.

Extraneous, of a foreign or strange Land.

Extraparochial, out of the Bounds of a Parish.

Extravagance, Excessiveness, not keeping within compass.

Extravasated, in *Anatomy*, is whatever is put or let out of the Vessels, as Blood out of the Veins, &c.

Extream and mean Proportion, a line is divided in *Extream* and mean Proportion, when the whole line is to the greater Segment, as the greater is to the less.

Extremity, the end, edge, brink or border of a thing: also distress.

Extricate. (Lat.) to rid out, to deliver, to disentangle or disengage.

Extrinsical, outward.

Extrusion, (Lat.) a thrusting out.

Extuberances, are swellings forth, or risings up in the Flesh, or other parts of the Body.

Extumescence, (Lat.) a swelling or rising up.

Exuberancy, abundance, plenty.

Exuberant, abundant, plentiful.

Exuccous, (Lat.) without Juice.

Exudation, a sweating out.

Exulceration, a Blistring or turning to an Ulcer. A solution of continuty, proceeding from some gnawing matter, and in soft parts of the Body is attended with a loss of their Quantity.

Exultation, (Lat.) a Rejoycing, a leaping for joy.

Exumbilication, a swelling of the Navel.

Exundation, (Lat.) an overflowing.

Exuper-

Exuperation, (Lat.) an excellency or surpassing.

Exustion, (Lat.) a burning, a setting on Fire.

Eye, in a Ship; the hole wherein the Ring of the Anchor is put into the Shank, is called the *Eye* of the *Anchor*; and the Compass or Ring which is left of the Strap to which any Block is seized, is also called the Eye of the Strap.

Eye, in Architecture, is the middle of the *voluta* of the Ionick Chapiter, which is cut in the form of a little Rose.

Eyrie, the Nest where Hawks sit and hatch their young.

Ezekiel's Reed, a scripture Measure of length of 1 English Foot, 11 Inches, and 328 decimal Parts.

F A.

FABLE, a Story devised for the sake of Instruction.

Fabricate, to make, to build, to frame, to invent.

Fabrick, (Lat.) a Shop or Work-house wherein any thing is framed. The Art of framing, or making, building, or proportioning. It is commonly used for a building, as a House, Church, &c. or any thing artificially made.

Fabrick-Lands, are Lands given for the Building or Repairing of any Church, College, &c.

Fabulator, (Lat.) a teller of Tales or Stories.

Fabulous, (Lat.) full of Lyes or Stories.

Facade, (Fr.) the out-side or fore-front of a House.

Face, in Architecture, is a flat Member which hath a great breadth and small Projecture, as in Architraves, &c. it is also taken for the Front or exteriour Part of a great Building which immediately presents it self to view.

Face of a Bastion, is the most advanced part of a Bastion towards the Field, or the distance comprehended between the Angle of the Shoulder and the Angle of the Flank.

Facetious, pleasant, or wittily merry.

Facil, (Lat.) easie, feasible, pliable.

Facility, (Lat.) easiness, gentleness, courtesie.

Facinorous, villanous, wicked.

Fact, a Deed, a Work, a thing done or made.

Faction, is the withdrawing of a smaller or greater number from the main Body, either of a Church or State, governing themselves by their own Counsels, and openly opposing the Established Government.

Factious, given to Faction.

Factitious, (Lat.) Artificial, done or made by Art; also counterfeited, or made like another.

Factor, (Lat.) a doer or maker.

C 5

maker. But most commonly it signifies an Agent for a Merchant beyond Sea, or one that trades for him.

Factory, any place beyond Sea where Merchants Factors reside.

Faculæ, are certain bright or shining Parts, which the Modern Astronomers have observed upon or about the Surface of the Sun.

Faculent, bright, clear.

Faculty, a Power or Ability to do or perform any Action. In Law, it is used for a Privilege or special Power granted unto a Man by Favour, Indulgence and Dispensation to do that, which, by the Common Law, he cannot do.

Facundity, (Lat.) Eloquence.

Fadom. See *Fathom*.

Faces, is sometimes used for Excrements, and sometimes for the gross Substance that settles after Fermentation, or remains after Distillation.

Fain, glad, desirous. *Spencer*.

Faint Action, in Law, is as much as Feigned Action, *viz.* such an Action as tho' the words of the Writ be true, yet for certain causes he hath no Title to recover thereby, whereas in a false Action the words of the Writ are false.

Faint Pleader, a false and deceitful Pleader.

Fair Pleader, a Writ upon the Statute of *Marlborough*, whereby it is provided, that no Fines shall be taken of any

Man for not pleading fairly.

Fairy, a Goblin or Phantasm. *Spencer*.

Faith, in general is an assent of the Mind to things whose truth only depends upon the Testimony of others. Christian Faith is an assent of the Mind to all things delivered in Holy Scriptures as the Testimony of God Almighty.

Faitours, Vagabonds. *Spencer*.

Faisable, (Fr.) that may be done, possible.

Falcation, (Lat.) a Mowing or cutting with a Bill or Hook.

Falcidian Law, a Law among the *Romans*, made in the time of the Consul *Falcidius*, which treated of the liberty every *Roman* Citizen ought to have in the disposal of his Goods.

Falcon, a piece of Ordnance whose Diameter at the Bore, is 2¾ Inches, weight 750 Pound, length seven Foot, load 2½ Pound, shot 2½ Diameter, and 2½ Weight; also a Hawk.

Falconer, one that tames, manages and looks after Hawks.

Falconet, a sort of Ordnance whose Diameter at the Bore is something more than two Inches.

Faldstool, a folding Stool.

Fallacious, deceitful, crafty.

Fallacy, Deceit, a crafty Device, Guile or Fraud.

Falling Sickness See *Epilepsie*.

Fallow-Colour, or Dear-Colour; also Ground left untill'd is said to lie fallow.

False-

False-Bray, in Fortification, is a small mount of Earth four Fathom wide, erected on the Level round the Foot of the Rampart, on that side towards the Field, and separated by its Parapet from the Berme and the side of the Moat. It is made use of to fire upon the Enemy when he is so far advanced that you cannot force him from off the Parapet of the Body of the Place.

False Claim, in Law, is where a Man claims more than his due.

False Imprisonment, is a Trespass committed against a Man by imprisoning him without a lawful Cause.

Falsification, a making false or not standing to one's word; a forgeing, a sophisticating.

Falter. Seee *Faulter*.

Fame, Report, Reputation good or bad.

Familiar, intimately acquainted, free; it is sometimes used substantively for a Spirit or a Devil.

Family, an House-hold; also a Stock or Kindred.

Famine, a great scarcity of Provisions.

Fanatick. See *Phanatick*.

Fane, (Gr. and Fr.) a Weathercock to shew what way the Wind stands.

Fantacy. See *Phantasy*.

Fantasm, Apparition.

Fantastical Ideas, are such

Fantastick, imaginary, full of whims.

Ideas as have no foundation in Nature, nor have any conformity with that reality of Being, to which they are tacitly referr'd as to their *Architypes*.

Fantome, a Specter, a Chimera, a vain Apparition, which we imagine we see, tho' in reality it exists no where but in our own disturbed Imagination.

Fapesmo, is a Technical word among the Logicians, denoting the fourth imperfect Mood of the first Figure of a Categorical Syllogism, wherein the first Proposition is an universal Affirmative, the second an universal Negative, and the third a particular Negative.

Farce, (Latt) a stuffing; also a sort of comical Representation, less regular than a Comedy, and stuffed with rambling and extravagant Passages of Wit.

Farcy, a Disease in a Horse, which is either the knotty, or the Water-farcy.

Fardle, a Bundle or Pacquet.

Fare, Diet or Provision; also the hire for passage by Water or Coach.

Farinaceous, mealy, or full of Meal, beflowered.

Farrago, (Lat.) a mixture of several Grains together, Mescelline.

Farraginous, of or belonging to a Farrago; *which see*.

Farreation, a joining in Marriage with the Ceremony of a Cake.

Farrier, one that shoes and cures Horses.

Farsang, is three of our English Miles, or a League among the *Persians*.

Farthing, the fourth part of a Penny.

Fascia, (Lat.) a Swathe or swadling Band: In Heraldry it signifies a *Fess*: In Architecture, the three Bands of which the Architrave are composed are called *Fascias*.

Fasciation, (Lat.) a swathing or binding up with swadling Bands.

Fascicular, belonging to a Bundle or Fardle.

Fascinate, (Lat) to bewitch, enchant, or charm.

Fascination, (Lat.) a bewitching, enchanting, or charming.

Fascines, or *Faggots*, in Fortification, are small Branches of Trees or Bavins bound up in bundles, which being mixed with Earth serve to fill up Ditches, &c.

Fashion-pieces, are those two Timbers which describe the breadth of the Ship at the Stern.

Fashionable, most in use.

Fasti, were days among the *Romans* that the Lawyers were permitted to plead in, like our Term-time; and they called their Vacations *Dies Nefasti*.

Fastidious, (Lat.) scornful, disdainful.

Fatal, pertaining to Destiny or Fate; unlucky, deadly.

Fatality, (Lat.) fatalness, also unavoidableness.

Fate, (Lat.) Destiny, that which must of necessity come to pass by God's secret appointment.

Fathom, (Sax.) a measure of six Foot. By this measure all Ropes and Cables at Sea are measured, and the depth of the Sea is sounded; also a Scripture Measure of 7 Feet, three Inches, and 552 decimal Parts.

Fatidick, a Fortune-teller.

Fatigable, (Lat.) which may be wearied or tired.

Fatigue, (Fr.) weariness, tediousness, trouble, toil.

Fatuate, (Lat.) to play the fool.

Faulter, to fail or stumble.

Favonian, (Lat.) belonging to the West Wind, favourable.

Favour, a Kindness or good Office done to any Person.

Favourite, one that enjoys the good Will of his Prince, of his Superiour, of his Mistress, &c.

Faust, (Lat.) lucky.

Fausebraye, in Fortification, a second Wall, or Rampart below the first that runs about the place for the defence of the Moat.

Fautor, a cherisher or favourer.

Fauxbourg, the Suburbs of a City.

Faun,

Fawn, to flatter or wheadle; also a young Deer.

Fay, Faith. *Spencer*.

Fealty, in Law, signifies an Oath taken at the admittance of every Tenant to be true to the Lord of whom he holdeth his Land.

Feasible, that may be done, easie to be done.

Feat, a notable Action or Deed; also neat, finical or trim.

Feaver, is a Fermentation or Inordinate Motion of the Blood, and a too great heat of it, attended with Burning, Thirst, and other Symptoms, whereby the œconomy of the Body is variously disturbed.

Feazing, at Sea, is the ravelling out of the Cable, or any great Rope at the ends.

Febricitate, to fall sick of an Ague or Feaver.

Febrifuge, a Medicine which cures an intermitting Fever.

Februation, (Lat.) a purifying or cleansing by Sacrifice.

Fecial, (Lat.) pertaining to the Herald at Arms, who denounces War or Peace. Among the Antient *Romans* there were twenty in number, the chief of which was called *Pater Patratus*.

Fecula, are dregs that subside in the squeezing of certain Vegetables.

Feculent, full of dregs.

Fecundity, (Lat.) Fruitfulness.

Fee, is in our Law an E-quivocal word, but most usually taken for an Estate of an Inheritance in Lands to one and his Heirs for ever, or to one and the Heirs of his Body. It is also used for the compass or extent of a Mannor; and in the common acceptation, it is taken for that consideration which is given to a Serjeant at Law or Counsellor or a Physician for their Counsel and Advice in their Professions.

Feeble, weak, infirm.

Fee Simple, is an absolute Estate that is given him in these Terms, *to him and his Heirs for ever*.

Fee-Tail, is a conditional Estate, that is, whereof we are seized to us and our Heirs with limitation.

Fee-Farm, is when a Tenant holds of his Lord in *Fee-Simple*, paying him any certain annual Rent as ½, a third, a fourth, &c. of the value of the Land.

Feign, to counterfeit.

Felapton, a Technical word, denoting the second Mood of the third Figure of a Categorical Syllogism, wherein the first Proposition is an universal Negative, the second an universal Affirmative, and the third a particular Negative.

Felicity, Happiness.

Fell, direful, outragious.

Fellmonger, a dealer in Skins.

Fellon, an Ulcer or Sore on a Finger.

Fellows, of which the Rim of a Wheel is made.

Felo de se, a Self-murderer.

Felony, in common Law, is accounted any Offence that is in degree next Petit Treason, and comprizeth divers particulars, as Murther, Theft, Killing of a Man's self, Sodomy, Rape, wilful burning of Houses, and such like.

Felt, a sort of Stuff of which Hats are made.

Fen, Moorish Ground.

Fence, an Enclosure.

Fend, for defend, is the Sea word for saving a Boat from being dashed against the Rocks, Shore, or Ships sides.

Feneration, (Lat.) Usury, or the practise thereof.

Feodum, in Law, any Fee, Benefit, or Profit.

Feoffment, in Law, signifies any Gift or Grant of any Honours, Castles, Mannors, Messuages, Lands, or other corporeal and immovable things of the like nature unto another in Fee Simple, that is to him and his Heirs for ever, by the delivery of seisin, and the possession of the thing given, whether the Gift be made by word or writing.

Feoffee, in Law, is he that is enfeoffed or to whom a Feoffment is made.

Feoffor, is he that gives or grants a Feoffment to another.

Feracity, (Lat.) Fruitfulness.

Feral, (Lat.) deadly, mortal, dangerous.

Ferdemoulin, a Term in Heraldry for a Milrind.

Ferial, belonging to Holy-days, idle, vacant.

Ferine, brutish, beastly, wild.

Ferity, (Lat.) Savageness, Brutishness, roughness of Temper and Disposition.

Ferizon, a Technical word, expressing the sixth Mood of the third Figure in Logick, where the first Proposition is an universal Negative, the second a particular Affirmative, and the last a particular Negative.

Fermentation, is an easie, gentle, and slow motion of the intestine or inward Particles of a mixt Body, arising usually from the operation of some active Acid, which rarifies, exalts, and subtilizes the soft and sulphurous Particles; as when *Leaven* or *Yeast* rarifies, lightens and ferments Bread and Wort.

Fern, a sort of Fewel.

Ferocity, Fierceness, Cruelty.

Ferruginous, that which hath in it something of the Nature of Iron; like to, or of the Colour of rusty Iron.

Ferry, (Gr.) a Passage to pass over the Water at.

Fertile, fruitful.

Fertility, Fruitfulness.

Fervency, (Lat.) Heat, Vehemency, Zeal.

Fervent, hot, vehement, zealous.

Fesse,

Feſſe, is one of the honourable Ordinaries in Heraldry, repreſenting a broad Girdle of Honour, which Knights at Arms were anciently girded withal; it poſſeſſeth the Center of the Eſcutcheon, and contains in Breadth one third part thereof.

Feſtination, a making haſt, or haſtening.

Feſtino, a Technical Word which the Logicians make uſe of to denote the third Mood of the firſt Figure of a Categorical Syllogiſm, wherein the firſt Propoſition is an Univerſal Negative, the ſecond a Particular Affirmative, and the third a Particular Negative.

Feſtival, a Solemnity or Day of rejoycing.

Feſtoon, (Fr.) a Garland or Border of Fruits and Flowers; eſpecially engraven or emboſſed Works, alſo a Noſegay.

Feſtucous, (Lat.) of or belonging to a Shoot or Stalk of a Tree or Herb.

Fetid, (Lat.) ſtinking or ſmelling ill.

Fetlock, the loweſt Joint of a Horſe's Leg.

Fetters, Chains for the Leg.

Feud, is a Profeſſion of unquenchable Hatred, till we be revenged even by the death of our Enemy.

Feude, the *Civilians* define it to be a Grant of Lands, Honours, or Fees, made either to a Man at the Will of his Lord or Sovereign, or for

the *Feudatories* own Life; or to him and his Heirs for ever, upon condition that he and his Heirs do acknowledge the Giver and his Heirs for their Lord and Sovereign, and ſhall bear Faith and true Allegiance to him and his for the ſaid Tenure, and ſhall do ſuch Service to him and his for the ſame as is between him and them. covenanted, or as is proper to the Nature of a *Feude*.

Fewel, combuſtible Matter.

Fibers, are round oblong Veſſels in an Animal Body, in which are convey'd the Animal Spirits to all the Parts of the Body.

Fibrous, full of Fibres.

Fickle, unſtable, inconſtant.

Fictile, (Lat.) made of Earth.

Fiction, (Lat.) a Lye, a Story, a Device.

Fictitious, diſſembled, feigned, counterfeit.

Ficus, are the external Protuberances of the *Anus*, commonly called the *Piles*.

Fidelity, Faithfulneſs, or a ſtanding to one's Oaths and Promiſes.

Fido, an Iron Pin uſed at Sea to ſplice or faſten Ropes together.

Fiduciary, taken ſubſtantively, is a Feoffee in Truſt, or one intruſted on condition to reſtore. Adjectively, truſty or ſure.

Fief, a Feodal Tenure, or Lands held by Fealty.

Fiend, an Evil Spirit.

Fieri facias, is a Writ judicial, that lieth at all times within the Year and Day, for him that hath recovered in an Action of Debt or Damages, to the Sheriff to command him to levy the Debt or the Damages of his Goods against whom the Recovery was had.

Fife, an Instrument for Wind Musick.

Fifth, a Term in Musick, the same with *Diapente*; which see.

Fights, in a Ship, are the waste Cloaths which hang round about her in a Fight, to hinder the Men from being seen by the Enemy.

Figment, a Fiction, Story, or Lye.

Figurate Numbers, are such as do or may represent some Geometrical Figure, in relation to which they are always considered.

Figurative, spoken by way of Figure.

Figure, in Mathematicks, is a Space terminated on all hands by Lines that are either streight or crooked, and accordingly is called either a Rectilineal, Curvilineal; or mixed Figure, if its Bounds be partly straight, partly crooked.

Figures Grammatical, are Digressions from the common and ordinary Rules of Construction, as when any word is omitted and left to be supply'd by the Reader or those we talk to.

Figures Rhetorical, are Ornaments of Elocution which adorn our Speech, or a garnishing of Speech when words are used for Elegancy in their Native Signification, as, *Latet omnis hora ut expectetur omnis hora.*

Filaments, (Lat.) are little, thin, slender Rags like threads, such as sometimes appear in Urine; also the small Fibres or Threads which compose the Texture of the Muscles; also the small Threads which compose the Beard of any Root are called Filaments.

Filazer, is an Officer in the *Common Pleas*, so called, because he files those Writs whereon he makes Process. There are fourteen of them in Number, in their several Divisions and Counties; they make out all Original Process as well Real as Personal and mixt.

Filch, to steal privately.

File, a Thread, Wire, &c. whereon Writs or other Exhibits in Courts are fastened; in a Military Sense it signifies a Row of Men standing one behind or below another.

Filet, a little Member in Architecture, which appears in the Ornaments and Mouldings.

Filial, (Lat.) belonging to a Son.

Pillemot, (Fr.) a Colour like that of a dead Leaf.

Fillet, in Heraldry, the fourth part of a Chief.

Film,

Film, a fine thin Skin enwrapping the Brain, and several other Parts of the Body; also that thin Skin which is usually seen at the Surface of Mineral Waters is called a Film, &c.

Filtration, (Lat.) is the passing a Liquor, (in order to purifie it) through a woollen Cloth, or usually through a Coffin of brown Paper.

Fimbriated, (Lat.) encompassed with a Hem or Edge; a Term in Heraldry.

Final, last, belonging to, or having an end.

Final Causes, are such great, wise and good Ends, as God Almighty, the Author of Nature, had in creating and proportioning, in adapting and disposing, in preserving and continuing all the several parts of the Universe.

Fine, a Mulct or Penalty; also a ceremonious conveiance of Lands, by acknowledging a perfect Agreement before a Judge.

Finite, that which hath fixt and determinate Bounds and Limits set to its Power, Extent, or Duration.

Finitor, the same with *Horizon,* which see.

Finours, of Metals, are such as purifie them from Dross.

Fireboot, a Competency of Firewood allowed to a Tenant of Lands.

Firkin, the fourth part of a Barrel.

Firmament, is by some used for the Orb of the fixed Stars; but most commonly for that space which is expanded and arched over us in the Heavens.

Firmness, Solidity, Constancy, Resolution.

First Fruits, are the Profits of every Spiritual Living for one Year.

Fiscal, belonging to the Fisque or publick Treasury.

Fishes, are pieces of Timber used to strengthen the Masts or Yards a-board a Ship, when they begin to Sail in a stress of Weather.

Fisque, (Lat.) the publick Revenue or Treasure: a Treasury, or Exchequer.

Fissure, (Lat.) a Cleft, a Division.

Fistula, a Pipe, or Flute; also a long Cavity, strait or winding about in any part of the Body, being a narrow and callous Ulcer of difficult Cure.

Fitchee Cross, in Heraldry, is a Cross, the lower part whereof is sharpened into a Point.

Fitz. (Fr. *Fils*) a word commonly added to the Sirname of several great Families of this Nation, descending from the *Norman* Race; as *Fitz Herbert, Fitz Williams,* i.e. the Son of *Herbert,* or the Son of *William;* answerable to the Hebrew *Ben,* and the Caldee *Bar,* &c.

Fixation, in Chymistry, is a making any Volatile, Spiritual Body endure the Fire, and not fly away, whether it it be done by often repeated Diſtillations, or Sublimations, or by adding ſome fixing thing to it.

Fixed Line of Defence, in Fortification, is a Line drawn along the Face of the Baſtion and terminated in the *Courtain.*

Fixed Stars, are ſuch as do not, like the Planets, change their Poſitions or Diſtances in reſpect of one another.

Fixity, is that Quality which makes any Body unfit to be evaporated, or exhailed; and to the conſtituting this Quality it is requiſite that the parts of the Body, to which it belongs, ſhould be pretty large, heavy and branched, or hooked; all which being put together, will render the Parts unfit for Avolition, or unfit to be carried off by heat.

Flabellation, (Lat.) a Fanning, an airing or giving wind unto.

Flaccid, (Lat.) withered, feeble, weak.

Flagellet, a Muſical Inſtrument.

Flaggs, on Board a Ship, are Colours, Ancients, or Standards which the Admirals of a Ship bear on their Tops.

Flaggon, a large Pot of Pewter or other Metal.

Flagg-ſtaff, is that long Staff or piece of Wood whereto the *Flag* is made faſt, and along which 'tis hoiſed up.

Flagitation, (Lat.) an earneſt intreaty or deſire.

Flagitious, (Lat.) Ungra-cious, wicked, Lewd, Villanous.

Flagrancy, (Lat.) a burning, flaming, or glittering; an ardent deſire.

Flagrant, burning, flaming, ſhining.

Flair, the Seamen ſay that the work doth *Flair over*, when a Ship being houſed in near the Water, a little above that the work hangs over a little too much, and ſo is let broader aloft than the proportion will allow.

Flambeau, a kind of Torch.

Flamma vitalis, the *vital Flame*, which ſome ſuppoſe reſides in the Heart, and is nouriſhed by the Air we take in by reſpiration.

Flanch, in Heraldry, an imbowed Line, beginning at the top, ſwelling into the middle, and drawn in at the bottom of either ſide of the Eſcutcheon.

Flank, in Fortification, is that part of the Baſtion which reaches from the Curtain to the Face, and defends the Face of the oppoſite Baſtion, as well as the Curtain.

Flask, in Heraldry, is an Ordinary made by one Arch Line drawn downwards to the *Baſe Point*, it ſeems to be the repreſentation of a Bow when bended, and they are always born double.

Flat, to flat a Ship, is to hale in the Fore-ſail by the Sheet as near to the Ship ſides as may be, which is called *flatting* the Fore-ſail.

Flats,

Flats, Banks of Sand which make the Sea shallow.

Flattery, fawning, false Praise.

Flatulent, windy or engendring Winds, as Meats which cause Wind are called *Flatulent Meats*.

Flavor, a certain Relish proper to Wine.

Flaw, a Crack, Chink, or Scar in any thing.

Fledged, when the Feathers of a young Bird are grown, and the Down gone off.

Fledwit, a Term in Law, signifying a Discharge or Freedom from Amerciaments, where one having been an Out-law'd Fugitive, cometh to the Peace of his Lord on his own accord.

Fleet, Swift, as a Dog, &c also a company of Ships at Sea.

Fleurette, in Heraldry, Bordered or set off with Flowers.

Flexanimous, (Lat.) having a flexible or easie Mind.

Flexible, that may be bent, pliant, tractable, of a compliant Temper.

Flexibility, (Lat.) aptness to bend or yield.

Flexion, (Lat.) a bending or bowing.

Flie, is that part of the Mariner's Compass on which the 32 Winds are drawn, and to which the Needle is fastened underneath.

Flinch, to give out or quit a Business.

Flippant, jocund, nimble Tongued, brisk.

Flitting, A frequent removing from place to place.

Floating Bridge, is a Bridge made in form of a Redoubt, consisting of two Boats covered with Planks, which ought to be so solidly framed as to bear both Horse and Cannon.

Floor, in a Ship, strictly taken, is so much only of her bottom as she doth rest upon when she lieth on Ground.

Florid, (Lat.) flourishing, or adorned with Flowers; a Discourse in which is display'd a great deal of Eloquence, is said to be a Florid Discourse.

Florinus, a Heretick who lived in the Second Century of Christianity; He taught that God did not only permit but do Evil.

Florist, one conversant or skilled in Flowers.

Flotes, are certain pieces of Timber joyned together with Rafters over-thwart, which serve to convey Burthens down the River with the Stream.

Flotson, or *Flotzam*, Goods which being lost by Shipwrack, and lie floating upon the Sea, are given to the Lord Admiral by his Letters patent.

Flouk of an Anchor, is that part which taketh hold on the Ground.

Flourets, little Flowers. *Spencer.*

Fluctuate, (Lat.) to be tossed to and fro, also to be wavering in Opinion.

Fluctu-

Fluctuation, a rifing or fwelling of the Waves, a toffing to and fro; alfo a wavering in Opinion.

Fluctivagant, (Lat.) toffed on the Sea, or floating on the Waves.

Fluency, readinefs of Expreffion, or volubility of Language.

Fluid Body, is a Body whofe Parts eafily give place, and move out of the way, by any force impreft upon them, and by that means do fo eafily move over one another.

Fluidity, feems to confift in this, that the Parts of any Body being very fine and fmall, are fo difpofed by motion and Figure, as that they can eafily flide over one another's Surfaces all manner of ways.

Fluores, (Lat.) by Mineral Writers, is ufed for fuch foft tranfparent fparry kind of Mineral Concretions as are frequently found among Ores and Stones in Mines and Quarries.

Flute, an Inftrument of Wind Mufick.

Flux, and *Reflux* of the Sea, is the Ebbing and Flowing of the Sea, occafioned by the univerfal Law of Gravitation.

Fluxibility, aptnefs to flow.

Fluxing. See *Saltvation*.

Fluxions, (Lat.) in Geometry, is a new and very great Improvement upon the Doctrine of *Indivifibles* and Arithmetick of *Infinites*, invented by the profoundly learned Sir *Ifaac Newton*.

Foeillation, (Lat.) a comforting or cherifhing.

Focus, of a Glafs, in Opticks, is that point where the Rays of the Sun are united after their Reflection or Refraction from the Glafs.

Focus of a *Parabola*, is a Point in the *Axis* of a *Parabola*, diftant from the principal *Vertex* by ¼ of the Principal *Parameter*, it is called the *Focus*, becaufe a Glafs ground in this form will burn in this Point.

Focus of the Ellipfis; this Figure has two *Foci*, which are two Points in the Tranfverfe *Axis*, from whence if you draw two Lines to any Point in the Curve, the fum of them is equal to the Tranfverfe *Axis*.

Focus of an Hyperbola, is a Point in the indeterminate *Axis*, the diftance whereof from the Center of the *Hyperbola*, is equal to a part of one of its *Affymptotes* comprehended between the Center and the Tangent to the *Vertex* of the indeterminate *Axis* which is perpendicular to that *Axis*.

Foeman, a Foe. *Spencer*.

Fodder, a courfer fort of Food for Cattel.

Faeculent, full of Dreggs.

Faecundity, (Lat.) Fruitfulnefs.

Faederal, belonging to a Covenant.

Faeneration, (Lat.) Ufury, or letting Money out to Ufe.

Faetus, (Lat.) is the Young of all kind of Creatures, more efpeespecially humane; immediately after the Conception, it is called an *Embrio*, but as soon as its Parts are perfectly formed, it is properly termed *Fœtus*.

Fogg, a thick Mist, sometimes taken for After-Pasture in Winter.

Foil, to overcome; also the name of an Instrument used in the Art of Defence.

Folcmote, or *Folkmote*, the County Court and Sheriffs turn; also a general assembling of the People.

Foliaceus, (Lat.) of, or like a Leafe.

Foliage, branched Work in Tapstery or Painting; also a kind of Ornament used in Cornices, Frizes, Chapiters of Pillars, &c.

Foliate Curve, is a particular Curve in Mathematicks so called.

To *Foliate* Looking-glasses, is to spread something on the back of them, thereby to make them reflect the Image.

Fomahant, a Star of the first Magnitude in *Aquarius*.

Fomentation, is the bathing any part of the Body with a convenient Liquor, which is usually a decoction of Herbs in Water, Wine or Milk; also applying of Baggs stuffed with Herbs and other ingredients, which is commonly called a dry *Fomentation*.

Fond, or *Fund*, a Bottom, Floor, or Foundation; also a Merchants Stock, be it Money or Money's worth.

Fondery, (Fr.) a Stilling-house; the Trade of melting Mettals.

Font, a place for administration of Baptism.

Fontanel, is an Issue made in found parts of the Body, to evacuate Humours, cure Diseases or prevent them; so called because it represents a little Fountain.

Foot, a measure of length containing 12 Inches.

Fop, a Fool, or one who is over nice and affected in his Dress, Speech and Behaviour.

Foramen, a hole.

Foraminous, (Lat.) that is full of holes.

Foraneous, pertaining to a Court or Market-place.

Force, in Common Law signifies unlawful violence.

Force, (in Mechanicks) which is also called Power, is whatever is or may be made the Primary terrestrial Cause of any motion of Bodies, as Weight, Water, Men, Horses, &c. in relation to the Body or Weight to be mov'd.

Forcible Entry, is a violent actual entry into a House, Land, &c.

Ford, a shallow place where a River is passable.

Forebode, (Sax.) to presage, also to prohibit.

Fore-castle, of a Ship, is that part where the Fore-mast stands, and is divided from the rest of the Floor by a Bulk-head.

Fore-closed, barred, quite excluded.

Fore-foot, a Sea Term for one

one Ships failing or lying a cross another's way.

Fore-hale, to drag, distress. *Spencer*.

Foreign Answer, is such an Answer as is not triable in the County where it is made.

Foreign Matter, is a matter triable in another County.

Foreign Plea, is a refusal of the Judge as Incompetent, because the matter in hand was not in his Precinct.

Fore-judged the Court, is when an Officer of any Court is expelled the same for some Offence, as for not appearing to an Action by Bill filed against him.

Fore-judger, in Law, signifies a Judgment whereby a Man is deprived, or put by the thing in question.

Fore-land, in Fortification, the same with Berme; *which fee*.

Fore-locks, in a Ship, are little flat Wedges like pieces of Iron, used at the ends of Bolts to keep the Bolts from flying out of the holes.

Fore-mast, a Mast in the Fore-castle or fore-part of the Ship.

Fore-prized, a Term in Conveyancing, which signifies excepting.

Forest, is a large Wood priviledged to hold the King's Game of all kind.

Fore-staff, is an Instrument used at Sea to take the Altitude of the Sun or Stars, with one's Face towards the Object.

Fore-stall, to prevent. *Spencer*

Fore-staller, one that buys Corn, Cattle, or other Merchandize by the way, as it comes towards the Fair or Market, in order to enhaunce the price, or sell it at a dearer rate.

Fore-said, forbidden. *Spencer*.

Fore-went, gone before. *Spencer*.

Fore-reach, the Seamen say one Ship fore-reaches upon another, when both failing together, she faileth better or out goeth the other.

Forfeit, to lose an Estate or Preferment for want of doing his Duty, or for some Crime committed.

Forfeiture, is the effect of transgressing a Penal Law.

Forge, a Furnace; also *verbally*, to frame, to counterfeit.

Forgery, is a counterfeiting; as of Writings, Coins, &c.

Forlorn, afflicted, miserable, lost, forsaken.

Form, (Lat.) among Philosophers, is that by which one Species of things is distinguished from another; or in a more extensive signification, it is the essential, specifical, or distinguishing modification of the matter of any natural Body, or other Substance, so as thereby to give it such a peculiar manner of Existence, and distinguish it from other Bodies or Substances.

Formal, punctual, precise.

Formalist, one that is very punctual or precise in his Actions or Words.

For-

Formation, (Lat.) a fashioning or framing.

Formee, a Term in Heraldry, the same with *Patee*.

Formidable, (Lat.) dreadful, to be feared, terrible.

Formulary, (Fr.) the stile or manner of proceeding in the Law, a precedent for doing any thing.

Fornication, Whoredom between unmarried Persons.

Forrage, (Fr.) is the Hay, Oats, Barley, Wheat, Grass, Fitches, Clover, &c. which is cut down and brought into the Camp by the Troopers for the subsistence of their Horses.

Forswat, over sweat, Sun burnt. *Spencer*.

Forswonk, over laboured. *Spencer*.

Fort, is a work environed on all sides with a *Moat*, *Rampart* and *Parapet*, the design of it is to secure some high Ground, or the passage of a River, to make good an advantageous Post; to fortifie the Lines and Quarters of a Siege, and several other things.

Fortification, is an Art shewing how to fortifie a Place, or make it strong; so that a small number of Men within may be able to defend themselves for a considerable time against the Assaults of a numerous Army without.

Fortin, a Term in Fortification, signifying Sconces or little Fortresses.

Fortitude, Valour, Stoutness; also a Virtue by which

a Man in the midst of pressing Evils, always does that which is agreeable to the Dictates of right Reason.

Fortress, a general Name for all places that are fortified, whether by Art or Nature.

Fort-star, is a Redoubt constituted by re-entring and salient Angles.

Fortuitous, happening by Chance, casual, accidental.

Fortunate, happy, lucky, prosperous.

Fortune, is that which happeneth by Chance and unexpected; Wealth, Honours, and other inconstant Blessings of this Life, are said to be Blessings of Fortune, also Luck.

Fossible, (Lat.) that may be dug out of the Earth.

Fossils, all Bodies whatever that are dug out of the Earth are by Naturalists commonly called by the general Name of *Fossils*.

Foster, to nourish.

Fotion, (Lat.) a cherishing.

Fougade, (Fr.) a kind of Mine, in which are Fireworks to blow any thing up.

Foul-Water, a Ship is said to make foul Water, when being under Sail, she comes into such shole or shallow Water, that tho' her Kiel do not touch the Ground, yet it goes so near it that the Motion of the Water underneath raises the Mud from the Bottom, and so fouls the Water.

Foun-

Foundation, the Ground-work of any Building, or other piece of Work.

Founder, he that erects or endows a Church or College, or leaves a Stipend for the reading of Lectures, &c.

Founder'd, is when a Ship by a leak becomes full of Water and perishes.

Fourneau, Powder-chamber, or *Chamber of a Mine*, is a Hole, or Cavity made under a Work, the Top of which is sometimes cut into several Points like Chimneys, to make more Passages for the Powder, to the end it may have its Effects on several sides at the same time.

Fraction, (Lat.) a break-ing; in Arithmetick it is a broken Number, or Unity divided into any determinate Number of Parts; as ½, ⅓, &c. are Fractions, or 1 divided into two parts, three parts, &c.

Fracture, in Surgery, is the breaking of a Bone in any part of the Body.

Fragility, Aptness to break, Brittleness.

Fragment, a broken part, or piece of any thing.

Fragrancy, a Sweetness of Smell.

Fragrant. smelling sweet.

Fraight of a Ship, is her Bur-den, or the quantity of Goods she can carry.

Frailty, weakness of Na-ture, aptness to Sin, &c.

Fraises, in Fortification, Stakes fixed in Bulwarks made of Earth, on the one side of the Rampart below the Parapet.

Frame, to shape or build; also a thing so formed.

Franchise, in Law, is ta-ken to be a Privilege or Ex-emption from ordinary Ju-risdiction, and sometimes an immunity from Tribute.

Franchise Royal, is where the King granteth to one and his Heirs that they shall be quit of toll.

Franciplegium, (Fr.) the ancient Custom for the Free-men of *England* at fourteen Years of Age to find surety for their Truth and Fidelity to the King, and good Be-haviour to their Fellow-Sub-jects.

Frangible, that may be broken.

Frank-Fee, in Law, is that which is in the Hands of the King or Lord of the Mannor, being antient demesne of the Crown; whereas that which is in the hands of the Tenant, is antient demesne only.

Frank-fold, is where a Lord hath benefit of folding the Sheep within the Mannor for manuring of his Lands.

Frank-Law, is taken for the free Enjoyment of all those Privileges which the Law permits to a Man not guilty of any hainous Offence.

Frank-Pledge, a Pledge or Surety for Freemen.

Frankincense, a Gum used in Physick; also for Perfu-mers.

Frantick, See *Phrenetick*.

Fraternal,

Fraternal, Brotherly.

Fraternity, Brotherhood ; also a Company of Men entered into a firm Bond of Society and Friendship.

Fratricide, a killing one's Brother, or he that kills his Brother.

Fraud, Deceit, Cunning, Craft.

Fraudation, a cheating, deceiving or beguiling.

Fraudulent, crafty, cunning, deceitful.

Fray, a Scuffle or Contention ; also a fretting in Cloth.

Fraying, a fcaring or frighting away.

Freak, a Conceit, Whimfey, or idle Fancy.

Free-booter, a Soldier who having Liberty to plunder ferves without Pay.

Free-hold, in Law, is that Land or Tenement which a Man holdeth in Fee, Fee-tail, or at leaft for Term of Life.

Freeze, a Term in Architecture. See *Frize*.

Frequent, often, ufual.

To *Frequent*, to go often to, to haunt, to go in great Companies to, &c.

Frefcades, (Fr.) Refrefhments ; as (in Summer-time) light Garments, cool Air, cool Places, cool Drinks, Shades overfpread with green Boughs, &c.

Frefco,(Ital.)frefh,cool,&c. as to walk or drink in *Frefco*, is to walk in the cool or frefh Air , to drink cool or frefh Wine ; alfo to paint in *Fre*-

fco is to paint on Walls newly cieled, that the Colours may fink in and become more durable.

Frefh Diffeifin, in Law, fignifies fuch a Diffeifin, as a Man may feek to defeat of himfelf, by his own Power, without the help of the King or Judges.

Frefh-Fine, is that which is levied within a Year paft.

Frefh-Force,is a Force done within forty Days.

Frefh-Shot, in the Sea Phrafe, is the falling down of any great River into the Sea, fo that the Sea has frefh Water a good way from the Mouth of that River.

Frefh Suit, in Common Law, is fuch a prefent and earneft Purfuit of an Offender, as never ceafes from the time of the Offence committed or difcovered, until he be apprehended.

Frett, in Heraldry, is a Field with feveral Lines running crofs one another.

Friable, is an Aptnefs upon rubbing to break, crumble, or divide into fmall parts.

Frication, (Lat.) a rubbing.

Friction, (Lat.) a rubbing ; 'tis much ufed in Mechanicks, and denotes the rubbing of the parts of an Engine one againft another, and according as thefe parts rub more or lefs they are faid to have a greater or lefs Degree of Friction.

Frigefaction, (Lat.) a making cold.

Frigeratory, (Lat.) a Place to make or keep things cool in.

Frigidity, (Lat.) Coldness.

Frigorifick, making or producing cold.

Friperer, one that cleanseth old Apparel to sell again.

Fripery, the Place where Friperers drive their Trade.

Frisk, to skip about in Merriment.

Frivolous, vain, silly, foolish.

Frize, in Architecture, is that round part of the Entablature, which is between the Architrave and the Cornice.

Frizzle, the curling or crisping of the Hair.

Frodmortes, is an Immunity or Freedom granted for Murther or Manslaughter.

Frolicksome, jocund, merry, gay, full of Play.

Frondose, leafy, or full of Leaves.

Frondosity, (Lat.) Leasiness or Aptness to bear Leaves.

Front, in Perspective is the Orthographical Projection of an Object upon a Parallel Plain.

Frontale, (Lat.) a Frontlet, or Attire for the Forehead.

Frontiers, the Borders or Limits of any Kingdom or Country.

Frontispiece, the Forefront of a House ; also the Title or first Page of a Book done in Picture.

Frenton, is a Part or Member in Architecture, which serves to compose an Ornament raised over Doors, Cross-work, Nitches, &c. sometimes making a Triangle, and sometimes part of a Circle.

Froward, peevish, fretful, surly.

Frowy or *Frowsy,* musty, mossy. *Spencer.*

Fructiferous, (Lat.) that which produces Fruit.

Fructifie, (Lat.) to bring forth Fruit.

Frugality, (Lat.) Thriftiness, Sparingness in Expences.

Fruitage, branched Work, or the Representation of Fruit in Sculpture and Painting.

Fruitery, a Place for Fruit.

Fruition, Enjoyment or obtaining.

Frustrate, (Lat.) to disappoint, to deceive.

Frustration, (Lat.) a Disappointment or deceiving.

Frustum, (Lat.) in Mathematicks, signifies a piece cut off, or separated from any Body, as the *Frustum* of a Pyramid or Cone is a part or piece cut off, (usually by a Plane parallel to the Base) and comprehended between the Base and the secant Plane.

Frutication, (Lat.) a sprouting out of young Sprigs, a springing forth.

Fucate, (Lat.) to colour, paint, or counterfeit.

Fucation, (Lat.) a colouring, painting or counterfeiting.

Fud-

Fuddle, to tipple, drink often.

Fuga Vacui, (Lat.) an Abhorrence of a *Vacuum*; which was a Notion of the Peripateticks, and some other old Philosophers; who believ'd, that several Effects which we daily see were owing to Nature's abhorring a *Vacuum*.

Fugile, an Imposthume in the Ears:

Fugitive, (Lat.) running away, a Renegade.

Fugitive Goods, are the proper Goods of him that flies upon Felony, which after the Flight lawfully found do belong to the King.

Fugue, (Fr.) a Chase of Musick, as when two or more parts chase one another in the same Point.

Fulciment, (Lat.) a Prop, or Underset; in Mechanicks it is the same with the Point of Suspension, or that Point upon which a *Libra* or *Vectis* plays or is suspended.

Fulgency, (Lat.) a shining or glistering.

Fulgent, (Lat.) shining, glistering.

Fulguration, Lightening; which is commonly by us observed to precede Thunder, tho' in Reality they are both together.

Fuliginous, (Lat.) sooty, or full of Smoak.

Fullonical, (Lat.) belonging to a Fuller, or one that is a Scourer of Cloth.

Fulminate, (Lat.) to strike with a Thunderbolt, to blast with Lightening.

Fulmination, (Lat.) a striking with a Thunderbolt or Lightening. In Chymistry, it is the same with Detonation; which see.

Fulvid, (Lat.) a deep yellow Colour.

Fumidity, (Lat.) Smoakiness.

Fumigation, (Lat.) a smoaking, or making one Body receive the Smoak of another, in order to impregnate it with the more volatile parts of the Body burnt.

Funambulation, (Lat.) a dancing upon a Rope.

Function, (Lat.) the Exercise or Execution of some Office or Charge.

Fund, Land or Soil; also the same with *Fond*, which see.

Fundament, (Lat.) Foundation; also the Breech or Seat is called the Fundament.

Fundamental, (Lat.) belonging to a Foundation.

Funebrous, (Lat.) mournful, sad, belonging to Funerals.

Funeral, (Lat.) belonging to a Burial; also the Burial it self.

Fungous, (Lat.) full of holes like a Mushroom.

Funicular, (Lat.) belonging to little Ropes.

Funk, a strong Scent or Smell; also a fungy Excrescence of some Trees dress'd to strike Fire on.

Furacity, (Lat.) Thievishness; or an Inclination to steal.

Dd 2   *Fur-*

Furbish, to polish or make bright.

Furfures, the Scales that fall from the Head, and sometimes from the Skin of the other parts of the Body, occasion'd by the Separation of the *Cuticula*, or scarf Skin from the *Cutis* or true Skin.

Furie, a violent Anger, or Rage.

Furies, three imaginary Fiends or Spirits in Hell, having Snakes growing on them instead of Hairs, whose Office is to torment the Souls of wicked Men; their Names were *Alecto*, *Megara* and *Tysiphone*.

Furle, a Sea-Term, signifying to wrap up and bind any Sail close to the Yard.

Furling Lines, are small Lines made fast to the Top-sails, Top-gallant Sails, and the Missen-yard Arms, to furle up those Sails.

Furlong, (Fr.) the eighth part of a Mile, or 120 Poles.

Furlough, a Licence granted by a superior to an inferiour Officer in War, to be absent some time from his Charge.

Furnace, an Oven; or that place where Chymists put the Fire.

Furniture, is often used in the same Sense with Ornament; thus, a House well *furnished*, or with good *Furniture*, is a House well adorned. The Furniture of a Dial, are the Lines that are drawn thereon, for Ornament.

Furole, (Fr.) a little Blaze of Fire appearing by Night on the Tops of Soldiers Lances, or at Sea on Sail Yards, where it whirles and leaps in a moment, from one place to another. If it be double it is lookt upon to be lucky, if single otherwise.

Furr, the Skins of several wild Beasts used for Warmth, Distinction and Ornament; also Furs in Heraldry are the doubling of the Mantlings in Coats of Arms, and sometimes used in the bearing.

Furring, of a Ship, is laying on double Planks on her sides.

Furrow, for the draining of moist Sands, or cast up by the Plow in Arables for securing the Seed from too much Water.

Furtive, (Lat.) done by Stealth, Secret.

Fuse, of a Bomb or Granado Shell, is that slender Tube or other Contrivance; which is of such a length or so proportioned, that being filled with wild-fire, or such like Composition, it may burn so long and no longer, as is the time of the Motion of the Bomb from the Mouth of the Bomb to the Place where it is to fall.

Fusibility, Aptness or Easiness to be melted.

Fusible, (Lat.) that is apt or easy to be melted.

Fusil, in Heraldry, is a Rhomboidical Figure more slender than a Lozenge.

Fusiliers,

Fusiliers, (in an Army) are the same with Musqueteers, so called from *Fusil*, which sometimes signifies a Musquet.

Fusilly, in Heraldry, is when the Field of an Escutcheon is divided throughout into Fusils.

Fusion, (Lat.) a melting; in Chymistry it is the melting or making fluid of Metals or Minerals.

Futility, (Lat.) Lightness, Vanity.

Futtocks, in a Ship are the compassing Timbers, which make her Breadth.

Futurity, Time to come.

G A.

G *Abel*, (Ital.) signifies a Rent, Custom, or Duty, yielded or done to the King, or any other Lord, not by Contract or Bargain, but imposed by the Will of the Lord.

Gaberdine, a coarse Frock such as Shepherds and Countrymen wear.

Gabions, in Fortification, signifies Baskets made of Osier Twigs equally wide at the top and bottom, about four Foot in Diameter, and from five to six high; which being filled with Earth, are sometimes used as Merlons for the Batteries, and sometimes as a Parapet for the Lines of Approach, when it is requisite to carry on the Attacks through a strong or rocky Ground, and to advance them with extraordinary vigour.

Gable end of a House, a Term in Architecture, signifying the top of a House; also the fore part or frontis piece.

Gablocks, false Spurs for fighting Cocks, made of Silver or Steel.

Gachal, a Jewish Measure of capacity for things dry, containing of our English Measure for Corn, 17 Pints, and 33 decimal Parts.

Gad, (old w.) to straggle.

Gadding, straggling.

Gage, (Fr.) in Law, is a Pawn or Pledge: To Gage a Vessel is to take the solidity of it. At Sea when a Ship is to the *windward* of another, she is said to have the *Weather-gage* of her. The Seamen call also, trying how much Water a Ship draws, *gaging*, or rather *gauging of her*; which is done by driving a Nail into a Pole near the end, and putting it down by the Rudder till it catch hold on it, for then as many Feet as the Pole is under Water is the Ship's *Gage*.

Gaianites, certain Hereticks that sprang from the *Eutychians*, who maintained, that after the Union of the two Natures in Christ, his Body was incorruptible, and that he suffered neither Hunger, Thirst, nor any other Infirmity to which Man is liable by natural necessity, but after another manner,

Gaiety, Chearfulnefs, Gallantry.

Gainage, in Common Law, is Land held of the bafer kind of Men or Villains.

Galactite, a kind of precious Stone of a Milk white Colour.

Galage, Shoo. *Spencer.*

Galaxy, in the Heavens, is that parcel of Stars, called the milky Way; it only cafts a whitenefs in the Sky to the naked Eye, but by the help of a Telefcope, an inumerable number of little Stars are difcovered, which appearing clofe together caufe that whitenefs which we fee, and from thence call the Milky Way.

Galt, is the Sea Word for the blowing of the Wind at Sea.

Galea, in Pharmacy, is a Pain in the whole Head.

Galenick Medicine, is that Phyfick which is grounded upon the Principles of *Galen*, a famous Phyfician of *Pergamus.*

Gall. See *Bile.*

Gallant, fpruce, neat, accomplifh'd, brave.

Galleon, (Sp.) a greater fort of Galley made ufe of in War.

Gallery, in a Ship, is that beautiful Frame which is made upon the Stern without board.

Gallery, in Fortification, is a covered Walk, the fides whereof are Musket Proof, confifting of a double row of Planks lined with Plates of Iron; the top being fometimes covered with Earth or Turf to hinder the effect of the artificial Fire of the Befieged.

Galliaffe, a great double Galley.

Gallicifm, (Lat.) a *French* Idiom, or fpeaking after the Idiom of the *French*.

Galligaskins, or *Galligafcoins*, a fort of Breeches firft in ufe among the Inhabitants of that part of *France* called *Gafcoin*.

Gallimaufry, a minced difh of feveral forts of Meats.

Gallon, an Englifh Meafure of capacity for Wine, containing 8 Pints, or 231 folid Inches.

Gallon, an Englifh Meafure of capacity for Corn, containing 272 folid Inches, and this is what is commonly called the *Winchefter Gallon*.

Gally, a Ship with Oars.

Galreda, a thick vicious Juice that is extracted by boyling from the grifly parts of Animals, and is ufually called a Jelly.

Gambado, (Ital.) a kind of Leather Inftrument affixed to the Saddle in the place of Stirrups, wherein we put our Leggs when we ride to preferve them from dirt or cold.

Camboles, (Ital.) are properly Gaines or tumbling Tricks plaid with the Legs.

Gammut, the firft Note in the ordinary Scale of Mufick; alfo the Scale it felf is

usually

ufually called by this name.

Gan, Began. *Spencer.*

Gang, a Company, a Crew, theCompany of Men that are put to Man a Ship's Boat.

Gang, go. *Spencer.*

Gang-way, fignifies all the feveral Entrances, Ways, or Paffages from one part of the Ship to the other.

Ganglion, is an Humour in the Tendinous and Nervous Parts proceeding from a fall, ftroke, &c.

Gangrene, is a cadaverous Corruption of a Part, attended with a beginning of Stink, Blacknefs and Mortification.

Gantlope, or *Gantlet*, (qu. *Ghentlope*) or Punifhment of Souldiers firft invented at *Ghent* in *Flanders*, derived from the Dutch *Gaen-looper*, that is, to take one's Heels or run, for the Offender is to run through the whole Regiment with his upper part naked, and every fellow Soldier to have a whip at him.

Ganymede, the name of a *Trojan* Boy; now it commonly fignifies any Boy loved for Carnal Abufe, or hired to be ufed contrary to Nature, to commit the Sin of *Sodomy*.

Gaol, a Prifon.

Gap, a Breach in a Hedge or Wall, &c.

Garbe, (Ital.) Comelinefs, Gracefulnefs, or good Fafhion; alfo a fharp or piquant Tafte, applied to Wine or Beer, that has a kind of pleafant piquantnefs in its Relifh. In Heraldry it fignifies a Wheat Sheaf.

Garble, (Ital.) to purifie or fort out the bad from the good; 'tis borrowed from the Druggifts and Grocers, who are faid to Garble their Spices; that is, to cleanfe them from Dirt and Drofs.

Garboard-Plank, the firft Plank of a Ship faftened on her Keel.

Garboard-Strake, is the firft Seam in a Ship next to her Keel.

Garboil, trouble, tumult.

Gardian, in general, fignifies one that hath the Cuftody or Charge of any other Perfon or Thing: But moft commonly it fignifies him that hath the Education or Protection of fuch People as are not of fufficient Difcretion to guide themfelves and their Affairs.

Gargareon, the Cover of the Wind-pipe, the fame with *Epiglottis*.

Gargarifm, a Mouth-Water, or a Liquid Medicine ufed to cleanfe the Mouth, by gargling or moving it up and down in theThroat without fwallowing.

Garget, a mortal Difeafe in Cattel.

Garland, in a Ship, is that Collar of Rope which is wound about the Head of the Main Maft to keep the Shrouds from galling.

Garnet, is a Tackle in a Ship, wherewith Goods are

D d 4   haled

haled or hoifed into, or out of a Ship.

Garnifh, (Fr.) commonly fignifies a certain Fee, or quantity of Good Liquor, which Prifoners either give their fellow Prifoners, or elfe their Keepers at their firft admittance into Prifon. The word properly fignifies a fur-nifhing, ftoring, or fupply-ing, and fometimes a giving affurance.

Garnifhee, a Term in the Court of *Guild-Hall*, fignify-ing the Party in whofe Hands another Man's Money is at-tached.

Garniture, Furniture of a Chamber.

Garrifon, is a certain num-ber of Officers and Soldiers that defend a Place.

Garrulity, (Lat.) babling, over much prating.

Garrulous, full of Talk or prating,

Gars thee Greet, makes thee Weep and Complain. *Spen-cer*.

Garter King at Arms, the chief of the three Kings at Arms; alfo a half Bend in Heraldry.

Gafcoyns, the inner parts of the Thighs of a Horfe.

Gafh, a wide Wound or Cut.

Gafp, a panting for Breath.

Gaftly, frightful, like a Gholt.

Gaftrick, (Gr.) belonging to the Belly.

Gaftromyth, (Gr.) one that fpeaketh inwardly, as out of his Belly,

Gaftromancy, (Gr.) divina-tion by the Belly.

Gaftrotomy, (Gr.) a cut-ting up of the Belly.

Gate, Goate. *Spencer.*

Gaudy, (from the Latin word *gaudium*) fignifies gay, fine; gaudy Days, are the Feftivals of the Inns of Courts and Colledges.

Gavel, in Law, fignifies Tribute, Toll, Cuftom, year-ly Rent, Payment or Re-venue.

Gavelet, is a fpecial and antient kind of *Ceffavit* ufed in *Kent*, where the Cuftom of Gavel-Kind continueth; whereby the Tenant fhall forfeit his Lands and Tene-ments to the Lord of whom he holdeth, if he withdraw from him his due Rents and Services.

Gavel-kind, (Sax.) in Law, fignifies a Cuftom whereby the Land of the Father is e-qually divided at his Death among all his Sons, or the Land of the Brother at his Death equally divided a-mong all his Brethren, if he have no Iffue of his own.

Gauging, is the Art of Measuring folid Bodies, but in particular thofe Concave Solids which Brewers ufe as Hogfheads, Tuns, Barrels, &c.

Gaulonites, were a certain Sect among the Jews, fo cal-led from one *Judas Gaulonites*, who, together with his Fol-lowers, oppofed the Tribute raifed by *Cyrenius* under *Au-guftus*.

Gay,

Gay, of a merry and pleasant Temper.

Gaynage, in Law, is most properly the Profit that comes by the Tillage of the Land held by the baser kind of Soke-men.

Gaze, to stare, look about.

Gazet, (Gr.) a certain *Venetian* Coin, scarce worth our Farthing; also the News Paper, or a Relation of the Occurrences of the Times.

Geat, a sort of Precious Stone or solid Bitumen, commonly called Black-Amber.

Gehenna, (Heb.) the Valley of *Hinnom*, where they sacrificed to *Moloch*; and Metaphorically it is taken for Hell.

Gelid, (Lat.) icy, cold.

Gemelles, the Term in Heraldry for bearing of Barrs by pairs or couples in a Coat of Arms, as in the Figure.

Gemellus, a Muscle of the Cubit.

Geminate, (Lat.) to double or encrease.

Gemination, a doubling.

Gemini, the third Sign in the order of the Zodiack.

Gemmery, a Cabinet to keep Jewels in, a Jewel House.

Gemmiferous, bearing, or bringing forth Jewels.

Gemmony, a place in *Rome* where condemned Persons were cast down by a pair of Stairs headlong into the *Tiber*.

Gendarme, (Fr.) a Man of Arms, one that serves in compleat Armour, and on a great Horse.

Gender, in Grammar, is the difference of Sex or Kind.

Genealogy, (Gr.) a description of one's Lineage or Pedegree.

General, common, of all sorts; also General Commanders.

Generated, begot or produced.

Generating, (Lat.) begetting or producing.

Generation, (Lat.) is the Production of any thing in a natural way which before was not in being.

Generical, (Lat.) belongning to a Genus or Kind.

Generosity, nobleness of Mind.

Generous, of a noble Mind or Blood.

Genesis, (Gr.) the same as Generation; in Geometry it is the formation of a Line, Surface or Solid, by motion or otherwise.

Genethliacal, belonging to the Calculation of Nativities.

Genethlialogy, (Gr.) a telling of Fortunes by the Calculation of Nativities.

Genethliaques, (Gr.) Books which treat of the foretelling of Men's Fortunes by the Calculation of Nativities.

Genial, full of Mirth, pertaining to Marriage.

Genicu-

Geniculation, a joynting.

Geniculum, in Botany, is the knot or joint in the Stalk of a Plant.

Genitals, the privy or generating Members of any Creature.

Genius, a good or evil Angel; also a Man's Nature, Fancy or Inclination.

Gentile, among the Jews all were Gentiles which were not of the twelve Tribes. Now commonly we call them Gentiles which profess not the Faith of Christ.

Gentilism, Heathenism, or the belief of the Gentiles.

Gentilitious, that belongs to a Stock, Kindred, or Ancestors.

Gentleman, a Person of worthy Extraction, or who is beholding for his Nobility, neither to his Employment, nor the Patents of his Prince.

Genuflexion, (Lat.) a bending of the Knee.

Genuine, (Lat.) proper, peculiar; also free from adulteration: Thus we say Genuine Wine, that is, unadulterated.

Genus, in Logick, is an Idea so universal that it extends it self, or may be predicated of other universal Ideas.

Geocentrick Latitude, of a Planet seen from the Earth, is its deviation from the Plane of the Ecliptick, and is measured by an Angle formed by two Lines, one of which is supposed to be drawn from the Earth to the Planet, and the other from the Earth to

that Point in the Ecliptick, where a Line drawn from the Planet perpendicularly to the Ecliptick, cuts it.

Geocentrick, any motion of the Planets that has, or is supposed to have the Earth for its Center.

Geodæsia, (Gr.) the Art of Surveying or Measuring Land.

Geodætical Numbers, are such as are considered according to those vulgar Names or Denominations, by which Money, Weights, Measures, are generally known, or particularly divided by the Laws and Customs of several Nations.

Geographical, belonging to Geography.

Geographical Mile, is the Sea Mile or *Minute*, being the 60th part of a Degree of a great Circle on the Surface of the Earth.

Geography, (Gr.) is a description of the whole Globe of the Earth, or known habitable World, together with all its Parts, Limits, Situations, and other remarkable things thereunto belonging.

Geomantie, (Gr.) a kind of divination by Points and Circles made on the Earth, or by opening the Earth.

Geometrical, belonging to Geometrie.

Geometrie, (Gr.) Originally signifies the Art of Measuring the Earth, or any distances or dimensions on, or within it; but now 'tis used for the Science of Extension, abstractedly

abstractedly considered without any regard to matter.

Geometrick Place, is a certain bound or extent wherein any Point may serve for the solution of a local or indetermin'd Problem. If a Problem be proposed with such a Latitude, as that it may be solved by any Point in such a *straight Line*, such *a Periphery of a Circle*, or *Ellipse*, such *a Parabola*, such *an Hyperbola*, &c. this was called *Locus ad Lineam*, and particularly *Locus ad Lineam Rectam*, *ad Circulum* (which are called *Loci Plani*) *ad Ellipsin*, *ad Parabolam*, *ad Hyperbolam*, (which are called *loci solidi*;) and so to any other more compounded.

Geoponical, belonging to the Art of Tilling or Manuring the Ground.

Geoponicks, (Fr.) the Art of Tilling or Manuring the Ground.

Georgians, a Sect of pernicious Hereticks; so called from one *David George*, born at *Delft* in *Holland*; he held that the Law and Gospel were unprofitable for the attaining Heaven, &c. that he was the true *Christ* and *Messias*, with such other damnable Tenets.

Gerah, (Heb.) the least Silver Coin among the Hebrews, valued at $\frac{13}{16}$ Penny.

Germanity, (Lat.) Brotherhood.

Germination, (Lat.) is the growing or sprouting out of Vegetables, or any part of them.

Gestation, (Lat.) a carrying or bearing.

Gesticulation, (Lat.) a representing any Man by Countenance, Hands, or other parts of the Body.

Gesture, Behaviour.

Geules, a Term in Heraldry, signifying a Vermilion Colour.

Gewgaws, Trifles for Children to play with; some say 'tis derived from the Latin word *Gaudere*, to rejoyce.

Ghittar, a sort of musical Instrument; heretofore very much in use among the *Italians* and *French*, and now of late among the *English*; some say 'tis derived from *Cithara* a Harp.

Gibbosity, (Lat.) a bunching out of the Back, or any other part of the Body.

Gibbous, bunchy, bossed; this word is most commonly apply'd to the Moon; for while she moves between her Quadratures and her Opposition to the Sun, she is said to be gibbous; for her enlightened part is bunched out or convex.

Gift-Rope, is the Boat-rope which is fastened to the Boat when she is swifted, in order to her being towed at the Stern of the Ship.

Gigantick, big-bodied, Giant-like.

Gigantomachy, (Gr.) the Ancient War of the Giants against Heaven, often spoke of by the Poets. *Gild,*

Gild, in Law, signifies a Tribute, or sometimes an A-merciament, and sometimes also a Fraternity or Company combined together with Orders and Laws made among themselves by the Prince's Licence.

Giglet or *Giglot*, an Old Word, signifying a wanton Woman or Strumpet.

Gimlet, a small Piercer to make holes with.

Gin, a Trap.

Gin, begin. *Spencer*.

Gingle, to make a tinkling Noise.

Ginglymus, is an Articulation of a Bone, when it both receives and is received.

Gipsous, (Lat.) belonging to Lime or Plaster.

Girding-Girt, the Seamen say a Ship is *girt*, or hath a *Girding-Girt*, when her Cable is so tite or strained that she cannot go over it with her Stern-port, but will lie a-cross the Tides.

Giste, (Fr.) a Bed or Couch to lie or rest on, hence come the *Gists* of the King's Progress, that is a Writing containing the Names of the Houses or Towns where the King or Prince intends to lie or rest every Night thro' his Progress.

Given, is a word used in Mathematicks, and signifies something which is supposed to be known; and a Magnitude may be given in three respects; either in *Specie*,

Magnitude, or *Position*. See *Euclid's Data*.

Gives, Fetters or Shackles.

Glacial, (Lat.) belonging to Ice, freezing, cold.

Glaciation, the turning of Water or any other Liquor into Ice.

Glacis, a sloaping Bank in Fortification, it signifies a very gentle Steepness, but is more especially taken for that which rangeth from the Parapet of the *Covered-Way* to the Level on the side of the Field.

Glade, an open and light Passage made thro' a Wood by lopping off the Branches of Trees along that way.

Gladiator, (Lat.) a Swordplayer or Fencer.

Glance, a casting the Eye.

Gland, a Kernel; also a Substance in the human Body of a peculiar Nature, whose principal Use is to secrete or separate the Fluids.

Glandage, Mastage, the Season of turning Hogs into the Woods; the feeding of Hogs by Mast.

Glanders, a Disease in a Horse, a dangerous running at his Nose.

Glandiferous, bearing Mast.

Glandulous, full of Kernels.

Glans, in Botany, is that which being contained within a smooth but hard Bark, and containing but one Seed hath its hinder part covered with a kind of Cup, while the fore part is bare, as Acorns,

corns, &c. but properly Glans is the Fruit without the Cup.

Glare, fierce Look, *Milt*.

Glaucoma, is a fault in the Eye, or a Transmutation of the Chryttalline Humour into a Gray or Sky Colour.

Glaze, to varnish.

Glean, to gather loose Ears after a Corn Field is reapt.

Glebe-Land, is most commonly taken for that Land, Meadow, or Pasture, which belongs to a Parsonage besides the Tythe.

Glee, (Old Word) Joy or Mirth. *Spencer*.

Glenoides, are two Cavities in the lower part of the firtt Vertebra of the Neck.

Glib, slippery, smooth, or easie.

Glimmering, a glancing or trembling Light.

Glifter, a Liquor made sometime with sodden Flesh, sometime with Decoction of Herbs, or other things which by a Pipe is convey'd into the lower Parts of the Body.

Glitter, and *gliitering*. *Spencer*.

Globe or *Sphere*, is a round solid Body, every part of whose Surface is equally distant from a Point within it called its Center; if it have the Places of the Earth delineated upon it in their natural Order and Situation, 'tis called a *Terreftrial Globe*; but if upon its Surface be drawn the fixt Stars and Conttellations, 'tis called a *Celeftial Globe*.

Globofe, globular, round like a Globe.

Globofity, Roundness.

Globules, little Globes.

Glomeration, (Lat.) a rolling or gathering into a round lump.

Gloomy, (Old Word) dusky, dark. *Milt*.

Glory, Honour, Renown, Reputation. It is also taken for the Joys of Heaven.

Glofs, a short Comment upon a Word or Text.

Glofary, a Dictionary, explaining the most obscure and difficult Words in a Language.

Glofographer, one that writeth a *Glofary*.

Glofocomium, is a Surgeon's Inftrument for broken Limbs, so called from the Shape of a Merchant's little Casket, which was formerly carry'd upon the Back.

Glottis, is the Chink of the *Larynx*, which is covered with the *Epiglottis*.

Glout, to look scurvily or sourly.

Glutæi, Muscles of the Buttocks.

Glutia, are two Prominences of the Brain called *Nates*.

Glutination, (Lat.) a joyning together with Glue.

Glutinofity, Clamminess, Gluiness.

Glutinous, clammy, gluish.

Glutos, is the greater Rotator in the upper part of the Thigh-bone, named *Trochanter*.

Glutted,

Glutted, satiated, filled. *Milt.*

Glyconick, a kind of Verse consisting of a Spondee and two Dactyles.

Gnathonical, playing the *Gnatho;* flattering, deceitful in words, soothing one's humour to get by him.

Gnathonize, to play the *Gnatho,* to flatter.

Gnavity, (Lat.) Activeness, Lustiness, Quickness.

Gnomological, (Gr.) belonging to the Art of Dialling.

Gnomon, in a Parallelogram, is a Figure made of the two Complements, together with either of the Parallelograms about the Diagonal, and is like a Carpenter's Square. In Dialling *Gnomon* signifies the Stile Pin or Cock of a Dial, the Shadow whereof pointeth out the Hours.

Gnomonice, or *Gnomonicks,* is the Art of Dialling.

Gnosimacti, a sort of Hereticks among Christians, who condemned all manner of Inquisition after Knowledge, believing it of no use to them, from whom God only required good Actions.

Gnosticks, a Sect of Hereticks sprung from one *Carpocras,* as 'tis generally thought about the Year of Christ, 125. in the time of Pope *Xistus* the first, and the Emperor *Adrian* the first; they arrogated to themselves a high Degree of Skill and Knowledge in all things, and therefore were called *Gnostici;* they held the Soul of Man to be of

God's Substance. They held two Gods, one good and the other bad; they denied the future Judgment, with other absurd Errors.

Goad, a Staff pointed with sharp Iron to drive Cattle with.

Goal, the end of a Race.

Goaring, the Seamen say a Sail is cut goaring, when 'tis cut sloping by degrees, and is broader at the Clew than at the Earing.

Goblet, a Drinking-Cup, commonly of Silver.

Goblin, Evil Spirit.

Gobonated, a Term in Heraldry, for a Bordure of this Form; which is neither *Checky,* nor *Counter-componed,* but

of a figure different from both.

Goggle-Eyed, having Eyes rolling and stairing out.

Golden Number. See Cycle of the Moon.

Golden Rule, otherwise called the *Rule of Three,* is a Rule in Arithmetick teaching how to find a fourth proportional to three Numbers given; and 'tis either *Direct* or *Inverse.*

Golgotha, (Syriack) a Place of dead Mens Skulls; it was at *Jerusalem* on the North side of Mount *Sina.*

Golps, Roundlets of the Purpure Colour in Heraldry.

Gomer, a Jewish Measure of Capacity for things dry, contain-

containing $5\frac{1}{10}$ Pints, 1 solid Inch, and 211 Decimal Parts of our *English* Measure for Corn.

Gomphos, is when the Pupil of the Eye going beyond a little Skin of the *Tunica Uvea* is like that swelling of hard flesh in the corner of the Eye called *Clavus*.

Gomphosis, is when one Bone is fastened into another like a Nail, as may be seen in the Teeth.

Gomorrhean, (from *Gomorrha*) a *Sodomite*, a Buggerer.

Gonagra, (Gr.) the Gout in the Knee.

Gonorrhea, (Gr.) a Disease called the running of the Reins; the Flux or flowing of the Seed, without any Erection of the *Penis*.

Good a bearing, or *good Behaviour*, in Common Law, signifies an exact Carriage and Behaviour of a Subject to the King and his Liege-People, whereunto Men upon their evil Course of Life, or loose Behaviour are sometimes bound. One bound to this is more strictly bound then to the Peace.

Goodlyhead, Goodness. *Spencer*.

Goos-Wing, in Navigation, is a Sail fitted up, so as the Ship sailing before the Wind, or with a quarter Wind, and in a fresh Gale, may make the more way.

Gore, a Term in Heraldry; *Goresinister* is an Abatement for Effeminacy or Cowar-

dice; the Dexter is sometimes used as a Charge.

Gorge, in Architecture, is the narrowest part of the *Tuscan* and *Dorick* Capital, lying between the *Astragal* above the Shaft of the Pillar and the Annulets.

Gorge, in *Fortification*, is the Entrance of the Platform of any Work.

Gorge of a Bastion, is nothing else but the prolonging of the Curtains from their Angle, with the *Flank* to the Center of the *Bastion* where they meet: But when the *Bastion* is flat its *Gorge* is a right Line, which terminates the Distance comprehended between two *Flanks*.

Gorged, the Heralds Term for the bearing of Crown, Coronet, or such like thing, about the Neck of a Lion, Swan, *&c.* for then they say the Lion or Cygnet is *gorged* with a Ducal Coronet, *&c.*

Gorgeous East, bright, gay, spritely Morning.

Gormandize, (Fr.) to play the Glutton.

Gors or *Goss*, the Shrub commonly called Furz.

Gortinians, a Sect in *New England*, not much differing from our Quakers, so called from *Samuel Gorten*, who was banished thence about the Year 1646.

Gospel, from the *Saxon* Word *Godspel*, which with them signified *The History of God*, or the good Tidings of God.

Gossomor,

Goſſomor, a kind of thin and Cobweb-like Exhalations, which fly abroad in hot Sunny-Weather.

Gothick, in Architecture, is an Order ſo far different from the Antient Propotions and Ornaments, that its Columns are either too maſſy in form of vaſt Pillars, or as ſlender as Poles, having Capitals without any certain Dimenſions carved with the Leaves of *Brank-Urſin, Thiſtles, Cole-worts*, &c.

Governant, (Fr.) a She Governor, a Governeſs.

Government, Rule, Dominion, either Supreme, or by Deputation; alſo the form or manner of Governing, whether Monarchical, *i. e.* that by Kings; Ariſtroratical, *i.e.* that by Principal, or Democratical, *i. e.* by the generality of the People.

Gout, a Diſtemper occaſioned by the defluxion of a ſharp Humour upon the Nerves and Tendons, and which is very painful.

Gracility, (Lat.) ſlenderneſs.

Gradation, (Lat.) an aſcending by degrees and ſteps.

Gradatory, (Lat.) a place to which we go up by ſteps, more particularly 'tis the aſcent out of the Cloyſter into the Choir of a Church.

Gradual, by degrees.

Graduate, ſignifies one that hath taken a Degree at ſome Univerſity.

Gradus, a Roman Meaſure of length containing 2 Engliſh Feet, 5 Inches, and 10 decimal Parts.

Grain, all ſorts of Corn, &c. alſo the ſmalleſt Weight in uſe among us, *viz.* the 20th part of a Scruple, or the 24th part of a Penny-weight Troy. The value of a Grain of Gold is twoPence of Silver half a Farthing; alſo three Grains of Barly in length make an Inch.

Gramineous, belonging to Graſs; Green, in Botany.

Gramineous Herbs, are ſuch as have a long narrow Leaf, and no foot Stalk,

Grammar, is the Art of Speaking and Writing any Language truly, ſo called from the Greek word *Gramma*, becauſe it treats primarily of the formation of Articulate Sounds, which are repreſented by Letters.

Granadier, one that throws Granadoes.

Granado, is a little hollow Globe or Ball of Iron, or other Metal, about two Inches and a half in diameter, which being filled with fine Powder, is ſet on fire by means of a ſmall Fuſee faſtened to the Touch-hole; as ſoon as it is kindled the caſe flies into many pieces, to the great damage of all that ſtand by.

Grand Cape, in Common Law, is a Writ that lieth when any real Action is brought, and the Tenant appears

pears not but maketh default upon the firſt Summons.

Grandeur, Greatneſs, Magnificence, Power.

Grandiloquence, (Lat.) greatneſs of Speech, a high Stile.

Grandinous, (Lat.) full of Hail, ſubject to Hail.

Grand-Sergeanty, is where one holds Lands of the King by Service which he ought to do in his own Perſon, as to bear the King's Banner or his Spear.

Grange, (Lat.) a great Farm which hath Barns , Stables , Stalls, and other Places neceſſary for Huſbandry.

Graniferous, (Lat.) bearing Grain.

Granivorous , (Lat.) are thoſe Animals that feed upon Corn and other Seed.

Grant, in Law, ſignifies a Gift in Writing of ſuch a thing as cannot conveniently be paſſed or conveyed by word only, as Rents, Reverſions, Services, Advowſons in Groſs, Common in Groſs, Tythes, *&c.* Or made by ſuch Perſons as cannot give but by Deed, as the King, and all Bodies Politick; which difference is often in Speech neglected, and then it is taken generally for any Gift whatſoever , made of any thing by any Perſon ; and he that *granteth* is called the *Grantor* ; and he to whom it is *granted*, it called the *Grantee*.

Granulation, (Lat.) in Chymiſtry, ſignifies pouring a melted Mettal drop by drop into cold Water, ſo that it may *granulate* or congeal into ſmall Grains.

Granule, (Lat.) a ſmall Grain.

Graphical, (Gr.) curiouſly deſcribed or wrought.

Grapnel, is a kind of Anchor for Boats or Gallies to ride by ; it differs from other Anchors, in that it has four Flukes and no Stock, tho' there are ſome with three Flukes, with which they uſe to *ſweep* for Hawſers or ſmall Cables. In Men of War Grapnels are uſed to be thrown into the Enemies Ship in order to catch hold of her.

Graſſation, (Lat.) a Robbing, Killing, Spoiling, or laying waſte.

Grateful , willing to reward or make amends for, thankful.

Gratiæ Expectivæ , were certain Bulls, by which the *Pope* uſed to grant *Mandates* for *Eccleſiaſtical* Livings before they became void.

Gratification, (Lat.) a rewarding or making amends for ſome piece of Service done.

Gratis, (Lat.) freely, for nothing, without Reward.

Grating, rough, harſh, diſagreeable.

Gratings, in a Ship, are ſmall ledges of ſawed Plank framed one into another like a Lettice or Priſon-Gate,

E e   lying

lying on the Upper Deck, between the Main-maſt and the Fore-maſt, ſerving for a defence in a cloſe Fight, as alſo for coolneſs and light.

Gratitude, (Lat.) a vertue which ſeeks to make returns for favours done.

Gratuitous, done for nothing, without any conſideration of Intereſt, freely beſtowed.

Gratuity, (Lat.) a free Reward.

Gratulation, (Lat.) a rejoycing in another's behalf, wiſhing of joy; alſo a thanking.

Graveolence, (Lat.) a rank, or ſtinking ſmell.

Gravid, (Lat.) great with Child.

Gravity, Weight, or that quality by which all heavy Bodies tend towards the Center of the Earth.

Gravity Specifick, is that which commonly proceeds from the denſities of Bodies, by which one Body weighs more, or is heavier than another Body of the ſame bulk.

Greaſe, Fat, moſtly that of the Inwards of an Animal.

Great Circles on the Sphere, are thoſe which divide it into two equal parts, or two Hemiſpheres, as the Equinoctial, the Meridian, the Ecliptick.

Greaves, Armour of the Legs.

Grecism, is ſomething ſpoke according to the Idiom of the Greek Tongue.

Gree, degree. *Spencer.*

Greek Church, differs from the Roman Catholick, 1. In denying the Holy Ghoſt to proceed from the Father and the Son. 2. In denying Purgatory, but praying for the Dead. 3. In believing that Holy Men enjoy not the Preſence of God before the Reſurrection. 4. In Communicating in both kinds; but uſing leavened Bread, and mingling warm Water with Wine, which both together they diſtribute with a Spoon. 5. Receiving Children of ſeven Years old to the Sacrament, becauſe they then begin to Sin. 6. Forbidding extream Unction, and fourth Marriages. 7. Admitting none to Orders but ſuch as are Married, and prohibiting Marriage to them that are actually in Orders. 8. Rejecting carved Images, but admitting the painted. 9. Obſerving four Lents in the Year. 10. Reputing it unlawful to faſt on *Saturdays.* Theſe, by ſome, are reputed to be the differences, tho' ſome make them otherwiſe.

Green Cloth, or *Counting-Houſe of the King's Houſhold*, is ſo called, becauſe the Table ſtands always covered with a *green Cloth.*

Green-wax, in Law, ſignifies the Eſtreats of Fines, Iſſues, and Amerciaments in the Exchequer under the Seal of that Court made in Green-wax to be levied in the County.

Greet,

Greet, Weeping and Complaint. *Spencer.*

Greeting, a familiar Salutation.

Gregorian-Year, is the Reformation of the *Kalendar* made by Pope *Gregory* the XIIIth. which we call the *New Stile*. See *Julian Account.*

Gremial, (Lat.) belonging to the Lap or Bosom.

Gride, pierced. *Spencer.*

Grim, Fierce, Rugged, Ghastly.

Grimace, (Fr.) a crabbed Look, or wry Face that is made, either through Pain, or by way of Scorn and Contempt of any one.

Gripe of a Ship, is the compass or sharpness of her *Stem* under Water, and chiefly towards the bottom of her *Stem*.

Gripe, also in the Sea Phrase, is used for a Ship's being apt to run her Head too much into the Wind, for then they say *she Gripes*.

Grizled, hoary, gray like a Badger.

Grobianism, (Fr.) slovenly behaviour.

Gromets, in a Ship, are small Rings fastend to the upper side of the Yard of a Ship by Staples to tie unto it, or to fasten the *Laskirs*.

Groom, a Servant of divers sorts, more especially belonging to the Stable.

Gross, thick, dull, uncouth ; also the number of 12 Dozen is called a Grofs.

Grotesques, (Ital.) Pictures representing odd sort of things without any peculiar sense or meaning, but only to please the Eye; and it is sometimes used for any mishapen thing.

Grove, a Copse or Spring of Wood.

Grovelling, lying on the Face, or with the Face to the Ground.

Grounding of a Ship, is bringing her a Ground in order to be trim'd and made clean.

Grounds, the Principles of any Science ; also the Settlings of Liquors.

Ground-Tackle, is the Sea Term for a Ship's Anchor, Cables, or whatever else is necessary to make her ride safe at Anchor in proper Ground.

Ground-Timbers, in a Ship, are those Timbers which lie on her Keel, and are fasten'd to it with Bolts through the *Keelson.*

Grudge, Hatred, ill Will.

Grumosity, (Lat.) fulness of Clods or Lumps.

Grumous, full of Clots or Lumps.

Gry, according to Mr. *Lock*, is a Measure containing $\frac{1}{10}$ of a Line, a Line $\frac{1}{10}$ of an Inch, an Inch $\frac{1}{10}$ of a Philosophical Foot, and a Philosophical Foot is $\frac{1}{3}$ of a Pendulum, whose *Diadromes* or Vibrations in the Latitude 45, are each equal to one Second of Time, or $\frac{1}{60}$ of a Minute.

Guarantee, (Fr.) a Person

agreed on to fee Articles performed in Treaties between Princes.

Guardant, the Herald's Term for a Lion born in a Coat of Arms, when his Face is turned towards the Spectator, and he appears in a posture of guard or defence of himself.

Gubernation, (Lat.) Government of a Ship, ruling, managing.

Gudgions, in a Ship, are the Eyes drove into the Stern-Post, into which the Pintles of the Rudder go to hang her on; also a Fish so called.

Guerdon, Reward. *Spencer*.

Guerite, is a sort of small Tower of Stone or Wood generally on the Point of a *Bastion*, or on the Angle of the Shoulder to hold a *Centinel*, who is to take care of the Fofs, and to watch and hinder surprizes.

Guest-Rope, is that Rope by which the Boat is kept from steeving or going too much in and out as she lies in the Tow of a Ship.

Gugaw, (Fr.) See *Gewgaw*.

Guebe, in Architecture, the fame with Gorge.

Guidon, the Standard or Colours of a Troop.

Guild, a Fraternity or Corporation.

Guile, Fraud, Deceit. *Milt.*

Guife, Custom, Carriage, Mode, Fashion.

Gules, so the *Heralds* call the red Colour in the Arms of Gentlemen;but in the Arms of the Nobility, 'tis called *Ruby*, and in that of the Prince 'tis call'd *Mars* : 'Tis expressed in Ingraving by perpendicular Strokes, or Hatches, thus.

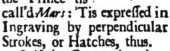

Gulf, in Geography, is a part of the Ocean or great Sea which runs up into the Land through narrow Passages, which are called *Streights*.

Gull, to Deceive, Cheat, or Cozen.

Gunter's Line, Quadrant, Scale and Sector, are all useful Mathematical Instruments, invented, or much improved by that Learned Mathematician Mr. *Edmund Gunter*, sometime Professor of Astronomy of *Gresham College*.

Gunwale, or *Gunnel* of a Ship, is that piece of Timber which reaches on either side of the Ship from the *half Deck* to the *Fore-Castle*.

Gusset, an abatement in *Heraldry*, formed of a Trave se Line drawn from the Dexter Chief, and descending perpendicularly to the extream base Parts, or contrary wife.

Gusto, Taste, Savour, or Relish.

Gutta Rosacea, is a redness with Pimples in the Nose and Checks, and sometimes in the whole Face.   *Gut-*

Gutta-Serena, is a dimnefs, or even a total lofs of Sight, caufed from a watery Humour flowing down from the Brain upon the Optick-Nerves.

Gutta, or Drops, in Architecture, are little parts like Bells, which to the number of fix are put below every *Trigliff*, in the Architrave of the *Dorick Order*.

Guttural, (Lat.) belonging to the Throat.

Guttural Letters, are Letters which are pronounced in the Throat.

Guve de Rond, in Fortification fignifies the fame as a *Single Tenaille*.

Guy, in a Ship, is any Rope ufed to keep off things from bearing or falling a-gainft the Ship fide, when they are to be hoifted in.

Gymnafticks, that Part of Phyfick which treats of the Rules that are to be obferved in all forts of Exercifes, in order to the Prefervation of Health.

Gymnofophifts, (Gr.) were certain Philofophers in *India* that went always naked, and lived folitary in Woods and Defarts, feeding on Herbs.

Gynæcia, (Gr.) in general, are the Accidents incident to Women, tho' by *Hippocrates* they are taken more ftrictly for the Courfes.

Gynecocracy, (Gr.) Feminine Rule, or the Government of a Woman.

Gyration, (Gr.) a turning round, a Dizzinefs.

Gyron, is an Ordinary in Heraldry, confifting of two ftrait Lines iffuing from divers Parts of the Efcutcheon, and meeting in the Feffe Point, thus:

HA

HAbeas Corpora, is a Writ that lies for the bringing in a Jury, or fo many of them as refufe to come upon the *venire facias*, for the Tryal of a Caufe brought to Iffue.

Habeas Corpus, is a Writ which a Man indicted of a Trefpafs before Juftices of Peace, or in a Court of any Franchife, and being apprehended and imprifoned for the fame, may have out of the *King's Bench* to remove himfelf thither at his own Charge, and to anfwer the Caufe there.

Habendum, is a word of Form in a Deed or Conveyance, every one of which muft have two Parts, *viz.* the *Premifes* and the *Habendum*.

Habere facias feifinam, is a Writ Judicial, which lieth where a Man hath recovered Lands in the King's Court, directed to the Sheriff, and commanding him to give *Seifin* of the Land recovered.

E e 3   *Habere*,

Habere facias vifum, is a Writ that lies in divers Cafes, where View is to be taken of Lands or Tenements in Queftion.

Habergeon, a fort of Armour.

Habilement, (Fr.) Apparel, Clothing, Attire, alfo Armour.

Hability, (Lat.) an Ablenefs, Fitnefs, or Capacity.

Habit, (Lat.) the outward Attire of the Body, whereby one Perfon is diftinguifh'd from another; alfo an Ufe or Cuftom.

Habitable, (Lat.) that may be inhabited or dwelt in.

Habitacle, (Lat.) a dwelling Place or Habitation.

Habitual, (Lat.) grown to a Habit by long Ufe, cuftomary.

Habitude, (Lat.) the State or Difpofition of the Body; Cuftom, Ufe.

Halofis, fome ufe for a reflected Inverfion of the Eyelid.

Hæmalops, (Gr.) the Extravafation of Blood about the Eye, occafioned by a Blow or Contufion, commonly called a *Blew Eye*.

Hæmatites, the Name of Bloodftones, of which there are divers forts, fome of them ftanching Blood by outward, others by inward Application.

Hæmatofis. See *Sanguification*.

Hæmodia, (Gr.) a painful Numbnefs of the Teeth occa-

fioned by the Irritation of the Membranes that furround their Roots, or the Nerves that are difperfed thro' their Subftance.

Hæmoptyfis, (Gr.) a fpitting of Blood from the Lungs.

Hæmorrhagia, (Gr.) is a Flux of Blood at the Noftrils, Mouth, or Eyes, &c.

Hæmorrhoides, (Gr.) are fwelling Inflammations in the *Rectum*, or about the Fundament.

Hærede abducto, is a Writ that lieth for a Lord, who having the Wardfhip of his Tenant under Age, by Right cannot come by his Body, for that he is conveyed away by another.

Hærede deliberando alii qui habet cuftodiam terræ, is a Writ directed to the Sheriff, willing to command one, having the Body of him that is Ward to another, to deliver him to him, whofe Ward he was by reafon of his Lord.

Hærefiarch, (Gr.) the chief Broacher and Maintainer of a Herefy.

Hærefy, (Gr.) a Divifion in the Church caufed by fome erroneous Opinion contrary to the Fundamental Points of Religion.

Hæretare, in Law, fignifies to give a Right of Inheritance, or make the Donation Hereditary to the *Grantee* and his Heirs.

Hæretico comburendo, is a Writ that lies againft him that is a Heretick. *He-*

Hasitate, to stick or stand at a thing, to doubt.

Hasitation, a standing at a thing, a doubting.

Haile, to haile a Ship is either to call her to know from whence she is, and where she is bound, or else to salute her and wish her Health.

Hale, to hale at Sea is the same as to *pull* a-shore.

Half-moon, in Fortification, is an Outwork that hath only two faces, forming together a Salient Angle, which is flanked by some part of the Place, and of the other Bastions.

Halieuticks, (Gr.) are Books treating of the Art of Fishing.

Halimote, a general Meeting of Tenants in a Court Baron ; also an Ecclesiastical Court.

Haliography, (Gr.) a Description of the Sea.

Halituous, (Lat.) that may be voided by Pores, vaporous.

Hallelujah. See *Allelujah.*

Halliards, in a Ship, are Ropes for hoising up all the Yards, besides the Cross-jack and Sprit-sail.

Hallow, to dedicate or consecrate to holy Uses.

Hallucination, (Lat.) a being mistaken or deceived in Judgment, an Errour of Opinion, a Blindness of Mind.

Halo, a certain Meteor in form of a bright Circle or Ring, that surrounds the Sun or Moon ; also a reddish Circle of Flesh surrounding each Nipple in the Breasts of a Woman.

Halt, to go lame, to stop or stay. It is used also in a Military Sense, upon a March.

Hamlet, a small Town, or Division of a Town.

Hammocks, are little hanging Beds used at Sea.

Hamper, a great Basket. *Comptroller* and *Clerk of the Hamper*, are Officers in the Court of Chancery ; also *to hamper* is used for to trouble or entangle.

Han, have. *Spencer.*

Hanse, (Fr.) a Society or Corporation of Merchants combined together for the good Usage and safe Passage of Merchandize from Kingdom to Kingdom.

Hans - en - Keldar, in the *Dutch*, is as much as *Jack in a Cellar*, and by a Metaphor is taken for the Child in a Woman's Belly.

Hansiatick, belonging to the *Hanse-Towns*, or *Hans-Merchants.*

Harass, (Fr.) to tire out, weary or disquiet.

Harbinger, an Officer that provides lodgings in a Prince's Progress.

Harbour, a safe riding for Ships ; also a lodging, a Place of Refuge, or retiring ; also a Deer is said to harbour when he goes to rest.

Hardy, accustomed to hardship.

Hariolation, (Lat.) a Sooth-saying.

Hariot, in Law, is taken for the beft Cattle that a Tenant hath at the Hour of his Death, due to the Lord by Cuftom.

Harmonia, in fome Anatomical Authors fignifies the joyning together the Bones of the Head.

Harmonical, Mufical; *Harmonical* Divifion of a Line is a Line fo divided, that the whole Line is to one of the Extreams, as the other Extream is to the intermediate part.

Harmony, is an agreeable or pleafing Union between two or more Sounds, continuing together at the fame time.

Harnefs, Equipments for a Trooper; alfo Furniture for a Horfe in a Coach or Waggon.

Harping Irons, are certain Irons to ftrike great Fifh withal, being at one end like a barbed Arrow, and having at the other end a Cord or Rope faftened to throw it withal.

Harpings, in a Ship, is properly her breadth at the Bow, tho' fome call the ends of the Bends Harpings.

Harpficord, a Mufical Inftrument like Virginals.

Harrow, an Inftrument in Husbandry to break Clods.

Hask, a Fifher's Rod or Basket. *Spencer.*

Hatches, of a Ship, are the Doors in the Midfhip by which any Goods of Bulk are let down into the Hold.

Hatchment, the marfhalling of feveral Coats of Arms in an Efcutcheon; alfo an Atchievement.

Hatchway, is that Place which is directly over the Hatches.

Haven, a Port or Harbour; alfo the Skin which Snakes caft Yearly is fo called.

Haunt, the Walk of a Deer, or the place where he frequents; alfo by a Metaphor applied to Men.

Havock, Deftruction, Ruin. *Milton.*

Hauriant, (Lat.) a Term in Heraldry, proper to blazon Fifhes when they are born in any Efcutcheon in an erect Pofture or ftanding upright, as if they were putting up their heads above Water to breath.

Haw, a fort of Berry growing on a white Thorn; alfo a Spot upon the Eye.

Hawkers, are certain deceitful Fellows, that go from place to place, buying and felling Brafs, Pewter, and other Merchandize, that ought to be uttered in open Market.

Hawm, the lower part of the Straw after the Ears are cut off.

Hawfer, is a kind of little Cable, ferving for many ufes on board a Ship.

Hawfes, of a Ship, are two round holes under her Head

or *Beak,* thro' which the Cables pass when she is at Anchor.

Hayboot, is used in Law for a Permission to take Thorns to make or repair Hedges.

Hayward, an Old Word for a Herdsman, sworn in a Court Baron for due Performance of his Office.

Hazzard, that which happens by chance (as we say) or without any apparent or necessary Cause; also Danger.

Head-land, in Navigation, is a Point of Land that lies farther out at Sea than the rest.

Head-lines, (in a Ship) are the Ropes of all Sails which are next to the Yards, and which fasten the Sails to the Yards.

Head-sails, are those Sails in a Ship which belong to the Fore-mast and Bolt-sprit, so called, because they govern the Head of the Ship.

Head-sea, is when a great Wave of the Sea comes right a Head of a Ship as she is in her Course.

Heady, stubborn, obstinate; also strong Liquors which fly into the Head.

Heame, Home. *Spencer.*

Hearse, (a Hulk) an empty Tomb or Monument for the dead; also the Litter wherein the Corps is carried.

Heath, a large open ground, so called from a Shrub of that Name, which frequently grows thereon.

Heave, at Sea, is to fling any thing over-board.

Heave Offerings, First-fruits paid to the Jewish Priests.

Heaulme, in Heraldry, is an Helmet or Head-piece.

Hebdomade, (Gr.) the number Seven, as seven Years, seven Weeks, but most commonly seven Days, or a Week.

Hebetude, (Lat.) Bluntness, Dulness.

Hebraism, an Idiom of the Hebrew Language.

Hecatomb, (Gr.) a Sacrifice wherein were killed a hundred Beasts.

Hectica, (Gr.) is a continued Fever arising from the very Habit of the Body, and introduced in a long time, and has so rooted it self into the very Constitution, that it is very difficult ever to cure, it is often accompanied with an Ulcer of the Lungs and a Cough.

Hederal, (Lat.) belonging to Ivy.

Hederiferous, (Lat.) bearing Ivy.

Hegemonica (Gr.) are the Principal Actions in a humane Body, as the Actions Animal and Vital.

Hegesians, a Sect of Philosophers, so called from *Hegesias* Scholar to *Parebates.*

Hegyra, a Term in Chronology, signifying the Epocha or account of Time, used by the *Arabians* and *Turks,*
who

who begin their Accounts from the Day that *Mahomet* was forced to make his Escape from the City of *Mecca*, which happened on *Friday*, *July* 16. *A. D.* 622.

Heidegiver, a Country Dance. *Spencer*.

Heir, in the Civil Law, is he who by Will succeeds in the whole Right of the Testator, as in Common Law Heir is he who succeeds by right of Blood in any Man's Lands or Tenements in Fee.

Heirloome, referr'd to in Principal.

Helchesaites, a Sect of Hereticks, sprung from one *Helchesaus*, who held it no Sin to deny *Jesus Christ* in the time of Persecution.

Helcydra, are certain little Ulcers thick and red, which send forth Matter.

Helcysm, the Froth and Filth of Silver, the Dross and Scum of that Metal.

Heliacal, (Gr.) belonging to the Sun ; *Heliacal Rising* of a Star is when a Star having been under the Sun's Beams, and consequently invisible, gets from the same so as to be seen again; *Heliacal Setting* is when a Star by the near approach of the Sun first becomes inconspicuous.

Heliconian, belonging to *Helicon* a Hill of *Phocis*, Sacred to the Muses.

Helicosophy, (Gr.) the Art of delineating all sort of *Spiral Lines in Plano*.

Heliocentrick Place of a Planet, is said to be such as it would appear to us, being beheld from the Center of the Sun.

Heliocentrick Latitude of a Planet, to an Eye placed in the Sun, is the distance of a Planet from the Ecliptick, and is measured by an Angle made by two Lines, one of which is supposed to be drawn from the Center of the Sun to the Center of the Planet, and the other from the Center of the Sun to that Point, where a Perpendicular let fall from the Planet, cuts the Ecliptick.

Helioscopes, a sort of Telescopes, so fitted as to observe the Sun without Detriment to the Eyes.

Helix, in Geometry the same with *Spiral*, in Anatomy it is the exteriour Brim of the Ear.

Hellenism, is the Imitation in Latin, or any other Language of the proper Idiom in the Greek Tongue.

Hellenistical Language, is that used in the Apocryphal Writings and the New Testament according to *Heinsius*.

Helm, in a Ship, is a piece of Timber or Beam fastened to the Rudder; in Chymistry it is the head of a Still or Alembick, so called because it is something like a Helmet or Head-piece.

Helminthagogues, are Medicines that expel Worms by Stool.

Helluation, (Lat.) a playing the *Helluo* or Glutton.

Helve,

Helve, the handle of a Hatchet or Ax.

Hematosis, (Gr.) Sanguification or turning into Blood.

Hemeralopia, or *Acies nocturna*, is when one sees better in the Night than in the Day.

Hemerobaptists, (Gr.) daily Baptists; a Sect so called because they did every day wash themselves.

Hemi, (Gr.) half, a word used only in Composition.

Hemicircular, half round.

Hemicrania, is a Pain in either part of the Brain.

Hemina, a *Roman* Measure of Capacity for things liquid, containing ½ Pint, and 24 Decimal Parts of a solid Inch, of our Corn Measure.

Hemiplegia, (Gr.) is a Palsie on one side below the Head, proceeding from an Obstruction in one part or other of the Spinal Marrow, or from a Blow.

Hemisphere, half a Globe or Sphere, cut by a Plain thro' the Center; the conspicuous Hemisphere is so much of the Heavens as is visible above our Horizon.

Hemistick, (Gr.) half a Verse.

Hemitritæus, an irregular intermitting Fever that returns every Day, and differs thus from a Quotidian, that the Fit comes twice every other Day.

Hemorrhagy, (Gr.) a Flux of Blood.

Hemorrhoid, (Gr.) a Disease in the Fundament commonly called the *Piles*.

Hendecagon, in Geometry, is a Figure of eleven sides.

Heniochus, one of the Northern Constellations.

Hent, caught. *Spencer.*

Hepatick, (Gr.) belonging to the Liver.

Hepaticus Morbus, a Disease so called.

Heps, the Black Thorn Berry.

Heptagon, (Gr.) in Geometry, is a Figure of seven sides and seven Angles; in Fortification it is taken for a Place that hath seven Bastions for its Defence.

Heptangular, that hath seven Angles.

Heptaphony, (Gr.) the having seven Sounds.

Heptarchy, (Gr.) a kind of Government where seven rule.

Hepthemimeris, is a *Cæsura* in a Latin Verse, where after the third foot there is an odd Syllable, which serves to help to make a Foot with the next Word.

Herald or *Harald*, with us signifies an Officer at Arms, whose Duty 'tis to denounce War, to proclaim Peace, or to be imploy'd by the King in Martial Messages, &c. they are Judges and Examiners of Gentlemens Arms, they marshal all Solemnities, at the Coronation of Princes, manage Combats, and the like; the three chief are called

led *Kings at Arms*, and of them *Garter* is the Principal instituted by *Henry* the Fifth, whose Office is to attend the Knights of the Garter at their Solemnities, and to marshal the Funerals of all the Nobility. The next is *Clarentius* ordained by *Edward* the Fourth, whose Office is to marshal and dispose the Funerals of Knights, Esquires, &c. thro' the Realm on the South side of *Trent*; the third is *Norroy*, whose Office is the same on the North side of *Trent* as that of *Clarentius* on the South.

Heraldry, the Art of Blazoning a Coat of Arms.

Herbage, in Common Law, signifies the Fruit of the Earth provided by Nature for the Cattle, also the liberty a Man hath to feed his Cattle in another Man's Ground; also what is customarily paid in lieu of Tythe for Pasture Ground.

Herbalist, one skill'd in the Nature and Temper of Herbs.

Herbiferous, (Lat.) bearing or bringing forth Herbs.

Herbulent, full of Herbs or Grass.

Herculeus Morbus, the same with *Epilepsy*; which see.

Hereditaments, in Law, are such things as descend to a Man and his Heirs by way of Inheritance, not falling within the Compass of an Executor or Administrator, as Chattels do.

Hereditary, (Lat.) that which passes from Family to Family, or from Person to Person, by right of a natural Succession.

Heresiarch, the chief of a Sect of *Hereticks*, or the Author of an *Heresy*.

Heresie, is a Separation made in Ecclesiastical Communion between Men of the same Religion for some Opinions, which those that make the Separation know are no way contained in the Rule of their Religion; as amongst those who acknowledge nothing but the Holy Scriptures to be their Rule of Faith, *Heresie* is a Separation made in their Christian Communion for Opinions known to be not contained in the express words of Scripture.

Heretick, a Person knowingly maintaining false Opinions against the Scriptures and Doctrines of the Church; or one who divides the Church into Parts, introduces Names and Marks of Distinction, and voluntarily makes a Separation because of such Opinions.

Herie, Worship. *Spencer*.

Herisson, in Fortification, is a Beam armed with a great quantity of small Iron Spikes or Nails having their Points outwards, and is supported by a Pivot upon which it turns, and serves instead of a Barrier to block up any Passage,

He-

Heritage , Inheritance by Lot or Succession.

Hermaphrodite, one that is both Man and Woman.

Hermetical Philosophy , is that which pretends to solve and explain all the *Phenomena* of Nature by the three Chymical Principles , Salt, Sulphur and Mercury.

Hermetical Physick, is that Hypothesis in Physick which refers the Causes of all Diseases to Salt, Sulphur and Mercury.

Hermetick Art, is the same with Chymistry.

Hermites , or Persons devoted to Religious Solitude.

Hermitage, (Lat.) a solitary Place, the Habitation of Hernia, properly the falling of the Intestines, Cawl, &c. by the Processes of the *Peritonæum* dilated into the Groin; also a Protuberance of the Navel.

Heroe, was in former Ages a great and illustrious Person; and although he was of a mortal Race, was yet esteemed by the People a partaker of Immortality, and after his Death was put among the Gods.

Heroick , (Lat.) Noble , Stately, Excellent, becoming a Hero.

Heroick Poem , so called, for that it sets forth the noble Exploits of Kings, Princes and Heroes.

Heroick Verse , the same with *Hexameter*, consists just of six Feet, without any certain Order, save that a *Dactyle* is commonly used in the fifth Place, tho' 'tis not always so, for sometimes a *Spondee* is found in the fifth Foot.

Herse, in Fortification , is a *Lattice* or *Portcullice* made in the form of a *Harrow*, and beset with Iron Spikes.

Herfillon, in Fortification, is a Plank struck with Iron Spikes for the same use as the *Herse*.

Heteroclites, in Grammar, are such Nouns as are of different *declensions* in one Number from what they are in the other.

Heterodox, (Gr.) differing in Sentiments or Opinion from the generality of Mankind.

Heterogenial , (Gr.) of a different Nature or Kind.

Heterogeneous Light, is that which consists of different degrees of Refrangibility, and *Heterogenial Particles* are such as are of different Kinds, Natures and Qualities.

Heteroscii, (Gr.) are such Inhabitants of the Earth, as have their Shadows falling but one way, as all those who live between the *Tropicks* and *Polar Circles*.

Hew, the rough cutting of Timber or Stone.

Hexacord, a certain interval of Musick commonly called a *Sixth*.

Hexaemeron, the Work of the six Days at the Creation.

Hexagon,

Hexagon, (Gr.) in Geometry, is a Figure of six Angles and six Sides.

Hexagonal, (Gr.) having six Angles.

Hexahedron, (Gr.) is a solid Figure of six equal sides or faces, and is the same with a *Cube or Dye*.

Hexameter Verse. See *Heroick Verse*.

Hexastick, (Gr.) a Stanza consisting of six Verses.

Hexastyle, an Ancient Building which had six Columns in the Face before and six also behind.

Hidder and *Shidder*, He and Shee. *Spencer*.

Hideous, affrighting or terrible to look at.

Hidroa, are Pimples about the secret Parts.

Hidronosus, a Feaver wherein the Patient sweats extreamly.

Hidrotick Medicines, are such as cause Sweating.

Hierarchy, (Gr.) an Holy Governance or Principality; also the Holy Order of Angels which consists of nine Degrees, *Seraphims*, *Cherubims*, *Thrones*, *Dominions*, *Principalities*, *Powers*, *Vertues*, *Arch-Angels* and *Angels*.

Hieroglyphicks, were certain mysterious Characters, or Letters used among the *Egyptians* wherewith they kept their Policy an Ethnick Secret; for they communicated the Secrets of Nature, and the particulars of their History and Morality only to

the Priests of the Sun; and those Men who were to succeed to the Crown or publick Ministry, and yet this was performed in a Cabalistick manner.

Hirographer, (Gr.) a writer of Divine things.

Hieronymians, an Order of Monks founded by St. *Hierom*.

Hight, named.

Hilarity, (Lat.) chearfulness, merriness.

Himple, (Sax.) to halt or grow lame.

Hin, a Jewish Measure of capacity for things Liquid, containing 1 Gallon, 2 Pints, $2\frac{1}{2}$ solid Inches of our Wine Measure.

Hine, or *Hind*, (Sax.) one of the Family, a Servant, especially for Husbandry.

Hippeus, a Comet which some make to resemble a Horse, but the shape of this kind of Comet is not always the same.

Hippocentaurs, (Gr.) Monsters feigned to be half Men half Horses.

Hippocras, a Wine made, percolated through Spices in a Flannel Bag, called *Hippocrates* his Sleeve.

Hippus, is an affection of the Eyes wherein they continually shake and tremble, and now and then twinkle as it happens in riding.

Hirculation, (Lat.) a Disease in a Vine when it bears no Fruit.

Hircus, a fixt Star, the same with *Capella*.

Hirst,

Hirst, or *Hurst*, a little Wood.

Hirsute, (Lat.) rough bristly, full of hair.

Hispid, (Lat.) rough, haired, shaggy, rough with Briars,

Historian, (Gr.) one that is vers'd in, or writes History.

Historical, belonging to History.

Historiographer, (Gr.) a writer of History, an Historian.

History, a Narration or Relation of things as they are, or of actions as they did pass.

Histrio, (Lat.) a Stage-Player, an Actor, a Booffoon.

Histrionical, Player-like.

Hitch, is the Sea word to catch hold of any thing with a Hook or Rope.

Hithe, (Sax.) a little Port or Haven, for loading and unloading Goods at; hence *Queen-hithe*, and the like.

Hoary, Gray-headed; also covered with Hoar-frost, mouldy.

Hobby, a little *Irish* Nag; also a kind of Hawk.

Hocus Pocus, a Juggler, one that shews Tricks by slight of hand.

Hodgee, (Perf.) a Priest or Holy Man among the *Persians*.

Hodge-podge, is Flesh cut to pieces and sodden together with Herbs; also a confused jumbling of different things together.

Hodiernal, (Lat.) belonging to the present Day or Time.

Hogan Mogan, (Dut.) High and Mighty, the Title of the States of the United Provinces.

Hogoo, (in the Fr. *Haut gout*) a high Taste or Savour, it is generally apply'd to any dish of Meat that has some more than ordinary Taste or Savour.

Hogshead, an English Measure of Capacity for things Liquid, containing 63 Gallons, or 14553 solid Inches.

Hoiden, an ill-bred clownish Wench.

Hoise, or *Hoist*, to heave or lift up; to raise up any thing into a Ship.

Hold of a Ship, is all that part of it which lies between the Keelson, and the lower Deck.

Hold off, is a Term used at Sea, about heaving in the Cable at the Capstan.

Hold-fast, a piece of Iron in the form of an S, fixed in a Wall to support it; also a Joyner's Tool.

Hollow Tower, in Fortification, is a Rounding made of the remainder of two Brisures to joyn the Curtain to the *Orillon*, where the small Shot are plaid that they may not be so much exposed to the view of the Enemy.

Hollow Square, is a body of Foot drawn up with an empty Space in the middle for the Colours, Drums and Baggage

gage, facing and covered by the *Pikes* every way to oppose the Horse.

Holocaust, (Gr.) a Sacrifice that's altogether burnt on the Altar.

Holometer, (Gr.) a Mathematical Instrument for measuring.

Holsom, so a Ship is said to be at Sea that will hull, trie, and rides well at Anchor without rolling.

Holt, (Sax.) a small Wood or Grove; hence came the name of the Street called *Holborn* in *London*.

Homage, is the Submission, Promise and Oath of Service and Loyalty, which a Tenant makes to his Lord when he is first admitted to the Land which he holds of the Lord in *fee*. In general 'tis taken for that Submission and Respect which an Inferiour pays to his Superiour.

Homager, one that pays Homage, or is bound to do so.

Home-stall, a Mansion-House, or Seat in the Country.

Homesoken, or *Homesakon*, (Sax.) freedom from Amercement for entring Houses violently, and without License, or a power to punish such an Offence.

Homicide, in Common Law, signifies the killing of a Man, and it is either *voluntary* or *casual*; *voluntary* is that which is deliberate and committed of a set Mind and

Purpose to kill, and that is either with precedent Malice or without; the former is *Murther*, the latter *Manslaughter*; *Casual*, is when the slayer kills a Man by pure mischance.

Homily, (Lat.) a Sermon, a Discourse, Conversation.

Homine Replegiendo, is a Writ to bail a Man out of Prison.

Homocentrick, (Gr.) having the same Center.

Homœomery, (Gr.) a likeness of Parts.

Homogeneal, (Gr.) of the same Kind or Nature.

Homogeneous Particles, are such as are all of the same Kind, Nature and Properties.

Homogenial Light,' is that whose Rays are all of one Colour and Degree of Refrangibility, without any mixture of others.

HomogeniumComparationis, is the absolute Number or Quantity in a Quadratick or Cubick Equation, and which always possesses one side of the Equation.

Homologation, (Gr.) an Admission, or Allowance, Approbation.

Homologous, (Gr.) agreeable, or like to one another; Homologous Terms in Proportionals, are Antecedents to Antecedents, and Consequents to Consequents; Homologous things, in Logick, are such as agree only in Name, but are of different Nature. *Ho-*

Homonymous , (Gr.) are things of the same Name but different Natures.

Homonymy, (Gr.) is when divers things are signified by one word.

Honesty , Purity of Manners.

Honey-Moon, the first Month of Matrimony, so termed from the first fondness of a new Married Couple.

Honour, in Common Law, is taken for the more noble part of Seigneury, on which other inferiour Lordships or Mannors depend by the performances of some Customs, or Services to the Lords of such *Honours*.

Honour Point, in Heraldry, is the upper part of an *Escutcheon*, when its breadth is divided into three parts.

Honourable, worthy of Honour, or that is possest of Honour.

Honourary, (Lat.) pertaining to Honour, done or conferred upon any one on account of Honour.

Hooks of a Ship, are all those forked Timbers which are placed directly upon the Keel, as well in her *Run* as in her *Rake*.

Hoord, or *Hord*, a Tribe, Clan, or distinct Company among the *Tartars*.

Hoplochrism, Weapon-Salve.

Horary, (Lat.) hourly, belonging to the Hours.

Hordeatum, (Lat.) a Liquid Medicine taken inwardly, prepared of Barley beat and boiled with other suitable and well strained Liquors.

Horizon of any place upon the Surface of the Earth, is that great Circle which in that place divides the conspicuous part of the Heavens from the inconspicuous.

Horizontal Line or Superficies, is a Line or Superficies parallel to the Horizon.

Horizontal Projection, is a Projection of the Globe upon the Plain of the *Horizon*. See *Projection*.

Horn-work, in Fortification, is an out-work which advanceth toward the Field, carrying in the fore part two Demibastions in the form of Horns.

Horological, pertaining to a Clock or Dial.

Horologiography, (Gr.) the Art of making Clocks, Dials, or other Instruments to shew the Time.

Horometry, (Gr.) the Art of measuring Time by Hours.

Horopter, in Opticks, is a right Line drawn through the Point of Concourse, parallel to that which joins the Center of the Eye.

Horoscope, is the degree of the Ascendant, or the Star ascending above the Horizon, at the moment you intend to predict any thing; also the whole Astrological Figure is called by this Name.

Horrent, horrible, abhorring. *Milton*.

F f   *Horrible*,

Horrible, (Lat.) hideous, frightful, exceſſive.

Horrid, (Lat.) terrible, dreadful.

Horrifica Febris, is that Fever in which the Patient is often ſeized with ſhaking Fits and horrible Agonies.

Horrour, (Lat.) Dread, Fright, ſhivering for Cold.

Horſe, is a Rope in a Ship made faſt to one of the Fore-maſt Shrouds, having a dead Man's Eye at its end, through which the Pendant of the *Sprit-Sail* Sheets is reeved.

Horſe-Shooe, in Fortification, is a Work ſometimes of a round, and ſometimes of an oval Figure, raiſed in the Ditch of a marſhy place, and bordered with a Parapet; 'tis made to ſecure a Gate, or to lodge Soldiers in to prevent ſurprizes.

Hortation, an exhorting or perſuading to a thing.

Horticulture, (Lat.) the Art of dreſſing Gardens.

Hoſanna, (Heb.) ſave we beſeech thee, a ſolemn Acclamation of the *Jews.*

Hoſpitable, (Lat.) that uſes Hoſpitality.

Hoſpital, (Lat.) a Houſe erected out of Charity for the Entertainment or Relief of the Poor, Sick, and impotent People.

Hoſpitalers, an Order of Knights that built an Hoſpital at *Jeruſalem* for entertainment of Pilgrims, whom they protected in their Travels.

Hoſpitality, the entertaining and relieving of Strangers.

Hoſpitious, that receives Gueſts friendly.

Hoſt, (Fr.) an Inn-keeper, or Land-lord; alſo the Conſecrated Bread at the Communion; alſo an Army, or great Body of Men.

Hoſtage, (Fr.) a Pawn, Surety, or Pledge.

Hoſtile, (Lat.) Enemy-like.

Hoſtility, Enmity, Hatred.

Hovel, a Covering of Hurdles for Cattle, a mean Building.

Hough, the Joint of the hinder Leg of a Beaſt.

Hounds, in a Ship, are holes in the Cheeks at the top of the Maſts, through which the Ties run to hoiſe the Yards.

Hour Circles the ſame with Meridians; *which ſee.*

Hour Circle, is a ſmall brazen Circle fitted on the Meridian, having the Pole of the World for its Center, divided into twenty four Hours, which in one Revolution of the Globe, are all pointed at with an *Index* for that purpoſe fitted on the *Axis* of the Globe.

Houſage, Money pay'd by Carriers or others, for laying up Goods in a Houſe.

Houſe, the Heavens are divided by Aſtrologers into 12 parts, called Houſes, each of which has a particular ſignification.

Houſed in, the Seamen ſay of a Ship, which after the breadth of her bearing, is brought in too narrow to her upper Works, that ſhe is *houſed in.*　　　　*Houſe,*

Houffe, or *Houfing*; (Fr.) a Cloth that Horfes wear behind the Saddle.

Howle, when the foot Hooks of a Ship are fcarfed into the Ground Timbers and boulted, and then the Plank laid on them up to the Orlop, the Carpenters fay they begin to make the Ship Howl.

Hubbub, a confufed Noife. *Milton*.

Huckfter, a Seller of Provifions or fmall Wares by Retail.

Huddle, Buftle, Diforder, *verbally*, to lay up things in a coufufed manner.

Hue, Colour, Countenance. *Milton*.

Hue and *Cry*, in Common Law, is a purfuit of one having committed Felony by the High-way, by defcribing the Party, and giving notice to feveral Conftables from one Town to another.

Huguenots, the nick Name of the *French Calvinifts*, from *Hugo* a great Leader and Writer among them; or from *Hugon*, a Gate in *Tours*, near which they affembled; or from *huc nos venimus*, the beginning of their Proteftation.

Hull of a Ship, is the Body of a Ship without her Rigging.

Hull, to float, to ride too and fro on the Water.

To ftrike a Hull; that is, in a Storm to lie clofely and obfcurely in the Sea, or tarry for fome Confort, bearing no Sail with the Helm *lafhed a Lee*.

To Hull, or *lie a Hull*, is faid of a Ship when either in a dead Calm, or in a Storm when fhe cannot carry them, fhe takes all her Sails in, fo that nothing but her Mafts, Yards, and Rigging are abroad.

Hullock, a Sea Term, and fignifies part of a Sail loofed (in a Storm) to keep the Ship's Head to the Wind.

Humane, (Lat.) belonging to Mankind; alfo Courteous, Affable.

Humanift, one skilled in Humane Learning.

Humanity, (Lat.) Manhood or the Nature of Man; alfo Gentlenefs, Courtefie, Affability; alfo Humane Learning.

Humectation, (Lat.) is the moiftening of any mixt thing in order to prepare it for fome Operation, or that its beft and fineft Parts may the better be extracted.

Humeral, (Lat.) belonging to the Shoulder.

Humid, moift, dewy. *Milt.*

Humidity, moifture, moiftnefs, dampnefs, a power of wetting.

Humiliate, to make low or humble.

Humiliates; a Religious Order inftituted in 1166, that led very ftrict and mortified Lives.

Humiliation, (Lat.) a making low, or humbling.

Humility , Humbleneſs ; Meekneſs ; alſo the Name of a Bird.

Humour, Moiſture, Juice ; alſo Temper of Mind, Fancy, Whim.

Humouriſt, (Lat.) one that is fantaſtick, full of Humours or odd Fancies.

Humourous, of, or belonging to Humours ; alſo fantaſtical, whimſical, wedded to a Humour.

Hundred, a part of a Shire, ſo called becauſe it conſiſted of ten Tythings, and each Tything of ten Houſholds.

Hundreder, he who has the Juriſdiction of an Hundred, holding its Court.

Hunks, a Miſer, covetous or niggardly Wretch.

Hurdles, in Fortification, are Twigs of Willows or Oſiers interwoven very cloſe together, and uſually laden with Earth, that they may ſerve to render Batteries firm, to conſolidate the Paſſages over muddy Ditches, &c.

Hurly-burly, Tumult, Uproar, or Crowd of People.

Hurricane, a violent Storm of Wind, which happens oft times in *Jamaica*, and ſome other part of the *Weſt Indies*, in the Months of *September* and *October*, and makes great havock of all that comes in its way.

Hurts, a Term in Heraldry. See *Balls*.

Huſſars, *Hungarian* Horſemen , ſo nam'd from the Shout they give at the firſt Charge.

Huſtings, a Court held before the Lord Mayor and Aldermen of *London*.

Hyacinth, (Gr.) Tenne or Tawney Colour in Noblemens Coats in Heraldry.

Hyades, ſeven Stars in the head of the Bull, that always bring Rain , by the Poets ſaid to be the Daughters of *Atlas*.

Hyaloides, the vitreous humour of the Eye.

Hybernal, (Lat.) belonging to the Winter.

Hydatides, (Gr.) watery Bliſters on the Bowels of Hydropical Perſons.

Hydatoides, (Gr.) is the watery humour of the Eye.

Hydra, (Gr.) a Southern Conſtellation, conſiſting of 26 Stars, and imagin'd to repreſent a Water Serpent.

Hydragogues, (Gr.) are Medicines which by Fermentation and Precipitation, purge out the watery humours.

Hydragogy, (Gr.) a conveying of Water by Furrows and Trenches.

Hydrargyre, the Chymiſts Name for Mercury.

Hydraulicks , the Art of making all ſort of Engines to carry or raiſe Water, or which are moved by Water and ſerve for other Uſes.

Hydraulo-Pneumatical Engines, are ſuch Engines as raiſe Water by means of the Spring of the Air.

Hydrography, (Gr.) an Art which teaches how to deſcribe and meaſure the Sea, giving

giving an Account of its Tides, Counter Tides, Bays, Gulfs, Creeks, &c. as also the Rocks, Shelves, Sands, Shoals, Promontories, Harbours, Distance from one Port to another, and other remarkable things on the Coasts.

Hydrographical Charts, are Sea Maps, delineated for the use of Pilots and other Mariners; wherein are marked all the Rhumbs or Points of the Compass, as also the Rocks, Shelves, Sands and Capes.

Hydromancy, (Gr.) Divination by Water.

Hydromel, (Gr.) Mead, is a Decoction of Water and Honey.

Hydromphalum, is a Protuberance of the Navel, proceeding from watery humours in the *Abdomen*.

Hydrophobia, (Gr.) is a Distemper highly convulsive, accompanied with Fury, and a shunning of Water and all things that are liquid, proceeding from the Bite of a mad Dog, or a Contagion Analogous to it.

Hydropthalmy, (Gr.) is when the Eye becomes so big that it almost starts out of its Orbit.

Hydropical, (Gr.) belonging to, or affected with the Dropsy.

Hydrops, (Gr.) a Dropsy, that is a Stagnation of the watery humour in the habit of the Body, or some Cavity of it.

Hydroscope, an Instrument for discovering the watery Steams in the Air.

Hydrostaticks, is that Part of Staticks which relates to the Gravities and *Equilibria* of Liquers, and also comprehends the Art of weighing Bodies in Water or some other Liquor, thereby to estimate their Specifick Gravities.

Hydroticks, (Gr.) are Medicines that produce sweating.

Hyemal, (Lat.) belonging to Winter.

Hygiastick, (Gr.) tending to preserve health.

Hygieina, that part of Physick that teaches to preserve health,

Hygrometer, (Gr.) an Instrument to measure the Moisture of the Air.

Hygroscope, (Gr.) the same with *Hygrometer*.

Hymen, is a circular folding of the inner Membrane of the *Vagina*, which being broke at the first Copulation, its Fibres contract in three or four Places, and form what *Anatomists* call *Glandulæ Myrtiformes*.

Hymenæan, belonging to *Hymen*, or Marriage,

Hymnigrapher, (Gr.) a Writer of Hymns,

Hypæthron, is an open Gallery or Building, the inside whereof is uncovered and exposed to the Weather; the Ancients gave this Name to all Temples which had no Roof.   F f 3   *Hy-*

Hypallage, (Gr.) or *Immutation*, a figure in Grammar wherein the Order of the Words is contrary to the meaning of them in Construction.

Hyberbaton, a Figure in Grammar, where there is too bold and frequent Transposition of Words.

Hyperbola, (Gr.) a Figure in Geometry, which may be formed by cutting a Cone parallel to its Axis.

Hyperbole, is a Figure which represents things greater, lesser, better, &c. than in Reality they are.

Hyperbolical, belonging to an *Hyperbole* or *Hyperbola*, exceeding Belief.

Hyperbolicum acutum, is a Solid made by the Revolution of the infinite *Area*, of the Space contained between the Curve and its *Assymptote* in the *Apollonian Hyperbola*, turning round that *Assymptote*, which produces a Solid infinitely long, which is nevertheless Cubable.

Hyperboreans, a certain People of *Scythia* so called.

Hypercatharticks, (Gr.) Purgers that work too long, and too violently.

Hypercriticism, a more than ordinary Judgment or Censure, over nice Criticism.

Hypercritick, (Gr.) a Master Critick or over critical.

Hyperdyssyllable, (Gr.) a Word of more than two Syllables.

Hyperoon, are the two holes

in the upper part of the *Ossa Palati*, which receive the pituitous humours from the mamillary Processes, and after they are separated discharge them at the Mouth.

Hyperphysical, (Gr.) that which is above Physicks or Natural Philosophy, Metaphysical.

Hyperthyron, (Gr.) in Architecture, is a large Table usually placed over Gates or Doors of the *Dorick Order*.

Hyphen, is an Accent in Grammar, that implies two Words are to be joyned together, as *Male-Sanus*.

Hypnotick, (Gr.) causing Sleep.

Hypocaust, (Gr.) a subterraneous Place, where there was a Furnace which served to heat the Baths of the Ancients.

Hypochondres, (Gr.) the lateral Parts of the Belly about the short Ribs, where lie the Liver, Stomach, and Spleen.

Hypochondriacal, belonging to the *Hypochondres*; also troubled with the Spleen or Melancholy.

Hypochondriacus Affectus, is a kind of convulsive Passion or Affection arising from the flatulent and pungent humours in the Spleen which afflict the nervous and Membranous Parts, Melancholy.

Hypochymy, a Suffusion, wherein Gnats, little Clouds, &c. appear to fly before the Sight.   *Hy-*

Hypocrisis, (Gr.) Diffimulation, feigned Holiness.

Hypocrite, (Gr.) properly fignifies one that affumes the Perfon or Gefture of another in order to difguife his own; but commonly is taken for a Diffembler, or one that would appear better than he is.

Hypocritical, belonging to a Hypocrite or Diffembler.

Hypogæum, a Place under ground: with Aftrologers, the fourth Houfe, or *Imum Cœli*.

Hypogaftrium, (Gr.) is the lowermoft Region of the *Abdomen*, reaching from three Inches below the Navel to the *Os Pubis*.

Hypomoclion, otherwife called the *Fulcrum* or Prop, in Mechanicks, is the fixed Point or the Center of Motion of a Body or Engine, by which it is fufpended, and on which it' refts in its Motion; thus in a Ballance, the Point on which the Beam moves, is the *Hypomoclion*.

Hypophthalmia, (Gr.) is a Pain in the Eye under the horny Tunick.

Hypophyllofpermous Plants, are fuch as bear their Seed on the backfides of their Leaves.

Hypopyon, is a gathering together of Matter under the horny Tunick of the Eye, which fometimes quite takes away the Sight.

Hypofpathifmus, is an Incifion in the Forehead, made by three Cuts or Divifions

where the *Spatula* is thruft in under the Skin.

Hypofphagma, is a Bloodfhot, from a Stroke upon the Eye.

Hypoftafis Urinæ, is that thick Subftance which generally fubfides at the bottom of Urine.

Hypoftatical Principles, are the three Chymical Principles Salt, Sulphur and Mercury, fo called by *Paracelfus* and his Followers.

Hypothenufe, (Gr.) in a right angled Triangle, is that fide which fubtends the right Angle.

Hypothefis, (Gr.) is a Suppofition; among Mathematical Principles *Poftulates* are fo called; the different Syftems of the World are alfo called by that Name.

Hypothetical, (Gr.) belonging to, or upon Suppofition.

Hypotrachelion, (Gr.) in Architecture, is the Top or Neck of a Pillar, or the moft flender part of it which touches the Capital.

Hypotypofis, (Gr.) is a lively and exact Defcription of any Object made in Fancy.

Hypfiftarians, Hereticks in the fourth Century of Chriftianity, who made a Mixture of the *Jewifh* Religion, and Paganifm; for they worfhipped Fire with the *Pagans*, and obferved the Sabbath and Legal Abftinence with the *Jews*.

Hysteralgia, (Gr.) is a Pain in the Womb, proceeding from an Inflammation.

Hysterica Passio, Fits of the Mother, is according to some, a Convulsion of the Nerves of the *Parvagum* and *Intercostal* in the *Abdomen*, proceeding from a pricking Irritation and Explosion of the Spirits.

Hysterical, (Gr.) belonging to the Womb.

Hysteromotocia, (Gr.) a cutting the Child out of the Womb.

Hysteron Proteron, (Gr.) a preposterous way of speaking or writing, expressing that first which shou'd be last.

Hysterotomy, (Gr.) a Dissection of the Womb.

Hythe. See *Hithe.*

J A.

Jabber, to talk Gibberish.

Jacent, (Lat.) lying along.

Jacinth, a precious Stone found in *Æthiopia*, whereof there are two kinds, the one of a Pale Yellow Colour, the other of a clear bright Yellow inclinable to red, which is accounted the better.

Jacobites, a Sect of Hereticks; who 1. Acknowledged but one Will, Nature and Operation in Christ. 2. Used Circumcision in both Sexes. 3. Sign'd their Children with the Sign of the Cross imprinted with a burning Iron,

4. Affirm'd Angels to consist of two Natures, Fire and Light.

Jacob's Staff, a Mathematical Instrument for taking Heights and Distances.

Jactator, (Lat.) a Boaster.

Jactitation, (Lat.) a vain boasting.

Jaculation, (Lat.) a shooting or darting.

Jaculatory, (Lat.) that which is suddenly cast from one like a Dart.

Jagged, dented, notched, cut like the Teeth of a Saw.

Jakes, an House of Office, a Laystall.

Jambes, (Fr.) is used with us for the Posts sustaining both sides of the Door; the side Posts of a Door.

Iambick, (Lat.) a Measure or Foot in a Verse, having the first Syllable short and the second long.

Janitor, (Lat.) the Keeper of a Door or Porter; also the lower Orifice of the Ventricle.

Janizaries, are the Turk's principal foot Soldiers that are of his Guard.

Jansenism, the Tenets of *Cornelius Jansenius*, Bishop of *Ypres*, who held St. *Augustin's* Opinion concerning Grace, and opposed the *Jesuits*.

Jansenist, a Follower of *Jansenius*.

January, the first Month of the Year, from *Janus*, an ancient King of *Italy*, deified after his Death.

Jargon,

Jargon, (Fr.) Gibberish, fuſtian Language, Pedlars French, a barbarous Jangling

Jarr, Quarrel, Strife, *Shakeſp.* verbally, to fall out, to diſagree.

Jaſper, a precious Stone, of divers Colours, but the beſt is green, tranſparent with red Veins, and ſhows faireſt being ſet in Silver.

Jaſponix, (Gr.) a kind of Jaiper of a white Colour, with red Streakes, not unlike the Nail of a Man's hand.

Iatromathematick, (Gr.) a Mathematical Phyſician, or a Phyſician who cures in a Mathematical Way.

Javelin, a ſort of Dart, or half Pike, 5½ Foot long, uſed anciently in War.

Jaundice, (Fr.) a Diſeaſe which makes the Patient look Yellow.

Jaunt, to trot or trudge up and down.

Ich Dien, (Sax.) I ſerve, a Motto of the Arms of the Prince of *Wales*, firſt aſſum'd by *Edward* the Black Prince.

Ichnography, in Perſpective, is the View of any thing cut off by a Plane Parallel to the Horizon, juſt at the Baſe or Bottom of it, and in Architecture it is taken for the Geometrical Plan or Platform of an Edifice, or the Ground Plot of a Houſe or Building, delineated upon Paper.

Ichthyology, (Gr.) a Diſcourſing or Deſcription of Fiſhes.

Icleped, called, or named.

Icon, (Gr.) a Cut or Picture, an Image, or the Repreſentation of a thing.

I cond, I learned.

Iconical, (Gr.) belonging to an Image.

Iconiſm, (Gr.) a faſhioning, a true and lively Deſcription.

Iconoclaſt, (Gr.) a Breaker or Demoliſher of Images; ſo were the Enemies to Image Worſhip called.

Iconography, a Deſcription by Pictures.

Icoſahedrum, (Gr.) is one of the Regular Bodies comprehended under 20 equal and Equilateral Triangles.

Icterical, belonging to, or troubled with the Jaundice.

Icterus, the Jaundice, is the changing the Skin into a Yellow Colour, from an Obſtruction of the *Ductus Choledicus*, or the Glandules of the Liver.

Idea, is properly the Image or Repreſentation of any ſenſible Object, tranſmitted into the Brain thro' the Organ of Sight or the Eye, but in a more general Senſe it is taken for the immediate Object of Underſtanding whatever it be.

Ideal, belonging to an Idea, imaginary.

Identical, that is the ſame.

Identitate nominis, is a Writ that lies for him who upon a *Capias* or *Exigent* is taken and committed to Priſon for another Man of the ſame Name.

Identity,

Identity, the Sameness of a thing.

Ides, eight Days in every Month so called; in *March*, *May*, *July* and *October*, these 8 Days begin at the eighth Day of the Month, and continue to the fifteenth; in other Months they begin at the 6ᵗʰ Day, and continue to the thirteenth. But here note, that the last Day only is called the *Ides*, and the first of these Days the eighth of the *Ides*, the second the seventh of the *Ides*, and so of the rest; therefore when we speak of the *Ides* of such a Month in general, it is to be understood of the fifteenth or thirteenth Day of that Month.

Idiocracy, (Gr.) the proper Disposition or Temperament of a thing or Body.

Idiom, the peculiar Phrase or manner of Expression in a Language; a Propriety in speaking.

Idiopathy, (Gr.) is a primary Disease, which neither depends on, nor proceeds from any other.

Idiosyncrasy, (Gr.) a Temperament peculiar to any particular Animal Body, whereby it hath either in Sickness or in Health, a peculiar Inclination or Aversion to or against some particular things.

Idiot, (Gr.) a private Person. (Lat.) an unlearned Man. In Law, a Natural, a Changeling.

Idiotism, (Gr.) the same that *Idiom*; also Simplicity.

Idol, (Gr.) an Image, or the Statue of some false Deity.

Idolatry, a worshipping false Gods, or paying Divine Honours to Idols, or false Representations.

Idolize, to be extremely fond, to dote upon.

Jear-Rope, is a piece of a Hawser fastened to the main Yard and fore Yard in great Ships; its Use is to help to hoise up the Yard, but more especially to succour the Ties and to keep the Yard from falling if they shou'd break.

Jehovah, (Heb.) the most sacred Name of God, denoting him, *Who is, Who was, and is to come.*

Jejune, (Lat.) hungry, barren, empty.

Jejunum, is the second part of the Intestines, beginning where the *Duodenum* ended, and is about 12 or 13 hands Breadth long.

Je-ne-scay-quoy, (four *French* words contracted as it were into one) signifies *I know not what.*

Jennet, a *Spanish* Mare. *Shakesp.*

Jentaculation, (Lat.) Breakfasting.

Jeofail, (in Common Law) is an Over-sight in Pleading.

Jeopardy, (Fr.) Danger or Hazard.

Jessant, in a Coat of Arms when a Lion or other Beast

is born over some Ordinary, as over a *Chief*, a *Bend*, &c.

Jesses, Ribbons hanging down from Garlands; also short Strops of Leather fasten'd to Hawks Legs, and so to the Varvels.

Jesuit, one of the *Society of Jesus*, founded by *Ignatius Loyola*, a *Spanish* Soldier.

Jesuitical, belonging to a *Jesuit*, subtle, deceitful.

Jet d'eau, is the *French* word for a Pipe of a Fountain, which throws up the Water to any considerable height in the Air.

Igneous, (Lat.) fiery.

Ignify, (Lat.) to set on fire.

Ignipotent, (Lat.) powerful in Fire.

Ignis-Fatuus, is a certain Meteor that appears chiefly in Summer Nights, for the most part frequenting Church Yards, Meadows, and Bogs, and consists of a somewhat viscous Substance or fat Exhalation, which being kindled in the Air, reflects a kind of thin Flame, yet without any sensible heat. This Meteor is called by the common People, *Will of the Wisp*, or *Jack with a Lanthorn*.

Ignition, reducing to Powder by means of Fire, Calcination.

Ignivomous, (Lat.) vomiting out Fire, or Flames of Fire.

Ignoble, (Lat.) of an obscure Birth, or of a base Spirit.

Ignominious, disgraceful, dishonourable, reproachful.

Ignominy, (Lat.) Infamy, Disgrace, Affront, Slander, Dishonour.

Ignoramus,(Lat.)is commonly used for a Fool or ignorant Fellow. It is also used by the Grand Inquest in the Inquisition of Causes Criminal and Publick, when they dislike their Evidence as defective or too weak to make good the Presentment; which Word being written upon the Bill, all farther Enquiry upon the Party is stopped.

Ignorance, (Lat.) want of Knowledge.

Ignoscible, (Lat.) fit to be pardoned or forgiven.

Jilt, a lewd Woman that cheats or disappoints, a Whore; verbally, to disappoint or cheat.

Ile, is the Cavity from the Thorax to the Bones of the Thighs.

Ileum, (Gr.) the third small Gut, named from its many turnings, twenty one Hands long, beginning at the *Jejunum*, and ending at the *Cæcum*.

Ilia, the Flanks; also the small Guts.

Iliacal, of, or belonging to the Flanks or small Guts.

Iliack-Passion, the same with *miserere*, or the twisting of the Guts.

Iliades, the Title of *Homer*'s Poem, whose Subject is the Destruction of *Troy*, which was called *Ilium*.

Il

Ilk, the fame. *Spencer.*

Illaborate, (Lat.) done or made without Labour or Pains.

Illachirimable, (Lat.) not capable of Weeping.

Illaqueate, (Lat.) to intangle or infnare.

Illation, (Lat.) an Inference, a Conclufion.

Illaudable, not worthy of Praife. *Milt.*

Illecebrous, (Lat.) that enticeth or allureth.

Illective, an Allurement, or Inticement.

Illegal, (Lat.) contrary to Law, unrightful.

Illegality, Unlawfulnefs.

Illegitimate, (Lat.) unlawful; alfo unlawfully or bafely born, a Baftard.

Illepid, (Lat.) unpleafant, dull in Converfation.

Illiberal, (Lat.) nigardly, ungenteel.

Illicit, (Lat.) unwarrantable, not allowed.

Illigation, an enwraping, or entangling.

Illimitable, that cannot be limited.

Illiquation, (Lat.) a melting down one thing in another, mingling earthly Bodies with metalline.

Illiterate, (Lat.) Unlearn'd.

Illogical, (Gr.) unreafonable, not agreeing with Rules of *Logick.*

Illucidate, to enlighten, to explain.

Illuminate, to Enlighten, to Beautifie, to lay Colours on Maps and Prints, to Gild and Colour the Initial Letters of Manufcripts.

Illumination, (Lat.) an enlightning.

Illuminative-Month, is that fpace of Time that the Moon is vifible or between one Conjunction and another.

Illuminators, Perfons that illuminated the Capital Letters of Manufcripts; hence the word *Limners.*

Illufion, (Lat.) a mocking or fcorning.

Illufory, mocking, deceitful.

Illuftration, a making clear, plain or evident.

Illuftrious, (Lat.) famous, renowned.

Image, (Lat.) an artificial refemblance either in Painting or Sculpture.

Imagery, Painted or Carved Work of Images, Tapeftry with Figures.

Imaginary, not real, fantaftick.

Imagination, (Lat.) is an application of the Mind to the Phantafin or Image of fome corporeal thing expreffed in the Brain.

Imaginative, of, or belonging to the Imagination.

Imbargo, (Span.) a ftop or ftay, a word ufed among the Merchants, when the Ships or Merchandizes are arrefted or detained upon any occafion.

Imbark, (Ital) to go aboard a Ship.

Imbafe, to mix with bafer Metal.

Imbattel, to put in Battle Array.

Imbecillity, (Lat.) weaknefs.

Imbellifh,

Imbellish, (Fr.) to adorn, to beautifie.

Imbellishment, Ornament.

Imbezzle, to consume or waste things entrusted, to pilfer or purloin.

Imbibe, (Lat.) to drink in.

Imbody, to make up several Ingredients into one Body; also to take or join it self with a Body.

Imbordering, in Heraldry, is when the Field and Circumference of the Field are both of one Metal, Colour, or Fur.

Imbossed Work, in Metal or Stone, is made with Bosses or Bunches.

Imbossing, Carving or Engraving that sticks out more or less, which by the *Italians*, is accordingly termed *Basso*, *Mezzo*, or *Aleto Relievo*.

Imbrew, to soak or steep.

Imbricated, (Lat.) a word used by some Botanists to express the Figures of the Leaves of some Plants which are hollowed within like an Imbrex or Gutter-Tile.

Imbroyl, (Fr.) to put into a combustion, or set together by the Ears.

Imbue, (Lat.) to season, as a Vessel.

Imitation, (Lat.) an acting or doing like another; a following of another's example.

Immaculate, without spot, or stain.

Immanity, fierceness, wildness, cruelty.

Immarcessible, never-fading, that cannot wither or decay.

Immaterial, that consists not of Matter or Body; also of little Moment or Consequence.

Immature, (Lat.) unripe.

Immediate, that which follows without any thing coming between.

Immedicable, which cannot be cured.

Immemorable, not to be remembred, not worth the remembrance, also past Memory, as also unspeakable.

Immemorial, out of Mind, or beyond the Memory of Man.

Immense, (Lat.) unmeasurable, exceeding great.

Immensity, (Lat.) infiniteness, vastness.

Immensurability, (Lat.) a being uncapable to be measured.

Immerse, to dip over Head and Ears.

Immersion, (Lat.) a dipping or plunging in some Liquor. In *Astron*, it is when a Star is hid in the Sun's Rays, or one Planet in the shadow of another.

Imminent, (Lat.) at hand, ready to come upon us, hanging over our heads.

Imminution, (Lat.) a diminishing or lessening.

Immission, (Lat.) a sending or putting in; a setting or grafting.

Immobility, (Lat.) unmoveableness, stedfastness.

Immoderate, (Lat.) observing no measure, unreasonable, intemperate beyond excess.

Immode-

Immoderation, Intemperance, Excefs.

Immodeft, (Lat.) Wanton, Impudent, Lafcivious, Malepert, Saucy.

Immolation, (Lat.) a facrificing or offering.

Immoral, of depraved Morals, contrary to good Manners.

Immorality, Lewdnefs, Prophanenefs, Debauchery.

Immorigerous, difobedient.

Immortal, (Lat.) everlafting, or which never dieth.

Immortality, (Lat.) a living for ever, everlaftingnefs.

Immovable, that cannot be moved.

Immunity, (Lat.) exemption from any Office, Freedom, Priviledge.

Immure, to enclofe between Walls.

Immutability, (Lat.) unchangeablenefs, eonftancy.

Immutable, (Lat.) unchangeable, conftant.

Immutation, (Lat.) a changing or altering.

Impacted, driven in.

Impair, to diminifh, or make worfe.

Impale, to fence about with Pales; alfo to drive a Stake through the Body, or to fpit upon a Stake.

Impaled, when the Coats of a Man and his Wife, who is not an Heirefs, are born in the fame Efcutcheon, they muft be marfhal'd in Pale, the Husbands on the right fide and the Wives on the left, and this the Heralds call *Ba-*

ron and *Femme* two *Coats impaled*.

Impanation, a being or exifting in Bread; a Term ufed in the *Lutheran* Doctrine of the Sacrament of the Lord's Supper.

Impanel. See *Empanel*.

Imparifyllabical, not of an equal number of Syllables in oblique Cafes.

Imparity, (Lat.) inequality, unevennefs.

Impark, to enclofe Ground for a Park.

Imparlance, in Law, is a motion made in Court upon account of the Demandant by the Tenant, or Declaration of the Plantiff by the Defendant, whereby he craveth Refpite or another Day to put in his Anfwer.

Imparfonee, inducted, or put in Poffeffion of a Benefice.

Impartial, favouring neither Party, juft, uprightly, difinterefted.

Impartiality, Difinterestednefs.

Impaffable, not to be paft through.

Impaffibility, an uncapablenefs of fuffering.

Impaffible, that cannot fuffer.

Impatronization, a putting into poffeffion of a Benefice.

Impeach, to hinder; alfo to accufe as guilty of the fame Crime.

Impeachment, Accufation, or Information againft one.

Impeccability, (Lat.) a being uncapable of Sinning.

Impeccable, that cannot Sin.

Impede, to hinder, let, or stop.

Impediment, Hinderance, Disturbance, Obstruction.

Impell, to drive, or thrust forward; to force or egg on.

Impend, to hang over one's Head; also to spend or lay out Money.

Impendent, hanging over Head, at Hand.

Impenetrability, unsearchableness; also in Natural Philosophy, it is the distinction of one extended Substance from another, so that two Bodies extended cannot be in one and the same place, but must of necessity exclude each other.

Impenetrable, (Lat.) that cannot be pierced, discover'd, or fathomed.

Impenitence, a want of Repentance.

Impenitent, who does not repent, or is not sorry for his Sins.

Imperative Mood, in Grammer, implies a Command to such a one to do such a thing.

Imperceptible, which is not to be perceived.

Imperfect Flowers of Plants, are such as want the *Petala*, or those finely coloured little Leaves which stand round and compose the Flower.

Imperfect Numbers, are such whose aliquot-parts taken together, do either exceed or fall short of that whole Number of which they are parts.

Imperfect Plants, are by the Botanists such as either really want Flower and Seed, or seem to want them.

Imperfection, the want of something that is requisite or suitable to the Nature of the thing.

Imperforable, (Lat.) not to be bored through.

Imperial, (Lat.) belonging to an Emperor or Empire.

Imperial Table, is an Instrument made of Brass, with Box and Needle to measure Land.

Imperialists, the Subjects or Forces of the *German* Emperour.

Imperious, Commanding, Lordly, Haughty.

Impersonal Verbs, are such as are used only in the third Person Singular.

Impertinence,--cy, Extravagance, Foolery, Nonsense.

Impertinent, not to the purpose, absurd, silly.

Impervious, (Lat.) through which there is no Passage.

Impetigo, the Itch.

Impetrate, (Lat.) to obtain by earnest Request or Intreaty.

Impetuosity, a driving headlong with great Force and Violence.

Impetuous, violent, rapid, vehement.

Impiety (Lat.) Ungodliness, Wickedness.

Impignoration, a laying in Pawn.

Impinge,

Impinge, (Lat.) to hit or strike against.

Impious, Wicked, Ungodly.

Implacable, (Lat.) not to be appeased or pacified.

Implanting, a setting or fixing into.

Implead, in Common Law, is to sue, or commence a Suit.

Implements, is used for things of necessary use in any Trade; also for the Furniture of a House.

Implication,(Lat.) a folding or wrapping within, an entangling; also a necessary Consequence.

Implicit, tacitly understood, intricate, following by Consequence.

Implicite Faith, is a Faith altogether upheld and solely built upon the Judgment and Authority of others.

Imploration, (Lat.) an Imploring and Beseeching.

Imply, to pre-suppose, to infold, or contain.

Implore, (Lat.) to beg or cry out for, earnestly to beseech or crave.

Impolite, not polished, rude, rough.

Impolitick, disagreeing with the Rules of Policy, imprudent.

Imporcation, (Lat.) a making a baulk or ridge in the Ploughing of Land.

Imporous, a Term used in Natural Philosophy, and signifies without Pores, or having no Pores.

Import, Sense or Meaning; verbally, to mean or signifie; to concern; also, to bring Goods into a Port.

Importance, (Fr.) Moment, Weight, Consequence, a carrying in it some weighty matter.

Important, of great Weight and Moment.

Importation, the bringing in of Merchandizes from foreign Countries.

Importunacy,--ity, an eager Pressing or urging, hard dunning.

Importunate, (Lat.) troublesome or wearying with too frequent or unseasonable Requests.

Importune, to teaz, or vex, to request earnestly and often.

Importuous, without Port or Harbour.

Impose, to enjoyn, to lay a Tax, to lay upon; also to Cheat. In Printing, to set in order the Pages, and fix them in the Chace.

Imposition, an Injunction, a Deceiving, an Assessment or Tax.

Impossibility, (Lat.) that which cannot be done.

Impost, (Fr.) signifies Imposition, Custom, Tribute, and more particularly the Tax received by the Prince for such Merchandizes as are brought into any Haven from other Nations.

Impostor, (Lat.) a seller of false Wares; a Deceiver or Juggler, a Cheat.

Imposture,

Impoftume; a quantity of evil Humours gathered together into one part of the Body; whereof there are two kinds, one, when enflamed Blood, turned to corrupt Matter, fills fome place; the other, when without any Inflammation, Nature thrufts thofe Humours into fome part fit to receive them.

Impofture, a Deceiver, a Cheat.

Impotency, weaknefs, want of Power or Strength.

Impotent, (Lat.) weak, unable, maimed.

Impoverifh, (Fr.) to make Poor.

Impound, to put into a Pound or Enclofure for fome Trefpafs.

Impracticable, that can't be done.

Imprecate, (Lat.) to Curfe, to call down Mifchief.

Imprecation, a Curfing, or wifhing Evil to.

Impregnable, (Fr.) when a Town is fo well fortified that it cannot be forced, we fay 'tis *impregnable*.

Impregnate, to make fruitful, to caufe to fwell.

Impregnation, a making fruitful: In Chymiftry, when any body hath drunk in fo much moifture, or fo much of any Liquor that it will hold no more, we fay it is impregnated with fuch a Liquor.

Imprefe, (Ita.) an Emblem, Device with a Motto.

Imprefs,(Lat.)Print,Stamp,

Image: *Verbally*, to Print, Stamp, or make an Impreffion upon; alfo to compel Men to enter into publick Service.

Impreffion, a Printing Stamp or Mark; an Impreffion of Books, is that number of Books which is ufually printed off at the fame time.

Imprefs Money, is Money paid to Soldiers before hand.

Imprime, to roufe a wild Beaft; alfo to make her forfake the Herd.

Imprimery, (Law Term) an Impreffion or Print; alfo the Art of Printing, or a Printing Houfe.

Imprimis, (Lat.) firft of all, in the firft place.

Imprifon, (Fr.) to put in Prifon or Gaol.

Imprifonment, the reftraint of a Man's Liberty, whether in the open Field, in the Stocks, or in the common Gaol.

Improbability, an unlikelinefs of being true, or which cannot be proved.

Improbable, unlikely, which has no likelihood of being true.

Improbate, (Lat.) to difallow, difpraife or diflike.

Improbation, (Lat.) a difallowing or difproving of.

Improbity, (Lat.) Wickednefs, Lewdnefs.

Improper, a word that does not agree with a thing, or exprefs it fufficiently, is faid to be improper. A Stile becomes obfcure and unintel-

  G g   ligible

ligible when it makes use of improper words.

Impropriation, (Lat.) is a Parsonage or Ecclesiastical Living that is in the Hands of the Laity, or which descends by Inheritance.

Impropriator, he that has possession of a Spiritual Living by Inheritance.

Impropriety of Speech, is when the Writer or Speaker does not make use of proper and significant words.

Improvident, (Lat.) unheedful, void of forecast.

Improvement, an advancing of Profits, a thriving, a benefiting in any kind of Profession.

Imprudence, (Lat.) a want of Precaution, Deliberation and Fore-sight of the Consequences of things.

Impudence, (Lat.) Shamelessness, want of Modesty.

Impugn, (Lat.) to contest a Doctrine or Thing, to endeavour to disprove it by Argument.

Impuissance, (Fr.) want of strength or means to succeed in an Affair.

Impulse, (Lat.) a thrusting, pushing, or driving forward.

Impulsion, (Lat.) a thrusting forward, a driving on.

Impulsive, that drives or thrusts forward.

Impunity, (Lat.) lack of Punishment, Pardon.

Impurity, (Lat.) Uncleanness.

Imputation, (Lat.) a laying to one's Charge.

Impute, to Ascribe, to Charge, to lay the Blame or Fault on one.

Inability, (Fr.) a not being able or capable.

Inaccessible, (Lat.) not to be come at.

Inadequate Ideas, are such as are but a partial and incompleat representation of those Archetypes or Images, to which the Mind refers them.

Inadvertency, (Lat.) a not sufficiently observing, a want of Heed or Care.

Inaffable, (Lat.) uncourteous, unpleasant in Conversation.

Inaffectation, (Lat.) carelesness, or freeness from vain Glory.

Inalieneable, which cannot be alineated or transferred to another by Law.

Inamissible, (Lat) that can't be lost.

Inamorato, (It.) a Lover.

Inamoured, fallen in Love.

Inanimate, (Lat.) without Life or Soul.

Inanition, Emptiness, Weakness, for want of Nourishment; also Emptying

Inanity, (Lat.) is the School Term for Emptiness, or absolute Vacuity, and implies the absence of all Body and Matter whatsoever.

Inappetency, (Lat.) want of a Stomach for Victuals.

Inarable, (Lat.) not arable, not to be ploughed.

Inarticulate, (Lat.) indistinct, confused, not articulate.

Inartificial,

Inartificial, (Lat.) withou Art, Unworkmanly, Artlefs.

Inaudible, (Lat.) not to be heard.

Inaugurate, (Lat.) to confult the Sooth Sayers; alfo to Dignifie or Ennoble one, to inveft one with a Place of Truft or Honour; alfo to Confecrate.

Inaurated, (Lat.) covered over with Gold, gilded over.

Inaufpicious, unlucky, illboding.

Inborow, and *Outborow*, an Office formerly for obferving and allowing the Paffage of thofe that travell'd to and again between *England* and *Scotland*.

Incalefcence, (Lat.) is the growing hot of a thing by fome internal Motion or Fermentation.

Incalefcent, a Term apply'd to a thing growing hot by fome internal Motion or Fermentation.

Incantation, an inchanting, or charming,

Incantator, an Inchanter or Charmer.

Incapacious, not fit or large enough to hold or contain a thing.

Incapacity, (Lat.) the not having Qualities or Parts fufficient or neceffary to be in a condition to do or receive a thing.

Incapacitate, to make uncapable, put out of Capacity.

Incarceration, Imprifoning.

Incarnate, to bring Flefh upon, or fill up with new Flefh.

Incarnation, a taking of Flefh, a bringing on of Flefh; alfo a deep, rich or bright Carnation Colour.

Incarnative, that caufes Flefh to grow.

Incartation, a Chymical Term, and fignifies the Purification of Gold by means of Silver and *Aqua Fortis*.

Incaftelled, (Fr.) narrowheel'd, or Hoof-bound.

Incendiary, (Lat.) a Firebrand, a fetter of Houfes on Fire, a fower of Divifion and Strife.

Incenfe, (Lat.) to fet on fire, to inflame, to ftir up to Anger; alfo the beft Frankinfcenfe, or a rich Perfume made ufe of for facred ufes.

Incenfory, a Cenfer or perfuming Pan.

Incentive, (Lat.) a ftirring up, or provoking, a motive.

Incentor, (Lat.) the fame as *Incendiary*; which fee.

Inception, (Lat.) a begining or enterprize.

Inceptive of Magnitude, is a word ufed by Dr. *Wallis*, expreffing fuch Moments or firft Principles as tho' of no Magnitude themfelves are yet capable of producing fuch.

Inceration, is a mixture of moifture with fomething that is dry, by a gentle foaking till the Subftance be brought to the confiftence of foft Wax.

Inceffant, (Lat.) continual, without ceafing.

Inceffantly, without ceafing.

Inceft, (Lat.) did fignifie all kind of Pollution or Uncleannefs committed by undoing or untying the Girdle called *Ceftus* or *Zona*; but now in a more ftrict acceptation it fignifies that kind of Uncleannefs which is comitted between two near of kin.

Inceftuous, given to, or guilty of Inceft.

Inchain, to put in Chains or Fetters.

Inchanter, a Wizzard, Sorcerer, or Conjurer.

Inchantment, a Charm.

Inchafe, to fet in Gold, Silver, &c.

Inchoate, (Lat.) to begin, or take his beginning.

Inchoation, (Lat.) a beginning any Work.

Incident, (Lat.) happening to, or falling out occafionally.

Incident, in Common Law, a thing neceffarily depending upon another as more Principal.

Incident Angle, or *the Angle of Incidence*, in Opticks, is that Angle which the incident or falling Ray makes with a Perpendicular erected at the Point of Incidence, or a that Point where the Ray meets the Body upon which it falls.

Incineration, is the reducing the Bodies of Vegetables and Animals into Afhes by a violent Fire.

Incipient, beginning.

Incircle, to encompafs.

Incifion, (Lat.) a cutting deep into a thing, a gafh.

Incifure, a Cut or Gafh.

Incitation, (Lat.) a ftirring up or provoking.

Incitement, Inducement, Motive.

Incivility, (Lat.) rudenefs in Words and Behaviour.

Inclemency, (Lat.) Unmercifulnefs, Unpitifulnefs, alfo Rigour, Sharpnefs.

Inclination, a bowing downward, a natural Difpofition to a thing.

Inclination, in Mathematicks, is taken for the leaning of Lines or Planes towards one another.

Inclofe, to furround with a Wall to fhut in, to fence about, to contain.

Incloyftered, fhut up in a Monaftery.

Include, (Lat.) to take in, to comprehend, to contain.

Inclufion, (Lat.) an inclofing or fhutting in.

Inclufive, that comprehends or takes in.

Incogitancy, (Lat.) a want of Thought, Rafhnefs, Inconfideratenefs.

Incogitative, not thinking, heedlefs, rafh.

Incognito, (Lat.) unknown.

Incoherent, that hangs, or agrees not well together.

Incolumity, (Lat.) Safety, Freedom from Danger.

Incombuftible, that cannot be burned or confumed by Fire.

Incom-

Incommensurable, that cannot be measured.

Incommensurable Quantities, are Quantities between which there is no common Measure of the kind can be found; thus the *Diagonal* and Side of a Square are incommensurable Lines. *In Power,* when between their Squares also there can be found no *Area* that can be a common Measure or exactly measure both, *&c. ad infinitum.*

Incommode, (Lat.) to cause an Inconvenience, to prejudice or hurt.

Incommodious, unprofitable, unfit, troublesome, offensive.

Incommunicable, not to be made common, or imparted to others.

Incompact, (Lat.) not close joyned or faftened together.

Incomparable, (Lat.) without compare, excellent.

Incompaffionate, void of Pity.

Incompatibility, (Lat.) Antipathy, Contrariety.

Incompatible, (Lat.) difagreeing, not enduring one another.

Incompenfable, (Lat.) uncapable of being recompenfed.

Incompetency, Infufficiency, Inability.

Incompetent, incapable, not qualified; unfit, improper.

Incompetible, unfuitable, that agrees not.

Incomplex, (Lat.) uncompounded, fingle, fimple.

Incompliance, a not confenting, or not bearing with.

Incompofed, not orderly,

uncouth, neglected, ill-favoured.

Incompoffible, that can't confift with.

Incompofure, Confufion, Diforder.

Incomprehenfible, that cannot be comprehended or conceived in the Mind.

Inconceivable, not to be conceived, or imagined.

Inconcinnity, (Lat.) an ill Grace, Unhandfomenefs, Difproportion.

Incongealable, (Lat.) that cannot be frozen.

Incongruity, (Lat.) a Difagreeablenefs, an Unfitnefs.

Incongruous, unfit, difagreeable.

Inconnexion, a Defect in joining things together, want of Coherence.

Inconfequency, Weaknefs of arguing, when the Conclufion follows not from the Premiffes.

Inconfequent, that does not follow.

Inconfiderable, (Lat.) of fmall account, not worthy of Regard.

Inconfiderate, (Lat.) rafh, unadvifed.

Inconfideration, Want of Thought.

Inconfiftence, a not agreeing, fuiting or comporting.

Inconfolable, (Lat.) that cannot be comforted.

Inconftancy, wavering, Unfteddinefs, Unchangeablenefs.

Inconftant, (Lat.) wavering, fickle, uncertain.

In-

Incontinency, (Lat.) a not containing one's self from unlawful Defires.

Incontinently, prefently, immediately.

Inconvenience, Trouble, crofs Accident, Difficulty.

Inconverfable, unfociable, unfit for Converfation.

Inconvertible, (Lat.) that can't be tranfpofed or converted.

Incorporate, (Lat.) to mix or unite two or more Subftances together; alfo to admit to a Society.

Incorporeal, (Lat.) without Body, or having no Body.

Incorporeity, the Condition of that which is incorporeal.

Incorrect, not correct, faulty.

Incorrigible, (Lat.) obftinate, paft Correction.

Incorruptible, (Lat.) not fubject to Corruption or Decay.

Incounter, Meeting, Fight.

Incraffation, (Lat.) a making thick or grofs.

Increate, (Lat.) not made, or created.

Incredible, (Lat.) not to be believed.

Incredulous, hard of Belief, that will not believe.

Increment, (Lat.) an Increafe, a growing or waxing bigger; a Term frequently ufed in the new Method of *Fluxions,* and fignifies the infinitely fmall Increafe of a Line growing bigger by Motion.

Increpation, (Lat.) Chiding, Rebuke.

Increffant, (Lat.) a Term in Heraldry, fignifying the Moon paft the New, and not come to the Full.

Incruftation, (Lat.) a making or becoming hard on the outfide like a Cruft, a rough cafting, a pargetting.

Incubation, (Lat.) a lying upon, a fitting, a Brooding.

Incubus, a Difeafe called the *Night Mare,* when a Man in his Sleep fuppofes he has a great Weight lying on him, and feels himfelf almoft ftrangled; in fuch fort that he can neither turn himfelf, fit up, nor call for Help.

Inculcation, (Lat.) a driving or thrufting in, a repeating often, and as it were beating into one's head.

Inculpable, (Lat.) unblameable, not to be blamed.

Incumbent, (Lat.) leaning, lying, or refting upon; alfo he that is in prefent Poffeffion of a Benefice.

Incumbrance, Hindrance, Clog.

Incur, (Lat.) to run upon or into, as to incur one's Difpleafure, is to difpleafe one.

Incurable, that can't be healed or cured.

Incurfion, (Lat.) a running into, or hitting againft; alfo an Inroad of Soldiers into an Enemy's Country.

Incurvation, (Lat.) a crooking or bending.

Incuffion, (Lat.) a violent fhaking or dafhing againft.

In

Indagation, (Lat.) a diligent searching or enquiring into.

Indecency, Unbecomingness.

Indecent, (Lat.) unbecoming, unfitting.

Indecimable, not Tithable, not liable to pay Tithes.

Indeclinable, (Lat.) not to be declined or shunned; also in Grammar, a Noun is indeclinable which varies not the Cases.

Indecorous, (Lat.) unhandsome, unseemly.

Indefatigable, (Lat.) unwearied not to be wearied.

Indefeasible, (Fr.) that can't be defeated, or made void.

Indefinite, (Lat.) is what has no Bounds or Limits determined, or what is considered as not having any.

Indelible, (Lat.) not to be cancelled or blotted out.

Indemnify, to save harmless.

Indemnity, (Lat.) an escaping harmless, a being saved from Danger or Harm.

Indemonstrable, that can't be prov'd or demonstrated.

Indented, a Term in Heraldry, when the out Line of a Bordure, out Line, &c. is in the form of the Teeth of a Saw.

Indenture, is a Writing comprising some Writing between two, and being indented in the top answerable to another that likewise contains the same Contract.

Independency, (Lat.) a not depending upon another, Absoluteness of one's self.

Independents, a Sect amongst us who first appear'd in *England* about the Year 1643. They hold that Churches should not be subordinate as Parochial to Provincial, and Provincial to National, but co-ordinate without Superiority.

Indetermined, not determined, not decided.

Index, a Token or Mark to shew and direct; also the Exponent of a Logarithm or Power is so called. See *Exponent*; also a Table of a Book.

Indication, a word used in Physick and Surgery, and signifies a Discovery of what is to be done, and what Course is to be taken for the Recovery of the Patient's Health; as if on Examination, bleeding be found necessary, they say bleeding is indicated.

Indicative Mood, in Grammar, is that Mood which barely affirms and no more.

Indicavit, is the Name of a Writ, by which the Patron of a Church may remove a Suit commenced against his Clerk from the Court Christian to the King's Court.

Indict, to impeach, accuse, to prefer a Bill against.

Indiction. See *Cycle of Indiction*.

Indictment, in Law, is a Presentment of those who

G g 4   have

have committed any illegal Trefpafs.

Indifference, as it is generally taken, fignifies a carelefs and unconcerned Way and Behaviour.

Indifferent, (Lat.) of fmall Concern, not material; cold, or without Affection; alfo pretty good, paffable, ordinary.

Indigence, (Lat.) Need or Want.

Indigent, (Lat.) needy, poor.

Indigitate, to point at, to fhew.

Indignation, (Lat.) Anger.

Indignity, (Lat.) Unworthinefs, Bafenefs, Infamy, Difgrace.

Indirect Practices, are ill Practices, or under-hand Dealings.

Indifcerpible, that can't be rent or divided.

Indifcretion, want of Difcretion or Prudence.

Indifcriminate, not feparated, diftinguifh'd, or differenced.

Indifpenfable, that cannot be difpenfed with, but is of abfolute Neceffity, and admits of no Excufe.

Indifpofition, (Lat.) a being difordered, or not in perfect Health.

Indifputable, not to be queftioned or difputed.

Indiffolvable, (Lat.) that cannot be diffolved.

Indiffoluble, (Lat.) that can't be loofed, broken, or undone.

Indiftinct, (Lat.) confufed difordered.

Indite, to compofe or deliver Matter to one that writeth; alfo the fame with *Indict*.

Individual, the fame, one only, not to be divided.

Indivifible, which cannot be divided.

Indivifibles, in Geometry, are fuch Elements or Principles as any Body or Figure may be fuppofed to be ultimately refolved into, as a Line into Points, a Surface into Lines, a folid into Surfaces.

Indocible, *Indocile*, that can't be taught, dull.

Indoctrinate, to teach, or inftruct.

Indolency, (Lat.) having no Apprehenfion of Grief, or feeling no Pain.

Indorfed, a Law Term, and fignifies writ on the backfide.

Indorfement, the Writing upon the back of a Conveyance, Obligation, or other Deed.

Indow, to beftow a Dower; to fettle Rents or Revenues upon.

Indraught, a Gulph or Bay that runs in between Lands.

Indubitable, not to be queftioned paft, all doubt.

Inducement, (Fr.) a Perfwafion or Motive to a thing.

Induciary, belonging to a Truce or League.

Induciate, immediate, next; as induciate Heir.

Indu—

Inducted, that has receiv'd Induction.

Induction, a leading into; in Logick 'tis taken for a kind of Argumentation or imperfect Syllogism; in Law it is taken for the giving Possession to an Incumbent of his Church, by leading him into it, and delivering him the Keys.

Indue, to qualify, supply, or furnish.

Indulgence, (Lat.) Fondness, Gentleness; also Pardon, Forgiveness.

Indult, or *Indulto,* a special Grant of the Pope to do or obtain something contrary to the Canon Law.

Indurable, tolerable, sufferable.

Induration, (Lat.) a making hard.

Industry, (Lat.) Pains taking, Labour, Diligence.

Inebriation, (Lat.) a making drunk, or being drunk.

Inedia, (Lat.) an abstaining from Meat, when one eats less than formerly.

Ineffable, unspeakable, that cannot be uttered or expressed.

Ineffective, of no effect, vain, fruitless.

Inefficacious, of no Force, or Virtue.

Inenarrable, (Lat.) that can't be related.

Ineptitude, (Lat.) Silliness, Fondness; also Unaptness.

Inequality, (Lat.) Unequalness, Unevenness.

Inergetical, sluggish, unactive.

Inerrable, that cannot err.

Inert, (Lat.) sluggish, unfit for Action.

Inescation, (Lat.) deceiving, inveigling.

Inescutcheon, in Heraldry, is an *Escutcheon* containing of the Field, and is born as an Ordinary, thus; *Ermin,* an *Inescutcheon Gules;* also an *Escutcheon of Pretence.*

In esse, (Lat.) in Being, Law Phrase, what is apparent and has a real Being.

Inestimable, which cannot, or is of too high a Price to be valued.

Inevitable, (Lat.) not to be shunned or avoided.

Inexcusable, (Lat.) not to be excused.

Inexhaustible, (Lat.) not to be drawn out or emptied.

Inexorable, (Lat.) that is not to be intreated, or will not be intreated, obdurate.

Inexpedient, not convenient or fit.

Inexperience, want of trying, or Skill.

Inexpiable, (Lat.) unappeasable, irreconcilable, not to be purged from Sin, never to be satisfied for.

Inexplicable, (Lat.) which cannot be unfolded or explained.

Inexpressible, that cannot be utter'd or expressed.

Inexpugnable, (Lat.) not to be taken, or won by force, impregnable. *Inex-*

Inextinguishable, not to be put out, or quenched.

Inextirpable, (Lat.) not to be rooted out.

Inextricable, (Lat.) that of which one cannot rid himself or get out of.

Inexuperable, (Lat.) that cannot be surpass'd or overcome.

Inextricable, not to be disentangled. *Milton.*

Infallibility, (Lat.) an Impossibility to be deceiv'd.

Infallible, that cannot be deceived.

Infamous, of evil Report, scandalous, base.

Infamy, (Lat.) Reproach or ill Report.

Infancy, (Lat.) Childhood.

Infangthefe, (Sax.) a Privilege of Lords of certain Manours to pass Judgment upon Theft committed by their Servants within their Jurisdiction.

Infante, all the Sons of the Kings of *Spain* and *Portugal* are so called, except the eldest, as the Daughters in like manner *Infanta.*

Infanticide, killing or murthering of Infants.

Infantry, the Footmen or Foot Soldiers of an Army so called.

Infatigable, (Lat.) not to be wearied or tired.

Infatuation, (Lat.) a besotting, or making foolish.

Infect, to communicate to another Corruption, Poison, or Pestilence.

Infection, (Lat.) Plague, Corruption.

Infectious, apt to infect, tainting, catching.

Infecundity, (Lat.) Barrenness, Unfruitfulness.

Infeeble, to weaken.

Infelicity, (Lat.) Unhappiness.

Infeoff, to unite, or joyn to the Fee.

Infeoffment, a Settlement in Fee.

Inference, a Conclusion, a Consequence, or a way of inferring.

Inferiour, (Lat.) lower, of a meaner Degree.

Infernal, belonging to Hell, low, neathermost.

Infernal Stone, a Caustick us'd by Surgeons; the *Lunar* Caustick.

Infertility, Barrenness, Unfruitfulness.

Infest, (Lat.) to hurt, trouble, indamage.

Infibulation, a buttoning, or Clasping.

Infidel, (Lat.) a Heathen, or one who believes nothing of the Christian Religion.

Infidelity, Unfaithfulness, a Failure in the Performance of a Man's Word or Oath.

Infinite, what hath no Bounds, Terms or Limits.

Infinitive Mood, in Grammar, is when a Verb is used so as to determine neither any particular Person nor Number.

Infinity, Endlesness, Unmeasurableness.

Infirmary, an Apartment for sick People, in a Monastery, or Hospital.

Infirmity,

Infirmity, weakness, indisposedness.

Infistulated, turn'd to, or full of Fistulaes.

Infix, to fix, or fasten into.

Inflammable, apt to catch fire.

Inflammation, a swelling with Heat, Redness, Beating, and Pain.

Inflation, (Lat.) a puffing up, a windy swelling.

Inflection, (Lat.) a bending; by the *Inflection* of the Rays of Light, is meant a bending or turning of them from their Rectilineal Course, which happens before they actually touch the Surfaces of Bodies or different Mediums. *Point* of *Inflection,* in Mathematicks, is that Point where the Curve begins to bend back again a contrary way to what it did before, or that Point where a Curve before concave towards its *Axis* begins to bend and grow convex towards the same *Axis.*

Inflexibility, Stiffness, Obstinacy.

Infliction, (Lat.) a laying a Punishment upon, a smiting.

Influence, (Lat.) a flowing or running into; most commonly taken for the effect which the heat of the Sun or Stars have upon things here below.

Influx, (Lat.) a flowing in.

Infold, to fold or wrap up.

Inforcement, a Constraining or Compulsion,

Information, (Lat.) informing or making known.

In forma Pauperis, is a having Clerks and Council assign'd without Fees, upon Affidavit made that your Debts being paid you are not worth five Pounds.

Informatus non sum, an Attorney's formal Answer in Court when he hath no more to say in defence of his Client.

Informed Stars, are such of the fixed Stars as are not cast into, or ranged under any form.

Informous, without Shape or Fashion.

Infortunes, Saturn and *Mars,* are so termed of Astrologers, because of their unlucky Influences.

Infranchise, (Fr.) to set free, to make a Free-man, to incorporate into a Society.

Infranchisement, a setting Free, Discharge, Release.

Infrangible, (Lat.) not to be broken, durable, strong.

Infrequent, (Lat.) uncommon, rare, seldom happening.

Infringe, (Lat.) to break to pieces, to break a Law, Custom or Privilege.

Infucation, (Lat.) a painting of the Face, a colouring or disguising.

Infuscation, a making dark or dusky.

Infusion, (Lat.) a pouring in; it is used in Physick for a steeping of Roots or Leaves, or any kind of Medicine in some liquid Substance for a certain

certain time, till the chiefest of their Virtue be drawn out.

Ingemination, (Lat.) a doubling or repeating one thing twice.

Ingenerated, (Lat.) not begotten.

Ingenio, a House or Mill where Sugar is made.

Ingenui, among the Romans were such as had been born Free, and of Parents that had been always Free.

Ingenuity, (Lat.) ingeniousness, wittiness.

Ingenuous, frank, sincere, plain.

Ingeny, (Lat.) Genius, Disposition, Parts, &c.

Ingested, (Lat.) put in.

Ingineer, is an able experienced Man, who by the help of Geometry delineates upon Paper, or marks upon the Ground all sorts of Forts and other Works, proper for Offence and Defence.

Inglorious, (Lat.) without Glory.

Ingot, a Wedg or Mass of Gold or Silver.

Ingraft, to let a Shoot into the Stock of a Tree, to implant, imprint, or fix.

Ingrailed, (Lat.) a Term in Heraldry; a Bordure *ingrailed*, is when the line of which the Bordure is made crooks inward toward the Field.

Ingrate, (Lat.) unthankful.

Ingratiate, to render acceptable.

Ingratitude, unthankfulness.

Ingredients, in Physick, are the several Parts or Simples that go to the making any Compound Medicine, and in general it signifies the constituent Parts or Principles of any mixed Body.

Ingress, in Astronomy, signifies the Sun's entring the first Scruple of one of the four Cardinal Signs; in general it signifies an entring into.

Ingressu, is a Writ of Entry whereby a Man seeketh entry into Lands and Tenements.

Ingross, to write over fair in great Characters; also to buy up all of a Commodity, to forestal.

Ingrosser, in Common Law, is one that buys Corn growing, or dead Victuals to sell again.

Ingurgitation, (Lat.) greedy swallowing, devouring.

Inhabitable, generally signifies not to be inhabited or dwelt in; tho' Inhabitant signifies one that dwells or inhabits in such or such a place.

Inherent, sticking to, or abiding in.

Inheritance, in Common Law, is a perpetuity of Lands and Tenements to a Man and his Heirs.

Inhesion, (Lat.) a sticking or cleaving unto.

Inhibition, a forbidding; in Law, it is a Writ to inhibit or forbid a Judge from further proceeding in a
Cause

Cauſe depending before him.

Inhoneſtation, (Lat.) a diſparaging or diſgracing.

Inhoſpitality, (Lat.) rudeneſs to Strangers, giving no entertainment to them.

Inhumanity, (Lat.) unkindneſs, cruelty, incivility.

Inhumation, (Lat.) a burying, or putting under Ground.

Injection, (Lat.) a caſting in : In Phyſick it is a caſting of any liquid Medicine into Wounds or Cavities of the Body by Syringe, &c.

Inimitable, (Lat.) not to be imitated or followed.

Iniquity, (Lat.) want of Equity, Injuſtice, Partiality.

Initial, (Lat.) beginning.

Initiate, to admit into any Order or Faculty, to enter or begin.

Initiation, the entring or admiting one into any Order or Faculty.

Injucundity, Unpleaſantneſs.

Injudicious, void of Judgment.

Injunction, (Lat.) an injoyning or commanding. In Common Law, it is a Writ grounded upon an interlocutory Order in Chancery, ſometimes to give Poſſeſſion to the Plaintiffs for want of the Defendants Appearance; ſometimes to the King's ordinary Court; and ſometimes to the Court-Chriſtian to ſtay Proceedings in a Cauſe upon Suggeſtions made, that the rigour of the Law, if it

take place, is againſt Equity and Conſcience in that Caſe.

Injurious, wrongful, againſt Right and Law.

Injuſtice, (Lat.) acting contrary to Juſtice ; unfair Dealing.

Inkindle, to light, to ſet on fire.

Inkling, an intimation, a hint.

Inlagary, in Common Law, is a reſtitution of one Out-law'd to the King's Protection, and to the Benefit or Eſtate of a Subject.

Inland, upon the main Land, far from the Sea.

Inlarge, to make large, to write or diſcourſe at large.

Inlay, a Term among Artificers, and ſignifies a laying of coloured Wood in Wainſcoat-works, Bedſteads, Scrutores, &c. or a laying of Gold and Silver in other Metals.

Inleaſed, (Fr.) catched in a Gin, ſnared, intangled.

Inlet, an Entrance or Paſſage into.

Inly, intirely, intimately. *Spencer.*

Inmate, a Lodger.

Inn, a Publick Houſe for entertaining Strangers or Travellers.

Inns of Chancery, Houſes appointed for young Students of Law, eight in number, *viz. Bernard's, Clement's, Clifford's, Furnival's, Lion's, New, Staple,* and *Thavy's Inn.*

Inns of Court, four other Houſes or Colleges for Entertainment

tertainment of Students in the Law, *viz. Gray's-Inn, Lincoln's-Inn*, and the Inner and Middle *Temples*, to which was added the Outer *Temple*.

Inn, to lodge at an Inn; also to lay up in a Store-House.

Innate, inbred; Innate Ideas or Principles, are Ideas or Principles stamped upon the Soul at its first make, and which it brings into the World with it.

Innavigable, that can't be sail'd on.

Innings, Lands by draining and banking gain'd from the Sea.

Innocence, (Lat.) Purity of the Soul.

Innocents-Day, the 28th of *December*, kept in remembrance of *Herod's* slaying the Children, call'd otherwise *Childermas*.

Innocuous, (Lat.) harmless, doing no hurt.

Innovation, (Lat.) a making new; also a bringing in of new Customs or Opinions.

Innoxious, harmless.

Innuendo, a word frequently used in Writs, Declarations and Pleadings, and its use is only to declare and ascertain the Person or Thing which was named or left doubtful before.

Innumerable, (Lat.) not to be numbred.

Inoculation, is a kind of Grafting by insertion of a Bud of one kind of Fruit Tree into the Bark of another, so as to make different kinds of Fruit grow on the same Tree, and the same common Sap supply them all.

Inodorous, without Scent, or Smell.

Inofficious, discourteous, disobliging.

Inopinate, (Lat.) sudden, unexpected.

Inordinate, out of Order, Extravagant, Immoderate.

Inorganical, wanting Organs or Instruments proper for any Motion or Operation.

Inosculation, the joining of the Mouths of the Capillary Veins and Arteries.

In Posse, (Lat.) in Law, that which is not, but may be.

Inquest, Search, Inquiry, especially made by a Jury; also the Jury it self.

Inquietude, (Lat.) restlesness, want of Repose or quiet of Mind.

Inquination, (Lat.) a staining or defiling.

Inquirendo, is an Authority given to a Person or Persons to inquire into something for the King's Advantage.

Inquisition, (Lat.) a diligent Search or Inquiry, a strict Examination; a Tribunal or Court erected by the Popes for the examining of those whom they call Hereticks.

Inqui-

Inquisitive, Curious, Prying.

Inquisitor, a Sheriff, a Coroner; also a Judge of the bloody Inquisition.

Inroad, Invasion of a Country.

Inrollment, a Regiſtring, Recording or Entring of any lawful Act in the Rolls of the Chancery, Exchequer, King's-Bench, or Common-Pleas, &c.

Insatiable, not to be satisfied.

Insatiate, or *Insatiable*, that can't have enough.

Insconsed, is part of an Army fortified with a Sconce or small Fort in order to defend some Pass.

Inscribe, to write in, to draw one Figure within another.

Inscription, (Lat.) a Title, Name, or Character Written or Engraven over any thing.

Inscrutable, (Lat.) not to be found out by searching; hidden, myſterious.

Insculp, to Engrave, Carve, or Cut.

Insect, the ſmalleſt ſort of Animal, as the Fly, Bee, or Ant, either not divided into Joints as other Creatures, or, as it were, divided between the Head and the Body.

Insectator, a Railer, a Slanderer, an Adverſary at Law.

Insection, (Lat.) a cutting into.

Insensate, ſenſeleſs, fooliſh.

Insensible, (Lat.) not to be perceived; also nor having any Senſe.

Inseparable, (Lat.) not to be ſevered or parted.

Insertion, (Lat.) a putting, planting, or grafting in.

Insiccation, (Lat.) a drying.

Insidious, (Lat.) deceitful, treacherous.

Insignificant, inconſiderable, uſeleſs, vain.

Insimulation, (Lat.) an accuſing or impeaching.

Insinuation, (Lat.) a winding one's ſelf in by degrees, a getting into Favour by degrees; also an Intimation or ſlight touch of a thing.

Insipid, (Lat.) without Taſte or Reliſh.

Insist, (Lat.) to urge, to ſtay upon.

Insition, the Botanick word for Grafting; it ſignifies in general, the inſertion and uniting of any Cyon, Bud, &c. into the ſubſtance of the Stock, and is of divers kinds.

Insociable, unconverſable, unfit for Society.

Insolation, (Lat.) a bleaching, or laying a thing in the Sun.

Insolent, (Lat.) Haughty, Proud, Preſumptuous.

Insoluble, (Lat.) that cannot be looſed or undone.

Insolvent, unable to pay.

Inspection, (Lat.) a prying or looking into narrowly.

Inspersion, (Lat.) a ſprinkling on.

Inspeximus, are Letters Patent, ſo called, becauſe they begin

begin after the King's Title with this word *Inspeximus*.

Inspiration, (Lat.) a breathing into; also a being mov'd by the Spirit and Finger of God to speak and act in an extraordinary manner.

Inspirit, to put Life or Courage into.

Inspissate, to thicken or make thick.

Instability, (Lat.) unsteddiness, inconstancy.

Installment, putting in possession of an Office or Benefice.

Instance, Entreaty, Motion; also an Example.

Instant, is such a part of Duration in which we perceive no Succession; or it is that which takes up the time of only one Idea in our Minds without the succession of another, wherein we perceive no Succession at all; a putting one into the Possession of a Place or Benefice.

Instauration, (Lat.) a restoring, renewing, repairing, re-edifying.

Instigation, (Lat.) a stirring or pricking on, an incouragement or inticement.

Instill, (Lat.) gently to infuse or pour in; also to infuse false Notions and Opinions.

Instinct, an inward stirring or Motion, a natural bent or inclination to a thing.

Institute, (Lat.) to Enact, Decree or Establish.

Institution, Establishment; also Teaching, Education; also putting a Clerk in possession of the Spirituality of a Benefice.

Institutions, Ordinances, Precepts, or Commandments, and particularly part of the first of the four Tomes of the Civil Law, and is a compendium of the Digest drawn into four Books, composed on purpose by the Emperor *Justinian* for the use of young Students.

Instructions, Directions in any Business.

Instrument, a Tool to work with; also a publick Act, Deed, or Writing.

Instrumental, (Lat.) belonging to an Instrument, Tool or Implement; also furthering or helping in the doing of a thing.

Insuccation, moistening of Aloes, &c. with juice of *Violets*, *Roses*, &c.

Insular, belonging to an Island.

Insult, (Lat.) to leap for Joy; also to domineer, to vaunt or vapour over one.

Insuperable, (Lat.) not to be vanquished or overcome.

Insupportable, (Lat.) not to be born or endured.

Insurance, Security given to make good Ships, Goods, Houses, &c.

Insurmountable, not to be overcome.

Insurrection, (Lat.) a rising against, a popular Tumult.

Intabulate, (Lat.) to write in Tables.

Intacta, (Lat.) are right Lines to which Curves do continually approach, and yet can never meet with them.

Integer, whole, intire; in Arithmetick, it fignifies a whole number in contradiftinction to Fractions, or broken Numbers.

Integral, whole.

Integration, (Lat.) a making whole.

Integrity, Honefty, Uprightnefs, Sincerity.

Integument, (Lat.) a Covering, a Cloak, a Difguife, or Pretence.

Intellect, (Lat.) the Faculty of the Soul which is ufually called the Underftanding.

Intellectual, (Lat.) belonging to the Intellect, Spiritual.

Intelligence, (Lat.) Knowledge, Underftanding; alfo the Correfpondence that Statefmen and Merchants hold in Foreign Countries; it is alfo taken for a Spiritual Being.

Intelligible, (Lat.) that may be underftood or apprehended.

Intemperance, (Lat.) unablenefs to rule and moderate a Man's Appetite and Lufts, immoderate Defire, Excefs.

Intemperature, an excefs of one or more Qualities in the Air, or Humours of Man's Body.

Intempeftive, (Lat.) unfeafonabley out of time.

Intendant, one that has the Infpection, Conduct and Direction of certain Affairs.

Intendment, Meaning, Purpofe.

Intenebrate, (Lat.) to endarken, or obfcure.

Intenerate, (Lat.) to make tender.

Intenfe, (Lat.) ftretched out to the utmoft, as intenfly hot, or intenfly cold, is hot or cold to a very great degree.

Intenfion, in Law, is a Writ that lies againft him, that enters after the Death of Tenant in Dower, or other Tenant for life, and holds him out in the reverfion or remainder.

Intenfion, in Natural Philofophy, fignifies the increafe of the Power, or energy of any Quality, as *Heat* and *Cold*, &c.

Intenfively, (Lat.) extreamly, in the higheft degree.

Intent, Meaning, Defign, Drift.

Intentional, belonging to the Intention.

Intercalation, (Lat.) is a putting in of a Day into the Month of *February* in Leap Year.

Intercede, (Lat.) to come between, to pray for one, or to ufe his Power and Intereft to procure one a Favour for another.

Intercepted-Axe, a Term in Conick Sections, and is the fame with *abfciffa*: In general this word fignifies taken up by the way; forestalled, incroached.

Intercession, an entreating in behalf of another.

Intercessor, (Lat.) a Pleader, or Mediator.

Interchange, to exchange between Parties.

Interchangeably, mutually, or by turns.

Intercision, (Lat.) a cutting off between or in the midst.

Interclusion, a shutting up, or stopping up between.

Intercolumniation, (Lat.) is the space or distance between the two Pillars of any Building.

Intercommoning, (Law Term) is for Cattel to feed promiscuously on two adjoyning Commons.

Intercostal, between the Ribs, as *Intercostal Veins* and *Arteries* are *Veins* and *Arteries* that run along the Intervals and Spaces between the lower and upper Ribs.

Intercourse, mutual Traffick or Correspondence.

Intercurrent, (Lat.) running between.

Interdict, (Lat.) an Ecclesiastical Censure whereby the Church of *Rome* forbids the Administration of the Sacraments, and the performances of Divine Service to a Kingdom, Province, Town, &c.

Interdicted of Water and Fire, were in old Time those who for some Crime were banished, which Judgment altho' it was not by express Sentence pronounced, yet by

giving order that no Man should receive such an one into his House, but deny him Fire and Water, the two necessary Elements of Life, he was condemned as it were to a Civil Death, and this was called *Legitimum exilium*.

Interemption, (Lat.) a killing or slaying.

Interess, or *Interest*, to concern.

Interest, Concernment, Advantage, Credit, or Power; also Money paid for the use of a principal Sum.

Interfector, (Lat.) the killer; in *Astrology*, a destroyingPlanet plac'd in the eighth House of a Figure, either five Degrees before or twenty after the Cusp.

Interfere, (Fr.) to rub or dash one Heel against another; also to hit or fall foul upon one another, to clash.

Interfluent, (Lat.) flowing between.

Interjacent, (Lat.) lying between.

Interjection, (Lat.) a casting between: In Grammer, an *Interjection* is an indeclinable word used in a Sentence to declare the Affections or Passions of the Mind, and to compleat the Sense of it.

Interim, the mean while: Also a certain Deed containing a mixt Form of Doctrine tendred by the Emperor *Charles* V. at *Augsburg*, to be subscribed by both Protestants and Papists, and to be observed ferved until a general Council.

Interiour, (Lat.) inward, being on the infide.

Interlace, (Fr.) to twine or twift, to infert, or put amongft.

Interlard, to ftuff lean Meat with Fat.

Interleave, to put blank Paper between the Pages of a Book.

Inierlined, written between the lines.

Interlocution, a fpeaking between, or interruption of another's Difcourfe. In Law, an intermedial Sentence before a final Decifion.

Interlocutory Order, is that which decides not the Caufe, but only fettles fome intervening Matter relating to the Caufe.

Interlopers, in Common Law, are thofe that without legal Authority intercept the Trade of a Company.

Interlucation, in Husbandry, a lopping off Branches, to let in light between.

Interlude, (Lat.) a Play or Comedy; that which is fung or acted between the Acts.

Interlunary, (Lat.) belonging to the Seafon between the going out of the Old and the coming in of the New Moon.

Intermeation, a flowing or paffing between.

Intermediate, that is, or lies between.

Intermeffes, Courfes fet on the Table between other Difhes.

Intermication, (Lat.) fhining between.

Interminable, boundlefs, endlefs.

Intermiffion, (Lat.) a putting between; alfo a defering, a leaving off to a while.

Intermitting Fever, the fame with Ague, fo called from its abating fome time, as one, two or three Days, and then returning again.

Intermixture, (Lat.) a mingling between, or amongft.

Intermural Space, a fpace between two Walls.

Internal, (Lat.) that is within, inward.

Internodium, in Botany, is the fpace contained between any two knots or joints of the Stalk of a Plant.

Internuntio, (Lat.) an Agent for the Court of *Rome* in the Courts of Forreign Princes, where there is no exprefs Nuncio in the fame.

Interpaffation, with Apothecaries, is ftitching of Bags at certain diftances, to keep the Medicines from falling together.

Interpellation, (Lat.) an interrupting or difturbing.

Interplication, (Lat.) an interfolding or folding between.

Interpolation, a furbifhing up of old things, new vamping up; alfo falfifying of an Original.

Interpofe, to put in or between for the reconciliation of two Parties.

Interpofition, (Lat.) an interpofing or putting between, an intermedling.

Interpretation, (Lat.) an Expounding, a Tranflating, a Commentary.

Interpunction, diftinguifhing by Pricks or Points, a Pointing.

Interre, to bury or lay under Ground.

Interregnum, (Lat.) the fpace of Government between the Death or Depofition of one King, and the Coronation or Election of another.

Interrogation, (Lat.) an asking or demanding a Queftion.

Interrogatives, in Grammer, are certain Particles which are made ufe of in the asking of a Queftion.

Interrogatories, Queftions put to Witneffes, that are examined.

Interruption, a troubling one in the midft of Bufinefs; a cutting one fhort in the middle of his Difcourfe; alfo Interruption is the fame with Disjunction of Proportion in Geometry.

Interfecants, in Heraldry, are pertranfient lines which crofs one another.

Interfection, (Lat.) a cutting in the midft; that point where two Lines, or that line where two Plains interfect one another.

Interfonant, (Lat.) founding between or in the middle.

Interfperfed, fprinkled here and there.

Interfperfion, (Lat.) a ftrewing or fcattering about.

Interfpinales Colli, are Mufcles of the Neck.

Interftellar, a word ufed by fome Authors to exprefs thofe parts of the Univerfe that are without and beyond our folar Syftem; and which are fuppofed as Planetary Syftems moving round each fixt Star, as the Center of their motion, as the Sun is of ours.

Interftice, (Lat.) a diftance or fpace between.

Interftitial, that hath a fpace between.

Intertrigo, is a cutting or fretting off of the skin of the Parts near the Fundament, or between the Thighs.

Interval, (Lat.) a fpace between, a paufe, a refpite; alfo the diftance or difference between any two Sounds, whereof one is more grave, and the other more acute.

Intervene, (Lat.) to come between.

Intervenient, (Lat.) coming or returning between.

Intervert, (Lat.) to turn afide, to convey a thing to his own ufe.

Interview, a meeting of great Perfons, a fight of one another.

Intervigilant, that is watchful, or that awakes now and then, or between whiles.

Inteftable,

Inteſtable, uncapable by Law to make any Will, or be taken for a Witneſs.

Inteſtate, a Man dying without making a Will, is ſaid to die *Inteſtate*.

Inteſtine, (Lat.) within, inward, lying within the Intrals, as inteſtine Motion is a motion of the inward parts of a Body.

Inteſtines, in Anatomy, are a long and large Pipe, which by ſeveral circumvolutions and turnings reaches from the *Pylorus* to the *Anus*; they are ſix times as long as the Body to which they appertain.

Inthral, to bring into Bondage, to Enſlave.

Inthronize, (Lat.) to inſtall in the Seat of Honour, to place in a Royal Throne.

Intimacy, ſtrict Friendſhip, great Familiarity.

Intimation, (Lat.) a hinting, ſignifying, or ſecret declaring.

Intimidate, (Lat.) to put in fear, to affrighten.

Intimidation, putting into fear, affrighting.

Intitulation, (Lat.) an Intitling, or adding a Title to a thing.

Intolerable, (Lat.) not to be born or endured.

Intonation, a giving of the Tone or Key by the Chanter to the reſt of the Choir.

Intoxicate, (Lat.) to Poiſon; alſo to Fuddle or make Drunk.

Intractable, (Lat.) not to be managed, wild, ſavage.

Intrado, (Spa.) an entrance to a place.

Intraneous, (Lat.) that is within, inward.

Intranſitive, (Lat.) in Grammar, that paſſes not from one to another; ſo a *Verb* is called when the Action paſſes not out of the Agent.

Intreague, is a Plot or Contrivance, or private Correſpondence which is unlawful; it is always uſed in a bad ſenſe.

Intrenched, an Army is ſaid to be intrenched when they have raiſed Works before them to fortifie themſelves againſt the Enemy, that they may not be forced to fight at a diſadvantage.

Intrenchments, are all ſort of Works made to fortifie a Poſt againſt an Enemy.

Intrepid, (Lat.) undaunted, without fear of danger.

Intrepidity, (Lat.) undauntedneſs.

Intricate, intangled, perplexed, difficult.

Intrigue, an intricacy, incumbrance; alſo a ſecret Deſign carried on with privacy.

Intrinſick, (Lat.) inward, ſecret, occult.

Introduction, (Lat.) a leading in; alſo a beginning or Preface to any Diſcourſe.

Introductory, that ſerves to introduce.

Introgreſſion, (Lat.) a going in.

Intromission, (Lat.) a letting or sending in.

Introruption, (Lat.) a rushing or breaking in by violence.

Introspection, (Lat.) a looking narrowly into.

Introsumption, a taking in, as of Aliment.

Intrude, to thrust rudely into a Company or Business.

Intrusion, (Lat.) a wrongfully thrusting into the Possession of a vacant thing; also a thrusting one's self into other People's Company, is called an *Intrusion*.

Intuition, (Lat.) a clear seeing into, a distinct beholding, or a perception of the certain agreement or disagreement of any two Ideas immediately compared together.

Intuitive, that beholds or considers.

Intumescence, (Lat.) a swelling, puffing, or rising up.

Invade, to set or come upon violently.

Invalid, (Lat.) weak, Feeble, of no Force or Strength.

Invalidity, (Lat.) Weakness, want of Force or Strength.

Invadiatus, in Law, is when one has been accused of some Crime, which being not fully proved, he is put *Sub debita fide jussione*, i. e. Suretyship.

Invariable, unchangeable, steadfast.

Invasion, (Lat.) an Assault or Attack.

Invected, a Term in Heraldry, and signifies the direct contrary to *Engrailed*; which see.

Invective, (Lat.) railing, sharp, virulent Words or Expressions.

Inveigle, (Dutch) to allure or entice.

Invendible, unseasonable, that can't be sold.

Invention, (Lat.) a finding out; also any thing found out is often called an *Invention*.

Inventory, (Lat.) is a Description or Repertory orderly made of all dead Mens Goods and Chattels prized by four or more credible Men, which every Executor or Administrator is bound to exhibit to the Ordinary at such time as he shall appoint the same.

Inversion, (Lat.) a turning inside out: Inversion, in Geometry, is when in any Proportion the Consequents are turned into Antecedents, and the Antecedents into Consequents.

Invest, (Lat.) to give or put into Possession; also to besiege a Place closely so as to stop all its avenues, and to cut off all Communication with any other place.

Investigation, (Lat.) a diligent searching into, or, as it were, tracing of a thing step by step. Among Mathematicians the analytical way of demonstration is often called by this Name.   *In-*

Investiture, a giving Livery of Seifin, a putting in Poffeffion.

Inveterate, confirmed by long ufe, grown into a Cuftom, waxed old.

Invidious, hated, envied or envious.

Invigilancy, want of watchfulnefs, careleffnefs.

Invigorate, (Lat.) to infpire with Life and Courage.

Invincible, (Lat.) not to be overcome or conquered.

Inviolable, (Lat.) not to be violated or broken.

Inviron, (Fr.) to incompafs or furround.

Invifible, (Lat.) not to be feen, or perceived with the Eyes.

Invitation, (Lat.) to bid or defire one to come, as to a Feaft, Ceremony, &c.

Inumbration, (Lat.) a cafting a fhadow upon.

Inundation, (Lat.) a Deluge, an overflowing with Water.

Inunction, a thorow anointing.

Invocation, (Lat.) a calling upon, a crying for help.

Invoice, is a particular of the Value, Cuftom and Charges of any Goods fent by a Merchant in another Man's Ship and configned to a Factor.

Involve, (Lat.) to wrap or fold in.

Involuntary, (Lat.) unwilling.

Involute and *Evolute* Figures in Mathematicks are Figures fo called.

Involution, in Algebra, is the raifing up any quantity affigned, confidered as a Root to any Power affigned.

Inurbanity, (Lat.) Incivility, clownifh Behaviour.

Inure, to accuftom; and in Law it fignifies to take effect, or be available.

Inufitate, (Lat.) not in ufe.

Inutility, (Lat.) ufeleffnefs, unprofitablenefs.

Invulnerable, (Lat.) not to be wounded.

Joanniticks, an Order of Monks that wear the Figure of a Chalice on their Breafts.

Jobb, a fmall piece of Work.

Jobber, an undertaker of fuch Work.

Joccofe, (Lat.) merry, pleafant, given to jefting.

Jocofity, (Lat.) jeftingnefs, drollery, a playing the wag.

Jocular, pleafant, merry, jocofe.

Jollity, Gaiety, Mirth, good Humour.

Jonick, belonging, or peculiar to the *Jonians*.

Jonick Mood, a light and airy fort of Mufick, of foft and melting Strains.

Jonick Order, in Architecture, is the form of a Column or Pillar invented by the *Jonians* in antient *Greece*, by way of Improvement of the Beauty of the *Dorick Order*, which, as it was taken from the Figure of a robuft Man's Body, and defigned to reprefent Solidity and

H h 4   Strength;

Strength; so the *Jonians* having more regard to Beauty, chose an Order of a more elegant Proportion, which occasion'd this Order to be called the *Femine Order*, and soon after sprung up to that of the *Caryatides*; the Pillars of this Order are commonly hollowed or channelled, and the Ornaments of the Capital are *voluta's*.

Jonthus, is a little hard, callous swelling in the Skin of the Face.

Joffing-block, a Block to get up on Horse-back.

Jouder, to chatter.

Jovial, pleasant, jolly, merry.

Jovisaunce, Joy, Sporting. *Spencer*.

Journal, (Fr.) a day Book; in Navigation, it is a Book wherein is kept an account of the Ship's way at Sea, the changes of the Wind, and several other remarkable Occurrences.

Journey, (Fr.) Travel by Land, properly of one Day.

Journey-Man, is one that works by the Day, but is now also applied to one that works for any longer time.

Joynder, in Law, is the the joyning of two Persons against a third in a suit of Law.

Joyning Issue, a Term in Common Law, the referring a matter depending in suit, or any Point thereof to the trial and decision of the Jury.

Joynt Tenants, in Common Law, are those that hold Lands or Tenements by one Title, or without Partition.

Joynture, in Law, is a Covenant whereby the Husband, or some other Friend in his behalf, assureth to his Wife in respect of Marriage, Lands or Tenements for her Life, or otherwise.

Joy, is a delight or pleasure of the Mind, founded in the consideration of some approaching Good which he is assured to possess.

Irascible, (Lat.) capable of Anger, or subject to Anger.

Ire, (Lat.) Anger, Wrath.

Irenarchs, (Gr.) Justices of the Peace; a military Officer among the *Romans*.

Irksome, tiresome, grievous. *Milt*.

Irony, is a Trope in Rhetorick by which we speak contrary to what we think by way of deriding or mocking him we argue or talk with.

Ironical, spoke by way of Irony.

Ironsick, in Navigation, a Ship or a Boat is said to be *Ironsick*, when her spikes are so eaten with Rust, and so worn away, whereby they make hollows in the Planks, whereby the Ship leaks.

Irradiate, (Lat.) to shine upon, to cast his Beams upon, to enlighten.

Irradiation, (Lat.) an enlightening.

Irre

Irrational, unreasonable, without Reason.

Irrational Numbers. See *Surd Numbers.*

Irreconcilable, (Lat.) not to be appeased or mitigated.

Irrecoverable, not to be recovered or got again.

Irrecuperable, (Lat.) wholly lost, not to be recovered.

Irrefragable, (Lat.) undeniable, invincible.

Irrefutable, (Lat.) that can't be confuted.

Irregularity, (Lat.) disorder; as it were a going without Rule; In the old Canon Law it is taken for an Impediment, hindring a Man from taking Holy Orders, as if he be base born, notoriously guilty of any Crime, maimed, or much deformed, &c.

Irreligious, prophane, without Religion or Fear of God.

Irremeable, (Lat.) that through which there is no returning back, or returning.

Irremediable, that can't be remedied, desperate, helpless.

Irremiscible, unremittable, unpardonable.

Irreparable, (Lat.) which cannot be repaired or made up again.

Irrepleviable, or *Irreplevisable*, that should not be set at large upon Sureties.

Irreprehensible, (Lat.) not to be reprehended or blam'd.

Irreproachable, that cannot be charged with any thing, against whom nothing can be alledged.

Irreprovable, unblameable, blameless.

Irresistible, that can't be opposed or withstood.

Irresolution, uncertainty, suspense; also want of Courage.

Irreverent, wanting Respect and Veneration for Sacred things and Holy Persons.

Irreversible, that cannot be repealed, recalled, or made void.

Irrevocable, not to be recalled or brought back.

Irrigated, (Lat.) watered.

Irrigation, (Lat.) watering of a Garden or Meadow; in Chymistry *Humectation*.

Irrision, (Lat.) laughing at, or mocking to scorn.

Irritation, (Lat.) a provoking or stirring up to Wrath.

Irroration, (Lat.) a besprinkling or bedewing.

Irruption, (Lat.) a breaking into by force or violence.

Isagogical, pertaining to an Introduction or Beginning.

Isagon, in Geometry, is sometimes used for a Figure of equal Angles.

Ischema, are Medicines that stop the Blood, i. e. by their binding and cooling Nature, either close up the openings of the Vessels, or stop the Fluidity or violent motion of the Blood.

Ischias, the Gout in the Hip.

Ischiatic

Ischiatical, (Lat.) that hath the Hip-Gout, or *Sciatica*.

Ischureticks, (Gr.) Medicines that remove a stoppage in Urine.

Ischuria, (Gr.) a stoppage or difficulty of Urine.

Isicle, a drop of Water frozen.

Isinglass, Fish-glue brought from *Island*, of use in Medicine.

Island, is a portion of Earth enclosed by the Sea or a River.

Islander, an Inhabitant of an Island.

Isochrone Vibrations of a Pendulum, are such Vibrations as are made in equal time, as are all the Vibrations or Swings of the same Pendulum, whether the Arks it describes be longer or shorter; also all the Vibrations of a Pendulum vibrating in a Cycloid, are Isochronal, or performed in equal times.

Isomeria, is a method of freeing an Equation from Fractions, which is done by reducing all the Fractions to one common Denominator, and then multiplying each Number of the Equation by that common Denominator.

Isoperimetrical Figures, are such as have equal Perimeters.

Isosceles, (Gr.) equal legged; so is a Triangle called that has two sides equal.

Issuant, a Term in Heraldry, when a Lion or other Beast is drawn in a Coat of Arms just issuing out of the bottom Line of any *Chief*, *Fesse*, &c. but if it come out of the middle of any Ordinary, they call it *Naissant*; that is, *Nascent*, just coming out as it were from the Womb.

Issue, Success, Event, Passage, Out-let; also a little Ulcer made by art for letting out bad Humours. In common Law, Children begotten between Man and Wife: Also Profits from Fines, or of Lands and Tenements; also a matter depending on suit.

Issue, verbally, to spring forth or sally out.

Issue out, to publish, or disperse; also to disburse.

Isthmus, in Geometry, is a little neck or part of Land joining a *Peninsula* to the *Continent*; in Anatomy, *Isthmus*, according to some, is that part which lies between the Mouth and the Gullet, like a neck of Land.

Italian, belonging to *Italy*.

Italick Letter, with Printers, is that whose Body stands not upright, but somewhat sloping.

Item, (Lat.) also, or in like manner: Also a Caution or Warning; also an Article of an Account.

Iterarium, a Surgeon's Instrument so called.

Iteration, (Lat.) a saying or doing the same thing over again.

Itinerant,

Itinerant, (Lat.) journeying.

Itinerary, (Lat.) belonging to a Journey; also a Note-Book wherein Travellers set down the Particulars of what they have seen and observed.

Jubilate, with the Roman Church, a Monk, Canon, or Doctor that has been fifty Years a Professor.

Jubilation, a solemn Rejoicing.

Jubilee, a Year of Rejoicing, celebrated every fiftieth Year among the *Jews*, in remembrance of their deliverance from *Egypt*. Among the Christians this Solemnity was first instituted by Pope *Boniface* the VIIIth. in the Year 1300, who ordained it to be kept every hundred Year. After this *Clement* VI. ordained it to be kept every 50th Year. *Sextus* the IVth. every 25th Year. It comes from the Hebrew word *Jobel*.

Jucundity, (Lat.) Mirth, Pleasantness.

Judaick, Jewish, belonging to the Jews.

Judaise, to hold the Customs, Religion or Rites of the Jews.

Judgment, in Law, is the Censure of the Judges so called, and is the very Voice and final Doom of the Law, and therefore is always taken for unquestionable truth.

Judgment, a Faculty of the Soul, is the putting *Ideas*

together or separating them from one another in the Mind, when their certain Agreement or Disagreement is not perceived, but presumed to be so; and if it so unites or separates them, as in reality things are, it is *right Judgment*.

Judicatory, a place of Judgment.

Judicature, a Judge's Place or Office.

Judicial, or *Judicary*, (Lat.) belonging to a Cause, Trial, or Judgment.

Judicious, of a good or nice Judgment.

Jugerum, a square Measure among the *Romans*, containing 28800 square Feet, or two English Roods, and 19 square Poles.

Jugular, (Lat.) belonging to the Throat.

Jugular Veins, the Veins that pass towards the Skull by the Neck, being of two sorts, either External or Internal.

Jugulation, (Lat.) a cutting any one's Throat.

Juke, or *Jug*, to Pearch or Roost as a Bird does.

Julap, is a sweet Potion, or a grateful Medicine composed of Distilled Water, Spirits, &c. sweetened to the Patient's Palate with Sugar, or some agreeable Syrup.

Julian Account, so called from *Julius Cæsar*, who forty Years before the Birth of Christ, observing the falseness of the Account then in use,

use; ordered the Year to consist of 365 Days, 6 Hours, (whereas before it only consisted of 365 Days) which six Hours added together, in four Years time made a Natural Day, which he order'd to be inserted at the end of *February*, so that every fourth Year contained 366 Days, and was thence called *Bissextile* or *Leap-Year*; because the sixth of the Calends of *March* was twice written, and the thing it self was called *Intercalation*. This Account for some time seem'd true enough: But in process of time, 'twas found not so well to agree with the motion of the Sun: for the true solar Year consists only of 365 Days, 5 h. 49' and 16", so that it falls short of the odd six Hours by 10'. 44". whereupon Pope *Gregory*, by the Advice of some other Mathematicians, corrected the Calender, making the Year to consist of 365 Days, 5 h. 49' and 12". (tho' it should be 16".) and that the vernal Equinox, which was on the 11th of *March*, ought to be reduced to the 21st of *March*, as it was at the time of the *Nicene Council*. He commanded 10 Days in *October*, viz. from the 4th to th 14th to be left out, so that the 4th Day of the Month was accounted for the 14th. Hence it comes to pass that the New or *Gregorian* Account is ten Days before the old or *Julian* Account.

Julian Law, a Law among the *Romans* which made Adultery Death.

Julus, the Botanick word for those *Catkins*, as some call them, or long Worm-like Tufts, which at the beginning of the Year grow out of Willows, Hazels, &c.

July, this Month was so called from *Julius Cæsar*, either because he was born in this Month, or because he triumphed in it after his Victory by Sea over *Cleopatra* Queen of *Egypt*, and her Husband *Mark Antony*; it was before called *Quintilis*, or the fifth Month accounted from *March*, the beginning of their Year.

Jumbals, a sort of sugar'd Past wreath'd into knots.

Jumble, to mingle, to confound, to shake.

Jument, (Lat.) a labouring Beast.

Jump, a Leap; also a kind of Bodice for Women.

Juncto, (Span.) a Meeting of Men to sit in Council; also a Cabal or Faction.

Juncture, (Lat.) a joyning or coupling together, a joint; also juncture of Time is the very nick of Time as we say, or the Critical Minute.

June, the fourth Month of the Year from *March*, so called, either from *Juno*, or *Junius Brutus*, who began his Consulship in that Month.

Junetia, a kind of Apple.

Junior,

Junior, (Lat.) younger in Age or Standing.

Junke, at Sea, is a piece of an old Cable.

Junket, to entertain with, or hunt after dainty Dishes.

Junkets, Cakes and Sweet-Meats, the Entertainments that Ladies give to one another.

Jupiter, (Lat.) a heathen God ; also a Planet the highest except *Saturn*.

Juration, (Lat.) swearing an Oath.

Jurats, are in the nature of Aldermen for the Government of their several Corporations.

Jurden, a sort of Urinal.

Juridical, (Lat.) belonging to the Law ; also actionable ; also just, judicial, orderly.

Jurisdiction, (Lat.) is a Dignity which a Man hath conferred on him to do Justice in Cases of Complaint.

Jurisprudence, (Lat.) skill of the Law.

Jurist, a Civilian, a Lawyer, one that writes of the Law.

Juris Utrum, a Writ that lies for a Possessor of a Living, whose Predecessor has alienated his Lands or Tenements.

Juror, (Lat.) is one of those twenty four or twelve Men which are sworn to deliver a Truth upon such Evidence as shall be given them touching the matter in question.

Jury, in Common Law, is either twenty four or twelve Men sworn to enquire of the matter of Fact, and declare the Truth upon such Evidence as shall be deliver'd them touching the matter in question.

Jury-Mast, at Sea, is whatever the Seamen set up in the room of a Mast lost in a Fight or a Storm.

Jussel, a Dish made of several Meats minced together.

Justice, is a rendring to every Man his own.

Justice, is one that is deputed by the King to do right by way of Judgment.

Justice of the Common Pleas, is a Lord by his Office, and with his Assistants originally did hear and determine all Causes at the Common Law ; that is, all civil Causes between common Persons as well Personal as Real.

Justice of the Forrest, or *Justice in Eyre of the Forrest*, is a Lord by his Office, and hears and determines all Offences within the Forest committed against *Venison* or *Vert*.

Justice of the King's Bench, is a Lord by his Office, and above all the rest, on the chief Justice in *England* : his Office is to hear and determine all Pleas of the Crown, viz. such as concern Offences committed against the Crown, Dignity and Peace of the King

King, as Treasons, Felonies, and such like.

Justices of Assizes, are those which by special Commission are sent into this or that County, to take Assizes for the ease of the Subjects.

Justices in Eyre, are those who are Commissioned to go into divers Counties to hear Causes, especially those that are termed *Pleas of the Crown*; and this was done for the People, who must otherwise have been forced to come to the *King's Bench*.

Justices of Gaol-Delivery, such as are sent with Commissions to judge Causes belonging to those that for any Offence are cast into Prison.

Justice of Nisi Prius, are now the same with *Justices of Assise*, so called from the words in the Adjournment.

Justices of Oyer and Terminer, were Justices deputed upon some special and extraordinary Occasion, to hear and determine some peculiar Causes.

Justices of Peace, are such as are appointed by the King's Commission to attend the Peace in the County where they dwell, whereof such, whose Commission begins *Quorum vos unum esse volumus* are called Justices of the Quorum.

Justicements, all things belonging to Justice.

Justiciary, an Administrator of Justice.

Justicies, a Writ directed to the Sheriff, for dispatch of Justice in some special Cause, of which he cannot by his ordinary Power hold Plea in his County Court.

Justification, a clearing, justifying, making good: In Common Law, it is the giving a good Reason for such and such a thing.

Justificators, Compurgators, such as by Oath justifie the Innocence, Report, or Oath of another; also Jury-Men.

Justifie, to clear one's self, to verifie, to prove. In *Divinity*, to make or declare just. In *Law*, to shew why an Act was done.

Justinians, a Religious Order founded in 1412, in St. *Justin*'s Abby at *Padua*.

Jutty, part of a Building that jutts, *i. e.* stands out beyond the rest.

Juvenile, (Lat.) youthful, sprightly, brisk, &c.

Juxta-Position, (Lat.) a laying by one another, a placing things close by one another's side.

Iwimpled, muffled.

K.

K Alender. See *Calender*.
Kalends. See *Calends*.

Kayage, Money pay'd for Wharfage.

Keckle, at Sea, is to wind a small Rope about the Cable or Bolt-Rope, to keep the Cables from gauling in the Hawse, or the Bolt-Rope from

from galling againſt the Ship's Quarters.

Kecks, dry Stalks or Sticks.

Kedge, to ſet up the Fore-Sail, Fore-top-Sail and Miſſen, and ſet a Ship to drive with the Tide, when in a narrow River we would bring her up or down, the Wind being contrary to the Tide.

Kedgers, ſmall Anchors uſed in calm Weather.

Keel, is the loweſt piece of Timber in a Ship in the bottom of her Hull, one end whereof is at the *Stern*, and the other at the *Stem*; alſo a Veſſel for Liquors to cool in.

Keel-Rope, a hair Rope running between the Keelſon and the Keel of a Ship, to clear the limberHoles when they are choaked up with Ballaſt.

Keelſon, the next piece of Timber in a Ship to her Keel, lying right over it next above her Floor Timbers.

Keen, ſharp, ſubtil, eager.

Keep, a ſtrong Tower in the middle of a Caſtle, the laſt reſort of the Beſieged.

Keeper of the Great Seal, is a Lord by his Office, and ſtiled *Lord Keeper of the Great Seal of* England, thro' whoſe Hands paſs all Chartrs, Commiſſions and Grants under the Great Seal; without which Seal, all ſuch Inſtruments are of no force by Law.

Keeper of the Privy Seal, is a Lord by his Office, through whoſe Hands paſs all Charters ſigned by the King before they come to the Great Seal, and ſome things which do not paſs the Great Seal at all.

Kembo, (from the *Ital. a-ſchembo*) *to ſet one's Arms a Kembo*, is to ſet them obliquely or a thwart.

Ken, (Sax.) Knowledge, Sight or View.

Kenks, at Sea, are doublings in a Cable or Rope when 'tis handed in or out ſo that it doth not run ſmooth.

Kennets, in a Ship, are ſmall pieces of Timber nail'd to the inſide, to which the *Tacks* or *Sheets* are *be-layed* or faſtened.

Kerchief, (from the *French couvre chef* to cover the Head) a linnen Cloth that Women wear on their Heads, and hence comes Handkerchief tho' improperly.

Kerne, a Churle or Farmer. *Spencer.*

Kerf, a Notch in Wood.

Kerſey, a ſort of courſe Woollen Cloth.

Keſar, among the antient *Britains*, is a King or Soveraign Prince.

Keſhitah, a *Hebrew* Coin, ſo named from the Image of a Lamb upon it, the ſame with *Gerah*.

Ketch, a Veſſel like a Hoy, but not ſo large.

Kevels. See Kenets.

Key, in Muſick, is a certain Tone whereunto every Compo-

Compofition, whether it be long or fhort, ought to be referred, and this *Key* is either flat or fharp, not in refpect of its own Nature, but with relation to the flat or fharp third which is joined with it.

Kibes, a painful fwelling with inflammation upon the Heels, often occafioned by Cold.

Kibfey, a fort of wicker Basket.

Kickfhaw, fome fmall and curious matter of Victuals.

Kidder, a Huckfter, or Carrier of Victuals to fell.

Kidnap, to entice or fteal away Children.

Kidnapper, one that makes a Trade of decoying young Children and others to fhip them for foreign Plantations.

Kidft, Knoveft. *Spencer.*

Kilderkin, a liquid Meafure of two Firkins or eighteen Gallons.

King, from the Dutch word *Koning*, to know, becaufe he ought to be the moft knowing of Men: He is defined in Law to be the principal Confervator of Peace within his Dominions.

King's Bench, is the Court or Judgment Seat where the King of *England* was wont to fit in his own Perfon, and therefore it was moveable with the *King's* Houfhold, and was called *curia domini Regis*, and *Aula Regia*.

King of Heralds, is an Officer at Arms, of which we have three, *Garter*, *Norroy*, and *Claremeieux*, whereof *Garter* is the principal, and is the fame with *Pater Patratus* among the *Romans*.

King's-Evil, a Difeafe, the Gift of curing which is afcribed to the Kings and Queens of *England* from *Edward* the Confeffor.

Kingdom, a Country or Countries fubject to a Soveraign Prince; alfo the three Orders of Natural Bodies, *Mineral*, *Vegetable* and *Animal*, are called Kingdoms by Chymifts.

Kintal, a Weight of about a hundred Pounds, more or lefs, according to the ufage of fundry Nations.

Kirk, Church. *Spencer.*

Kirtle, a kind of fhort Jacket.

Kit, a Pocket-Violin; alfo a Pail.

Knap-fack, a Bag at a Soldier's Back.

Knave, a Rogue, a Villain; tho' of Old this word was not ufed as a word of Difgrace, but as the Name of fome kind of Servant or Lacquey.

Knave-line, is a Rope in a Ship faftened to the crofs Trees, whence it comes down by the *Ties* to the *Ramhead*, and there it is reeved through a piece of Wood, and fo brought down to the Ship's fide, and there hailed up taught to the Rails; 'tis ufed to keep the Ties and Hallyards

yards from turning about one another, as they will do when new and firſt uſed.

Kneck, in the Sea Language, is the twiſting of a Rope or Cable as it is veering out.

Knees, are pieces of Timber in a Ship, bowed like a Knee, which bind the Beams and Futtocks together, being bolted ſtrongly into them both.

Knee-Timber, is the cutwater of a Ship.

Knell, the ſound of a Bell, a Paſſing-Bell.

Knettles, in the Sea Phraſe, are two pieces of Spun Yarn put together untwiſted.

Knight, *fore Knight and main Knight*, are ſhort pieces of Wood, commonly carv'd with a Man's Head upon them, wherein are four Shivers a piece, three for the Hallyards, and one for the top Ropes to run in.

Knight, in the Latin *Eques*, ſignifies a Soldier or Horſeman; but now 'tis uſed for a Title of Dignity, of which there are ſeveral Orders.

Knights Batchelours, the loweſt but antienteſt Order of Knight-hood: It cometh from the *Germans* among whom it was an old Cuſtom, as ſoon as any one was judged capable of managing Arms, either for the Prince or Father of the Perſon or ſome other of his Relations, to give him a Shield and a Javelin; as the *Romans*

did the *Toga virilis*, to thoſe they thought fit for publick Employment; after which he was accounted a Member of the Commonwealth. It was alſo an old Cuſtom to honour Men with the Girdle of Knight-hood, and he who received was ſolemnly to go to Church and offer his Sword upon the Altar, and vow himſelf to the Service of God. Afterwards Kings us'd to ſend their Sons to the Neighbouring Princes to receive Knight-hood of them.

Knight Banneret, is a Knight made in the Field by cutting off the point of his Standard and making it a Banner, and is allowed to diſplay his Arms in a Banner in the King's Army. They that are created under the Standard of the King perſonally preſent take place of Baronets.

Knights Baronet, is a late Order erected by King *James*, who for ſeveral disburſments towards the Plantation in *Ulſter*, created divers into this Dignity, and made it Hereditary by his Letters Patents to be ſeen in the Rolls: And theſe *Baronets* were to have the Precedency in all Writings, Seſſions and Salutations before all Knights of the *Bath*, *Knights Batchelors* and *Bannerets*, except thoſe above mentioned.

Knights of the Bath, an Order of Knights created within the Liſts of the *Bath*, who bathed themſelves, and uſed

many

many Religious Ceremonies the Night before their Creation.

Knights of the Carpet, an Order of Knights made out of the Field, so called, because when they receive their Order they kneel upon a Carpet.

Knights of the Garter, or *St. George*, an Order of Knight-hood instituted by *Edward* III; some say upon the account of good Success in a Skirmish, wherein the King's Garter was used for a Token: Others say that the King after his great Success, dancing one Night with his Queen and other Ladies, took up a Garter that one of them dropt, whereat some of the Lords smiling, the King said, that ere long he would make that Garter to be of high Reputation, and shortly after he erected the Order of the BlewGarter, which consists of twenty six Martial Nobles, whereof the King used to be the Chief, and the rest to be either of the Realm, or Princes of other Countries; they always wear the *George* and Star.

Knights of the Order of St. John of Jerusalem, an Order erected about the Year 1104, but suppress'd in *England* towards the latter end of King *Henry* the VIII's time for adhering to the Pope.

Knights of the Temple, or *Knights Templars*, an Order of Knight-hood erected by Pope *Gelasius*, or, as some say, *Baldwin* II. about the Year 1117; their Office and Vow was to defend the Temple, Sepulchre, and Christian Strangers, and entertain these charitably, and conduct them in their Pilgrimage through the Holy Land. But growing vicious after two hundred Years, they were supprest by Pope *Clement* V. and their Substance given to the Knights of Rhodes, and other Religious Orders.

Knights of the Round Table, King *Arthur*'s Knights, a Brittish Order, the most antient, they say, of any in the World.

Knights of the Shire, two Knights or Gentlemen of worth that are chosen by the Free-holders of every County that can dispend forty Shillings *per Ann.* and be resident in the Shire.

Knight-Marshal, an Officer of the King's House, who hath the Jurisdiction and Cognizance of any Transgression; as also of all contracts made within the King's House and Verge.

Knights of Calatrava in *Spain*, an Order erected by *Alonzo*, the ninth King of *Spain*, conferred upon certain *Cavalleroes* who went out of Devotion to succour *Calatrava* against the *Moors*; they wore a red Cross on the left Breast.

Knights of the holy Sepulchre, an Order of Knight-hood instituted ftituted by St. *Hellen*, a Brittish Lady, and confirmed by the Pope, after fhe had vifited *Jerufalem* and found the Crofs of our Saviour.

Knights Teutonick, a mixed Order of Hofpitallers and Templars, to whom the Emperor *Fred.* II. gave *Pruffia*, on condition they fhould fubdue the Infidels, which accordingly they did. The Elector of *Brandenburg* was at laft fole Mafter of their Order, for at firft they had three.

Knights of Rhodes, (now of *Maltha*) fprung from the Hofpitallers after they were forced out of the Holy Land, and having held *Rhodes* 200 Years, they were driven out thence by *Solyman*; then the Emperor *Charles* the Vth. gave them *Maltha*, paying a *Falcon* annually for a Heriot, which is paid yearly to the King of *Spain*.

Knights of the Order of St. Maurice and Lazaro, an Order inftituted in the Year 1119, and the Duke of *Savoy* was confirmed their grand Mafter.

Knights of the Annunciada, an Order of Knight-hood in *Savoy*, erected in the Memory of the Annunciation of the Bleffed Virgin. There are fourteen in number who wear a Coller of Gold, and the Virgin *Mary*'s Medal.

Knights of St. Jago, or *St. James*, a Spanifh Order, inftituted under Pope *Alexan-*

der III. They obferve St. *Auftin*'s Rules, their great Mafter is next to the King in State, and hath 150 thoufand Crowns for his yearly Revenue.

Knights of the Pear-Tree, or *St. Julian*, inftituted in the Year 1179, called afterwards Knights of *Alcantara* in the Kingdom of *Leon*.

Knights of San Salvador in *Arragon*, an Order inftituted by *Alphonfo*, in the Year 1118.

Knights of Montofia, an Order of Knight-hood in the Kingdom of *Valentia*.

Knights of Jefus Chrift, a Portugal Order of Knighthood.

Knights of the Broom-flower, erected by St. *Lewis* with this Motto *exaltat humiles*.

Knights of the Order of *Chriftian Charity*, made by *Henry* III. for the Benefit of poor Captains and maimed Soldiers.

Knights of the Order of the Virgin Mary in Mount Carmel, an Order inftituted by *Henry* IV. in the Year 1670, confifting of 100 French Gentlemen.

Knights of the Rue, or of St. *Andrew*, a *Scotifh* Order of Knight-hood.

Knights of the Order of the Dragon, an Order in *Germany*, erected by *Sigifmund* the Emperor upon the Condemnation of *John Hus* and *Jerome of Prague*

Knights of the Order of Auſtria and Carinthia, or of St. *George,* inſtituted by the Emperor *Frederick* III. firſt Arch-Duke of *Auſtria.*

Knights of the Order of the white Eagle, erected in *Poland* by *Ladiſlaus* V. in the Year 1325.

Knights of St. Stephen, made by *Coſmo* Duke of *Florence,* An. 1501, in honour of Pope *Stephen* the IXth.

Knights of St. Mark, a *Venetian* Order.

Knights of the Elephant, a *Daniſh* Order.

Knights of the Sword and Baudrick, a *Swediſh* Order.

Knights of la Calza, or of the *Stockin,* a *Venetian* Order.

Knights of St. George, an Order of Knight-hood in *Geneva.*

Knights of San Maria De mercede, a *Spaniſh* Order.

Knights of the Golden Fleece, an Order inſtituted by *Philip* Duke of *Burgundy,* upon his marrying *Iſabel* the Daughter of *Portugal.* This Order wear a great Collar of double *Fuſils,* interwoven with Stones and Flints darting Flames of Fire, with this Motto, *Ante ferit quam flamma micet.* This Order conſiſts of thirty; of which the King of *Spain* is chief.

Knights of the Militia Chriſtiana, a late Order of Knight-hood in *Poland.*

Knights of Nova Scotia in the *Weſt Indies,* erected by *James* I. King of *Great Brit-*

tain ; this Order wear an Orange Tawny Ribbon.

Knights of the order of Genette, is the moſt antient Order of Knight-hood in *France,* erected by *Charles Martel,* after the beating of the *Saracens* in a great Battel at *Tours,* Anno 782.

Knights of the Dog and Cock, an Order of Knight-hood inſtituted by *Philip* I. of *France.*

Knights of the Star, an Order of Knight-hood in *France* ; thoſe of the Order have this Motto, *Monſtrant regibus aſtra viam.*

Knights of S. Michael the Arch-Angel, an Order of Knight-hood inſtituted by *Lewis* An. 1469; of their Order there are ſix and thirty, of which the King is Chief.

Knights of the half Moon or Creſcent, an Order inſtituted by *Kenier* Duke of *Anjou* when he conquered *Sicily,* with this Motto *Los,* i. e. Praiſe.

Knights of the Lilly in Navarre, a French Order of Knight-hood.

Knights of the Thiſtle in the Houſe of Bourbon, a French Order who conſtantly bear this Motto, *Nemo me impune laceſſit.*

Knights of Orleance, or the *Porcupine,* a French Order with this Motto, *Cominus & Eminus.*

Knights of the Ear of Corn, or *de l'Eſpic,* or of the *Ermin,* an Order inſtituted by *Francis* V. in *Bretaign,* in the Year 1450.   *Knights*

Knights of the Golden Shield, an Order created by *Lewis* II. whereon there was a Bend with this Motto *allons, Let us go* to the defence of our Country.

Knights of St. Magdalen, a French Order of Knight-hood, inſtituted by St. *Lewis* againſt Duels.

Knights du S. Eſprit, or of the *Holy Ghoſt,* an Order created by *Henry* III. at his return from *Poland,* who was both Born and Crowned King of *France* on *Whitſonday;* this, tho' a Modern Order, is the moſt uſed now in *France.*

Knight Service, was a Tenure whereby ſeveral Lands in this Nation were held of the King, which draw after it *Homage, Eſcuage, Wardſhip, Marriage,* &c.

Knipperdolings, Hereticks ſo called from their Ringleader, who appeared in *Germany* about the time of *John* of *Leyden.*

Knots, at Sea, the Diviſions of the Log-line, uſually ſeven Fathom, or fourty two Foot aſunder.

Kolliarion. an Attick Meaſure of Capacity, either for things liquid or things dry; for things liquid, it contains $\frac{1}{72}$ of a Pint, and 04 decimal Parts of a ſolid Inch of our Wine Meaſure; for things dry it contains $\frac{1}{144}$ of a Pint, and 004 decimal Parts of a ſolid Inch of our Corn Meaſure.

L.

LAbarum, the Standard carried before the *Roman* Emperors in War, and adored by the Soldiers; being a long Spear with a Staff a-croſs at top, from which hung down a rich Purple Standard, richly adorned with Gold and Precious Stones.

Labefaction, (Lat.) a weakning or enfeebling, a deſtroying.

Label, is a large thin Braſs Ruler, with a ſmall Sight at one end, and a Center-hole at the other: Alſo a Term in Heraldry denoting the Eldeſt Brother, and is that which hangs down with three Points from the File in the top of an Eſcutcheon.

Labial, (Lat.) pertaining to the Lips. Labial Letters are ſuch, as in their pronunciation, require chiefly the Lips to form their ſound.

Labels, Ribbands hanging down on each ſide of a Miter, Crown, or Garland of Flowers; alſo narrow ſlips of Paper or Parchment by which Seals are hang'd to Writings. In *Heraldry,* Lines that hang down from the File in the top of an Eſcutcheon, and make a diſtinction for the Elder Brother.

Laborant, one that aſſiſts, or works under a Chymiſt, whilſt about an Experiment.

Laborariis, a Writ lying against such as refuse to serve, tho' they have not wherewithal to live; or against one that refuses to serve in Summer where he serv'd in Winter.

Laboratory, a Room fitted on purpose for Chymical Operations, and furnished with variety of Furnaces and Instruments fitted to that Art.

Laborious, that works hard, or takes much pains; also toilsome, difficult.

Labyrinth, a Maze, or a place full of turnings and windings; an intricate or obscure Matter or Business.

Lacerate, (Lat.) to tear or pull in pieces.

Laceration, (Lat.) a tearing or pulling in pieces.

Lac Lunæ, is the Chymists word for a fat, porous, friable Earth, insipid, but dissolvable in Water.

Laches, (Fr.) in Common Law, negligence, slackness.

Lachesis, one of the three Destinnes, and a kind of Deity among the Pagans, who, as they say, Spins the Thread of Man's Life.

Lachrymation, (Lat.) a weeping or shedding of Tears.

Lachrymatories, small Earthen Vessels, in which in old time, the Tears of surviving Friends were reposited and buried with the Urns and Ashes of the Dead.

Lacken, despised; also lessened.

Laconick, concise, brief: Thus one who speaks concisely and pithily is said to have a *laconick* way of speaking.

Laconism, (Gr.) a brief way of speaking after the manner of the *Lacedemonians.*

Lactary, (Lat.) a Milkhouse, or Dary-house.

Lactation, sucking of Milk as a Child.

Lactea Via. See *Galaxy.*

Lacteal, Milky, belonging to Milk.

Lacteal Veins, are slender pellucid Vessels, dispersed in great numbers through the Mesentery, and appointed for the carrying of the *Chyle.*

Lactifical, that breeds Milk.

Lactucimina, the same with *Aphthæ.*

Lacunar, in Architecture, is an arched Roof or Cieling, more especially the Planking or Flooring above the Porticoes.

Ladders, in a Ship, are usually three, the *Entring Ladder,* made of Wood, the *Gallery Ladder,* made of Ropes, and the *Boltsprit Ladder* at the Beak Head, which are only used in great Ships.

Ladle, an Instrument at Sea to load great Guns with.

Lagan, is those Goods which the Seamen cast out of the Ship in danger of Shipwrack.

Lagh, the Law; hence Saxonlage and such like.

Laghslite,

Laghflite, a breach of the Law, or the Punifhment for it.

Lagophthalmy, (Gr.) a Difeafe in the Eyes which makes the Patient fleep with his Eyes open.

Laical, (Lat) belonging to Laymen, or fuch as have nothing to do in the Miniſterial Function.

Laick, a Perfon not engaged in the Miniſtry, or who has not taken Holy Orders.

Lake, is a fmall Collection of deep ſtanding Water, entirely furrounded with Land, and having no viſible communication with the Sea.

Laity, the ſtate of Men not in Orders; the common People not in Orders.

Lambative, a Pectoral Medicine, to be taken or licked off the end of a piece of Lichoris-ſtick.

Lambdacifm, (Gr.) a fault in fpeaking, by infiſting too much on the Letter L.

Lamdoides, is the backward Suture of the Brain, fo called from its refembling the Letter *Lambda*.

Lambent, licking; alſo touching gently.

Lamella, little thin Plates of Mettal; alſo little thin Plates conſtituted by a Network of very finall Fibres, of which the Shells of Shell-Fiſhes confiſt.

Lamentable, (Lat.) mournful, pitiful.

Lamentation, a bewailing, a moanful Complaint.

Lamina, the Plates or Tables of the Skull, of which there are two in number.

Lammas-Day, the firſt day of *Auguſt*, ſo called from Tithe-lambs the Prieſts received on that Day.

Lampadias, (Lat.) a kind of bearded Comet, ſomething like a burning Lamp, being of ſeveral ſhapes; for ſometimes its flame or blaze runs tapering upward like a Sword, and ſometimes is double or triple pointed.

Lampoon, a Poem wherein a Perfon is treated with Reproach and Ridicule; *verbally*, to write ſuch a Poem.

Lancepefade, (Fr.) one who has command of ten Soldiers, an under Corporal.

Lancet, a Surgeon's Inſtrument uſed in the letting of Blood, in cutting of Fiſtulas, &c.

· *Landcape*, a narrow piece of Land that runneth farther into the Sea than the reſt of the Continent.

Land-Fall, a Sea Term, ſignifying to fall in with the Land; thus when a Ship expects to fee Land in a little time and does ſo, they ſay, they have made a good *Land-Fall*.

Land-gable, or *gavel*, a Quitrent for the Soil of a Houfe, Ground-Rent.

Land-lay'd, they ſay the Land is lay'd, when a Ship

is juft got out of the fight of Land.

Land-lock'd, a Ship is faid to ride *Land-lock'd* when fhe is at Anchor in fuch a place that there is no point open to the Sea, fo that fhe is fafe from Wind and Tide.

Land-mark, a Boundary fet up between Lands; alfo with Sailers, 'tis a Mountain, Steeple, or the like, whereby the Pilot knows how they bear by the Compafs.

Land fhut in, is when another Point of Land hinders the Sight of that which a Ship came from, then they fay, that the Land is fhut in.

Land-to, is when a Ship lies fo far from the Shoar that fhe can but juft ken Land, then fhe is faid to be *Land-to*.

Land-turn, the fame off the Land by Night, as a Brieze is off the Sea by Day.

Land-Skip, a defcription of the Land as far as it can be feen above our Horizon by Hills, Vallies, Cities, Woods, Rivers, &c. all that in a Picture which is not of the Body or Argument (which denote the Perfons) is called by this name of *Land-Skip*.

Landgrave, one that has the Government of a Province in *Germany*; a Count or Earl.

Langrel-Shot, a kind of Shot ufed at Sea, made of two Bars of Iron, with a joint in the middle, to which at each end is faftned half a a Bullet of Lead or Iron.

Language, a fet of articulate Sounds or Words which particular People agree upon to exprefs their thoughts by.

Langued, a Term in Heraldry, it comes from the French word *Langue*, a Tongue.

Languid, (Lat.) weak, faint.

Languifh, to grow faint or weak, to fall away, to grow worfe and worfe.

Languor, (Lat.) faintnefs, weaknefs, feeblenefs.

Laniation, (Lat.) a flaughter, a butchering or tearing to pieces.

Laniferous, (Lat.) Wool-bearing, or that bears Wool.

Lanigerous, bearing Wool or Down.

Lanis de crefentia walliæ traducendis abfque cuftuma, is a Writ that lieth to the Cuftomer of a Port for the permitting one to pafs over Wools without Cuftom, becaufe he hath paid Cuftom in *Wales* before.

Lank, flender, lean.

Lanniers, or *Lanniards*, in a Ship, are fmall Ropes received into the dead Mens Eyes of all the Shrouds, whofe ufe is to flacken or fet taught the Shrouds.

Lanfquenet, a *German* Foot Soldier; alfo a Game at Cards.

Lanuginous, downy, or covered with a foft Down or Wool-like Subftance.

Lapicide, a Stone cutter.

Lapidary,

Lapidary, (Lat.) one that pollishes or works in Stones, a Jeweller.

Lapidary Verses, are of a middle nature between Verse and Prose, such as are cut in Monuments.

Lapidation, (Lat.) a stoning to death.

Lapidescent, (Lat.) that which can turn any Body into a stony Nature, Thus those Waters which have stony Particles dissolved and swimming in them, and in their Course or Motion, deposite them in the Pores of Sticks, Leaves, &c. and by this means petrifie them, are called *Lapidescent Waters*.

Lapidification, in Chymistry, is the converting any Substance to Stones, by dissolving any Metal in some corrosive Spirit, and then boiling the Dissolution to the consistence of a Stone.

Lapse, a Slip or Fall.

Laqueus, in Surgery, is a Band so tied, that if it be attracted or pressed with weight it shuts up close.

Larboard, the left Hand side of a Ship, when one stands with his Face toward the Stem.

Larbord Watch. See *Watch*.

Larboard the Helm. See *Port*.

Larceny, in Law, is a wrongful taking away another Man's Goods with a design to steal them: If the things stolen exceed the value of twelve Pence, 'tis called *Theft simple*, if not *Petit Larceny*.

Lard ; to *lard* a Hair or Fowls, is to stick little slices of Bacon in them.

Lardoon, a small slip of Bacon proper for larding.

Lare, (Lat.) an Idol which the Heathens worshipped, sometimes taken for a God of the Fields or Ways, sometimes for a Houshold God.

Large, the greatest measure of musical Quantity, containing two Longs, one Long, two Briefs, one Brief, two Semibriefs.

Large, the Seamen say a Ship sails large when she goes neither before the Wind, nor upon a Wind, but, as it were quarterly between both.

Largess, a free Gift, a Dole, or Present.

Larmier, a flat square Member in Architecture, which is placed on the Cornice below the *Cymatium*, and jets out farthest, being so called from its use, which is to disperse the Water, and cause it to fall from the Wall drop by drop, or, as it were, by Tears: The word comes from the French word *Larme* a *Tear*.

Larvated, (Lat.) one that hath a Vizard on, disguised.

Laryngotomy, (Gr.) a cutting of the Larynx.

Larynx, (Gr.) the Top or Head of the *Aspera Arteria*, or Windpipe.

Lascivious, wanton in Behaviour, lustful.

Lash,

Lash, is the Sea Term for binding to the Ship's side, Muskets, Buts of Water or Beer, pieces of Timber, &c.

Lashers, the Ropes which bind fast the Tackles and the Breechings of the Ordnance when they are made fast within Board.

Lask, one that is loose in the Belly, or troubled with a *Diarrhea*.

Laskets, or *Latches*, at Sea, are small lines, like loops, fastened by sowing into the *Bonnets* and *Drablers* of a Ship, in order to lace the *Bonnets* to the *Courses* or *Drablers* to the *Bonnets*.

Lasking, when a Ship sails not either by a Wind, or straight before it, but quartering between both, she is said to go *Lasking*, which is the same with Veering.

Lassitude, (Lat.) weariness, laziness; a Disease like the Green Sickness.

Lastage, Custom at some Markets for carrying of things; also a Duty paid for Wares sold by Last; also Ballast of a Ship.

Latches. See *Laskets*.

Latched, catched. *Spencer*.

Latent, (Lat.) lying hid.

Lateral, (Lat.) belonging to the sides of any thing.

Lateral Equation, in *Algebra*, is an Equation which hath but one Root, or wherein the highest Power of the unknown quantity, is of one dimension only.

A Latire, (Lat.) on the side. *Legate a latere*, is a Title given to those Cardinals whom the Pope sends to Courts of foreign Princes.

Lathe, (Sax.) a great part or division of a County, sometimes containing three or more Hundreds.

Latinism, a speaking after the Idiom of the Latin Tongue.

Lation, (Lat.) is the translation or motion of a Body from one place to another.

Latitat, is a Writ whereby all Men in personal Actions are called Originally to the *King's Bench*; and it hath this name as supposing the Defendant doth lurk and lie hid.

Latitude, (Lat.) breadth, largness, wideness.

Latitude of a place on the Earth, is the distance of that place, either North or South from the Equinoctial, and 'tis measured by that Ark of the *Meridian* of the place, that is intercepted between the Place and the Equinoctial.

Middle Latitude, is half the Sum of any two given Latitudes.

Difference of Latitude, is the *Northing* or *Southing* of a Ship, or the way gained, to the *Northward* or *Southward* of the Place she departed from.

Latitudinarians in Religion, are those who profess a freedom, and, as it were, a more than ordinary Latitude in their Principles and Doctrines.

La-

Latrant, (Lat.) barking, Snarling.

Latrocination, (Lat.) a robbing, plundering, pillaging.

Latten, Iron tinned over.

Latus Rectum, an imaginary Line belonging to the Conick Sections.

Latus Tranfverfum, a Line belonging to the Ellipfis and Hyperbola.

Latus Primarium, a Line belonging to a Conick Section.

Lavation, (Lat.) a washing, a cleanfing of Metals or Minerals from the Filth.

Laud, Praife, Commendation, Lavifh, Prodigal, Extravagant.

Laudable, (Lat.) worthy of Praife or Commendation.

Laudanum, a Medicine extracted out of the finer and purer part of Opium mixed with Water and Spirit of Wine, and then evaporated to its due confiftence.

Lauds, (Lat.) Praifes read or fung laft in either Morning or Evening Service.

Laver, (Lat.) a Veffel to wafh in.

Launce, or *Launch*, among Seamen, to put out, to place or beftow, to leave off.

Laund, or *Lawn*, in a Park, is plain untilled Ground.

Laureat, Crowned with Laurel, wearing a Garland of Bays. *Laureated Letters*, were Letters bound up in Leaves, which the *Roman* Generals fent to the Senate when their Contents were

Victory and Conqueft. *Poet Laureat*, is he (who as principal Poet in his Country) was wont to be Crowned with a Garland of Laurel.

Laurel, a Tree; figuratively, Triumph, Victory.

Law, in general is a Rule of acting or not acting, fet down by fome intelligent Being, having Authority for fo doing.

Law of Reafon, is the Sentence which Reafon gives concerning the goodnefs of thofe things one is to do.

Laws of Nature, are thofe Laws of motion, by which natural Bodies are governed in all their Actions upon one another.

Laws of Nations, are either *Primary* or *Secundary*; the *Primary* are fuch as concern Embaffage, and fuch as belong to the courteous Entertainment of Strangers, and fuch as ferve for the commodious Traffick of one Nation with another, and the like; and the *Secundary* Laws are fuch as concern Arms.

Laws of Motion, oftentimes ufed in the fame fenfe with *Laws of Nature*; tho' moft commonly *Laws of Motion* are thofe Laws which two Bodies ftriking one againft another, obferve before and after the fhock.

Laws of the twelve Tables, were, by order of the *Roman* State, compil'd from thofe of *Solon* and others, engrav'd on twelve Tables of Brafs,

Brafs, and committed to the Care of the *Decemviri*, thence call'd *Decemviral Laws*.

Lawn, a kind of fine Linnen; also a great Plain in a Park; also a Plain between two Woods.

Laxation, (Lat.) a loofening or eafing.

Laxatives, or *loofening Medicines*, are thofe which with their benign Particles foftning and fcouring the Guts, cleanfe them of their Excrements.

Laxe, loofe, flack, weak.

Laxity, loofnefs.

Lay the Land, to *lay the Land*, at Sea, fignifies to fail out of fight of Land.

Lay-ftall, a place to lay Dung, Soil, or Rubbifh on.

Lazar, a Leper, one full of Sores and Scabs.

Lazaret, (Ital.) an Hofpital.

Leachery, Luft, Luftfulnefs.

League, from the Greek word *Leucos* white, becaufe in old time they placed white Stones at every League's end from the City. The Englifh and Italian Miles are both the fame, and two of thefe make a French League; three and fomewhat more make a Spanifh League; a League at Sea is commonly reckoned three Englifh Miles.

League, a Covenant or an Agreement made between Princes.

Leap-Year, every fourth Year, named from Leaping, as it were, one Day further

than other Years. See *Biffextile*,

Leafes, in Law, fignifies a Demife or letting of Lands or Tenements, Right, or common Rent, or any Hereditament unto another for term of Years or Life, or a Rent referved.

Leaffee, or *Leffee*, the Party to whom a Leafe is granted.

Leaffor, or *Leffor*, the Perfon that lets a Leafe.

Leaven, a piece of Dough falted and foured to ferment and relifh the whole lump.

Leaver, a bar of Wood or Iron to lift or bear up a Weight.

Lecanomancy, a fort of Divining or Sooth-faying by Water in a Bafon.

Lectern, (Fr.) the Reader's Desk in a Church.

Lectiftern, (among the antient *Romans*) the folemn Ceremony of trimming and fetting out a Bed, not for Repofe but Repaft, wherein they laid the Images of their Gods reared up upon Bolfters and Pillows.

Lecturer, (Lat.) a publick Profeffor; a Reader of *Lectures*, that is, certain Portions of an Author or Science read in the publick Schools: 'Tis now frequently ufed for a Minifter who Preaches in the Afternoon, having no other Benefit befides the free Gifts of the People.

Ledges, in a Ship, are fmall pieces of Timber lying a-thwart Ships from the *Waft-Trees*

Trees to the *Roof-Trees*, which serve to bear up the *Nettings* or *Gratings* over the half Deck.

Lee, a word differently used at Sea, but generally it signifies the part opposite to the Wind.

Lee Shore, is that on which the Wind blows.

A Lee the Helm, by this they mean, put the Helm to the Leeward side of the Ship.

Lee Watch, a Word of Command to the Men at the Helm, and is as much as to say, take care that the Ship don't go to the Leeward of her Course.

Leeward-Ship, one that is not fast by a Wind, or which doth not sail so near the Wind to make her way so good as she should. To lay a Ship by the Lee, is to bring her so that all her Sails may be flat against her Masts and Shrouds, and that the Wind may come right upon her Broad-side.

Leefe, deare. *Spencer*.

Leet and *Court Leet*, is a Court out of the Sherif's turn, and enquires of all Offences under the degree of high Treason that are committed against the Crown and Dignity of the King.

Leetch of a Sail, signifies the outward edge or skirt of the Sail from the Earing to the Clew, or rather the middle of the Sail between these two.

Leetch Lines, are small Ropes in a Ship, whose use is to hale in the Leetch of the Sail when the Top-sail is to be taken in.

Legacy, a Gift bequeathed by a Testator in his Will to any private Person, or to a Corporation.

Legal, (Lat.) according to Law, lawful.

Legality, (Lat.) Lawfulness.

Legatary, vid. *Legatee*.

Legate, (Lat.) an Ambassador or Envoy, in general, but 'tis now restrained to one sent from the Pope to some foreign Prince or State.

Legatees, those Persons who haves Legacies left them in a Will, are called Legatees.

Legatine, belonging to a Legate.

Legend, (Lat.) a writing; also the words that are about the edge of a piece of Coin. The *Golden Legend* is the Title of a Book containing the Lives of the Saints.

Legendary, belonging to a Legend; also fabulous.

Leger-Book, a Register belonging to Notaries and Merchants.

Legedermain, (Fr.) flight of Hand, Couzenage, Jugling Tricks.

Leggs of the Martnets, are those small Ropes in a Ship which are put through the *Bolt Ropes* of the *Main* and *Fore-Sail* in the *Leetch* of each.

Leggs of a Triangle, are any two sides of a Triangle, when the third is considered as a Base.   *Legible*,

Legible, (Lat.) that may be read.

Legion, (Lat.) an Army or Band of Men. The exact number of Foot in such a Batallion *Romulus* fixed at three thousand; tho' *Plutarch* assures us, that after the Reception of the *Sabines* into *Rome*, he encreased it to six Thousand. The common number afterwards in the time of the free State was four Thousand. In the War with *Hannibal* it arose to five thousand; after this, 'tis probable they sunk to about four Thousand, or four Thousand two Hundred again; the Horse required to every Legion were three Hundred.

Legionary, belonging to a *Roman* Legion.

Legislative, (Lat.) that hath Power or Authority to make or give Laws.

Legislator, a Law-giver, a Law-maker.

Legitimate, (Lat.) lawful, done according to Law and Right. Legitimate Children are those which are born in Matrimony.

Legumen, in Botanicks, is that Species of Plants which we call Pulse, and they are so called because they may be gathered with the Hand without cutting.

Leman, a Concubine, a Harlot.

Lemma, in Mathematicks, is a Proposition which serves previously to prepare the way for the demonstration of some Theorem, or for the construction of some Problem.

Lemnian, of *Lemnos*, an Island; as *Leminan* Earth.

Lenientia, loosening Medicines. See *Laxatives*.

Lenity, mildness, softness, gentleness.

Lenitive, or *Lenient*, (Lat.) of a softning or an assuageing Nature.

Lens, in Opticks, is a small *Convex* or *Plano Convex*, a Concave, or *Concavo* Convex Glass.

Lent, in the old *Saxon*, signifies the *Spring*, and thence has been taken in common Language to signifie the *Spring Fast*, or the time of Humiliation generally observed before *Easter*.

Lenta Febris, the slow or lingring Fever, which proceeds from some hidden Putrefaction sticking to some Bowel, so that its Substance is almost corrupted: Such a Fever is often bred in the Consumption of the Lungs, and degenerates into a Hectick.

Lentes, a Roman Weight which contains $\frac{85}{112}$ gr. being reduced to our English Troy Weight.

Lentigines, are what we call Freckles.

Leo, is the fifth of the twelve Signs of the Zodiack reakoning from *Aries*.

Leomine, Cruel, Savage, of a Lion-like Nature.

Lepid, pleasant, jocose.

Lepido-

Lepidoides, is the scaly Suture of the Scull.

Leporine, (Lat.) belonging to a Hare.

Leprosy, is a dry Scab, whereby the Skin becomes scaly like a Fish.

Leptology, (Gr.) in Rhetorick, is a description of minute and sordid things.

Leptuntica, are attenuating cutting Medicines which part or cut the viscuous Humours with their sharp Particles.

Lepus, a Southern Constellation consisting of thirteen Stars.

Lere, Lesson to learn. *Spencer*.

Lesser Circles of the Sphere, are those which divide the Globe into two unequal halves.

Lessian Diet, a moderate Diet, from *Lessius* a famous Physician.

Lessor and *Lessee*. See *Lease*.

Leteeh, a Jewish Measure of Capacity for things dry, containing 16 Pecks, 26 solid Inches. and 52 decimal Parts of the English Corn Measure.

Lethal, (Lat.) Mortal, deadly.

Lethality, (Lat.) Mortality, Frailty.

Lethargy, (Lat.) a Disease caused by cold flegmatick Humours oppressing the Brain in such sort, that the Person can do nothing but Sleep, whereby he becomes forgetful, and, in a manner, loses both his Reason and all his Senses.

Lethargick, that is troubl'd with a Lethargy.

Lethiferous, (Lat.) that bringeth Death, deadly.

Letters Patent, are Writings sealed with the Great Seal of *England*, whereby a Man is authorized to do or enjoy any thing, that otherwise of himself he could not.

Letter of Attorney, is a Writing authorizing an Attorney, that is, a Man appropriated to do a lawful act in our stead.

Letters of Mart, are Letters that authorize any one to take by force of Arms those Goods which are due by Law of *Mart*.

Letter-Founder, one that Casts the Types or Characters for Printers.

Lettered, Learned; Book *Lettered*, that is, with its Title on the Back in Golden Letters.

Levant, the Eastern parts of the Continent are so called, as *Asia*, &c.

Levant and *Couchant*, in Law, is when Cattle have been so long in another Man's Ground, that they have lain down and are risen again to feed.

Levantine, of, or belonging to the East.

Levari Facias, is a Writ directed to the Sheriff for levying of a sum of Money upon Lands and Tenements of him that hath forfeited a Recognisance.

Levari

Levari facias damna difcif-toribus, is a Writ directed to the Sheriff for levying of Damages, wherein the *Difcifor* hath formerly been condemned to the *Difcifee.*

Levari facias refiduum debiti, is a Writ directed to the Sheriff, for the levying the Remnant of a Debt upon Lands and Tenements, or Chattels of theDebtor that he hath in part fatisfied before.

Levatory, a Surgeon's Inftrument to elevate the depreffed Cranium.

Leuce, is a cutaneous Difeafe, when the Hair, Skin, and fometimes the Flefh underneath, turns white, the Flefh being pricked, is not fenfible, nor emits Blood, but a milkySubftance; it differs from *Alphus,* in that it penetrates deeper.

Leucoma, a white fcar in the Horney Tunick of the Eye.

Leucophlegmatick, a Perfon troubled with a pituitous Dropfy, or a Dropfy that feizes the whole Body.

Lvel, an Inftrument ufed by Carpenters, and other Artificers to try whether Plains, Boards, or pieces of Timber lie Horizontal; alfo a Mathematical Inftrument whofe ufe is to find the true level, in order to convey Water to fupply Towns, make Rivers navigable, drein Boggs, *&c.*

*Levellers,*People who would have all things common.

Lever, rather. *Spencer.*

Lever, is one of the Mechanical Powers, and is nothing but a Ballance refting inftead of hanging on a certain determinate Point, called its *Fulcrum* or *Hypomocleon,* and fo lifting up any given Weight; another difference between this and the common Ballance, is, that in the common Ballance, the Center of motion is in the middle, but it may be in any Point in the Lever.

Leveret, a young Hare.

Leviathan, a Whale, or, as fome think, a huge Water Serpent; fometimes 'tis taken for the Devil.

Levigation, (Lat.) a making plain or fmooth.

Levigation, in Chymiftry, is the grinding any hardMatter to a very fine, or, as they fay, an impalpable Powder upon a Marble.

Levin, Lightning. *Spencer.*

Levity, (Lat.) lightnefs, or the want of weight in any Body when compared with another that is heavier.

Levy, (Fr.) in Common Law, it fignifies to erect or fet up; alfo to tax or gather Money.

Lex talionis, (Lat.) a Law of Recompence, or a Law which rendreth one good or ill turn for another.

Lexicon, (Gr.) a Dictionary, a Collection of the words of any Language.

Ley, (Fr.) the Law.

Lhan, (Brit.) a Church.

Libation

Liard, a French Farthing, a small piece of Money worth three *Deniers*. See *Deniers*.

Libation, a Ceremony practised in the Sacrifices of the *Pagans*, wherein the Priest poured down Wine, Milk, and other Liquors, in honour of the Deity to whom he sacrificed after he had first tasted a little of it.

Libel, (Lat.) a little Book; also a scandalous and invective Pamphlet, secretly spread abroad and publish'd unlawfully; also an Original Declaration of any Action in the Civil Law.

To *Libel one*, to set forth Libels against, to defame or slander.

Libella, a Roman Coin. See *As*.

Libellatici, were those Christians, who, that they might not be forc'd to Idol Worship, gave up their Names in Petitions, or subscrib'd to pay a Fine.

Libellous, slanderous, abusive; of the Nature of a Libel.

Libera chasea habenda, a Writ judicial, granted to a Man for a free Choice belonging to his Mannor, after he hath by a Jury proved it to belong to him.

Liberal, bountiful, generous, free; also honourable, genteel.

Liberal Arts and Sciences, are those that are suitable for Gentlemen to exercise; as mechanick Trades and Handicrafts are for meaner People.

Liberality, a Vertue whereby a Man freely bestows upon others Money, &c. according to his Ability.

Liberate, set free or at liberty, deliver'd.

Liberate, (Lat.) is the name of a Warrant issuing out of Chancery, for Payment of a yearly Pension, or other sums granted under the Great Seal, or sometimes to the Sheriff for Delivery of Lands or Goods taken upon Forfeits of Recognizance: It lies also to a Jailer for delivery of a bailed Prisoner.

Libertas, (Lat.) freedom, leave; a privilege by Grant or Prescription to enjoy some extraordinary Benefit.

Libertate Probanda, a Writ for such as were challenged for Slaves, and offered to prove themselves free.

Libertatibus allocandis, a Writ for a Citizen (impleaded contrary to his Liberty) to have his Privilege allow'd.

Libertatibus exigendis in itinere, is a Writ whereby the King willeth the Justices in *Eyre* to admit of an Attorney for the defence of another Man's Liberty before them.

Libertine, among the Romans, was the Child of one that had been made Free; but now 'tis frequently used for one of a loose and debauched Life and Principles.

Libertines, a Sect of Christian Hereticks sprung from one

K k

one *Quintin* a Taylor, and one *Copin*, who about 1525, divulged their Errors in *Holland*. They maintain'd that whatsoever was done by Men, was done by the Spirit of God; and from thence concluded there was no Sin but to those that thought it so. They affirm'd, that to live without any Doubt or Scruple, was to return to the state of Innocency.

Libertinism, the state of him that of a Slave is made Free; the Divines thus define it, Libertinism is nothing else but a false Liberty of Belief and Manners, which will have no other dependance but on particular Fancy and Passion.

Liberty, (Lat.) Freedom, which is a Power a Man has to do or forbear any particular Action as seems good to him.

Libidinous, full of Lust, Incontinent, Sensual.

Libitinarii, were those among the *Romans* that furnished what was necessary in Funerals; with us they are called *Undertakers*.

Libra, the Ballance; one of the twelve Signs of the Zodiack exactly opposite to *Aries*, and the sixth from it.

Libra, a Roman Weight, which being reduced to our Troy Weight, contains 10 Ounces 18 pw. 13½gr.

Libra Medica, the Physicians Pound, it contains twelve Ounces.

Libration, (Lat.) a weighing or ballancing; but 'tis most commonly used for the motion of swinging in a Pendulum.

Library, a Study or place where Books are kept.

Licence, (Lat.) Liberty, Permission, Power, Leave. *Verbally*, to grant a Licence, to give Leave or Power, to Authorize.

Licence to Arise, is a Liberty or Space given by the Court to a Tenant in a real Action (*essoined de malo lecti*) to arise or appear abroad.

Licentiate, (Lat.) one that hath full Licence or Authority to practise in any Art.

Licentious, of a loose Carriage and Behaviour.

Lich-fowl, are certain unlucky Birds, as the Night-Raven, and Scrietch-Owl; from *Lich* a *Saxon* word that signifies a Carcass.

Lichas, a Grecian Measure of length, containing 7 Inches, 5546⅔ decimal parts of our English Measure.

Lichenes, are certain Asperities of the Skin, and, as it were, Tumours which itch much, and, as it were, send forth Matter:

Licitation, (Lat.) a setting out to be sold to the highest bidder, an Auction.

Lickorish, loving dainty or sweet things.

Lictors, among the Romans, were Sergeants or Beadles who carried the *Fasces* before the Supreme Magistrates ftrates; and befides this, they were the publick Executioners in fcourging and beheading.

Lidford-Law, is to hang one firft and judge him aftewards. 'Tis fo named from *Lidford*, a Town in *Cornwal*. The like is faid of *Halifax* in *Yorkfhire*.

Lietf, or *Leof*, (Sax.) rather.

Liege, (Fr.) is fometimes for *Liege Lord*, and fometimes for *Liege Man* : *Liege Lord* is he that acknowledgeth no Superiour ; *Liege Man* is he that owneth Allegiance to his *Liege Lord*.

Liegancy, is fuch a Duty or Falfty as no Man may owe or bear to more than one Lord ; alfo the Territories or Dominions of the *Liege Lord*.

Lienteria, is a kind of Loofenefs, where the Meat or Aliment taken in is fent out of the Body before it be altered, or at leaft before it be digefted.

Lieu, (Lat.) in the place or ftead.

Lieutenancy, or *Lieutenantfhip*, the Office of a Lieutenant.

Lieutenant, (Fr.) one that fupplies the Place and reprefents the Perfon of the Prince, or others in Authority ; as the Lord Lieutenant of *Ireland*, or of a County.

Lieutenant General, (in an Army) is a Commander next to a General ; in Battel he commands one of the Wings or Lines; upon a March, a Detachment or flying Camp, and a particular quarter of a Siege.

Lieutenant General of the Artillery, is next to the General of the Artillery, and fupplies his Place in his Abfence.

Lieutenant Colonel (of Horfe, Foot, or Dragoons) is next in Office to the Colonel, and commands in his Abfence.

Lieutenant of a Troop or Company, is next to the Captain, and commands in his Abfence.

Lieutenant of a Ship, is next to the Chief Commander or Captain.

Lieutenant of the Tower of London, he is next in place to the Conftable, and in his Abfence acts with as full Power as he. By his Office he is in Commiffion of the Peace for *Middlefex.*, *Kent* and *Surry*; and has 200 *l. per Ann.* befides other Fees and Perquifites.

Life Rent, in Law, is a Rent or Exhibition which a Man receives either for Term of Life, or for Suftentation of Life.

Lifts, are Ropes in a Ship belonging to the Yard Arms of all Yards, whofe ufe is to make the Yards hang higher or lower.

Ligament, in Anatomy, is a Part, of a middle Subftance betwixt a Cartilage and a Membrane, appointed for the

the tying of sundry parts together: Those which tie Bones together are void of Sense, but those that knit other parts together, are (duly) sensible.

Ligation, (Lat.) a binding or tying.

Ligatures, in Mathematicks, are compendious Notes or Characters, by which are represented the Sums, Differences, or Rectangles of several Quantities.

Ligg, *so laid*; lye so faint. *Spencer*.

Light Homogeneal, or similar and uniform Light, is that whose Rays are equally Refrangible.

Light Heterogeneal, is that whose Rays are unequally Refrangible.

Like signs, &c. are Signs of the same Nature, either all , + or all—

Light-Horse, are such Horse-men as are not in Armour; in *England* all are so called besides the Troops of Life-Guards.

Ligula, a Roman Measure of Capacity for things Liquid, containing ¼ of a Pint 117½ decimal Parts of a solid Inch of our Wine Measure. Also a Roman Measure of Capacity for things dry, containing ¼ of a Pint, and 61 decimal Parts of a solid Inch of our Corn Measure.

Limation, a filing or Polishing.

Limb, is a part of the Body; also the outermost Edge or Border of any thing.

Limbus Patrum, (Lat.) a place where the Antient Patriarchs, after their decease, were supposed to reside, 'till the coming of our Saviour.

Limit, a Border, Bound, or Boundary. *Verbally*, to set Bounds, to confine, to stint.

Limitation, (Lat.) a stinting or setting of Bounds.

Limitation of Assize, is a certain time set down by Statute wherein a Man must alledge himself, or his Ancestor to have been seized of Lands sued for by a Writ of Assize.

Limn, to paint in water Colours.

Limonade, a cooling Liquor of Lemons, Water, and Sugar.

Limosity, (Lat.) Muddiness.

Limp, supple, limber. *Verbally*, to halt.

Limpheducts, in Anatomy, are small Pipes consisting of an exceeding thin and pellucid Coat, conveying the Liquor called *Lympha* into the Mass of the Blood.

Lympid, clear, bright, pure, transparent.

Linch-Pins, are those Pins that keep on the Trunks or Wheels of the Carriage of a piece of Ordnance.

Line, is a row of words in Writing or Printing. In Geometry, 'tis a length without breadth and depth, form'd by the motion of a Point. In Measuring, 'tis ¹⁄₁₂ of an Inch: Also the Flax Plant.

Line

Line of Measures, a Line in the *Stereographick Projection* of the *Sphere.*

Line in Fortification, is a Line drawn from one Point to another in delineating a Plane upon Paper.

Line Capital, is that which is drawn from the Angle of the *Gorge* to the Angle of the Baftion.

Line of Defence, is that which reprefents the courfe of the Bullet, or any fort of Fire-Arms, more efpecially of a Mufquet Ball, according to the fituation which it ought to have to defend the Face of the Baftion.

Line of Defence Fixed or Fichant, is that which is drawn from the Angle of the Curtin to the flanked Angle of the oppofite Baftion.

Line of Defence Rezant, is a Line drawn from a certain point of its Curtin which rafeth the Face of the oppofite Baftion, this is called alfo the Line of Defence ftringent or flanking.

Lines of Approach or of Attack, is the Work which the Befiegers carry on under covert to gain the Moat and the Body of the Place.

Line of Circumvallation, is a Line or Trench cut by the Befiegers within Cannon-Shot of the Place, which rangeth round their Camp, and fecures its Quarters againft the relief of the Befieged,

Line of Contravallation, is a Ditch bordered with a Parapet, which ferves to cover the Befiegers on the fide of the Place, and to cover the Sallies of the Garrifon.

Lines within fide, are the Moats toward the place to prevent the like Sallies.

Lines without fide, are the Moats toward the Field, to hinder Relief.

Lines of Communication, are thofe that run from one Work to another.

Line of the Bafe, is a right Line which joins the Points of the two neareft Baftions.

To line a Work, is to ftrengthen a Rampart with a firm Wall, or to encompafs a Moat or a Parapet with a good Turf, *&c.*

Line Horizontal, is a Line drawn parallel to the Horizon.

Line Horizontal in Dialing, is the common Section of the Horizon and Dial-Plane.

----In Perfpective, it is the common Section of the Horizontal Plane, or that of the Draught or Reprefentation, and which paffes through the principal Point.

Line Geometrical, in Perfpective, is a right Line drawn any how on the Geometrical Plain.

Line Terreftrial, in Perfpective, is a right Line wherein the Geometrical Plain and that of the Picture or Draught interfect one another.

Line of the Front, in Perspective, is any right Line parallel to the Terrestrial Line.

Line vertical, in Perspective, is the common Section of the vertical Plain, and of the Draught.

Line of Station, in Perspective, according to some Writers, is the common Section of the Vertical and Geometrical Planes. Others, as *Lamy,* mean by it the perpendicular height of the Eye above the Geometrick Plane. Others, a Line drawn on that Plane, and perpendicular to the Line expressing the height of the Eye.

Line Objective, is the Line of an Object from whence the Appearance is sought for in the Draught or Picture.

Line of Direction, of any Body in motion, is either that according to which it moves, or that according to which the force was impressed upon it.

Line of swiftest Descent, is a Line in which a heavy Body, by the force of its own Gravity, shall descend from one Point as *A* to another Point as *B,* (both placed in some Vertical Plane) in the shortest time possible, and such a Line is proved to be the common Cycloid.

Lines Horary, or *Hour Lines,* in Dialing, are the common interfections of the Hour-Circles of the Sphere with the Plane of the Dial.

Line Substilar, is that Line on which the Stile or Cock of the Dial is erected, and is the Representation of an Hour Circle perpendicular to the Plane of that Dial.

Line Equinoctial, in Dialling, is the common Intersection of the Equinoctial and Plane of the Dial.

Lines, in the Art of War, signifie the Position of an Army ranged in the Order of Battel.

Lineal, belonging to a Line; that is, or goes in a Right-Line.

Lineament, (Lat.) the Feature or Proportion of any thing drawn out in Lines.

Lingel, a little Tongue.

Linger, to be tedious, or long a doing; to languish for droop.

Lingots, in Chymistry, Iron Moulds of divers Figures for casting melted Metals into.

Linguacity, a being full of Tongue or Talk, Talkativeness.

Linguist, a Person skillful in Tongues and Languages.

Liniment, an external Medicine of a middle Consistence between an Oil and an Ointment.

Linsey-Woolsey, ony Stuff or Cloth that is partly Linnen, and partly Wollen.

Lioncels, the Heralds Term for Lions, when there is more than two of them born in any Coat of Arms and no Ordinary between them; and

and 'tis all one with a small or young Lion.

Lipopfychy, (Gr.) a small Swoon, or imperfect *Syncope*; which see.

Lipothymy, a fainting or swooning away, being also an imperfect *Syncope*.

Lippitude, (Lat.) a waterishness of the Eyes, a looking bloodshot or blear Eyed.

Liquable, (Lat.) that may be melted or dissolved.

Liquation, or *Liquefaction*, (Lat.) a melting or dissolving.

Liquefy, (Lat.) to make Liquid, to melt, to become Liquid.

Liquid, (Lat.) moist, soft, fluid.

Liquidescency, aptness to melt or grow soft.

Liquids, are such Bodies as have all the Properties of Fluidity.

Lispound, a foreign Weight of fifteen or sixteen, and sometimes twenty Pounds.

List, a Scrowl of the Names of several Persons of the same Quality or imploy'd in the same Business.

List, or *Lists*, a place enclosed or railed in for Tournaments, and other Exercises.

List, in Architecture, is a strait upright Ring which runs round the lower part of any of the Columns just above the *Tore*, and next to the Shaft or Body of the Pillar.

Listel, a small Band, or a kind of Rule in the moulding

of Architecture; also a space between the chanelling of Pillars.

Listless, careless, heedless, uneasie.

Litation, (Lat.) a sacrificing.

Litany, a part of the Liturgy or Common-Prayer so called; the word signifies Prayer or Supplication.

Literal, (Lat.) belonging to Letters.

Literate, (Lat.) Learned, skill'd in Letters.

Literature, (Lat.) knowledge in Letters, Learning.

Litharge of Gold and Silver, is the scum to be taken off in the Purification of those Mettals by a Spoon, or other Instrument.

Lithiasis, (Gr.) the breeding of the Stone in the Kidneys or Bladder.

Lithomancy, (Gr.) divination by casting Pebble Stones, or by the Load Stone.

Lithontripticks, (Gr.) are Medicines which break the Stone either in the Kidneys or in the Bladder.

Lithotomy, in Surgery, is the cutting the Stone out of the Bladder; also a Mason's Work-house or Quarry.

Litigation, (Lat.) a contending, wrangling, or Quarrelling.

Litigious, quarrelsome, full of dispute and wrangling.

Litispendence, the time of depending of a Law-Suit.

Litmoss-blew, a sort of blew Colour used in Painting and Limning.

Litotes, or *diminutio*, is a Term in Rhetorick, by which we speak less than we think.

Littoral, belonging to the Shore.

Liturgy, (Gr.) signifieth in general any publick Office, but particularly Divine Service, or a Form of Publick Prayers.

Livery, (Fr.) hath three Significations; in one it is used for a suit of Cloth or Stuff that a Gentleman giveth to his Servants or Followers. In the second it signifies a Delivery of Possession. And in the third signification Livery is the Writ which lies for the Heir to obtain the Possession or Seisin of his Land at the King's Hand.

Livery of Seisin, is a delivery of Possession of Lands, Tenements, or other things Corporeal, unto one that hath Right; or a probability of Right to them.

Livid, black and blew, or a kind of Leaden or dead blewish Colour, caused in any part of the Body by a blow or stroke given; also envious, malicious.

Livre, (Fr.) signifies a Pound; 'tis in value 1 s. 6 d. Sterling. In *Leghorn*, a Livre is only 9 d. in value.

Lixiere, a Term in Fortification, the same with *Berme*, which see.

Lixiviate, or *Lixivious*, be-

longing to, or proceeding from Lye; as *fixt Salts*.

Lizard-Point, the utmost Southwest Point of the Lands end in *Cornwall*.

Load-Star; that is leading Star; the North Star that guides the Mariners.

Load-Stone, i. e. Leading Stone, because it directs Sailers. 'Tis of a dark rusty Colour, and endu'd with the faculty of attracting Iron and Steel, whereby it is of admirable use to Mankind. See *Magnet*.

Loam, grafting Clay, Morter of Clay and Straw.

Lobby, a sort of Passage Room or Gallery.

Lobes, the several Divisions of the Lungs or Liver.

Local; is whatever is supposed to be tied or annexed to any particular place.

Local Medicaments, are those which are applied outwards as Plaisters, Ointments, &c.

Local Problem, is such an one as is capable of an infinite number of Solutions, i. e. which may be done an infinite number of different ways, insomuch that the Point which resolves the Problem when it is in Geometry, may be indifferently taken within a certain Extent, which may be a Line, a Plain, or a Solid.

Locality, (Lat.) the being of a thing in a place.

Location, (Lat.) a letting out to hire.

Lochia,

Lochia, are the Natural Evacuations of Women in Child-bed after the Birth of the *Fœtus*, and the exclusion of the Membranes called *Secundina*, or the after Birth.

Locker, a Pigeon-Hole; in a Ship, 'tis a kind of Box or Chest made along the side of a Ship to put or stow any thing in.

Locket, a set of Diamonds, or other Jewels; also that part of a Sword's Scabbard, where the Hook is fastned.

Lock-spit, a Term in Fortification, signifying the small Cut or Trench made with a Spade, to mark out the first Lines of any Works that are to be made.

Locomotive, (Lat.) so is that Faculty termed which produces Motion from one place to another.

Loculamentum, in Botanicks, is a little distinct Cell or Partition within the common *Capsula Seminalis* of any Plant.

Locus, or the place of any Body, is either Absolute or Relative.

Locus Absolutus, or place absolute of a Body, is that part of the absolute and immovable Space or extended Capacity to receive all Bodies which this individual one takes up.

Locus Relativus, is that apparent and sensible place in which we determine a Body to be placed with regard to other contiguous or adjacent Bodies.

Locusta, in Botany, are the Beards and Pendulous Seeds of Oats, and of the *Gramina Paniculata*.

Locution, (Lat.) a saying or speaking.

Lodemanage, is the hire of a Pilot for conducting a Ship from one place to another.

Lodesman, a Pilot that guides Ships in and out of Harbours, and about the Coasts.

Lodgment, in Military Affairs, is sometimes an Encampment made by an Army; but most commonly 'tis a Work raised with Earth, Gabions, Fascines, Wool-Packs, or Mantlets to cover the Besiegers from the Enemies Fire.

Log, a Jewish Measure of Capacity for things Liquid, containing ? of a Pint, and 1½ solid Inches of our Wine Measure.

Log, a Board a Ship, is a piece of Wood about seven or eight Inches long, of a triangular Form, with as much Lead in one end thereof as will serve to make it swim up-right in the Water, and at the other end is fastened to the Log-Line.

Log-Line, is a small Line having the Log tied to one end, the use whereof is to keep an account, and make an Estimate of the Ship's way.

Log-Board, is a Board or Table divided usually into five

five Columns; the first contains the Hours of the Day from Noon to Noon; in the second is placed the Ship's Course; in the third and fourth Column is placed the Distance run in Knots, Fathoms, and half Fathoms, or sometimes Feet; and in the fifth is placed the Winds, Weather, Accidents, &c.

Log-Wood, or *Block-Wood*, a sort of Wood much used in Dying, otherwise called *Campechio*. from a Town of that name in *Yucatan* in *Northern America*.

Logarithms, are Numbers that are *Indexes* or *Exponents* of Ratio's, as is easily seen from these two Series,

$$0 \quad 1 \quad 2 \quad 3 \quad 4$$
$$1 \quad a \quad aa \quad aaa \quad aaaa$$

where 0, 1, 2, 3, 4, are the Logarithms of 1, a, aa, aaa, &c. which latter Series of Terms are very often more compendiously writ thus, $1^0, a^1, a^2, a^3, a^4$, &c. and now 'tis plain that the Logarithms or *Exponents*, 0,1,2,3,4, are also the Exponents of the Ratio's of any of the said Terms to 1. Thus the Ratio of a^2 to 1, is $\frac{a^2}{1}$ or a^2; so that a^3 being the Ratio of a^3 to 1, 2 is the Exponent of that Ratio; and the Ratio of a^3 to 1, is a^3, whose Exponent is 3; and this is what is meant by the definition, that Logarithms are Numbers which are *Indexes* or *Exponents* of Ratio's.

Logarithmick Line, is a Curve : whose Ordinates taken to equal parts of the *Axis* are Geometrically proportional.

Logarithmick Spiral, is a sort of Spiral which we may conceive to be formed much after the same manner with other Spirals. Thus suppose the Radius of a Circle move uniformly through the Circumference, while a certain Point moves from the extremity of this Radius towards the Center, with a motion retarded in a Geometrick Proportion, the track of this Point will form the *Logarithmick Spiral*.

Logical, belonging to Logick, agreeable to the Rules thereof.

Logician, one that studies Logick, or is skillful in it.

Logick, is the Art of thinking right, or well using our rational Faculty; and the Power or Force of Reason unassisted by Art, is called Natural Logick.

Logist, an expert Accomptant, or one skill'd in casting Accompts.

Logistica, the Logarithmick Line; *which see*. Also *Algebra*, or Numeral Arithmetick.

Logistical Arithmetick, sometimes signifies the Arithmetick of Sexagesimal Fractions used by Astronomers in their Calculations.

Logographer, (Gr.) a Lawyer's Clerk, or a writer of Books of Accounts.

Lege.

Logomachy, (Gr.) a verbal Strife, a contention in words.

Loimography, (Gr.) a de-scription of pestilential Dis-eases.

Lollards, so were those of the Reformation called for-merly in *England*, from one *Walter Lollard* their first Lea-der.

Lome, Clay, Mortar.

Lombar, or *Lombard*, a Bank for Usury or Pawns, so call'd from the *Lombards* that were much given to U-sury.

Lombar-House, a House in which several sorts of Goods are stowed, in order to be exposed to Sale.

Lonchites, a Species of Comets resembling a Lance or Spear, its Head is of an Elliptick Form, and its Tail or Stream of Rays, ve-ry long, thin, and pointed at the end.

Long, is a Musical Note, equal to two Briefs.

Long Accent, in Grammer, shows the Voice is to stop at the Vowel that has that mark.

Long Boat, is the largest and strongest Boat belonging to a Ship, that can be hoist-ed a Board of her; its use is to bring any Goods, Provi-sions, *&c.* to or from her; or on occasion to land Men any where, and particularly to weigh the Anchor.

Long-primer, are Printers Types, one size bigger than *Brevier.*

Longanimity, (Lat.) Long-suffering, Forbearance, great Patience.

Longevity, (Lat.) length of Life.

Longimetry, is the Art of measuring Length and Di-stances.

Longitude, (Lat.) signifies length of any thing that is measurable, as of Place, Mo-tion, Time, *&c.*

Longitude, in Geometry, is an Arch of the Equator comprehended between the first Meridian, and the Me-ridian of the place you en-quire after, and shows how much one place is more Ea-stern or Western than the other.

Longitude of the Stars, is reckoned in the Ecliptick from the first degree of *Aries* to the last of *Pisces*, and this by great Circles of the Sphere passing through the Poles of the Ecliptick; so that the Ark of the Ecliptick inter-cepted between the first de-gree of *Aries*, and that Cir-cle which passes through the Center of the Star, is the Longitude of the Star.

Longitude, in Dialing, the Arch of the Equinoctial in-tercepted between the substi-lar Line of the Dial, and the true Meridian, is called the Plane's difference of Lon-gitude.

Longitudinal Suture, that Seam of the Head which runs along between the Coronal and Lambdoidal Sutures.

Loof,

Loof, or *Loof*, of a Ship, is that part of her a-loft which lies juft before the *Cheft-Trees*.

Loof-Hook, a Tackle with two Hooks; one of which is to hitch into the Crengle of the Main and Fore-Sail, and the other likewife to hitch into a Strap, or Pulley-Rope, that is let into the Chefs-Tree, and fo down the Sail; its ufe being to fuccour the Tackles in a large Sail.

Loof-Pieces, are thofe Guns which lie at the Loof of the Ship.

Loof-Tackle, is a fmall Tackle ferving to lift all fmall Weights in or out of a Ship.

Loof, or *Luff*, is alfo a word ufed in *Conding* of a Ship, as *Loof, Keep your Loof*, that is, keep the Ship near the Wind.

Loof up, that is, keep nearer the Wind.

To Loof into a Harbour, is to fail into it clofe by the Wind.

To fpring the Loof, is when a Ship that before was going large before the Wind, is brought clofe by the Wind.

Loom, the Looming of a Ship is her Perfpective, as fhe appears at a diftance great or little.

Loom-Gale, is a gentle, eafie gale of Wind in which a Ship can carry her Top-fails.

Loop-Holes, are holes made in the Coamings of the Hatches for clofe Fights, and other conveniencies.

Loquacious, (Lat.) full of talk, prating, tattling.

Loquacity, (Lat.) Talkativenefs, or a being given to much Talking.

Lord, a word of Honour, fometimes attributed to thofe who are noble by Birth or Creation; fometimes 'tis a Title given by the Courtefie of *England* to the Sons of Dukes and Marqueffes, and Eldeft Sons of Earls; and fometimes 'tis given to Perfons on the account of their Office or Employment.

Lord of the Geniture, (in Aftrology) is the Planet of the greateft ftrength in the Figure of a Nativity, and fo becomes principal fignificators of the Temperament, Manners, Difpofition of Body, &c.

Lord Mefne, the owner of a Manour that has Tenants holding of him in Fee, who yet holds of a fuperiour Lord, or Lord Paramount.

Lord of the Hour, a Planet that governs one twelfth part of the Day, or of the Night, both which are divided into twelve equal parts, called *Planetary Hours*, which are longer or fhorter as the Days or Nights lengthen or fhorten.

Lore, (Sax.) Learning, Skill, *Spencer*.

Lorel, Devourer, a crafty Fellow. *Spencer*.

Lorication, (Lat.) Harneffing, or Arming with a Coat of Mail; alfo filling of Walls with Morter; alfo covering

covering glass Chymical Vessels with Clay to arm them against the naked Fire.

Lorne, left, lost. *Spencer.*

Losenger, a Lyer or Flatterer. *Chaucer.*

Lot, when any thing is shared among several Persons, the shares are often call'd *Lots*.

Lotion, (Lat.) a *Washing*: In Chymistry and Pharmacy, 'tis the washing or cleansing any Medicine in Water; as the *Lotion of Antimony*, &c. Also a particular Remedy between a Fomentation and a Bath, which is used for washing Head, Hands, or other distempered Part.

Lotterie, a Play of Chance, in the nature of a Bank, wherein are put Lots of Goods or Sums of Money, which are mixed with many more blank Lots, of which every one buys as many as he pleases; which done the Lots are drawn out at a venture, and has the value of the Lot he draws.

Lough, Irish word for a Lake; also a Term in Falconry.

Low-Bell, a Device to catch Birds.

Low-beller, one that goes a Fowling with a Light and a Bell.

Lower Flank, or *Retired Flank*. See *Flank.*

Low-masted, or *Under-masted*, so is a Ship said to be, when her Mast is too small or too low, to carry Sail enough.

Lowr, to frown, to look sour or grim; also to begin to be overcast with Clouds.

Loxodromick, or *Rhumb-Line*, is an irregular Curve winding about the Convex Surface of the Globe, whose Nature is such, that any Point taken therein, lies in one and the same Quarter and *Plaga* from all the other Points of that Curve whatsoever.

Loxodromicks, is the Art of oblique sailing by the Rumb, which always makes equal Angles with every Meridian, *i.e.* when you sail, neither directly under the Equator, nor under the same Meridian, but obliquely or a-cross them.

Loxodromick-Line, is the Line of the Ship's way, when she sails upon a Rumb oblique to the Meridian.

Loxodromick-Tables, are the Tables of Rhumbs, or the traverse Tables of Miles with the difference of *Latitude* and *Longitude.*

Loyal, (Fr.) Honest, Trusty, Faithful.

Lozenge, is that Figure in Heraldry, which in Geometry is called a Rhombus, *i.e.* a Parallelogram whose sides are all equal to one another, and Angles unequal, *Thus*: In this Figure, all unmarri'd Gen-

tle-

tlewomen and Widows do bear their Coats of Arms, becaufe, as fome fay, 'twas the Figure of the *Amazonian Shield*; or as others, becaufe 'tis the Antient Figure of the Spindle.

Lubber, a mean Servant that does all bafe Services in a Houfe.

Lubricitate, (in Phyfick and Philofophy) to make flippery.

Lubricity, (Lat.) Slipperinefs.

Lubricous, (Lat.) flippery, uncertain.

Lucid, (Lat.) clear, bright, fhining; Lucid Body, is a Body that emits Light.

Lucida Carona, a fixed Star of the fecond Magnitude in the Northern Garland, whofe *Longitude* is 217°. 38'. *Latitude*, 44°. 23'. *Right Afcenfion* 130°. 11'.

Lucida Lyra, a fixed Star of the firft Magnitude in the Conftellation of *Lyra* whofe *Longitude* is 10°. 43'. *Latitude*, 61°. 47'. *Right Afcenfion* 276°. 27'. and *Decli*. 38°. 30'.

Lucidity, (Lat.) brightnefs, fhining.

Lucifer, (Lat.) light bringing; fo *Venus* is called in the Morning when fhe rifes before the Sun.

Luciferians, a fort of Hereticks, fo called from their Author *Lucifer of Cagliari*, who lived about the Year of Chrift 365. It is faid that they held that the Soul of Man was propagated out of

the Subftance of his Flefh, &c.

Luciferous, bringing Light, giving Infight into.

Lucrative, gainful, profitable.

Lucre, (Lat.) Gain or Profit.

Luctation, (Lat.) a wreftling or ftruggling.

Lucubration, (Lat.) ftudying or working by Candle Light.

Luculency, (Lat.) clearnefs, plainnefs, brightnefs, beauty.

Luculent, (Lat.) full of light, clear, beautiful, famous.

Ludicrous, (Lat.) pertaining to Play or Mirth, Mocking, Light, Childifh.

Ludification, (Lat.) a mocking or deceiving.

Lues Deifica, or *Sacra*, the Falling-Sicknefs.

Lues Venerea, the *French-Pox*, is a malignant and contagious Diftemper communicated from one to another by Coition or other impure Contact, proceeding from virulent Matter, and accompanied with many illSymptoms, fuch as Gonorrhæa, the falling of the Hair, Spots, Swellings, Ulcers, Pains in the Bones, &c.

Luff, (Sea-Term) the fame as Loof: which fee.

Lugubrous, or *Lugubrious*, mournful, forrowful.

Lukewarm, between hot and cold, indifferent, carelefs.

Lumbago,

Lumbago, (Lat.) is a pain in the Muscles of the Loins.

Lumbar, or *Lumbary*, (Lat.) belonging to the Loins.

Lumbares Arteriæ, (in Anatomy) are *Arteries* which arising from the *Aorta*, spread themselves over all the parts of the Loins.

Lumbaris Vena, a Vein that rises from the descending Trunk of the *Vena Cava*, sometimes one, sometimes two or three, and is then usually divided into *Lumbaris Superior* and *Inferior*, which are bestowed on the Muscles of the Loins.

Lumbrical Muscles, are four Muscles in each Hand, and as many in the Feet, by reason of their smallness and shape resembling Worms.

Lumbrical, (Lat.) like unto, or resembling a Worm.

Luminaries, (Lat.) Lights, Lamps; also the Sun or Moon are so called by way of Eminence for their extraordinary Lustre, and the great Light they afford us.

Luminous, (Lat.) that which emits Light, full of Light.

Lunacy, Frenzy or Madness, happening according to the Course of the Moon.

Lunar, belonging to the Moon, which in Latin is called *Luna*.

Lunar Months, are either *Periodical*, *Synodical*, or *Illuminative*; which see under these words.

Lunar Cycle. See Cycle of the Moon.

Lunaticks, People that are disordered or mad at a certain time of the Moon.

Lunations of the Moon, are the time between one New Moon and another.

Lunes, in Geometry, are Figures in the form of a Crescent or half Moon, made by the Arks of two intersecting Circles.

Lunettes, in Fortification, is a small Work raised sometimes in the middle of the Foss before the Curtin, forming an Angle; its Terreplain rising but a little above the Surface of the Water about twelve Foot broad, with a Parapet of eighteen Foot. There is another sort of *Lunettes* which are larger, and raised to cover the Face of a half Moon.

Lungis, a slim Slow-back, a drowsy or dreaming Fellow.

Lungs, that part of an Animal which is the Instrument of Respiration, and is nothing else but a Collection of membranous Vesicles heaped one above another, and interlaced with Branches, Arteries and Veins.

Lunt, a Match to fire Guns withal.

Lupia, is a Tumor or Protuberance about as big as a small sort of Bean.

Lupus, (Lat.) a Southern Constellation, consisting of two Stars.

Lupus,

Lupus, a sort of a Canker in the Thighs and Leggs.

Lurcher, one that lies upon the Lurch, or upon the Catch ; also a kind of hunting Dog.

Lurid, pale, wan.

Luft of a Ship ; the *Ship has a Luft to the Starboard, or a Port* ; that is, she is inclined to *Heel* that way.

Luftration, (Lat.) a viewing on every side; also a purging by Sacrifice, used by the *Romans* after they had done numbring of the People, which was done every five Years.

Luftre, a shining, or brightness ; also among the Romans *Luftrum* was used for the space of five Years.

Luftring, or *Lute-ftring*, a kind of glossy Silk.

Lutation, in Chymiftry, is a cementing of Chymical Veffels close together.

Lute, a musical Instrument: In Chymiftry it is that wherewith the Chymifts join together the Necks of the Retorts and Receivers, or wherewith they coat over the Bodies of Glass Retorts, to save them from being melted in a very vehement Fire.

Lutheranifm, the Doctrine of *Martin Luther*, who being an *Auguftin* Frier, separated from the Church of *Rome* about the Year 1115.

Lutherans, the Followers of *Luther*.

Luxation, (Lat.) is the diflocation, difplacing or putting any Bone or Joint out of place.

Luxury, (Lat.) all fuperfluity and excefs in Carnal Pleafure ; fumptuous Fare, Riot.

Luxuriant, or *Luxurious*, Riotous, given to Excefs or Debauchery.

Lycanthropia, (Gr.) a Madnefs proceeding from the bite of a mad Wolf, wherein Men imitate the howling of Wolves.

Lydian Mufick, doleful and lamentable Mufick.

Lye under the Sea, is faid of a Ship when her Helm is lafh'd faft a-Lee, and she lies so a-Hull that the Sea breaks upon her Bow or Broadfide.

Lye a Hull. See *Hull.*

Lye a Try. See *Try.*

Lygmos, (Gr.) the Hickup.

Lymphatick, allayed or mixed with Water ; also mad, furious.

Lynceous, quick fighted ; from *Lynceus*, one of the Argonauts of a very quick fight.

Lypyria, is a Term some Phyficians give to any kind of Fever attended with an *Erifypelas* ; which fee.

Lyra, the Harp, a Conftellation in the Northern Hemifphere confifting of thirteen Stars.

Lyrick Verfes, are Verfes made to be fung to the Harp or Lute, fuch as are the Odes of *Horace*, *Pindar*, &c.

MAC, a Son in *Irifh*; 'tis added to the beginning of many Sirnames, as *Mac-Donald*, &c.

Macaronique, (Fr.) a fort of Burlefque Poetry wherein the Native Words of a Language are made to end in a Latin Termination; alfo a confufed heap of many feveral things.

Macerate, (Lat.) to make lean or bring down; alfo to fteep or foak.

Maceration, (Lat.) a making lean, weakning or bringing down. Alfo foaking or fteeping in fome Liquor.

Machiavilian, politick, crafty, fubtil; from *Machiavel* the *Florentine*.

Machinate, to contrive, plot, or hatch.

Machine, any Inftrument made ufe of for the examining the Weight, or facilitating, or ftopping the Motion of Bodies.

Machines fimple, are the *Ballance*, *Leaver*, *Pulley*, *Wheel*, *Wedge* and *Screw*.

Machines Compound, are fuch as are compounded or made out of the Simple ones.

Machination, (Lat.) an Engine; alfo a Plotting or laying an evil defign againft any one; alfo a Device or Invention.

Macilent, lean, thin, lank.

Macrocofm, (Gr.) the great World, is the whole Univerfe in contradiftinction to *Microcofm*, which is commonly taken for the Body of Man.

Macrology, a Rhetorical Figure, it fignifies a prolixity in fpeaking; or a Speech containing more Words than are juft and neceffary.

Mactation, (Lat.) a killing or committing Slaughter.

Maculation, (Lat.) a ftaining or defiling with fpots.

Maculatures, wafte or blotting Papers.

Madam, (Fr.) *i. e.* my Lady; a Title due to Perfons of Quality.

Madefaction, (Lat.) Wetting or Moiftning.

Mademoifelle, anfwering to Miftrefs in *Englifh*, is a Title given to Wives and Daughters of bare Gentlemen in *France*.

Madriers, a Term in Fortification, fignifying long Planks of Wood very broad, ufed for fupporting the Earth in Mining, in carrying on a *Sap*, in making *Coffers*, *Caponiers*, *Galleries*, and many other ufes at a Siege. They are likewife ufed to cover the Mouth of *Petards* after they are loaded, and fixed with the *Petards* to the Gates or other places defigned to be broke open. When the Planks are not ftrong enough they are doubled with Plates of Iron.

Madrigal, (Ital.) a kind of *Italian* Air or Song.

Mads, a Difeafe in Sheep.

Meander, a Matter full of

A a a   Intricacy

Intricacy and Difficulty, so called from a River in *Phrygia* that has many Turnings in its Course.

Meandring, proceeding with many Turnings.

Maffle, to Stammer, or Stutter; to utter one's Words confusedly.

Magazine, (Fr.) a Publick Storehouse, most commonly 'tis apply'd to War, and signifies a place where all sorts of Stores are kept, where *Guns* are Founded, and where the *Carpenters*, *Wheel-wrights*, *Smiths*, *Turners*, and other Handicrafts are constantly employed in making all things belonging to an *Artillery*, as *Carriages*, *Waggons*, &c.

Magellanick, belonging to, or found out by *Ferdinand Magellan* a *Portugese*; as the *Magellanick Streights*.

Magical, belonging to Magick.

Magician, (Pers) the *Persians* call those *Magos* or *Magicians*, whom the Greeks call *Philosophos*, the Latins *Sapientes*, the Gauls *Druids*, the Egyptians *Prophets*, or *Priests*, the Indians *Gymnosophists*, and we English *Wise-men*, *Wizards*, *Cunning-men*, or *Conjurers*.

Magick, (Gr.) is taken mostly in a bad Sense for the Black-Art, dealing with Familiar Spirits, Conjuring, Sorcery, Witchcraft.

Magick-Lanthern, a little Optick Machine; by the means of which are represen-

ted on a Wall in the dark many Phantoms and terrible Apparitions which are taken for the Effect of *Magick* by those that are Ignorant of the Secret.

Magisterial, pertaining to or done by a Master or Magistrate. Also imperious, haughty.

Magistery, Mastership, the Rule or Office of a Master. In *Chymistry* it is sometimes used for *Fine-Powders*, and sometimes for *Resins* and *Resinous Extracts*.

Magma, the Dregs that are left after the straining of juices.

Magna Charta, the Great Charter containing a Number of Laws ordained in the 9th year of *Henry* the third, and confirmed by *Edward* the first containing the Sum of all the written Laws of England.

Magnanimity (Lat.) greatness of Mind, Courage.

Magnanimous, of great Courage, or Spirit, Generous, Brave.

Magnet or *Load-stone*, is a Fossil approaching to the Nature of Iron-Oar and endowed with the Property of attracting Iron, and of both pointing it self, and giving the Virtue to a Needle touched by it of Pointing to the Poles of the World.

Magnetism, is the Power a Loadstone has of attracting Iron.

Magnetical Amplitude, is an Arc of the Horizon intercepted

ted between the Sun in his Rifing or Setting and the *Eaſt* or *Weſt* Point of the Compaſs.

Magnetical meridian, is a great Circle paſſing through the Magnetical Poles, to which Meridians the Compaſs hath reſpect.

Magnetical Azimuth, is an Arc of the Horizon intercepted between the *Magnetical meridian*, and the Sun's *Azimuth* Circle.

Magnificat, the Song of the bleſſed Virgin, ſo call'd from its firſt Word in the *Latin*.

Magnificence, (Lat.) a largeneſs of Soul in conceiving and managing great things; Grandure.

Magnifie, to make things ſeem bigger than they really are, as by *Microſcopes*; to cry up, to praiſe highly.

Magniloquence, a lofty and high way of ſpeaking, high vaunting talk.

Magnitude, Largeneſs, Bigneſs, Greatneſs; with reſpect to the Stars, 'tis divided into 6 Degrees, as when we ſay Stars of the *firſt, ſecond, third*, &c. Magnitude.

Mahometan, a Follower of the Doctrine of *Mahomet*.

Mahometiſm, is the Religion invented by *Mahomet*.

Mahone, a ſort of large *Turkiſh* Veſſel, reſembling a Galleaſs.

Majeſty, Authority, Power, Grandure, Venerableneſs.

Mail, an Iron Ring for Armour; alſo a ſpeck on Birds Feathers; alſo a Port-manteau,

or Trunk to travel with for carrying Letters or other things.

Maile, a ſmall Piece of Money, thence uſed to ſignifie Rent, not only that paid in Money, but that in Grain.

Maim or *Mayhim*, in Common Law, ſignifies a Corporeal Hurt by which a Man loſeth the uſe of any Member, that is, or might be any defence to him in Battel.

Main, chief, principal; alſo the long Hair of a Horſe's Neck; alſo the Main is the Middle of Sea or Land.

Main-maſt of a Ship, is a long piece of round Timber ſtanding upright in the middle or waſt of the Ship; it carries the *Main-Yard*, and *Main-Sail*, and is uſually 2½ the length of the *Midſhip-Beam*.

Main-top-maſt is one half the length of the Main-maſt, and the *Top-gallant-maſt*, half the length of the *main-top-maſt*, the firſt is made faſt or ſecure unto the Head of the Main-maſt, and the Main-top-gallant-maſt, is faſtned to the Head of the Main-top-maſt.

Mainour, manour, or *meinour*, in the Law is a thing that a Thief taketh away or Stealeth; and to be taken with the Mainour is to be taken with the thing ſtolen about him.

Mainpernable, ſignifies Bailable or that may be bailed.

Mainpernors, are thoſe Perſons to whom a perſon is delivered out of Cuſtody or Priſon

son, upon Security given either for appearance or satisfaction.

Mainprise in Law, signifies the taking or receiving a Man into Friendly custody, that otherwise is or might be committed to Prison, upon security given for his forth-coming at a day assigned.

Maintain, to give a livelyhood to, to keep in repair, in a good condition, to uphold, defend, or make good the truth of a thing which he affirms.

Maintenance, in Law is a seconding or upholding a Cause depending in Suit between others, either by disbursing Money, or making Friends for either Party towards his help.

Main-Body of the Army, is the Body of Troops that Marches between the Advance and Rear Guards. In a Camp it is that part which is encamped between the *right* and the *left Wing.*

Main-guard, or grandGuard is a Body of Horse posted before the Camp for the safety of the Army. In Garrison it is that Guard to which all the rest are subordinate.

Major, (Lat.) greater, bigger. In *Logick* the first Proposition of a Syllogism ; also one come of Age.

Major, of a *Regiment of Horse or Foot,* is the next Officer to the *Lieutenant-Colonel,* and is generally made from the Eldest *Captain,* he is to

take care that the Regiment be well exercised, that they be drawn up in good order at a *Review,* or upon a Parade, or any other Occasion, to see it march in good Order, and to rally it in case of its being broke.

Major-domo, (Ita.) the Steward of a great Man's House, Master-Houshold.

Major-General, is the next Officer to the *Lieutenant-General* ; when there are two Attacks at a Siege he commands that on the Left. His chief Business is to receive the Orders every Night from the *General,* or in his absence from the *Lieutenant-General* of the Day ; which he is to distribute to the *Brigade-majors,* with whom he is to regulate the *Guards, Convoys, Parties, Detachments,* and appoints the Place and Hour of their Rendezvous.

Major of a Brigade, either Horse or Foot, is an Officer appointed by the *Brigadeer* to assist him in the Business of his Brigade, and acts in his Brigade the same that a *Major-General* does in the Army.

Majority, the greater Number or Part ; also one's being of Age.

Make, a Word frequently used in the Law, signifying to perform or Execute.

Make-bate, a causer and promoter of Quarrels.

Malacia, is a depraved Appetite which covets those things which are not fit to

be

be eaten, alſo a tenderneſs of Body.

Malaſtica or *Emollientia*, are things which ſoften the parts by a moderate heat and moiſture, by diſſolving ſome of them, and diſſipating o-thers.

Mal - adminiſtration, Miſ-demeanor in a Publick Em-ploy.

Malady, (Fr.) Diſeaſe, Sick-neſs, Indiſpoſition.

Malanders, a Diſeaſe in the Fore-legs of a Horſe.

Malapert, Saucy, Impu-dent.

Malaxation, is the mixing of Ingredients, whereof ſome are dry, ſome ſoft or liquid, with the Hand or Peſtle into a Maſs, for Pills, or Plaiſters.

Maldiſant, (Fr.) a back-biter, an evil-ſpeaker.

A Male, a kind of Sack or Budget from the Greek word μαλλοl Fleece, becauſe they uſed to be made of Sheeps Skins.

Malecontent, (Lat.) diſcon-tented, now often apply'd to Rebels, to factious or ſediti-ous People.

Malediction, (Lat.) an Evil-ſpeaking, or curſing.

Malefactor, (Lat.) evil-doer an offender.

Malefice, a ſhrewd turn, an evil Deed.

Maleficence, Miſchievouſneſs.

Malevolence, (Lat.) an ill-will.

Malfeaſance, a doing of E-vil.

Malicious, (Lat.) delighting in miſchief, ſpiteful.

Malign, evil, miſchievous-

Malignant, hurtful, noxi-ous, bad; alſo an ill-affected Perſon.

Malignant Diſeaſe, is that which rages more vehement-ly, and continues longer than its nature uſually permits it to do, as in a Peſtilential Fe-ver, &c.

Malignity, Hurtfulneſs, Miſ-chievouſneſs.

Malleable, is that which will bear being hammer'd, and ſpread being beaten. Gold has this Quality in a very great degree, for 'tis the moſt *ductil* and *malleable* of any Mettal.

Maltraited, (Fr) abuſed, ill dealt by.

Malum mortuum, the dead Diſeaſe, is a ſort of Scab, ſo called becauſe it makes the Bo-dy appear black and mortified.

Malverſation, (Fr.) ill con-verſation, miſdemeanor, miſuſe.

Mamaluks, Light Horſe-men, an Order of valiant Souldiers, that were the prin-cipal ſupport of the *Saracens* in Egypt.

Mammiform Proceſſes, two Apophyſes of the Bone of the back part of the Scull.

Mammillary Artery, it ſup-ſupplies the Breaſts, and comes from the Subclavian Branch of the aſcending *Aorta*.

Mammillary Proceſſes, two Protuberances of the parietal Bones reſembling the Teats of a Cow.

Mammock, a Fragment, Piece, or Scrap.

Mam-

Mammon, (Syriack) signifies Riches, or the God of Riches.

Mamon r. ft. a Worldling, or one that seeks after Riches.

Mammooda, a Coyn among the East Indians of equal value with our Shilling.

Man a *Ship* or *Fleet*; is to provide them with a sufficient number of men for an Expedition.

Man the *Capftan*; that is, have all hands neceffary to heave the Capftan-Bars; See *Capftan*.

Man the *Top* or *Yard*; that is, when the men are commanded to go up to the *Top* or *Yard* for some particular Service.

Man the fide or Ladder, that is, when an Officer or any Person of Fashion, is at the Ship fide ready to come Aboard, the men are commanded to wait and help him up the fide.

Manacle, to bind with *Manacles*, Hand-Fetters.

Manage, (Fr.) an Academy for Exercises, such as Riding the Great Horse, Dancing, Fencing, &c.

Management, Ordring, Conduct, or Difcretion in Orders.

Manation, (Lat) a Flowing or Running.

Manche, (Fr) a Sleeve. In Heraldry, the Figure of an ancient Sleeve in Efcutcheons, fee *Maunch*.

Manchet, a fine fort of fmall Bread.

Mancipate, (Lat.) to deliver

poffeffion, to give the right to another, to fell for money.

Mancipation, (Lat.) a parting with a thing and giving it up to another; a manner of felling before witneffes by Seifing and delivery with fundry Solemnities and Ceremonies.

Manciple, a Caterer, or one that in Colledges or Hofpitals buys Victuals, and common Provifion into the Houfe.

Mandamus, is a Writ that goes to the Efcheator for the finding an Office after the Death of one that dy'd the King's Tenant: There is alfo another *Mandamus* granted upon a motion out of the *King's-Bench*; one to the Bifhop, to admit an Executor to prove a Will, or grant an Adminiftration; another to command Corporations to reftore Aldermen and others to Offices out of which they are unjuftly put.

Mandatary, in Law, is he to whom a Charge or Commandment is given, alfo he that obtains a Benefice by a *Mandamus*.

Mandate, a Commandment, a Meffage, a Commiffion; alfo a Commandment of the King or his Juftices, to have any thing done for difpatch of Juftice.

Mandibular, (Lat.) belonging to the Jaw.

- *Mandilion*, (Fr.) a kind of Military Garment, a loofe Caffock.

Mandorin,

Mandorin, the Title of a great Lord or Governour among the *Chinese Tartars*.

Mandy-Thursday, is the *Thursday* before *Easter*, quasi, *Dies Mandati*, from our Saviour's Charge to his Disciples of Celebrating his Supper.

Maneh, a Jewish Weight, which being reduced to our English Troy Weight contains 3 Pound, 9 Ounces, 10 Penny-Weight, 17½ Grains; the same with *Mina Hebraica*; which see.

Manes, has two significations amongst the Ancients; 'tis commonly taken for departed Souls, tho' 'tis sometimes used for Hell.

Manger, in a Ship, is a Circular place made with Planks fastned on the Deck right under the *Hawses*, for to receive the Sea-water beating in at the *Hawses* in a stress of Weather.

Mania, a sort of Madness, is a deprivation of Imagination and Judgment, with great Rage and Anger, and most commonly without a Fever.

Maniack, afflicted with, or belonging to Madness.

Manicheans, a sort of Hereticks so called from one *Manes*, who pretended himself to be the Apostle of Christ, and that he was the Comforter our Saviour promised to send. He held that there were two Principles, the one good from whence proceded the good Soul of Man, the other bad, from whence proceeded the evil Soul, and likewise the Body with all corporeal Creatures. He forbad his Disciples to give Alms to any that were not of his own Sect.

Manica Hippocratis, or *Hippocrates's* Slieve, is the Chymists word for a Woollen Sack or Bag, in the Form of a Pyramid, wherewith Wines, Medicines, and other Liquors, are strained.

Maniple, a Word used amongst Physicians, signifying as much of Herbs, or any other thing, as can be held in one's hand; also an Ensign of a Band of Souldiers.

Manipular, belonging to a Maniple.

Manner, (Fr.) is used to signifie a peculiar way of Managing one's skill in Painting, Sculpture, Singing, or Playing on an Instrument.

Mannopus, in Common Law signifies Goods taken in the Hands of an Apprehended Thief.

Manor, from the French *Manoir*, Habitation. This Word was brought in by the *Normans*. The constitution of a *Manor* was this, the King granted to some Baron, or Military Man, a certain Circuit of Ground for him and his Heirs to dwell upon, and to enjoy, holding some part in Demesn to their own Use and Occupation, and letting out other parcels to free and Servile Tenants, who were to do their Suit and Service at the Court of the said *Manor*, now called the Lord's Court, or Court Baron. It was also sometimes used simply for the Court or Mansion of the Lord.

Mansion, a tarrying, a waiting, an abiding; 'tis commonly taken for the Lord's chief dwelling House within his Fee.

Manslaughter, in Common Law, is the unlawful killing of a Man without prepensed Malice.

Mansuete, Gentle, Courteous, Meek, Mild, Tractable.

Mansuetude, Gentleness, Courteousness, Meekness.

Mantelets, in Fortification, are great Planks of Wood, of about five foot high, and three Inches thick, which serve at a Siege to cover the men from the Enemies fire, being pushed forward on small *Trucks*.

Mantle, in Heraldry, is that appearance of the foldings of Cloth, Flourishing or Drapery, that is in any Atchievment drawn about a Coat of Arms.

Manual, (Lat.) belonging to the Hand or performed by the Hand.

Manualist, a Handicrafts-Man, or Artificer.

Manucaption, (Lat.) a taking by the hand; also a Writ that lies for a man, who taken upon suspicion of Felony, and offering sufficient Bail for his Appearance, cannot be admitted thereto by the Sheriff, or other having power to admit of Main-prise.

Manuduction, (Lat.) a leading or guiding by the Hand.

Manuel, a small Book easily carried in one's Hand, or Pocket.

Manufacture, (Lat.) handywork, or what is made by Hands.

Manumission, (Lat.) a making of a Servant Free, the giving him his Freedom, a discharge or dismission from serving any longer.

Manumit, to give Liberty to a Bond-Man.

Manure, Dung, Marl, &c. for fatning Ground; verbally, to fatten or Till the Ground, or Labour it with the Hand.

Manuscript, (Lat.) any thing written by Hand; a written Copy of any Book.

Manutenentia, a Writ used in Case of Maintenance.

Manworth, the Price of a Man's Head, which was pay'd to the Lord for killing his Vassal.

Map, is a description of the Earth, or some particular part thereof, projected upon a plain *Superficies*; describing the Form of Countries, Rivers, situation of Cities, Hills, Woods and other things of Note.

Marasm, a Consumption, in which the sick Person wastes away by degrees.

Marasmodes, is the Term for a Fever which at last ends in a Consumption.

Maravedis, a very small *Spanish* Coin, 35 of 'em not amounting to above 6 pence.

Marcessible, apt or easy to rot or putrify.

Marcgrave, (Ger.) a Count or Earl of the *Marches*, or Frontiers.

March, from *Mars* the 3d. Month of the Year; among the *Romans* 'twas formerly the First, and is so in some Ecclesiastical Computations, beginning the Year on the 25 of the Month.

Marchant, one that Trades and deals into Foreign Countries, exports the Products of his own, and imports the Commodities of other Nations or Countries.

Marchasite, is the general Term for a Mineral Body having in it some Metalline Parts, though the Quantity of them be often so small that they cannot be separated from the Mineral Body.

Marcid, (Lat.) withered, rotten, feeble.

Marcionists, ancient *Hereticks*, so called from *Marcion*, a Stoick, who denied Christ was the Son of God.

Marforio, a famous Statue in *Rome* opposite to *Pasquin*, on which are fix'd commonly Answers to the Satyrical Questions fastned on the Latter.

Margin, the Brink or Brim of a thing; also the outermost part of the Leaves of a Book, on which there is nothing Printed, at least nothing belonging to the Body of the Book.

Marginal, belonging to the Margin, written in the Margin.

Marinade, (Fr.) in Cookry, is pickled Meat, either of Flesh or Fish.

Marinated, pertaining to the Sea, tasting of Saltness.

Marine, (Lat.) of or belonging to the Sea.

Mariner, a *Seaman* or one that belongs to the Sea.

Mariola, (in ancient Writers) a Shrine or Image of the Blessed Virgin.

Marisca, a great unsavoury Fig. Also the Hemorrhoids or Piles.

Maritagio amisso per defaltam, a Writ for a Tenant in Frank-marriage to recover Lands, &c. out of which he is kept by another.

Maritagium, (Lat.) Old Law Term; the lawful joyning of Man and Wife; the right of bestowing a Ward, or Widow in Marriage: Lands given in Marriage: also the Dower or Portion receiv'd with the Wife.

Marital, (Lat.) belonging to an Husband or Marriage.

Maritima Angliæ, the Profits accruing to the King, from the Sea, anciently collected by Sheriffs, and afterwards granted to the Admiral.

Maritime, belonging to or near the Sea.

Mark, an Earldom in *Germany*.

Mark-Penny, a Penny pay'd at *Maldon* in *Essex*, for laying Pipes or Gutters into the Street. *Mark-*

Mark-weight, a Forreign Weight commonly of 8 Ounces: and *Mark*-Pound is two such Marks.

Marle, a chalky Earth used in soiling of Land.

Mar-line, a small line of untwisted Hemp, very pliable and well Tarr'd, serving to seize the ends of Ropes, and keep them from Ravelling out; or the Straps at the Arse (or lower End) of the Blocks.

Marline a Sail, that is, when the Sail is rent out of the *Bolt-Rope* to make it fast, with *Marline* put through the Eyelet Holes made in it for that purpose, to the *Bolt-Rope* till it can be mended.

Mar-line-Spike, is a little piece of Iron to splice small Ropes together; as also to open the *Bolt-Rope* when the Sail is sowed into it.

Marmalet, or *Marmelade*, a Confection made of Quinces: from *Marmelo* a Quince in the *Portugueze*.

Marmorean, (Lat.) of marble, like Marble in colour, hardness, &c.

Marmorata aurium, Earwax.

Marmoset, a kind of black Monky with a shaggy Neck: Also a kind of Grotesk Figure in Building.

Maroncan Wine, a sort of Wine that is extraordinary strong.

Maronites, a Christian People that dwell towards Mount *Libanus*, so called from one *Maron* who was formerly the

Head of them; they are also said to have sometime followed the Errors of the *Jacobins*, *Nestorians*, and *Monothelites*; but they afterwards separated from them.

Marque, in ancient Statutes signifies Reprisal.

Marquess, a Nobleman between a *Duke* and an *Earl*.

Marquetry, a Joyner's chequer'd inlaid Work, with wood of divers forts and colours, wrought into the shape of Knots, Flowers, and other things.

Marquisate, a Marquiship or the Jurisdiction of a *Marquess*.

Marrow, a fat Substance in the Hollow of Bones: Also a Fellow, (spoken of *Gloves*, *Shoes*, &c)

Mars, War, or the God of War; also one of the seven Planets placed next above the Earth.

Marsh, is a standing Pool, or Water mixed with Earth, whose Bottom is very dirty; which dries up and diminishes very much in the Summer.

Marshal, (in the *German* Language signifies Master of the Horse) there are several Officers which bear this name, as,

Lord or *Earl Marshal* of *England*, whose Office consists chiefly in War and Arms.

Marshal, of the King's House, whose special Authority is in the King's Palace to hear and determine all Pleas of the Crown, and to punish
faults

faults committed within the Verge, and to hear and judge of Suits between those of the Kings-Houshold, &c,

Marshal of the *Exchequer*, is he to whom the Court committeth the Custody of the King's Debtors during the Term time for securing the Debts.

Marshal of the *Kings-Bench*, who hath the Custody of the Prison called the *Kings-Bench* in *Southwark*.

Marshal of the Ceremonies, who is to receive Commands from the Master of the Ceremonies, or Assistants, and to do nothing without his Order.

Marshal at Sea, one who punishes Offences committed there, and sees Justice executed; as Ducking at the Yard's Arm, Haling under the Keel, setting in the Bilboes, &c.

Marshal, is also a Military Officer in every Regiment and Company, whose Office is to see to Prisoners of War, and to execute all Sentences or Orders of the Council of War upon the Offenders.

Marshal of France, is the highest Preferment in the Army or in the Fleet, it is the same with Captain General. When two or more Marshals are in one Army the Eldest Commands.

Marshal de Camp, is in *France* the next Officer to the *Lieutenant-General*, and is the same as a Major-General with us.

Marshalling a Coat of Arms, (in Heraldry) signifies the due and proper joyning of several Coats of Arms in one and the same Shield or Escutcheon; together with their Ornaments, Parts, and Appurtenances.

Marshalsee, the Court or Seat of the Marshal.

Marsupialis, or *Bursalis*, a Muscle of the Thigh, arising from the *Os Ilium*, *Ischium* and *Pubis*, and inserted into the upper Part of the great *Trochanter*, it hath its Name from its doubled Tendon resembling a Purse, and is called *Obturator Internus*; its Office is to draw upwards the Thigh-bone.

Mart, a great Fair or Market.

Mart-Town, a large Town in which is some great Fair, frequented by People of several Nations for Commerce and Trade; as *Franckfort* on the *Main* in *Germany*.

Marten or *Martern*, a little Creature like a Ferret, of a rich Furr, whose Dung smels like Musk.

Martial, Warlike, Valiant, belonging to War; also, Born under the Planet *Mars*: Also, that partakes of the Nature of Iron or Steel.

Martial law, is the Law of War depending on the King's Pleasure; or his Lieutenant, or the General or his Officers in War.

Martingal, a Thong of Leather fastned at one End to the

the Girts under the Horfe's Belly, and at the other to the Mufs-roll, to prevent his rearing.

Martnets, at Sea are fmall Lines made faft to the Leetch of the Sail, and reeved thro' a Block at the Top-Maft-Head, and fo they come down by the Maft to the Deck, they ferve in Furling the Sail to bring that part of the Leetch which is next the Yard-Arm, clofe up to the Yard, fo that the Sail may be furled up the better.

Top-Martnets, are thofe which belong to the *Top-fails*.

Top the Martnets, that is, hale them up.

Martyr, one that bears witnefs to the truth at the Expence of his own Life.

Martyrology, (Gr.) a Book that treats of the Acts, Names and Sufferings of the Martyrs.

Mafcarade, (Fr.) a Mask or Mummery, which fee.

Mafcle, a Term in Heraldry for a bearing of this Figure ;

Gules a Chevron Ermin between three *Mafcles Argent*, by the Name of *Bellgrave*.

Mafculine, of the Male

kind : Alfo manly, couragious, lofty.

Mafora, or *Mafforah*, the Criticifms of *Jewifh* Doctors, on the *Hebrew* Text of the Bible, fhewing the various Readings, how often any Word occurs ; yea even the number of Verfes, Words, and Letters.

Mafs, a Word ufed in natural Philofophy to exprefs the Quantity of Matter in any Body.

Mafs, amongft Latin Authors is generally ufed to fignifie all kinds of Divine Service, or a Leffon of that Service ; but in a more ordinary ufe, efpecially in the Church of *Rome* it fignifies an Oblation which they call *Mafs*, and very frequently their Liturgy or Church Service.

Maffeters, (Gr.) Mufcles of the lower Jaw, which with the Temporal Mufcles, move it to either fide, and forwards.

Maft, the Fruit of the Oak, Beech, Chefnut, &c. Alfo part of a Ship, fee *Main-maft*, *Fore-maft*, &c.

Mafter of the Armory, one that has the care and overfight of his Majefties Armour.

Mafter of the Ceremonies, the King's Interpreter who introduceth Ambaffadors, &c.

Mafters of the Chancery, are Affiftants to the Lord-keeper in matters of Judgment ; of thefe there are 12 in Number the Chief of which is called the Mafter of the Rolls.

Mafter

Master of the Horse, is he that hath the Rule and Charge of the King's Stable.

Master of the King's Houshold, hath generally the Title of Lord high Steward of the Kings Houshold.

Master of the King's Musters, or *Muster-Master-General*, is one who takes care that the King's Forces be compleat, well Armed and Trained.

Master of the Ordnance, who hath care of all the King's Ordnance and Artillery.

Master of the Rolls, Assistant to the Lord Chancellour of *England*, and in his Absence hears Causes, and gives Orders.

Master de Camp in *France*, is he who commands a *Regiment* of Horse, being the same as a *Colonel* of *Horse* with us.

Master de Camp General, is likewise a Post in *France* being the next Officer over all the *Light-horse*, and commands in the Absence of the *Colonel General*.

Mastication, (Lat.) chewing, is an action whereby we break the Meat into pieces with our Teeth, and mix it with the Saliva, in order to its being more easily digested and turned into Chyle.

Masticatories, are Medicines designed to provoke Spitting.

Mastoides, (Gr.) certain Muscles that bend the Head, arising from the Neck-Bone, and Breast-Bone, and terminating in the Mammillary Pro-

cesses; Also any Processes shap'd like Teats.

Mates at Sea; are Assistants to the several Officers aboard a Ship.

Mater-Dura, a strong Membrane next to the Skull encompassing the Brain and *Cerebellum*, having four Cavities, that supply the Place of Veins.

Mater-Pia, a thinner and finer Membrane immediately investing the Brain and *Cerebellum*, very full of Blood-Vessels.

Materia medica, is whatever is used in the Art of Medicine for the prevention or cure of Diseases.

Material, of or belonging to Matter.

Materiality, a being Material.

Maternal, (Lat.) Motherly, relating to a Mother.

Mathematicks, (Gr.) the Sciences of Magnitude and Numbers, or of Quantity continued or discrete.

Mathematical, belonging to the *Mathematicks*.

Mathurins, a Religious Order founded by *Innocent* III. for the Redemption of Christian Captives out of *Turkish* Slavery.

Matras, is a long strait-necked Vessel of Glass frequently used by Chymists in Distillations, and when they are fitted to the Nose of an *Alembick* they are called *Receivers*, because they receive the Matter, which the Fire forces over

ver

ver the Helm or Head of the Still.

Matrice, that part of the Womb where the Child is conceived.

Matricide, a killing or killer of his Mother.

Martriculate, to Regifter Names. It comes from *Ma-ter* a Mother, for then are young Schollars in a Univerfity faid to be matriculated, when they are Sworn and Regiftred into the Society of their fofter Mother of Learning the Univerfity.

Matrimonial, of or belonging to Matrimony or Wedlock.

Matron, a Grave Mortherly Woman.

Matter or *Body*, is an Impenetrable, divifible, folid and paffive Subftance, extending it felf into Length, Breadth and Thicknefs.

Matter in *Deed*, in Law, is a Truth to be proved tho' not by any Record.

Matter of *Record* in Law, is that which may be proved by fome Record.

Mattins, (Lat.) Morning-Prayer; alfo one of the Canonical Hours in the *Roman* Church.

Mattrefs, (Fr.) a kind of Quilt filled with Cotton or Wool; a Flock-Bed.

Matts, on *Board a Ship*, are a kind of thick Clouts, Wove out of thick Yarn, Sinnet or Thrums to preferve the *main* and *Fore-yards* from galling againft the *Mafts* at the *Tyes*.

and at the *Gunnel* of the *Loof*.

Maturation, (Lat.) a ripening; or the action of growing Ripe.

Mature, ripe, perfect.

Maturity, (Lat.) the juft Ripenefs of any Fruit; and by Analogy, the arrival of any thing to its juft degree of perfection.

Matutina, belonging to the Morning.

Maudlin, maudled, half drunk, or out of order with Drink, Tipfie.

Mauling of Hawks, is pinioning their Wings.

Maugre, (Fr. Malgre) in fpight of one's Teeth, as I'll do this thing, maugre fuch an one, *i. e.* I'll do it in fpight of fuch an one's Teeth.

Maunch, the Figure of an Ancient Slieve fo called by the Heralds, and is born in many Gentlemens Efcutcheons, and the Figure of it is thus;

Maundring, grumbling, muttering or growling.

Maufoleum, a Famous Tomb that Queen *Arthemifia* made for her Husband *Maufolus*, reckoned one of the Wonders of the World. Whence any fumptuous and ftately stately Monument or Sepulchre may be so called.

Mawks, a dirty nasty slut.

Maxilla, (Lat.) the Jaw-bone, of which there are two, *superior* the upper, and *inferior* the lower.

Maxillar, belonging to the Jaw-bone.

Maximis & minimis, a method which Mathematicians use for the Resolution of a great many perplext Problems, especially such wherein is required a *maximum* or a *minimum,* the *greatast* or *least* quantity attainable in such a Case.

Maxims, see *Axioms.*

May ; a Maid. *Spencer.*

Mayor, the Chief Magistrate of a City.

Maze, an Astonishment,

Mazarines, little Dishes to be set in the middle of a larger one, for Ragoos or Fricassies: Also a kind of small Tarts filled with Sweetmeats.

Mazer, a Cup. *Spencer.*

Meagre, (Fr.) Scraggy, lean, mere Skin and Bone.

Mean Diameter, (in Gauging) is a Geometrical mean between the Diameters at Head and Bung in a close Cask.

Mean, in Law signifies the middle between two extreams, and that either in Time or in Dignity.

Mean Anomaly, in Astronomy. See *Anomaly.*

Mean Proportional Geometrical, is a Quantity which is

as big in respect of a third Term as the first is in respect of it.

Mean Proportional Arithmetical, is a Quantity which exceeds or is exceeded by a third Term as much as it exceeds or is exceeded by the first.

Meander, properly a winding River in *Phrigia.* Hence any oblique turning or crooked winding is called *Meander.*

Means continual, when one Root or first Number is multiply'd by it self, and the Product again multiply'd by it self, and this last Product multiply'd by it self, and so on; the Numbers between the first and last are *Continual-Means.* Thus 2 multiply'd by it self is 4, and 4 squared is 16, which in like manner squared is 256: here 4 and 16, are Continual Means between 2 and 256.

Mease, (Lat.) a Mansion-House ; also a Measure of Herrings containing 500.

Measure, is some certain Quantity or Quantities fixed and agreed upon, whereby to estimate the Quantity, the Length, Breadth, Thickness or capacity of other things by.

Measure in *Musick,* is a Quantity of the length and shortness of Time, either with respect to natural sounds pronounced by the Voice ; or Artificial drawn out of Musical Instruments, which Measure

is

is adjusted in variety of Notes by a constant Motion of the Hand or Foot, *down* or *up*, is called a *Time* or *Measure* whereby the length of a *Semibreve* is measured, which is therefore the *Measure Note*, or *Time Note*.

Meatus, a Moving or Course, a Passage or Way; the Pores of the Body.

Meatus Auditorius, the Auditory Passage beginning from the Hollow of the Ear, and ending at the *Tympanum*.

Meatus Urinarius, the Passage whereby the Urine is conveyed from the Bladder.

Mechanick, frequently signifies a Handy-crafts-man, or a Trades Man; also belonging to Mechanicks.

Mechanicks, is a Mathematical Science which treats of Motion as it is produc'd by determinate powers, and of the forces that are requisite to produce or stop such and such Motions.

Mechanick Powers, or Principles are usually reckoned six. 1. the *Libra* or *Ballance*, 2. *Vectis* or *Leaver*, 3. *Trochlea* or *Pulley*, 4. *Cochlea* or *Screw*, 5. *Axis in Peritrocheo* or *Windlace*, and 6. *Cuneus* or *Wedge*.

Mechanical Solution of a *Problem*, is such an one as is done by any Line that is not a Geometrical one.

Mechanick Demonstration, is that whose Ratiocinations are drawn from Rules of Mechanicks.

Meconium, properly an O-

piate, or the condensed juice of Poppies.

Medals, are pieces of Mettal like Money Stamped or Coined upon some extraordinary Occasion, to perpetuate the Memory of some Great and Eminent Person, or of some considerable Victory, or other publick Benefit to a Nation or People.

Medallions, are large Medals Coined not as current Money, but upon some special Extraordinary Occasion.

Meddled, mingled, *Spencer*.

Medewife, (Saxon) a Woman of Merit from whence comes our word *Midwife*.

Mediastinum, is a sort of Membrane, that standeth in the middle of the Breast, and divideth its Cavity into two Partitions, *viz.* a right and left.

Mediation, (Lat.) a dividing in the middle, an intreating or beseeching; an intercession, an arbitrating a Controversie.

Medietas Linguæ, or *Partyjury*, is a Jury impanelled upon any Cause wherein a Stranger is Party, wherein one half consists of Denizens, and the other of Strangers.

Mediety, the Moiety or half a thing.

Mediator, he that intercedes or intreats for another.

Medicable, that may be healed or cured.

Medicament, a Medicine, Drugg, Physick, or Salve.

Medicine,

Medicine, or Phyfick is an Art affiftant to Nature and defigned for the preferving of Health in Humane Bodies as much as is poffible by the Ufe of convenient Remedies.

Medimnus, (Gr.) an Attick Meafure of Capacity for things dry, containing 4 Pecks, 1 Gallon, 1 Pint, and 53 decimal Parts of a folid Inch of our Englifh Corn Meafure.

Medio acquittando , is a Writ Judicial, to diftrain a Lord for the *acquitting a mean* Lord, from a Rent which he formerly acknowledged in Court not to belong to him.

Mediocrity, (Lat) a mean, Indifferency, Moderation.

Medifance, (Fr) evil fpeaking, obloquy, reproach.

Mediterranean, (Lat.) Inland, fhut up between the Lands.

Meditullium, the middle of any thing ; alfo the fpungy Subftance betwixt the two Tables of the Scull.

Medullar, belonging to the Marrow.

Meed, Reward.

Meen, (Fr) the Air, the Countenance or Pofture of the Face.

Megacofm, (Gr.) the Great World.

Megrim, a Difeafe which caufeth great Pain in the Temples and forepart of the Head.

Meint, mingled. *Spencer.*

Meiofis, (Gr.) A diminution, or making a thing lefs than it is, which is done by using eafier Terms then the Matter requires.

Meiny, the many, Multitude. *Spencer.*

Mela, a Surgion's Inftrument to Probe Ulcers or draw a Stone out of the Yard.

Melancholy, black Choler caufed by aduftion of the Blood ; alfo fadnefs, penfivenefs, folitarinefs.

Melanagogues, Medicines againft Melancholy.

Melaffes, the drofs of Sugar commonly called Treacle.

Melchifedecians, a Sect of Hereticks that held *Melchifedeck* to be the Holy Ghoft.

Melchites, certain Chriftians in *Syria*, under the Patriarch of *Antioch*, who had their Name from the *Syriack* Word *Melchi*, which fignifies a King, becaufe they were wont to obey the Emperour's Orders in Religious Matters.

Melicratum, is a Drink made one part of Honey, and eight parts of Rain Water.

Melioration, (Lat) a making better, or improving.

Melius Inquirendo , is a Writ that lieth for a fecond Inquiry of what Lands and Tenements a Man died feized , where partiality was fufpected upon the Writ of *Diem claufit extremum.*

Melliferous , (Lat.) that brings or bears Honey.

Mellification, (Lat) a making of Honey.

ellifluous, that out of which Honey flows ; alfo Eloquent of Speech.

    B b b   *Melling.*

Melling, Medling, *Spencer.*

Melody, (Gr.) Harmony, sweet Singing.

Melpomene, one of the nine Muses, to whom is attributed the Invention of Tragedies, Odes, and Songs.

Membrana Adiposa, a Term in Anatomy, is that covering of Fat which lieth under the skin, and by some is taken to be a covering altogether distinct from the *membrana Carnosa* that lieth under it.

Membrana Carnosa, the *Carnous membrane* is only properly so called in Brutes in whom it is truly Fleshy and Muscular; but in Man on account of the fat that adheres to it, it ought to be called *Adiposa* rather than *Cannosa.*

Membrana Nictitans, a thin Membrane of a Purplish or Reddish Colour, which is found in the Eyes of several Beasts and Birds, serving to cover and defend their Eyes from Dust.

Membrane, in Anatomy, is a common Appellation to all coverings that invest the solid parts of the Body, or contain the fluid Humours; also a skin of Parchment.

Membranous, belonging to a Membrane.

Membred, in Heraldry, is applyed to those Birds which are either whole footed, or which have no Tallons.

Memoires, (Fr.) remarkable Observations.

Memorable, (Lat.) easie or worthy to be remembred.

Memorandum, (Lat.) a short Note or Token of something to be remembred.

Memorial, (Lat.) that which puts one in Mind of a thing, or brings it into Memory.

Memory, is that Faculty of the Soul which repeats things perceived by former Sensations, or is the calling to mind known and past things.

Menaces, angry and threatning Expressions.

Menacing, threatning, swaggering, or huffing.

Mendicant, (Lat.) begging, or one that Beggs.

Mendication, (Lat.) a Begging.

Mengrelians, Circassians, of the Greek Religion, save that they Baptize not their Children till eight years old.

Menial, (Lat.) belonging to Walls, *a menial Servant,* is a Servant that lives within the Walls of his Master's dwelling House.

Meninges, are the thin skins that cover the Brain, they lie immediately within the Skull, and are two in Number, the *Dura mater,* and *Pia mater,* or the *Crassa meninx,* aod *tenuis meninx.*

Meniscus Glasses, are those which are convex on one side, and concave on the other.

Meniver, a sort of Furr, being the Skin of a Milkwhite Creature in *Muscovy;* as others think the skin of a Squirrel's Belly.

Menno-

Mennonites, a certain Sect of Anabaptists in *Holland*, so called from one *Mennon Simon* of *Frisia*, who lived in the 16th Century; and held very different Tenets from the first Anabaptists.

Menopegia, a sharp pain in the Head, affecting one single Place.

Menow, (Fr.) a little fresh-water Fish, a Cackrel.

Menses, (Lat.) the same with *Menstrua*.

Menstrua, the monthly Flowers of Women; for when Accretion draws to a Period, and the Blood which was wont to be spent in the encrease of the Body, being accumulated, distends the Vessels, it breaks forth once a Month at those of the Womb, because of all the Veins in the Body which stand perpendicularly to the Horizon, these are without Valves.

Menstrual, (Lat.) monthly.

Menstruous, (Lat.) abounding with, or belonging to Monthly Terms or Flowers.

Menstruum, the Chymical Word for a dissolving Liquor; some Chymists gave it this Name, because they pretend that a compleat dissolution cannot be performed in less then 40 Days; which Period they call the *Philosophical Month*.

Meusurability, is a fitness in a Body, whereby it may be apply'd or conformed to a certain Measure.

Mensuration, is a finding the Length, Surface, or Solidity of Quantities in some certain known Measures.

Mental, (Lat.) thought or kept in the Mind.

Mention, (Lat.) a speaking, or taking notice of, a Naming.

Menuet, (Fr.) a kind of *French* Dance, or the Tune of it.

Mephitical, Stinking, Noxious, Poisonous.

Meracity, (Lat.) pureness, without mixture.

Mercantile, Merchant like, belonging to Merchants, dealing in the way of Merchandize.

Mercator's Chart or *Projection*, is a Projection of the Face of the Earth in *Plano*; wherein the Degrees upon the Meridian increase towards the Poles in the same Proportion that the Parallel Circles decrease towards them.

Mercature, Trade of Merchandize.

Mercenary, (Lat.) one that works and labours by the day for a Lively-hood; also one that is easie to be corrupted, and that will be hired to an ill act for the sake of Gain.

Mercer, a dealer in Silks and Stuffs in *London*; in the Country they Trade also in all sorts of Linnen, Woollen, and Grocery Ware.

Mercery, Mercers Goods.

Merchandise, formerly were all Goods and Wares exposed to sale in Fairs and Markets, and therefore *Merchant*

B b b 2

chant originally was not con-
fin'd to Traffiquers in Forreign
Commodities, but extended
to all fort of Traders, Pedlars, Buyers and Sellers.

Merchant, a Trader by
Wholefale, chiefly in Forreign
Commodities.

Merchant-man, a Ship fitted out for a trading Voyage.

Mercurial, belonging to,
or mixt with *mercury*; alfo
ingenious, brisk, lively; alfo
maggoty, whimfical.

Mercury, a Heathen Deity,
which conducted the Souls of
the Deceafed into Hell, and
had Power to take them out a-
gain, as the Pagans believed.
Befides he was over and above
all reputed the God of Eloquence.

Mercury, alfo fignifies one of
the Planets in place next to
the Sun. Alfo,

Mercury, according to the
Chymifts, is the third of their
Hypoftatical Principles, and is
the fame with what we call
Spirit. Mercury alfo fignifies
Quickfilver, and in this fenfe
'tis very frequently taken by
thofe which treat of Hydro-
ftaticks, and Experimental
Philofophy.

Mercury-Women, Women
that fell News-books and
Pamphlets to the Hawkers.

Merdiferous, (Lat.) bearing
Dung.

Mere, a Pond, Lake, or
Pool; alfo a Boundary or
Line, dividing Plough'd
Lands.

Meretricious, (Lat.) Who-
rifh, belonging to a Whore.

Meridian, (Lat.) is a great
Circle paffing through the
Poles of the World, and both
the *Zenith* and *Nadir*, croffing
the *Equinoctial* at right Angles, and dividing the Sphere
equally into a *Weftern* and
Eaftern Hemifphere. Its Poles
are the *Eaft* and *Weft* Points
of the *Horizon*; 'tis called Meridian, becaufe when the Sun
comes to this Circle, 'tis then
Meridies or *Mid-day*.

Meridian Altitude of the *Sun*
or *Star*, is the Altitude of the
Sun or *Star* when they are in
the Meridian of the Place, or
an Ark of the Meridian Intercepted between the Ho-
rizon and the *Sun* or *Star*.

Meridian-line on a Dial,
is a right line arifing from the
Interfection of the Meridian
of the Place with the Plane of
the Dial.

Meridian Magnetical, fee
magnetical meridian.

Meridional diftance, is the
difference of *Longitude* between *the Meridian* under
which the Ship is at prefent,
and any other fhe was under
before.

Meridional-Parts, *minutes*
or *miles*, are the Parts by
which the *meridians* in
Wright's or *Mercator's Chart*,
do encreafe as the Parallels
of Latitude decreafe.

Merifmus, (Gr.) Divifion,
a difpofing things in their proper places.

Merit, (Lat.) defert, alfo to
deferve. *Merito-*

Meritorious, full of desert.

Merlon, is that part of the Parapet which is terminated by two *Embraffures* of a *Battery*, so that its Height and Thicknefs is the fame with that of the Parapet, but its breadth is ordinarily nine Foot on the infide, and on the outfide. It is better of Earth, than of Stone, becaufe they are apt to fly.

Mermaid, i. e. Sea-maid, a Sea-Monfter, refembling a Woman from the Waft upwards, and thence downwards a Fifh.

Merfion, (Lat) a ducking, drowning or overwhelming.

Mefaraick, (Gr.) of or pertaining to the *mefentery*.

Mefenterick, the fame with Mefaraic.

Mefentery, (Gr.) is a Membranous part fituate in the middle of the lower Belly, ferving not only for conveying fome Veffels to the Inteftines and others from them, but tying moft of the Guts together fo Artificially, that for all their manifold windings, they are not entangled and confounded.

Meskite, (Ar.) a Church or Synagogue with the *Turks* and *Moors*.

Mefn, a Lord of a Manor, who holds of a fuperior Lord, though he has Tenants under himfelf; alfo a Writ that lies where there is a Lord, Mefn, and Tenant.

Mefnagery, (Fr.) Husbandry or Houf-wifry.

Mefnalty, the right of the Mefn Lord.

Mefocolon, that part of the Mefentery which is join'd to the Colon and the beginning of the fteight-Gut.

Mefolabium, a Mathematical Inftrument for finding mean Proportionals.

Meffalians, a fort of Hereticks under the Empire of *Conftantius*, who were alfo called *Euchites*; they held that Prayer alone was fufficient inftead of all other good Works.

Meffenger, one that goes between Party and Party, to deliver Bufinefs in Writing: 'tis a Name given to feveral Officers in civil Affairs.

Meffias, (Heb) the fame with *Chriftos* in Greek, i. e. anointed. Our Saviour is often fo called in the Holy Scriptures.

Meffile or *Miffil*, (from *mifceo* to mingle) a kind of Bearing in Heraldry, becaufe of the Intermixture of one colour with another.

Meffor, (Lat.) a Reaper or Mower.

Mefforious, (Lat.) belonging to Reaping.

Meffuage, in Common-Law, a Dwelling-houfe, with fome Land adjoyning, a Garden, Curtilage, Orchard, and all other Conveniencies belonging to it.

Meftizo's, the Breed of *Spaniards* with *Americans*.

Metabafis,(Gr.) a Tranfition, or paffing from one thing to another.

Metabole, (Gr.) an Alteration or Change ; in Physick a Change of Time, Air or Diseases.

Metacarpus, the four Bones that sustain the Fingers, joining to those of the *Wrist* at the other End.

Metachronism, (Gr.) an Error in Chronology or reckoning of time, either reckoning under or over.

Metacondyli, the utmost Bones of the Fingers.

Metalepsis, (Gr.) a participating, the continuation of a Trope in one word through a Succession of significations.

Metaleptick, as Metaleptick Motion, the transverse Motion of the Muscles.

Metalline, (Lat.) pertaining Metals.

Metallist, one that is skill'd in the Nature of Metals, and in Working upon them.

Metallurgy, (Gr.) is the Working or operation upon Metals in order to render them hard, bright, beautiful, Serviceable or useful to Mankind.

Metamorphists, a Name given in the sixteenth Century to those Sacramentarians, who affirmed that the Body of Jesus ascended into Heaven, wholly Deified.

Metamorphize, (Gr.) to transform or change the form or shape of a thing.

Metamorphosis, (Gr.) a changing of one shape into another.

Metangismonites, a sort of Hereticks in Christianity, so denominated from the Greek Word ἄγγος a Vessel, who say, that the Word is in his Father as one Vessel is in another. The Author of this Opinion is unknown.

Metaphor, a Trope in Rhetorick, by which we put a strange and remote Word, for a proper Word by reason of its resemblance with the thing of which we speak ; as smiling Meadows, a youthful Summer, &c.

Metaphorical, pertaining to, or spoken by way of *Metaphor*.

Metaphysical, supernatural, belonging to *Metaphysicks*.

Metaphysicks, (Gr.) a Science which treats of *Entity* and its Properties, But the Philosophy of the Schools being now in a great measure rejected, 'tis commonly taken for the Science of Immaterial Beings.

Metaplasmus, (Gr.) a Figure in Rhetorick, wherein Words or Letters are transposed, or placed contrary to their usual Order.

Metaptosis, (Gr.) is the degenerating of one Disease into another, as when a *Quartan-Ague* degenerates into a *Tertian*, &c.

Metastasis, a Figure in Rhetorick, In Physick it is when a Disease goes from one part to another ; which happens to Apoplectick People, when the Matter which affects the Brain,

Brain, is tranflated to the Nerves.

Metatarfus, is compofed of five fmall Bones, connected to thofe of the firft part of the Feet.

Metathefis, (Gr.) Tranfpo-fition; is when one Letter is put for another.

Metecorn, a Portion of Corn given by the Lord of a Ma-nor, as an Encouragement of Work or Labour.

Metegavel, a Rent paid in Victuals, which formerly was cuftomary, till chang'd into Money by *Henry* I.

Metempfychofis, (Gr.) a Tranfmigration, or paffing of the Soul out of one Body into another, whether of Man or Beaft.

Meteorology, (Gr.) a Dif-courfe of Meteors.

Meteorofcopy, (Gr.) the part of Aftronomy that treats of fublime heavenly Bodies, di-ftance of Stars, &c.

Meteors, (according to *Def-cartes*) are certain various Impreffions made upon the Elements, exhibiting them in different Forms, and are fo called from their Elevation becaufe for the moft part they appear to be high in the Air, of which fort are, *Ignis Fatu-us*, *Trabs*, *ignis Pyramidalis*, *draco volans*, *capra faltans*, &c.

Metheglin, (from the La-tin word *mulfum*) is a kind of drink made of Herbs, Honey, Spice, &c.

Method, (Gr.) is an apt dif-pofition of things, or a placing them in their natural Order, fo as to be eafieft underftood or retained.

Methodical, belonging to Method; faid of one that ob-ferves, or any thing wherein a Method is obferved.

Metonick-Year, (fo called from one *Meton* who invented it) is the fpace of 19 years, in which the Lunations re-turn and begin as they were before.

Metonymy, (Gr.) a putting one name for another, a Fi-gure when the Caufe is put for the Effect, the Subject for the Adjunct, or contra-rily.

Metopa, in Architecture, is the interval or fpace between every Triglyph in the Frize of the *Dorick* Order.

Metopofcopy, (Gr.) the Art of telling mens Natures or Inclinations, by looking on their Faces.

Metrenchyta, is an Inftru-ment wherewith Liquours are injected into the Womb.

Metretes, (Gr.) an Attick Meafure of Capacity for things Liquid containing 10 Gallons, 6 Pints, 1 folid Inch, and 554 decimal parts of our Englifh Wine Meafure.

Metrical, (Lat.) belonging to *Meter* or Verfe.

Metropolis, (Gr.) the Chief or Mother City of a Pro-vince.

Metropolitan, belonging to a Metropolis; alfo an Arch-bifhop is fo called, becaufe his *See* is in the Metopolis, or Mother City of the Province.

Mettle, Vigour, Fire, Sprightliness, Briskness.

Mew, a fort of Coop for Hawks.

Mezzo-tinto, (Ital.) middle Tincture, a way of Engraving Pictures on Copper-Plates.

Miasma, (Gr.) is a contagious Infection in the Blood and Spirits, as in the *Plague*, &c.

Micel-Gemotes, (Sax.) great Councils of Kings and Noblemen, a general or great Affembly.

Michaelmas, the Festival of the Archangel *Michael*, on *September* 29.

Mickle, much.

Microcausticks, (Gr.) are Instruments contrived to magnifie small sounds.

Microcosm, (Gr.) the Body of Man is called the little World, as a kind of *Compendium* of the greater.

Microcosmography, (Gr.) a description of the little-world, *viz.* Man.

Micrometer, an Astronomical Instrument, used to find the Diameters of the Stars or Planets.

Microphones,, see *Microcausticks*.

Microscope, is an Optical Instrument, which magnifies any Object extreamly, and thereby helps us to discover the Minute Particles of which Bodies are composed, and the curious Frame and Contexture of them.

Midding, a Dunghil.

Middle-Latitude-Sailing, is a method of working the several Cafes in Sailing, nearly agreeing with *Mercator's* Way, but without the help of *Meridional Parts*.

Midriff, a Skin or Membrane which parts the Cavity of the *Thorax*, from that of the Abdomen or lower-belly.

Midship-men, are *Officers* on Board a Ship, who affist on all Occasions; both in Stowing and Rummaging the Hold, and Sailing the Ship; they are generally Gentlemen upon their Preferments; having served the limited time in the *Navy* as Volunteers.

Midsummer-Day, the Feast of St. *John Baptist*, June 24.

Mien, the same with *Meen*.

Migration, (Lat.) a removing or shifting from place to place.

Mildew, a Dew which falling on Wheat, Hopps, &c. hinders their growth by its clammy Nature, unless 'tis washt off with Rain.

Mile, a fort of measure of length; an English Mile contains 1056 English Paces, or 1760 Yards; and the Roman Mile 967 Paces, or 1607 English Yards.

Mile Eastern, see *Eastern-mile*.

Militant (Lat.) going to War, fighting; *Church-militant*, is the Church here on Earth, subject to Trials, Combats and Temptations.

Mili-

Military, belonging to Souldiers, or War.

Military Architecture, the same with Fortification; which see.

Military Execution, is the ravaging and deſtroying a Country for Contribution.

Militia, (Lat.) Warfare, Souldiery, the Imployment and Furniture of War; alſo ſuch in any Nation as are train'd up for the defence of it.

Milky-way, is a broad white Path or Track in the Heavens, which is diſcovered to be nothing elſe, but an Infinite number of ſmall Stars, which being inviſible to the naked Eye, cauſe that whiteneſs which we ſee in the Heavens.

Mill-Ree, i. e. a Thouſand Rees, a *Portugueſe*, Coin, worth 6 *s*. 8 *d*. ½. Sterling.

Millenarians, a party of Chriſtians who do believe that after the general or laſt Judgment the Saints ſhall live a Thouſand Years upon Earth, and Enjoy all manner of Innocent ſatisfaction; alſo they believed that in Hell there was a ceſſation of Pain once in a Thouſand Years.

Millener, one that ſells Ribbons, Gloves, Womens Head Attire, &c.

Miller, the Male among Fiſh.

Million, (Lat.) the Number of ten hundred thouſand.

Milt, the Spleen; alſo the ſoft Roe of Fiſhes.

Mimick, a Jeſter, or one that counterfeits the Geſtures or Countenances of others.

Mimical, apiſh, given to Imitate.

Mimoſis, (Gr.) Imitation; a Figure in Rhetorick, when the Words and Actions of other Men are counterfeited or repreſented.

Mina Attica Communis, the common Attick *mina*, a weight, which being reduced to our Engliſh *Troy*, contains 11 Ounces, 7 Penny weight, 16½ gr.

Mina Attica medica, a weight that contained 1 Pound, 2 Ounces, 17⅐ gr. *Troy*.

Mina Ægyptiaca, contained 1 Pound, 3 Ounces, 3 Penny Weight, 13 gr. being reduced to Engliſh *Troy*-Weight.

Mina Antiochica, a Weight that contains 1 Pound, 3 Oun. 3 Penny Weight, 13. gr. *Troy*.

Mina Cleopatræ Ptolemaica, contains 1 Pound, 4 Ounces, 7 Penny Weight, and 20 gr. *Troy*.

Mina Alexandrina Dioſcoridis, contains, 1 Pound, 6 Ounces, 4 Penny Weight, 6 gr. *Troy*.

Mina Hebraica, being reduced to the Engliſh Standard, is worth 6 Pound, 16 Shillings, 10½ Penny.

Mina, among the Grecians, was about 3 Pound 4 Shillings and 7 Pence of our Money.

Mince,

Mince, to cut very small; also to diminish a Matter, or not to speak out plain.

Mine in Fortification, is an Ouverture made in a Wall or other Place, which is designed to be blown up with Powder, it is composed of a *Gallery* and a *Chamber*. The *Gallery* is the first Passage made under Ground, being no higher, nor broader, than to suffer a man to Work on his Knees. The *Chamber*, is the small space at the end of the *Gallery*, like a small *Chamber*, where the Barrels of Powder are deposited for blowing up what is proposed to be sprung.

Mine-Dial, a Box and Needle, with a Brass-Ring divided into 360 parts, and several *Dials* marked on it, for the use of Miners.

Minerals, are hard Bodies dug out of the Earth, or Mines, (whence the Name) being in part of a Metalline, and in part of a Stony Substance, and sometimes with some Salt and Sulphur intermixed with the other.

Mineralist, one skilful in Minerals.

Miniature, the Art of drawing of Pictures in little, which is many times done with *minium* or Red-Lead; (from whence the Name.)

Minim, a Term in Musick, signifying half a *Semibreve*.

Minim Friers, an Order of Monks founded by *Francis de Paul.*

Minima Naturalia, are such Particles of Matter, which though they have each a determinate Shape and Bulk, yet are too minute to be singly sensible: they are supposed to be indivisible, and are what in another word are called *Atoms.*

Miniments, or rather *Muniments* in Law, are the Evidences or Writings whereby a Man is ennabled to defend the Title of his Estate.

Minion, is a piece of Cannon, carrying a Ball of 4 Pound Weight; the Diameter of its Bore is 3 Inches 1/2, and the length of the Piece, about six Foot and a half.

Minion, (Ital.) a Darling or Favourite; one much esteemed and belov'd of a great Person.

Minister, (Lat.) a Servitour, Waiter or Attendant; also an Assistant, Furtherer or Helper.

Ministerial, belonging to a Minister.

Ministry, (Lat.) Service or charge in any Employment, but used more especially for the *Priestly-Function.*

Minnekins, the smallest sort of Pins; also small Catgut-strings for Musical Instruments,

Minnow, the same with *Menow.*

Minor in Law, is one in Nonage, Minority, or Under-Age, or more properly an Heir Male or Female, before they come to the Age of one and Twenty. *Mi-*

Minoration, (Lat.) a making less, or diminishing.

Minority, (Lat.) Nonage, or being under Age.

Minors, Minorites, Minor-Friers, the Friers of the Order of St. *Francis*.

Minster, (Sax.) a Monastery; hence *Minster* a Church, so called becaufe it formerly belonged to fome Monaftery.

Minftrel, a Player on a Mufical Inftrument, a Fidler or Piper.

Mint, a Place where Mony is Coined.

Minute, little, fmall.

Minute, is the 6oth part of an Hour; alfo (in Geometry) the 6oth part of a Degree.

Minutes, the firft Draughts of Writings; alfo the Abftract of a Judge's Sentence; fhort Notes of any thing.

Miracle, according to the Divines, is a Work effected in a manner unufual, or different from the common and regular method of Providence, by the Interpofition either of God himfelf, or of fome intelligent Agent Superiour to Man, for the Proof or Evidence of fome particular Doctrine, or in Atteftation to the Authority of fome particular Perfon.

Miraculous, belonging to a Miracle.

Mirifical, wonderfully done, ftrangely wrought.

Mirke, dark, obfcure. *Spencer*.

Mirmillion, a Challenger at Fighting with Swords, one fort of Gladiators.

Mirobalans, a kind of Plumbs ufed in Medicine.

Miroar or *Mirrour*, (Fr.) a Looking-glafs.

Mifanthropy, (Gr.) a Man-hating, a flying the Company of Men.

Mifadventure, in Law, fignifies the killing of a Man partly by negligence, and partly by chance, as by throwing a Stone carelefly, fhooting an Arrow, and the like.

Mifcarriage, Folly, Ill-behaviour, Ill-fuccefs of Bufinefs; alfo the untimely bringing forth of a Child.

Mifcellaneous, (Lat.) mixt together without order.

Mifcellanies, Collections of feveral different Matters.

Mifconftruction, the miftaking the Senfe of Words fpoken; moft commonly for the worfe.

Mifcreance, mif-belief, difpraife, *Spencer*.

Mifcreant, (Fr.) an Infidel or Unbeliever.

Miferable, wretched, diftreffed, unfortunate.

Mifcrere, a Title given to he fifty firft Pfalm.

Miferere mei, a moft violent Pain in the Guts, proceeding from an Inflammation thereof, or Involution, and the Periftaltick Motion inverted. Whence the Excrements are difcharged by the Mouth.

Miferecordia, in Law, is ufed for an Arbitrary Amerciament impofed

impofed on any for an Offence; for where the Plaintiff or Defendant in any Action is amerced, the Entry is *ideo in miferecordiâ*; it is fo called, becaufe it ought to be very moderate and lefs than the Offence.

Mifery, (Lat.) wretchednefs, fad Condition, that merits Compaffion.

Misfeafor, Mifdoer, Trefpaffer.

Mifinterpret, to give a wrong Senfe, to Interpret ill.

Mifnomer, (Fr.) a mifterming, or mifcalling, ufing of one Name or Term for another.

Mifogamy, (Gr.) a Marriage hating.

Mifogynift, (Gr.) Womanhater.

Mifprifon, (Fr.) a Term in Law fignifying neglect or overfight.

Miffal, a Book containing the Ceremonies of Popifh Mafs, a Mafs-Book.

Miffen-maft of a Ship, ftands aft in the fternmoftpart of the Ship; in fome great Ships there are two of thefe; that next the *Mainmaft* is called the *main-miffen*, and that next the Poop, the *Bonaventure-miffen*. The length of the *miffen-maft*, is by fome accounted the fame with the *main-top-maft* from the *Quarter-deck*; or half the length of the *main-maft*, and half as thick.

Miffen, Note, that when this word is ufed at Sea, by it

they always mean the Sail. *Set the Miffen*; that is, fit the *miffen-fail* right as it fhou'd ftand. *Change the Miffen*; that is, bring the *miffen-yard* over to the other fide of the Maft; *Peck the Miffen*, that is, put the *miffen-yard* right up and down by the Maft. *Spell the Miffen*; that is, let go the Sheet and peck it up.

Miffen-Sail, and *miffen-top-fail*, are thofe Sails that belong to the *miffen-yard*, and *miffen-top-fail-yard*. See *Yard*.

Miffil, (Lat.) a Dart, Stone, Arrow, or other thing thrown or fhot.

Miffionaries, perfons fent; commonly fpoken of Priefts fent to unbelieving Countries, to convert the People to Chriftianity.

Miffion, (Lat.) a fending away, licence or leave to depart.

Miffeve, fent, caft, hurled.

Mifter, Need, want.

Mifunderftanding, a not underftanding aright; alfo a Jealoufie and Sufpicion among Friends, tending to a rupture of Friendfhip.

Mifwent, gone aftray, *Spencer*.

Mif-woman, a Whore or lewd Woman. *Chaucer*.

Mite, a fmall Coin, about ⅓ of a Farthing; alfo the 24th part of a Grain Weight.

Mitella, is the Surgeon's Term for the Swath that holds up the Arm when it is hurt or Wounded.

Mithri-

Mithridate, an Electuary, which is a special Preservative against Poison, having its Name from *Mithridates* King of *Pontus*.

Mitigate, (Lat.) to assuage, pacify, or make quiet.

Mitral, belonging to a *Mitre*.

Mitral Valves, two Valves or Skins at the Orifice of the Pulmonary Vein, in the left Ventricle of the Heart, for hindring the Blood's returning to the Lungs, having their Name from the resemblance of a *Mitre*.

Mitre, a Pontifical Ornament, and 'tis the same with regard to a Bishop, as a Crown to a King.

Mittendo manuscriptum pedis finis, is a Writ judicial, directed to the Treasurer and Chamberlain of the Exchequer, to search and transmit the Foot of a Fine from the Exchequer to the Common-Pleas.

Mittimus, a Writ by which Records are transferr'd from one Court to another; also a Justice's Warrant to a Gaoler to receive and keep an Offender.

Miva, in Pharmacy, is the Flesh or Pulp of a Quince boiled up with Sugar into a thick consistence.

Mixen, a heap of Dung, a Dung-hill.

Mixt Body, in Chymistry and natural Philosophy, is a Body not mixt or compounded by Art, but by Nature, as Minerals, Vegetables, and Animals from which by Chymistry different Substances can be separated.

Mixt Number, is one that is part Integer and part Fraction as $2\frac{1}{4}$.

Mixt Angle in Geometry, is one which is formed by one right line, and one Curved one.

Mixt Figure, in Geometry, is a Figure which is bounded by lines partly right and partly crooked.

Mixture, (Lat.) a mingling of several things together.

Mixmor, (Span.) a dungeon.

Mizzle, to rain in small Drops.

Moat, in Fortification, the same with *Ditch* or *Foss*, is a depth or Trench round the *Rampart* of a Place, to defend it, and prevent surprizes; the Brink of the *Moat* next the *Rampart* is called the Scarp, and that opposite on the other side, is called the *Counterscarp* which forms a *Reentring Angle* before the Center of the *Curtin*.

Mobb, *Mobile*, the Tumultuous Rabble, the giddy Multitude, or Dregs of the People.

Mobby, a Drink made of Potatoe-roots, much used in *Barbadoes*.

Mobility, (Lat.) a Power of moving or being moved.

Mochel, or Mickle much, *Spencer*.

Mock-

Mockadoes, a kind of Wollen Stuff.

Modality, a School Term, fignifying the manner of a thing in *abftracto*.

Modder, a young Girl.

Mode, (Lat.) a manner of a thing; alfo the Fafhion of the time.

Model, the fhape or defign of any thing in little.

Moderata Mifericordia, in Law, is a Writ for the abating an immediate Amerciament.

Moderation, Temperance, Difcretion, Government.

Moderator, (Lat.) a difcreet Gouernour; a decider of any Controverfy.

Modern, (Lat.) new, of late time.

Modefty, (Lat.) Bafhfulnefs, Refervednefs.

Modicum, (Lat.) a fmall matter, a little pittance.

Modification, (Lat.) a qualifying, meafuring or limiting.

Modillions, in Achitecture, are little Brackets which are often fet under the Cornices, more efpecially in the *Corinthian* and *Compofit* Order, and ferve to fupport the Projecture of the *Larmier* or *Drip*.

Modiolus, *Trepanum*, or *Anabaptifton*, is an Inftrument which the *Surgeons* ufe in profound Corruptions, Contufions, Cuts and Fractures of the Bones of the Head.

Modifh, according to the Fafhion.

Modius, a Roman Meafure of capacity for things dry, which being reduced to the Englifh Corn Meafure, contains 1 Peck, 7 folid Inches, and 68 decimal Parts.

Modo & forma, are Words in Procefs and Pleadings, ufed by the Defendant when he denies the thing charged.

Modulation, (Lat.) Tuneing, Compofing in Mufick, Setting of Notes.

Module, a Meafure in Architecture, commonly half the Diameter of the Pillar at the lower end, in the Tufcan, and in the Dorick Order; but in others the whole Diameter, it is commonly divided into 60 parts called Minutes, except in the Dorick,

Modus decimandi, is when either Land, a Sum of Money, or Yearly Penfion is given to the Parfon, &c. by Compofition, as Satisfaction for his Tythes in kind.

Mohair, a Stuff of Silk and Hair.

Moietie, (Fr.) is one half of any thing divided into two equal parts.

Moineau, is a *French* Term for a little flat Baftion, raifed upon a *Re-entring Angle* before a *Curtin*, which is too long between two other *Baftions*.

Mokel, (Sax.) much.

Mokes, the Mefhes of a Net.

Moky, Cloudy.

Molar Teeth, Grinders or Cheek-Teeth.

Molar,

Molar, (Lat.) belonging to a Mill.

Molaſſes, the refuſe Syrup in boiling of Sugar.

Mole, a Rampart, Peer, or Fence againſt the force of the Sea ; alſo a ſpot on the Skin; alſo a Mooncalf, or piece of unſhapen Fleſh brought forth inſtead of a Child ; alſo a litle Creature that lives underground.

Moleſtation, (Lat.) a vexing or putting to trouble.

Moliminous, having, uſing, or requiring much ſtrength.

Moline, a Term in Heraldry, and ſignifies a Croſs of this Figure.

Moliniſts, the Followers of *Molina* a *Spaniſh* Jeſuit, Profeſſor of Divinity at *Coimbra* in *Portugal,* in his Opinions about *Grace* and *Free-will.*

Molition, an Attempting or Endeavouring.

Mollient, ſoftening, mollifying.

Mollify, to ſoften, to make ſupple, effeminate, &c.

Mollification, a making ſoft, ſupple, effeminate, &c.

Moloch, called alſo *Milchom* ; as God of the *Ammonites* and *Moabites,* to whom they were wont to ſacrifice their Children.

Moloſſus, the Foot of a Latin Verſe of three Syllables,

when they are all long.

Mome, a mere Drone, or dull Fellow without life.

Momentany, (Lat.) that laſts but a Moment, of ſhort continuance.

Moments, are ſometimes taken for the leaſt and moſt inſenſible parts of Time ; in natural Philoſophy.

Moment, commonly ſignifies the Motion of any Body, which is always as the Matter of that Body multiplied into it's celerity.

Monachal, (Lat.) belonging to a Monk.

Monaciſm, the State and Condition of Monks in General.

Monadical, belonging to Unity.

Monads, Units.

Monarchicals, certain Chriſtian Hereticks about the Year 196, who acknowledged but one perſon in the Holy Trinity, and ſaid, that the Father was Crucified.

Monarchy, is that Form of Government, where one perſon only Rules.

Monaſterians, ſee *Anabaptiſts.*

Monas, (Gr.) Unity, or the number one.

Monaſtery, is an Abbey, or ſolitary place where Monks live.

Monaſtick, belonging to a Monk or Abbey.

Mond, the World, Men, Folks; alſo a Golden Globe, one of the Enſigns of an Emperor.

Mone.

Monetagium, the right of Coining Money.

Monger, (Sax.) a Merchant anciently, but now added to the Names of feveral forts of Commodities, it fignifies a Dealer in the refpective Commodities, as *Iron-monger*, *Wood-monger*, &c.

Monition, (Lat.) a Warning or Admonition.

Monitor, (Lat.) an Admonifher, Warner, or Councellor.

Monk, one that lives in a Monaftery, under a Vow to obferve the Rules of the Founder.

Monks-feam, with Sailors is when the Selvedges of Sails are laid a little over one another, and fewed on both fides.

Monochord, a kind of Inftrument, anciently of fingular ufe in the Regulation of Sounds; but fome appropriate the Name of *Monochord* to an Inftrument, that hath only one String, as the *Trumpet marine*.

Monochromaton, (Gr.) a kind of Picture all of one Colour.

Monocolon, the *Inteftinum*, *Cæcum*, or Blind-gut.

Monocular, (Lat.) having but one Eye.

Monody, (Lat.) a Mournful or Funeral Song, where one Sings alone.

Monodical, (Lat.) pertaining to a *Monody*, or Funeral Son.

Monogamy, (Gr.) a Marrying one Wife and no more during life.

Monogram, (Gr.) a Letter that ftands alone; *monogrammick Picture*, is a Picture only drawn in Lines without Colours; alfo a Writing or Sentence in one Line or Verfe.

Monologue, frequently fignifies a Dramatick Scene, where onely one Actor fpeaks.

Monology, (Gr.) fpeaking alone, or always in the fame tone; alfo a long Difcourfe to little purpofe.

Monomachy, (Gr.) a fingle Combat or Fighting of two Hand to Hand

Monomial, (Gr.) having one only Name; in Mathematicks it is a Magnitude of one Name, or one only Term.

Monopetalous Flowers, (in Botany) are fuch as tho' they may be feemingly cut into 4 or 5 fmall *Petala*, or Leaves, are yet all of one piece, and which falling of all together have their Flower in one piece.

Monoplegy, a fharp Pain affecting one fingle place of the Head.

Monophagy, (Gr.) a Feeding alone, or on one fort of Meat.

Monopoly, is when a Man ingroffes, or gets Commodities into his Hands, in fuch a Fafhion that none Sell them, or gain by them but himfelf.

Monopolift, (Gr.) he that doth fo ingrofs Commodities, or he that hath the Grant of a *Monopoly*.

Monopteron, a kind of round Temple, having its Roof only

ly

ly supported by Pillars, and having but one Wing or Isle.

Monoptick, (Gr.) that sees only with one Eye.

Monoptote, (Gr.) a Word having but one Case.

Monosyllable, (Gr.) that hath but one Syllable.

Monothelites, a Sect of Christian Hereticks, who denied two Wills, and two different Operations of our *Saviour Jesus Christ*, and so received *Eutyches* his first Errors, *Theodorus* Bishop of *Phorane* was the Author of that Sect in the seventh Century. These Hereticks were also named *Monophysites*, *Egyptians* and *Schismaticks*.

Monotriglyph, a Term in Architecture, signifying the space of one *Triglyph* between two *Pilasters*, or two Columns.

Monsoons, are Periodical Winds in the *Indian Sea*, that is, Winds that blow half the Year one way, and the other half on the opposite Points; and those Points and Times of shifting are different, in different parts of the Ocean; and in some places 'tis constant for three Months one way, then three Months more the contrary way, and so all the Year.

Monster, (Lat.) any thing against or beside the common Course of Nature; a mis-shapen living Creature, that degenerates from the Right and Natural Disposition of its Parts.

Monstrable, (Lat.) that may be shewed or declared.

Monstrans de droit, in Law, signifies a Suit in *Chancery*, for the Subject to be restored to Lands and Tenements which he shews to be his Right, though by Office found to be in the Possession of another lately dead; by which Office the King is entitled to a Chattel, Freehold, or Inheritance in the said Lands.

Monstrans de faits ou Records, *shewing of Deeds or Records*, is thus; upon an Action of Debt brought upon an Obligation, after the Plaintiff hath declared, he ought to shew his Obligation; and so it is of *Records*.

Monstraverunt, in Law, is a Writ that lies for Tenants of *Ancient Demesne*, being distrained for the Payment of any Toll or Imposition, contrary to their Liberty which they do or should enjoy.

Monstrosity, (Lat.) which is done contrary to the Ordinary course of Nature: Monstrousness.

Monstrous, of, or like a Monster, prodigious, excessive.

Mont-Pagnote, or *Post of the Invulnerable*, is an Eminence chosen out of the *Cannon-shot* of the place besieged, where curious persons post themselves to see an Attack, and the manner of the Siege, without being exposed to danger.

Montanists, an Heretical Sect founded by one *Montanus*, who audaciously proclaimed himself to be the Comforter promised by Christ, condemned second Marriages as Fornication, permitted the dissolution of Marriage, &c.

Montanous, beloging to the Mountains.

Montesiasco, a rich Wine made at *Montesiascone*, a small City in *Italy*.

Montero, (Span.) a sort of Cap, us'd by Hunters, Horsemen, and Sea-men.

Monteth, a scallop'd Bason to cool Glasses in.

Month, properly speaking, is the time in which the Moon runs through the Zodiack, and therefore is accounted by the Motion of the Moon.

Month Synodical, see *Synodical Month*.

Month Periodical, see *Periodical Month*.

Month Solar, see *Solar Month*.

Month Astronomical, see *Astronomical Month*.

Month Civil, see *Civil Month*.

Monticles, (Lat.) little Mountains.

Monticulous, full of Monticles.

Montivagant, wandring on Mountains.

Monument, (Lat.) a Memorial for after Ages, a Tomb, Statue, Pillar.

Mood, Humour, Temper, Disposition.

Mood, in *Musick*, signifies certain Proportions of the Time or Measure of Notes, of which there are four. 1. *The Perfect of the more*, 2. *The perfect of the Less*, 3. *The imperfect of the More*, 4. *The imperfect of the Less*. Besides these, there were five other Moods relating to *Tune* amongst the *Grecians*, having their Names from several Countries, *viz.* the *Dorick*, *Lydian*, *Jonick*, *Phrygian*, and *Æolick* Moods; which see in their Places.

Moods in Grammer, determin the signification of *Verbs* as to the manner and circumstances of the Affirmation.

Moon, one of the seven Planets, being the secondary Planet of the Earth, in whose Motion there is wonderful Irregularities and Inequalities. It's periodical Revolution with respect to the fixt Stars, is in 27 Days, 7 Hours, 43 Minutes; but its Synodical, with Relation to the Sun, is 29 Days, 12 Hours, and ¼ of an Hour.

Moon-calf, a false Conception.

Moon-ey'd, one that sees better by Night than Day.

Moor, signify'd formerly a Heath or barren space of Ground; but is now commonly taken for a Marsh, or Fen; Also a Native of *Mauritania* in *Africk*.

Moor, to Moor a Ship, is to lay out her Anchors, so as is most convenient for her safe and secure riding. A Ship is not said to be *moored*, unless

less she has at least two *Anchors* out.

Moors-head, in Chymistry, is the Head of a Copper, Glass-Still or Alembick, which is luted on to the Body or Cucurbit, and hath a Beak, Nose or Pipe, to let the raised Spirit run down into the Receiver.

Moose, a Beast as big as an Ox, slow of Foot, and headed like a Buck, frequent in *America.*

Moot, is a Term used by the Lawyers, and signifies that Exercise or Arguing of Causes, which young Students perform at appointed Times, the better to enable them for Practice, and the defence of Clients Causes.

Mope, one Stupid, or Sottish.

Mopsical, mop-ey'd, that sees not well.

Moral, (Lat.) pertaining to Manners, Civility, or the Conduct of Human Life.

Moral of a Fable, the Application of it to Mens Lives and Manners.

Morals, Manners, Principles of one's Life, Thoughts, Designs, or Inclinations; also the Doctrine of Manners, Moral Philosophy.

Moralist, one skill'd in Morality, one of good and sound Principles of Dealing between Man and Man.

Morality, the same with *Morals.*

Morality, or moral Philosophy, is an Art which gives Rules, and lays down Methods concerning Manners, Behaviour, and the Regulation of the Actions of Man, only as he is Man.

Morass, a Moorish Ground, a Marsh, Fen, or Bog.

Moratur, or *demoratur in Lege,* signifies as much as *he demurs,* because the Party goes not forward in Pleading, but rests upon the Judgment of the Court in the Point, who deliberate, and take time to argue and advise thereupon.

Morbid, (Lat.) sickly, subject to Diseases.

Morbifick, (Lat.) that causeth Disease or Sickness.

Morbilli, the Measles.

Morbulent, (Lat.) full of Diseases, Sickly.

Mordacity, (Lat.) Bitingness, Sharpness; a corroding Quality, which with its Acid Particles corrodes and divides continuous Bodies; also Bitterness of Speech, Detraction.

Moresk-Work, (in Carving or Painting) is an antick Work after the manner of the Moors, consisting of several Pieces, in which is no perfect Figure, but only a rude resemblance of Men, Birds, Beasts, Trees, and jumbled together.

Morigerous, (Lat.) Obedient Dutiful.

Morion, (Ital.) a sort of Steel-Cap or Head-piece in use formerly.

Morisco, (Span.) a Moor, also a Morris (or Moorish) Dance.

Morking, (with Hunters) a wild Beast, dead by Sickness, or Mischance.

Morling, Wool got from off a Dead Sheep.

Morococks, a sort of Strawberry found only in *Virginia* and *Maryland*.

Morology, (Gr.) a foolish speaking.

Morosity, (Lat.) Frowardness, Peevishness, Averseness to please.

Morose, froward, testy, hard to please.

Morphew, a kind of white scurf upon the Body, from the French words *mort feu*, (a dead Fire.)

Morris-Dance, an Antick Dance performed by five Men, and a Boy in a Girl's Habit, with his head gaily trim'd up.

Morse, a Sea-Ox, being an Ampibious Creature of the bigness of an Ox, tho' more like a Lion, with Teeth like an Elephant's, and as large, a Skin twice as thick as a Bull, and short Hair'd like that of a Seal.

Mortal, (Lat.) deadly; also subject to Death.

Mortality, (Lat.) frailty, a state subject to decay or death.

Mortar-piece, is a short piece of Artillery, of a wide Bore, serving to throw *Bombs*, *Carcasses*, *Fire-pots*, and other sort of *Fire-works*, as likewise Stones.

Mort d' Ancester, is a Writ that lieth where a Man's Father, Mother, Brother or Uncle dies seized of Land, and a Stranger abutteth, or entereth the Land.

Mortgage in Law, signifies a Pawn of Lands or Tenements, or any thing movable, laid or bound for Mony Borrowed, to be the Creditor's for ever, if the Money be not paid at the Day agreed upon ; he that pledgeth this Pawn or Gage, is called the *Mortgager*, and he that taketh it the *Mortgagee*.

Mortiferous, (Lat.) Deathbringing, deadly.

Mortification, (Lat.) i. e. a making dead, vexation and trouble befalling a Man when disppointed or cross'd. In *Divinity*, a subduing of the Flesh, by Abstinence and Prayer: in *Surgery*, loss of Life in a Member ; in *Chymistry*, Alteration of the outward Form in Metals, Minerals, &c.

Mortise, with *Carpenters*, is a Hole cut in a Piece of Wood, to let in the Tenon of another.

Mortmain, (Fr.) an Alienation of Lands or Tenements, (with the King's Licence of *Mortmain*, to a Corporation or Fraternity, as Bishops, Parsons, &c.

Mortrell, a Mess of Bread and Milk, that was allowed to poor People in Hospitals.

Mortuary, is a Gift left by a man at his death, to his Parish Church, for the Recompence

pence of his Perſonal Tythes and Offerings, not duly paid in his life time.

Mortuum caput, ſee *Caput mortuum.*

Moſaical, of, or belonging to *Moſes.*

Moſaique, or *Moſaick Work,* is a moſt curious Work, wrought with Stones of divers Colours, and divers Mettals, into the ſhape of Knots, Flowers and other things, with that nicety of Art, that they may ſeem all to be one Stone, or rather the Work of Nature than Art; others deſcribe it to be a kind of Painting in ſmall Pebbles, Cockles and Shells of divers Colours, and of late, likewiſe with pieces of Glaſs Figured at Pleaſure; an Ornament of much Beauty and duration, but of moſt uſe in Pavements and Floorings.

Moſchc or *Moſque,* a Name given to Publick places, where the Mahometans meet to pray, from the Arabick word *Meſged,* that properly ſignifies a place of Worſhip.

Moſs, a kind of ſpongious or downy vegetable Subſtance, that grows upon Trees, Stones, and ſome Earths in various Forms and Shapes.

Moſſes, mooriſh, or boggy Places.

Moſſy, full of, or like unto Moſs.

Moſtick, the ſtick which Painters reſt upon, when at Work.

Mote, (Sax.) an Aſſembly, or Meeting, a Court of Judicature.

Mother, the Womb, or a Diſeaſe in that part; alſo Dregs of Ale, Beer, Oyl, &c.

Mother Tongues, are ſuch Languages as ſeem to have no dependence upon, derivation from, or affinity with one another; of which *Scaliger* affirms there are eleven only in Europe. The *Greek,* the *Latin,* the *Teutonick* or *German,* the *Sclavonick,* the *Albaneſe* or *Epirotick.* The *European Tartar* or *Scythian,* the *Hungarian,* the *Finnick,* the *Cantabrian,* the *Iriſh,* and the old *Gauliſh* or *Brittiſh*; to this number ſome add four others, the *Arabick,* the *Cauchian,* the *Illyrian,* and the *Jazygian.*

Motet, (Fr.) a Verſe in Muſick, a Stanza of a Song; alſo a ſhort Poeſie.

Motion, is by Philoſophers defined to be a continual and ſucceſſive Mutation of Place.

Motion Abſolute, is a Mutation of abſolute Place, and its celerity is meaſured according to abſolute ſpace.

Motion relative, is a Mutation of Relative Place, and its celerity is meaſured by Relative ſpace.

Motion equably accelerated, is ſuch, whoſe velocity increaſeth equally in equal Times.

Motion equably retarded, is whoſe velocity decreaſes equally in equal Times, till the Body come to reſt.

Motive, moving; also a moving Cause or Argument.

Motivity, the Power of moving.

Motley, mixt.

Motte, night. *Spencer.*

Motto, (Ital.) a Word; but in a restrained Sense it is properly taken for the Word or short Sentence, apply'd to an *Impress* or *device*, see these Words. There are also *Motto's* belonging to the Coats of Arms, of most of the Nobility and Gentry.

Movable Feasts, are those Festivals, which though they are celebrated on the same Day of the Week, have no fixed seat in the Calendar, but in several Years happen on several Days of the Month, as *Easter, Whitsontide, &c.*

Movement, the same with what is called an *Automaton*, and with us signifies all those parts of a Watch, Clock, or any such curious Engine, which are in Motion, and which by that Motion carry on the Design, or answer the end of the Instrument; also Motion, Moving.

Movent, that which moves or gives motion, moving.

Mould, a Form in which any thing is cast, the Hollowness in the upper part of the Head; also Earth for Plants to grow in.

Moulder, to fall to Dust; to consume or waste away.

Mouldings, of a Gun or Mortar, are all the eminent Parts, as Squares or Rounds which serve generally for Ornament, as the *Breech mouldings; muzzle mouldings, &c.*

Moulinet, a French Term signifying a *Turn-style*; 'tis used in the Mechanicks, and signifies a *Roller*, which being crossed with two *Levers*, is usually apply'd to *Cranes, Capstans*, &c. to heave up Stones, Timber, &c.

Moult, or *Moulter*, to shed the Feathers as Birds do.

Mound, in Heraldry, signifies a Ball or Globe with a cross upon it; also a Fence or Hedge.

To Mount the Guard, is to go upon duty; to *Mount a Breach*, is to run up it, or to Attack; to Mount the Trenches, is to go upon Guard in the Trenches.

Mount, a Hill or Mountain; a piece of Ground in a Garden raised higher than the rest. In *Fortification* a heap of Earth on which is a Parapet to cover the Cannons planted on it.

Mountain of Piety, a Stock of Money that was raised by Contribution, laid up to be lent on Occasion to poor People ruin'd by the Extortion of the Jews.

Mountainous, Hilly, full of Mountains.

Mountebanck, (Ital.) *Mountimbanco*) a cousening Drugseller, a base deceitful Merchant (especially of Apothecaries Druggs) who by his Impudence puts of his counterfeit Stuff to the common People.

Moxa,

Moxa, a fort of Indian Mofs, ufed againft the Gout.

Moyeneau, (Fr.) in Fortification is a little flat *Baftion,* raifed upon a *Re-entring Angle* before a *Curtin,* which is too long between two other *Baftions.* It is commonly joyned to the *Curtin,* but fometimes feparated by a *Fofs,* and then it is called a *Detatched Baftion.*

Mucilage, (in Pharmacy) is a vifcous Extraction made of Seeds, Roots, Gums, &c. with water.

Mucilaginous Glands, are Kernels about the Joynts, that feparate a flimy Matter for lubricating of 'em.

Mucid, (Lat.) hoary, mufty, mouldy.

Mucous, full of flime or Snot.

Mucronated, is whatever Ends or Terminates in a point like that of a Sword.

Mucronatum Os, the lower End of the Breaft Bone, pointed like a Sword.

Mudereffes, Perfons among the *Turks,* that teach Scholars the publick Service, for which they are paid out of Revenues of Mofques.

Muffle, in Chymiftry, is the cover of a *Teft* or *Coppel,* which is put over it in the Fire.

Muffler, a piece of Cloth, to be tyed about the Chin.

Mufti, the Principal Head of the Mahometan Religion, or Oracle of all doubtful Queftions in their Law, and is a Perfon of great Efteem and Reverence amongft the *Turks.*

Muggletonians, the Followers of *John Muggleton,* a Journey-man Taylor, who with one *Reeves,* fet up for a great Prophet, about the year 1657. pretending to abfolute Power of Saving and Damning whom they pleas'd.

Mulatto, one born of Parents, of whom one is a Moor, and the other of another Nation.

Mulciber, Vulcan, the God of Fire.

Mulct, (Lat.) a Penalty, or Fine of Money or Amerciament.

Muliebrity, (Lat.) Womanifhnefs, foftnefs, effeminacy.

Mulier, in common Law, is a Son born in Wedlock, with relation to one born before it of the fame Man or Woman, who muft yield the Inheritance to the younger.

Mulierofity, unlawful defire of Women.

Mulierty, the State of a *Mulier* or lawful Iffue.

Muller, the Stone which one holds in their Hand, with which they grind upon a Porphyry.

Mullet, in Heraldry, fignifies a Star of five Points, and is ufually the difference or diftinguifhing mark for the third Brother or Houfe.

Mulfe, (Lat.) Water and Honey fod together, alfo fweet Wine.

Mulſulmans, (Arab.) the Turks or Mahometans ſo called; the Word ſignifies as much as a People faithfull in their Law or Religion.

Multa, or *Multura Epiſcopi*, a Fine given to the King, that the Biſhop might have Power to make his laſt Will and Teſtament, and to have the Probate of other Mens, and the granting Adminiſtrations.

Multangular, (Lat.) Figures having many Angles.

Multatitious, gotten by Fine or Mulɗt.

Multifarious, of divers or ſundry ſorts.

Multiform, of many Forms, *Milton.*

Multilateral, (Lat.) Figures that have many ſides.

Multinomial Quantities compoſed of ſeveral Names, or monomes joyned by the Signs + or — thus, $m+n-n+p$, and $a-d+c-d$, are Multinomials.

Multinominal, (Lat.) having many Names.

Multiparcus, bringing forth many at a Birth.

Multiple, one number is ſaid to be multiple of another when it contains it, a certain number of times without any Remainder.

Multiplec, a greater number containing a leſs, a certain Number of Times without a Remainder.

Multiplication, (Lat.) is the finding a number equal to the Product of 2 other num-

bers, which is done by taking one ſo often as there are units in the other, thus if 4 were to be multiply'd by 2, the Product will be had by adding 4 as often to it ſelf, as there are Units in 2, ſo that 'tis 8.

Multiplication of lines, is to make a Rectangle under the two lines given to be multiply'd.

Multiplicand, is the Quantity that is multiply'd.

Multiplicater, is the Quantity that multiplieth.

Multiplicity, much variety, a great deal.

Multiply, to encreaſe the Number of a Thing.

Multipotent, (Lat.) able to do much.

Multiſcious, knowing much.

Multiſonant, (Lat.) that hath many or great Sounds.

Multitude, (Lat.) a great Number.

Multivagant, (Lat.) wandring or ſtraying much abroad.

Multivious, (Lat.) that hath many ways, manifold,

Multivolent, (Lat.) of many Minds, Mutable.

Multure, Griſt, alſo the Toll or Fee of a Miller for Grinding.

Mumble, to mutter or growl; alſo to chew awkwardly.

Mummer, a Masker, one in Maſquerade.

Mummery, (Fr.) a Perſonating others in a Mask or Antick Habit.

Mummy,

Mummy, (Lat.) Bodies anciently Embalmed, brought out of *Egypt, Arabia, Syria,* and kept in Libraries or Studies by way of Rarity; also a Pitchy fort of a Substance fold by Apothecaries, either from Bodies embalmed in *Arabia,* or made of Jews-lime and Bitumen.

Mumper, a gentle Beggar.

Mumps, a fort of Quinfey or fwelling of the Chaps.

Muncerians, a fort of Rebellious Anabaptifts in *Germany,* fo called from one *Muncer,* their Founder and General.

Mundane, (Lat.) worldly, or belonging to the World.

Mundanity, (Lat.) Worldlinefs.

Mundatory, fee *Purificatory.*

Mundbretch, (Sax.) a breach of the King's Peace, an Infringement of Privileges; alfo a breaking of Enclofures.

Mundivagant, (Lat.) wandring about the World.

Mundifying, Purifying, Cleanfing.

Muneration, (Lat.) a recompencing or rewarding.

Municipal, enjoying, or belonging to the Freedom of a City.

Municipal-Laws, are fuch Laws as the Inhabitants of a Free Town or City enjoy.

Munificence, (Lat.) Bountifulnefs, Liberality.

Munificent, Bountiful, Liberal.

Muniment, a Fortification, Fence or Fortrefs.

Muniment-Houfe, an Apartment in Cathedrals, Caftles, &c. for keeping Seals, Charters, Evidences, &c.

Muniments, in Law, are taken for fuch Authentick Deeds and Writing, as a man can defend the Title to his Land or Eftate by.

Munite, (Lat.) fenced, made ftrong.

Munition, a Bulwark, or Fortification, Defence; alfo Ammunition.

Munition-Ships, are thofe which have Stores on Board, to fupply the neceffaries required by a Fleet of Men of War at Sea.

Mur, a great Cold, the Pofe.

Murage in Law, is a Toll or Tribute to be levyed for Building or repairing Publick Walls, and is due either by grant or Prefcription. It feems alfo to be a Liberty granted, by the King, to a Town for gathering Money towards Walling it.

Mural, (Lat.) belonging to a Wall.

Mural Crown, a Reward the Ancient Romans gave thofe Souldiers, who firft Scalled the Walls and entred the Enemies City.

Murcid, (Lat.) cowardly, unadvifedly, flothfully.

Murder, in Law, is a Wilful killing of a Man upon premeditated Malice.

Murderers, are fmall Pieces of Ordnance, either of Brafs or Iron.

Murderous,

Murderous, bloody-minded, cruel.

Mure up, to wall up, or ftop up with Bricks, Stones, &c.

Murenger, an Officer to o-verſee a Wall.

Murex, a Fiſh with the Liquor of which they anciently died Purple; alſo the Colour it ſelf.

Muring, in Architecture, is the raiſing of Walls.

Murmur, a buzzing or humming Noiſe of People diſcontented.

Murmuring, grumbling, muttering, repining; alſo the Purling of Brooks and Streams.

Murnival, (Fr.) the Number Four; Four of a ſort at Cards, as 4 Kings, 4 Aces, &c.

Murrain, a waſting Diſeaſe among Cattle, the Rot.

Murrey, dark brown, or dun Colour.

Muſach Caſſa, a Cheſt or Church-Box in the holy Temple of *Jeruſalem*; wherein Kings were wont to caſt their Offerings.

Muſaph, a Book among the Turks that contains all their Laws.

Muſcadel or *Muſcadine*, a rich Wine brought from *Candy*, having the Flavor of Musk.

Muſcat, a delicious Grape, taſting richly of Musk.

Muſcheto, a kind of Inſect ſomewhat reſembling a Gnat.

Muſcle, is a diſſimilar or Organical Part, (framed of its proper Membrane, Fibrous Fleſh, a Tendon, Vein, Artery, and Nerve) appointed by Nature to be the compleat Inſtrument of local Motion; alſo a Shell-Fiſh.

Muſcle-vein, is twofold, one ariſing from the Muſcles of the Neck, called *Superior*; the other from thoſe of the Breſt, and is nam'd *Inferior*.

Muſcous, (Lat.) Moſſy or full of Moſs.

Muſcular, of, belonging, or like unto Muſcles.

Muſculous, belonging to, or full of Muſcles.

Muſes, certain ſuppoſed Divinities among the Heathens, and made to be the Daughters of *Jupiter* and *Mnemoſyne* (they are nine) to whom the Invention of Sciences are attributed, *viz. Clio*, *Urania*, *Calliope*, *Euterpe*, *Erato*, *Thalia*, *Melpomene*, *Terpſicore*, and *Polyhymnia*. The Poets made *Parnaſſus* to be their Reſidence, as alſo *Helicon* with *Appollo*, conſecrated ſeveral Fountains to them, as alſo the Palm, and the Lawrel.

Muſhroom, an imperfect Plant of a ſpongy Subſtance, which grows up to its Bulk of a ſudden; in a Figurative Senſe, 'tis us'd for an Upſtart.

Muſical, belonging to Muſick, Harmonious.

Muſician, one skill'd in Muſick.

Muſick, one of the ſeven Sciences term'd *Liberal*, belonging to the *Mathematicks*,
which

which confiders the Number, Time, and Tune of Sounds, in order to make delightful Harmony.

Mufing, Paufing, Thinking upon, Studying.

Musk, or, as the Indians call it, *Pat*, is a Perfume growing in a little Bag or Bladder, within an Indian Beaft, like a Roe or wild Goat.

Musket, (Fr.) the Taffel, or Male of a Sparrow-hawk; alfo that well-known fort of Fire Arms, that are to carry a Ball about an Ounce weight.

Musketoon, a Blunderbufs, a fhort Gun of a large Bore, for carrying many fmall Bullets.

Muforites, certain *Jews* who reverenced *Rats* and *Mice*.

Mufqueteer, is a Foot *Souldier* armed with a *Mufquet* or *Firelock*, *Sword*, *Bayonet*, &c.

Mufquet-Baskets, in Fortification, are Baskets of about a Foot and half high, and 8 or 10 Inches Diameter at the Bottom, and a Foot or more at the Top; they are fill'd with Earth, and placed on low Parapets, or Breaft-works, or on fuch as are beaten down, that the Mufqueteers may Fire between them, and yet be pretty well fecured againft the Enemies Fire.

Mufroll, the Nofe-band of a Horfe Bridle.

Mufs, fcramble, as to *make a Mufs*, to make People fcramble by throwing things in a Crowd.

Muffack, a Drink much ufed in *China*.

Muffitation, (Lat.) a mumbling, muttering, or fpeaking between the Teeth.

Muffulmans, the fame as *Mulfulmans*, which fee.

Muft, (Lat) fweet Wine, newly preft from the Grape.

Muftachio, or *Muftache*, Greek μύςαξ, French, *Mouftache*; that part of the Beard which grows upon the upper-Lip.

Muftaphis, Doctors or Prophets, men of great regard or Learning among the Turks.

Mufter, a Review of Military Forces, in order to take account of their Numbers, Condition, Arms and Accoutrements.

Muftering, taking a Review of Forces; alfo gathering together.

Mufter-Mafter-General, an Officer that takes an Account of every Regiment, as to their Number, Horfes, Arms, &c.

Mufter of Peacocks, a Term for a Flock of Peacocks.

Mufter-Rolls, Lifts of the Souldiers in every Troop, Company, Regiment, &c.

Mutability, Changeablenefs, Inconftancy.

Mutable,(Lat) changeable, or fubject to change.

Mutation, (Lat.) a changing.

Mute,(Lat.) Dumb, Speechlefs; alfo Dung of Birds

Mute Letters, in Grammar, Letters yielding no Sound of themfelves without Vowels.

Mute

Mute Signs, such as are named from Creatures without Voice; as *Cancer, Scorpio, Pises.*

Mutes, certain dumb Persons kept in the Grand *Signior's Seraglio,* serving as Executioners for straggling Offenders.

Mutilate, (Lat.) to maim, cut off, diminish, take away or make imperfect.

Mutilation, (Lat.) a maiming, or curtailing of any thing.

Mutinous, rebellious, seditious, apt to revolt.

Mutiny, (Fr.) a Sedition, especially among Souldiers.

Mutineer, a Seditious Person.

Mutter, to speak confusedly through the Teeth.

Mutual, (Lat.) a like on both sides, interchangeable from one to another.

Mutule, in Architecture, is a kind of Square Modillion, set under the Cornice of the *Dorick* Order.

Muzzle, the Snout of an Ox, Lyon, Tiger, or the like ; also a Halter for tying about a Horse's or Mule's Nose; also the Mouth of a Gun.

Muzzle mouldings of a Gun, is the Ornament round the Muzzle.

Mysterism, (Gr.) a wiping one's Nose, also in Rhetorick a closer kind of *Sarcasm.*

Mydryasis, (Gr.) is too great a dilation of the Pupil of the Eye, which dims the Sight, because then the Eye receives too much Light.

Mynchen, (Sax.) a Nun, or vailed Virgin, whence comes *Mincing.*

Myography, (Gr.) a Description of the Muscles, by Writing or Cuts.

Myology, a Discourse of the Muscles.

Myopia, Pur-blindness.

Myotomy, Dissecting of Muscles.

Myrinx, the Tympanum, or Drum of the Ear.

Myrrhe, an *Arabian* Gum of a Colour between white and red, 'tis often used in Physick, and is of an opening, cleansing, and dissolving Nature.

Myriad, (Gr.) ten Thousand.

Myrrhine, of or belonging to Myrrh.

Myrtle, a little low Tree growing in hot Countries, having small dark Leaves ; 'tis a Tender Plant, and not able to endure Cold. The Roman Captains us'd to wear it, Garland-wise, in Triumph when they had obtained a Victory without Slaughter of men.

Myropolist, (Gr.) one that Sells sweet Oyntments, Oils, or Perfumes.

Mystagogical, belonging to a *Mystagogue.*

Mystagogue, (Gr.) one that interprets Mysteries or Ceremonies ; also he that hath the keeping and shewing of Church Reliques to Strangers.

Mystical, Mysterious, secret, hidden, obscure.

Mysterious, the same that *Mystical*.

Mystery, (Gr.) a Secret, a thing Concealed; also any particular Art or Trade is so call'd.

Mythological, belonging to Mythology.

Mythologist, one skilled in *Mythology*.

Mythology, the History of the Fabulous Deities and Heroes of Antiquity, and the Explanation of the Mysteries of the old Pagan Religion.

N

NAam, in Law, signifies a Distress, or the taking another Man's Goods. And *Lawful Naam*, is a reasonable Distress to the value of the thing distrained for.

Nab, to surprize, or take napping; also to cog a Die.

Nabal, a proper Name, us'd appellatively for a Miser or Churl.

Nadir, is that Point in the Heavens which is directly under our Feet; and 'tis Diametrically opposite to the *Zenith*, or the Point over our Heads.

Nænia, Funeral Songs, or Songs which were wont to be sung in old time at the Funerals of the Dead.

Naiant, or Natant, (swimming) is the proper Term in Heraldry, to blazon Fishes in an Escutcheon, when they are drawn in an Horizontal Posture, or transversly a cross the Escutcheon; but if they are erect 'tis called *Haurient*.

Naiades, false Goddesses believed by the Poor Heathens to preside over Fountains and Rivers, and to whom they paid some sort of Worship.

Naif, (Fr.) that looks quick and natural, a Term apply'd to Jewels.

Nailing of Cannon, is driving Iron Spikes by main force into the Vent or Touch-hole, which renders the Cannon inserviceable, till the Spike be either got out, or a new vent drill'd.

Naissant, i. e. *Nascent*, just new born; in Heraldry it signifies a Lion or other Beast, appearing to be Issuing, or coming out of the middle of any *Fess* or other ordinary.

Naked Fire, in Chymistry, is an open Fire, or one not penned up.

Nakib escree, the Head or Superiour of the *Emirs* or *Mahomets* Race; who hath Sergeants and Officers under him, and is vested with so absolute an Authority over them, that he extends it to Life and Death at pleasure, though he will never scandalize this pretended Seed to execute or punish them.

Namation, (Law-Term) a Distraining, or taking a Distress.

Nap, the tufted surface of Cloth, also a short Sleep.

Napæa,

Napæe, Nymphs or Fairies of the Wood.

Naperie, (Fr.) Linnen for the Table, Houfhold Linnen.

Napier's Bones, certain numbering Rods, of Paft-board, Wood, or Ivory, for performing fpeedily feveral Arithmetical Operations, invented by my Lord *Napier* Baron of *Merchifton* in *Scotland.*

Napthe, a kind of Marle or chalky Clay, which takes fire eafily.

Narciffine, (Gr.) pertaining to a white Daffodil.

Narcofis, is a Privation of Senfe, as in a Palfie, or in taking of Opium, &c.

Narcotical, (Gr.) ftupifying, or benumming, taking away Senfe.

Narrator, (Lat.) a Relater, or Teller.

Nas, has not, *Spencer.*

Nafcalia, are little Globular Bodies, which on fome occafions, are apt to put into the Neck of the Matrix.

Naffip, a Word ufed by the *Mahometans* to fignifie Fate or Deftiny, which according to their falfe belief is, in a Book written in Heaven, containing the good and ill Fortune of all Men, which can no way be avoided.

Natagai, an Idol worfhipped by the Heathen *Tartars,* and thought to be the God of the Earth, and all living Creatures.

Natalitious, (Lat.) belonging to the Nativity or Birthday.

Natation, a Swimming.

Nates Cerebri, two Protuberances of the Brain behind the *Thalami Nervorum Opticorum,* that grow to the upper part of the Marrowy Subftance.

National, that which concerns or belongs to a whole Nation.

Native of fuch a Place, is the being Born in fuch a Place.

Nativity, (Lat.) Birth, firft, Entrance into the World; among *Aftrologers,* the true Time of one's Birth, or a Figure of the Heavens caft for that time.

Natta, is a great foft Tumor, with Pain and Colour, which grows moft ufually in the Back, but fometimes in the Shoulders.

Natural, belonging to Nature; alfo a Fool.

Natural-Day, the fpace of 24 Hours.

Natural-Year, one Revolution of the Sun, or 365 days, and almoft 6 Hours.

Natural-Philofophy, (the fame with Phyficks) is that Science which contemplates the Powers of Nature, the Properties of Natural Bodies, and their mutual action one upon another.

Naturalift, one skill'd in Natural Philofophy.

Naturalization, is when an Alien-born-fubject is made a Natural Subject, and this muft be done by Act of Parliament.

Nature, (Lat.) a peculiar Difpofition of *Parts* in fome particular

particular Body ; alfo the U-niverfal Difpofition of all Bo-dies ; alfo the Effence of any thing with its Attributes ; al-fo Condition, Difpofition, Hu-mour.

Naval, (Lat) belonging to a Ship or Navy.

Nave, that part in the Mid-dle of a Wheel, where the Spokes are fixed; alfo the main Part or Body of a Church.

Naufrage, Shipwrack.

Navicular, (Lat.) pertaining to a fmall Ship.

Navigable, (Lat.) where Ships may pafs, that will bear a Ship or Boat.

Navigation, (Lat.) is the Art of Carrying or Condu-cting a Ship at Sea, by the helps af Charts, Compaffes, &c. but particularly by the Affiftance of Trigonometry ; taking Obfervations, &c.

Naulage, (Fr.) the Fraight, or Paffage Money for go-ing over the Sea, or a Ri-ver.

Naumachy, (Gr.) a Sea Fight, or Battel at Sea.

Naufeate, (Lat) to have an Appetite to Vomit ; alfo to loath or abhor.

Naufeoufnefs, Loathing, is an earneft endeavour to Vomit, with Sicknefs and un-eafinefs.

Nautical, belonging to Ships or Marriners.

Nautical Chart, fee *Chart.*

Nautical Compafs, fee *Com-pafs.*

Nautical Planifphere, is the

Defcription of the Terreftrial Globe upon a Plane for the ufe of Marriners, and is ei-ther *the Plane Chart*, or *Mer-cator's Chart*, which fee.

Navy, a Fleet or Company of Ships.

Nazarites, the Names of certain Perfons under the *Jew-ifh* Law, who made a Law to abftain from the Fruit of the Vine, from fhaving their Heads, or cutting their Hair, and from polluting themfelves by the dead, unlefs it were for their Father and Mother, and that either for a Term of Time, or to their Lives End.

Ne, nor, not, *Spencer.*

Ne admittas, is a Writ di-rected to the Bifhop, at the Suit of one who is Parfon of any Church, and he doubts the Bifhop will collate one his Clerk, or admit ano-ther Clerk prefented by ano-ther Man to the fame Bene-fice; then he that doubts it, fhall have this Writ, to for-bid the Bifhop to collate or admit any to that Church.

Neal, or *Anneal*, to make a Metal fofter or lefs brittle, by heating in the Fire.

Nealed, if the *Sounding be nealed to*; that is if it be deep water, clofe the fhore ; or if the Lee-fhore be Sandy, Clayey, Oafie, or Foul and Rocky Ground.

Neap Tides, are the Tides when the Moon is in the fecond and laft Quarter ; being nei-ther fo high nor fo fwift as the Spring Tides.   *Near,*

Near, no Near, a Word of Command from him that Commands the Ship, to the Man at the Helm, ordering him to let her fall to the Leeward.

Neat, any kind of Beeves, as Ox, Cow, Steer, or Heifer.

Nebulose, the Heralds give this Name to the Out-line of any Bordure, Ordinary, &c. something resembling the Figure of Clouds.

Nebulous, (Lat.) Cloudy, Misty, Foggy.

Necessary, (Lat.) needful, unavoidable.

Necessitate, (Lat.) to force, to compell.

Necessitous, indigent, needy, poor.

Necessity, (Lat.) constraint, force ; also want, Indigence.

Necromancer, (Gr.) a Conjurer, Magician, or Wizard.

Necromancy, (Gr.) a Divination by calling up Dead Mens Ghosts, or the Devil ; also Conjuration in General.

Necromantick, belonging to *Necromancy.*

Nectar, (Gr.) a Pleasant Liquour, feigned by the Poets, to be the Drink of the Gods.

Nectarean, sweet as *Nectar,* Divine.

Nefandous, Horrible, Hainous, Mischievous, not to be mentioned or spoken of.

Nefarious, cursed, unworthy to live, wicked.

Negation, (Lat.) a Denying, a Gainsaying.

Negative, (Lat.) Denying, or Gainsaying.

Negative Quantity, in Algebra, is a Quantity with a Negative Sign prefixed, thus —*ab* is a— Negative Quantity.

Negative Sign, in Algebra is thus marked (—) and is directly contrary to Affirmative ones.

Neglect, (Lat.) want of care, Omission, Disregard.

Negligence, want of care, heedlesness.

Negoce, (Lat.) Treading, Dealing, Business.

Negotiation, a Merchandizing or Trafficking ; the Management of Publick Treaties and Affairs.

Negro, (Ital.) a Neger or Blackmore.

Neif, (Fr.) in the common Law signifies a Bondwoman.

Ne injustè vexes, a Writ forbidding the Lord to distrein, the Tenant having formerly prejudiced himself by doing or paying more than he needed.

Nemesis. the Goddess of Revenge, called also *Adrastia.*

Nemestrinus, from *Nemus* a Grove, the Heathen Deity of the Forests and Woods.

Neomenia, the new Moon, or the begining of the Lunar Month.

Neophitæ, (new set Plants) a Name given to those Christians who had lately quitted
Judaism,

Judaism, or Paganism, to embrace Christianity.

Nephalia, certain Feasts and Sacrifices of the Greeks, called the Feast of sober Men, because at them they offered Mead instead of Wine.

Nephela, are little white spots upon the Eyes; also little Clouds, as it were, that Swim in the middle of the Urine; likewise little white spots in the Surface of the Nails like little Clouds.

Nephritick, (Gr.) troubled with a Disease in the *Reins;* also that which is good against such Disease.

Nephritis, is a Pain in the Reins, proceeding either from an ill Disposition, or an Inflammation, or from the Stone and Gravel accompanied with Vomiting and stretching of the Thigh.

Nephrotomy, an Opening, or Cutting up of the Kidneys.

Nepotation, (Lat.) Riotousness, Luxury.

Nepotism, the State of a Nephew, or other Relation, a Word us'd chiefly with regard to the Pope's Relations.

Neptune, the God of the Sea.

Neptunian, belonging to Neptune, or to the Sea.

Neread, a Mermaid, or Fish, the upper part of which is like a Beautiful Woman, and the rest like a Fish.

Nereides, (Gr.) Sea-Nymphs, or Fairies.

Nereus, one of the Heathen Deities of the Sea; they make him to have fifty Daughters called *Nereides,* which indeed are no more then so many particular Seas being parts of the main Sea it self.

Nerves, are whitish round Vessels, taking their Origin from the Medullar Substance of the Brain (taken largely) and the spinal Marrow, conveying thence animal Spirits to all the Parts of the Body, for their Sense and Motion respectively.

Nervosity, fulness of Nerves or Sinews, Strength, Vigour.

Nervous, full of Nerves; strong.

Nescious, (Lat.) Ignorant.

Nestorians, the Followers of *Nestorius,* that held there were two Persons in Christ, and that the Holy Spirit proceeded only from the Father.

Nettings, in a Ship, are small Ropes seiz'd together grating-wise with Rope-yarn, and sometimes made to stretch upon the Ledges from the Waft-trees to the Rouf-trees, from the Top of the Forecastle to the Poop; and sometimes are laid in the waft of a Ship to serve instead of *Gratings.*

Nettle, to sting with Nettles; also to nip, teaz, or vex.

Neurodes, a sort of lingering Fever.

Neurology, (Gr.) is a Description of, or Discourse on the Nerves of a human Body.

D d d   *Neuro.*

Newroticks, are Remedies against Diseases in the Nerves.

Neurotomy, (Gr.) a Section, or cutting of the Nerves.

Neutral, (Lat.) belonging to neither.

Neutrality, a not siding with either Part, Indifferency.

New-Years-Gift, a Custom among us, which came first from the Ancient Romans; for the Knights used every Year on the first Day of *January* to offer New-Years-Gifts in the Capitol to *Augustus Cæsar,* though he were then absent.

Newel, a Novelty. *Spencer.*

Nicean, or *Nicene,* of, or belonging to *Nice,* a City of *Bithynia.*

Nicete, (Fr.) Sloth, Idleness, Simplicity; hence our word Nicety, which we commonly use for Coyness, Daintiness, Curiosity.

Niche, in Architecture, is a Gavity in the Wall of a Building to place a Statue in.

Nicholaitans, Hereticks who are supposed to have risen in the Christian Church, during the time of the Apostles, and are taken to be the Fathers of the Gnosticks; they held it lawful to have their Wives common.

Nicodemites, a Sect in *Switzerland,* named from professing their Faith in private like *Nicodemus.*

Nicotian, (Fr. *Nicotiane*) Tobacco; so called from *John Nicot,* who first sent it into *France* from *Portugal,* where he was Ambassadour for the French about the Year 1560.

Nictation, (Lat.) a winking or twinkling with the Eyes.

Nidgeries, (Fr.) Fopperies, Fooleries, Trifles.

Nidget, an Idiot, Ninny, or mere Fool.

Nient comprise, in Law, is an Exception taken to a Petition as unjust, because the thing desired is not contained in that Act or Deed, whereon the Petition is Grounded.

Night-mare, see *Incubus.*

Nigheth, draweth near. *Spencer.*

Nigrefaction, (Lat.) the Action of making black.

Nigrefy, to make black.

Nigromancy, the same with *Necromancy,* which see.

Nihil or *Nichil,* is a word which the Sheriff answers, that is opposed concerning Debts illeviable, and that are nothing worth, by reason of the insufficiency of the Parties from whom they are due.

Nihil dicit, in Law, is a failing to answer the Plea of the Plaintiff by the Day assigned; which if he do judgment passes against him in course by *nihil dicit;* that is, because he says nothing in his own defence why it shou'd not.

Nihil capiat per breve, the Judgment given against the Plaintiff.

Nim, to Filch, or take by Stealth.

Nimbi-

Nimbiferous, that brings Storms or Tempests.

Nippers, are small short Ropes with a little Truck at one end, and sometimes only a Wall-Knot; they serve to help to hold off the Cable from the *Main* or *Jeer Capstan*, when 'tis so slimy, so wet or so great, that they cannot strain it, to hold it off with their bare Hands. Also a Surgion's Instrument made use of in Amputations.

Nis, is not, *Spencer*.

Nisi prius, is a Writ Judicial, which lies in a Case where the Inquest is pannelled and returned before the Justices of either Bench; the one party or other making Petition to have this Writ for the ease of the Country.

Nitid, (Lat.) bright, neat, clean.

Nitre, is a Salt impregnated with abundance of Spirits out of the Air, which do render it volatile.

Nitrous, full of Nitre, or Nitrous Particles.

Nival, or *Niveus*, pertaining to Snow, white as Snow.

Nixidii, certain Divinities Worshipped by the Heathen *Romans*, and supposed by them, to be the helpers of Women in their Child-bed-throws.

Nobility, (Lat.) the being remarkable or well-known, Fame, Reputation, Renown, Glory, Nobleness of Birth.

Nobless, (Fr.) the Nobility, the State of a Nobleman.

Nocent, (Lat.) hurtful.

Nocive, (Lat.) hurtful.

Noctambulo, (Lat.) one who walks in his sleep.

Noctiferous, (Lat.) Night-bringing.

Noctivagrant, (Lat.) wandring by Night.

Nocturlabe, an Instrument to find the Motion of the North Star about the Pole.

Nocturn, a part of Church Service for the Night.

Nocturnal, (Lat.) belonging to the Night; also the Name of an Instrument for observing the Stars.

North Star, is higher or lower than the Pole at all Hours of the Night.

Nocti-luca, is one of the two kinds of Phosphorus, and is a self-shining Substance, and requires the being exposed to light to make it luminous.

Nocument, (Lat.) hurt or damage.

Nocuous, hurtful.

Nodes, in Astronomy signify the Points of Intersection of the Orbits of the Planets with the Ecliptick, and the Point where a Planet passes out of the Southern Latitude into the Northern is called the North *Node*, or ascending *Node*, and on the contrary where it passes from the North to the South, is called the Southern or descending *Node*.

Nodous, knotty, full of knots.

Noli me tangere, a fort of Canker in the Face, especially above the Chin ; also a piece of Flesh in the Nostrils which often stops the Wind, and the more it is touched the worse it grows.

Nome, deep rotten Ulcers in the Mouth.

Nomarchy, one that has Pre-eminence in Ministration of Laws.

Nombril, (Fr.) a Navel; in Heraldry it signifies the lower part of an Escutcheon divided broad-ways into three even parts ; the *Fesse* being the middle, and the *Honour Point* the upper Part.

Nomenclator, (Lat.) a Cryer in Court.

Nomenclature, (Lat.) the Office of a Cryer in Court ; also a Set of Names, or a Catalogue of useful and significant words in any Language.

Nominal, (Lat.) belonging to a Name.

Nomination, (Lat.) a nameing or appointing.

Nomographer, (Gr.) a Writer of the Law, a Ligiflator.

Nomothesie, (Gr.) the making, publishing or proclaiming a Law.

Nomparel, a very small fort of Printing Letter.

Nonability, in our Law, is an Exception against any Person that disables him to Commence a Suit.

Nonage, a Term in Law, signifying all that Time of a Man's Age, under One and Twenty in some Cases, and Fourteen in others, as Marriage.

Nonagesimal Degree, is the highest Degree, or 90th. Degree of the Ecliptick.

Nonagon, a Figure of nine Sides and Angles.

Non-claim, a Man's not claiming within the Time limited by Law, as within a Year and a Day, &c.

Non compos mentis, that is, not of sound Memory or Understanding, or one that is not in his right Wits, and signifieth in Law, first, an Ideot Born ; Secondly, one that by accident looseth his Memory and Understanding ; Thirdly, a Lunatick; and Fourthly a Drunkard.

Non-conformist, one that does not comply with, spoken especially with regard to an establish'd Church.

Non distringendo, a Writ containing under it divers particulars, according to divers Cases.

Non-entity, in Philosophy, denotes a Thing not in Being.

Nones of a Month, are the next Days after the Calends, which is the first Day; in *March*, *May*, *June* and *October*, the *Romans* accounted six Days of *Nones*, but in all the rest of the Months but four.

Non est culpabilis, in Law, signifies the General Plea to an Action of Trespass, whereby the Defendant doth absolutely deny the Fact imputed

imputed to him by the Plaintiff.

Non est Factum, is an Answer to a Declaration, whereby a Man denieth that to be his Deed, whereupon he is Impleaded.

Non Implicitando aliquem de libero tenemento sine brevi; is a Writ to Inhibit Baliffs, &c. from Distraining any man without the King's Writ touching his Freehold.

Non liquet, it appears not, it is not clear; also a Verdict given by the Jury, signifying that the Matter was to be deferred to another Day of Trial.

Non Molestando, is a Writ that lieth for him which is molested contrary to the King's Protection granted him.

Non-natural, (Physical term) so are things call'd that enter not into the Nature of Diseases, though Causes of them.

Non Obstante, notwithstanding; a Word frequently used in our Statutes, Patents, &c.

Non Organical, so Anatomists call that part which has an Use, but performs no Action.

Nonpareil, that has no equal, not to be parallel'd.

Non Plevin, Law-Term, us'd when Land is not Replevy'd in due time.

Nonplus, (Lat.) no more; a Term often used when a man can say no more, nor answer, an Objection; then we say he is at a Nonplus, to

puzzle, to vex, to gravel, to balk.

Non-principiate, having no begining.

Non procedendo ad Assisam Rege inconsulto, is a Writ to stop the Tryal of a Cause appertaining unto one that is in the King's Service, &c. untill the King's Pleasure be further known.

Non Residentia pro Clericis Regis, is a Writ directed to the Ordinary, charging him not to molest a Clerk employ'd in the King's Service by reason of his *non-Residence*.

Non-Residence, in Law, is when Spiritual Persons are not resident upon, but absent themselves from their Benefices; for *Personal Residence* is required of Ecclesiastical Persons.

Non sanæ Memoriæ, in Law, is an Exception taken to an Act declared by the Plaintiff or Defendant to be done by another, whereupon he grounds his Plaint or Demands; and the Effect of it is, that the party that did that Act, was Mad or not well in his

Non-suit, in Law, is Renouncing of the Suit by the Plaintiff, when the matter is so far proceeded in, as that the Jury is ready to deliver their Verdict.

Non sum Informatus, an answer made by an Attorney, who is commanded by the Court to say something in behalf of his Client, by which he is deemed to have nothing to say for his Client, and so Judgment passes against him.

Non Tenure, an Exception to a Court, or Declaration by saying, he holds not the Lands contained therein.

Non Term, the time of the King's Peace, Vacation time.

Nonupla, a quick time in Musick peculiar to Gigs and such like; having nine Crotchets between Bar and Bar.

Nook, a Corner. *Milt.*

Norbertines,, Monks founded by *Norbert*, Bishop of *Magdeburg* in 1120, called also *Premonstratenses*.

Normal, (Lat.) a word frequently used in the Mathematicks, and signifies the same with *perpendicular*.

Norrey or *Norroy*, that is north King, the third of the three Kings at Arms, whose Office is the same on the North-side of *Trent*, with that of *Clarenceux* on the South.

Northern Signs of the Ecliptick or Zodiack, are those six Signs which constitute that Semicircle of the Ecliptick which inclines to the Northward of the Æquator.

Northing, (at Sea) is the difference of Latitude a Ship makes in Sailing to the Northward.

North-Pole, a Point in the Northern Hemisphere of the Heavens, 90 Degr. every way distant from the Equinoctial.

North-Star, or *North-Pole-*

Star, is in the Tail of the *Ursa-minor*, and it is so called, as being not above two Degrees and a half distant from the Pole, and seems to the naked Eye, as if in the same Place.

Nosocomium, is an Hospital for Poor Sick People where they are attended and cured if possible.

Nostoch, the stinking, tawny Gelly of a fallen Vapour, or (by Dr. *Charleton*) the Nocturnal Solution of some Pletthoretical and Wanton Star.

Notable, (Lat.) remarkable, extraordinary, great.

Notary, a Scribe, or Scrivener, that takes Notes and short Draughts, of Contracts, or other Instruments.

Notation, (Lat.) a Marking, or putting a Mark upon a thing. In *Algebra*, Notation is the representing Quantities by Letters of the Alphabet, or a calling them by those Names.

Note of a Fine, a Brief of a Fine, made by the Chirographer before it be engross'd.

Notes, brief Remarks upon an Author for the better understanding him. Also in Musick, Notes are Terms to distinguish the Degrees of Sound in Tuning, and the Proportion of Time thereunto belonging.

Notification, (Lat.) an Information or Advertisement.

Notion, (Lat.) a Conception or Idea.

Notional, belonging to a Notion.

Notoriety, plain Evidence of a Matter of Fact.

Notorius, (Lat.) manifest, evident.

Novacula, a Surgion's Knife, the Shape whereof differs according to the difference of Operations.

Novatians, a fort of Hereticks, who held that Persons who had fallen into any open Sin, ought to be received into Communion without the impofing of any Penance; they are fo called from one *Novatus* their Founder, who lived about the Yerr, 215.

Novation, (Lat.) the entring into a New Obligation in Law, to take off a former; alfo the transferring an Obligation from one Perfon to another.

Novator, (Lat) he that maketh a thing New; a changer of the State, an Ufurper.

Novels, 168 Volumes of the Civil Law, added to the Codex by the Emperor *Juftinian*; alfo little Romances.

Novel Affignment, in Law, is the *Affignment* of time, place or the like, otherwife than it was before affigned.

Novelty, whatever is new, what we have not feen before.

November, fo called from its being the ninth Month from *March*, which began the *Roman* Year.

Novenary, (Lat.) belonging to, or confifting of nine.

Novennial, (Lat.) of nine Years.

Novenfiles, among the Heathen *Romans*, were Heroes newly received into the number of their Gods; or elfe the Gods of the Provinces and Kingdoms which the *Romans* had Conquered, and to which they offered Sacrifices, under the Name of the *Dii Novenfiles*.

Novercal, (Lat.) of, or belonging to a Stepmother.

Novice, a young beginner in any Art or Profeffion.

Novitiate, the time wherein one is a Novice.

Novity, (Lat.) Newnefs.

Nould, would not. *Spencer*.

Noun (in Grammar) is the firft Part of Speech, denoting a Word whereby any thing is Named; as a *Stone*, a *Sound*, a *Colour*, &c.

Noxious, (Lat.) hurtful, noifome, offenfive.

Nubecula, (Lat.) are little light Particles, which mutually, but loofly clofe with one another, and fwim upon the Urine.

Nubilous, (Lat.) Cloudy, Gloomy.

Nucamentum, in Botanicks, the fame with *Julus*.

Nucha, is the hinder part or the Nape of the Neck.

Nuciferous, (Lat.) Nut-bearing, or producing Nuts.

Nuciofity, Purblindnefs.

Nucleus, is the edible part of the Kernel of any Nut, which is contained within the Skin of the Kernel; also by some Astronomers it is used for the Head of a Comet, and by others for the central Parts of any Planets. In Architecture, it is the middle part of the Flooring of the Ancients, consisting of Cement, which they put betwixt a Lay or Bed of Pebbles cemented with Mortar made of Lime and Sand.

Nudation, (Lat.) a making bare or naked.

Nude, (Lat.) naked: *Nude Contract*, in Law, is a bare promise of a thing without any consideration.

Nude matter, in Common Law, is a naked Allegation of a thing done, to be proved only by Witness, and not either by Record, or other, speciality by writing under Seal.

Nudity, (Lat.) Nakedness. Among Painters, a Picture representing a naked Person.

Nugation, (Lat.) a Trifling.

Nugator, (Lat.) a Trifler.

Nuisance, (Fr.) hurt, Offence, Damage, Trespass. In Law, it is where any Man erects any Wall, stops any Water, or doth any thing upon his own Ground to the Unlawful hurt or annoyance of his Neighbour.

Nullifidian, one of no Religion, or no Honesty, one of no Faith.

Nullity, the being null, void, or of no effect.

Nullo, a Cypher standing for nothing.

Number, is a Collection of Units.

Numeral, (Lat.) of, or belonging to Number.

Numeration, the Art of reading or expressing any Numbers set down in Figures, and is commonly taught as the first Rule in Arithmetick.

Numerator, of a Fraction, is a Number which expresses the Number of the Parts of the Unity, or the whole, you make use of in any Fraction, as in $\frac{1}{4}$, 3 is the Numerator, as telling you after you have divided 1, or the whole into 4 equal parts, how many of those parts must be taken, *viz.* 3 of them.

Numerical, belonging to Number; also particular, individual.

Numero, (Lat.) in Number, a Term prefix'd by Merchants, Physicians, or others, to a certain Number of things, mark'd thus, N°.

Numerous, abounding in Number, great, manifold.

Nun, (*nonna q. non nupta.*) is a Holy or Consecrated Virgin, or a Woman that by Vow has bound her self to a single and chaste Life, in some place and Company of other Women separated from the World, and devoted to an especial Service of God by Prayers, Fastings, and such like Holy Exercises.

Nuncheon, an Afternoon's Repast.

Nunciature, the Office of a *Nuncio*; also a Report, or Message.   *Nuncio,*

Nuncio, the Pope's Ambaſſador is called by this Name, *viz.* the Pope's *Nuncio,*

Nuncupation, (Lat.) a Naming, or calling by Name.

Nuncupative, (Lat.) called, named, expreſly declared by word of Mouth.

Nundinal, (Lat.) belonging to a Fair or Market.

Nuper Obijt, is a Writ that lies for a *Co-heir,* being deforced by her Co-parcener of Lands or Tenements, whereof any of their Anceſtors died ſeiz'd of an Eſtate in Fee-ſimple.

Nuptial, (Lat.) pertaining to a Wedding or Marriage.

Nuptialiſt, a Bride, Bridgroom, or one that makes Matches.

Nurture, a nouriſhing, a teaching of good Manners.

Nuſance, (Law-term) Annoyance, when a Man does any thing on his own Ground, to the Damage of his Neighbour; alſo an Aſſiſe, or a Writ that lies for ſuch an Offence.

Nutation, (Lat.) a Nodding.

Nutriment, (Lat.) nouriſhment.

Nutrition, is a Natural Increaſe, whereby that which continually decays of any corporeal Subſtance is repaired by convenient Nouriſhment.

Nutritious, (Lat.) nouriſhing, or cheriſhing.

Nutritive, (Lat.) apt to nouriſh, or that ſerves for nouriſhing.

Nux, is a ſort of Pain in the Head, which afflicts a Place as big as a Nut.

Nychthemeron, is the ſpace of 24 Hours, or an entire Day and Night.

Nyctalopia, is firſt a dimneſs of the ſight in the Night, or in dark places, without any impediment in the light; or Secondly, a dimneſs in the Light, and clear ſight in the Night, or in ſhady places.

Nyctelia, Feaſts of the Heathens in Honour of their falſe God *Bacchus,* and ſo called becauſe they were celebrated in the Night.

Nymph, (Gr.) a Bride, or new Married Wife.

Nymphal, belonging to the Nymphs.

Nymphotomy, a cutting of the *Nymphæ.*

Nymphs, falſe Deities believed by the Heathens to preſide over Waters, Rivers and Fountains, Foreſts and Trees.

O

OAkum, or *Oaklam,* are old Ropes untwiſted and torn in pieces, and pull'd again out into looſe Hemp, like Hurds of Flax; that it may be driven into the Seams, Trennels, and rends of a Ship, to ſtop, or prevent a Leak.

Oazy, Oazy Ground, that is ſoft, ſlimy, or muddy Ground, which is bad Anchoring Ground, becauſe the Anchor cannot hold firm, but will be apt to give way in bad Weather; but ſuch Ground is good to bring a
Ship

Ship a Ground upon, becaufe fhe can there Dock her felf and lye foft.

Obambulate, (Lat.) to walk about, or up and down.

Obduction, (Lat.) a covering or laying over.

Obdurate, (Lat.) hardned; alfo unrelentiug, obftinate.

Obedientials, (Lat.) thofe that Execute an Office under Superiours, and with Obedience to their Commands.

Obeifance, (Fr.) Obedience, a dutiful obferving of, an Obfequious yielding to.

Obelisk, is a Magnificent high piece of folid Marble or other fine Stone; having ufually four Faces, and leffening upwards by degrees till it ends in a Point like a Pyramid, and the difference between an *Obelisk* and a *Pyramid* is this; an *Obelisk* is all of one entire Stone or piece, and therefore not fo high as a Pyramid, which confifts of divers Stones.

Oberration, (Lat.) a running up and down, a wandring about.

Obequitate, (Lat.) to ride about.

Obefe, (Lat.) fat, grofs.

Object, any thing which is oppofed to our fight, or any other of our Senfes, is frequently called by this Name.

Object-glafs, of a Telefcope or Microfcope, is that Glafs which is placed at that end of the Tube which is next the Object.

Objection, (Lat.) a cafting

againft, or a laying to one's Charge.

Obit, (Lat.) a coming to or meeting; alfo Death, Difeafe, or fetting or going down of the Sun, &c. alfo a Funeral Song or an Office for the Dead.

Obituary, a Regifter-Book, in which the Friers in a Monaftery enter the Obits of their Benefactors.

Objuration, (Lat.) a binding by Oath.

Objurgation, (Lat.) a chiding, reproving, rebuking, or blaming.

Objurgatory, (Lat.) Pertaining to chiding, or rebuking.

Oblat, a Souldier difabled in the Prince's Service, that had the Benefit of a Monk's Place given him in an Abbey; alfo the Maintenance it felf.

Oblata, is a Word ufed in the *Exchequer,* fignifying old Debts brought together from precedent Years, and put to the prefent *Sheriff's* charge.

Olation, (Lat.) an Offering; more efpecially that which is offered by Religious Perfons to the Church, or to pious ufes; alfo a Toll or Subfidy.

Oblectation, (Lat.) Recreation, Delight, Pleafure.

Obligation, (Lat.) a Binding or Obliging ones felf to any thing by Word or Writing; alfo a Bond containing a Penalty with a Condition annexed, either for

Payment

Payment of Money, performance of Covenants or the like.

Obligatory, (Lat.) binding, or laying an Obligation.

Obligee, a Person to whom a Bond, or obligatory Writing is made.

Obliging, civil, courteous.

Obligor, one that enters, or is entred into a Bond for Payment of Money, &c.

Oblimation, (Lat.) a Plaistering or Daubing over.

Oblique, crooked, awry.

Oblique Ascension, see *Ascension*.

Oblique Descension, is that Point in the Equinoctial which Sets with the *Sun* or *Stars*, or any Point of the Heavens in an Oblique Sphere.

Oblique Sphere, is when the Pole is elevated any number of Degrees less then 90.

Oblique Sailing, is when the Ship runneth upon some Rhumb between any of the four Cardinal Points, making an Oblique Angle with the Meridian, and then she continually changes both Longitude and Latitude.

Obliquity, (Lat.) Crookedness.

Obliteration, (Lat.) a blotting out, a Cancelling or Abolishing.

Oblivion, (Lat.) Forgetfulness, Unmindfulness.

Oblong, in Geometry, is the same with a Rectangle Parallelogram, whose sides are unequal.

Obloquy, (Lat.) a speaking evil against any one, a backbiting, a slandring.

Obmutescence, (Lat.) a being silent, a holding one's Peace.

Obnoxious, (Lat.) guilty, or faulty, liable to Punishment.

Obnubilate, to make dark with Clouds, to obscure.

Obnunciate, (Lat.) to tell or shew ill Tidings, or things unpleasant and unlucky.

Obreption, (Lat.) creeping or steeling in.

Obreptitious, that has cunningly stollen upon, obtained after a cunning Manner.

Obrogate, (Lat.) to check or interrupt one in his Tale; to Obrogate a Law, is to proclaim a contrary Law for taking away the former.

Obscene, (Lat.) Filthy, unclean, unchast, dishonest.

Obscenity, Filthiness, Uncleanness.

Obscura Camera, in Opticks, is a Room darkned, all but in one little Hole, in which is placed a Glass to transmit the Rays of Objects to a piece of Paper, or White Cloth.

Obscure, (Lat.) dark.

Obscurity, (Lat.) Darkness.

Obsecration, (Lat.) a Beseeching or Praying earnestly.

Obsequies, (Lat.) Funeral Rites or Solemnities.

Obsequious, (Lat.) Dutiful, careful to please, Submissive.

Obser-

Obfervable, fit to be obfer- ved.

Obfervance, (Lat.) Perfor- mance; alfo Refpe&, Regard.

Obfervant, that has regard to, or refpectful.

Obfervation, (Lat.) a watch- ing, guarding, looking after; alfo noting, marking.

Obfervatory, a place where Aftronomical Obfervations are made.

Obfeffed, (Lat.) befet, haun- ted with an evil Spirit.

Obfeffion, (Lat.) a Befieging or compaffing about.

Obfidional, belonging to a Siege; whence an Obfidio- nal Crown, was a Crown gi- ven to him that relieved a City or Town befieged.

Obfigillation, (Lat.) a fea- ling up.

Obfolete, (Lat.) grown out of ufe, or difufed.

Obftacle, (Lat.) as it were a ftanding againft, a let or hindrance that Obftucts the Succefs of any Defign.

Obftetrication, (Lat.) a play- ing the Midwife, or doing the Office of a Midwife.

Obftinacy, (Lat.) a ftub- born refolvednefs to do any thing right or wrong; a fix- ednefs in the maintaining an Opinion though never fo much againft Reafon.

Obftinate, ftubborn; fee *Obftinacy*.

Obftipation, (Lat.) a ftop- ping up chinks.

Obftreperous, (Lat.) full of Noife, or that makes a great Noife.

Obftruct, (Lat.) to ftop up, or hinder.

Obftruction, (Lat.) a ftop- ping up, the hindrance of a- ny thing from proceeding in its due courfe.

Obftupefaction, (Lat.) a ftupe- fying, aftonifhing, or making abafhed.

Obtemperate, (Lat.) to o- bey.

Obtenebration, (Lat.) a ma- king dark or cloudy.

Obteftation, an Injunction in earneft and folemn words, as it were a calling God to witnefs.

Obtrectation, (Lat.) a ca- lumniating or back-biting.

Obtrude, (Lat.) to force upon, to impofe.

Obturation, (Lat.) a ftop- ping, fhutting or clofing up.

Obtufe, (Lat.) blunt, having a dull point or edge; alfo heavy or dull witted.

Obtufe Angle, an Angle greater than a right Angle.

Obvallation, (Lat.) incom- paffing with a Trench.

Obvention, (Lat.) a com- ing againft, a meeting with.

Obventions, *Church-fees*, or Spiritual Revenues.

Obviate, (Lat.) to meet with one; alfo to refift or withftand.

Obvious, meeting in the Way, or coming toward; al- fo eafie to be found or under- ftood.

Obulus, a *Grecian* and *Ro- man* Weight, containing $9\frac{3}{11}$ Grains *Troy*; alfo a *Grecian* Coin

Coin worth 1 Penny 1½ Farthings of our Money.

Obumbration, (Lat.) a shadowing over, or obscuring.

Occasion, a proper Season, fit and convenient to do any thing; also a Cause.

Occasional, belonging to Occasion; also casual.

Occator, a Heathen Deity, and reputed to be the President of that part of Husbandry, which consists in Breaking the Clods and Harrowing the Ground.

Occecation, (Lat.) a Blinding.

Occident, is the West Quarter of the Horizon.

Occidental, (Lat.) Westward, Western.

Occipital, belonging to the hinder part of the Head.

Occision, (Lat.) a Killing.

Occisor, a Killer.

Occlusion, (Lat.) a shutting up fast, a stopping.

Occular, see *Ocular*.

Occult, (Lat.) secret or hidden.

Occult Qualities, the common *Asylum* of the Ignorance of the Ancient Philosophers, whenever they could give no account of any *Phenomenon*, rather than they would seem to appear wholly Ignorant of the matter, us'd to say 'twas by an *Occult Quality*.

Occultation, in Astronomy, is the time when a Star or Planet is hid from our sight by the Interposition of the Body of the Moon, or some other Planet between it and us.

Occupant, one that takes Possession, a Possessor.

Occupation, (Lat.) an using; also an Imployment or Trade. In Law, it signifies the putting a man out of his Freehold in Time of War.

Occupative, employed, used or Possessed.

Occupavit, is a Writ that lieth for him which is ejected out of his Land or Tenement in time of War.

Occur, (Lat.) to meet; to come in the way, or to offer it self.

Occurence, a casual adventure, rencounter, or conjuncture of Affairs.

Occursion, an occurring, or meeting.

Ocean, (Gr.) is that vast collection of Waters, which encompasses the whole Earth, and into which other lesser Seas do run.

Oceanous, belonging to the Ocean.

Ochlocracy (Gr.) a Form of Government, wherein the multitude, or common People bear Rule.

Octagon, (Gr.) a plain Figure in Geometry consisting of eight Angles.

Octahedron, a Solid Figure in Geometry consisting of eight sides; and this is one of those five Bodies, which are commonly call'd the Platonick, or Regular Bodies.

Octangular, (Lat.) having eight Angles.

Octant,

Octant, an Aspect when a Planet is distant the eight part of a Circle, or 45 Deg. from another.

Octastyle, a Building with eight Pillars in Front.

Octave, or *Diapason*, an Interval in Musick, whose terms are as 2 to 1.

Octavo, (Lat.) a Book is called an Octavo, whose Leaves are each of them the eight part of a Sheet, or wherein a Sheet is foulded into eight parts.

Octennial, (Lat.) containing the space of eight Years, or which is performed every eight Year.

October, (Lat.) the eight Month from *March*.

Octonary, belonging to the Number Eight.

Octogenary, (Lat.) that is, Eighty Years Old.

Ocular, (Lat.) belonging to the Eyes or Sight.

Ocular demonstration, is that Evidence which we have of any thing by seeing it done or performed with our own Eyes.

Oculist, one skill'd in curing the Diseases of the Eyes, or in preserving the Eye-sight.

Odaxismus, is the Itching of the Gums when Children breed Teeth.

Ode, a Poem that is Sung to the Harp, or a Copy of Lyrick Verses.

Odius, (Lat.) hateful, detestable.

Odium, (Lat.) the Censure, or blame that is incident to a Fault.

Odontalgia, (Gr.) the Toothach.

Odor, (Lat.) signifies sometimes the *Sense of Smelling*; but 'tis used more generally and more properly for those agreeable and disagreeable *Effluvia*, which are emitted by those Bodies which are Odorous, or which cause in us the Sense of Smelling.

Odoriferous, (Lat.) Smell-bearing, or which causes theSense of Smelling, sweet-smelling.

Odorous, that has a Smell or Scent.

Oeconomical, (Gr.) of, or belonging to *Oeconomy*.

Oeconomist, one that Governs or Rules a Family.

Oeconomy, (Gr.) the Ordering of a House or Family; also Thriftiness, good Husbandry.

Occumenical, General, Universal, belonging to the whole World.

Oedastine, that is cunning in the Knowledge of Weights and Measures.

Oedema, is sometimes taken for any Tumour; but more strictly for a white, soft, insensible Tumour, proceeding from pituitous Matter heaped up together.

Oesophagus, (Gr.) the Gullet, or a long, large and round Canal, descending from the Mouth, to the left Orifice of the Stomach; 'tis this through which the Meat passes from the Mouth to the Stomach.

Offal,

Offal, Refuse, or Dross.

Offals, Garbage, or Fragments of Meat.

Offence, a fault, transgression.

Offend, to transgress, hurt, or displease.

Offensive, hurtful, displeasing.

Offering, a Sacrifice, or any thing offered to the Gods.

Offertory, (Lat.) a Place where Offerings are kept.

Office, signifies not only that Function, by Virtue whereof a Man hath some Imployment in the Affairs of another, but also an Inquisition made to the King's Use, of any thing by virtue of his Office who enquireth.

Officiate, (Lat.) to perform an Office.

Officious, (Lat.) ready to do one a good Office, Serviceable, or very Oblinging.

Offing, is the Sea-mensterm for an open Sea, a good distance from the Shore, where there is deep water, and no need of *Pilot* to Conduct the Ship into the Port or Harbour; also the middle Part of any Stream is called *Offing*.

Offward, that is, contrary to the Shore. *The Ship Heels offward*, is when a Ship being a ground heels towards the Water-side.

Offuscation, (Lat.) a shadowing, a making dark or dusky.

Ogdastich, (Gr.) an Epigram, or Stanza of eight Verses.

Ogive, in Architecture, a Member of a Moulding, consisting of a round and a hollow.

Ogle, to eye one, to look often and earnestly upon a Person.

Ogresses, a Term in Heraldry, the same with *Pellets*.

Oker, a Colour used in Painting.

Oleaginous, (Lat.) Oily, or belonging to the Nature of Oil.

Olfactory, (Lat.) pertaining to the Sense of Smelling.

Oligarchical, (Gr.) belonging to an Oligarchy.

Oligarchy, (Gr.) a Form of Government, where the Supreme Power is lodged in the Hands of a few Principal Persons.

Oligotrophy, (Gr.) is a decrease of Nutrition, or a very small one.

Olla Podrida, (Sp.) a hotchpotch of several Meats together.

Olympiad, the space of four compleat Years; an Account of Time much used by the Ancient *Grecians*. The first Olympiad happened, *A. M.* 3174, and this way of Reckoning was brought in by *Iphitus*, taking it's rise from the *Olympick-Games*.

Olympick Games, were first instituted by *Pelops*, and then renewed by *Atreus* and *Hercules*, and celebrated every fifth Year in Honour of *Jupiter Olympius*, in the Plains of of *Elis*, a City of *Peloponesus*, near the Town of *Olympia*. Thefe Games were continued with great Solemnity for five days, in five kinds of Exercifes, *viz.* Leaping, Running, Wreftling, Quoiting, and Whorlbats. The Names of the Conquerours were fet down on publick Record, but the Prize they won was only a Garland of Olive Branches.

Olitory, a Kitchen-Garden of Herbs, Roots, &c. for Food.

Ombiaffes, the Names of the Priefts and Doctors of the falfe Religion, which obtains in the Ifle of *Madagafcar*, who are fomewhat of the Nature of thofe whom they call *Marabants* at *Cape verde*, i. e. Phyficians and Soothfayers or Magicians.

Omega, the laft Letter of the Greek Alphabet; alfo Metaphorically the End of a thing.

Omen, (Lat.) a Sign or Token of good or bad Luck.

Omentum, the Caul, fo called from the Latin Word *Omen*, becaufe the Soothfayers ufed to Divine by it; it is a double Membrane, arifing from the *Peritonæum*, fpread upon the Inteftines or Guts; in *Englifh* 'tis commonly called the Net.

Omer, a Meafure among the *Hebrews*, that contain'd about three Pints and a half.

Ominate, to forebode, or fore-fhew.

Ominous, ill-boading, or portending ill-luck, for 'tis rarely ufed in a good Senfe.

Omiffion, (Lat.) a neglecting, or letting a thing pafs.

Omnifarious, (Lat.) divers, fundry, of all forts.

Omniparent, (Lat.) bearing, or bringing forth all things.

Omnipotent, (Lat.) allmighty, or which has a Power to do all things poffible.

Omniprefent, (Lat.) that is every where prefent.

Omnifcient, (Lat.) that knows all things.

Omnivagant, (Lat.) wandring every where or in all Places.

Omnivorous, that eateth, or devoureth all fort of things.

Omphalocele, (Gr.) is a Rupture about the Navel, to wit when the Cawl or Inteftines are Protuberant in that Part.

Onerando pro rata Portionis, is a Writ that lies for a Joint-Tenant, or Tenant in Common, that is diftrained for more Rent than his Proportion of the Land cometh to.

Onerary, (Lat.) ferving for Burthen or Carriage.

Onerate, to load.

Onomancy, (Gr.) a Divination by Names.

Onomatopeia, (Gr.) a Figure in Rhetorick, and is the feigning of a Name from fome kind of Sound.

Onprefs, downward.

Onflought, (Dutch) ftorming, a fierce Attack upon a place.

Onyx,

Onyx, a Precious Stone, somewhat like the Colour of a Man's Nail; also the same with *Hypopyon,* or the gathering together of Matter under the *Tunica cornea* of the Eye.

Oozy, moist, wet or plashy.

Opacity, (Lat) Non-transparency, not transmitting of Light.

Opacous, (Lat) shady, obscure, dark; and the reason why some Bodies are Opacous, is probably because their Pores are oblique and crooked, and hinder the Rays of Light from freely permeating and passing through them, as they do through those Bodies which are transparent.

Opal, (Gr.) a Precious Stone of divers Colours, wherein appear the fiery shining of the *Carbuncle,* the Purple Colour of the *Amethyst,* and the Greenness of the *Emerald* very strangely mixt together.

Open-theoff, (Sax.) open or plain Theft.

Open-Flank, in Fortification, is that part of the Flank which is covered by the *Shoulder* or *Orillion.*

To Open Trenches, is the first breaking of Ground by the Besiegers in Order to carry on their Approaches towards a Place.

Opera, is a sort of Solemn Entertainment of Musick upon the Theatre or Stage, and is very common in *France* and *Italy.*

Operation, (Lat.) a labouring or working. 'Tis frequently used in Chymistry and Surgery, and signifies a Chymical Process, or any thing performed by the Hand of a Surgion.

Operator, (Lat.) a Workman.

Operculum, (Lat.) a Cover.

Operose, (Lat.) Laborious, Busie, Active; That requires much Labour, Pains, or Diligence; that about which much Workmanship is employ'd, well wrought.

Ophiasis, (Lat.) is a Disease where the Hairs grow thin, and fall off here and there, so that they leave the Head spotted like a Serpent.

Ophites, a sort of Hereticks that lived in the second Century; 'tis said they honoured a Serpent, and when their Priests celebrated their Mysteries, they made a Serpent come out of a Hole, which after it rolled it self over the things that were to be offered in Sacrifice, they said that Jesus Christ had sanctified them, and then delivered them to the People who Worshipped them.

Ophineus, one of the Northern Constellations the same with *Serpentarius.*

Ophthalmicks, (Gr.) are such Medicines as are good for Diseases in the Eyes.

Ophthalmy, (Gr.) an Inflammation of the Coats of the Eye, Blood-shot.

Opiates, are Medicines made of *Opium*, or something of the same Nature with it, designed to cause sleep, and to ease Pain.

Opine, to think, to be of Opinion.

Opiniative, (Lat.) that stands in his own Opinion, wedded to, or stiffly persisting in his own Opinion.

Opiniotists, a Name given in Pope *Paul's* time, to a Sect that boasted of affected Poverty, and held there could be no Vicar of Christ on Earth that did not practice this Vertue.

Opinion, (Lat.) Mind, Thoughts, Belief. In *Philosophy* it signifies an Assent of the Mind built upon probable Reasons.

Opinionate, see *Opiniative*.

Opisthotonus, is a kind of Cramp, or stretching of the Muscles of the Neck backwards.

Opitulation, (Lat.) a helping, or aiding.

Opium, the Juice of black Poppies.

Oppignoration, (Lat.) a Pawning, or laying in Pledge.

Oppilation in Physick, an Obstruction or Stoppage.

Oppletion, (Lat.) a filling up.

Opponent, (Lat.) an Adversary in Disputation.

Opportune, (Lat.) fit, seasonable, convenient.

Opportunity, occasion or fit-

ness of time and place.

Opposite, (Lat.) contrary, over against.

Opposite Angles, in Geometry, are two Angles joyned point to point, or touching one another with their points only.

Opposites, (in *Logick*) are things opposed, either relatively, as Master and Servant; or privatively, as Light and Darkness; or contrarily, as Knowledge and Ignorance.

Opposition, (Lat.) a contrary setting against; also a Resistance; in Astronomy, 'tis that Position or Aspect of the Stars or Planets, when they are six Signs, or 160 Degrees distant from one another.

Oppression, (Lat.) is a pressing or crushing down, an enslaving or getting under his power by force.

Opprobrious, (Lat.) reproachful, taunting, disgraceful to him, of whom 'tis said.

Opprobrium, (Lat.) a Reproach or Taunt.

Optative-Mood, (in *Grammer*) is that Mood whereby we express a desire that such a thing may happen; and therefore there is usually an Adverb of wishing connected with it as *utinam*, &c.

Opticks, (Gr.) is a Science that treats of Sight in General, and of every thing that is seen with direct Rays, explaining by Physical Principles joyned with Geometry, the reason of the different appearances

OR

pearances that may happen from some Object.

Optick Place of a Star or Planet, is that Point or Part of it's Orbit which is determined by our sight when the Star is there; and this is either *true*, when the Observers Eye, is supposed to be at the center of the Earth or Planet he Inhabits, or *apparent* when his Eye is at the Circumference of the Earth.

Option, (Lat.) a Choice or Election, a Wish. In a Law-sense, when a new Suffragan Bishop is Consecrated, the Arch Bishop of the Province, by a customary Prerogative, claims the Collation of the first vacant Benefice in that See, at his Choice, term'd therefore *The Arch-Bishop's Option.*

Oppugn, (Lat.) to assault, besiege, or fight against; to oppose, confute, or reject.

Opsimathy, (Gr.) a learning late.

Opsonation, (Lat.) a Catering.

Optable, (Lat.) desirable.

Optimacy, is where the Rule or Government is lodg'd in the Nobles.

Opulency, (Lat.) riches, wealth, plenty.

Opuscle, a small Work.

Or, (Fr.) in Heraldry, is the Colour of Gold; 'tis represented in Engraving by small Points or Pricks, thus.

Or in Valdarno, a Vale on the Banks of the River *Arno.*

Oracle, (Lat.) an Ambiguous and Obscure Answer which the Heathen Priests made to the People concerning things to come, by making them believe that God spoke by their Mouths.

Oracular, belonging to an Oracle.

Oral, (Lat.) belonging to the Mouth, or delivered by Word of Mouth.

Oranoco, that is, bright and large, the common sort of Tobacco in *Virginia* is so called.

Oration, (Lat.) a Discourse, or Speech.

Orator, a Person skill'd in Rhetorick, an Eloquent Person.

Oratorians, an Order of Regular Priests establish'd *Anno* 1564, by *Philip Nereius* a *Florentine*, nam'd from the Oratory of St. *Jerome* in *Rome*, where they us'd to pray.

Oratory, (Lat.) the same with Eloquence, which see.

Orb, a hollow Sphere.

Orbation, (Lat.) a taking away, or depriving.

Orbicular, round, in the Fashion of a Ball, or Globe.

Orbis magnus, is the Orbit of the Earth in its Annual Revolution, which is round the Sun.

Orbit, of any Planet, is the Curve that it describes in its Revolution round its central Body.

Ee e 2   *Orbity,*

Orbity, (Lat.) the want of Children on the Parents part; or the want of Parents on the Childrens Part; any want or privation.

Orcheſtre, the place where the Chorus Danceth, or where Muſitians ſit.

Ordalian-Law, a Law which eſtabliſh'd the Ancient way of Tryals by Fire and Water, call'd Ordeal.

Ordeal, (in the *Saxon* Judgment,) certain particular ways of Tryal, by which Perſons accuſed of Crimes, were obliged to clear themſelves, as by Camp-fight, Duelling, &c.

Fire-Ordeal, when the party accuſed, undertook to prove his Innocence by walking blindfold and barefoot, over red-hot Plough-Shares.

Water-Ordeal, a Purgation, by putting one's Arms into boiling Water. Theſe Tryals were inſtituted long before the Conqueſt, and continued in force till the Reign of King *John*, when they were abrogated, and utterly condemned by Pope *Stephen* the Second.

Order of Battel, is a diſpoſition of *Batallions* and *Squadrons* of an Army in one or more Lines, according to the Nature of the Ground, either to engage an Army, or to be reviewed by the General.

Order in *Architecture*, is a Rule for the Proportion to be abſerved in the erecting of Pillars, and for the form of certain parts appertaining to them.

Ordinal, belonging to Order; as Ordinal Numbers, which expreſs the Order of things as, firſt, ſecond, &c.

Ordinance, a Law or Statute.

Ordinary, in the Civil Law, is any Judge that hath Authority to take Cognizance of Cauſes in his own Right, as he is a Magiſtrate, and not by deputation. But in the Common Law it is taken for him that hath exempt and immediate Juriſdiction in Cauſes Eccleſiaſtical.

Ordinaries, in *Heraldry*, are the Charges that properly belong to that Art, being commonly uſed therein. They are generally call'd *Henourable*, and are nine in Number, *viz.* the *Croſs*, *Chief*, *Pale*, *Bend*, *Feſſe*, *Eſcutcheon*, *Chevron*, *Saltier*, and *Bar*, which ſee in their proper places.

Ordinate, a Term frequently uſed in Conick Sections, and ſignifies a line drawn thro' any Diameter of any of the 3 Sections, parallel, to a Tangent to the Vertex of that Diameter thro' which 'tis drawn.

Ordination, (Lat.) an appointing; or admitting into Holy Orders.

Ordinatione contra ſervientes, is a Writ that lieth againſt a Servant for leaving his Maſter.

Ordnance, all ſorts of great Guns uſed in War; alſo all ſorts forts of *Stores* or *Arms* belonging either to offence or defence.

Ordonance, in Architecture, is the giving to all the parts of an Edifice the juſt Quantity and Dimenſions, which they ought to have according to the Model.

Ordure, filth, the Dung of Man or beaſt.

Orexis, the natural Appetite of Meat.

Organical Part, is that part of an Animal, or Vegetable Body, which is deſigned for the performing ſome particular Action.

Organization, (Lat.) the forming of Organs or Inſtrumental Parts.

Organized, furniſhed with proper Organs.

Organs, Inſtruments; the parts of an Animal Body, fitted as Inſtruments to diſcharge any particular Office or Function.

Orgaſmus, is an *Impetus* and quick Motion of the Blood and Spirits; as when the Animal Spirits ruſh violently into the Nerves.

Orgia, a Term made uſe of by the Heathens, whereby to expreſs the Feaſts and Sacrifices of their falſe God *Bacchus*, which were more particularly celebrated upon Mountains by raving Women called *Bacchanales*.

Orgues, in Fortification, are many Harquebuſſes linked together, or divers Muſquet Barrels laid in a row, with

in one wooden Stock, ſo that they may be diſcharged either all at once or ſeparately.

Orgia, a *Grecian* Meaſure of Length, which being reduced to our *Engliſh* Meaſure contains 6 Feet, and 525 decimal parts of an Inch

Orient, (Lat.) the Eaſt, or the Eaſtern part of the Horizon.

Oriental, belonging to the Eaſt,

Orifice, (Lat.) the Mouth, Entry, or Brim of any thing; more eſpecially that of a Vein, Tube, Wound, &c.

Origeniſts, a Sect of Hereticks, ſo called becauſe they maintained ſome Errors drawn from *Origen*'s Book concerning Principles.

Origin, (Lat.) the firſt riſe or ſource of a thing.

Original, a firſt Draught, or Pattern of a thing.

Originalia, in the Treaſurer's Remembrancer's Office in the *Exchequer*, are Records or Tranſcripts ſent thither out of the *Chancery*, and are diſtinguiſhed from *Recorda*, which contain the Judgments and pleading in Suits try'd before the Barons of that Court.

Orillon, in Fortification, is a Maſs of Earth faced with Stone, built on the Shoulder of a *Cazemated Baſtion*, to cover the *Cannon* of the retired *Flank*, and hinder it's being diſmounted by the Enemies Cannon.

Orion,

Orion, a Southern Conftellation confifting of 39 Stars.

Orifons, (Fr.) Prayers.

Orle, is an Ordinary in Heraldry, almoft of the Figure of an *Inefcutcheon*, only it is voided fo that the Field appears through, as in the Figure.

Orle, in Architecture, the fame with *Plinth*, which fee.

Orlope, the Seamen call by this Name, the fpare Deck in a great Ship, reaching from the Main-Maft to the Miffen ; and in a three-deck'd Ship the fecond and loweft Deck are someties called *Orlopes*.

Ornament , an Embellifhment, any thing that fets off another, or makes it appear to advantage.

Ornaments, in Architecture, are the *Architraves*, *Frizes*, and *Cornices* of feveral Orders; alfo the Carvings of the Mouldings, as *Leaves*, *Chanellings*, *Wreaths*, *Ovals*, *Chaplets*, *Trefces*, *Feftochs*, *Flowers*, *Rofes*, &c.

Ornithology, (Gr.) is a defcription of the feveral Natures and kinds of Birds.

Ornithomancy, (Gr.) Divination by the flight of Birds.

Oroboides, a fubfiding in Urine, like to a kind of Pulfe ca'led *Vetches*.

Orphan, (Gr.) a Fatherlefs Child.

Orphanifm, (Gr.) the State of a Fatherlefs Child.

Orpiment, a Yellow kind of Arfenick.

Orteil, in Fortification, is the fame with *Berme*, which fee.

Orthodoron, a *Grecian* Meafure of Length, containing in *Englifh* Meafure 8 Inches, $3101\frac{9}{77}$ Decimal Parts.

Orthodox, (Gr.) that believes aright.

Orthodoxy, (Gr.) Soundnefs of Judgment, true Belief.

Orthodromiques, (Gr.) is the Art of Sailing in the Ark of fome great Circle.

Orthodromy, a Courfe of a Ship when fhe Sails in a Line which is the fhorteft diftance between two Points on the furface of the Globe.

Orthogonal, (Gr.) right angled.

Orthographical, (Gr.) belonging to *Orthography*.

Orthographical Projection of the Sphere, is the Delineation of the Sphere upon a Plane that cuts it in the middle, the eye being fuppofed at an infinite diftance from it.

Orthography, (Gr.) in Grammer, is Writing and Spelling any Language truly, according to its juft Etymologies and Proprieties.

Orthography, in Mathematicks, is the true Delineation of the Fore-right Plane of any Object.

Orthography, in Architecture, fignifies the Model, Platform and delineation of the Front of a Houfe to be built.

Ortho-

Orthography, or Profile, in Fortification is the representation of a Work, shewing its breadth, thickness, height and depth, so as it wou'd appear, if cut perpendicularly on the Horizontal line, from the uppermost to the lowest of its parts.

Orthopnœa, (Gr.) an ill respiration when the Person affected cannot breath but with his Neck erect.

Orvietan, a kind of Electuary good against Poison, and nam'd from the Inventer.

Oryal, a Porch, Cloister, or arched Room in a Monastry.

Oscillation, (Lat.) a swinging up and down, a vibrating like the Pendulum of a Clock.

Oscitancy, (Lat.) Sluggishness, Negligence.

Oscitation, (Lat.) Yawning, is a certain light convulsive motion of the Muscles which open the lower Jaw of the Face.

Oscula, (Lat.) are the openings of Vessels in an Animal Body at their Ends.

Osculation, (Lat.) a kissing, or embracing.

Ossicle, (Lat.) a little bone.

Ossiculum, amongst the Botanists, is the Stone of a Cherry, Plum, or such like Fruit.

Ossuary, (Lat.) a Charnel house, or place where dead Mens Bones are kept.

Ostensive demonstrations, are such as plainly and directly demonstrate the truth of any Proposition.

Ostentation, (Lat.) vain-Glory, excessive Boasting, making a fair shew outwardly.

Ostentative, apt to boast, or make a shew of.

Osteology, (Gr.) is a description of Bones.

Ostiary, (Lat.) a Porter, or door keeper.

Ostocopi, are Pains in the Bones, or rather in the Membranes and Nerves about the Bones, for Bones as such are insensible.

Ostracism, a Ten Years Banishment among the *Athenians,* which was done by delivering a Shell (*Ostracos*) with the condemned Person's Name written in it; this Custom was invented not so much to punish Offences, as to abate the immoderate Power of Noblemen. 'Twas first ordained by *Clistenes,* who for his Labour was first condemned.

Ostrogoths, those *Goths* who came out of the East, and invaded the Southern and Western parts of the Empire.

Otacausticks, (Gr.) are Instruments which help to improve the sense of hearing.

Otalgia, (Gr.) is a pain in the Ears.

Otenchyta, an Auricular Clyster, a little Syringe or Squirt which injects Medicines into the Ears.

Otica, Medicines against Distempers of the Ears.

Ottoman, belonging to the *Turks;* as the *Ottoman Empire.*

Oval, (Lat.) of the shape of an Egg, see *Ellipsis.*

E e e 4   *Ovation,*

Ovation, a petty Triumph for a Victory gain'd with little or no Slaughter.

Ovaria, are the Testicles of Females, and are so called because they resemble, and have the same use as the Lathers or Collections of Eggs in the Bodies of Fowls.

Ovelty of Services, in Law, signifies equality of Services, as when the Tenant Paravail, owes as much to the Mesne, as the Mesne does to the Lord Paramount.

Over-bear, to prevail over, to oppress or Crush.

Overgast, overgrown with *Grass*. Spencer.

Over-haile, draw over. *Spencer.*

Over-Rake, when a Ship riding at Anchor, doth so over-beat her self into a head-Sea, that she is washed by the Waves breaking in upon her, then they say the Waves do Over-Rake her.

Over-set, to over-turn, a Ship is *Overset*, when shes is turn'd over on one side.

Overture, an opening or disclosing of a Matter; a Proposal; also a Flourish of Musick before the opening of the Scenes in a Stage-Play.

Overt, (Fr.) open, manifest.

Overt-act, in the Sense of the Law is a plain matter of Fact, serving to prove a Design.

Over-weening, presumptuous, self-conceited, having too great an Opinion of one's self.

Over-went, over-gone. *Spencer.*

Oviparous, (Lat.) Egg-bearing: *Oviparous Animals*, are such as lay Eggs.

Ounce, is 20 Penny-weight, or 480 Grains *Troy*. The *Roman* Ounce is the twelfth part of an *As*.

Ounding, (old word) rising like Waves.

Ouranography, (Gr.) a description of the Heavens.

Ousted, (Fr.) Law-word, removed, or put out; as *ousted out of Possession*.

Ouster-le-main, (Fr.) is a Writ directed to the Escheator, to deliver Possession out of the King's hands, to the party that Sues.

Outfangthef, (Sax) a Privilege enabling a Lord to bring to a Trial in his own Court, any Man living in his own Fee that's taken for Felony in any other Place.

Out-Law, signifies one deprived of the Benefit of the Law, and out of the King's Protection.

Out-Lawry, is the loss of the Benefit of a Subject, *i. e.* the King's Protection.

Out-licker, is a small Piece of Timber made fast to the Top of the Poop, and so stands out-right a Stern; at the outmost end thereof there is a hole, into which the standing part of the Sheet is reeved through the Block of the Sheet; and then again reeved through another Block which is seized close by the end of this *Out-licker*,   *Out-*

Outrage, (Fr) a grievous Injury or Affront, a violent Affault.

Outragious, cruel, fierce, highly injurious.

Out-riders, in Law, are Bailiffs Errant, employed by the Sheriffs, to ride to the fartheſt places of their Country, to ſummon perſons to their County or Hundred-Courts.

Outward flanking Angle, is the Angle comprehended between the two flanking lines of defence.

Out-works, in Fortification, are Works of ſeveral ſorts which cover the Body of the Place; as *Ravelins, Half-moons, Tenailles, Horn-works, Crown-works, counter-guards, Envelopes, Swallow-Tails, Lunetts,* &c.

Ouverture, ſee *Overture.*

Owler, is one that conveys Wool or other prohibited Goods by Night to the Sea-ſide to be Ship'd off, contrary to Law.

Owelty, in Law, is when there is Lord, Meſne, and Tenant; and the Tenant holds of the Meſne by the ſame Service, that the Meſne holds of the Lord above him.

Oxelæum, (Gr.) a mixture of Vinegar and Oyl.

Oxycrat, a Remedy made of Vinegar and Water to allay the heat of Inflammations.

Oxydercia, (Gr.) are Medicines which quicken the fight.

Oxygal, (Gr.) is ſowre Milk.

Oxygon, (Gr.) an acute angled Triangle.

Oxygonial, acute-angular.

Oxymel, a Syrup made of Honey, Vinegar and Water.

Oxyregmia, (Gr.) is an acid ſower Belch from the Stomach.

Oxyrrhodinum, is Vinegar of Roſes mixed with Roſe-Water.

Oyer, (Fr.) *i. e.* to hear, a Term us'd formerly for what we now call Aſſizes.

Oyer and *Terminer,* a ſpecial Commiſſion granted to certain Judges to hear and determine Criminal Cauſes.

Oyer de Record, is a Petition made in Court, that the Judges for better Proofs ſake, will be pleaſed to hear and look upon any Record.

Oyes, (Fr.) hear ye, a word uſed by publick Cryers when they make Proclamation of any thing.

Ozoena, is an old ſtinking Ulcer in the inſide of the Noſtrils, taking its Name from its fulſome ſmell.

P

*P*Abulum, (Lat.) food for Cattle or Beaſts, Fodder, Forage, Fuel.

Pacation, (Lat.) an appeaſing, pacifying or aſſwaging.

Pace, an Engliſh Meaſure of Length, containing five Foot.

Pachamacac, the Name whereby the *Peruvians* call God, the Creator of the World, beſides whom they worſhip

worſhip the Sun and many other imaginary Deities.

Pacification, (Lat) Peace-making, Mediation.

Pacifick, (Lat.) making peace, or appeaſing.

Pacify, (Lat.) to make peace, or appeaſe.

Paction, (Lat.) a Bargain, Covenant or Agreement.

Pactitious, done by Bargain or Agreement.

Pad, to rob upon the Road.

Padder or *Foot-pad,* one that Robs on theHigh-way onFoot.

Paean, a Hymn or Song of Praiſe made to *Apollo*, at ſuch time as any Plague or Peſtilence raged.

Paedagogue, (Gr.) a School-maſter.

Paganiſm, the Principles and Practices of the Pagans.

Pagans, Gentils, Heathens.

Page, a young lad attending upon a Perſon of Quality.

Pageant, a Triumphal Chariot, or Arch, or other pompous Device, uſually carried about in publick Shows.

Pageantry, Pomp, Show, or Oſtentation.

Pagod, (q. d. the Pagan's God) an Idol worſhiped by the Heathens in *India*, *China*, &c.

Pain fort & dure, in Law ſignifies an eſpecial Puniſhment for him that being Arraigned of Felony, refuſes to put himſelf upon the Ordinary Tryal of God and his Country, and thereby ſtands mute by the Interpretation of the Law.

Painter-ſtainer, is one that Paints Coats of Arms, and other things belonging to Heraldry.

Painting, the Art of repreſenting things in their proper Colours, and Figures.

Paiſage, a Draught of any part of a Country, a Landskip.

Palace, the Court or Manſion of a Prince.

Palanka, a piece of Fortification made of Poles or Stakes.

Palanquin, (Sp.) a Chair of State, in which great Perſonages of *Eaſt-India*, are carried on Mens Shoulders.

Palatable, (Lat.) Pleaſant or agreeable to the Taſt.

Palate, (Lat.) the upper part of the Mouth, which becauſe it reſembles the Roof of an Houſe, is called the *Roof* of the Mouth.

Palatinate, the Country or Seat of a Count *Palatine,* or chief Officer in the Palace or Court of an Emperour or Soveraign Prince.

Palatine-Mount, one of the ſeven Hills of *Rome,* on which ſtood the Royal Manſion-houſe ; from whence comes the Word *Palace,*

Pale, (Lat.) a Stake. In *Heraldry,* 'tis one of the eight Honourable Ordinaries, it conſiſts of two Lines drawn perpendicularly from Top to Bottom of the Eſcutcheon, and takes up the third part of it thus ;

He

He bearth *Gules*, a *Pale Or*.

Pales, the Heathen Goddess of Shepherds, beloved by *Apollo*.

Paleſt or *Doron*, a *Greek* Meaſure of four Fingers Breadth.

Palfrey, (Fr.) a Horſe of State, decked with rich Trappings; alſo a Pacing Horſe. *Shakeſp.*

Palici, certain Heathen Deities famous in *Sicily*.

Palindrome, (Gr.) a Verſe or Sentence which is the ſame read Backward as Foreward. Alſo a Relapſe into a Diſeaſe.

Palinode, (Gr.) a Recantation, or unſaying what one had ſpoken or written before.

Pall, the Cloth or Velvet that covers the Coffin at a Funeral. Alſo an Ornament made of Lambs Wool which the Pope beſtows on Archbiſhops, &c. Alſo a Mantle worn by the Knights of the moſt Noble Order of the Garter on ſolemn Occaſions. In *Heraldry* they have a kind of Croſs, which they call by this Name, and they deſcribe it thus. He beareth *Gules*, a *Croſs Pall Argent*.

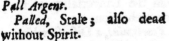

Palled, Stale; alſo dead without Spirit.

Pallet, is the moiety, or half of the *Pale*, and muſt never be charged with any thing either quick or dead.

Pallet, at Sea, is a Room within the Hold of a Ship, cloſely parted from it, in which by laying ſome Pigs of Lead, a Ship may be ſufficiently Ballaſted without loſing Room in the Hold, which will therefore ſerve for ſtowing the more Goods.

Palliate, to cloak or diſguiſe.

Palliation, (Lat.) a cloaking or diſguiſing; *Palliation* of a Diſeaſe, is a giving eaſe to incurable Diſeaſes by applying preſent Remedies.

Pallification, a Term us'd by ſome Writers of Architecture ſignifying Piling or ſtrengthning the Ground-work with Piles.

Pallifadoes, in Fortification, are ſtrong wooden ſharp pointed Stakes, about eight foot long, of which three foot is ſunk into the Ground, ſet up half a foot ſometimes one above another with a Croſs piece of Timber that binds them together; they ſometimes ſtand erect, and ſometimes obliquely pointing towards the Enemy.

Pallor, (Lat.) a pale Colour, paleneſs, wanneſs.

Palm, the inner part of the Hand; the Meaſure of an Hand's Breadth, three Inches. Alſo the white Bud of Sallies or Withy that comes before the Leaf. *Verbally*, to Juggle

Juggle in one's Hand, to cog or cheat at Dice.

Palmer, (Sp.) a Pilgrim that carries a Bough or Staff of *Palm* in going to visit the Holy places.

Palmister, one skill'd in Palmestry.

Palmistry, the Art of telling Fortunes by certain lines or marks on the *Palms* of one's Hand.

Palpable, that may be ealy felt, or perceived.

Palpitation, (Lat.) a panting, or beating quick like that of the Heart.

Palter, to prevaricate, or deal indirectly.

Paltry, sorry.

Paly. a Term in Heraldry, when an Escutcheon is divided into 6, 8 or 10 even divisions *Pale-wise*, 'tis always Blazoned Paly of 6, 8, 16, &c. Pieces; but if the Number be odd, then the Field is first named, and the Number of the Pales specified.

Paly Bendy, is when a Coat is divided both *Pale* and *Bendwise*, as here. The Field *Paly Bendy*, *Pearl* and *Emerald*.

Pamper, to indulge.

Pamphlet, (Du. *pampier paper*) a stitched Book or a Libel.

Pamphleteer, one that writes or deals in Pamphlets.

Pan, a Heathen *Egyptian* Deity, worshipped under the Shape of a Goat, reputed to be the God of Shepherds, and also considered as the God of Nature.

Pan of a *Bastion*, is the same with the Face of a Bastion, which see.

Panacea, (Gr.) an *Universal Medicine*, or a Medicine that cures all Diseases in all circumstances, Ages, and Constitutions, of which divers are to be met with in Books of Chymistry.

Panado, (Sp.) a sort of Gruel made of Crums of Bread boiled in Water with Currans, Sugar, &c.

Panch, in Navigation, are broad Clouts, woven of Clouts and Sinnets together, to save things from gauling and fretting.

Panchymagogues, (Gr.) are Universal Purgative Medicines that expel all kinds of Humours.

Pancreatick, belonging to the Sweet-Bread.

Pandalea, as the modern Physitians call it, is the same with a solid Electuary, but that it remains intire, for the Sugar being rightly boiled, is let grow hard.

Pandects, (Gr.) Books that handle all Subjects, or all the parts of the Subject whereof they treat; also a Volume of the Civil Law, so called from the Universality of its Comprehension.

Pandemius, a Disease which is universally rife in any place,

Pander,

Pander, (in *Dutch* one that takes Pawns) a Pimp or male Bawd.

Pandiculation, (Lat.) is the reſtleſneſs, ſtretching, and un-eaſineſs that uſually accompanies the cold fit of an Inter-mitting Feaver.

Pandore, a kind of Muſical Inſtrument.

Panegyrick, (Gr.) a Speech delivered before a ſolemn aſ-ſembly of People ; or an O-ration of Thanks and Praiſe to an Emperour, Prince, &c.

Pauegyriſt, one that makes Panegyricks, or a Perſon skill'd in that way of Wri-ting.

Pangs, the Agonies of death, or throws of a Woman in Labour.

Panick Fear, a ſudden and diſtracting fear without known cauſe, anciently ſaid to be inflicted by the God *Pan*.

Panicula, a Term in Bota-ny for a ſoft kind of woolly Beard or String, on which the Seeds of ſome Plants do hang pendulous as in Reeds, Millet, &c.

Pannade, (Fr.) the curve-ting or Prancing of a luſty Horſe.

Pannage, (Fr.) the feeding of Swine upon maſt in the Woods, or Money paid for ſuch a Licence ; alſo a Tax upon Cloth.

Pannel, a Pain or Square of Wainſcot, &c. Alſo a Saddle for carrying Burdens on Horſe-back. Alſo a Roll of Paper or Parchment with the Names of the Jurors re-turned by the Sheriff.

Pannicle, (Lat.) a little Clout or Rag.

Panniculus carnoſus, is a fat ſort of Membrane, in ſome part thick and Muſculous, and in others thin, with ma-ny ducts of fat in it ; it co-vers the whole Body.

Pannier-man, he that winds the Horn, or rings the Bell in the Inns of Court.

Panoply, (Gr.) compleat Ar-mour or Harneſs.

Panſelene, (Gr.) the full Moon.

Panſophy, (Gr.) Wiſdom or Knowledge in all things.

Pantais, is a Hawk's hard fetching of Wind.

Pantaloon, a ſort of Gar-ment formerly worn, conſiſt-ing of Breeches and Stock-ings faſtned together, and both of the ſame Stuff.

Pantarb, a Precious Stone ; in Engliſh called the Stone of the Sun.

Panters, Nets or Toils to catch Deer.

Pantheology, (Gr.) the whole Sum of Divinity.

Pantheon, (Gr.) an Ancient Temple in *Rome*, dedicated to all the Heathen Gods ; and ſince by Pope *Boniface*, the fourth, to the Virgin *Mary*.

Pantler, an Officer that keeps the Bread in a King's Court, or Houſe of a Noble-man.

Pantofle, (Fr.) a Slipper for wearing in a Chamber.

Pantometer,

Pantometer, a Mathematical Instrument for Measuring all sorts of Angles, Lengths, Hights, &c.

Pantomime, an Actor of many Parts in one Play; one that can represent the Gesture and Counterfeit the Speech of any Man.

Pantry, a Room or Closet where Bread and cold Meat are kept.

Panurgy, (Gr.) craft, or skill in all kinds of matters.

Panus, a sort of Botch, or sore under the Arm-pits or Jaws, Ears and Groins, to wit in the Glandulous parts.

Papacy, (Lat.) the Dignity of a Pope, or Popedom.

Papal, (Lat.) belonging to a Pope.

Papaverous, (Lat.) belonging to a Poppy.

Papian Law, a Law made among the old *Romans*, against a single Life, and that if any forbore from the Priviledges of Parents, and had no Children; the People (who was the common Father of all) shou'd inherit their Goods.

Papilionaceous Flower of a Plant, is by the Botanists accounted such an one as represents something of the Figure of a Butter-fly with its wings display'd.

Papillary, belonging to, or like unto a Teat or Nipple.

Papist, one that acknowledges the Pope, and owns the Popish Religion.

Pappose, (Lat.) downy or full of down.

Pappus, in Botany, is that soft light Down which grows out of the Seeds of some Plants, such as *Thistles*, *Hawkweed*, &c. which buoys them up so in the Air, that they can be blown any where by the Wind.

Par of Exchange, is when one to whom a Bill is payable, receives of the Acceptor, just so much Money in Value as to Weight and Fineness, as was pay'd to the Drawer by the Remitter.

Parable, (Gr.) a continued Similitude, or Comparison.

Parabola, (Gr.) a Mathematical Figure, whose primary property is, that the squares of its Ordinates are in proportion to one another as their respective Abscissæ, or the Ordinates themselves are to one another in a *Subduplicate ratio* of their Abscissæ.

Parabola cubical, see *cubical Paraboloid*.

Parabolical, belonging to a Parable or *Parabola*.

Parabolism, in Algebra, is the Division of the Terms of an Equation, by the known Quantity (when there happens to be one) that is involved or multiply'd into the first Term.

Paraboloid, is a solid formed by the circumvolution of a Parabola about its Ax.

Paracelsian, a Physician that follows the Method of *Paracelsus*, and his manner of curing, which was by exceeding strong Oyls and Waters,

ters, extracted out of the Natures of Things.

Paracentesis, (Gr.) is a Perforation of the Chest or Abdomen.

Parachronism, (Gr.) an Error in Chronology, a mistaking the time of any action or adventure in History.

Paraclete, (Gr.) an Advocate or Comforter, an Epithet attributed to the Holy Ghost.

Parachynanche, an Inflammation with a continual Fever, and difficulty of Breathing excited in the outward Muscles of the Larynx.

Paracium, the Tenure between Parceners, *viz.* that which the youngest owes to the eldest.

Paracmaftical, (Lat.) pertaining to a kind of continual hot burning Fever, wherein the heat when 'tis at greatest, by little and little diminisheth, till it totally ceaseth.

Parade, (Fr.) a great show or appearance; especially of Military Officers in a rich Garb, or of Souldiers at a set time to receive Orders.

Paradiaftole, (Gr.) a distinction in Rhetorick, an inlarging of a matter by Interpretation.

Paradise, (Gr.) a place of Pleasure. The Garden of Eden.

Paradigm, (Gr.) a Pattern or Example.

Paradox, (Gr.) a strange sentiment, and one that is contrary to common Opinion.

Paradoxal or *Paradoxical*, belonging to a Paradox.

Paradrome, (Gr.) an open Walk or Gallery that hath no shelter over head.

Parænetical, (Gr.) apt to perswade, admonishing.

Parage, (in Law) Equality of Name, Blood or Dignity; but especially of Land in dividing an Inheritance. Hence comes to *Disparage*.

Paragoge, (Gr.) a Figure in Rhetorick, whereby a Letter or Word is added at the end of a Word, as *potirier* for *potiri*.

Paragon, (Fr) a compeer an equal; also a Peerless Dame or one without compare.

Paragraph, (Gr.) the smaller Section of a Book where the line Breaks off; or what is comprehended between one Break and another.

Paralipomenon, (Gr.) left out, omitted, not spoken of; There are two Books in the old Testament so called; because some things are related there, which are omitted in other places.

Parallactical, belonging to a Parallax.

Parallax, (Gr.) is the difference between the true place of a Planet and it's apparent one; or the difference between that place among the fixed Stars which a Planet appears to have to an Eye placed upon the Surface of the Earth, and that it wou'd seem to have to an Eye placed at the Center.   *Paral-*

Parallax of Longitude, is the difference between that place in the Ecliptick which a Planet appears to have to an Eye placed upon the Surface of the Earth, and that which it won'd seem to have to an Eye placed at the Center.

Parallax of Latitude, is the difference between the true and apparent Latitude of a Planet, as it is observed from the surface of the Center.

Parallax of Right Ascension, is the difference between the true and apparent right Ascension of a Planet.

Parallax of declination, is the difference between the true and apparent declination of a Planet.

Parallel, (Lat.) equally distant every where; also like or resembling.

Parallel Lines, are lines that always keep an Equal distance from one another.

Parallel Sphere, is that Position of the Sphere which has one Pole in the *Zenith*, and the other in the *Nadir*, and the Equinoctial is the Horizon.

Parallels of Altitude, or Almacanters, on the Globe, are such Circles as are drawn Parallel to the Horizon.

Paraellels of Latitude, on the *Terestrial Globe*, are Circles Parallel to the Equinoctial; and on the *Celestial*, Circles parallel to the Ecliptick.

Parallel, in Geography, a space of the Terrestrial Globe,

compriz'd between two Circles parallel to the Equinoctial; between which in the longest Day of Summer there is a variation of a quarter of an Hour.

Parallelism, is the being Parallel, as the *Parallelism* of the Earth's *Axis*, is its keeping in a Position always Parallel to it self.

Paralipsis, a Figure in Rhetorick, whereby we pretend to desire to have omitted what we say, as *I am willing to forget the wrong which my Enemy hath done me*, &c.

Parallelogram, (Gr.) in Geometry, is a Plane Figure bounded by 4 right lines; whereof those which are opposite are parallel to one another.

Parallelogramick, belonging to a Parallelogram.

Parallelopiped, (Gr.) is a solid Figure contained under six Parallelograms the opposite sides of which are equal and Parallel; or 'tis a Prism whose Base is a Parallelogram.

Parallelopleuron, (Gr.) an Imperfect Parallelogram, or kind of Trapezium; two of whose opposite sides are Parallel, but the other two not Parallel.

Paralogism, (Gr.) a fallacious or deceitful way of Arguing.

Paralysis, (Gr.) the *Palsey*, is an entire loss of voluntary motion, or sense, or both, either in all the Body or in some part, caused either from an Obftruction or Contufion of the Nerves.

Paralytick, troubled with, or fick of a Palfey.

Paraments, (Fr.) an Ornament for an Altar; alfo Robes of State. *Chaucer.*

Parameter, an imaginary line belonging to the Conick Sections; in the *Parabola,* 'tis always a third Proportional to any Abfciffa and its refpective Ordinate; But in the *Ellipfis* and *Hyperbola* the Parameter belonging to any Diameter, is a third Proportional to that Diameter, and its conjugate Diameter.

Paramount, above all, without any equal; in our Law, it fignifies the Supreme Lord of the Fee.

Paramour, an he or fhe Lover; a Sweet-heart.

Paranymph, (Gr.) a Brideman, or Bridemaid; alfo one who makes a Speech in Commendation of one that commences Doctor in an Univerfity.

Parapet, in Fortification, is an Elevation of Earth, defigned for covering the Souldiers from the Enemies *Cannon* or *fmall Shot,* wherefore its thicknefs is from 18 to 20 Foot; it is 6 foot high on the infide, and 4 or 5 on the fide next the Countrey. So that this difference of Heights form a kind of *Glacis* above, from whence the Mufqueteers mounting the *Banquet* of the *Parapet* may eafily fire into the Moat, or at leaft upon the Counterfcarp.

Paraphanalia, or in the Civil Law *Paraphernalia,* are thofe Goods a. Wife brings her Husband over and befides her Dowry and Marriage Money; as Furniture for her own Chamber, her own Apparrel, and Jewels if fhe be of Quality; all which fhe muft have and not the Executors of the Husband.

Paraphimofis, is a Fault of the Yard, when the *Praeputium's* too fhort; alfo a narrownefs and contraction of the Womb.

Paraphlegia, a Palfie, which feizeth all the parts of the Body below the Head, through an obftruction of the Spinal Marrow.

Paraphrafe, (Gr.) is the expreffing of a Text in plainer Words, and fomewhat more largely and more accommodated to the Reader's Capacity.

Paraphrenitis, a Madnefs accompanied with a Continual-Fever, by reafon of fome matter that lies in the *Cerebellum,* whereby the Animal Spirits cannot flow, and thence the *Midriff* and *Lungs* are troubled.

Paragbrofyne, is a flight fort of doating in the Imagination and Judgment.

Parafang, a Scripture Meafure of length, being 4 *Englifh* Miles, 153 Paces, and 3 feet.

Parafelene, a Mock-Moon.

Parafite, (Gr.) a Flatterer, fmell-feaft, or Spunger.

F f f   *Parafi-*

Parafitical, belonging to a *Parafite*. *Parafitical* Plants, are fuch as live upon the Stock of others, as *Mifletoe*, *Mofs*, &c.

Parafol, (Fr.) a fort of fmall Canopy or Umbrello, that is carried to keep off the Rain, &c.

Parafynanche, is an Inflammation of the Mufcles of the upper part of the *Oefophagus*, with a continued Fever.

Parathefis (Gr.) a putting to ; alfo in Printing the Matter contained within two Crotchets.

Paravaile, in common Law fignifies the loweft Tenant, or him that is Tenant to one that holdeth his Fee over another ; and is called Tenant Paravaile, becaufe it is prefumed he hath Profit, and Availe by the Land.

Parboil, to boil but in part.

Parbuncle. (a Sea Term) a Rope doubled about a Cask to hoife it up.

Partel, Part, Bundle, Sum.

Parcel, at Sea to *Parcel a Seam*, is after a *Seam* is chaulked to lay over it a narrow piece of Canvafs, and pour on it hot Pitch and Tar.

Parceners, according to common Law, are where one feized of an Eftate of Inheritance, hath Iffue only Daughters, and dies and the Lands defcend to the Daughters, and they are called Parceners and are but as one Heir. *Parceners* according to cuftom, are ; where a Man feized of Lands in Gavel-kind, and hath Iffue divers Sons, and dies, then the Sons are Parceners by the Cuftom.

Parco fracto, is a Writ that lies againft him that violently breaketh a Pound, and taketh out Beafts thence, which for fome Trefpafs done upon another Man's Ground are lawfully impounded.

Pardie, }
Perdie, } verily. *Spencer.*

Pardonable, to be pardoned, or that may be pardoned.

Parenchymous Parts of the Body, by the old Anatomifts are reckoned fuch flefhy parts of it as fill up the Interftices between the Veffels, and not confifting of Veffels themfelves, which is a miftaken notice for the whole Body is little elfe but a Collection of Veffels.

Parentation, (Lat.) Performance of Feafts, Sacrifices, and other folemn Rites, at the Funeral of Relations.

Parenthefis, (Gr.) a Claufe put into the middle of a Sentence, which being left out the Senfe remains entire, and is thus mark'd, ( )

Parenticide, one that kills, or the killing of Father or Mother.

Parget, in Architecture, is the Plafter of a Wall.

Parhelion, (Gr.) a Mock-Sun.

Parifthmia, are two Glandules of the Mouth ty'd together by a flender Production.

Parifylla-

Parisyllabical, (Lat.) of, or consisting of an equal Number of Syllables.

Paritour, see Apparitour.

Parity, (Lat.) Equality or Evenness.

Park of Artillery, is the place appointed for the Encampment of the Artillery, which is generally the Rear of both Lines of an Army.

Park of Artillery, at a Seige, is a Post fortified out of Cannon Shot of the Place Besiegd, where the Cannon, Artificial Fires, Powder, and other Warlike Ammunition are kept, and Gaurded only by Pikemen, to avoid Casualties which may happen by Fire.

Park of Provisions, is a place in the Camp on the Rear of every Regiment, which is taken up by the Suttlers, who follow the Army with all sort of Provisions, and sell them to the Souldiers.

Parley, (Fr.) a Conference, in order to surrender a Place upon Terms.

Parliament, (Fr.) the General Assembly of the Estates of a Kingdom, to make or correct Laws, and to debate Matters touching the Common Wealth. In England it consists of three Estates, viz. King or Queen, Lords Spiritual, and Commons.

Parliamentary, conformable to the Methods of Parliament.

Parlous, a fictitious word, and signifies shrew'd, notable.

Parochial, of, or belonging to a Parish.

Paræmia, a Proverb.

Parole, (Fr.) a Word or Promise; when a Prisoner of War is permitted to go into his own Country upon his Promise to return, he is said to go upon his Parole.

Paronychia a Whitlow, is a preternatural Swelling in the Fingers and very troublesome. It is caused by a sharp malignant Humour, which sometimes gnaws the very Bone it self.

Parotides, are Glandules behind the Ear; also a swelling of those Glandules.

Paroxysm, (Gr.) the Access or Fit of an Ague or Fever.

Parrets, in a Ship; are Frames made of Trucks, Ribs, and Ropes, which go round the Masts, and made fast to the Yard that they may slip up and down the easier; and with the help of the Brest-Ropes keep the Yards close to the Masts.

Parricide, (Lat.) a Murtherer of his Father, Mother, or any of his near Kindred.

Parsimony, (Lat.) thriftiness,

Parsimonious, (Lat.) living, frugal, thrifty.

Parson, is the Law-Term for a Minister of a Parish-Church.

Parsonage, a Parson's Cure; or a Spiritual Living composed of Glebe-Land, Tythe, and other Oblations of the

People, separate or dedicate to God in any Congregation, for the service of the Church there, and for the Maintenance of the Minister to whose Charge the same is committed.

Parterre, (Fr.) a Garden with Knots or Figures, a Flower Garden.

Partial, (Lat.) that sides too much with a Party.

Partiality, (Lat.) a siding too much with a party ; a being more on one side then the other.

Participate, (Lat.) to partake of.

Participation, (Lat.) a partaking, or sharing of a thing.

Participial, belonging to a Participle.

Participle (Grammatical Term) one of the eight Parts of Speech, named from its partaking both of the Noun and of the Verb.

Particles, (Lat.) are small minute parts of Matter.

Particular, (Lat.) proper, peculiar, singular, extraordinary, intimate, apart. *Substantively,* an Inventory of Goods, a certain circumstance.

Particularize, to insist on the *Particulars,* or produce particular Instances.

Parties, in Law, are those which are named in a Deed, or Fine as Parties to it.

Partile Aspect, the most exact and full Aspect possible.

Partisan, a Favourer or Abetter of a Party. In *War,* one that Commands a Par-

ty. Also a Weapon like a Halbard.

Partition, (Lat.) a parting, sharing or dividing. Also that which divides a Room.

Partitione faciendâ, is a Writ that lies for those, who hold Lands or Tenements *pro indiviso,* and wou'd sever to every one his part, against him or them that refuse to joyn in Partition as Co-partners.

Partners, in a Ship, are strong pieces of Timber, bolted to the Beams incircling the Masts, to keep them steady in their Steps. These *Partners* are also at the second Deck for the same purpose.

Partnership, a joyning with some other Person in some affair or concern.

Parturient, (Lat.) travailing, being in Labour, or ready to bring forth.

Party Jury, or half Tongue ; *i. e.* a Jury of half Englishmen and half Foreigners, Impanelled for the Trial of a Criminal of a Foreign Nation.

Parvity, (Lat.) littleness, smalness.

Parvo nocumento, in Common Law, is a Writ of Nuisance, which see.

Parvum & Crassum, is the fourth Pair of Muscles of the Head.

Parylis, is an Inflammation, Rottenness, or Excrescency among the Gums.

Paschal, belonging to the *Jewish* Passover.

Paschal,

Paſchal Rents, are Rents or Annual Duties, paid by the Inferiour Clergy to the Biſhop, at their *Eaſter Viſitations*.

Pas de ſouris, a French Term in Fortification, the ſame with *Berme*, which ſee.

Paſquil, a ſlanderous Libel poſted up for publick view, ſo called from *Paſquin*, a Statue in *Rome*, upon which Satyrical Papers are uſually fix'd, and father'd on him as Author. Hence

Paſquinade, a Satyrical Invective or Libel.

Paſſade, (Fr.) Alms or Benevolence to a Paſſenger. Alſo the Courſe of a Horſe forwards and backwards on the ſame Plot of Ground; alſo a Paſs or Thruſt in Fencing.

Paſſagio, is a Writ directed to the Keeper of the Ports, to permit a Man to paſs over that hath the King's Licence.

Paſſant, the Term in Heraldry for a Lion born in an Eſcutcheon in a walking poſture. In moſt other Beaſts this is called *Tripping*.

Paſſarado, in a Ship, is a Rope, whereby all the ſheat-Blocks of the Main and Fore-Sails are haled down *Aft*. The clew of the *Main Sail* to the *Main Maſt*, and the clew of the Fore-Sail to the *Cat-Head*.

Paſſenger, one that Paſſes or Travels by Land or Water.

Paſſibility, (Lat.) an aptneſs or capacity to ſuffer.

Paſſion, (Lat.) in general ſignifies ſuffering; alſo tranſport of Mind.

Paſſionate, haſty, ſubject or inclinable to Anger.

Paſſive, ſuffering or bearing, able or diſpoſed to ſuffer. *Paſſive Principles* in Chymiſtry, are Water and Earth, either becauſe their parts are at reſt, or not moved ſo rapidly as thoſe of Spirit, Oil and Salt, and ſo hinder their Motion.

Paſſport, a Licence granted by any one in Authority, for the ſafe Paſſage of any Man from one place to another.

Paſſus, a *Roman* Meaſure of length, containing 4 feet, 10 Inches, 02 decimal parts.

Paſtills, are a kind of Comfits made up in little Rolls.

Paſtination, the opening, looſening, and preparing of the Earth for planting.

Paſtoral, (Lat.) belonging to a Shepherd, or Rural Life, whence Paſtoral Song; alſo an Epithete apply'd to a Curate.

Paſturage, the ſame with Paſture Ground, or Ground for the feeding of Cattle.

Patacoon, a *Spaniſh* Coin worth about 4 s. 8 d.

Patee, a Term made uſe of by the Heralds for a Croſs of this Figure. The Field is ſable *a Croſs Patee*, *Argent*.

Patefaction, (Lat.) a making open ; also a discovering or making manifest.

Patents, see *Letters Patents.*

Patentee, is he to whom the King grants his Letters Patent.

Paternal, of or belonging to a Father, Fatherly.

Pathetick, or *Pathetical*, moving or that stirs up the Affections.

Pathognomonick, (Gr.) is a proper and inseperate Sign of such or such a Disease.

Pathology, (Gr.) is that part of Physick that treats of the Causes and differences of Diseases.

Patience, a Vertue enabling to bear Afflictions with courage and resolution.

Patonce the Heralds term for one of their Crosses of this Figure. *Gules, a Cross Patonce, Argent.*

Patriarch, (Gr.) a chief Father, or the first Father of a Family or Nation, in which sense the Jews reckoned *Abraham, Isaac,* and *Jacob.* Also it is a Dignitary in the Church above an Arch-Bishop, of which there were anciently five, viz. at *Rome, Constantinople, Alexandria, Jerusalem,* and *Antioch.*

Patriarchate, the Jurisdiction of a Patriarch.

Patricians, were the most Noble among the *Romans,* being come of Senatours and the Founders of their Commonwealth.

Patrimony, (Lat.) an Inheritance or Estate left by a Father to his Son.

Patriot, a Father of his Country or Publick Benefactor.

Patripassians, a sort of Christian Hereticks who said that the Father and the Holy Ghost suffered as well as the Son.

Patrocination, a patronizing, protecting or defending.

Patroll, is a Night Watch, of about 5 or 6 Men commanded by a *Sergeant*, who are sent from the Guard to walk in the Streets and prevent disorder.

Patron, a powerful Friend, Protector, or Advocate. He, who hath the *Jus Patronatus* or the right of Advowson of a Church , which was at first acquired, by endowing a Parochial Church at the foundation of it with Manse and Glebe , which Endowment was generally made by the Lord of the Mannor ; to which Piety we owe the Original of Lay-Patrons.

Patronage, the Office of a Patron ; also Care, Protection.

Pavan, a grave sort of Dance ; also the slowest sort of Instrumental Musick.

Paucity, (Lat.) small number, fewness.

Pavice, is a piece of defensive Armour which the Ancients wore in the Wars, it was

was the largeſt ſort of Buck-
lers, whoſe two ſides bended
inwards, like the Roof of a
Houſe, or a Shed of Boards
for Souldiers, and ſo it diffe-
red from a *Target*.

Pavilion, (Lat.) an old
Term for a Tent of War.

Paunch, is Matts made of
Sinnet, faſtened to the main
and fore Yards, to keep them
from galling againſt the Maſts.

Pawl, a ſmall piece of Iron
bolted to one end of the
Beams of the Deck, cloſe by
the Capſtan, but yet ſo eaſily
that it can turn about. It's
uſe is to ſtop the Capſtan
from turning back by being
made to catch hold of the
Whelps.

Pawn-Broker, one that lends
Money on any ſort of Goods.

Paying, the Seamens Term,
for laying over the Seams of
a Ship a Coat of hot Pitch.

Payable, to be paid, or that
muſt be pay'd.

Peaceable, of a quiet Temper and Diſpoſition; not given
to ſtrife and War.

Peaking, of a puling ſickly
Conſtitution.

Pean, in Heraldry, is when
the Field of a Coat of Arms
is *Sable* and the Powderings
Or.

Peaſant, (Fr.) a Country-
Man, a Country Clown, or
Boor.

Peccadillo, (Span.) a ſmall
Fault or Crime.

Peccant, (Lat.) Sinning; alſo thoſe Humours of the Body, which contain ſome ma-

lignity, or which are too Exuberant are called *Peccant*.

Peccavi, (Lat.) I have done
amiſs.

Peck, an *Engliſh* Meaſure
of Capacity for Corn, containing 2 Gallons, or 544½ ſolid Inches.

Pechys, a *Grecian* Meaſure
of Length, which being reduced to the *Engliſh* contains
one Foot ſix Inches, and 1312
Decimal Parts.

Pecten Arboris, is the Grain
of the Wood of any Tree.

Pectorals or *Pectoral Medicines*, are ſuch as are uſed in
Diſeaſes of the Breaſt, for attenuating, or thickning or
allaying the Heat thereof, and
rendering the Matter which
cauſes Coughing, fit to be Ex-
pectorated or ſpit out.

Peculation, a Robbing or
Cheating of the Publick.

Peculiar, particular, or
ſingular; alſo a *Peculiar*, is a
Pariſh or Church exempt from
the Ordinary, and the Biſhop's
Courts.

Pecuniary, (Lat.) of, or belonging to Money.

Pedagogue, (Gr.) an Inſtru-
ctor or Teacher of Youth.

Pedal, belonging to, or containing a Foot in Meaſure.

Pedant, a paltry School-
maſter; a conceited pretender
to Schollarſhip, and one who
values himſelf mightily upon
his Scraps of Latin.

Pedantick, imitating a Pedant.

Pedantry, is the ridiculous
way and humour of a Pedant.

Pedee, a Foot-boy, a Drudge.

Pedestal in Architecture, is the Foot or Basis of a Pillar, and is different according to the several Orders of Architecture.

Pediculus, in Botany, is the Foot-stalk of any Leaf, Flower or Fruit.

Pedigree, Descent from *Ancestors*, Stock, Race.

Pediment, in Architecture, the same with Fronton, which see.

Pedo-baptism, (Gr.) Infant-baptism, the baptising of Children.

Pedrero, a small piece of Ordnance used at Sea.

Peek, a Grudge.

Peere, (Fr.) a Fortress made against the force of the Sea, for the better securing Ships that lie at Harbour in any Haven.

Peers, *q. pares*, Equals; so the House of Lords in Parliament, is called the House of *Peers*.

Pegasus, the Winged Horse, a Northern Constellation of 23 Stars.

Pelagiæ, a Term used by some Natural Historians, to express such Sea Shell-fishes, as never or very rarely are found near the Shores, but always reside in the deep, and in those parts of the Bottom of the Sea which are farthest from Land.

Pelagians, the Followers of *Pelagius*, or *Morgan a Britain*, who denyed Original Sin, and held many other erroneous Opinions.

Pelicoides, the Name of a sort of a mixt Figure in Mathematicks.

Pelidnus, a Black and Blue Colour in the Face, frequent in Melancholick Men.

Pellets, a Bearing in Heraldry.

Pelican, is a kind of double Vessel, which the Chymists used in Circulations.

Pellicle, (Lat.) a little Skin, or thin Rind.

Pellucid, (Lat.) clear, bright, transparent, or shining thro'.

Pemphigodes Febris, is a spotted Fever; some say a Windy and Flatulent Fever.

Penal, (Lat.) that inflicts Punishment, as the *Penal Laws* against Papists, &c.

Penalty, a Fine imposed by way of Punishment.

Penance, a sort of Mortification practised among Roman Catholicks

Pencil, a small Instrument of Bears, Ermins, or Hogs-Hairs, put into Quills of several sizes, for Drawing, Painting, &c.

Pendants or *Streamers*, are those long Colours which are hung at the Heads of the Masts, or at the Yard-arm-Ends. Their use is chiefly for Ornament, and sometimes for distinction of Squadrons.

Pendent, (Lat.) hanging, bending.

Pendulous, hanging down; also doubtful.

Pendulum, (Lat.) is a weight hanging at the End of a String,

String, Chain or Wire, by whose Vibrations or Swings too and fro, the parts or differences of time are measured.

Penetrable, (Lat.) that may be penetrated, pierced or dived into.

Penetrate, (Lat.) to pierce or dive into.

Penetration, (Lat.) a piercing or diving into. Penetration of Bodies, a Philosophick expression for two Bodies being in the same Place, so that the parts of one do every where penetrate into, and adequately fill up the dimensions or places of the parts of the other, which is a contradiction.

Peninsula, (Lat.) a Track of Land surrounded with Water except in one place, where it is joyned to the Continent by a narrow Neck of Land.

Penitence, Repentance, which consists in being sorry for one's Sins, and resolving amendment of Life.

Penitent, repenting, sorrowful for having done amiss. *Substantively* a Person so affected.

Penitential, belonging to Repentance. *Substantively*, a Penance Book.

Penitentiary, a Priest that imposes Penance on an Offender, as he thinks fit; also a place for hearing Confessions.

Pennant, in a Ship, is a short Rope made fast at one end to the Head of the Mast, or to the Yard-Arm, with a Block at the other end, and a Shiver to reeve some running Rope into; and all the Yard-Arms except the *Missen* have *Pennants*.

Pennata folia, (Lat.) Winged leaves, which the Botanists reckon such as grow directly one against another on the same Rib or Stalk.

Penny-Weight, an English Troy Weight containing 24 Grains.

Pension, a Salary or Yearly allowance.

Pensioner, one that receives a Pension.

Pensive, (Fr.) sad, heavy, sorrowful, thoughtful.

Pent Ypent, shut up. *Spencer*.

Pentagon, (Gr.) in Geometry, is a Figure having five sides, and five Angles.

Pentagonal, (Gr.) belonging to a Pentagon, or having five sides and five Angles.

Pentameter, (Gr.) a Verse consisting of five feet.

Pentapetalous Plants, are such as have a Flower consisting of five Leaves.

Pentasticks, (Gr.) Stanza's, consisting of five Verses; also Porches having five Rows of Pillars.

Pentateuch, (Gr.) the five Books of *Moses*; also any Volume consisting of five Books.

Pentecontarch, (Gr.) a Captain that hath the Command of 50 Men.

Pentecost, or Whitsuntide, so called in the Greek from

in being the 50th day after *Easter*.

Pentiveme, (Gr.) a Gally that hath five Oars to a Seat, or five Men to an Oar.

Penumbra, in Astronomy, is a faint kind of Shadow, or the utmost edge of the Perfect Shadow, which happens at the Eclipse of the Moon.

Penurious, extream needy and necessitous, that wants necessaries; also niggardly.

Penury, (Lat.) extream want of necessaries.

Peptick, that serves to concoct or digest.

Pepuzians, a sort of Christian Hereticks, that sprung from the *Montanists*, whose Errors they follow'd; they were so called from *Pepuza* a Town in *Phrygia*, which they named *Jerusalem*, whither they invited all men to present themselves. They appeared in the second Age.

Peradventure, perchance, or by chance.

Peraction, (Lat.) an accomplishing, performing or ending of a thing.

Peracute, (Lat.) very sharp.

Peragration, (Lat.) a Travelling or Wandring about; a Progress, a Ramble.

Perambulation, a walking or travelling about; also a Surveying.

Perambulation of the Forest, is the walking of Justices or other Officers about the Forest, in order to take a sort of Survey, and set down its Bounds and Limits.

Perambulatione facienda, is a Writ directed to the Sheriff, commanding him to make Perambulation, and set down the Bounds of two or more Mannors, whose Limits are not so well known.

Perceptible, (Lat.) that may be perceived, or understood.

Perception, (Lat.) is the clear and distinct apprehension of Objects offered to us, without inferring any Judgment concerning them.

Perceptivity, a Power of Perception or thinking.

Perch, a Measure, by our Statute Law of 16 Foot and a half.

Percolation, (Lat.) a Term in Chymistry, signifying a straining through.

Percontation, an asking of Questions, a strict enquiry.

Percussion, (Lat.) the hitting or striking of one Body against another.

Perdition, (Lat.) Ruin or Destruction.

Perdonatio utlagariæ, is a Pardon for him who for contempt in not coming to the King's Court is Out-law'd, and afterwards of his own accord, yieldeth himself to Prison.

Perdue, (Fr.) lost; also secret, hidden.

Perduration, a continuing or lasting very long.

Peregal, equal. *Spencer.*

Peregrine, (Lat.) a Foreigner, an Out-landish Man.

Peregrina-

Peregrination, (Lat.) Travelling in Foreign Countries.

Peremptory, (Lat.) express, final, determinate, positive.

Peremptorily, positively, absolutely.

Perennity, (Lat.) lastingness, long Continuance, Perpetuity.

Perfection, (Lat.) Accomplishment, Excellency. The State or Condition of that which is perfect.

Perfidious, (Lat.) false, treacherous, deceitful.

Perforate, (Lat.) bored or pierced through.

Perforation, (Lat.) a boaring through.

Perforated, (Lat.) boared through; the Armorists use it to express the passing or penetrating of one Ordinary thro' another as thus; He beareth Or a Bend Ermine perforated through a Cheveron Gules.

Perfrication, a rubbing or chafing throughly or all over.

Perfunctorily, (Lat.) slightly or carelesly.

Perfunctory, (Lat.) slight or careless.

Periamma, (Gr.) is a Medicine which being tied about the Neck is believed to expel Diseases.

Pericardium, (Gr.) a double membrane that surrounds the whole Substance of the Heart.

Pericarpium, (Gr.) a Me-

dicine apply'd to the Wrists to cure an Ague, &c.

Pericranium, (Gr.) is a Membrane which infolds the Skull, and covers it all except just where the Temporal Muscles lie.

Perigæum or *Perigee*, (Gr.) when a Planet is in its nearest distance to the Earth, it is said to be in its *Perigæum* or *Perigee*.

Perihelion, (Gr.) when a Planet is nearest to the Sun, it is said to be in its *Perihelion*.

Perillous, dangerous or full of danger.

Perimeter, (Gr.) the Bound of any Figure, or that line which encompasseth it.

Perinde valere, a Term used in the *Ecclesiastical Law*, signifying a dispensation granted to a Clerk, that being defective in his Capacity to a Benefice, or other Ecclesiastical Function, is *de facto*, admitted to it.

Perinæum, a Ligamentous Seam between the *Scrotum* and Fundament.

Period, a full Stop at the end of any Sentence. In chronology, it signifies a Revolution of a certain Number of Years. In Astronomy, it is taken for the entire Revolution of a Planet.

Periodical, of or belonging to a Period, that goes or comes by Course.

Periodical Month, is the space of Time, in which the Moon finishes her Revolution round

round the Earth, or the time she spends in going from any Point in the Zodiack till her return to the same Point again, and is something less then 27¼ Days.

Periæci, (Gr) are such Inhabitants of the Earth as live under the same Parallel, but at two opposite Points of this Parallel, or at the 2 Extreamities of a Diameter of the Parallel, and these have the *Seasons* of the Year the same, or the same Seasons at the same time, but Day and Night at different times.

Periostium, (Gr.) a thin Membrane, immediately enwarpping almost all the Bones in the Body, except the Teeth, those of the Ear, &c.

Peripatevicks, (Gr.) the Disciples and Followers of *Aristotle*.

Periphery, (Gr.) the Circumference of a Circle; sometimes 'tis used, tho' improperly, in the same sense with Perimeter.

Periphrasis, (Gr.) a Circumlocution, or expressing a thing or Person by many Words.

Periphrastical, (Gr.) belonging to a *Periphrasis*, or spoken by way of *Periphrasis*.

Peripneumonia, (Gr.) is an Inflammation of the Lungs and Breast, accompanied with a sharp Fever, a Cough, an an Heavy Pain.

Periptere, in Architecture, is a place encompassed with Columns without, and with a kind of Wings about it.

Periscii, are those who have their Shadows cast on all sides of them the same Day, that is, their Shadows go round them in a Day, and such are the Inhabitants of the Frigid Zone.

Perissology, a Discourse stuffed with unnecessary and superfluous Words.

Peristaltick, (Gr.) that hath force to strain, gripe or press together. Amongst Physitians it is commonly apply'd to the quibling motion of the Guts.

Peristyle, in Architecture, is a place encompassed with Pillars standing round about within side.

Peritonæum, (Gr.) a Membrane covering the whole Abdomen on the inside and the Entrails on the out.

Peritrochium, (Gr.) in Mechanicks is a kind of Wheel, or circular Frame of Wood, placed upon an Axis or Cylinder round which a Rope is wound, in order to raise a Weight.

Perjury, a Crime committed, when a Lawful Oath is administered by one in Authority, to a Person in any Judicial proceeding, who Sweareth absolutely and falsly in a matter material to the Cause in Question.

Permanent, durable or constant,

Permeate, (Lat.) to penetrate into, or pass through the Pores of any Body.

Permea-

Permeation, (Lat.) a going or paſſing through; the paſſing of any thing through the Pores of another Body.

Permiſſion, (Lat.) is that Leave or Liberty, which a Superiour grants to an Inferiour to do a thing.

Permutation, (Lat.) an Exchanging one thing for another; alſo in Mathematicks, 'tis the ſame with *Alteration*, or *Alternate Proportion*, which ſee.

Permutatione Archi-Diaconatus, & Eccleſiæ eidem annexæ cum Eccleſia & Præbenda, is a Writ to an Ordinary, commanding him to admit a Clerk to a Benefice, upon Exchange made with another.

Permute, to exchange.

Pernicious, (Lat.) deſtructive, miſchievous, or hurtful.

Pernio, is a Preternatural ſwelling cauſed by extream cold in the Hands and Feet, and which at laſt breaks out.

Pernour of Profits, in Law, is a taker of Profits.

Peroration, (Lat.) the concluſion, or laſt part of an Oration.

Pependicular, (Lat.) that is directly down right; in Geometry, one right line is perpendicular to another, or one Plane perpendicular to another Plane, when it ſtands right upon it, and leans no more one way than it does another.

Perpetrate, (Lat.) to effect, perform, go through with; or commit a Crime.

Perpetual, (Lat.) that does not ceaſe, continual, Everlaſting, endleſs.

Perpetuate, (Lat.) to make perpetual.

Perpetuity, a continual laſting; it is alſo uſed in Law, where an Eſtate is ſo deſigned to be ſettled in Tail, that it cannot be undone or made void.

Perplex, (Lat.) intangled, twiſted together, intricate difficult, doubtful.

Perquiſite, a caſual Profit or gain, that ariſes by an Office, &c.

Perſcrutation, (Lat. a ſearching throuly, or into the depth of a thing.

Perſecute, (Lat.) to follow hard after, to vex, trouble, or oppreſs.

Perſecution, (Lat.) a following hard after any one with a deſign of doing him hurt; a vexing or troubling Men for the ſake of Religion.

Perſeverance, (Lat.) conſtancy, firmneſs, reſolution to abide in any way of living or in any Opinion.

Perſevere, (Lat.) to continue or be ſtedfaſt in a thing.

Perſeus, a Conſtellation in the Northern Hemiſphere.

Perſiſt, to abide, hold on, or continue.

Perſick Order of Architecture, is where the Bodies of Men ſerve inſtead of Columns to ſupport the *Entablature*.

Perſona

Perfonable, a Law Term, fignifying, inabled to hold Plea in Court ; as he was made Perfonable by Parliament ; that is, he was made able to ftand in Court.

Perfonable, comely.

Perfonage, an Honourable Perfon.

Perfonal, of or belonging to a Perfon. *Perfonal Tythes*, are Tythes of things acquired by Labour of his own Perfon, as Buying, Selling, Merchandife, &c.

Perfonate, to act, or reprefent a Perfon.

Perfpective, is an Art which gives Rules for the reprefenting of Objects on a Plain Superfice , after the fame manner as they wou'd appear to our fight, if feen through that Plain, which is fuppofed as tranfparent as Glafs.

Perfpicacious, (Lat.) quickfighted, or of a quick apprehenfion.

Perfpicuous , (Lat.) that which is fo clear and tranfparent as that the light may be feen freely through it.

Perfpicuity , (Lat.) clearnefs ; or plainnefs in writing and fpeaking.

Perfpiration, (Lat.) a breathing through.

Perfuafive or *Perfuafory*, that is apt to perfuade.

Pert, openly, apert. *Spencer*.

Pertica; a fort of Comet.

Pertinacious, (Lat.) (*i. e.* that holds faft) obftinate, ftubborn, or ftiff in Opinion.

Pertinence , (Lat.) fitnefs, patnefs, fuitablenefs.

Pertinent, (Lat.) fit, pat, fuitable, to the purpofe.

Pertnefs, brisknefs.

Perturbation, (Lat.) difquiet, diforder, trouble of Mind.

Perverfe, froward, or crofsgrained.

Perverfion, (Lat.) a feducing.

Perverfity, or *Perverfenefs* , (Lat.) Frowardnefs, ill-Nature, Crofsnefs.

Pervert, (Lat.) to turn upfide down, to debauch or feduce.

Perveftigation, (Lat.) a diligent fearch, or inquiry.

Pervicacious, (Lat.) wilful, head-ftrong, ftubborn.

Pervicacy, (Lat.) Stubbornnefs, Wilfulnefs.

Pervious, (Lat.) eafie to be paffed through.

Perufe, to look, or read over.

Peruvian Bark, is the Bark of a Tree, that comes from *Peru* in *America*, a Remedy for Agues and intermitting Fevers ; its call'd alfo *Quinquina*, and *Jefuits Bark* or *Powder*.

Pes, or Foot, a *Roman* Meafure of Length, containing 11 Inches, and 604 decimal Parts of our Meafure.

Pefage, a Cuftom pay'd for weighing of Goods.

Peffary, an oblong Medicine to be thruft up into the Neck of the Womb.

Pefter, to embarafs, plague or trouble.

Peftiferous,

Pestiferous, (Lat.) that brings or causes the Plague.

Pestilent, plaguy, mischievous, dangerous.

Pestilential, that partakes of, or are nearly related to the Plague, as *Pestilential Fevers*, &c.

Petala, (Gr.) a Term in Botany, signifying those fine coloured Leaves that compose the Flowers of all Plants.

Petalism, a five Years Banishment among the *Syracusians*, inflicted by writing the Person's Name on an Olive Leaf.

Petard, a Hollow Engine made of Metal, in Form of a high-crown'd Hat, from 7 to 8 Inches deep, and 5 broad at the Mouth. 'Tis charged with Powder beaten very small, and fixed to a thick Plank called the *Madrier*, in order to break open the Gates, &c.

Petechealis, is a malignant Fever, which makes the Skin look as though it were flea-bitten.

Petit Treason, in common Law, is when a Servant kills his Master, a Wife her Husband, a Secular or Religious Man, his Prelate or Superiour to whom he ows Faith and Obedience.

Petitio principii, is a precarious supposing a thing to be true, or taking it for granted, which is expresly denied, and ought to be proved; and this is what is called *Begging the Question*.

Petition, (Lat.) a Request of an Inferiour to a Superior, especially one in Authority.

Petrifaction, (Lat.) is the changing any Body into a Stony Substance, when it had no such Nature before.

Petrify, (Lat.) to make or turn into Stone.

Petrobrusians, the Followers of *Peter Bruis* a Priest, who departed from the Church of *Rome* about the Year 1126. They were against Infant Baptism, rebaptizing such as had been Baptiz'd in Infancy; and are by the *Romish* Writers charged with sundry Errours.

Petronel, a sort of Harquebuss or Horse-man's Gun, Named from its hanging at the Breast.

Pettifogger, an Ignorant Practitioner in the Law.

Pettish, waspish, peevish, froward.

Petulancy, (Lat.) sauciness, malapertness, wantonness.

Petty, (Fr.) little, small, inconsiderable.

Petty Larceny, small Theft. See *Larceny*.

Petulant, (Lat.) saucy, wanton, malepert.

Pevetts, the Ends of the Arbor of any Wheel in a Watch, which are the smallest Parts of it.

Pevet-holes, the Holes in which the Pevets run.

Phacos, a spot in the Face like a Nit.

Phænomenon, (Gr.) a Term frequently used in Natural-Philoso-

Philofophy, and fignifies any Appearance, Effect or Operation of a Natural Body, which offers it felf to the confideration and folution of a Natural Philofopher.

Phagedena, is an Exulcerate Cancer.

Phagedenick-Water, in Chymiftry, is a mixture of fublimate and Lime-water.

Phalacrofis, is the falling of the Hair.

Phalangofis, a fault in the Eye-lids, when there are 2 Rows of Hair, or when the Hair grows inwards and is troublefome to the Eyes.

Phalanx, (Lat.) a Military Squadron of 8 Thoufand Footmen, fet in fuch array that they might encounter their Enemies, Foot to Foot, Man to Man, and Shield to Shield.

Phanatick, one that pretends to Revelations and new Lights, one that has vain Vifions or Apparitions.

Pantaftical, (Gr.) full of Fancys or Whims.

Phantafy, (Gr.) an inward Senfe or Imagination, whereby things are reprefented to the Mind, or imprinted on it.

Phantome, an Apparition, or Ghoft.

Pharingæus, a Mufcle of the Pharinx, dilating it in diglutition.

Pharinx, in Anatomy, is the upper end of the Gullet.

Pharifaical, belonging to the *Pharifeei*, a Sect of the *Jews*, named from the He-brew Word *Pharefh* to feparate. They apply'd themfelves to the Study of the Law in a fpecial Manner; pretending to more Holinefs than others.

Parmaceutick, belonging to Drugs, or Medicines.

Pharmacopæa, (Gr.) the Doctrine or Defcription of things Medicinal for Curing Difeafes.

Pharmacopolift, (Gr.) a Seller of Medicines, an Apothecary.

Pharmacum, (Gr.) is any fort of Medicine againft a difeafe.

Pharmacy, (Gr.) the Art of Preparing Medicines, or Phyfical Remedies, the Apothecaries Art.

Pharfang, or *Parafang*, a Meafure of way amongft the *Perfians* of 30, 40, or 60 Furlongs, altering with Time and Place.

Phafes, the Appearances, or the manner in which things fhow themfelves to us; thus in Aftronomy, it fignifies the feveral Appearances in which fome of the Planets fhew themfelves to us, *viz.* Horned, halved, Gibbous, and with a full Light.

Pheon, in Heraldry is the Barbed head of a Dart or Arrow, and is ufually of this Figure. *Sable a Fefs Ermin* between 3 *Pheons*.

Phial,

Phial, a little Glafs-Bottle.

Philanthrophy, (Gr.) is a love for Mankind in General, Humanity.

Philauty, (Gr.) felf-love.

Philology, (Gr.) the love of Difcourfe or Learning; the Study of Humanity, or of the Liberal Sciences.

Philofopher, (Gr.) one skill'd in Philofophy.

Philefophy, (Gr.) the love or defire of Wifdom; the knowledge of Divine and Humane Things; being chiefly of two forts *viz.* Natural and Moral, wh ch fee.

Philter, a Medicine, or Charm to procure Love; a Love-potion, or Love Powder.

Phlebotomy, (Gr.) opening of a Vein with a Lancet to difcharge fome of the Blood.

Phleborragia, (Gr.) the breaking of a Vein.

Phlegm, (Gr.) a flimy Excrement of the Blood, often caufed by too much nitrous Air. Alfo a Watry Diftilled Liquor oppofite to a Spirituous Liquour. Alfo thofe Clouds that appear in diftilled Waters. 'Tis fometimes by Phyfitians ufed for an Inflammation.

Plegmagogues, (Gr.) Medicines to drive away Phlegm.

Phlegmafia, an Inflammation, heat or burning.

Phlegmatick, (Gr.) that is much troubled with Phlegm.

Phlegmon, a hot Tumour proceeding from an over af-

fluxion of Blood to any part.

Phlogofis, a light Inflammation of the Eyes, with a fmall pain and rednefs.

Phlyctæna, is a Pimple in the Skin; alfo a little Ulcer in the Corneous Tunick of the Eye.

Phonicks, fee *Acoufticks*.

Phofphorus, (Gr.) the Morning Star, or *Venus*; alfo a Chymical Preparation that fhines in the Dark.

Photinians, a fort of Chriftian Hereticks, fo called from *Photinus* Bifhop of *Sirmich*, who renewed the Errors of *Sabellius*, *Samofatenus*, *Cerinthius* and *Ebion*, and added that Jefus Chrift was not only mere Man, but began to be the Chrift, when the Holy Ghoft defcended upon him in *Jordan*.

Phrafe, (Gr.) an Expreffion, or manner of Speech.

Phrafeology, (Gr.) a Book of Phrafes.

Phrenetick, (Gr.) poffeffed with a Phrenfie.

Phrenfie, (Gr.) is a Dotage with a continued Fever, often accompanied with Madnefs and Anger, proceeding from too much heat of the Animal Spirits, and not from an Inflammation of the Brain as the Ancients believed.

Phricodes, is a Terrible Fever wherein men are apt to Fancy terrible things.

Phrocion, a Star of the fecond Magnitude in the Conftellation *Canis minor*.

Phrygian

Phrygian Mood, a Warlike kind of Musick fit for Trumpets, Hautboys, &c. Also a sprightly Measure in Dancing.

Phthisick, (Gr) a Consumption of the whole Body, arising from an Ulceration of the Lungs, accompanied with a slow continued Fever, ill smelling Breath and Cough.

Phylacteries, (Gr.) scrolls of Parchment, in which the Ten Commandments or some Passages of Scripture were writ, worn by the *Pharisees,* on their Fore-heads, Arms, and Hem of their Garments; also Preservatives against Poison.

Physical, natural; belonging to Natural Philosophy, or the Art of Physick.

Physick, the Art of curing Diseases, or Medicines prepared for that purpose.

Physicks, (Gr.) is the speculative knowledge of all Natural Bodies, and of their proper Natures, Constitutions, Powers and Operations.

Physiognomer or *Physiognomist,* one versed or skilled in *Physiognomy.*

Physiognomy, (Gr.) an Art which teacheth to guess at the Natures, Conditions, and Fortunes of Persons by a view of their Face, Body, &c.

Physiology, (Gr.) *Physioks,* or Natural Philosophy, is the Science of Natural Bodies, and their various *Affections, Motions,* and Operations.

Phytology, a Discourse or Treatise of Plants.

Piaster, an *Italian* Coin, about the value of our Crown.

Placular, (Lat.) that hath power to purge or clear a man from some Sin or Offence.

Piazza, (Ital.) a broad open Place, as a Market-Place, &c. also corruptly, the Walks about it set with Pillars.

Pica, a Printing Letter of which there is 3 sorts, small, great, and double.

Pickage, a Term in Law, Money paid at Fairs, for breaking the Ground to set up Booths or Stalls.

Pickaroon, a kind of Pirate-Ship.

Pickeer, (Ital.) to skirmish, as Light-horse men do before the main Battel begins.

Picket, in Fortification, is sometimes used for a Stake sharp at one end, to mark out the Ground and Angles of a Fortification, when the Engineer is laying down the Plan of it.

Pied, spotted, or speckled.

Piedouche, in Architecture, is a little square Base smoothed and wrought with Mouldings, serving to support a *Bust,* or Statue drawn half way, or any small Figure in Relief.

Piedroit, in Architecture, is a Square Pillar, differing from a Pilaster in this respect that it hath no Base nor Capital.

Pia-Powder-Court, (Fr. the dusty-foot-court) a Court held in Fairs, to yield Justice to Buyers and Sellers, and to redress disorders committed in them.

Piety,

Pitty, Devotion, Godliness, Natural-Love for Country, Parents, or Relations.

Piger Henricus, a very slow distilling Chymical Instrument.

Pight, pitched, settled. *Spen.*

Pigment, (Lat.) a kind of Painting wherewith Women colour their Faces; also deceit, guile.

Pigneration, (Lat.) a Pawning or taking Pawn.

Pile, in Heraldry, is an Ordinary, consisting of a twofold line, formed after the manner of a Wedge. The Pile is born *invected*, engrailed, &c. like other Ordinaries, and  issues indifferently from any Point of the Verge of the *Escutcheon*. As he beareth a *Pile Gules*.

Piles, a Disease in the Fundament.

Pilgrim, (Ital.) one that Travels upon account of Religion, to visit holy Places, to pay his Devotion to the Relicks of Dead Saints, &c.

Pillage, (Fr.) to plunder, rifle, or rob.

Pillaster, (Fr.) in Architecture, is a square Pillar, that usually stands behind a Column to bear up Arches; it has a Base and a Capital as a Pillar has.

Pillow, is that piece of Timber whereon the Bow-sprit rests at its coming out of the Hull aloft, close by the Stem.

Pilot, is one employ'd to conduct Ships into Roads or Harbours, or over Bars and Sands, or through winding Channels. 'Tis also taken commonly for the Steersman.

Pilotage, the Office of a Pilot or Steersman.

Pimp, a Procurer of, or attendant upon Whores.

Pindarick, in Imitation of *Pindar*, whose Strains were lofty, and almost Inimitable.

Pinguedinous, (Lat.) fat, rude, gross, unweildly.

Pinion, the Wing of a Fowl; also a Nut or lesser Wheel of a Clock or Watch, that plays in the Teeth of another.

Pink, is a sort of Ship, Masted and Rigg'd like others; the Sides of it bulge out very much, which makes this sort of Ship very difficult to be boarded, and also renders it fit to carry great Burdens.

Pinnace, is a small Vessel with a square Stern, going with Sails and Oars, and carrying three Masts; they are used as Scouts for Intelligence, for Landing of Forces and the like.

Pinnacle, the Battlement, or highest Top of a great Building or Spire. Figuratively Eminency or Height.

Pinnata folia, in Botany are such Leaves of Plants as are deeply jagged, cut or indented in, and which have their parts resembling Feathers.

Pint, an *English* Wine Measure, contains 28¾ solid Inches; also an *English* Corn

Mea-

Meafure containing 343⅟₅ folid Inches.

Pintles, are the Hooks by which the Rudder hangs to the Stern-poft.

Pioneers, are fuch Labourers as are taken up for the ufe of an Army, to caft up Trenches. and undermine Forts.

Picus, (Lat.) Godly, Religious, Devout.

Piquant, (Fr.) Pricking, fharp, ftinging, quick-tafted.

Pique, the fame with Peek, or grudge.

Pirate, one that Robs on the Sea, having no Authority from any Prince or Republick.

Piratical, belonging to a Pirate.

Pifcary, a place where Fifh is kept or fold, a Fifh-Market. In Common Law, a liberty of Fifhing.

Pifces, (Lat.) the laft of the Twelve Signs of the Zodiack.

Piftole, a Foreign Coin worth 17 s. Sterling.

Pit-fall, a fort of Gin or Trap to catch Birds.

Pittance, (Fr.) a fmall Portion ; a fmall Allowance of Bread and Bear, or other Provifion to any pious Ufe, efpecially to the Religious for an Augmentation of their Commons.

Pituite, (Lat.) Phlegm, or Rheum, Snivel, Snot.

Pituitous, (Lat.) full of Phlegm.

Pityroides, a fettling in the Urin like Bran.

Placable, (Lat.) eafie to be pacify'd, or appeafed.

Placaert, (Du.) a *Dutch* Ordinance or Proclamation.

Placard, (Fr.) a *French* Edict, Order or Bill pofted up; in our Law, a Licence to maintain unlawful Games.

Place, the Place of any Body in a Philofophick Senfe, is that Part of Space which it takes up, and is either Abfolute or Relative.

Place Abfolute of a Body, is that part of abfolute fpace which that Body takes up.

Place Relative of a Body, is the apparent or fenfible Pofition of any Body, according to the Determination of our Senfes, with refpect to other contiguous or adjoyning Bodies.

Place of Arms, in General, is a ftrong City which is pitched upon for the Magazine of an Army. In Fortification, a *Place* ufually fignifies the Body of a Fortrefs.

Place of Arms in a Garrifon, is a large open fpot of Ground in the middle of the City, for the Garrifon to Rendezvous in, upon any fudden Alarm, or other Occafion.

Place of Arms of a Camp, is a fpacious Piece of Ground at the Head of a Camp, to draw out themfelves in Line of Battel, for a Review or the like.

Place Geometrick, is a certain Extent, wherein each
Point

Point may indifferently solve an *Indetermined Problem*, when it is to be resolved Geometrically.

Place Plane, is such a Problem, when the Point that resolves it is in the Periphery of a Circle.

Place Simple, is such a Problem when the Point resolving it is in a Right Line.

Place Solid, is such a Problem, when the Point that resolves it is in one of the Conick Sections.

Place surfolid, is when the Point is in the Circumference of a Curve of an higher Gender then the Conick Sections.

Placenta, is a thick Cake which grows upon the outside of the *Chorion*, in Proportion as the *Fœtus* grows.

Placitator, a Pleader.

Placitum, a Sentence of the Court, an Opinion, an Ordidinance or Decree: *Placita*, in common Law, signifies Pleas or Pleadings.

Pladarofis, are little Tumors which grow under the Eye-lids.

Plagiary, (Lat.) or Bookthief, one that Steals other Peoples Works, and puts them out under his own Name; but more properly it signifies one that Steals People out of one Country and sells them into another.

Plain Chart, is a Plat or Chart used by Seamen having the Degrees of Longitude thereon made of equal length with those of Latitude.

Plain Sailing, is the Art of finding all the various Motions of a Ship on a Plane, where all the Meridians are made Parellel, and the Parallels at right Angles with the Meridians, and the Degrees of each Parallel equal to those of the Equinoctial; which though false in it self, yet in some Cases does well enough.

Plain Table, an Instrument used in surveying of Land.

Plaint or *complaint* in Law, is the exhibiting any Action personal or real in Writing.

Plaintiff, in Law, is one at whose Suit a Plaint is made.

Plan, a Draught Model, or Ground Plot.

Plancher, (Fr.) a Planck, or Board.

Plantal, causing to sprout, or grow.

Plane, in Geometry is a surface, whose parts are equally disposed between its Extremities, so that there are no risings nor fallings, but it is perfectly even without any manner of Roughness or Asperity.

Plane Horizontal, is such an one as is parallel to the Horizon.

Plane Vertical, is a Plane that is perpendicular to the Horizon.

Planetary, belonging to a Planet or Planets.

Planets,

Planets, (Gr.) are the *Erratick* or *Wandring* Stars which are not, like the fixed ones, always in the same Position to one another. Of these are 6 Primary ones *Mercury*, *Venus*, The *Earth*, *Mars*, *Jupiter* and *Saturn*; and 10 Secondary ones which have hitherto been taken notice of, the *Moon*, the 4 Satellits of *Jupiter*, and the five belonging to *Saturn*.

Planet-Struck, blaited, stunned or amazed.

Planimetry, (Gr.) the Art of Measuring all sorts of Plane Surfaces.

Planisphere, the Sphere or Globe, described or projected upon a Plane Surface.

Plantar, (Lat.) belonging to the Sole of the Foot.

Plantation. a Colony, or Settlement of People in a Foreign Countrey.

Plasm, (Gr.) a Mould in which any Mettal or such like running Matter, which will afterwards harden, is Cast.

Plastick, pertaining to the Art of making or forming things of Earth.

Platform, in Fortification, is an Elevation of Earth, on which Cannon is placed; also a sort of *Bastion*, made on a re-entring Angle, when its two Faces make a right-line.

Platform, in Architecture, is a Row of Beams that support the Timber-work of any Roof, and lie on the Top

of the Wall, where the Entablature ought to be raised; also a kind of Terrass Walk on the Top of a Building.

Platform, is a place on the Lower Deck of a Man of War, abaft the Main Mast behind the Cock-pit.

Platonick Love, is a love abstracted from all corporeal gross Impressions, and sensual Appetite, and consists in Contemplation and *Ideas* of the Mind, not in any Carnal Fruition, so called from *Plato* the Divine Philosopher.

Platonick Bodies, in Mathematicks, are the five regular Bodies, *viz.* the *Tetrahedron*, the *Cube*, the *Octahedron*, the *Dodecahedron*, and the *Icoshedron*.

Platonick-Year, is every 36000th Year, when some Philosophers imagin'd all Persons and things should return to the same State as they now are.

Platoon, (Fr) a small square Body of *Musqueteers*, such as is used to be drawn out of a *Battalion* of foot, when they form the hollow square to strengthen the Angles.

Plats, (a Sea Term) certain flat Ropes to keep a Cable from galling.

A *Plaudite*, (Lat) Clapping of Hands in Token of Approbation.

Plausible, (Lat.) acceptable, received with applause and favour; also seemingly fair and honest.

Plea,

Plea, Excuse, in Law, is that which either party, alledgeth for himself in Court. *Common Pleas*, are such as are held between common People. Pleas of the Crown, are all Suits in the King's Name against his Crown and Dignity.

Plebeian, (Lat.) belonging to the common People; also mean, base, vulgar.

Pledge, (Fr.) a Surety; whence to Pledge in drinking, is to be Surety, or to ingage that he shall receive no harm whilst he is drinking, occasioned by a Practice of the *Danes* heretofore in this Kingdom, who frequently used to Stab the Natives as they were drinking.

Pledgit, is a flat Tent made not to enter into, but to be laid upon a Wound or other Sore.

Plegiis acquietandis, is a Writ that lies for a Surety, against him for whom he is Surety, if he pay not the Money at the Day.

Pleiades, (Gr.) the seven Stars in the Neck of the Bull are called by this Name.

Plenarty, in Law, is directly opposite to Vacation, and signifies the filling up of a vacant Benefice.

Plenary, (Lat.) full entire, or perfect.

Plenilunary, (Lat.) of, or pertaining to the full Moon.

Plenipotentiary, (Lat.) a Commissioner that has full Power and Authority from his Prince, to treat with o-

ther Princes or States about a Peace, &c.

Plenist, a Philosopher that admits no *Vacuum*.

Plenitude, (Lat.) fulness.

Pleonasm, (Gr.) a Figure whereby something superfluous is added.

Plerotica, (Gr.) are Medicines that Breed Flesh, and fill up Wounds.

Plesance, Pleasure, Delight.

Plethorick, full of Humours, Pursey.

Plethory, (Gr.) in Physick, is a fulness or abounding of Humours.

Plevin, (Fr.) in Common Law, a Warrant, or Assurance.

Pleurisy, (Gr.) is an Inflammation of the Membrane *Pleura*, and the Intercostal Muscles, accompanyed with a continued Fever, and Stitches in the side, difficulty of Breathing, and sometimes spitting of Blood.

Pliable, (Fr.) flexible, easy.

Plica, an Epidemical Disease in *Poland*.

Plight, State of Body; also Condition. *Milton*.

Plight, to engage, or promise solemnly.

Plinth, in Architecture, is the lowermost part of the foot of a Pillar, being in the form of a Tile or square Brick.

Platton, a small square Body of Musqueteers. See *Platoon*.

Plow, is an Instrument made of Box or Pear-Tree, used by the Seamen for taking the Altitude of the Sun or Stars, in order to find the Latitude of the Place.

Plumage, the Feathers of a Bird, or a Bunch of Feathers.

Plumb-line, the fame with perpendicular, which fee.

Plume, is the Botanifts Term for that part of the Seed of a Plant which in its growth becomes the Trunk.

Plunder, (Du.) to rob or take away by violence in time of War.

To *Plunge*, to dip over Head and Ears in Water.

Plural, (Lat.) belonging to many.

Plural Number, (in Grammer) is that whereby mention is made of more than one, as Men, Beafts, &c.

Plurality, more than one, greater Part, or greater Number.

Pluries, is a Writ that goeth out in the third Place, after two former Writs that had no effect; the firft is called *Capias*, the fecond *alias*, and the third *Pluries*.

Fluvial, a Prieft's Veftment or Cope.

Pluvious, (Lat.) rainy, fhowery.

Pneumatick, (Gr.) belonging to Wind, Air, or Spirits.

Pneumatick Engine, that Engine which is commonly colled the Air Pump.

Pneumatocele, (Gr) is a Windy Rupture, when the Skin of the Scrotum is diftended with Wind.

Pneumatodes, is a fhort breathing.

Pneumacofis, (Gr.) is the Generation of Animal Spirits, which is performed in the Cortical Subftance of the Brain.

Podagrical, having the Gout in the Feet.

Podefta, a kind of Magiftrate in feveral Cities of Italy.

Poem, a compofition in Verfe, a Copy of Verfes.

Poefie, Poetry or a Poet's Work; properly it fignifies a contexture of Poems or Poetical pieces.

Poetical, or *Poetick*, that has the Air and Character of Poefy.

Poetical rifing and fetting of the Stars, is either *Cofmical*, *Acronycal*, or *Heliacal*, which fee.

Point, in Mathematicks, is the beginning of Magnitude and is conceived fo fmall, as to have no dimenfion at all.

Point blank, Pofitively, directly.

Point, in Navigation, fignifies 11 Degrees, 15 Minutes, or one 32d part of the Compafs.

Point of Land, the Extremity of a Cape, or Headland at Sea.

Point of Incidence, in Opticks, is that Point on the furface of a Glafs or other Body, on which any Ray of Light falls.

Point of Inflection of a Curve, fee *Inflection*.

Point in, when 2 Piles are born in a Coat of Arms, fo

as

as to have their Points meet, they say he beareth 2 *Piles in Point.*

Pointing the Cable; is untwisting it at the End, and lessening the Yarn, and twisting them again, and making all fast with a piece of Marline, and this is to keep it from ravelling out.

Poise, to weigh with the Hand, to bring into an *Equilibrium.*

Poitral, a Breast-plate, or the Breast-leather of a Horse.

Poitrel, a Tool for graving.

Polar, belonging to the Poles.

Polar Circles, are two lesser Circles of the Sphere, Parallel to the Equinoctial, one 23 Degrees from the North Pole, and the other 23 Degr. from the South Pole.

Polarity, the Property of the Load-stone of pointing to the Poles.

Poles, of the World; the two ends of the Axis, or right line, about which the Sphere is conceived to move or turn, are called its Poles, the one whereof is called the *Arctick,* and the other the *Antarctick.*

Poles, of a Circle on the Sphere, are two Points on the Surface of the Sphere, equally distant from the Circumference of that Circle; thus, the Poles of the World, are the Poles of the Equinoctial, and the Zenith and Nadir the Poles of the Horizon.

Poles of a Dial, are the Zenith and *Nadir* of that place in which that Dial wou'd be an Horizontal one.

Polemians, a Sect of Christian Hereticks, the Followers of one *Polemius* about the Year 373; the principal of whose Errors, was the mixture which he said there had been between the Word and the Flesh. These Hereticks were confounded with the *Apollinarians.*

Polemical, belonging to that part of Theology which relates to controversy, which because of the Jarrs and Squabbles that usually arise about controverted Points, is called *Polemicks,* or *Polemical Divinity.*

Policy, craft, subtilty; or a prudent managing of Affairs; also the Art of Governing a Kingdom or Common-wealth.

Policy of Insurance, an Instruments or Writing given by Insurers to make good the thing Insured.

Polish, (Lat.) to smooth, to make clear or bright, to burnish; also to civilize; to refine one's Manners.

Polishable, that may be polished.

Polite, neat, accurate, genteel, or well-bred.

Political, belonging to Policy.

Politician, a States-man.

Politick, crafty, prudent; or belonging to civil Government.

Politicks,

Politicks, the Art of Government, or Books which treat upon those Subjects.

Polity Ecclesiastical, Church-Government.

Poll, a Head; also a setting down the Names of those that have a right to Vote in Elections, or to take a Poll at an Election; also to shave the Head.

Pollinctor, an Embalmer of Dead Bodies, an Undertaker.

Pollution, (Lat.) Uncleanness.

Pollux, a fixed Star in *Gemini* of the second Magnitude.

Poltron, (Fr.) a Coward, a Hen-hearted Fellow.

Polyacausticks, (Gr.) are Instruments contrived to multiply sounds.

Polygamy, (Gr.) a Marriage contracted by one Man with several Wives together.

Polygamists, (Gr.) a sort of Christian Hereticks, who said it was lawful for a Man to have as many Wives as he pleased. Their Patron was *Bernardine Ochimus*, who lived in the Sixteenth Century.

Polygarchy, a Government which is in the Hands of many.

Polygon, in Geometry, is a Figure of many Angles.

Polygram, (Gr.) in Geometry, is a Figure consisting of many Lines.

Polyhedron, (Gr.) in Geometry, is a Figure contained under, or consisting of many sides.

Polynomial, (Gr.) of many Names; in Algebra *Polynomials* are Quantities composed of several *Monomials*, joy'd together, by the Signs more or less, as $a + m + n - p$.

Polypetalous, (Gr.) having many Leaves. In Botany, a *Polypetalous Flower*, is a Flower which consists of more than six distinct Flower-leaves.

Polypus, is a swelling in the Hollow of the Nostrils.

Polyscopes, (Gr.) or *Multiplying Glasses*, are such as represent to the Eye one Object as many.

Polyspast, in Mechanicks, is an Engine consisting of several Pulleys.

Polyspermous, (Gr.) having many Seeds; in Botany, *Polyspermous Plants*, are such Herbs or Plants as have at least more than four Seeds in each Flower.

Polysyllable, a Word of many Syllables, or that hath many Syllables.

Polytheism, (Gr.) a holding many Gods, or that Religion which teaches to worship, and pay Adoration to several Gods.

Pomey, (in *Heraldry*,) is the Figure of an Apple or Ball, which must always be drawn of a green Colour.

Pomiferous, (Lat.) Apple-bearing, as a Pomiferous Tree, is a Tree that bears Apples or Pears.

Pommel,

Pommel, the round Knob on a Saddle-Bow, or on the Hilt of a Sword, (Verbally) to bang or beat soundly.

Pomp, (Lat.) State or Grandure, such as is used in solemn Shews.

Pompets, Printers Balls wherewith they put the Ink on the Letters.

Pompous, stately or sumptuous.

Ponder, (Lat.) to weigh in the Mind, or to consider.

Ponderosity, (Lat.) Heaviness, Weight.

Ponderous, (Lat.) Heavy, Weighty.

Pondus, (Lat.) a Term frequently used in Mechanicks, and signifies that dead weight apply'd to one end of a *Libra* or *Vectis.*

Pone, is a Writ, whereby a cause is removed from a County or Inferiour Court into the Common-pleas.

Pone per Vadium, is a Writ to the Sheriff to take surety of one for his appearance at a day assigned.

Ponendis in Assisis, is a Writ founded upon those Statutes, which shew what Persons Sheriffs ought to impannel upon Assises and Juries, and what not.

Ponendum in Ballium, is a commanding a Prisoner to be bailed, in Cases Bailable.

Ponendum Sigillum ad Exceptionem, a Writ willing the Justices to set their Seals to Exceptions brought by Defendants.

Poniard, (Fr.) a Dagger.

Pontage, (Lat.) a Contribution for the repairing or re-edifying of Bridges; also a Bridge-Toll.

Pontifical, (Lat.) belonging to an High-priest, Pope, or great Prelate.

Pontificalia, Pontifical Ornaments, wherein a Bishop performs Divine Service, which when he has on, he is said to be in *Pontificalibus.*

Pontoon, a Bridge of Boats.

Poop of a Ship, is the highest or uppermost part of her Hull or Stern.

Pope, (Gr.) signifies Father, and is a Name that was anciently given to all Bishops; but about the end of the Eleventh Century, *Gregory* 7. order'd the Name of Pope shou'd peculiarly belong to the Bishop of *Rome.*

Popery, the Popish or *Roman*-Catholick Religion.

Poplitick, belonging to the Ham.

Poppæan Law, a certain Law amongst the *Romans,* against single Life.

Populace, or *Populacy,* (Fr.) the common or meaner sort of People.

Popular, belonging to, or in request among the common People.

Population, (Lat.) an unpeopling, a laying waste.

Populous, full of People.

Pores, are small Interstices, or Vacuities between the Particles

ticles of Matter that conftitute every Body, or between certain Aggregates and Com-binations of them.

Porifm, in Mathematicks, is a General Theorem, found out by means of, and drawn from, another Theorem already demonftrated.

oriftick Method, in Mathematicks, is a Method whereby is determined, when, and what way, and how many different ways a Problem may be refolved.

Poroticks, Medicines that turn fome of the Nourifhment into hard Matter.

Porous, full of Pores.

Porocele, is a Rupture proceeding from Callous Matter or the Stone.

Porphyry, a kind of reddifh Marble, finely ftreaked with white Veins.

Porrection, a ftreatching out, or reaching forth.

Port, a Haven; alfo the Court of the *Grand Seignior*.

Port the Helm, is a Word of Command at Sea, to him at the Helm to put it to *Larboard*, and the Ship will go to *Starboard*.

Ports, are thofe Holes in a Ship's fide through which the Great Guns are put.

Port-laft, the fame with the Gun-wale of a Ship.

Port-fale, Sale of Fifh, as foon as brought into Harbour; alfo a publick Sale to fuch as bid moft.

Portable, (Lat.) that may be carried or born.

Portage, Money paid for Carriage.

Portal, a leffer gate.

Portative, that may be carried.

Portcullice, (Fr.) a falling Gate or Door, let down to keep the Enemies out of a City.

Portend, to forebode, forefhew, or betoken.

Portentous, monftrous, betokening or foreboding fome future ill or mifchance.

Porters of the Verge, certain Officers that bear white Wands before the Judges.

Portgreve, the chief Magiftrate in fome Sea-Port-Towns.

Portico, in Architecture, is a long place covered over either with a Vaulted or plain Roof, and fupported with Pillars.

Portioners, the feveral Minifters that ferve a Perfonage alternately or by turns.

Portlinefs, a being *portly*, majeftical or comely.

Portmote, is a Court kept in Sea-Port-Towns.

Portraiture, a Picture or Draught.

Portray, to draw the reprefentation or Picture of a thing.

Pofition, the State of a Queftion or Argument to be debated; alfo, in Natural Philofophy, it is an Affection of Place, and expreffes the manner of any Bodies being in a Place; alfo a Rule in Arithmetick.

Pofitive

Positive, absolute, peremptory.

Posse Comitatus, i. e. Power of the County, signifies the Assistance of all Knights, Gentlemen, Yeomen, Labourers, &c. above the Age of fifteen within a County.

Possession, (Lat.) an absolute Possession, in common Law, is taken for Lands and Inheritance, or for the actual injoyment of them.

Possessive, (Lat.) belonging to Possession.

Possible, that may be done, or may happen.

Postage, Money paid for the Carriage of Letters.

Post-date, to post-date a Writing is to date it some time after the real Date thereof.

Post-fine, a Duty belonging to the King for a Fine formerly acknowldged.

Post Term, 20 d. taken by the *Custos Brevium*, of the Court of Common Pleas, for filing any Writ after the Term.

Postea, a Record of the Proceedings, upon a Trial by *Nisi-prius*.

Posterity, Off-spring, or those which shall be Born in future Ages.

Posteriors, (Lat.) the backparts.

Posteriour, that comes after, later.

Postern, is a small door in the *Flank* of a *Bastion*, or other part of a Garrison, to march in and out unperceived by the Enemy, either to relieve the Works, or to make Sallies.

Posthumous, that is Born or published after the Death of the Father or Author.

Postick, behind, or on the back-side; added or done after.

Postil, a short Note, or Explication on a Text.

Postillon, (Fr.) a Post's guide or forerunner; also he that leads or rides upon one of the foremost of the Coach Horses when there are six.

Postmeridian, (Lat.) done in the Afternoon.

Postpone, (Lat.) to set behind, or make less account of.

Postscript, (Lat.) something added at the end of a Writing.

Postventional, coming, or come after.

Postulates, in Mathematicks, are such easie and self-evident Suppositions as need no Explication or Illustration to render them intelligible.

Postulation, (Lat.) a requiring or demanding.

Posture, the motion and carriage of the Body, or the state of Affairs.

Posy, a Nosegay; also a Motto for a Ring.

Potable, (Lat.) that may be drunk.

Potans or *Potence*, is that Stud in a Pocket Watch, wherein the lower Pevet of the Verge plays, and one of the Crown Wheel runs.

Potency,

Potency, (Lat.) Power.

Potent, Powerful, able;
In Heraldry
Potent or *Potence*, is a
Cross formed
into
this Figure.
This Form
reprefents,

the upper end of a Crutch, for
anciently Crutches were called *Potents*.

Potentate, a Soveraign
Prince, or a Perfon of great
Power and Authority.

Potential, a Word ufed in
Metaphyficks, and fignifies
having a Power or Poffibility
of acting or being.

Potion, (Lat.) a Medicinal
Mixture to drink, or a Phyfical drink.

Potulent, (Lat.) that may
be Drunk; alfo half Drunk.

Pouch, a Bagg. Pouches in
a Ship, are fmall Bulk-heads,
made in the Hold of a Ship,
to ftow Goods that they may
not fhoot from one fide to
the other.

Poultice, a kind of Phyfical
Decoction, apply'd outwardly to a part, to affwage Swellings or Inflammations.

Pounce, the Talon of a Bird
of Pray. Alfo a Powder,
which rubb'd on Paper, makes
it bear Ink.

Poundage, a Subfidy granted the King (of twelve pence
in the Pound) of all Merchandife imported or Exported.

Pounder, one that puts Cattel in a Pound. Alfo a great

Gun, as a *Ten-pounder*, that
is a Cannon carrying a Ball
that weighs ten pound.

Pour fair Proclamer, &c.
a Writ commanding the
Mayor, &c. to proclaim that
none caft filth into Ditches or
other places adjoyning.

Pour Party, to make *Pour
Party*, in Law, is to fever and
divide thofe Lands that fall
to Parceners, which before
Partition they held joyntly and
pro indivifo.

Pourfuivant, (Fr.) a Follower; alfo the King's Meffenger on fpecial Occafions.

Pourveyance, is the Providing Corn, Fuel, Victual, and
other neceffaries for the King's
Houfe.

Purveyour, an Officer of the
King or Queen, that provideth Corn and other Victuals
for their Houfe.

Pous, a Grecian Meafure
of Length, containing one
Foot, 0875 decimal parts of
an Inch of our *Englifh* Meafure.

Pouffe, Peafe. *Spencer*.

Power, Ability, Force, Authority.

Power, in Algebra, is the
Refult or Product of a certain Number of Multiplications, where the Multiplyer, is the fame quantity, continually.

Power in *Mechanicks*, is any
thing that is apply'd to any
Engine to move therewith any Weight.

Poynings Law, an Act of
Parliament, whereby the laws
of

of *England* became of force in *Ireland*, so called from Sir *Edward Poyning* then Lieutenant of *Ireland*.

Practicable, (Lat.) that may or can be done.

Practical, of or belonging to *practice*.

Practice, custom, use; or the actual Exercise of any Art or Science.

Practitioner, one that Practises in the Law.

Prædatory, belonging to Robbing, Pillaging, or Plundering.

Præpuce, the Fore-skin that covers the *Glans* of the Yard; also the fore-part of the *Clitoris*.

Pretorian, belonging to a *Prætor*. See *Pretor*.

Pragmatical, over-busy in other Mens Affairs, Saucy, Arrogant.

Prance, is for a Horse to tread loftily and wantonly.

Prank, an unlucky Trick.

Pratique, the same as *Practick*; also among the Merchants a Licence to Traffick.

Pravity, (Lat.) crookedness, deformity, naughtiness, a Corruption of Manners.

Preamble, (Lat.) a Prologue, or Preface.

Prebend, originally an Endowment in Land, or Pension Money given to a Cathedral or Conventual Church *in Prebendam*, that is for the maintenance of a secular Priest, or Regular Canon, who was a *Prebendary*, as supported by the said *Prebend*.

Precarious, got by Favour, or held at another's Will and Pleasure.

Precaution, a Forewarning, a Caution given or taken beforehand.

Precedaneous, that which goes before.

Precede, (Lat.) to go before, or excel.

Precedent, (Lat.) going before; also an Example.

Prece partium, in Law, is the continuance of a Suit by the consent of both parties.

Precellency, Excellency above another thing.

Precentor, he that begins the Tune in a Cathedral.

Precept, (Lat.) Instruction; In Law, it is sometimes taken for a Command in Writing sent out by a Justice of Peace, for the bringing of a person or Records before him; sometimes it signifies the Provocation whereby one Man incites another to commit a Felony as Theft, Murder, &c.

Preceptive, belonging to Precepts.

Preceptor, a Tutor, a Master, a Teacher.

Precession, (Lat.) an Advancing, or going before.

Precinct, a certain parcel of Land encompassed with some River, Hedge, &c. to distinguish it from other Lands; or a particular Jurisdiction comprehending several Parishes.

Precious, (Lat.) of great Price or Value.

Precipice,

Precipice, (Lat.) a steep Place dangerous to go upon, a down-right pitch or fall.

Precipitant, rash, unadvised, dangerous.

Precipitate, (Lat.) to hurl or cast down headlong, to do unadvisedly or rashly. This Name is also given by Chymical Writers to the Mercury dissolved in Acid *Menstruums*, and then afterwards precipitated down to the bottom in Form of a fine Powder.

Precipitation, in Chymistry, is the falling down of the Particles of any Metalline or Mineral Body, which are kept suspended in that *Menstruum* which dissolved it, by the pouring in of some *Alkalizate*, or other contrary Liquor, more easie for the *Menstruum* to dissolve.

Precise, stiff, formal, exact, particular, scrupulous.

Precisian, one that is over scrupulous in point of Religion.

Precognition, fore-knowledge, or knowing beforehand.

Preconceived, conceived, or taken up before-hand; as a preconceived Opinion, &c.

Precontract, a Contract made before another, or a former Bargain.

Precursor, (Lat.) a forerunner.

Predatory, (Lat.) of, or belonging to robbing.

Predecessor, (Lat.) he that was in Place or Office before one.

Predestinarian, (Lat.) one that believes *Predestination*.

Predestinate, to decree or ordain what shall come after.

Predestination, (Lat.) a preappointing, a fore-ordaining, or designing before what shall come after.

Predetermin, to determine before-hand.

Predial Tithes, are those which are paid of things arising and growing from the Ground only.

Predicable, in Logick, is a common Word or Term that may be attributed to more than one thing.

Predicament, in Logick, is a certain Class, or determinate Series or Order in which simple Terms or Words are ranged; of these they usually account 10 Heads, *viz.* Substance, Accident, Quantity, Quality, Relation, Action, Passion, the Situation of the Bodies as to Place, their Duration as to Time, and their Habit or External Appearance. In the Vulgar Sense to be in the same Predicament, is to be in the same State or Condition.

Predicant, (Lat.) Preach-ching; as *Predicant Friers*, i. e. such as are allowed to Preach.

Predicate, the latter Term of a Logical Proposition.

Predicate, (Lat.) to publish, to tell openly, also to affirm any thing of a Subject.

Prediction,

Prediction, (Lat.) a Fore-telling of things to come.

Predispose, to dispose before-hand.

Predominant, (Lat.) bearing chief sway, or Over-ruling.

Predominate, (Lat.) to over-rule.

Predy, a Sea Term, signifying the same with ready.

Pre-elected, elected or chosen before-hand.

Pre-eminence, great Honour, Prerogative, a right of Excellency, account before, place above another.

Pre-eminent, Eminent above the rest, or above others.

Pre-emption, (Lat.) a first Buying, or Buying before others.

Pre-engagement, an Engagement before-hand.

Pre-exist, to exist, or have a Being before.

Pre-existence, is an existing before.

Preface, (Lat.) a Prologue, a preparatory Speech, or Discourse which shews the Design of a Book, &c.

Prefatory, like a Preface, or in the Form of a Preface.

Prefecture, (Lat.) the Government or chief Rule of a City or Province.

Prefer, (Lat.) to esteem above, to promote or advance; to bring in.

Preference, a choice of one before another.

Preferable to be preferred or made choice of before another.

Prefigure, to represent by Figure afore-hand.

Prefix, to fix or place before, to appoint before-hand.

Pregnancy, (Lat.) a being pregnant, or great with Child; also subtilty, acuteness. And *Pregnant* frequently signifies of a Prompt and ready Wit.

Pregustation, (Lat.) a fore-tasting.

Prelection, (Lat.) a Lecture; a publick Discourse on an Art or Science.

Prejudication, a judging before-hand; whence comes the Word

Prejudice, which properly speaking, is a rash Judgment before the Matter be duly weighed, considered of, or heard; a being prepossessed; also an Injury or Damage.

Prejudicial, disadvantageous or hurtful.

Prelate, a dignified Clergyman, as an Arch-Bishop, or Bishop.

Prelibation, (Lat.) a Fore-taste.

Preliminary, Prefatory, or set at the entrance; as a *Preliminary* Discourse, &c.

Prelude, (Lat.) a Flourish of Musick before the Playing of a Tune, or an entrance into a Business.

Preludious, preparatory.

Premature, (Lat.) ripe before due Time and Season, untimely, coming too soon.

Premeditate, (Lat.) to think of before-hand.

Premise, (Lat.) to speak of before by way of Preface.

H h h   *Premises*,

Premises, what was just spoken of, rehearsed or mention'd before.

Premium, (Lat.) a Reward; amongst the Merchants it is that Sum of Money which the Insured gives the Insurer for the Insuring the safe return of any Ship or Merchandise.

Premonish, to forewarn.

Premonstratenses, an Order of White Friers, observing St. *Augustine*'s Rule.

Premunire, is the Punishment of the Statute of *Premunire,* by which the Usurpations of the Pope, and other Abuses were restrained; the Penalty was Banishment, Forfeiture of Lands, Goods, Chattels, &c. Hence to incur a *Premunire,* is to involve one's self in Trouble.

Premunition, (Lat.) a Fortifying or Fencing before-hand.

Prender, is the Power or Right of taking a thing before it is offered.

Prender de Baron, is usually taken in Law for an Exception, to disable a Woman from pursuing an Appeal of Murder against the Killer of her former Husband.

Prenomination, (Lat.) a Naming before.

Prenotion, (Lat.) a foreknowing of a thing, foreknowledge.

Pre-occupation, a Possessing before-hand; a seizing before-hand; also a preventing.

Pre-ordain, to ordain before-hand.

Preparation, a preparing, or making ready before-hand; also Provision made for some Design or Enterprize.

Prepensed, (Fr.) fore-thought, premeditated; as prepensed Malice.

Preponderate, (Lat.) to outweigh; or be of greater Importance.

Preposition, (Lat.) i. e. a putting before; also a part of Speech in Grammer.

Prepossess, to prejudice, or perswade one into Opinions, without giving him leave to judge whether they be right or no.

Preposterous, the Order of which is inverted; topsy-turvey, or having the wrong end forward.

Prepuce. See *Prapuce.*

Prerogative, a peculiar Preeminence or Authority above others, or a special Priviledge.

Prerogative Court, is the Court wherein all Wills are proved, and all Administrations taken that belong to the Arch-Bishop by his *Prerogative.*

Presage, (Lat.) to apprehend before-hand, Divine, Fore-tell or Betoken.

Presbyter, a lay-Elder, the Parish Priest in opposition to the Chaplain or Curate.

Presbytery, the Church-Government, or Principles of the Presbyterians.

Presbyterians, a Sect of Christians, who assert that the Government

vernment of the Church appointed in the New Testament is by Presbyters, that is Ministers and Ruling Elders, and that there is no Order in the Church Superiour to that of a Presbyter, and that all Ministers being Ambassadors of Christ, are equal by their Commission.

Prescience, (Lat.) fore-knowledge.

Prescind, (Lat.) to cut before, to divide or break first.

Prescribe, to order, appoint, or limit.

Prescription, (Lat.) appointment or limitation; also a Claim upon account of long possession.

Presentation, in Law, is the Act of a Patron, offering his Clerk to the Bishop to be instituted in a Benefit of his Gift.

Presentee, the Clerk so presented.

Presentment, a mere denunciation of the Jurors or other Officers, without information of an Offence inquirable in that Court.

Preservation, (Lat.) a keeping or saving.

Preservative, a preserving Remedy, or a Remedy made use of to keep off a threatning Disease.

Preside, (Lat.) to have Authority or Rule, to have the Protection and Tuition of any thing; to be chief in an Assembly.

Presidency, the Office or Dignity of a President.

President, a Governour or Overseer; also an Example or Instance.

Presidy, (Lat.) a Garrison or Succour.

Pressure, an urging Affliction, or Misfortune.

Prestation-money, Paid yearly by the Arch-deacons to their Bishops.

Prest-money, is earnest-money given to an Imprested Souldier or Sea-man.

Prestigiation, (Lat.) a juggling, or cousening.

Prestigious, (Lat.) deceitful.

Presto, (Span.) quickly.

Presumption, (Lat.) a taking upon one's self, a being proud or arrogant.

Presumptuous, proud, self-conceited.

Presuppose, to suppose before-hand.

Pretence, (Lat.) a Cloak or Colour for any thing.

Pretension, a Claim or Title to a thing.

Preterition, (Lat.) passing by.

Pretermission, (Lat.) an omitting, a leaving out, a letting a thing pass.

Preternatural, contrary to the Course of Nature; Extraordinary.

Pretor, was anciently the chief Ruler of any Province or Countrey subject to the *Roman* Empire; he had supream Authority not only in Military Affairs, but in Matters of Judicature.

Prevalent, powerful.

Prevaricate, (Lat.) to betray one's Cause to the Adversary, to play faft and loofe, to deceive.

Prevarication, (Lat.) deceit, double-dealing.

Preventer-Rope, (Sea-Term) a fmall Rope made faft over the *Ties* to fecure the Yards.

Primæval, (Lat.) of ancient Time.

Primary, (Lat.) chief, principal.

Previous, that leads the way, or goes before.

Priefe, Proof. *Spencer*.

Prier, one that fearches into other mens Bufinefs.

Prieft, (Heb.) one that is fet apart to offer Sacrifices, and perform other facred Rites. Among Chriftians, a Clergyman next in Dignity to a Bifhop, whofe Office it is to teach and inftruct the People, committed to his Charge by the Bifhop of the Diocefs, in the whole Doctrine of Chriftianity as delivered in the Scriptures.

Prieft-hood, the Order or Office of a Prieft.

Primacy, the Office and Dignity of a Primate.

Primage, a Duty paid to the Mariners for the loading of a Ship, at the fetting forth from any Haven.

Primate, or *Metropolitan*, the firft or chief Arch-Bifhop.

Prime, (Lat.) firft chief.

Prime Numbers, in Arithmetick, are thofe which have no other common Meafure befides Unity, as 8, 15, &c.

Prime of the Moon, is the *New Moon* at her firft appea-

ring, or about three Days after the Change, when fhe is faid to be *primed*.

Primigenious, (Lat.) firft in its kind, Original.

Priming Iron, an Iron made ufe of in Priming of a great Gun.

Primitive, (Lat.) of, or belonging to the firft Age.

Primogeniture, (Lat.) the Firft-birth; alfo a being Eldeft or Firft-Born.

Primordial, (Lat.) of, or belonging to the firft beginning.

Primum Mobile, in the *Ptolemaick* Aftronomy, is the outermoft Sphere, or the fartheft from the Center, containing all the other Spheres within it, and giving Motion to them, from whence its Name, turning its felf, and them quite round in the fpace of 24 hours.

Principal, the chief or head.

Principal, in common Law, is the fame with *Heirloome*.

Principality, the Dominions of a Prince; alfo one of the Orders of Angels.

Principles, in Sciences, are common or felf-evident Notions; in *Mathematicks*, there are reckoned three forts; *Definitions, Axioms*, and *Poftulates*, which fee.

Printing, this Art was firft invented, as fome fay by *Lawrence Cofter* of *Haerlem*, or as others fay by *John Guttembarg* of *Strasburg*, and was brought very early into *England* by *Caxton* and *Tourner*, whom K. *Henry* 6th. fent on purpofe to learn it. One of the firft printed red Books now Extant is *Tully's Offices*, 1465 kept in the *Bodleian* Library at *Oxford*.

Prior, the Head of a Priory.

Prioress; a Nun next in Order to an Abbess.

Priority, (Lat.) a being before. In Law, it is an Antiquity of Tenure in comparison of another not so Ancient, as to hold by Priority, is to hold of a Lord more anciently than of another.

Priorship, the Office and Quality of a Prior.

Priory, a sort of Benefice; also a Monastery.

Prisage, the King's Custom, or share of Lawful Prizes, which is usually $\frac{1}{15}th$.

Priscillianists, certain Christian Hereticks, Followers of one *Priscillian* a *Spaniard*, who besides those of the *Gnosticks*, taught several other Errors.

Prise, (Fr.) the Act of taking; also a Prize.

Prism, in Geometry, is a solid Body that has two Bases Equal and Parallel one to another.

Pristine, (Lat.) ancient, accustomed, wonted or former.

Privacy, secresie.

Privado, (Span.) a private Friend.

Privateer, a Pirate-ship.

Privation, (Lat.) a depriving, or taking away; lack or want.

Privative, (Lat.) that deprives, or takes away.

Privilege, (i. e. a private or particular Law) a special Prerogative or Preheminence,

or a particular Advantage which a Private Man or a particular Corporation enjoys above others.

Privity, private knowledge.

Privy, Secret, particular, conscious of, or accessory to.

Privy Seal, a Seal the King useth to such Grants as pass the Great Seal, and sometimes in things of less moment that never come to the Great Seal.

Probability, (Lat.) likelyhood, appearance of truth. Mr. *Lock* defines it to be the appearance of the Agreement or disagreement of two Ideas, by the Intervention of Proofs whose connexion is not constant and immutable, or at least is not perceived to be so, but is, or appears for the most part to be so, and is enough to induce the Mind to judge the Proposition to be true or false, rather than the contrary.

Probate of *Testaments*, proving of Wills in the Spiritual Court, either in common form by the Executors Oath, or, to avoid future debate, by Witnesses also.

Probation, (Lat.) a proving or trying; as of those who are about to take a degree in the Univerfity.

Probationer, a Schollar that undergoes a Probation.

Probator, in Law, is an Accusor, or one who undertakes to prove a Crime charged upon another.

Probe, a Surgeon's Instrument to search a Wound.

Probity, uprightnefs, honefty.

Problem, is a Propofition which relates to Practice, or which propofes fomething to be done; as to biffect a given Line, to draw a Circle thro' any 3 Points given.

Problematical, belonging to a Problem.

Procacity, (Lat.) Malepertnefs, Saucinefs.

Procatarctick, (Gr.) which foregoeth, or gives beginning to another, or which is outwardly impulfive to action.

Procerity, (Lat.) Heigth, Talnefs, Length.

Procefs, (Lat.) the manner of proceeding in every Caufe, whether Perfonal or Real, Civil or Criminal. In Chymiftry, *Procefs*, is the whole exact Courfe of any Operation or Experiment ; alfo the continued Order of things.

Proceffion, (Lat.) a proceeding, a going on ; a folemn March of the Clergy and People in the *Romifh* Church ; alfo the Vifitation of the Bounds of a Parifh in *Rogation Week*, performed by the Minifter, fome of the Principal Inhabitants and Children.

Proceffional, pertaining to procefs, proceeding, or Proceffion.

Proceffum continuando, a Writ for the continuing of a Procefs after the Death of the Chief Juftice, &c.

Prochein amy, in common Law, fignifies him that is next of Kin to a Child in his Nonage, and is in that refpect allowed by the Law, to deal for him, manage his Affairs for him, &c.

Prochronifm, (Gr.) an Error in Chronology, or the computation of time, and is a fetting things down before the real time they happened in.

Procidence, (Lat.) a falling down of a thing out of its place.

Prociduous, that falls out of his place.

Procidentia Ani, is a falling out of the lower end of the *Rectum Inteftinum*, and is very ufual in Children.

Procidentia uteri, is a relaxing of the inner Tunick of the *Vagina* of the Womb.

Proclamation, is a notice publickly given of any thing whereof the King thinks fit to advertife his Subjects.

Proclamation of a Fine, is a notice given openly and folemnly, at all the Affizes in the Country within one Year after the Engroffing it.

Proclamation of Rebellion, is a proclaiming publickly that a Man fhall be reputed a Rebel, unlefs he render himfelf by a Day affigned.

Proclivity, (Lat.) an aptnefs, propenfity, or, Inclination to a thing.

Proconful, a *Roman* Magiftrate fent to govern a Province with Confular Power.

Procraftinate, (Lat.) to put off from Day to Day, to delay or defer.

Procreation, (Lat.) a begetting, or bringing forth.

Proctor, one that undertakes to manage a Cause in the Ecclesiastical Court.

Proctors of the Clergy, Deputies chosen by the Clergy of every Diocess to sit in the Lower-house of Convocation.

Procuracy, the Deed or Writing whereby one is made a Procurator.

Procuration, a Power by which one is intrusted to act for another.

Procurator, (Lat.) a Factor or Sollicitor, one that looks to another man's Affairs; also he that gathers the Fruits of a Benefice for another Man.

Procuratory, the Instrument whereby any Person constitutes or appoints his Proctor to represent him in any Court or Cause.

Prodigal, lavish, wastful, riotous.

Prodigious, contrary to the Course of Nature, Monstrous, Excessive.

Prodigy, a wonderful and unnatural accident or thing.

Prodromus, a fore-runner;

Prodromus morbus, is a Disease that fore-runs a greater, as the straitness of the Breast, predicts a Consumption.

Produce, the same as *Product*; also verbally to draw out.

Product, the Quantity arising from, or *Produced* by the Multiplication of two or more Numbers or Lines one by another,

Production, (Lat.) a bringing forth or lengthening.

Productive, capable of bringing forth, or apt to bring forth.

Proem, (Gr.) a Preface, or a beginning any Matter.

Proecthosis, (Gr.) in Rhetorick is a Figure, by which the Speaker produces a Reason to clear or defend himself.

Profanation, (Lat.) an unhallowing or polluting, or turning holy things to common use.

Professed Monk, or Nun, one that having made the Vow, is admitted of a Religious Order.

Profane, (Lat.) unholy, wicked, unhallowed, not sacred.

Profession, (Lat.) a declaring openly, a protesting, acknowledging, owning; also the Condition of Life; or calling a Man is of.

Professor, a Publick Reader in an University, or College.

Professorship, the Office of a Professor.

Proffer, Offer, Attempt. In a Law sense, the Time for taking the Accounts of Sheriffs, and other Officers in the Exchequer, viz. twice a Year.

Proficient, (Lat.) one that has made a good progress in any Art or Science.

Profil, in Painting signifies properly a Head or Face set sideways, which, as on Coins, is said to be *in Profil*, or sideview. Also a Draught representing the Breadth, Depth, and Heigth of a Building or

Fortification, but not the Length. Also improperly 'tis taken for the Out-lines of any Figure.

Profit, (Fr.) Gain, Advantage, Interest.

Profitable, beneficial, useful.

Profligate, (Lat.) wicked, lew'd, or debauch'd to an high Degree.

Profluence, (Lat.) a flowing plentifully, abundance, store of.

Profound, (Lat.) deep; also great or eminent.

Profundity, (Lat.) depth, deepness.

Profundus Musculus, a Muscle that bends the Fingers.

Profuse, (Lat.) lavish, wastful, riotous.

Profusion, (Lat.) lavishness, or a squandring away of Money.

Prog, to use all endeavours to get or to gain.

Progenitour, (Lat.) Ancestor, Forefather.

Progeny, (Lat.) on Offspring or Issue.

Prognosis, (Gr.) Fore-knowledge, Fore-boding: In *Physick*, 'tis the same as *Prognostick Sign*; which see.

Prognosticate, (Lat.) to foretell things to come.

Prognostication, a Foretelling, or Conjecturing.

Prognosticks, (Lat.) Signs or Tokens of something to come.

Program, (Gr.) an Edict or Proclamation set up in a publick Place. Also a Bill

posted up, or delivered by Hand to give notice of something to be performed in a College.

Progress, (Lat.) a proceeding, or going forward in any undertaking.

Progression, (Lat.) a going on; In Mathematicks it is a Consequence or Train of Quantities, which follow one another, and keep a certain reason or proportion among themselves.

Progression Arithmetical, is a Consequence or Train of Numbers, or other Quantities in continued Arithmetical Proportion; which is when they proceed by equal Differences, increasing or decreasing.

Progression Geometrical, is a like Train of Numbers or Quantities in Geometrical Proportion continued, which is when they proceed by equal *Ratio's*, whether increasing or decreasing.

Progressive, that goes on.

Prohibition, (Lat.) a forbiding or hindring.

Prohibitory, that prohibits, forbids or hinders.

Project, any thing thrown or cast with a force; also a Contrivance.

Projectile, the same as project, any thing thrown or cast with a force.

Projection, in Chymistry, is putting any matter to be *calcined*, or *fulminated* into the Crucible, Spoonful by Spoonful.

Projection

Projection of the Sphere, is a deſcribing of the Lines and Circles of the Sphere, or ſo many of them as is requiſite *in plano*, or on a flat ſurface.

Projection Orthographick, ſee *Orthographick Projection*.

Powder of Projection, a ſort of Matter much boaſted of by ſome Alchymiſts, pretending to have the Philoſophers Stone, who ſay 'tis the Seed of Gold it ſelf, which it will multiply, ſome ſmall quantity being uſed for that Purpoſe.

Projection Gnomonick, is where the Plain of Projection is parallel to a great Circle of the Sphere, the Eye being ſuppoſed to be in the Center of the Earth.

Projectour, one that Projects, or Contrives any Deſign.

Projecture, in Architecture, is the Jutting or Leaning out of any Part of a Building, the coping of a Wall, &c.

Pro in diviſo, is a Poſſeſſion of Lands or Tenements, belonging to two or more Perſons, whereof none knows his ſeveral Portion.

Prolegomena, preparatory Diſcourſes, which the Reader ought firſt to be acquainted with, the better to underſtand any Book or Science.

Prolepſis, (Gr.) a Figure by which we prevent what might be objected by the Adverſary.

Prolepticus, is a Diſeaſe always anticipating, or ſeizing the Patient ſooner the next Day than it did the Day before.

Prolific, (Lat.) apt to breed, or fit for Generation; Fruitful.

Prolix, (Lat.) long; tedious or large in Speech.

Prolixity, (Lat.) tediouſneſs, or length of a Diſcourſe.

Prolocutor, (Lat.) one that Speaks out, or at length; alſo the Speaker or Chair-man of each Convocation-houſe, or of a Synod.

Prologue, (Gr.) a Preface, a Speech before a Play.

Prolongation, a delaying, lengthning or ſpinning out of a thing.

Promenade, (Fr.) a Walk in the Fields.

Prometheus, (Gr.) a certain Conſtellation or Cluſter of Stars.

Prominence, the jutting or ſtanding out of any thing.

Promiſcuous, (Lat.) mingled together, or confuſed.

Promiſe, (Lat.) a verbal aſſurance to do any thing.

Promiſſory, belonging to a Promiſe.

Promontory, (*quaſi mons in mare prominens*) a high Hill lying out a great way into the Sea.

Promoters, are ſuch as (for reward) complain of Offenders.

Promotion, Preferment, Advancement.

Prompt, (Lat.) ready, or quick in doing of a thing. *Verbally*, to tell or whiſper, to put one upon.   *Prompti-*

Promptitude, (Lat.) Readiness, Quickness.

Promptuary, (Lat.) a Storehouse, a Buttery.

Promulgation, (Lat.) the Act of Promulging.

Promulge, (Lat.) to noise abroad, to publish or proclaim.

Pronaos, (Lat.) a Term used in Architecture for a Church-Porch, or a *Portico* to a Pallace or spacious Building.

Prone, (Lat.) bending forward, or hanging the Face downwards; also inclined to.

Pronominal, (Lat.) belonging to a Pronoun.

Pronotary, see *Protonotary*.

Pronoun, one of the Grammatical Parts of Speech, which is set before, or stands for a Noun.

Pronunciation, (Lat.) utterance of speech, speaking out, one's delivery.

Propagate, (Lat.) to cause to multiply or increase, to spread abroad.

Propagation, (Lat.) a spreading abroad, or encreasing; also the Generation and Multiplication of Creatures.

Propelled, (Lat.) driven or thrust afar off or forwards.

Propense, prone, inclinable to.

Propensity, (Lat.) an Inclination of Mind, readiness, proneness.

Proper, peculiar, fit, convenient, tall, &c.

Proper Fraction, (in Arith.) is a Fraction less than Unity.

Proper Navigation, is the Guiding of a Ship to a proposed Harbour, where the Voyage is perform'd in the vast Ocean.

Property, the highest Right a Man can have to any thing; also Quality.

Prophasis, is a Fore-knowledge in Diseases, also an Occasion or antecedent Cause.

Prophesy, to tell of things to come, or to expound divine Mysteries.

Prophet, (Gr.) one that foretells future Events; a Person ordain'd by God to reveal his Will, warn of approach-Judgments', expound Scriptures, &c.

Prophetical or *Prophetick*, of or belonging to Prophesy.

Prophylattica, is a Part of Physick called *Hygieina*, which gives notice of future and imminent Diseases.

Propinquity, (Lat.) nearness, nighness.

Propitiate, to atone, pacify or appease.

Propitious, (Lat.) favourable, kind, merciful.

Proplasm, a Mould in which any Metal or soft Matter is Cast.

Proplastice, the Art of making Moulds for casting any thing.

Proportion, in Mathematicks, is a similitude or likeness of *Ratio's*, and is either *Geometrical*, *Arithmetical*, or *Harmonical*.

Proportion Geometrical, is a similitude of Geometrical *Ratio's*; thus these 4 Numbers, bers,

bers, 2, 4, 8, 16, are in Geometrick Proportion, becaufe the *Ratio* of 2 to 4, is the fame with that of 8 to 16.

Proportion Arithmetical, is a fimilitude of Arithmetical *Ratio's*; thus, 3, 7, 9, 13, are in Arithmetick Proportion, becaufe the Arithmetick *Ratio* of 3 to 7, is the fame with that of 9 to 13, the Excefs in each being 4.

Proportion Harmonick, is that wherein the firft Term is to the laft in a Geometrick *ratio*, equal to that of the difference of the two firft to the difference of the two laft.

Proportionable, agreeable to the Rules of Proportion.

Propofition, is a thing propofed to be proved, made out or demonftrated; alfo any thing that is predicated of any Subject.

Propound, (Lat.) to fet on foot, or propofe.

Proprietary or *Proprietor*, an Owner, or one that has a property in a thing.

Proptofis, (Gr.) is the falling down of fome part; as of the Eye, the Cawle, &c.

Prorogation, a deferring or putting off, efpecially faid of a Seffion of Parliament, put off by the King or Queen to a certain Time; in which Cafe all Bills pafs'd in either, or both Houfes, that have not had the Royal Affent, muft begin again at the next meeting. 'Tis not fo in an Adjournment.

Prorogue, to put off till another time.

Profaick, in Profe, or belonging to it.

Profcribe, (Lat.) to banifh, to outlaw one; alfo to fequefter and feize one's Eftate; alfo to poft up in Writing and publifh any thing to be fold.

Profcription, (Lat.) a Banifhment, Outlawry; a Confifcation and Sequeftring of Goods, and fetting them to publick Sale.

Profecute, (Lat.) to carry on a Defign, to Sue one at Law.

Profecution, Purfuit, Continuance.

Profelyte, (Gr.) a Stranger converted to our Religion.

Profodia, (Gr.) that part of Grammer which teaches to Accent right, or rightly to diftinguifh Syllables into long and fhort.

Profopopeia, (Gr.) a violent Rhetorical Figure wherein the Speaker addreffes himfelf to things inanimate, as if they were living, and makes them fpeak as if they had Souls.

Profpect, a View afar off, a Defign or Aim.

Profpective Glafs, a Glafs fet in a Frame, to view things at a diftance.

Profphyfis, (Gr.) a growing together; as when two Fingers grow into one.

Proftapherefis, in Aftronomy, is the difference between the true and mean Motion of the Planets.

Proftata, a Term in Anatomy, is a Conglomerate Gland

Gland fituated at the neck of the Bladder.

Profternation, (Lat.) an O-verthrowing, a beating or ftriking down.

Proftitute, (Lat.) to 'expofe, or fet open to every one that comes.

Proftitute, taken Subftan-tively, fignifies a *common Har-lot*.

Proftitution, a Harlot's let-ting out the Ufe of her Body for Hire.

Proftomia, the red-tin-ctured part of the Lips.

Proftrate, (Lat.) laid flat, along.

Proftrate, to throw one's felf down, or caft down to the Ground.

Proftration, (Lat.) a lay-ing flat along; a falling at one's Feet.

Protection,, (Lat.) a Guar-ding or being guarded.

Protervity, (Lat.) Peevifh-nefs, Waywardnefs, Froward-nefs.

Proteft, a Declaration a-gainft a party, for non-Pay-ment of a Bill of Exchange.

Proteftantifm, the Prote-ftant, or the Reformed Reli-gion.

Proteftants, Profeffours of the Reformed Religion, fo called becaufe they publickly pro-tefted to appeal from the Emperour *Charles* V. 's De-crees, to a General Council; which was made at *Spires* in *Germany*, A. D. 1529.

Proteftation, a free Decla-ration of one's Mind,

Proteus, a Sea-Deity, feig-ned by the Poets to change himfelf into what Shape he pleafed.

Protocol, the firft Draught of a Deed, Contract, or In-ftrument.

Protomartyr, (Gr.) the firft Martyr, or Witnefs, as *Abel* in the Old Teftament, and *St. Stephen* in the New.

Protonotary, a chief Scribe or Secretary; a chief Clerk of the King's Bench and Common-pleas; the former of which Records all civil a-ctions in that Court; as thofe in the Common-pleas (who are three in Number) enter and enroll all Declarati-ons, Pleadings, Affifes, Re-cognizances, in the fame Court, and make out all Ju-dicial Writs.

Protopathia, (Gr.) a Pri-mary Difeafe not caufed by another.

Protoplaft, (Gr.) firft for-med or made; alfo the firft framer of all things.

Prototype, (Gr.) an Ori-ginal *Type*, or firft pattern.

Protract, (Lat.) to delay or prolong.

Protractor, a Mathemati-cal Inftrument to lay down Angles.

Protraction, a putting off, deferring, or delaying.

Protrude, (Lat.) to thruft or pufh forwards.

Protuberance, (Lat.) a ri-fing or fwelling out; alfo the Procefs of a Bone.

Protuberant, (Lat.) swelling or bunching out.

Proveditor, (Ital.) *i. e.* a Provider, is a great Military Officer in *Italy.*

Provender, (Fr.) Food for Cattel.

Proverb, (Lat.) a common, or old saying.

Proverbial, (Lat.) belonging to a *Proverb,* that is, an old pithy saying.

Provide, (Lat.) to furnish with, to take care of, to prepare.

Providence, (Lat.) foresight, or fore cast ; more especially the fore-sight of God and his Government, of all created Beings.

Provident, having good fore-cast, wary, saving.

Providential, belonging to, or happening by Divine Providence.

Province, (Lat.) a considerable part of a Country; also the Jurisdiction of an Archbishop.

Provincial, (Lat.) of, or belonging to a Province ; also (amongst Friers) the chief of their Order in such a Province.

Provining, (Fr.) the Setting of Vine Branches in the Ground, to take Root.

Provision, any thing got or procured, which is necessary for the Subsistance of Life.

Proviso, (Ital.) a Caveat or Condition made in any Writing, without the Performance of which, the Writing becomes void.

Provocation, (Lat.) an incensing, urging, stirring up, or exciting.

Provocative, apt to provoke, or stir up.

Provost, (Fr.) a President of a College, a chief Magistrate of a City, &c.

Provost Marshal, an Officer for seizing and securing Deserters, and other Criminals, as also to set Rates on Provisions in the Army. Also an Officer in the Royal Navy, who has care of Prisoners taken at Sea.

Provostship, a Provost's Office or Dignity.

Prow, the fore-part of a Ship, that part of the forecastle which is Aloft and not in the Hold.

Prowess, (Fr.) Valour, a Valiant Act, an Exploit.

Prowl, to go about Pilfering, to gape for Gain.

Proximity, nearness, Neighbourhood, Kindred, Alliance.

Proxy, one that does the part of another, or acts for him in his absence.

Prudence, a Vertue which teaches us to act with deliberation and advice.

Prudential, partaking of Prudence.

Prune, to cut off superfluous Branches, or Roots from Trees. Also when a Hawk picks her self, she is said to *Prune.*

Pruni-

Pruniferous Trees, are such whose Fruit has a Stone in the middle.

Prurient, (Lat.) Itching, or having an Itching desire.

Prutenick Tables, certain Astronomical Tables for finding the Motions of Heavenly Bodies.

Psalm, (Gr.) a Hymn upon sacred Subjects.

Psalmody, (Gr.) a singing of Psalms; a Singing and Playing on a Musical Instrument.

Psalmography, (Gr.) a writing of Psalms.

Psalter, (Gr.) a Collection of *David*'s Psalms, a Book of Psalms.

Psaltery, (Gr.) a kind of Musical Instrument with ten Strings, somewhat like a Harp, but more pleasant.

Psammismus, a Bath of dry and warm Sand, to dry the Feet of Dropsical Persons.

Pseudodipteron, an ancient Form of a Temple, surrounded with one Row of Pillars only, though placed at the usual distance of 2 Rows of Pillars.

Pseudography, (Lat.) false-writing, a Counterfeit Hand.

Pseudology, (Gr.) a false speaking, or lying.

Pseudonymous, Gr. that has a Counterfeit Name.

Pseudo-Stella, (Gr.)(Lat.) in Astronomy, is a kind of Comet or *Phænomenon*, newly appearing in the Heavens like a Star.

Pseudo - Martyr, (Gr.) a false-witness, a counterfeit Martyr.

Psoropthalmy, (Gr.) an Inflammation of the Eyes with Itching.

Psyllica, are cooling Medicines against the Scab.

Ptarmica, are Medicines which cause sneezing.

Ptisana, a kind of cooling drink made of Barley, Liquorish, Raisins, &c. good for People in a Fever.

Ptylosis, a Disease when the Brims of the Eye-lids being grown thick, the Hairs of the Eye-brows fall off.

Publican, a Farmer of publick Revenues, Customs or Rents.

Publication. (Lat.) a making publick, or giving open notice of a thing.

Pucker, to shrink up, or lie uneven.

Pucelage, (Fr.) Virginity, Maiden-head.

Pudder, Noise, Bustle.

Puddings, are Ropes nailed to the Arms of the Main and *Fore-yards*, near the Ends, at some distances from one another, whose use is to save the Robbins from galling, or wearing upon the Yards when the Top-Sails are haled home.

Pudicæ Plantæ, the same with sensitive Plants.

Pudicity, (Lat.) Chastity, Modesty.

Puerile, boyish, childish,

Puerility, (Lat.) Childishness, Boyishness.

Puer-

Puerperial, belonging to Childbirth.

Pugil, a handful; or according to some as much as may be taken up between the Thumb and 2 Fingers.

Puisne, the Lawyers Term for younger.

Puissant, (Fr.) powerful or mighty.

Puissance, (Fr.) Power, Force, Might.

Pullet, is a Room within the Hold of a Ship, in which Pigs of Lead, or such like weighty things are put, to Ballast the Ship, without the loss of much Room.

Puling, sickly, weakly, crasy.

Pulley, one of the Mechanick Powers, a well known Instrument.

Pulley-piece, an Armour for the Knee; also that Part of a Boot which covers the Knee.

Pullulate, (Lat.) to spring up, or bud forth; to encrease, to multiply.

Pulmonary, (Lat.) belonging to the Lungs.

Pulpit, (Lat.) the higher part of the Stage on which the Musicians were; also a Desk to Preach, or make an Oration in.

Pulp, the Fleshy part of Fruits, Roots, or other Bodies.

Pulse, in Natural Philosophy, is the Stroak with which any Medium is affected by the Motion of *Light*, *Sound*, &c. also a General Name for all sorts of Grain, which are contained in Cods, Husks, Shells, &c.

Pulsion, (Lat.) a driving, or impelling of any thing forward.

Pulverisation, (Lat.) a reducing to Powder.

Pulverulent, (Lat.) full of dust or Powder, dusty.

Pump-Brake, at Sea, is the Handle of the Pump.

Pumpe's-can, is the Bucket whereby they pour Water into the Pump, to fetch it, and make it work when 'tis to be used.

Pump's-vale, the *Trough* by which the Water runs from the Pump along the Ship's sides.

Pun, to quibble, or play with Words.

Punchion, an *English* Measure of Capacity, a Wine Measure, containing 1¼ Hogshead, or 84 Gallons.

Punctilio, (Ital. a little point,) a nice Point; also a thing of no moment, an insignificant trifle.

Punctual, that does a thing as it were to a Point given.

Punctuation, the Method of Pointing, and making stops in Writing.

Puncture, a Prick, or Pricking.

Pundbrech, (Sax.) an unlawful taking of Cattel out of the Pound.

Pundle, an ill shap'd and ill dressed Creature; as, *she is a very Pundle*.

Pungency, Pricking, or Sharpness.

Pungent,

Pungent, (Lat.) sharp, pricking.

Punic, of, or belonging to the *Carthaginians*.

Punic Faith, Falshood, Perjury, which the *Carthaginians* were greatly guilty of.

Puny, (from the Fr. *Puisne*) younger, born after.

Pupil, (Lat.) the Apple of the Eye ; also an Orphan under age, or the Disciple of a College-Tutor.

Punctum Saliens, is a little Cloud, or Speck in an Egg, out of which the *Embrio* is formed.

Purchase, at Sea, signifies to draw in.

Pure, (Lat.) simple, uncompounded, chaste, clean, downright.

Purfle, a sort of Trimming for Womens Gowns ; also an Ornament about the edges of Musical Instruments, such as Viols, Violins, &c.

Purflew, (in *Heraldry*,) to express *Ermines, Peans*, or any other Furrs, when they make up a Border round a Coat of Arms. Thus 'tis said, *he bears Gules a Bordure purflew verry*, meaning that the Furr of the Bordure is *Verry*.

Purgation, (Lat.) a clearing one's self of a Crime.

Purgative, that has a cleansing Faculty.

Purgatory, a Purgation, or State of Cleansing or Purging; an imaginary Place of Purgation for the Souls of the Faithful, according to the *Roman Catholick* Creed.

Purge, to cleanse the Body from ill Humours by Medicines ; also to clear one's self.

Purification, a purifying, cleansing or refining ; to purify a Mettal, is to purge or cleanse it from the mixture of all other Mettals.

Purificatory, a Linnen-Cloth, with which the *Romish* Priest wipes the *Chalice*.

Purify, to make pure or clean ; also to separate the impurer from the purer Mettals.

Puritans, a Nick-name imposed on the Dissenters from the Church of *England*.

Purloin, (Fr.) to pilfer or steal.

Purlue, (Fr.) all that space that is severed by Perambulations from the Ancient Forest.

Purpure, or *Purple*, in *Heraldry*, a Colour consisting of much Red, and a little Black : In the Coats of Noblemen, it is called *Amethyst*, and *Mercury* in those of Sovereign Princes. 'Tis express'd in Engraving by Lines drawn athwart the Escutcheon,  beginning at the *Dexter Point*, thus,

Purport, Meaning, the Tenour or Substance of a writing.

Purser, is an Officer in a King's Ship, who has the Charge change of the Victual, receives it, takes care that it be good in Condition, and well lay'd and stowed. He keeps a *List* of the Ship's Company, and sets down exactly the days of each Man's admittance into pay, *&c.*

Pursevant, (Fr.) a King's Messenger upon special Occasions.

Pursuance, what follows, Consequence, a Pursuing.

Pursuant, following, according, or agreeable to.

Pursuit, running after; Diligence or Trouble to get any thing.

Pursy, over-fat, short or broken-winded.

Purvey, to provide.

Purveyance, the providing Corn, Fuel, Victuals, *&c.* for the King's House.

Purveyor, an Officer to whom is committed the Purveyance.

Purview, the Body of an Act of Parliament, beginning with, *Be it Enacted.*

Purulent, (Lat.) full of Corrupt Matter, Mattery.

Pusillanimity, (Lat.) Faintheartedness, want of Courage or Generosity.

Pusillanimous, (Lat.) Fainthearted, Cowardly.

Pustules, Blisters, Pushes.

Putage, (Fr.) Fornication on a Woman's side; Whoredom.

Putative, (Lat.) reputed, supposed, commonly taken for.

Putid, (Lat.) stinking, nasty; affected, unpleasant.

Putrefaction, (Lat.) a slow kind of Corruption of Bodies, wrought generally by the Air, or some other Fluids penetrating the Pores of Bodies, loosening and dislocating their Parts, and so altering their texture.

Putrid, (Lat.) rotten.

Putrify, to corrupt or rot, to grow rotten.

Puttocks, (a Term in Navigation,) are small *Shrouds* which go from the Main, Fore, and Missen-Masts to the Round-Top of those Masts; for where the *Shrouds* come near the Top, they fall in so much that one cou'd not get into the Top without the help of the Puttocks.

Putty, Powder of Calcin'd Tin; also a Composition used by Painters to fill up holes in Wood.

Puzzle, a Dirty Slut; also Difficulty or Trouble.

Pyebald, a Horse of two Colours, as some part White, and the others Bay, Iron-gray, or Dun-colour.

Pycnostyle, in Architecture, is a Building, the Pillars whereof stand so very close, that their distance from one another, is only a Diameter, and a half of the Column.

Pygmies, certain Fabulous People, said to be but from one to three Cubits high, and to be continually at War with the Cranes. Their Women

men have Children at five Years of Age, and are old at Eight.

Pylorus, (Gr.) the lower Orifice of the Ventricle, which lets the Meat out of the Stomach into the Inteſtines.

Pyramid, (Gr.) a ſolid Figure, terminated by Triangles, and ending in a Point at the *Vertex*, the Baſe whereof may be any Plane Rectilineal Figure.

Pyramidoid Parabolick, is a ſolid Figure in the Mathematicks, formed by placing the Squares of the Ordinate Applicates one upon another, and ſo that the Axis ſhall perpendicularly paſs through all their Centers.

Pyramidal, belonging to, or in the form of a Pyramid.

Pyreticks, (Gr.) Medicines that Cure Feavers.

Pyretology, a Diſcourſe, Deſcription, or Treatiſe of Fevers.

Pyromancy, (Gr.) a Divination by means of Fire.

Pyrotechny, (Gr.) the ſame with Chymiſtry; alſo the Art of making of Fireworks.

Pyroticks, in Phyſick, are Medicines, which being apply'd to the Body grow violently hot, and conſequently cauſe Redneſs, Bliſter, Ripen, Rot, &c.

Pyrrhoniſm, the Doctrine of *Pyrrho* the *Greek* Philoſopher, the firſt founder of the *Scepticks*, who taught that

there was no Certainty of any thing.

Pyrrichus, the Foot of a *Latin* Verſe, conſiſting of two Syllables, and both ſhort.

Pythagorean Syſtem, the ſame with that of *Copernicus*, in which the Sun is ſuppoſed to be at Reſt, and the Earth and the reſt of the Planets to move round him.

Python, a Venomous Serpent; alſo a Familiar Spirit, or one poſſeſt with it.

Pythoneſs, a Woman poſſeſs'd with a Familiar, or Prophecying Spirit, a Sorcereſs, or Witch.

Pyx, the Veſſel wherein the Hoſt is kept in Popiſh Churches.

Q.

Quack, a Mountebank, or ignorant Pretender to the Art of Phyſick.

Quadrageſima-Sunday, the firſt Sunday in *Lent*, ſo called as being about 40 Days from *Eaſter*.

Quadran or *Cadran*, (Fr.) the Dial-Plate of a Clock or Watch; a Sun-dial. In *Poetry* a *Stanza* of four Verſes.

Quadrangle, a Figure in Geometry, having four Angles.

Quadrangular, having four Angles, or in the Form of a Quadrangle.

Quadrant, (Lat.) the fourth part of a Circle, and from thence the Name of a Mathematical Instrument, of great use in Practical Geometry, Astronomy, &c.

Quadrantal, of, or belonging to a Quadrant; also four Fingers thick.

Quadrat, (Lat.) a Square, or Figure whose Sides are equal, and Angles right.

Quadrate, (Lat.) to agree, or answer.

Quadratick, square; as *Quadratick Equations,* are Square Equations, or such, wherein the highest power of the unknown Quantity is a Square.

Quadrature, (Lat.) squaring; as the *Quadrature* of any *Curvilineal,* or *mixed* Figure in Mathematicks, is the finding a Square equal to the Area of it.

Quadriennial, (Lat.) of four Years.

Quadrilateral, (Lat.) having four sides.

Quadrin, (Fr.) a Mite, a small piece of Money in value about a Farthing.

Quadripartite, (Lat.) divided into four parts.

Qudrireme, (Lat.) a Galley with four Oars on a side, or rather one wherein every Oar hath four men to draw it.

Quadrisyllable, consisting of four Syllables.

Quadrivial, (Lat.) consisting of four ways or turnings.

Quadruped, (Lat.) a four footed Beast.

Quadrupedal, (Lat.) having four Feet, or four Foot long.

Quadruple, (Lat.) fourfold.

Quadruplicate, (Lat.) said of a thing folded or repeated four times.

Quaff, to drink greedily and largely. *Milt.*

Quail, to curdle as Milk does.

Quaint, neat, polite, elegant.

Quakers, a Sect of Christians appearing first in the North of *England* about the Year 1650; They say that the Holy Spirit enjoyns them to use *Thee* and *Thou,* or the Plain Language; and that *Quaking* (from whence their Name) is sometimes used by the Power of God, and justify their Extravagant Emotions from Texts of Scripture; They suppose new Revelations still continued, and that their Ministers may thus supernaturally be enlightned up to the Degree of Prophesy and Vision; They suffer Women to speak in their Assemblies, &c.

Qualification, a particular Faculty or Endowment

Qualify, to give one a Qualification, to make him fit; also to appease or pacifie.

Quality, in General, signifies any Property or Affection of any Being, whereby it affects our Senses so and fo, and acquires fuch and fuch a Denomination.

Qualm, a fainting fit.

Quam diu fe bene gefferit, a formal Claufe in the grant of Offices, and is no more than what the Law wou'd have implied if the Office were granted for Life.

Quandary, (Fr. *Qu'en diray-je*, what fhall I fay to it) a Study or Doubt what to do.

Quantity, is any thing that is fufceptible of more or lefs, of Number or Meafure.

Quantity difcrete, is that whereof the parts are not u-nited together by a common *Vinculum*, or Band as *Number*.

Quantity continued, is that whereof the Parts are knit together within fome common Term or Terms; as *Magnitude*.

Qantum meruit, in Law, is an Action of the Cafe grounded on a Promife of paying a Man fo much as he fhou'd deferve.

Quarantain, (Fr.) the fpace of 40 Days; alfo the Benefit which the Law of *England* allows to the Widow of a Land Man Deceafed, of continuing 50 Days after his Deceafe, in his Capital Meffuage or chief Manfion-houfe; alfo a denying Entrance to thofe Perfons, who are fuppofed to come from an Infected place, till forty days be expired.

Quare ejecit infra Termi-

num, a Writ for a Leffee caft out of his Farm before his Term is expired.

Quare infpedit, a Writ for one difturbed in the right of his purchafed Advoufon, againft him that difturbs him.

Quare Incumbravit, a Writ againft the Bifhop, conferring a Benefice within fix Months after its Vacancy, while two others are contending in Law for the Right of prefenting.

Quarrel, Strife, Difpute; a Pain of Glafs. In *Law*, any Action Real or Perfonal.

Quarry, a Place whence Stones are digged. Among Hunters, the Reward given to Hounds. In *Falconry*, any Fowl flown at, and kill'd.

Quartan Ague, is when the Fit returns every fourth Day.

Quartation, a way of Purifying Gold, by melting three parts of Silver with one of Gold, and then cafting the mixture into *Aqua fortis*, which diffolves the Silver, and leaves the Gold in a black Powder at the Bottom.

Quarter, in Heraldry, is a Partition made of juft a fourth part of the Field, thus; He beareth *Argent*, a *Quarter Gules*.

Quar-

Quarter of a Ship, is that part of the Ship's Hull which lies from the Steerage-Room to the Transom.

Quarter, an *English* Measure of Capacity for Corn, containing 8 Bushels, or 64 Gallons.

Quarter, in a Military Sense, denotes the good treatment given to a vanquished Enemy; also the Ground a Body of Men is Encamped upon.

Quarters, the Place or Places where Troops are lodg'd during the Winter.

Quarter-master, in the Land Forces, is one whose Office it is to see out for good Quarters, either for the whole Army, or any part thereof.

Quarter-Masters, Aboard a Ship, are Officers whose Business is Rummaging, Stowing, and Trimming the Ship in the Hold; to overlook the Steward in his delivery of Victuals to the Cook, and in Pumping and drawing out Beer or the like, and also to mind the Ship's Loading.

Quartering; *the Ship goes Quatering*, that is, she goes upon a Quarter-Wind; or she goes neither by a Wind, nor before a Wind, but betwixt both.

Quarter-Deck, of a Ship, is that aloft the Steerage, reaching to the round house.

Quartile Aspect, of the Planets, is when they are a Quarter, or a fourth part of a Circle distant from each other.

Quarter-Sessions, a Court held quarterly by the Justices of the Peace in every County.

Quarterige, Money paid Quarterly.

Quarto, (Lat.) a Book whereof every four Leaves make a Sheet.

Quash, to spoil, frustrate, or defeat.

Quasi-modo-Sunday, Low-Sunday, being the next after *Easter*. 'Tis so nam'd from the first Words of a *Latin* Hymn us'd that Day at Mass.

Quassation, (Lat.) a shaking, or brandishing.

Quaternion, any thing containing the Number of four; a Pile of four Souldiers.

Quatrain, a Staff of four Verses; a *French* Farthing.

Quaver, a Measure of Time in Musick, being half a Crotchet.

Que estate, in Law, is a Plea whereby a Man Intitling another to Land, saith, that the same Estate he had, he had it from him.

Queach, a thick bushy Plot of Ground, a place of Shrubs or Brambles.

Quean, a Drab, a nasty Slut.

Queer, (Canting Word) odd, fantastical, sorry.

Queint, strange, fine. *Spencer*.

Quell, to restrain, keep under, or stop, to conquer, to subdue. *Spencer*.   *Quem*

Quem redditum reddat, a Writ to Cause a Tenant to Attorn.

Queme, please. *Spencer.*

Quene, a Term used by Heralds for the Tail of a Beast.

Querela coram Rege & Concilio, a Writ calling one to justify a Complaint made before the King and Council.

Querent, an Inquirer; one that comes to consult an Astrologer.

Querimonious complaining, bewailing.

Querk or *Quirk*, a Cavil, Shift, or Fetch.

Quern, a Hand-mill.

Querpo. See *Cuerpo.*

Querulous, apt to complain, full of Complaint.

Quested, among *Astrologers*, is that which is inquired after.

Querries, from the French *Ecurie*, a Stable, Persons who are conversant in the Queen's Stables, having the Charge of her Horses committed to them.

Querry, a Prince's Stables. A *Gentleman of the Querry*, one of those, whose Office 'tis to hold the Queen's stirrup, when she mounts.

Query, Question, Proposition, Doubt.

Quest, search after. *Milt.*

Quest, certain Persons chosen Yearly in every Parish, to enquire into Abuses and Misdemeanours, especially

such as relate to Weights and Measures.

Questus, in Law, 'is that Land, which does not descend by Hereditary right, but is acquired by our own Labour and Industry.

Questus est Nobis, a Writ against him to whom the thing is alienated that causeth the Nusance.

Quéue d' Hironde, (Fr.) in *Fortif.* a Swallow's Tail, a sort of Out-work, whose Sides open and spread towards the Head or Campaign, and draw close or narrow at the Gorge.

Quia improvide, a *supersedeas*, granted, where a Writ is erroneously sued out.

Quiddity, (Lat.) the Essence or Being of a thing; also a Querk, or subtle Question.

Quid pro quo, in Law, is the Reciprocal Performance of both parties to a Contract.

Quietism, the Doctrine of the Quietists.

Quietists, a Sect of Religious Persons amongst the *Roman* Catholicks, who teach that Religion consists in the Rest, and internal Recollection of the Mind.

Quietus, an Acquitance given Accomptants in the Exchequer; also *quietus est*, granted the Sheriff, discharges him of all Accounts due to the King.

Quindecagon, a plain Figure of 15 Angles, and consequently 15 Sides.   *Quin-*

Quinquagesima-Sunday, or *Shrove*-Sunday, so called from its being the fiftieth Day before *Easter*.

Quinqueangled, or *Quinqueangular*, (Lat.) having five Angles.

Quinquennial, (Lat.) of five Years continuance.

Quinquepartite, (Lat.) divided into five parts.

Quinquereme, (Lat.) a Galley made with five Oars on a Side, or five Men to an Oar.

Quinquina, See *Jesuits Powder*.

Quinsy, a Disease in the Throat.

Quintain, (Fr.) a sport yet in use at Marriages in *Shropshire* and elsewhere in which running a Tilt on Horse-back with Poles against a thick Post fix'd in the Ground, who breaks most Poles has the Prize, formerly a Peacock, now a Garland.

Quintal, a hundred Pound Weight.

Quintessence, a certain subtle and spirituous Substance, extracted out of Minerals, &c. by Chymical Operations.

Quintessential, belonging to Quintessence.

Quintile, that Position of 2 Planets, which are distant from one another 72 Degrees, or a fifth part of a Circle.

Quintilians, Christian Hereticks, the Disciples of *Montanus*, so called from *Quintilla*,

whom they followed as a Prophetess; they made the Eucharist of Bread and Cheese, from whence they got the name of *Artotyrites*, and among them the Women were Priests and Bishops.

Quintuple, five-fold, or five times as much as another.

Quinzain, a Staff of fifteen Verses.

Quip, a Jeer, or Flout.

Quinzieme, or *Quinzime*, (Fr.) *i. e.* a fifteenth; 'tis a certain Tax so called, because raised on a fifteenth Part of Men's Lands or Goods. See *Fifteenth*. Also the fifteenth Day after any Festival.

Quire, that part of a Church where divine Service is performed; also the quantity of 25 Sheets of Paper.

Quit-claim, in Law, is the Releasing of a man from any Action one hath, or might have against him.

Quit-rent, a small Rent of acknowledgment, payable by the Tenant of most Mannors.

Quittasole, (Span.) an Umbrello.

Quitter, the Matter of a Sore or Ulcer.

Quiver, a Case for Arrows; *Verbally*, to shiver, or shake.

Quo jure, a Writ to compel one to shew by what right he challenges common of Pasture.

Quo minus, a Writ against the Grantor, making such wast in his Woods, that the Grantee cannot enjoy his grant

grant of House-bote, and Hay-bote (or for any, that pays the King a Fee-farm Rent) against another for Debt or Dammage.

Quo Warranto, a Writ against him that usurps a Franchise of the King's; or him that intrudeth himself as Heir into Land.

Quod Clerici non Eleganter, a Writ for a Clerk, who by reason of his Land, is like to be made Bailiff, Beadle, Reeve, &c.

Quod Clerici beneficiati, a Writ to exempt a Clerk of the Chancery from Contribution towards the Proctors of the Clergy in Parliament.

Quod ei de forcat, a Writ for the Tenant in Tail, Tenant in Dower, or Tenant for Term of Life, having lost by default, against him that recovered, or against his Heir.

Quod permittat, a Writ for his Heir that is Disseized of his Common of Pasture against the Heir of the Disseisor.

Quod persona nec Prebendarii, a Writ that lies for spiritual Persons, that are distreined in their Spiritual Possessions for the payment of a Fifteenth with the rest of the Parish.

Quodlibet, (Lat) i. e. what one calls a Quiddity, a Querk or Fetch.

Quodlibets or *Quodlibetical Questions,* are Questions ingeniously disputed *pro* and *con*

in the Schools of an University; whereof one may take which side he pleases.

Quoil, at Sea, a Rope or a Cable laid up round, one Fake (or turn) over another, so that they may the more easily be stowed out of the way, is said to be *Quoiled* up.

Quoin, a Wedge fastned on the Deck, close to the Breech of the Carriages of the great Guns, to keep them firm up to the Ship's sides.

Quorum, (Lat.) as Justices of the *Quorum,* so called because some Matters of Importance cannot be transacted without their Presence or Assent.

Quota, a share of Contribution.

Quotation, a Quoting or Citing.

Quote, to cite, alledge, or bring in an Author or Passage.

Quotidian, (Lat.) dayly, or that comes daily.

Quotient, in Arithmetick, is that Number which arises by dividing the Dividend by the Divisor.

Queyl. See *Quoil.*

R

R.

R *Aabbeting*, is the letting in of the Planks of the Ship into the Keel, which in the Rake and Run of the Ship is hollowed away that the Planks may join closer together.

Rabbin, a Doctor or Teacher of the Jewish Law.

Rabbinical, belonging to a *Rabbi* or *Rabbin*.

Rabid, (Lat.) mad, furious.

Rabinet, a small sort of Ordnance between a Falconette and a Base, seldom used.

Radiation, (Lat.) a sending forth Beams of Light.

Radiant, (Lat.) bright, shining, casting forth Rays of Light.

Radiating Point, a word frequently used in Opticks, and is that Point from whence the Rays of Light issue, or are darted out.

Radical, (Lat.) belonging to the Root.

Radical Moisture, the Fundamental Juice of the Body, said to nourish and preserve the natural Heat, as Oil does a Lamp.

Radical Sign, the Sign of the Root of any Number or Algebraick Quantity, as √ is the mark which expresses the Root, &c.

Radicated, (Lat.) rooted, or that has taken Root.

Radicle, a Term in Botany,

and denotes that part of the Seed of a Plant, which upon its Vegetation becoms its Root.

Radius, in Geometry, is a Right-line drawn from the Center of a Circle to its Circumference.

Rag-Bolts, Iron Pins in a Ship, with Barbs on each side to keep them from coming out.

Raffle, a Game with three Dice, wherein he that throws the greatest Pair, or Pair Royal, wins.

Raft, bereft, deprived. *Spen.*

Raggamuffin, a sorry rascally Fellow.

Ragguled, a Term in Heraldry, used when the Outlines of an Ordinary are ragged or notched after an irregular manner, wherein it differs from Indented: As, he bears *Sable*, a *Cross Ragguled, or*

Ragoo, (Fr.) an high seasoned dish of Meat, after the French manner.

Raillery, (Fr.) a close or secret Jibe, pleasant drolling or playing upon another in Discourse.

Rake of a Ship, is so much of her Hull as hangs over both ends of her Keel.

Rake of the Rudder. See Rudder.

Raked Table. See *Table*, a Term in Architecture.

Rally, (Fr.) to reunite, or
A a a a　　　　gather

gather together scattered Forces; also to play upon any one, or jeer him.

Ramadam, the *Mahometans* Lent, rigidly kept by them.

Ramage, Boughs or Branches of Trees; also wild, coy.

Rams Head, in a Ship, is a great Block, belonging to the Fore and Main Halliards; it has in it three Shivers, into which the Halliards are put, and at the end of it in a hole are reeved the *Ties.*

Ramification, a Collection of small Branches, issuing out of one large one.

Rammer, a piece of Wood fitted to the Diameter of the Bore of a Gun, stuck upon a Staff, and used in driving home the Charge and the Wadding.

Rammish, smelling rank like a Ram or Goat.

Rampant, ramping, wanton. In Heraldry, it is when a Beast of Prey is reared on its hinder Legs in a fighting posture.

Rampart, in Fortification, is a heap of Earth raised round a place, capable of covering the Buildings from view, and of resisting the Cannon of an Enemy, as likewise of raising of those that defend it, that they may discover the Country about it.

Rancour, Malice or inveterate Hatred.

Random, without aim, rashly, inconsiderately.

Range, to put things in order, to dispose them in a convenient manner; also in Gunnery 'tis the distance of the flight of a Shot made at any degree of Elevation.

Ranges, in a Ship, are two pieces of Timber going a-cross from side to side; one aloft on the Fore-Castle, a little abaft the Fore-Mast, and the other in the Beak-Head, before the Mouldings of the Bow-Sprit.

Ranger, of the Forest, is one whose Office is to walk daily through his Charge to see, hear, and enquire, as well of Trespasses as Trespassers in his Bayliwick; to drive the Beasts of the Forest out of the Disforested into the Forested Lands: and to present all Trespasses of the Forest.

Rank, smelling strong, overgrown. *Shakespear.*

Ransack, to rifle.

Ransom, to redeem.

Rapacious, Ravenous; Extorting, Greedy, Devouring.

Rape, the Act of violence committed upon the Body of a Woman; also a division of a County.

Rapid, swift, that has a violent and impetuous Motion.

Rapidity, or *Rapidness*, (Lat.) quickness, hastiness, swiftness.

Rapine, (Lat.) Robbery, Pillaging, taking by Violence.

Rapparees,

Rapparees, a fort of Robbers in *Ireland* fo called.

Rapfody, (Gr.) a Connection together, or a Repetition of a vaft number of Heroick Verfes; but more commonly it fignifies a tedious and impertinent fpinning out of a Difcourfe to no purpofe, or benefit to the Reader.

Raptu Hæredis, a Writ for the taking away an Heir.

Rapture, an Exftafy or Tranfportment.

Rare, (Lat.) thin, feldom, excellent; Rare Bodies in a Philofophick Senfe, are fuch whofe Parts are not fo clofely connected together, but take up more room in proportion to their Matter than other Bodies do.

Rarefacientia, or *Rarifying Medicines*, are fuch as by difperfing the Humours, enlarge the Pores of the Body.

Rarefaction, (Lat.) a feparating the Parts of a Body, and making them take up more Room than they did before.

Rafant Line of Defence, is a Line drawn from a Point in the Curtin, razing the Face of the Baftion, and therefore fhows how much of the Curtin will clear and fcower the Face.

Rafpatory, a Surgeon's Inftrument to fcrape or fhave filthy or fcabby Bones with.

Rafure, fhaving or fcraping; alfo a dafh through Writing.

Ratafia, (Fr.) a delicious Liquor made of Apricocks, Cherries, or other Fruit with their Kernels bruifed and infufed in Brandy.

Ratally, according to a Rate.

Rate Tythe, is when Sheep or other Cattle are kept in a Parifh for a lefs time than a Year, the Owner muft pay Tythe for them *pro rata*, according to the Cuftom of the Place.

Rathe, quickly; alfo to chufe. *Spencer*.

Ratification, (Lat.) a confirming or eftablifhing.

Ratio, or *Reafon*, in Geometry, is the mutual Habitude or Relation of two Magnitudes of the fame kind to one another, in refpect of their quantity.

Ratiocination, a rational Debating, Arguing, or Difputing, a Reafoning.

Ration, a Proportion of Meat, Drink, or Forage, given to Seamen or Soldiers to fubfift themfelves and their Horfes for a Day.

Rationabili parte bonorum, a Writ for the Widow claiming the Thirds.

Rationabilibus Divifis, a Writ for the rectifying the Bounds of two Seigniories.

Rational, reafonable.

Rational Quantities, are thofe between which there is any expreffible Reafon or Proportion.

Rationale, the Breft Plate of the Jewifh High Prieft;

Aaaa2   alfo

also a Rational Account.

Rat-lines, or *Rat-lings*, at Sea, are those Lines which make the Ladder-steps, to get up the Shrouds and Puttocks.

Ravage, (Fr.) to spoil or make havock.

Raucity, Hoarsness.

Ravelins, are Works raised on the Counterscarp, before the Curtin of a Place, and serve to cover the Gates of a Town and the Bridges: They consist of two Faces, forming a Salliant Angle, and are defended by the Faces of the Neighbouring Bastions.

Ravendii, a wicked Sect of the *Mahometans* or Hereticks, who allowed of the Transmigration of Souls, &c.

Ravish, to deflower or commit a Rape.

Reach, in Navigation, is the distance between any two Points of Land that lie in a Right Line one from the other.

Re-adjourn, to adjourn again.

Re-admission, an admitting again.

A Real, a Spanish Coin worth six Pence.

Realgal, (Arab.) red Arsenick.

Reality, real Existence.

Ream, a quantity of Paper consisting of twenty Quires.

Re-ascend, to ascend, or get up again.

Reason, (Lat.) Thinking; 'tis that Faculty of the Soul whereby we judge of things; the Exercise of that Faculty; also Argument, Proof, Cause, Matter, Account.

Reasonable, conformable to the Rules of Reason, Just, Equitable.

Re-assemble, to summon again, or meet together again.

Re-assume, to assume again, or take to himself or upon himself again.

Re-attachment, a second Attachment of one formerly attach'd and dismiss'd the Court without Day.

Re-baptize, to Baptize again.

Re-bate, to Channel, to Chamber, to Blunt, to Check; also to discount in receiving Money, as much as the Interest comes to for the time 'tis pay'd before it becomes due; also to set a Mark of Dishonour in an Escutcheon.

Rebatement, an Abatement in Accounts, as a Person to whom Money is due at such a time, makes an Abatement provided it be paid before the time.

Rebellion, (Lat.) a rising against, or taking up Arms against the supream Power.

Rebound, to leap back again.

Rebuff, a notable Repulse or Opposition.

Rebus, a Device represented in a Picture, with a short Sentence alluding to one's Name.

Rebusses,

Rebuſſes, in Heraldry, are ſuch Coats as bear a reſemblance to the Sir-Name of the Perſon, as three Caſtles for *Caſtleton*, &c.

Rebutter, (Fr.) is when the Donee repelleth the Heir by virtue of a Warrantee made by the Donor.

Recantation, (Lat.) an unſaying or retracting what one has formerly ſaid or written.

Recapitulate, to rehearſe briefly the Heads of a former Diſcourſe.

Recaption, in Law, a ſecond diſtreſs of one formerly diſtrained for the ſame Cauſe; alſo a Writ lying for the Party thus diſtrain'd.

Recede, (Lat.) to go back, or retire.

Receit, an Acquittance for Money received; alſo a preſcribed Remedy.

Recent, (Lat.) new, freſh, lately done.

Receptacle, (Lat.) a place to receive or keep things in.

Receptaculum Chyli, is a Cavity into which all the lacteal Veins empty themſelves.

Reception, (Lat.) a receiving or entertaining any Perſon.

Receptive, apt or fit to receive or hold.

Receſs, (Lat.) a withdrawing or retreating; alſo a place of retreat or retirement.

Receſſion of the Equinoxes, is the going back of the Equi-

noctial Points every Year about 50 Seconds.

Recheat, the name of thoſe Leſſons which Hunters wind upon their Horn, when they have loſt their Game.

Recidivus Morbus, a Relapſe or falling back into the ſame Diſtemper in which he was before.

Recipe, (Lat.) i. e. take, a Phyſician's Bill ordering what Medicines the Apothecary ſhould make up for a Patient.

Recipients or *Receivers*, in diſtillation, are thoſe Veſſels, which are luted to the Beak or Noſe of an Alembick, Retort, &c. to receive the matter which is raiſed or forced over the Helm by the Fire.

Reciprocal, (Lat.) mutual, interchanging.

Reciprocation, (Lat.) an interchanging or returning like for like.

Reciſion, a cutting or paring off, a diſanulling or making void.

Recital, a Rehearſal, a reading over aloud; alſo a ſaying without Book.

Reck, to reckon, to care. *Spencer*.

Reclaim, to reduce to Reaſon, or amendment of Life; alſo to tame a Hawk.

Reclination of a Plane, in Dialling, is the quantity of Degrees, which any Plane lies or falls backwards from the truly upright or vertical Plane.

A a a a 3   *Recluſe*,

Recluse, (Lat.) closely kept in or shut up; and 'tis sometimes taken substantively for a Monk confined to his Monastery.

Recognizance, (Fr.) in Law, is a Bond or Obligation of Record, testifying the Recognizor to owe the Recognisee a certain sum of Money, and is acknowledged in some Court of Record, or before some Judge, Master of the Chancery, or Justice of Peace, &c.

Recognitione adnullanda, &c. a Writ for the disannulling a forced Recognisance.

Recognize, (Lat.) to call or bring to remembrance, to take notice of, to know again.

Recognition, (Lat.) Acknowledgement, Review, or Examination.

Recognitors, a word often used for the Jury Impannelled upon an Assize.

Recollection, is a searching after and bringing to mind those Ideas of which the Mind had formerly thought.

Recollects, a Branch of the Franciscan Friers, that go bare Foot and wear high Sandals.

Recommence, to begin again or a new.

Recommendation, (Lat.) a commending or setting forth any Person to another.

Recompence, Reward, Requital.

Reconcilable, that may be reconciled.

Reconcilation, a making

those Friends that are at variance, or bringing into Favour again.

Recondite, (Lat.) secret, hidden.

Re-conduct, to conduct back again.

Record, in Law, is an authentick and uncontrollable written Testimony, contained in Rolls of Parchment, and preserved in Courts of Record.

Recordare facias, a Writ directed to the Sheriff to remove a Cause from an inferiour Court, to the King's-Bench or Common-Pleas.

Recorder, a judicious Person for the most part well vers'd in the Law, whom the Major, or other Magistrate of any City or Town Corporate, having a Court of Record, associates to himself, for his better direction in the Execution of Justice, and Proceedings according to Law.

Recordo & processu mittendis, a Writ to call a Record, and the whole Process, out of an Inferiour into the King's-Bench-Court.

Recoverable, that may be recovered.

Recovery, in a legal Sense, is an obtaining any thing by Judgment or Trial at Law.

Recount, to relate.

Recoupe, (Fr.) in Law, is a quick and sharp Reply to a peremptory Demand, and used by Lawyers to defalk or discount.   Re-

Recourse, Application, Refuge, Address; also Passage, Return.

Recoyl, (Fr.) to give back, as Cannon does when fired.

Recreant, a Coward, or faint hearted Fellow.

Recreation, (q. d. a creating a new) a refreshing, diverting, or delighting.

Recredentials, an Answer to the Credential Letters of an Ambassador.

Recrement, (Lat.) any superfluous Matter in the Blood, or Body, or any of its parts: In the Plural 'tis used for such Juices as are separated in the several Glands of the Body for proper and particular uses, as the Spirits, the Lympha, the Gall, &c.

Recriminate, (Lat.) to charge one's Accuser, or lay the Fault that he is accused of to him that accuses him.

Recrimination, an Accusation, in which the Party accused charges his Accuser for the same Fact.

Recrudescence, a growing raw or sore.

Rectangle, in Geometry, is a Parallelogram, the Angles whereof are right.

Rectangular, (Lat.) Right-Angled.

Rectification, (Lat.) in Chymistry, is the distilling over again any Spirit, in order to make it more fine and pure.

Rectification of Curves, in Mathematicks, is the assigning or finding a straight Line equal to a curved one.

Rectilineal, (Lat.) Right-lined; a *Rectilineal Figure*, is a Figure, the Perimeter whereof consists of Right-Lines.

Rectitude, (Lat.) rightness, straightness; also uprightness, honesty.

Recto, a Writ of Right, trying both for Possession and Property, and if the Cause be lost there is no Remedy.

Recto de dote, a Writ whereby a Woman demands her whole Dowry.

Recto de dote unde nihil habet, a Writ whereby a Woman having a Dowry assured she demands her Thirds.

Recto de rationabili parte, a Letter for a Coparcener to recover his share.

Recto de advocatione Ecclesiæ, a Writ for him that claims the Advowson to himself and his Heirs in Fee.

Recto de custodia Terræ & Heredis, a Writ for a Guardian in Soccage, or appointed by the Ancestor's Will against a Stranger that enters upon the Land, and takes the Body of the Heir.

Recto quando dominus remisit, when the Lord, in whose Seigniory the Land lies, remits the Cause to the King's Court.

Recto sur disclaymer, is a Writ that lies when a Lord avows upon his Tenant, and the Tenant disclaimeth to hold of him, upon which the disclaimer shall have this

Writ; and if the Lord aver and prove that the Land is held of him, he shall recover the Land for ever.

Rector, (Lat.) a Governour; also the Parson of a Parish Church.

Rectory, a Parish Church, with all its Rights, Glebes, Tythes, &c.

Rectus in Curia, signifies one that stands at the Bar, and no Man objects any thing against him; also one that reversed the Outlawry, and can participate of the benefit of the Law.

Rectum, in Anatomy, is the last of the Intestines; it is a Hands breadth and a half long, and its Cavity about three Fingers in Diameter.

Recumbency, a relying or depending upon.

Recuperation, a recovering.

Recur, (Lat.) to run back or return.

Recurrent Nerves, a Branch of the *Par vagum* first descending, and after ascending, and imparted to the *Larynx*, whence they are call'd *vocal*.

Recursion, a running back,

Recurvated, bending back.

Recusant, a Roman Catholick, so called from his refusing to submit to the Discipline of the Reformed Churches. But in Law this word comprehends all those who refuse to Communicate with the Church of *England*.

Reddendum, a word used substantively for the Clause of a Lease, &c. whereby the Rent is reserved to the lessor.

Reddition, (Lat.) in Law, an acknowledgement that the Land or thing demanded belongs to the Demandant, or at least does not belong to himself.

Rede, warne, tell. *Spencer*.

Redeem, (Lat.) to purchase again, to recover, to deliver, to ransom.

Re-deliver, to give up again.

Re-demand, to ask or require again.

Redemption, (Lat.) a ransoming or delivering.

Redent, in Fortification, is a sort of a toothed Work, in form of the Teeth of a Saw, with salient and re-entring Angles, to the end that one part may defend the other.

Redevable, (Fr.) indebted, beholden to.

Redintegration, (Lat.) a restoring any mixt Body, the form whereof is destroy'd, to the same Nature and Constitution which it had before.

Redisseisin, a second Disseisin.

- *Redituaries*, are a Branch of the *Franciscan* Friers.

- *Redolent*, (Lat.) smelling sweetly, perfumed.

Redonation, a restoring or giving back that which was taken away.

Redouble, to double again, to encrease, to grow more violent.

Redoubted,

Redoubted, dreadful, much feared.

Redoubts, are square Works of Stone raised without the Glacis of a Place, about Musket Shot from the Town, with a Foss round them, having Loop-holes for the Musqueteers to fire through; sometimes they are of Earth, having a defence only in Front, surrounded with a Parapet and Foss, both the one and the other serve for detatched Guards to interrupt the Enemies Works.

Redound, to turn to, or light on.

Redubbers, are such as buy stollen Cloth, knowing it such, and turn it into some other Form or Colour that it may not be known.

Reduce, (Lat.) to back, or bring into subjection,

Reduce a Place, is to oblige the Governour to surrender it to the Besiegers by Capitulation.

Reduct, a Military Term, signifying an advantageous piece of Ground, entrenched and separated from the rest by a Foss, to retire to in case of surprize.

Reduction, (Lat.) a reducing or bringing back.

Reduction of Money, is a reducing a higher Denomination into a lower, as Shillings into Pence or Farthings; or a lower into a higher, as Farthings into Pence and Shillings.

Reduction of Equations, in Algebra, is the reducing them into a proper Order or Disposition for a Solution.

Redundancy, (Lat.) an overflowing, abounding, or exceeding.

Reduplication, (Lat.) a redoubling, a Figure in Rhetorick, wherein a Verse or Sentence ends with the same word that the following begins.

Reduplicative, that redoubleth, or may be doubled often.

Ree, a *Portuguese* Coin, forty of which are equivalent to six Pence.

Re-edifie, to build up again.

Reef, when part of the Sail below is rolled up that it may not draw so much Wind, that which is rolled up is called a Reef.

Reefed Top-Mast, is when the lower part of the Top-Mast being crack'd and cut off, the remainder is set in the Step again.

Reek, Steam or Vapour.

Re-entring Angle, in Fortification, is what points inwards to the Body of the place; such is the Angle of the Counterscarp before the Center of the Curtin.

Re-entry, in Law, is the resuming or taking again that Possession which he had lately forgone.

Re-establish, to establish, or settle again.

Reeve, (Sax. a Governor,) the Bailiff of a Franchise or Mannor.

Reeve,

Reeve, in Navigation, is to draw a Rope through a Block to run up and down.

Re-examination, (Lat.) a second examination.

Refectory, the Room where Friers and Nuns eat together.

Refel, (Lat.) to disprove, confute, or prove false.

Referee, an Arbitrator to whom a Law-Business is referred.

Reference, a mark in a Book directing the Reader to the Margin, or to some other place; also the giving up of a Matter to be determin'd by Arbitrators.

Refine upon, to handle nicely, to make critical Remarks.

Reflection, in Natural Philosophy, is the regress or return that happens to a moving Body, upon its meeting another Body which it cannot penetrate.

Reflection, in Mataphysicks, is the notice which the Mind takes of its own Operations and the manner of them.

Reflection, in the common acceptation of the word, signifies a Censure.

Reflexibility, (Lat.) an aptness or capacity of being reflected.

Reflux of the Sea, is the ebbing of the Water off from the Shore.

Reform, (Lat.) to put in an old or better Form, to mend, to rectifie Abuses; also to take up, or return from ill Courses. In a Military Sense 'tis to reduce a Body of Soldiers, either by disbanding the whole, and putting them into other Bodies, or only a part, and retaining the rest.

Reformado, (Span.) an Officer, who having lost his Men, is continued in Pay as an inferiour Soldier; also a Volunteer in a Man of War.

Reformation, the amendment of an Error or Abuse.

Refractory, (Lat.) wilful, obstinate, stubborn, unruly.

Refraction, (Lat.) in a Philosophick Sense, is the incurvation or change of determination in the Body moved, which happens to it just when it enters, or in some cases rather before it enters a different Medium.

Refraction Astronomical, is that Refraction produced by the Atmosphere, whereby a Star appears more elevated above the Horizon then really it is.

Refrangibility of the Rays of Light, is their disposition to be refracted or turned out of their way, in passing out of one transparent Body or Medium into another.

Refrangible, (Lat.) whatever is capable of being Refracted.

Refresh, (Fr.) to recruit one's self; to renew or revive.

Reflet, the Burden of a Song or Ballad.

Refrigerative, (Lat.) a Physical Term, signifying cooling.

Refrige-

Refrigeratory, (Lat.) any Plate or Vessel used for cooling, but more particularly it is taken for a Vessel like a Pail, placed about the Head of an Alembick or Still; 'Tis usually filled with cold Water, that so the head of the Still may not grow hot.

Refuge, (Lat.) a place of safety to fly to.

Refugee, one that flees from his Country.

Refulgency, (Lat.) brightness, splendor.

Refund, to pay or give back Money that one has laid out.

Refutatio Feodi, a Civil Law Term, signifying the loss of a Feudal Tenure by Forfeiture, either by not performing the Service required, or committing some villanous Act against the Lord or Soveraign.

Refutation, (Lat.) a disproving by Argumentss, what has been alledged by another.

Regal, Royal, Kingly, belonging to a King or Queen.

Regale, (Fr.) to fare like a Prince; to entertain or treat nobly.

Regalia, the Rights of a King, or the Ensigns of the Soveraign Dignity.

Regalio, a sumptuous Entertainment.

Regardant, in Heraldry, a Lyon or such kind of Beast of Prey painted looking behind him.

Regarder, a Forest Officer, whose Business it is to make the Regard of the Forest, and over-look all the other Officers.

Regel, or *Rigel*, a fixt Star of the first Magnitude in *Orion's* Foot.

Regency, the Goverment of a Kingdom during the Minority of a Prince by one or more of the Subjects.

Regeneration, a New and Spiritual Birth.

Regent, one that governs a Kingdom during the minority and incapacity of the King.

Regicide, (Lat.) the Murder or Murtherer of a King.

Regimen, Government, Rule. Among Physicians, it signifies a method in Diet, Exercise, &c. to be observ'd by a Patient.

Regiment, is a Body of Men either Horse or Foot, Commanded by a Colonel, Lieutenant Colonel, and Major; each Regiment of Foot is divided into Companies, but the number of Companies differs; tho' in *England* our Regiments are generally thirteen Companies, one of which is always Grenadiers. *Regiments of Horse*, are most commonly of six Troops, but some of nine. Dragoon Regiments are generally in time of War eight Troops, and in time of Peace but six. Some *German* Regiments consist of 2000 Foot, and the Regiment of *Picardy* in *France* of of 6000, being 120 Companies, at 50 in a Company.

Regio Assensu, a Writ whereby the King or Queen gives the Royal Assent to the Election of a Bishop.

Region, a Country, or a large extent of Land, inhabited by many People of the same Nation; also a particular extent of the Air.

Register, a Book of Records, or the Person that keeps it.

Registers, in a Chymical Furnace, are holes left in the sides of a Furnace with Stopples to them, to let in, or keep out the Air, according as the Fire is required to be more or less intense.

Regorge, to cast up or vomit.

Regrater, (Fr.) a Huckster, or one that trims up old Wares for sale; but now it is commonly taken for him that buys and sells any Wares or Victuals in the same Market or Fair, or within five Miles thereof.

Regress, (Lat.) a coming back, or coming in.

Regret, (Fr.) Desire; also Grief, Sorrow, Repentance; also Unwillingness, Reluctance.

Regular, (Lat.) conformable to Rule.

Regular Body, in the Mathematicks, is a Solid, the Surface whereof is composed of equal and similar Figures.

Regular Figures, in Geo-metry, are such, the sides whereof, and also the Angles, are equal to one another.

Regulate, (Lat.) to set in Order, to maintain good Discipline, &c.

Regulator, one that regulates or directs: In a Watch 'tis the Ballance or Pendulum Spring.

Regulus, *Regule*, in Chymistry, is the purest part of any Mettal or Mineral, when the Fæces or Dregs are separated or taken away.

Regurgitate, (Lat.) to swallow again.

Rehabilitation, a re-enabling or restoring to a former Ability.

Rehearse, to tell, relate, or repeat.

Rejection, (Lat.) a casting off or slighting.

Re-imbark, to take Shipping again.

Re-imburse, to pay back again.

Re-impression, a second Edition of a Book.

Reinard, a word used in Burlesque Poetry for a Fox.

Re-inforce, to strengthen again, to recruit.

Re-ingage, to ingage again.

Re-ingratiate, to get into Favour again.

Re-instate, to restore to the same state.

Re-joynder, in Law, is an Answer or Exception to a Replication; first the Defendant puts in an Answer to the Plantiff's Bill, which is sometimes called an *Exception*, and the Plantiff's Answer to that is called a *Re-joynder*.

Re-iterate, (Lat.) a saying or doing the same thing over and over again.

Relais, a French Term in Fortification, the same with *Berme*; which see.

Relapse, (Lat.) a falling or sliding back, most commonly into a Disease or fit of Sickness.

Relation, a Rehearsal of some Adventure, Battel, Siege, &c. also Respect or Comparison; also a Kinsman.

Relative, having relation or nearness to some other thing.

Relative Gravity, the same with Specifick Gravity; *which see.*

Relaxation, (Lat.) a respit or breathing time; also a dilatation of Parts or Vessels.

Relay, (in Hunting) the setting of fresh Dogs upon a wild Beast.

Release, in Law, an Instrument whereby Estates, Rights, Titles, Entrys, Actions, and other things, are sometimes Extinguished, sometimes transferred, sometimes abridged, and sometimes enlarged.

Release, in the common acceptation of the word, signifies a Discharge; and to *Release* is to Discharge and set at Liberty.

Relegation, in Law, is a Banishment for a certain time.

Relent, to wax soft; also to grow pitiful and compassionate.

Relevation, a raising or lifting up again.

Relevish, in Law, is to admit one to main-Prise upon Surety.

Relict, a Law Term for a Widow.

Relief, charitable Assistance, Comfort, Supply. See *Relievo*.

Relievo, (Ital.) is the protuberant jetting or standing out of any Figures or Images above the Plain on which they are formed, and 'tis distinguish'd into *Basso*, when it rises but little, and *Alto*, where it rises much or after the Life.

Religion, is properly the Worship given to God; but 'tis also applied to the Worship of Idols and false Deities.

Relinquish, (Lat.) to forsake or part with.

Reliquary, (Fr.) a Shrine or Casket where Relicks are kept.

Reliques, something preserved either of the Body or Cloaths of deceased Saints.

Relish, to give or to have a good Taste; to approve, to be agreeable.

Relive, live again. *Spencer*.

Reluctancy, a wrestling or striving against, unwillingness.

Remainder,

Remainder, i. e. that which is left: In a Law-sense, an Estate limited in Lands, Teniments and Rents, to be enjoy'd after the expiring of another particular Estate.

Remains, what is left of a Person or Thing.

Remancipate, to sell or return a Commodity to him that first sold it.

Remand, to command back again, or send back again.

Remark, Observation, taking notice of; also Note or Worth.

Remedy, Physick, Medicine; also Help, Means of Redress.

Remembrance, is when the Idea of something formerly known returns again to the Mind.

Remembrancers of the Exchequer, are three Clerks there.

Reminiscence, (Lat.) is the power which the Soul hath of recollecting it self, or calling again to remembrance such Ideas or Notions as it had really forgot.

Remisness, slackness, carlesness.

Remission, forgiveness; also an abatement of the Power, or efficacy of Quality.

Remit, (Lat.) to send back, to slacken, forgive, &c.

Remitter, in a legal sense, is to restore a Man to his best and most antient Title.

Remnant, that which is left of any thing.

Remonstrance, (Lat.) a Warning, Admonition, Declaration, a showing or giving Reasons.

Remonstrants, or *Arminians*, a Party of Christians first so called in *Holland*, and who took the name of Remonstrants from a writing call'd a Remonstrance, that was presented to them by the States of *Holland*, 1609, wherein they reduced their Doctrines to those five Articles.

I. That God in Election and Reprobation had regard on the one side to Faith and Perseverance, and on the other side to Incredulity and Impenitence.

II. That Jesus Christ died for all Men without exception.

III. That Grace was necessary for the application of one's self to Good.

IV. That yet it did not act in an irresistible manner.

V. That before affirming that the Regenerate cannot totally fall off; this Question ought more accurately to be examined.

They were also called *Arminians*, because that *Arminius*, professor of Divinity at *Leiden*, was the first that opposed the then received Sentiments of *Holland* of an absolute Predestination.

Remorse, the check or sting of Conscience.

Remote, (Lat.) far distant.

Remount, (Fr.) to set or get up again.

Remune-

Remunerate, (Lat.) to reward or requite.

Renal, (Lat.) belonging to the Reins or Kidneys.

Rencounter, (Fr.) an unexpected Adventure, and accidental Scuffle; a meeting by chance of two adverse Parties.

Rendevous, or *Rendezvous*, (Fr.) a place appointd for meeting, or a meeting place for an Army.

Rents, the Seams between the Planks of a Ship.

Renegade, or *Renegado*, a Soldier that revolts to the Enemy, and metaphorically one that has Apostatized from the Christian Religion.

Renitency, (Lat.) a resistance, or striving against.

Renovation, (Lat.) a renewing, a making new.

Renown, (Fr.) Fame, great Reputation.

Rent, a Sum of Money issuing yearly out of Lands and Tenements.

Renversed, (Fr.) over-turned, turned upside down, perverted.

Renversion, in Heraldry, is two fold; 1. When a Man bears in his own Escutcheon another renversed, and this is due to one that treats a Maid or Widow rudely or uncivilly, or, as some say, deflowers her only; and also to one that runneth away from his Soveraign's Banner. 2. When a Man's own Escutcheon is entirely *Renversed*, which is due to a Traitor.

Renunciation, (Lat.) a renouncing, disclaiming, or utterly denying.

Reparation, (Lat.) a mending of things fallen to decay, a making satisfaction for damages done, &c.

Reparatione facienda, a Writ when one Joint-Tenant is willing to repair, and the other not, against those which are not.

Repartee, (Fr.) a quick Reply, a sharp Answer.

Repartition, (Lat.) a dividing or sharing again.

Repast, (Lat.) properly a feeding or eating again; but commonly it signifies a single Meal.

Repeal, to abrogate or disannul.

Repell, (Lat.) to beat or drive back.

Repellent Medicines, are such as by stopping the Heat and Afflux of Humours, and by shutting up the Pores with their coldness, decrease the swelling of a Part, and drive the Humours another way.

Repeople, to stock with People again.

Repercussion, (Lat.) a driving back, or striking back.

Repertory, a Book wherein things are methodically placed for the more ready finding.

Repetition, (Lat.) a saying over again.

Repleader, in Law, is to plead against that which was once pleaded before.

Replegiare,

Replegiare, in Law, is to replevy or redeem a Diſtreſs, by putting in legal Security.

Replegiare de averiis, a Writ to releaſe Cattle diſtreined upon ſurety to anſwer the Suit.

Replenish, to fill.

Replete, (Lat.) full or filled, repleniſhed. *Milton.*

Repletion, (Lat.) a being ſtuffed or filled; a Surfeit.

A *Replevin*, or *Replevy*, the releaſing of Cattle or other Goods diſtrained by vertue of a Writ called *Replegiare de averiis*, or *Replegiari facias*, upon ſurety to anſwer the Diſtreiner's Suit.

Replevish, to let one to Mainpriſe or Bail.

Replevy, to recover by a Replevin.

Replication, (Lat.) the Plaintiff's Reply to the Defendant's Anſwer.

Report, in Law, is a publick relation of Caſes judicially argued, debated, reſolved, or adjudged; alſo a Relation of the Opinion or Judgment of a Referee upon any Caſe of Difference referred to his Conſideration by a Court of Juſtice, moſt commonly the Chancery.

Repoſitory, (Lat.) a Store-houſe or place where things are laid up and kept.

Reprehend, (Lat.) to find fault with or reprove.

Repreſentation, a making a reſemblance or likeneſs of any thing.

Repreſentative, one that repreſents another Perſon.

Reprieve, a reſpit of a Malefactor from Execution.

Reprimand, (Lat.) a Check or Reproof.

Re-print, to Print again.

Repriſes, in Law, are yearly Deductions out of a Mannor, as *Rent-charge*, *Rent-ſeek*, &c.

Repriſal, the Right of Repriſal or Law of Mark, by which he that has Injuſtice done him in another Country, redreſſes himſelf by Goods belonging to Perſons of that Country, taken within his own Bounds.

Reproach, to upbraid, to twit, to tax, or lay to ones's Charge.

Reprobate, a lewd or profligate Wretch.

Reprobation, (Lat.) a caſting out of Favour, or Rejecting.

Reptils, are all thoſe creeping Animals, which reſt upon one part of their Body, whilſt they advance the other forward, as Adders, Snakes, Worms, &c.

Republican, a Commonwealths-Man, or one that loves that ſort of Government.

Republick, a Commonwealth, a Government where many bear Rule, a free State.

Repudiate, (Lat.) to reject, put away, or divorce.

Repugnancy, (Lat.) averſneſs, oppoſition, contrariety.

Repugnant, contrary to.

Republication,

Repullulation, a budding forth again.

Repulse, (Lat.) a being driven back, a Denial.

Repute, or *Reputation*, (Lat) Credit, Esteem.

Repute, to think, count, or look upon.

Requiem, (Lat.) *i. e.* Rest, a Mass for the Souls of deceased Persons.

Requital, Reward, Acknowledgement.

Requisite, (Lat.) necessary.

Re-salutation, (Lat.) a saluting again.

Resceit, in Law, is an admission or receiving a third Person to plead his Right in a Cause formerly commenced between other two; as if a Tenant for Life brings an Action, and he in reversion comes in, and prays to be received to defend the Land, and to plead with the Demandant.

Rescind, (Lat.) to cut off, to disannul, to repeal.

Rescissory, making void, or repealing.

Rescous, or *Rescue*, in Law, is a resistance against Lawful Authority.

Rescript, a writing that is in answer to a Letter, Petition, Writ, &c.

Rescussor, is he that commits such a *Rescous*.

Re-search, strict Inquiry, diligent seeking after.

Resemblance, likeness, agreeableness.

Resent, to be sensible of, or to stomach an Affront.

Reservation, (Lat.) a reserving or keeping in store.

Reserved, grave, close, not free in Discourse.

Reset, the receiving or entertaining an Out-law'd Person.

Resiance, (Fr.) a Man's abode or continuance in the same place.

Resilence, (Lat.) the same as *Resiance*, only 'tis more peculiarly used for the continuance or abode of a Parson or Vicar upon his Benefice.

Residentiary, one that resides in his Benefice.

Residual. See *Apotome*.

Residue, the rest, the remainder.

Resignation, (Lat.) a giving up, or surrendering; in Law it is used for the giving up of a Benefice into the Hands of the Ordinary.

Resignee, the party to whom a thing is resigned.

Resigner, the Person resigning.

Resiliency, or *Resilition*, a leaping back, recoiling, or rebounding.

Resinous, yielding Rosin, or of the nature of it.

Resipiscence, i. e. a becoming wise again, Repentance, Amendment.

Resistance, (Lat.) a withstanding or opposing; a defending a Man's self against the force of one that assails him.

Res Naturales, or natural things are three, Health, the

Causes

Caufes of Health, and its Effects.

Res non Naturales, or things not Natural, are fix, Air, Meat and Drink, Motion and Reft, Sleeping and Waking, the Affections of the Mind, Things that are lett out of, and Things retain'd in the Body.

Refolvents, Medicines that refolve or difperfe.

Refolves, the Debates of the Houfe of Commons.

Refolution, a full purpofe or intent to do a thing; alfo Affurance, Boldnefs, or Courage.

Refonant, (Lat.) founding back again, refounding.

Refort, concourfe or meeting together, refuge.

Refound, (Lat.) to ring again.

Refpiration, or *Breathing*, is an alternate Dilation and Contraction of the Cheft, whereby the Air is taken in by the Wind-Pipe, and by and by is driven out again.

Refpite, a Law Term for delay, forbearance, or continuance of time.

Refplendent, bright, glittering.

Refpondent, (Lat.) he that anfwers the Opponent in Difputations and Interrogatories.

Refponfalis, in Law, is he that appears in Court for another at a day affigned.

Refponfible, liable or able to anfwer or give account.

Reftagnation, (Lat.) an overflowing, or running over.

Reftauration, (Lat) a reftoring, or re-eftablifhment.

Reftinction, a quenching or putting out.

Reftipulation, a mutual Engagement between Parties.

Reftitution, (Lat.) fignifies the yielding up again or reftoring of any thing unlawfully taken from another; alfo a reftoring one unlawfully diffeifed.

Reftitutione Extracti ab Ecclefia, is a Writ to reftore a Man to the Church, which he had recovered for Sanctuary.

Reftitutione Temporalium, a Writ for a Bifhop to recover the Temporalities or Barony of his Bifhoprick.

Reftive, or *Refty*, ftubborn, head ftrong.

Reftorative, a Medicine to reftore Health.

Reftraint, is when any Action is hindred or ftopped contrary to Volition or Preference of the Mind.

Reftriction, (Lat.) the fame as Reftraint.

Reftrictive, or *Riftringent*, Terms ufed in Phyfick, and fignifie of a binding quality.

Refult, (Fr.) the upfhot of a bufinefs.

Refume, (Lat.) to take up again; as to take up a Difcourfe, &c.

Refummons, a fecond Summons to anfwer an Action.

Refumption, in Law, is the taking again into the King's Hands

Hands what he had granted upon surprize.

Resurrection, (Lat.) a rising again from the Dead.

Retail, to sell by Retail, is to sell Goods by small parcels.

Retaining Fee, a Fee given to a Serjant or Councellor at Law, to keep him from pleading for the adverse Party.

Retaliate, (Lat.) to return like for like.

Retarde, (Lat.) to stop, hinder, or delay.

Retardation, (Lat.) a hindering or delaying.

Retchless, sloathful, lazy, careless.

Retentive, apt to retain or hold in.

Reticence, (Lat.) concealment, passing over in silence.

Retiformis Tunica, a Coat of the Eye, so called, because it resembles a Net, which covers the bottom of the Cavity of the Eye, it is a fine Expansion of the medullary Fibres of the Optick Nerve upon the Surface of the glassy Humour, as far as the *Ligamenta Ciliaria*; 'tis on this Coat that the Impressions of Objects are made.

Retinue, a train of Attendants.

Retirade, in Fortification, is a Trench with a Parapet; but *Retirade compure* is commonly taken for a Retrenchment formed by the two Faces of a Re-entring Angle in the body of a place, after

the first Defence is ruined, and the Besieged oblig'd to abandon the Head of the Work without quitting it entirely.

Retort, in Chymistry, is a Vessel used for distillations of Oils, and volatile Salts, and also of acid Spirits.

Retort, (Lat.) to turn, or throw back, to return.

Retract, to recant, to revoke what one has said or written.

Retraxit, an Exception against one that had withdrawn his Action, saying in open Court he will proceed no farther.

A Retreat, (Fr.) a Retirement.

Retrench, (Fr.) to cut off, to abridge, diminish, or lessen; also to cast up a Retrenchment.

Retrenchment, in Fortification, is any Work raised to cover a Post, and fortifie it against an Enemy; but 'tis more particularly a Ditch bordered with a Parapet, and secured with *Gabions* or *Bavins* laden with Earth.

Retribution, (Lat.) a giving back, a making Recompence or Requital.

Retrieve, (Fr.) to find again, to get again, to recover.

Retroaction, a driving back.

Retrocession of the Equinoxes. See *Retrogression.*

Retroduction, a leading or bringing back.

Retrogradation, (Lat.) a going backward.

     Retro-

Retrograde, in Astronomy, a Planet is so called, when it appears to move contrary to the succession of Signs, as from the second degree of *Aries* to the first.

Retrogression. See *Retrogradation*.

Retrospection, a looking back.

Retrase, hidden.

Return, a Certificate of what is done in the execution of Writs, &c.

Returno Habendo, a Writ for the return of the Cattle (distreined and replevied) to him that has proved his distress Lawful.

Returnum averiorum, a Writ for the return of the Cattle to the Defendant, when the Plaintiff doth not declare.

Returnum Irreplegiable, a Writ for the final restitution of Cattle to the Owner found by the Jury to be unjustly distrained.

Reveal, (Lat.) to discover, to lay open.

Revels, Dancing, Masking, Diceing, acting Comedies or Farces, and such like Sports.

Revelation, (Lat.) a discovering or laying open, or revealing.

Revenues, yearly Profit of Land, Money, or Offices.

Reverberate, to reflect, strike, or beat back again: In Chymistry, is to cause the Flame of the Wood or Coals that's lighted in the Furnace, to beat back upon the Vessel by means of a Dome placed over it.

Reberberatory, a kind of Chymical Furnace.

Revere, to stand in Reverence, to honour with awful Respect.

Reverse, that is on the Back or behind. *Verbally*, to repeal, or abolish.

Reversion, a returning, a coming back again.

Review, a second looking over.

Revisal, a second Examination.

Revise, to view over again.

Revocation, (Lat.) a calling back, or repealing.

Revolution, (Lat.) a rolling back; a notable turn of Affairs, or change of Government.

Rhabdology, the Art of computing or numbering by *Napier*'s Rods, or *Napier*'s Bones.

Rhachitis, the Spinal Marrow; also a Disease among the *English* commonly call'd the *Rickets*.

Rhagades, in Latin, *Scissura*, *Rima*, Chinks, Clefts, which as they happen in other parts of the Body, so they may happen in the Fundament, or sphincter Muscle closing the Fundament.

Rhapsody, (Gr.) a confused Collection of Poems, &c.

Rhegma, (Gr.) a breaking or bursting of any part, as of a Bone, the inner Rim of the Belly, the Eye, &c.

Rhetorians, Hereticks in the fourth Age, who maintain'd
that

that all Hereticks had Reason on their fide, of what Sect foever they were.

Rhetorical, belonging to Rhetorick, Eloquent.

Rhetoricate, to fpeak, like an Orator, to ufe Rhetorical Figures.

Rhetorications, turns of Rhetorick, empty Reafonings.

Rhetorician, an Orator, or one well skill'd in the Art of Rhetorick.

Rhetorick, (Gr.) the Art of fpeaking well or Eloquently.

Rheum, a defluxion of Humour from the Head upon the Parts beneath, as upon the Eyes or Nofe.

Rheumatick, belonging to a Rheumatifm; alfo troubled with Rheum.

Rheumatifm, a wandering pain in the Body, often accompanied with a fmall Fever, Swelling, Inflammation, &c.

Rhine-land-Rode, is a meafure of two Fathom or 12 Foot ufed by the Dutch Ingineers.

Rhine-Grave, is a Title belonging to the Count *Palatine* of the *Rhine* in *Germany*.

Rhinenchytes, is a little Syringe to inject Medicines into the Noftrils.

Rhomboides, a kind of Mufcle-Fifh. In *Geometry* a quadrilateral Figure, whofe Sides and Angles are only equal; alfo a Mufcle of the *Scapula*, named from its Figure.

Rhombus, (Gr.) a Paralle-logram which has all its Sides equal but not all its Angles.

Rhyos, a Difeafe of the Eyes, caufed by confuming of the Caruncle, or fmall piece of Flefh in the great corner of the Eye, fo that it can no longer contain its Liquor.

Rhyptica, fcouring Medicines which cleanfe away filth.

Rhythmical, belonging to, or made in Rhyme.

Rhytidofis, a wrinkling of any part.

Rialto, is a ftately Marble Bridge in *Venice*, where Merchants meet about Bufinefs.

Ribaldry, (Ital.) debaucbery, or obfcene Talk.

Ribbon, a Term in Heraldry, and fignifies the eighth part of a Bend; it is born a little cut off from the out Lines of the Efcutcheon thus. He beareth *or* a *Ribbon Gules*.

Rib-roaft, to beat or bang one foundly.

Ribs of a Ship, are the Timbers of the Futtocks when the Planks are off; fo called becaufe they bend like Ribs of a Carcafs.

Riddance, clearing, or difpatch.

Ride, a Ship is faid to Ride when her Anchors hold her faft, faſt, ſo that ſhe drives not by the force of the Wind or Tide.

Ride a-croſs, is when ſhe Rides with her Main-yards and Fore-yards hoiſted up to the Hounds, and both Yards and Arms top'd a like.

Ride-a-thwart, is to Ride with her ſide to the Tide.

Ride betwixt Wind and Tide, is to Ride ſo as the Wind has an equal force over her one way, and the Tide the contrary way.

Ride-Wind-Road, or to *Ride a great Road*, is to Ride ſo as the Wind has more power over the Ship than the Tide.

Ride Hawsful, or *to Ride a-ſtreſs*, is when in a ſtreſs of Weather the Ship falls ſo deep into the Sea with her Head that the Water runs in at her Hawſes.

Ride a Portoiſe, is when the Yards of a Ship are ſtruck down upon the Deck, or when they are down a Portlaſt.

Rideau, in Fortification, is a riſing Ground or Eminence, comanding a Plain, which is ſometimes near Parallel to the Works of a Place; alſo a Trench covered with Earth in form of a Parapet to cover the Soldiers.

Riders, in a Ship, are great pieces of Timber bolted on to ſtrengthen her where ſhe is too weakly built.

Ridicule, (Lat.) Jeſt, Mockery. a Laughing-ſtock.

Ridiculous, fit to be laughed at.

Riens Arriere, a kind of Plea uſed to an Action of Debt upon Arrearages of Account, whereby the Defendant does alledge there is nothing in Arrear.

Riens perdiſcent, is a form of Pleading when an Heir is ſued for a Debt of his Anceſtor, and hath not Aſſets in his Hand, nor any Lands liable to be extended.

Rife, frequently, common.

Rigging of a Ship, is all the Cordage or Ropes whatſoever belonging to her Maſts or Yards, or any part about her. *A Ship is well rigged* when ſhe has all her Ropes of a fit ſize and proportion to her Burden.

Right Aſcenſion. See *Aſcenſion*.

Right-Sphere, is that which has the Poles of the World in its Horizon, and the Equator in the Zenith.

Right the Helm, a Sea Phraſe ordering the Man at the Helm, to keep the Helm even with the middle of the Ship.

Right-Line, is that which lies equally between its Points, or according to ſome, the ſhorteſt that can be drawn between two Points.

Righteous, Juſt, Upright, Equitable.

Rightful, grounded on Right, Lawful.

Rigid, (Lat) ſtiff, ſtrict, ſtern or auſtere.

Riglet,

Riglet, (in Printing) is a small Rule for dividing Chapters, &c.

Rigols, a sort of Musical Instrument used in *Flanders*.

Rigour, severity of Manners and Disposition.

Rigour of the Law, is the severity of the Law.

Riot, Rout, Rabble or Tumult: In Law, it denotes the forcible doing of an unlawful act by three or more Persons met together for that purpose.

A Ripier, one that brings Fish from the Sea Coasts to sell in the Inland Parts.

Risible, (Lat.) capable of Laughing.

Rising Timbers in a Ship, are the Hooks placed on her Keel.

Risings in a Ship, are those thick Planks which go Fore and Aft on both sides under the ends of the Beams and Timbers of the second Deck, Half-Deck, and Quarter-Deck, and on them the Beams and Timbers of the Deck do bear at both ends by the Ship's side.

Risk, or *Risco*, a Hazard, a dangerous Accident.

Risus Sardonius, a convulsive kind of Grinning, caus'd by a contraction of the Muscles on both sides of the Mouth.

Rite, (Lat.) an Order to be observed on solemn Occasions; a Church Ceremony.

Ritornello, (Ital.) the repeating of six Notes at the end of a Song, or of a Couplet of Verses at the end of a Stanza.

Ritual, a Book of the Rites or Ceremonies of the Church.

Rivage, (Fr.) Bank, Shore; also a Toll sometimes pay'd for the passing of Boats over some Rivers.

Rival, (Lat.) a Competitor, or one that pursues the same thing with another, chiefly in Love Affairs.

Rive, to cleave asunder.

Rivulet, a small River or Brook.

Rix-Dollar, a German Coin worth about 4 s. 6 d.

Road, is a place near the Land where Ships may ride at Anchor.

Robbins, in a Ship are those small Lines which make the Sails fast to the Yards, being reeved into eyelet Holes in the Sail, under the Head Ropes for that purpose.

Robust, (Lat.) strong like Oak, strong limb'd, hardy.

Roche-Alom, is a very stiptick mineral Salt found in the Veins of the Earth in many places of Europe.

Rochet, a sort of Surplice or Ornament worn by Bishops.

Rodomontado, (Ital.) a vainglorious boasting.

Rogation-Week, the next Week but one before *Whitsuntide*, having its Name from the Supplications enjoin'd at that time.

Roist, to swagger or boast.

Bbbb4   *Roll*,

Roll, in Law, is a Schedule of Paper or Parchment, which may be turned or wound up in the fashion of a Pipe.

The Rolls, the Office where the Chancery Records are kept.

Roman Catholicks, are such as embrace the Doctrines of the Church of *Rome,* and are so called from their boasting themselves to be the only true Members of the Catholick or Universal Church.

Roman Order of Architecture, the same with the Composit ; *which see.*

Romance, (Fr.) a feigned Story about amorous Adventures and Intreagues.

Romanist, one of the Church of *Rome,* a Papist.

Romantick, belonging to a Romance, Fictitious.

Rompee, a Term in Heraldry, signifying a Chevron born of this Figure. He beareth a *Chevron Rompee between* 3 *Mullets.*

Rondel, in Fortification is a round Tower sometimes erected at the Foot of the Bastions.

Ronts, young Bullocks. *Spencer.*

Rood, a square measure, containing ¼ of an Acre of Land, or 40 square Polls, or 1210 square Yards.

Roof-Trees, in a Ship, are small Timbers that bear up the Gratings from the Halfdeck to the Fore-castle, and are supported by Stantions.

Rook, a known Bird ; also a Cheat, or Sharper.

Root, in Arithmetick, is a Number considered in order to be multiplied once or more times by it self, to make thereby Products called Powers.

Rope-Yarn, the Yarn of any Rope untwisted.

Rope-yard, the place where Ropes are made.

Rorid, (Lat.) dewy, moist.

Rosary, a place where Roses grow ; also a short Prayer Book said with Beads containing 15 *Pater-nosters,* and 150 *Ave-maries,* and used by the Confraternity of the Rosary instituted by St. *Dominick.*

Rosi-Crucians, are Chymists who call themselves Brothers of the Holy Cross.

Rosin, an oily Juice that runs out of some Trees.

Rostrum, in Chymistry, is the Nose of an Alembick.

Rotundity, (Lat.) roundness.

Rotation, (Lat.) a turning round like a Wheel.

Rotator Major & Minor, are two *Apophyses* in the upper part of the Thigh-bone called *Trochanters,* in which the Tendons of many Muscles are terminated.

Rotundus, a Muscle of the *Radius,* serving to turn the Hand downwards.

Rove,

Rove, to ramble, to have rambling Thoughts or Discourse.

Roulade, (Fr.) a Trill, Quavering or Trilling.

Roundelay, or *Roundell*, a *Shepherd's* Song sung by several in their turns, or as in a round.

Round-House, in a Ship, is the uppermost Room or Cabbin on the Stern of the Ship where the Master lies.

Round-Head, opposed to a Cavalier in the late Civil Wars, one of the Parliament Party, who usually wore short Hair.

Route, (Fr.) Road, Way, especially that which military Forces are to march thro'.

Rowel, in Surgery, a skain of Silk or Thread drawn through the Nape of the Neck.

Rowle, in a Ship, is a round piece of Wood or Iron wherein the Whip goes, being made to turn about that it may carry over the Whip the easier from side to side.

Rowse in, at Sea, signifies to hall in, or pull in; but it properly belongs to the Cable or Hawser.

Royal Parapet, in Fortification, is a Bank about three Fathoms broad and six Foot high, placed upon the brink of the Rampire towards the Country, to cover those who defend the Rampire.

Royal Society, a Society incorporated by King *Charles* II. under the name of President, Council and Fellows of the Royal Society of *London*, for the improvement of Natural Philosophy.

Royalty, Royal Dignity, Kingship.

Royalties, or *Royal Rights*, according to the Civilians, are six in number, the Power of Judicature; the Power of Life and Death; Power of War and Peace; Goods that have no Owners; Coyning of Money; and levying Taxes.

Rubican, a true mixt Roan Horse.

Rubicund, (Lat.) ruddy; Blood-red.

Rubiginous, (Lat.) rusty, foul.

Rubigo, or *Mildew*, is a Disease which happens to Plants.

Rubrick, the directions given in the Liturgy; so called, because formerly written or printed in red; the Office it self being done in black Letters; it is now printed in Italick Letter; also any Title or Sentence in red Letters.

Ructation, or *Belching*, is a depraved motion of the Stomach, occasioned by an effervescence there, whereby Vapours and Flatulent Humours are sent out at the Mouth.

Rudder of a Ship, a piece of Wood hung on the Stern-Posts by Hooks and Hinges, and by this the Ship is directed and turned at Pleasure.

Rudder

Rudder-Irons, are the Checks of that Iron whereof the Pintle is part, which is faſtened and nailed down about the Rake of the Rudder.

Rudiments, (Lat.) are the Principles or firſt Grounds of an Art.

Ruffian, an Aſſaſſin, a deſperate Villain.

Ruffle, to wrincle, to diſorder or make one chafe.

Rugitus, (Lat.) an efferveſcence of Chyle and Excrements in the Blood, whereby Wind and other motions are excited in the Guts, and rowl up and down, the Excrements finding no paſſage either upwards or downwards.

Rugoſiſty, (Lat.) ruggedneſs, a being full of wrinkles, plaits, or furrows.

Rumbs, are the Points of the Compaſs, and ſometimes the Road a Ship makes at Sea by following one of the Points of the Compaſs.

Ruminant, chewing the Cud.

Rummage, to remove Lumber out of one place into another.

Run of a Ship, is ſo much of her Hull as is always under Water.

Rundles, in Heraldry, ſignifies Balls or Bullets.

Rung-Heads, are thoſe Heads of the Ground-Timbers of a Ship which are made a little bending to direct the Sweep or Mould of

the Futtocks and Naval Timbers.

Rungs, in a Ship, are thoſe Timbers which conſtitute her Floor.

Ruptory, a Cauſtick, or a corroſive Medicine.

Rupture, (Lat.) a Breach of Friendſhip, of a Bone, &c.

Rural, (Lat.) belonging to the Country.

Ruſtical, (Lat.) clowniſh, unmannerly.

Ruſticated, made, or become clowniſh.

Rut, the Copulation of Deer, wild Boars, &c.

Ruthful, pitiful, compaſſionate.

S.

SAbbathians, a ſort of Chriſtian Hereticks, ſo called from one *Sabathius* a Jew, and afterwards an Heretical Biſhop of the fourth Century.

Sabbatarians, a Name about an Age ago given to ſome Anabaptiſts who obſerved the Saturday like the Jews.

Sabbath-days-Journey, in Scripture is 729 Engliſh Paces and 3 Feet.

Sabeans, the name of a Chriſtian Sect, patch'd up of *Chriſtianiſm, Judaiſm, Mahometaniſm,* and Heatheniſh Superſtition: They receive Baptiſm in Commemoration of *John's* Baptizing, but do not adminiſter it in the name
of

of the Holy Trinity. They own four Sacraments, Baptism, the Eucharist, Orders and Matrimony; their Ministers as well as Laicks, are allowed each of them two Wives.

Sabellians, a Sect of Christian Hereticks, the followers of one *Sabellius*, who taught that there was no distinction between the Persons of the Trinity, but that they were all one, as the Body, Soul and Spirit make but one Man.

Sable, the Heralds Word for a black Colour in the Arms of Gentlemen, but in those of the Nobility they call it *Diamond*, and in the Coats of Sovereign Princes *Saturn*. 'Tis expressed in Engraving by strokes drawn perpendicularly a-cross, thus. Also a rich Fur.

Sabliere, a Sand-Pit, or Gravel-Pit.

Sacerdotal, (Lat) Priestly, belonging to a Priest.

Saccophori, a Sect of *Messalian* Hereticks, so called from their frequently covering themselves with great Sacks.

Sacculi Medicinalis, little Physical Bags filled with several Simples, and applied to the Part affected.

Sacculus Chyliferus, is the common Receptacle of the Chyle.

Saccus, sometimes signifies the Gut called Rectum.

Sacrament, (Lat.) signifies a military Oath; but as now used, 'tis *An outward and visible Sign of an inward and Spiritual Grace.*

Sacramental, belonging to a Sacrament.

Sacramento Recipiendo, quod vidua Regis, &c. a Writ or Commission to one, for taking an Oath of the King's Widow, that she may not marry without the King's Licence.

Sacred, (Lat.) Holy, that deserves Veneration, not to be injured.

Sacrilege, is an alienation to prophane and common Purposes, of what was given to Religious Persons and to Pious Uses. The stealing of things out of a Holy Place, Church-Robbing.

Sacrum os, is the broadest of all the Bones in the Back, and sustains all the other *Vertebræ*.

Sadduces, an Heretical Sect among the antient Jews, who denied the Existence of the Spirits, the Immortality of the Soul, and the Resurrection of the Body.

Sadducism, the Principles and Doctrines of the *Sadduces*.

Saffron of Gold, or *Aurum Fulminans*, is a Chymical Preparation of Gold that fired, makes an Explosion like Gun-Powder.

Sagacious, quick-sighted, subtle, shrewd, apprehensive.
Sagacity,

Sagacity, sharpness of Wit, quickness of Apprehension or Understanding.

Sage, (Lat.) Wise, Prudent; Sublantively, a wise Man, or great Philosopher.

Sageness, Gravity or Prudence.

Sagitta, a Constellation in the Northern Hemisphere.

Sagitta, in Mathematicks, is the versed Sine of any Arch or Circle.

Sagittalis Sutura, is that Suture of the Skull which begins at the Coronal, and ends at the Lambdoidal Suture.

Sagittarius, the name of one of the Signs of the Zodiack.

Saick, a sort of Merchant Ship, used chiefly in the Mediterranean.

To Saigner a Moat, to drain the Water by conveyances under Ground that it may be more easily passed over, after having cast Hurdles on the Mud that remains.

St. Antony's Fire. See Erisypelas.

Sail, in a Ship, is made of several pieces of strong Cloth, and fastened to the Yards and Stays; and every Yard in a Ship hath its proper Sail belonging to it.

Saker, a sort of Cannon, and is of three sorts.

Saker extraordinary, is 4 Inches Diameter at the Bore, 10 Foot long, its load is 5 Pounds, Shot 3 Inches ¼ Diameter, and something more than 7 Pound Weight.

Saker Ordinary, is 3 Inches ½ Diameter at the Bore, 9 Foot long, its load 4 Pounds of Powder, Shot 3 Inches ¼ Diameter, and 6 Pound Weight.

Saker the least size, is 3 Inches ½ Diameter at theBore, 8 Foot long, its load near 3 Pounds and a half, Shot 4 Pound ¼ Weight, and 3 Inches Diameter.

Salacious, (Lat.) Lustful, Leacherous, Wanton.

Salade, among the Romans was antiently a slight Covering for the Head, which the light Horse-men wore.

Salamander, a spotted Creature like a Lizzard, that will for some time endure the flames of Fire.

Salamander's Blood, a name the Chymists give to the red Vapours, which in distillation of Spirit of Nitre, towards the latter end, do fill the Receiver with red Clouds.

Salary, (Lat.) at first signified the Rents or Profits of a Sala or House; but now it signifies any Wages or annual Allowance.

Saliant Angle, is what advances with its Point towards the Country; such is the Angle of the Counterscarp before the Point of the Bastion.

Salient, (Lat.) the Heralds Term for a Lyon in a leaping posture.

Saline, saltish, of a Saltish Nature.

Salique

Salique Law, a Law whereby the Crown of *France* cannot be inherited by a Woman.

Saliva, (Lat.) the Spittle.

Salivation, is an evacuation of Spittle, by Salivating Medicines, which are commonly Mercurial Preparations.

Sallow, pale.

Sally, is when the Besieged march out of the Garrison, to attack the Besiegers in their Works, to nail their Cannon, and to hinder the Progress of their Approaches.

Salt, the third of the five Chymical Principles, and 'tis of three sorts *Fixt*, *Volatile*, and *Essential*.

Saltation, (Lat.) a Dancing or Leaping.

Saltier, the name of one of the Ordinaries in Heraldry in the form of St. *Andrew's* Cross.

Salva Gardia, is a security given by the King to a Stranger, fearing the violence of some of his Subjects, for seeking his Right by Course of Law.

Salvage Money, a Recompence allow'd by the Civil Law to a Ship that has saved or rescu'd another from Enemies or Pirates.

Salvatory, a Surgeon's Box for holding several sorts of Salves, Ointments and Balsams.

Salubrity, (Lat.) wholsomness, Healthfulness.

A Salvo, a caution or reserve.

Salutary wholesome, sound, profitable.

Salutation, the formal act of shewing Respect and Civility either in Words or Ceremonies.

Salutiferous, bringing Health or Safety.

Samaritans, a People of *Samaria*, a Country and City of *Syria*; also a Sect among the Jews, who rejected all the Scripture, save only the five Books of *Moses*, denied the Resurrection, but held there were Angels.

Samplar, from *Exemplar*, a Pattern or Copy to imitate, a Model or Draught.

Sanative Waters, are the Mineral Waters of any kind.

Sanctification, (Lat.) a Sanctifying or making Holy.

Sanction, (Lat.) a decreeing, enacting or establishing any Decree or Ordinance; also the Decree or Ordinance it self.

Sanctuary, a Holy or Sanctified Place; in the old Law 'twas the most holy Place of the Jewish Tabernacle; also a place privileged by the Prince for the Safe-guard of Offenders Lives, or a Place of Refuge.

Sanctum Sanctorum, was the holiest place of the Jews Temple, where the Ark was kept, and whereunto none entred but the High Priest, and he but once a Year.

Sandal, a rich Wear for the Feet used by Roman Ladies;

dies; also a kind of Shoe open at top and faftened with Latchets.

Sandarack, is the name which fome Chymiſts give to red Arſenick.

Sangiack, a Turkiſh Governour, next in Dignity to *a Beglerbeg*.

Sanctification, (Lat.) is the turning of Chyle into Blood, which is performed in all the parts of the Body, and not in any one particular part.

Sanguinary, Bloody, Blood-thirſty or Cruel.

Sanguine, (Lat.) the Heralds Term for the Colour uſually called *Murry*, or a dark brown Colour; alſo of a ruddy Complexion.

Sanhedrim, (Heb.) the fupream Council or Court of Judicature among the Jews, confiſting of the High-Prieſt, and ſeventy Seniors or Elders. This was, as it were their Parliament to confult about and decide the greateſt Matters that could ariſe in their Eccleſiaſtical or Civil Commonwealth.

Sanity, (Lat.) Health, Soundneſs.

Saphæna, is the Vein of the Leg, or crural Vein.

Saphatum, is a dry Scurf in the Head.

Sapience, ſolid Wiſdom. *Milton*.

Saporific, (Lat.) cauſing Taſte, as *Saporifick Particles* are fuch as occaſion that Senſation which we call Taſte.

Saporous Bodies, are fuch as afford fome fort of taſt when touched with the Tongue.

Sapp, is the digging deep under the Earth, in finking lower by degrees to paſs under the Glacis, and open a way to come under cover to the paſſage to the Moat.

A Sapphire, a Precious Stone a deep Skie-colour.

Saraband, a fort of Muſical Compoſition in Triple-time; alſo a Dance in the fame meaſure.

Sarcaſm, (Gr.) a bitter jeſt, a biting ſcoff or taunt.

Sarcaſtical, Scoffing, Satyrical.

Sarcling-time, (from the Fr. *Sarcler* to rake or weed) is the time when the Country-man weeds his Corn.

Sarcocele, in Phyſick, is a Rupture which couſiſts in a fleſhy Excreſcence of the Teſticles.

Sarcæpiplocele, a carnous omental Rupture.

Sarcoma, a fleſhy Excreſcence in the Noſtrils.

Sarcomphalum, is a fleſhy Excreſcence of the Navel.

Sarcoticks, are thoſe Medicines which fill up Wounds with Fleſh.

Sarculation, (Lat.) plucking up of Weeds.

Sardonian Laughter, is an involuntary Laughter, or a convulſive Diſtortion of the Muſcles of the Mouth in which the Patient appears to laugh.

Sardonix, a Precious Stone partly

partly of the colour of a Man's Nail, and partly of a Cornelian Colour.

Sarplar of Wool, or a half Sack, contains 40 Tod.

Sarrasin, in Fortification, is a kind of Portcullice, otherwise called a Herse hung over the Gate of a Town.

Sartorius, a Muscle of the Leg by which we throw one Leg over the other, or a cross the other.

Satanical, belonging to *Satan,* Devilish.

Satellites, the small secundary Planets that move round *Jupiter* and *Saturn* are so called, the Moon likewise in the same sense is a *Satellite* to the Earth.

Satiate, to satisfie, clog or glut.

Satiety, (Lat.) fulness or glutting.

Satisfactory, (Lat.) sufficient, or which satisfies.

Satrapy, (Pers.) a Lieutenancy, a Dutchy.

Saturity, fulness, excess.

Saturn, one of the Planets the most remote from the Sun, according to some 71 times, and according to others 91 times bigger than the Earth.

Saturnine, of a melancholy Disposition.

Satyr, a kind of Poetry, sharply inveighing against Vice and vicious Persons.

Satyrical, belonging to Satyr, sharp, severe.

Satyrs, certain paltry *Demi-Gods,* said to dwell in Woods and Deserts, represented like a horned Man with Goats Feet.

Savage, (Fr.) wild, fierce, barbarous.

Savana's, (Span.) Pasture Grounds in *America* for feeding Deer and other Cattel.

Saucisse, is a long train of Powder sewed up in a roll of pitched Cloth, of about two Inches diameter; the use of it is to fire Mines.

Saucissons, are Faggots or Fascines, made of great boughs of Trees bound together; the use whereof is to cover Men, or to make Epaulments.

Saxifrage, i. e. Breakstone, a kind of Herb.

Scabrous, (Lat.) rough, unpolished, rugged.

Scalado, in Fortification, is the mounting of a Wall of a fortified Town or Castle, with scaling Ladders.

Scale of the Gamut or *Musical Scale,* is a kind of Diagram consisting of certain Lines and Spaces whereby an artificial Voice or Sound may either ascend or descend.

Scalenous Triangle, one that has its three sides unequal to one another.

Scaleni, three Muscles of the *Thorax,* so called from the inequality of their sides.

Scalprum, (Lat.) a Surgeon's scraping Iron with which he scrapes rotten Wounds.

Scamble, to rove or wander up and down.

Scambl-

Scambling Town, a Town wherein the Houses stand at a great distance.

Scamilli Impares, in Architecture, are certain Blocks or Zocco's which serve to elevate the rest of the Members of anyColumn orStatue, which was placed before the Horizon.

Scamnum Hippocratis, an Instrument of six Ells long, an Instrument for setting of Bones.

Scandal, (Gr.) Stumbling-block or Offence, ill Name, bad Example, Shame.

Scandalize, to give Offence, raise a Scandal.

Scandalum Magnatum, (Lat.) a Writ to recover Damage from wrong done to a Peer or any great Officer of the Realm, by scandalous Reports, &c. also the wrong that is done.

Scanned, enquired into, disputed. *Milton*.

Scarfed, at Sea, signifies pieced, fastened or joined in.

Scarification, (Lat.) is an Incision of the Skin with a Penknife or Lancet.

Scarp, in Fortification, is the inward Slope of the Moat or Ditch of a Place ; *i. e.* the Slope of that side of the Ditch, which is next to the Place, and looks towards the Field ; also the Foot of the Rampart Wall, or the sloaping of the Wall from the bottom of the Work to the Cordon on the side of the Moat.

Scarpe, in Heraldry, is the Scarf which Military Commanders wear for Ornament, as he beareth *Argent, a Scarpe Azure*.

Scaramouch, the Name of a famous *Italian* Buffoon, who acted in *London*, Anno 1673.

Scarf-Skin, is the outmost Skin of a Man's Body which serves to defend it, and being full of Pores evacuates Sweat.

Scate, a kind of Pattens to go upon the Ice.

Scathe, loss, hinderance. *Spencer*.

Scavenger, (Dut.) a ParishOfficer that takes care to pare away the Dirt, and cleanse the Streets.

Scenes, the changing of Persons in every Act of a Comedy ; also the Pictures representing Landskips, Buildings, &c. round about the Stage.

Scenography, in Architecture and Fortification, is the representation of a Building or Foretress, as they are represented in Perspective.

Scepter, a King's commanding Staff, and born by him when he appears in Ceremony; 'tis one of the Badges of the Royal Dignity.

Sceptical, (Gr.) of that Sect of Philosophers called *Scepticks*.

Septicism, (Gr.) the Doctrine and Opinion of *Scepticks*.

Scepticks, were a Sect of Philosophers, who maintained that there is nothing certain, and no real Knowledge at all to be had, but a Man ought to doubt of and disbelieve every thing; *Pyrrho* was the Author of this Sect.

Scedule, a scroll of Paper or Parchment.

Scheme, (Gr.) the outward fashion of any thing; it commonly signifies a Mathematical Figure, and is taken in the same sense with *Diagram*.

Schirras, is a hard, livid Swelling, that resists the Touch, and is without Pain.

Schism, is properly a division in, or separation from the Christian Church, without any just cause.

Schismatick, a separatist, or one that separates from the Christian Church, without any just cause.

Scholastick, of or belonging to the Schools.

Scholastick Divinity, relates to controverted Points, such as are usually disputed in Schools.

Scholiast, one that writes Scholiums.

Scholium, a Gloss, a brief Exposition or short Comment.

Sciatica, (Lat.) the Gout in the Hip.

Science, is Knowledge founded upon clear, certain, and self-evident Principles.

Sciography, (Gr.) is the Art of Shadows or Dialing; also in Architecture, the draught of a Building cut in its length and breadth, to show the inside of it.

Sciolist, a Smatterer in any kind of knowledge.

Scioptrick, is a Sphere or Globe of Wood, with a circular hole through it, and a *Lens* placed therein; 'tis so fitted, as that like the Eye of an Animal it may be turned round every way; and 'tis used in making the Experiments of the darkened Room.

Scire facias, a Writ calling one to shew, why Judgment pass'd at least a Year should not be executed.

Scleropthalmy, (Gr.) is a hard blearedness of the Eyes, accompanied with Pain.

Scleroticks, (Gr.) or hardening Medicines, are such as unite the Parts more firmly among themselves.

Scloopomachærion, is a Surgeon's Knife with which Wounds of the *Thorax* are widened, and also larger swellings opened.

Sconces, in Fortification, are small Forts, built for defence of some Pass, River, or other Place.

Scoper-Holes, in a Ship, are holes made through the side,

close to the Deck, to carry off the Water that comes from the Pump, or any other way.

Scorbutick, troubled with, or subject to the *Scurvy*.

Scorpion, one of the twelve Signs of the Zodiack thus marked ♏.

Scot, (Fr.) a Part, Portion, Shot, or Reckoning; and according to some, 'tis a certain Custom, or common Tillage made to the use of the Sheriff and his Bailiffs.

Scotia, in Architecture, is the same with *Trochile*.

Scotomy, (Gr.) dizziness or swiming of the Head, is when the Animal Spirits are so whirled about, that external Objects seem to turn round.

Screen, to keep off the heat of the Fire, or defend from heat.

Scribler, a sorry Writer, or a very bad Author.

Scribes, a powerful Sect among the Jews, who expounded the Law to the People, upon which account they were called Doctors of the Law, and Lawyers.

Scriptulum, a Grecian and Roman Weight, containing 18 $\frac{3}{14}$ when reduced to Troy Weight.

Scriptural, belonging to the Holy Scriptures.

Scripturist, is one who grounds his Faith on Scripture only.

Scrobiculis Cordis, the Heart Pit, is a Cavity of the Breast a little above the Region or Place of the Heart.

Scrotum, in Anatomy, is that Bag which contains the Testicles of the Male, which is composed of two Membranes besides a Scarf Skin.

Scrowles, a Term in Architecture. See *Volutes*.

Scudds before the Wind, runs before the Wind. *Shakespeare*.

Scrutiny, (Lat.) a strict search or enquiry into a thing.

Scutage, (Lat.) from *Scutum*, a Shield, whereon they formerly wore a Device or military distinction, whence *Scutum armorum* a Coat of Arms. All Tenants who held from the King by military Service, were bound to attend personally in Wars and Expeditions, or for default of Personal Service, a *Scutage* or Composition Tax on every *Scutum Militare*, or Knights Fee, was asserted and levied for the King's use.

Scuttles, are little square holes, cut in the Deck, big enough to let a Man through; they serve to let People down below on occasion, or from Deck to Deck.

Scurrility, (Lat.) Buffonry, Scoffing, or saucy Jesting.

Scurrilous, Railing, or saucily Abusive.

Sea, is that general Collection of Waters which encompasseth the Earth, and has different names according to the different Countries it washes.

Sea's,

Seah, a Hebrew Measure of Capacity for things liquid, containing 2 Gallons, 4 Pints, and 5 solid Inches, when reduced to our English Measure.

Sea-gates, among Sea-men, are the Waves and Billows of the Sea.

Sea-Yoke, is two Blocks seized to the end of the Helm, one on each side, with two small Ropes reeved through them, which they call Falls, and which are fastened to the sides of the Ship, some Men stand at each Tackle and govern the Ship according to direction.

Sea-drags, are whatever hangs over the Ships in the Sea, as Shirts, Coats, and the like.

Sea Chart. See *Chart*.

To Seal Hermetically, is to stop the Mouth or Neck of a glass Vessel with a pair of Pincers heated red hot.

Seams of a Ship, are places where her Planks meet and join together.

Seasonable, opportune or convenient.

Secant, cutting, or which cuts another, also a Line which cuts a Circle.

Secession, (Lat.) a going aside, as the Secession of a Parliament.

Seclude, (Lat.) to shut forth or turn out.

Second, the sixtieth part of a Minute.

Second Deliverance, a Writ that lieth after the return of Cattle replevied, for the replevying of the same Cattle again by reason of some default in the Party that replevied.

Secondary Circles, with reference to the Equinoctial, are Hour Circles; and with reference to the Ecliptick are Circles of Longitude of the Stars; and with reference to the Horizon are Azimuths or Vertical Circles; by the help of these *Secundary Circles*, all the Points in the Heavens are referred to the Equinoctial, Ecliptick, or Horizon.

Secondary Planets, are such as move round others as the Centre of their motions, such is our Moon, the *Satellites* of *Jupiter* and *Saturn*.

Secondary of the Counters, the next Officer to the Sheriffs of *London*.

Secretary, one that is imployed in writing Letters, Dispatches, &c.

Secretion, (Lat.) is the seperation of one Fluid from another in the Body of an Animal or Vegetable.

Sectary, (Lat.) i.e. separating, or setting a part from others; one that adheres to any Sect, i.e. Faction or Party.

Section, a word frequently used in Mathematicks, and is that Point in which two Lines intersect or cut one another, that Line in which two Surfaces cut one another, or that Plane in which a Plane cuts a Solid.

     Sector,

Sector, a Portion of a Circle, comprehended between two Radii and an Ark of a Circle.

Secular, (Lat.) Temporal; of or belonging to this World.

Secular Priest, is one that takes upon him the care of Souls, and does not live under any Rules of Religious Orders.

Secundans, a word made use of by Dr. *Wallis* in his Arithmetick of Infinities, and denotes a series of the Squares of Arithmetick Proportionals, beginning from nothing.

Secundine, the After-Birth, or the three Membranes wherein the Child is wrapped whilst it is in the Womb, and which are excluded after the Child is born.

Securitate Pacis, a Writ against him that threatens another with Death or Danger.

Security, (Lat.) safety; also surety for the Payment of Money; also carelesness, or a being without any fear of danger.

Sedate, (Lat.) quiet, composed, undisturbed.

Se defendendo, a Plea for killing one in his own defence; yet must he procure his Pardon from my Lord Chancellor, and forfeit his Goods to the King.

Sedentary, (Lat.) that is much given to sitting.

Sediment, (Lat.) the settlement, or dregs of any thing.

Sedition, (Lat.) Mutiny, Strife, popular Tumult.

Seduce, to lead a Man astray into Error, to entice him to Wickedness.

Sedulous, diligent, careful, industrious.

Seel, at Sea has much the same signification with *Heel*, for as a Ship is said to *Heel*, when she lies down constantly or steadily on one side, so she is said to *Seel* when she tumbles on one side violently and suddenly.

Segment, (Lat.) a part cut off; as a *Segment* of a Line is a part of that Line cut of; a *Segment* of a Circle, is a Figure terminated by a right Line less than the Diameter and the Circumference, and 'tis only a part cut off the Circle.

Seignior, (Fr.) in Law, a Lord of the Fee, or of the Mannor.

Grand Seignior, that is, *Grand Lord*, a Title given to the Turkish Emperor.

Seigniory, (Fr.) a Lordship, or the Jurisdiction of a Lord.

Segregation, (Lat.) a separating from the rest of the Flock, a parting.

Segreiant, in Heraldry, are Griffins drawn in a Salient or Leaping Posture.

Seiant, (i. e. sitting) the Heralds Term for a Lion or other Beast when it is drawn in an Escutcheon, sitting like a Cat with his Feet strait.

Seisin,

Seifin, a Law Term for Poffeffion.

Seifina habenda, a Writ for delivery of Seifin to the Lord of the Land or Tenements, after the King hath had the Year, Day and Wafte.

Seizing, in the Sea Language, is the fame as faftening.

Semblance, refembling, likenefs. *Milton.*

Semeiotica, is that part of Phyfick which treats of the figns of Health and Sicknefs.

Semets, are the Apices of the Attire of a Plant.

Semi-Arrians, the Arrian Sect was divided into two principal Parties, the one of which fticking more clofely to the Opinion of their Mafter maintained that the Son of God was unlike the Father; and the other refufed to receive the word *Confubftantial*, yet acknowledged the Son of God of a like Subftance or Effence with the Father, and therefore were called *Semi-Arrians.*

Semi-brief, a Note in Mufick, containing two Minims, four Crotchets, &c.

Semi-circle, half a Circle, or a Figure contained between the Diameter of a Circle and half the Circumference.

Semi-colon, half a Colon, a Point of diftinction in Writing or Printing, thus marked (;).

Semicupium, is a Bath, in which the Patient is only up to the Navel in Water.

Semi-diameter, in Geometry, is a Line drawn from the Centre of a Circle to its Circumference.

Semi-diapafon, a Term in Mufick, fignifying a defective or imperfect *Octave.*

Semi-diapente, in Mufick, is an imperfect Fifth.

Semi-ditone, in Mufick, is the leffer Third, having its terms as fix to five.

Seminal, (Lat.) belonging to Seed.

Seminary, a Seed-Plot or Nurfery of Plants; alfo a College of young Students.

Semi-Pelagians, a fort of Chriftian Hereticks, who endeavoured to find a Mean between the *Pelagians* and the Orthodox. They agreed with the *Pelagians* in the Power of Free-Will, at leaft as to the beginning of Faith and Converfion.

Sempiternal, (Lat.) perpetual, endlefs.

Senate, properly the fupreme Council among the antient *Romans*, or the place where they affembled; a Parliament, or the Bench of Aldermen in a City.

Senator, a Member of the Senate, an Alderman.

Send, at Sea, a Ship is faid to Send much when fhe falls deep a Stern, or a Head into the hollow between two Waves.

Senefcent, (Lat.) waxing Old, growing in Years.

Senior, (Lat.) the Elder.

     Sen-

Sensation, (Lat.) is that perception which the Mind has when any Object strikes the Senses.

Sensitive Plants, are such as contract their Leaves or Flowers when touched, as if they were really sensible of the Contact.

Sensory, is that place of the Brain where Sensation is performed.

Sensuality, Libertinism, the gratifying of the Senses, or satisfying the Appetite.

Sententious, full of Sentences, *i. e.* grave or wise Sayings.

Sentiment, (Fr.) Opinion, Judgment.

Sentinel, (Fr.) a Sentry, a common Soldier appointed to stand and watch in a certain place.

Separability, (Lat.) a possibility of being separated.

Separable, (Lat.) that may be separated.

Separate, (Lat.) distinct or particular.

Separatist, a Schismatick, or one that separates himself from the Church without any lawful Reason.

Septangular, (Lat.) that hath seven Angles.

September, (Lat.) a Month so called, because 'tis the seventh from *March*.

Septemfluous, (Lat.) divided or flowing into seven Streams.

Septempedal, (Lat.) belonging to 7 Feet, or 7 Foot long.

Septenary, (Lat.) of or belonging to the number seven.

Septennial, (Lat.) of the Space or Age of seven Years.

Septennarius, a Constellation in the Northern Hemisphere.

Septentrio, (Lat.) the North.

Septentrional, (Lat.) Northern.

Septica, are those things which, by a malignant sharpness, rot and corrupt the Flesh.

Septuagenary, (Lat.) belonging to the number 70.

Septuagesima, the third Sunday from the first Sunday of *Lent*, so called, because 'tis about seventy Days from *Easter*.

Septuagint, or *Septuagint-Bible*, the *Greek* Translation of the Old Testament, by the 72 Jewish Elders, at the appointment of *Ptolemy Philadelphus*, King of *Egypt*.

Septum Cordis, the fleshy part that divides the right Ventricle of the Heart from the left.

Sepulchral, belonging to a Grave or Funeral.

Sepulchre, (Lat.) a Grave or Tomb.

Sepulture, (Lat.) Interment, Burial.

Sequel, (Lat.) what follows; a Consequence or Conclusion.

Sequence, a following in Order.

Sequester, or *Sequestrate*, (in the Civil Law) is when a Widow disclaims to have any thing to do with the Estate of her deceased Husband,

band. In the Common Law, it fignifies to feparate a thing in difpute from the poffeffion of the contending Parties, or the true Proprietor or Owner.

Sequeftrator, the third Perfon to whom the thing in Controverfie is committed.

Sequeftro habendo, a Writ for the diffolving the Bifhop's Sequeftration of the Fruits of a Benefice, &c.

Seraglio, the Palace of the Grand Seignior.

Seraph, one of an Order of Angels, plurally called *Seraphim*. Milton.

Seraphical, or *Seraphick*, belonging to a Seraphim, or one of the higheft Order of Angels.

Serapies, Houfhold Gods of the antient *Ægyptians*, fome of whofe Idols they placed in their famous Pyramids, their Office being according to them, to preferve the Corps depofited there, and tranfport their Souls to Heaven.

Serafquier, a Generaliffimo or Commander in chief of the Turkifh Forces.

Sere, withered. *Spencer*.

Serenade, (Fr.) Night Mufick, play'd by a Lover at his Miftreffes Door, or under her Window.

Serene, (Lat.) clear, fair, without Clouds.

Serenity, (Lat.) clearnefs of the Sky, calmnefs of Mind; alfo a Title given to fome Princes, or Chief Ma-

giftrates of Commonwealths.

Sergeant at Law, is the higheft degree taken in that Poffeffion, as a Doctor in the Civil Law.

Series, (Lat.) is an orderly Procefs or Continuation of things one after another.

Serious, (Lat.) fober, grave, important, fincere.

Sermocination, (Lat.) talking, or holding a Difcourfe.

Seron, a certain variable Weight, of Almonds, 2 C. of Annis-feeds, from 3 to 4 C. of Caftle-foap from 2½ C. to 3¼ C.

Serofity, (Lat.) waterifhnefs; alfo the watery part of the Blood.

Serous, belonging to the *Serum*, waterifh.

Serpentine, (Lat.) of or belonging to a Serpent. In Chymiftry, 'tis that long winding Worm of Lead or Pewter, which is placed in a Tub of Water in the diftillation of Spirits.

Serration, in Surgery, the fawing of a Bone,

Servage, Service.

Serve, to ferve a Rope, in the Sea Language, is to lay upon it fpun Yarn, a piece of Canvafs, or the like, to keep it from fretting or galling in any place.

Servile, belonging to a Servant or Slave, flavifh.

Servitiis Acquietantibus, is a Writ judicial, that lies for one diftrained for Service, for the acquittal of fuch Services.

Servitour, a serving Man or Waiter.

Servitude, Bondage, Slavery, Thraldom.

Serum, is a watery fort of a Liquor; it is the vehicle of the Blood; and 'tis that watery part that separates from the Blood, after any Person is let Blood, and the Blood has stood for some time.

Sesqui, (Lat.) as much and half as much.

Sesquialteral ratio, of two Quantities, is when the first is to the latter, as one and a half to one.

Sesquipedal, (Lat.) containing a Foot and a half in length.

Sesquiquadrate, an Aspect of the Planets, when at the distance of four Signs and a half.

Sesquiquartan, containing another thing once, and a fourth part more.

Sesqui-quartile, a new Aspect of the Planets when they are distant 135°.

Sesqui-quintile, an Aspect when two Planets are distant 108°.

Session, or *Sitting*; as a Session of Parliament; the *Quarter* or *General Sessions* are the Assizes that are held four times a Year in all the Counties in *England*, to determine Civil and Criminal Causes.

Sestertius, a Roman Coin worth a Penny, 3¼ Farthings of our Money.

Sestertium, among the Ro-

mans was 8 *l.* 1 *s.* 5 *d.* 2 *f.*

Set taught the Shrouds, is to make the Shrouds stiffer when too slack.

Sethians, Christian Hereticks, a Branch of the *Valentinians*; they held that *Cain* and *Abel* were created by two Angels, and that the latter being killed, the supreme Power would have *Seth* made as a pure Original; and that the Angels by their mutual Impurities drew on the Flood which destroyed their wicked Offspring; but some of them having crept into the Ark, gave a new Origin to wicked Men.

Seton, is a kind of Issue made by running a Needle through the Skin, in the Neck or elsewhere, and keeping it open by a Skean of Thread, Silk, &c.

Several Tail, is that whereby Land is given or entailed severally, to two Men and their Wives, and to the Heirs of their Bodies begotten.

Several Tenancy, is a Plea or Exception taken to a Writ that is laid against two as joint, which are several.

Severance, is the singling or severing of two that are joined in a Writ.

Severe, (Lat.) strict, rough, stern, harsh, crabbed.

Severians, Hereticks that condemn'd Marriage and eating of Flesh.

Sewn, the Ship is Sewed, that is when a Ship at low Water

Water comes to lie dry on the Ground.

Sewel, a Term used by Hunters, and signifies any thing hanged up to keep a Deer from entring a place.

Sewer, an Officer that ushers in the Meat of a King or Nobleman.

Sextarius, a Roman Measure of Capacity for things Liquid, which being reduc'd to our Wine Measure, contains 1 Pint, 5 solid Inches, and 636 decimal Parts; also a Measure for things dry, containing 1 Pint, and 48 decimal Parts of an Inch, of our Corn Measure.

Sexagenary, (Lat.) belonging to the number sixty.

Sexagesimal Fractions, such as have 60 always for their Denominator.

Sexangle, in Geometry, a Figure consisting of six Angles.

Sexennial, of six Years continuance.

Sextain, a Stanza of six Verses.

Sextans, an Astronomical Instrument, which is the sixth part of a Circle.

Sextile, the Position or Aspect of the Planets, when 60° distant from one another.

Sextry, a Vestry.

Shackles, in a Ship, a kind of Rings that serve to shut up the Ports.

Shagreen, out of Humour, Vexed; also a kind of Leather.

Shallop, (Span.) a light Ship or Bark made to attend great Vessels.

Sham, false, pretended; *verbally*, to put a Trick on one.

Shamade, a beat of the Drum for a Parley.

Shammy Leather, is made of wild Goat Skins tanned.

Shank, in a Ship, is a short Chain fastened under the Fore-Mast-Shrouds by a Bolt to the Ship's side, it serves to make fast the Anchor at the Bow.

Shapournett, in Heraldry, is a sort of Cap which is born in some Coats of Arms.

Shear, at Sea, is to swing too and again, the Ship Shears, i. e. goes in and out, and not right forward.

Shear-Hooks, Irons fixed in the Yard Arms to cut the Enemies Shrouds.

Sheat Anchor, the biggest Anchor in a Ship.

Sheathing of a Ship, is caseing that part of her which is to be under Water, with something to keep the Worms from eating into her Planks; 'tis usually done by laying Tar and Hair mixed together all over the old Planks, and then nailing on thin new Boards.

Sheats, are Ropes bent to the clew of the Sails; also those Planks under Water, which come along the Ship's Run, and are closed into the Stern-Post.

Sheen,

Sheen, fair, shining. *Spen.*

Sheers, are two Mast Yards or Posts set up an end, and at a pretty distance at the bottom, and seiz'd a-cross one another near the top; they serve to take in or let out a Mast, or else to hoise in or out into Boats that have no Masts, such Goods as are to be taken in.

Shield, defend. *Spencer.*

Shekel, a Jewish Weight, containing 9 Penny Weight, and 2½ Grains; also a Jewish Coin worth 2 Shillings 3½ Pence of our Money.

Sheer o'er, clear, over. *Milton.*

Shekle, or *Sickle*, a Jewish Silver Coin, value about 2 s. 6 d. English; there was also a common *Shekle* of half that value; and another *Gold-Shekle*, worth 1 l. 16 s. 6 d.

Shelf, a board fix'd to a Stall for laying things upon; also the Till of a Printing-Press; also a heap of Sand in the Sea.

Shend, blamed. *Spencer.*

Sherbet, a pleasant Drink made of Lemmon Juice, Sugar, Amber, &c. in great vogue among the *Turks* and *Persians.*

Sheriff of a County, from the Saxon word *Shire-reve*, that is, *Governour of the Shire*, a chief Magistrate in every Shire, nominated by the King: But there are two in *Middlesex*, chosen by the Citizens of *London.*

Sheriffalty, the Office of a Sheriff, or the time during which that Office is held.

Shewing, in Law, is to be quit of Attachments in any Court, and before whomsoever in Plaints *Shewed* and not avowed.

Shiboleth, an Hebrew word, by the pronounciation of which the *Gileadites* discovered the *Ephraimites* to be their Enemies, and not the *Gileadites* as they pretended; and hence the word is usually taken for a word of trial, to discern Citizens from Aliens, Friends from Foes, &c.

Shieve, to fall a-Stern. Sea Term.

Shifters, are those Men aboard a Man of War, who are employ'd by the Cooks to shift or change the Water in which the Flesh or Fish is put and laid for some time, in order to fit it for the Kettle.

Shingle, a Lath or piece of Wood to cover Houses with.

Shire, or *County*, a tract of Land, from the *Saxon Scyran* to divide.

Shivers, in a Ship, are those little round Wheels in which the Rope of a Pully or Block runs.

Shoale, in the Sea Language, is the same as *Shallow.*

Shock, an Encounter, or Fight; also the meeting together of two hard Bodies.

Shole, a multitude, properly of Fish. *Spencer.*

Shot

Shot of a Cable, is the splicing two Cables together that a Ship may ride safe in deep Water, and in great Roads.

Shooting-stick, a Wedge, commonly of Box, wherewith Printers lock up their Pages in the Chase.

Shouldring, in Fortification, is a Retrenchment opposed to the Enemy, it is also a square *Orillon.*

Shot for Ordnance, whereof there are several sorts, *viz. Cross-bar-Shot, Trendle-Shot, Chain-Shot, Case-Shot,* and *Round-Shot;* which see in their places.

Shoulder of a Bastion, is where the Face and the Flank meet.

Shrine, a kind of Coffer or Box to keep Relicks in.

Shrivel, to wrinkle, to run up in wrinkles or scrolls.

Shrove-tide, or *Shrove-Tuesday,* seven Weeks before *Easter,* taking its Name from the old Saxon word to *Shrive,* is to confess, because at that time Confession of Sins was usually made in order to a more Religious Observation of *Lent* season immediately following.

Shrouds, are great Ropes in a Ship that go up on both sides of all the Masts except the Bowsprit.

Shuddering, shivering, trembling. *Milton.*

Sib, a Kin, of Kind. *Spen.*

Sibil. See Sybil.

Siccity, (Lat.) dryness.

Sickle, a sort of Reaping-Hook.

Sicut alias, is a second Writ sent out when the first was not executed.

Sideration, (Lat.) blasting of Trees with the Eastern Wind, or excessive Heat; a being Planet-struck.

Sides-men, or *Quest-men,* those that are Yearly chosen according to the custom of a Parish, to assist the Church-Warden in enquiring.

Sidereal, belonging to the Stars.

Sideral-Year, is the space of Time, in which the Sun going from one fixed Star, returns to the same again; it consists of 365 Days, 6 Hours, and nearly 10 Minutes.

Side-lays, in Hunting, are Dogs laid in the way to be let loose at a Deer as he passes by.

Siege, is the encamping or sitting down of an Army before a Place, in order to take it either by Force or Famine.

Sigmoides, are the Apophyses of the Bones representing the Letter C of the antient *Greeks;* also the Valves of the great Artery that hinder the Blood from returning from the Heart.

Signal, a word frequently used at Sea, and signifies a Sign, which is most commonly made by putting out such Colours, or such a Light, firing one or more Guns, &c. to give notice or advice to the rest.

Signa-

Signalize, to do fome remarkable Action, to render a Man's Life remarkable and famous.

Signature, (Lat.) one's Hand or Mark fet to a Writing ; a Signing ; alfo among Printers, the Mark or Letter they fet at the bottom of every printed Sheet, as A, B, C, &c. to tell the Quires by, and diftinguifh one Sheet from another, is called the Signature.

Signet, a Seal fet in a Ring.

Significabit, a Writ for the imprifoning him that ftands obftinately excommunicate forty Days.

Significant, that expreffes much, or is to the purpofe, clear, effectual.

Signification, (Lat.) Meaning, Senfe.

Signifie, to mean, to intimate, to notifie, to prefage.

Signs of the Zodiack, are Conftellations which are fuppos'd to refemble living Creatures, and are twelve in number, *viz. Aries, Taurus, Gemini, Cancer, Leo, Virgo, Libra, Scorpio, Sagittarius, Aquarius, Pifces*

Silence, (Lat.) Peace; not fpeaking or making a noife.

Silentiary, a Gentleman-Ufher, who takes care that good Order and Silence be kept at Court, or elfewhere.

Siker, furely. *Spencer.*

Siliquous Plants, are fuch as are of the Leguminous Kind whofe Seed is contain'd in Husks, Cods, or Pods.

Sillabub, a well known Drink; 'tis figuratively ufed for a florid, but frothy and empty Difcourfe.

Sillon, in Fortification, is a Work raifed in the middle of a Fofs to defend it when it is too wide; it has no particular Form, being fometimes made with little Baftions, Half-Moons, Redans, which are lower than the Works of the Place, but higher than the Covert-way : This word is feldom ufed being now called *Envelope.*

A Similar Part, in Anatomy, is that, which tho' it be cut, or divided into feveral pieces, yet they will be all of the fame Nature, Subftance, and Denomination with one another, and with the whole; as every Portion or Particle of Bone, is Bone.

Similar Figures, in Geometry, are fuch, the Angles whereof are refpectively equal, and the fides about thofe equal Angles proportional.

Simile, (Lat.) a Similitude, or Comparifon.

Similitude, (Lat.) Likenefs, Comparifon, Refemblance.

Similitudinary, belonging to, or exprefs'd by way of Similitude.

Simitar, a kind of broad Sword much ufed in *Turkey* and *Perfia.*

Simoniacal, belonging to Simony, or done thereby.

Simony,

Simony, the buying or selling of Church-Livings, or other Spiritual Things for Money; 'tis so called from *Simon Magus*, who offered Money to the Apostles, that he might have power to give the Holy Ghost to any he should lay his Hands on.

Simple Problem. See *Problem*.

Simple Quantity, in Algebra, is such on one which does not consist of more parts than one connexed by the Signs + or —

Simpler, or *Somplist*, one that has skill in Simples.

Simples, Physical Herbs or Drugs.

Simpleton, a silly and half witted Person.

Simplicity, (Lat.) Singleness, plain Dealing, downright Honesty; also Silliness, Foolishness, Indiscretion.

Simpling, gathering of Simples or Physical Herbs in the Fields.

Simulation, (Lat.) a feigning, a counterfeiting, a colour of Pretence.

Sinapism, (Lat.) a Medicine made of Mustard, wild Radish and Leaven.

Sincere, (Lat.) honest, true, free, open.

Sincerity, (Lat.) Uprightness, Plainness, Honesty.

Sine, in Geometry, is a Right Line drawn from one of the Extremities of an Ark, perpendicular to the Diameter which passes thro'

the other Diameter of the same Ark.

Sine-complement of an Arch, is the Sign of what that Ark wants of 90 Degrees, or what it is greater than 90 when it exceeds them.

Sine assensu Capitali, in Law, is a Writ against him that alienates Lands without consent of his Chapter or Covent.

Sine die, dismiss the Court.

Singultus, or the Hickup, is a convulsive motion of the Midriff, caused by tough and irregular Particles forcing it to this disordinate motion.

Singular, particular, special, extraordinary.

Sinister, unlucky, unfortunate, indirect, unjust. In Heraldry, sinister side of an Escutcheon is the left side.

Sinnet, a Line made of Rope-Yarn, the use whereof is to serve Ropes, &c. to keep them from galling.

Si non omnes, a Permission for some Commissioners, when all cannot meet to finish a Business.

Sinuosity, (Lat.) a being full of Turnings or Windings; also a Cavity or Hollowness.

Siphon, an incurvated or crooked glass Tube.

Sire, Father, the Male Parent of Men or Animals. *Milton*.

Si recognoscant, a Writ against the Debtor, having
acknow-

acknowledged the Debt before the Sheriff.

Sirens, Sea-Monsters or Merchants, that used to allure Men by singing sweetly.

Sirius, a Star of the first Magnitude in the Constellation *Canis Major*.

Sirones, little Pushes in the Palm of the Hand and Sole of the Foot, containing small Insects or Worms.

Site, or *Scite*, (Lat.) the standing or seating of any Place or Territory.

Sithence, since, after. *Spen.*

Situation, the manner of being seated, a Seat.

Skatch, is to stay or stop a Wheel of a Cart, Waggon, or other Carriage, by putting something under it.

Skegg, in a Ship, is that small and slender part of the Keel, which is cut slanting, and left a little without the Stern-Post.

Skeleton, of a Man or Animal, is when the Bones are cleaned, and put together again in their natural Order and Position.

Sketch, a rude Draught; *verbally*, to chalk out or design.

Skiff, is the least of Ship-Boats.

Skirmish, a small and disorderly Encounter of a few Men.

Skittish, wanton, frisking.

Skulk, to lie hid, or lurk here and there.

Skuppers. See *Scoper-holes.*

Slab, a Puddle.

Slabby, plashy, dirty.

Slaken, quench. *Milton.*

Slam, the winning of all at Cards.

Slander, Backbiting, or speaking Evil.

Slatch, when any Rope or Cable hangs slack, the Seamen call the middle part which hangs down, the slatch of the Cable or Rope.

Sleepers, in a Ship, are Timbers lying before and aft in the bottom of a Ship, as the Rung-heads do.

Slings, at Sea, are made of Ropes spliced into themselves at either end, with one or more Eyes, according to the nature of the thing to be slung.

Sloops, are Vessels attending our Men of War, and generally of about 66 Tuns, carrying about 35 Men, and commonly two Guns.

Slops, a sort of wide Breeches worn by Seamen.

Slouth, Hunting term, a Herd of some sorts of wild Beasts.

Slug, a kind of heavy great Gun; a sort of Shot; a heavy sailing Ship.

Smacks, are small Vessels with one Mast which attend on Men of War in carrying the Men or Provisions Aboard.

Smattering, a tincture of slight knowledge.

Smegmatick, belonging to Soap, of a scouting quality.

Smiting

Smiting-Line, in a Ship, is a small Line fastened to the Misen-Yard-Arm, below at the Deck, and is always furled up with the Misen-Sail even to the upper end of the Yard, and from thence it comes down to the Poop. It serves to loose the Misen-Sail without striking down the Yard.

Smuggle Goods, to steal them in without paying Custom.

Smutty, full of Smut; also Obscene, or full of Ribaldry.

Snaffle, a kind of Bridle or Bit for a Horse.

Snap, is the noise of any thing brittle, that breaks all at once.

Snatch-block, is a great Block with a Shiver in it cut through one of its Cheeks for the more ready receiving in of any Rope; for by this Notch the middle part of a Rope may be reeved into the Block without passing it endwise.

Sneaks or *Sneakesby*, a sorry, sneaking Fellow, that hardly dares appear.

Sneb, Check, Rebuke. *Spencer.*

Snudge, an old close fisted Curmudgeon.

Sobriety, a Vertue that moderates the Appetite in Eating and Drinking.

Soc, (Fr.) a Plough-Share; also a Power or Liberty of Jurisdiction.

Soccage, in Law, is a Te-nute of Lands by, or for certain inferiour Services of Husbandry to be performed to the Lord of the Fee.

Sock-mans, or *Soak-mans*, are such Tenants as hold their Lands and Tenements by *Socage* Tenure.

Sociable, (Lat.) that delights in, or is fit for Society.

Society, (Lat.) Company or Fellowship.

Socinians, an Heretical Sect of Christians, so called from one *Socinus* the Author of it, who died in 1604. He asserted that Christ was mere Man, and had no manner of Existence before *Mary*. He denied the personality of the Holy Ghost; also Original Sin, Grace and Predestination, the Sacraments and Immensity of God.

Socque, a Sandal, wooden Patten or Clog.

Sodality, (Lat.) Society, Fellowship.

Sodomite, a Person given to *Sodomy* or Buggery, the Sin of *Sodom* the chief of the five Cities in *Palestine* which was destroy'd by fire from Heaven; the Territory where it stood being swallowed up in the Brimstone Lake, commonly called the dead Sea.

Sofa, a kind of Alcove used in the Eastern Country; 'tis an Appartment raised about two Foot higher than the Floor of the Room, furnished with rich Carpets and Cushions, for Entertain-ment

ment of the moſt honourable Perſons.

Soil, Ground conſidered as to its Quality or Situation : Country.

So-journ, to ſtay in a place.

To Solace, to comfort or re-create a Man's ſelf.

Soleus, a Muſcle that helps to extend the Foot.

Solar, (Lat.) belonging to the Sun.

Solar Year, is the time the Sun employs in going thro' the Zodiack, which is about 365 Days, 5 Hours, 49 Minutes, 16 Seconds. It is ſomething longer in finiſhing the **Solar Aſtral Year,** or the **Sidereal Year** ; which ſee.

Solar Month, in Aſtronomy, is that time in which the Sun runs over one ſide of the Zodiack.

Soldan, a Mahometan Prince.

Soldier, one that ſerves in Wars, from the French word **Solde,** which ſignifies the Pay that is given for ſuch Service.

Soleciſm, an incongruity of Speech contrary to Grammar Rules; the word is derived from the **Soli** a People of **Cilicia** in **Greece,** who being tranſplanted into the leſſer **Aſia,** loſt the purity of their Mother Tongue, and were noted for their rude and barbarous Expreſſions.

Solemn, that is celebrated or done in due Order at ſome certain time.

Solemnize, to celebrate.

Sole-Tenant, is He or She that holds only in His or Her own Right without any other joined.

Solid, (Lat.) Maſſive, Strong, Subſtantial, Sound.

Solid, in Geometry, is the third Species of Magnitude, having three Dimenſions, length, breadth and thickneſs.

Solid-Angle, is an Angle contained under more than two Plane Angles not plac'd in the ſame Plane, but meeting in one and the ſame Point.

Solid Number, is ſo called by way of Analogy , and is any three Numbers multiplied by one another.

Solidation, a making firm or ſolid, a ſoldering.

Solidity, (Lat.) firmneſs, ſoundneſs ; alſo ſoundneſs of Judgment.

Soliſidian, (Lat. from **Sola fides**) one that holds Faith only without Works neceſſary to Salvation.

Soliloquy, (Lat.) a meditating alone with one's ſelf.

Solitary, lonely, without Company.

Solitude, (Lat.) a Deſart or uninhabited Place ; alſo a Retirement, or ſolitary Life.

Sollicitation, a ſolliciting or entreating earneſtly, an importuning or preſſing ; alſo a managing of a Law Suit.

Sollicitor at Law, is a Perſon employed to take care of and follow Suits depending

ing in Courts of Law or E-
quity.

Sollicitous, full of Care and
Fear; much troubled or con-
cerned about a Bufinefs.

Sols or *Sous,* a French
Coin of 12 *Deniers,* whereof
20 make a *Livre* ; value 3¾
Farthings Englifh.

Solstice, is when the Sun
enters the Tropical Points ,
where he feems for fome days
to be at a ftand. There are
two *Solstices,* the *Estival* or
Summer Sollistice when the
Sun enters *Cancer* the 11th of
June ; and the Hyemal or
Winter *Solstice* on the 11th of
December when he enters *Capricorn.*

Solsticial Point, the fame
with *Solstice* ; which fee.

Solvable, that may be folv-
ed, or that is able to pay.

Soluble, (Lat.) that may
be unloofed, or diffolved.

Solvendo esse, in Law, fignifies that a Man hath wherewith to pay, or is a Perfon
Solvent.

Solvent, able to pay ; alfo
the fame with *Dissolvent,* being any corrofive Liquor or
Menftruum that will diffolve
Bodies.

Solutio Chymica, is a refolv-
ing any Body into its Chymical Principles, which are
Spirit, Salt, Sulphur, Earth
and Water.

Solutio continui, is a folution
of the unity and continuity
of Parts ; as in Wounds,
Ulcers, &c.

Solution, in Mathematicks,

is the anfwering any Que-
ftion, or the refolution of a-
ny Problem.

*Solutione feodi militis Parlia-
menti,* a Writ for the Knight
of a Shire to recover his allowance if it be denied.

Solutive, (Lat.) that loofens
the Belly.

Some deale, fomewhat in
part. *Spencer.*

Somniferous, (Lat.) caufing
or bringing Sleep; as *Somniferous Medicines* are fuch as
caufe Sleep.

Sonorous, (Lat.) founding
or making a noife. *Milton.*

Sooth-fayer, any Perfon
that foretells the things to
come by the Heavens or the
effects of Nature.

Sooter, fweet. *Spencer.*

Soph, a Sophifter; *which
fee.*

Sophi, (Arab.) a Title of
the fupreme Monarch of *Perfia,* equivalent to King or
Emperor.

Sophism, (Gr.) a Cavil, a
fubtil, but falfe and deceitful Argument.

Sophister, a cunning and
cavilling Difputer, a prating Caviller.

Sophistical, belonging to a
Sophifm, captious, deceitful.

Sophisticated, (Lat.) counterfeited, debafed, or adul-
terated , ufually fpoken of
Wines, Chymical Prepara-
tions, &c.

Sophistry, the art of deceiving by falfe Argument.

Soporiferous, (Lat.) bringing Sleep; as *Soporiferous Medicines*.

Sorbonists, are the Doctors and Batchelors of Divinity of the College of *Sorbon* in *Paris*, so called from one *Robert de Sorbon*, who was one of the Almoners and Preachers of St. *Lewis* the IXth. King of *France*, and the Donor and Institutor of this College, about the Year 1264.

Sordid, foul, filthy; also base, niggardly.

Sorites, (Gr.) a kind of Argument, consisting of divers Propositions, in which the Predicate of the former is still made the Subject of the latter, till in Conclusion the last Predicate is attributed to the first Subject.

Sorrance, a Horse's Disease.

Sortilege, (Lat.) Divination by Lots; also Sorcery.

Soveraign, Independent, Supreme, Chief or Excellent.

Sound, in Geometry, any great inlet of Sea between two Head-lands.

Sounding a Sea, is trying the depth of the Water with a Line and Plummet.

Source, (Fr.) the Spring-head of a River, or the place from whence it takes its rise; also the Original or Cause of a thing.

Souvenance, remembrance. *Spencer*.

Spacious, (Lat.) wide, large.

Spagyrick Art, (Gr.) the same with Chymistry; *which see*.

Spagyrist, (Gr.) a Chymist.

Spahies, or *Spachies*, (Per.) are the great *Turk's* Horsemen or Cavalry, armed for the most part with Bow, Mace, Launce, Harquebuse, and Scimeter.

Span, an English Measure of length of 3 Palms, or 9 Inches; also a Scripture Measure of length, consisting of 10 Inches, and 944 decimal parts.

Spangle, a small thin piece of Gold or Silver.

Spangling, glittering. *Mil.*

Spanking, fine, jolly, spruce.

Sparadrapum, a piece of Linnen tinged on both sides, either with a thick Ointment or Plaister.

Spare-Deck, the uppermost Deck in some great Ships, call'd also the Orlope, lying between the Main and Missen-Masts.

Spars, are certain Stones found in Lead-Mines like Gems, but not so hard.

Spasin, Convulsion and Weakness in the Nerves. *Mil.*

Spasmotick, troubled with the Cramp.

Spasmedicks, (Gr.) are Medicines against Convulsions.

Spasmus, (Gr.) any Convulsive motion.

Special, particular, singular, or excellent.

Specialty, in Law, is a Bond or Bill, &c.

Species,

Species, (Lat.) a kind or sort.

Species, in Algebra, are those Letters or Marks which represent the quantities in any Equation or Demonstration.

Species, in Medicine, are the simple Ingredients out of which compound Medicines are made.

Specification, (Lat.) an expressing, declaring, or particularizing.

Specifick, is in general whatever is peculiar to any distinct Species of things.

Specifick Medicines, are such as have a peculiar vertue against some Disease.

Specifie, to particularize or mention in express terms.

Specimen, (Lat.) an Example, Proof, essay, or Pattern.

Specillum, a Surgeon's Instrument usually called a Probe whereby he searches the Depths, Windings, &c. of Wounds and Ulcers.

Specious, fair in appearance, plausible.

Spectacle, (Lat.) a publick or solemn Show.

Spectator, (Lat.) a beholder or looker on.

Spectre, (Lat.) a frightful Apparition, a Vision, a Spirit.

Speculation, (Lat.) spying, a watching on a high Tower, or other Place; a Discovery; also Contemplation.

Speculative, belonging to Speculation.

Spell, (Sax.) a Word Saying; but 'tis now ta for a Charm or Amulet.

Spell, a Sea word, sig fying to let go the Sheets a Bowlings of a Sail (chi the Missen) and Bracing Weather Brace in the Wir that the Sail may lie loose the Wind.

Spent, at Sea, is the san as broken down, as a Ma or Yard is said to be *Spen* that is, broken down by fo Weather.

Sperm, (Gr.) the natura Seed of any living Creature.

Spermatick Vessels, are thof Arteries and Veins whicl bring the Blood to, and con vey it from the Testicles.

Sphacelus, is a sudden extinction of Life and Sense in every part.

Sphænoides, a Bone of the *Cranium*, common both to the Skull and upper Jaw.

Spænopalitinus, is a Muscle of the *Gargareon*.

Sphere, or *Globe*, is a solid conceived to be formed by the Circumvolution of a Semicircle round about its Diameter, which for that reason is called the Ax of the Sphere.

Sphere Right. See *Right Sphere.*

Sphere Oblique. See *Oblique Sphere.*

Sphere Parallel. See *Parallel Sphere.*

Spherical, belonging to or round like a Sphere.

Spherical Projection, is the Art of defcribing on a Plane the Circles of the Sphere, or any parts of them in their juft Pofition and Proportion.

Spherical Triangle, is a Portion of the Surface of a Sphere, included between the Arks of three great Circles of the Sphere.

Spherical Angle, is the mutual Aperture or Inclination of the Arks of two great Circles of the Sphere meeting in a Point.

Spheroid, a Solid which may be conceiv'd to be formed by the Circumvolution of a Semi-Ellipfe about one of its *Axes*. If the Circumvolution be performed about the longeft Ax, 'tis called an *Oblong Spheroid*, but if about the fhorteft, it is called a *Prolate Spheroid*.

Spheroidical, belonging to, or of the Figure of a *Spheroid*.

Sphincter, a Mufcle that contracts the Gullet, Anus, Bladder, &c. alfo a large, thick, flefhy Mufcle encompaffing the Anus.

Sphygmica, that part of Phyfick which treats of Pulfes.

Spikes, in a Ship, are large, long Iron Nails, with flat Heads, ufed to faften the Planks and Timbers of a Ship.

Spiking up the Ordnance, is faftening a Coin with Spikes to the Deck clofe to the Breech of the Carriages of the great Guns, that they may keep clofe and firm to the Ship's fide, and not break loofe when the Ship Rolls.

Spina dorfi, are the hinder Prominencies of the *Vertebræ*.

Spinalis Colli, a Mufcle accompanying the Spiues of the Neck.

Spindle, in a Ship, is the fmalleft part of a Ship's Capftan which is between the two Decks.

Spine, (Lat.) is the Backbone, or that long jointed Bone that goes down the Back.

Spinfter, a Law Term, being an addition ufually given to unmarried Women, from the Vicount's Daughter downwards.

Spindle, an Inftrument ufed in Spinning; alfo the main Body of the Capftan; alfo the Arbor of a Wheel in Clock or Watch.

Spinofity, (Lat.) difficulty, Intricacy; properly, a having of Thorns or Prickles.

Spiral Line, in Geometry, is a Curve Line which may be conceived to be thus generated; fuppofe a right Line of any determinate Magnitude to be fixed at one of its Extremities, and equally to move round that end as a Center, till fuch time as it comes to the Pofition from whence it fet out; alfo let the central Point be fuppos'd to flow equally along the moving Right Line, and come to the other Extremity at the fame time that the Line finifhes finishes its Revolution; this Central Point by this compound motion, will describe a Curve Line, which is called a *Spiral Line*; of this sort of Curve Lines there may be an infinite variety according to the Laws of these two generating motions.

Spiration, breathing.

Spire, a Steeple that rises tapering gradually, and ends in a sharp Point; also a heap of Corn or Grass.

Spirit, the same what the Chymists call *Mercury*, is one of the five Principles which may be separated from a mixt Body by Fire; 'tis subtil, penetrating, and hath its Particles in a very quick motion; also in a Metaphysical sense, it signifies an immaterial Substance: also Liveliness, Vigour, Courage.

Spiritual, Ecclesiastical, in opposition to Temporal; also Pious, Devout.

Spiritualities, the Spiritual Revenues of a Prelate, or those he receives from a Bishop, as the Profits arising from Visitation, Ordaining and Instituting Priests, &c.

Spiritualization, a Chymical Term, is the extraction of the most pure and subtil Spirits out of natural Bodies.

Spirituous, full of Spirits.

Spissitude, (Lat.) thickness, grossness.

Spithame, a Grecian Measure of length, which contains 9 Inches and 0656; decimal Parts when reduced to

our English Measure.

Splanchnia, are Medicines proper against Diseases of the Intestines.

Splanchnology, (Gr.) a Discourse or Treatise of the Intrails.

Spleen, is a Receptacle for the Salt and Earthy Excrements of the Blood, that there, by the assistance of the Animal Spirits, it may be volatilized, and returning into the Blood may help its fermentation.

Splendent, (Lat.) bright shining.

Splendid, (Lat.) Glorious, Noble, Magnificent, Stately.

Splendour, great Light, or Brightness; also Glory Magnificence.

Spleniatick Artery, an Artery which ends in the Spleen.

Splenical, belonging to, or proper for the Spleen.

Splice, a Sea Term, is to untwist two ends of Ropes, then twist them both together, and fasten them one into the other.

Split, the Seamen say a Sail is *Split* that is blown to pieces.

Spoliation, (Lat.) in Law, is a Writ that lieth for one Incumbent against another in any case where the right of Patronage cometh not in debate.

Spondee, is a Foot of a Latin Verse consisting of two Syllables and both long.

Sponsion, (Lat.) an Engagement or Promise.

Sponsor, an Undertaker or Surety for another, a God-Father.

Spontaneous, (Lat.) voluntary, free.

Spooming, or *Spooning*, when a Ship being under Sail in a Storm at Sea, cannot bear it, but is forced to put right before the Wind without any Sail, then they say the Ship *Spooms*.

Sporadici Morbi, are those Diseases which (tho' different in Nature) seize several People at the same time, and in the same Country.

Sprain, a violent Contorsion of the *Tendons* of the Muscles by a sudden accident.

Spright, a Phantom, a Spirit, a Hobgobling.

Spring a Mast, when a Mast is only crack'd but not broken in any part of it, then 'tis said the Mast is sprung.

Spring a Leak, is said of a Ship that begins to Leak.

Spring-Tide, is the encreasing higher of a Tide after a dead Neap, which is about three or four Days before the Full or Change of the Moon; but the highest Spring-Tide is three Days after the Full or Change.

Springy Bodies, or *Elastick Bodies*, are such as having had their Figure changed by the Stroke or Percussion of another Body, or some other way, can recover again their former Figure.

Sprit-Sail, the Sail which belongs to the Bolt-Sprit-Mast.

Spun-Yarn, is Rope-Yarn, whose ends are beaten or scraped thin, and so spun one piece to another that it may be as long as is necessary.

Spurious, base Born, or Counterfeit; that is not genuine or of the right Stamp.

Spurkets, are the spaces betwixt the Timbers along the Ship's side, in all parts betwixt the upper and lower Futtocks, or betwixt the Rungs fore and aft.

Spume, (Lat.) Fome or Scum.

Squab, little and fat, or thick and short.

Squabbled Letters, among Printers, are those Letters or Lines which are fallen out of order in a Form before it be Imposed.

Squadron, (Fr.) a certain number of Soldiers ranged into a square Body; but most commonly 'tis used for a particular detachment of Ships of War, or one of the three Bodies, which, in order of Battel, compose the Van, Centre and Rear.

Squalid, Nasty, Stinking, Ugly. *Milton*.

Square, in Geometry, is a Right-lin'd Figure consisting of four equal sides, and as many Right Angles.

Square Number, is any Number

Number multiplied into it self, as 9 is the Square of three.

Squinsey, or Quinsey, a Swelling and Inflammation in the Throat.

Stability, (Lat.) firmness.

Stadium, is a Roman Measure of length, containing 125 Geometrick Paces, or 120 English Paces, 4 Feet 4 Inches and a half; also a Scripture Measure of length containing 145 English Paces, 4 Feet, and 6 decimal Parts.

Stadios, a Grecian Measure of length the same with Stadium.

Stagma, are juices of Plants mixt together in order to Distillation.

Stagnate, to lie still as Water does in Ponds, or to want a free Course, as the Blood when grown too thick.

Stalactite, a sort of stoney, sparry, Icycles which hang down from the Tops of Arches of Grottos, Caves, and from the Roofs of the Buildings and Capitals of the Pillars of such Places as are built over the Thermæ or hot Springs.

Stallage, a customary Rent paid in Fairs and Markets, for the liberty of a Stall or Standing, by those Traders who exposed their Goods to sale in the said Stall.

Stamina, (Threds) in Botany, are those little small Threds or Capillaments which grow up within the Flowers of Plants, encom-

passing round the Style, and on which the Apices grow at their Extremities.

Stammer, to stutter or falter in Speech.

Stanch, good, sound, downright, substantial, solid.

Stanchions, in a Ship, are those Timbers, which being set up Pillar-wise, do support and strengthen the wast Trees.

Standard, (Fr.) the chief Ensign of an Army, belonging to the King or General; also the standing Measure of the King or State, to which all Measures are framed; also the standing Allay of Gold and Silver as it is settled in the King's Mint.

Standing part of the Sheat, is that part which is made fast to a Ring at the Ship's Quarter.

Standing-Ropes, are those which do not run in any Block, but are set tau't, or let slack as occasion serves.

Standing part of a Tackle, is the end of the Rope where the Block is seized or fastened.

Stank, weary, faint. Spen.

Stannaries, the Mines and Works wherein Tin is digged and purified.

Stanza, (Ital.) a staff of Verses, being an intire Strain.

Stapes, a little Bone in the Ear resembling a Stirrup.

Staphyloma, a Disease in the Eye, affecting the two Tunics; the Cornea and Uvea.

D d d d 4   Staple,

Staple, a City or Town, where Merchants lay up Commodities; a publick Store-house. Hence *Staple Commodities* are any good saleable Commodities, tho' formerly restrained to some of the principal ones of *England*.

Starboard, the Right-hand side of a Ship, as Larboard is the Left.

Stater Aureus, a Grecian Gold Coin, worth 16 Shillings, one Penny and 3 Farthings of our Money.

Stater Cyzicenus, a Grecian Gold Coin, worth 18 Shillings, and one Penny of our Money.

Stater Philippicus, & *Stater Alexandrinus*, of the same value with *Stater Cyzicenus*.

Stater Daricus, worth 1 Pound, 12 Shillings, and 3 Pence halfe Penny of our Money.

Stater Crasius, a Golden Coin of the same value with *Stater Daricus*.

Statical, belonging to *Staticks*.

Staticks, is a Science which teaches the knowledge of Weights, of Centres of Gravity, and the Equilibrium of Bodies.

Station, a place where a Man fixes himself and his Instruments, to take Angles or Distances, as in Surveying, &c. also a Post, Rank, or Condition.

Stationary, a Planet is said to be Stationary, when to an Eye, placed upon the Earth, it appears for some time to stand still, and not to go forward in its Orbit round the Sun.

Stationer, one that deals in Paper, a Paper Merchant.

Statuary, a Carver of Statues.

Statue, a standing Image of Wood, Stone, Brass, &c.

Statute, (Lat.) signifies a Decree or Act of Parliament; also a kind of Bond; as *Statute-Merchant*, so called because those Bonds are made according to the form of certain Statutes; also Petit Sessions kept yearly for the disposing of Servants.

Statute-Staple, Bonds made and acknowledged in manner directed by the Statutes.

Statuto Stapula, a Writ for the Body and Goods of him that forfeits the *Statute-Staple*.

Statuto Mercatorio, a Writ for the Imprisoning of him that has forfeited a *Statute Merchant*, until the Debt be satisfied.

Statutum de Laborariis, a Writ against Labourers that refuse to work.

Stays, in a Ship, are Ropes whose use is to keep the Mast from falling aft, and they belong to all Masts, Topmasts, and Flag-staffs, except the Sprit-sail Top-mast.

Steady, is a word of Command to the Man at the Helm, to keep the Ship right upon that Point he Steers by, and not to make Yaws in or out.   *Stea-*

Steatocele, is a Rupture or Tumor in the *Scrotum* of a fatty or Suet-like Confiſtence.

Steatoma, is a preternatural Swelling.

Steccado, (Span.) the Lifts, a place railed in for beholding a Combat or Duel. In *Fortification*, a ſort of Pale or Fence before Trenches.

Stede, (old word) Place.

Steed, a Horſe.

Steel, is made by ſtratifying of Plates of Iron in a large Furnace, with the Horns or Hoofs of Animals, under which is made a vehement Fire; thus is Iron calcined; but when red hot and near melting, the Plates are ſuddenly dipt in cold Water, and ſo become Steel.

Steer, a Bullock or young Ox.

Steer, to Steer a Ship, is to guide or direct her Courſe by the Helm.

Steerage, is that part of the Ship next below the Quarter-Deck, before the Bulk-Head of the great Cabbin : Here, in moſt Ships of War, ſtands the Steers-man, or he that guides the Helm or Rudder of the Ship.

Steeve, the Seamen ſay the Bow-ſprit or Beak-head of the Ship does Steeve, that is, it either ſtands too upright, or not ſtrait enough forward.

Steganography, (Gr.) is the Art of ſecret Writing, only known to the Perſons correſponding with one another.

Stegnoſis, in Phyſick, is a conſtriction or ſtopping up of the Pores.

Stellate Plants, in Botany, are ſuch as have their Leaves growing on the Stalks at certain Intervals in the form of a Star.

Stellionate, all kind of Cozenage in buying and ſelling.

Stellar, (Lat.) ſtarry, pertaining to a Star.

Stelliferous, (Lat.) Star-bearing, ſtarry.

Stem, the Stalk of an Herb, Flower, or Fruit; the Stock of a Tree; alſo a Race or Pedigree.

Stem of a Ship, main Stem is that great piece of Timber which is wroughtcompaſſing, and ſcarfed at one end into the Keel of the Ship, and comes bending right before the Fore-Caſtle.

Stem, to ſtop, or put a ſtop to.

Stentorian Voice, a roaring Voice, ſo called from *Stentor* a *Greek* mention'd in *Homer*, whoſe Voice was as loud as that of fifty Men together.

Stentoro-phonick-Tube, is a Speaking Trumphet, ſo called from one *Stentor* a *Grecian*, who is ſaid to have had a louder Voice than fifty Men together.

Step, that piece of Timber in a Ship whereon the Maſts or Capſtans do ſtand at bottom.

Stercoration, (Lat.) a dunging.

Stereobata,

Stereobata, in Architecture, is the *Greeks* word for the first beginning of the Wall of any Building, and immediately standing on the Foundation.

Stereography, (Gr.) is the Art of representing Solids on a Plane.

Stereographick Projection of the Sphere, that Projection of the Sphere upon a Plane, where the Eye is supposed to be in the Surface of the same Sphere it projects.

Stereometry, (Gr.) an Art teaching how to measure all sorts of Solids.

Steril, barren or unfruitful.

Sterling, (Sax.) a Rule or Standard. Sterling Money seems to be that sort of Coin, which for Metal and Value is a common Standard of all current Money.

Stern, severe, crabbed, grim, surley; also fell, sturdy. *Spencer.*

Stern of a Ship, is properly the out-most part of a Ship abaft, tho' generally speaking, 'tis all the hinder-most or aft-most part of a Ship.

Stern-fast, is some fastening of Ropes, &c. behind the Stern of a Ship, to which a Cable or Hawser may be brought or fixed, in order to hold her Stern fast to a Wharf.

Stern-Post, is a great Timber let into the Keel of the Stern of the Ship, somewhat sloping, into which are fa-

stened the After-Planks, and on this Post hangs the Rudder by its Pintles and Gudgeons.

Sternum os, the Breast-Bone.

Sternutation, or *Sneezing*, is a forcible driving out of the Head some sharp Matter, which vellicates and disturbs the Nerves and Fibres.

Steven, noise. *Spencer.*

Steward, is a word of different significations, but is always taken for an Officer of high Account within his Jurisdiction; whereof the Chief is *High Steward of England.*

Steward, of a Ship, is he that receives all the Victuals from the Purser, and is to see it be well stored in the Hold.

Stigmatize, (Gr.) to mark with a hot Iron, as we commonly do Rogues at a Gaol-delivery, to set a mark of Infamy upon.

Stile, in Dialing, is the Gnomon or Cock of a Dial that casts the shadow upon the Hour-lines.

Stillatitious Oils, in Chymistry, are such as are extracted out of mixed Bodies by the force of Fire.

Stilletto, an Italian Dagger or Tuck.

Stilling, a Stand or wooden Frame to set a Vessel on in a Seller.

Stimulate, (Lat.) to move or stir up, to spur or egg on.

Stipendiary, one that takes Wages, a Pensioner.

Stiptick,

Stiptick, or *Stiptical*, (Gr.) stopping or binding, a word used in Physick.

Stipulate, to agree upon Causes and Conditions to be inserted in a solemn Contract between Parties; to Covenant or Bargain.

Stirrup of a Ship, is a piece of Timber put on upon a Ship's Keel, when some of her Keel happens to be beaten off, and the Carpenter cannot come conveniently to put or fit in a piece.

Stithy, a Smith's Anvil; also a Disease in Oxen.

Stoaked, when in a Ship the Water in the bottom cannot come to the Well of the Pump, they say the Ship is a *Stoak*, or *Stoaked*.

Stoccado, (Span.) a Stab, or Thrust with a Weapon.

Stocks, is a Frame of Timber and great Posts made a Shore, to build Pinnaces, Ketches, Boats, and such small Crafts, and sometimes small Frigates; hence we say, a *Ship is on the Stocks* when she is a building.

Stoical, belonging to, or of the humour of the Stoicks.

Stoicks, a Sect of Philosophers at *Athens*, whereof *Zeno* was the chief; they held a Wise Man ought to be free from all Passions, never to be moved either with Joy or Grief, and esteeming all things to be ordered by an inevitable necessity of Fate. They were so called from the Greek *Στοα*, a Porch, because *Zeno* taught his Followers in a common Porch of the City.

Stolones, are the Suckers which grow from the Root of any Tree, and if not cut off hinder its thriving.

Stomach, that part in the Body which digests the Food; also the Appetite, or a testy and refractory Humour.

Stomachful, (Lat.) dogged, peevish, loath to submit.

Stomachick, belonging to, or good for the Stomach.

Stone-henge, an admirable pile of Stones on *Salisbury-Plain*.

Stooping, in Falconry, is when a Hawk upon Wing at the height of her pitch, bendeth down violently to strike the Fowl.

Stopper, is a piece of Rope in a Ship, having a wail-Knot at one end, with a Lannier spliced into it; and at the other end 'tis made fast in the place where 'tis to be used; it serves to stop the main Halliards or the Cable.

Storm, a Military Term, and signifies furiously to attack; also a Tempest of Wind and Rain.

Stounds, Fits. *Spencer*.

Stour, a Fit, an Assault. *Spencer*.

Stowage, the putting of Goods into the Hold of a Ship.

Strabismus, Squinting, is occasioned by a fault in the Muscles which move the Eye.

Strain,

Strain, Tune, flight of Speech or Eloquence; *Verbally*, to pass Liquor through a Sieve, or other Strainer; to raise the Voice, to endeavour greatly.

Strait, or *Streight*, is a narrow Arm of the Sea shut up on both sides by the Land.

Strake, in a Ship, is a Seam between two Planks; the *Ship heels a strake*, that is, the Ship hangs or inclines to one side the quantity of a whole Planks breadth.

Strand, (Sax.) the bank of the Sea, or of a River; hence the *Strand* in *London*, because it lies by the *Thames*-side.

Stranded, is when a Ship is run a Ground and so perishes.

Strangury, a Disease wherein one makes Water by drops, very hardly and with great pain.

Strap, in a Ship, is the Rope which is spliced about any Block, and made with an Eye to fasten it any where on occasion.

Strappado, (Ital.) a kind of Rack, a Punishment inflicted by drawing the Criminal up on high with Arms tied backwards.

Strapping, huge, lusty, bouncing.

Strata, a Term made use of by some Naturalists, and signifies several Layers or Beds of different kinds of Earthy Matter, lying over another.

Stratagem, (Gr.) witty shift or contrivance in War.

Stratarithmetry, (Gr.) the Art of drawing up an Army, or any part of it, in any Geometrical Figure assigned.

Stratification, (Lat.) a Term in Chymistry, and is a putting different matters Bed upon Bed, or one Layer upon another, in a Crucible, in order to calcine a Mettal or Mineral.

Stratocracy, (Gr.) Military Government, or a Commonwealth that is governed by an Army, or by Soldiers.

Streamer, a Flag, or Pendant in a Ship.

Strenuous, (Lat.) vigorous, stout, valiant, active.

Stress, main Point in a Business; also storm or foul Wrather at Sea.

Stricken, advanced.

Strict, (Lat.) close, exact, positive, rigid, or severe.

Stricture, a Spark from a red hot Iron; 'tis mostly used in a figurative sense.

Strike, has several significations at Sea; a *Ship strikes* when in a Fight, or on meeting with a Man of War, she lets down or lowers her Top-sails, at least half Mast high, which signifies that she yields or submits, or pays her devoir to that Man of War she passes by. She is also said to strike when she touches ground in shoal Water. *Strike the Top-Mast*, that is, take it down.

Stria, amongst Naturalists, are the small hollow Channels or Chamfering, which

which are found in Shells of Cockles, &c.

Strip, as *the Chafe ſtrips himſelf into ſhort and fighting Sails*; that is, puts out his Flag in the Main-Top, his Colours in the Poop, his Streamers at the Yard-arm; Furls his Sprit-ſail; Peeks his Miſen, and ſlings his Main-Yard; in which caſe the Chaſer muſt provide himſelf to fight.

Stromatics, (Gr.) Books of ſeveral ſcattered Subjeĉts.

Structure, (Lat.) a Fabrick or pile of Building.

Strumatick, that has the Impoſtume *Struma*, which is a Wen or Swelling in the Neck and Arm-holes, wherein are, as it were, hard Kernels cloſed in the Skin.

Stud of Mares, is a ſtock of breeding Mares from the Saxon *Stodmyra, equa ad fœtum.*

Stupea, in Surgery, a piece of Linnen dipt in a Liquor, and applied to the Part affected.

Stupendious, (Lat.) prodigious or wonderful.

Stupefaction, (Lat.) a making ſtupid, dull, or ſenſeleſs.

Stupid, (Lat.) blockiſh, dull, or ſenſeleſs.

Stupor, (Lat.) lack of Senſe or Feeling; Unſenſibleneſs, Stupidity.

Stygian, belonging to the River *Styx*; alſo Infernal, Helliſh.

Style, in Botany, is that middle prominent part of

the Flower of a Plant which adheres to the Fruit or Seed.

Stylobata, in Architecture, is the Pedeſtal of a Column or Pillar.

Stylo novo, the new computation of Time, according to the *Gregorian* Account; *which ſee.*

Styloceratohyoides, are Muſcles of the *os Hyoides*, which draw upwards the Tongue and *Larynx*, as alſo the Jaws in deglutition.

Stylogloſſum, is that pair of Muſcles which lift up the Tongue.

Stylopharyngæus, is a pair of Muſcles that dilate the Gullet and draw the *Fauces* upwards.

Stymma, in Phyſick is that thick Maſs which remains after the ſteeping of Herbs, Flowers, &c. and preſſing out their Oils.

Styptick. See *Aſtringents.*

Suada, the Goddeſs of Eloquence among the *Romans.*

Suaſory, (Lat.) that tends to perſuade.

Subaction, (Lat.) a bringing under or ſubduing.

Subaltern, (Lat.) that ſucceeds by turns, or that is placed under another.

Subclavian Veſſels, are the Veins and Arteries that paſs under the *Clavicles.*

Subcontrary Poſition, of two ſimilar Triangles, is when they are ſo placed as to have the Angle at the Vertices common, and yet their Baſes not parallel.

Subcontrary

Subcontrary Propofitions, in Logick, are fuch as differ in Quality, and agree in Quantity.

Subcutaneous, (Lat.) lying under the Skin.

Subdelegate, to fubftitute, or appoint another to act under himfelf.

Subdivide, (Lat.) to divide the parts of any thing already divided.

Subduction, (Lat.) the fame with *Subtraction*; which fee.

Subduple, the fame as a half, thus, 2 is *Subduple* of 4.

Subjoin, to annex, join, or add to.

Subjugate, (Lat.) to bring under Yoke, to fubdue.

Subitaneous, (Lat.) done fuddenly or haftily.

Sublimate, corrofive, a Preparation in Chymiftry, whereby *Mercury* is impregnated with Acids, and then fublimed up to the top of the Veffel.

Sublimation, (Lat.) an operation in Chymiftry, whereby the finer and more fubtile Parts of a mixt Body are feparated from the reft, and carried up in the form of a fine Powder to the top of the Veffel.

Sublime, (Lat.) high, lofty, great.

Sublunary, (Lat.) below the Moon, as are all things in the Earth, or in the Atmofphere thereof.

Submultiple Number, or Quantity, is that which is contained in another Number or Quantity, a certain number of times exactly.

Subordinate, (Lat.) appointed or placed in order under another.

Suborn, to bring in a falfe Witnefs, to prepare or inftruct him under-hand.

Sub-pœna, a Writ to call a Man, under the degree of Peerage, into *Chancery*, in fuch Cafe only where the Common Law fails, and has made no Provifion; alfo a Writ for the calling in of Witneffes to teftifie.

Subfcription, (Lat.) a figning or fetting one's Hand at the bottom of a Writing.

Subfequent, (Lat.) that follows after.

Subfervient, helpful.

Subfidy, in Law, fignifies an Aid, Tax, or Tribute, granted to the King, for the urgent occafions of the Kingdom.

Subfide, (Lat.) to reft or fall down to the bottom, as heavy Bodies do in Water, &c.

Subfiftence, a Livelihood, or that which preferves the Life of a living Creature by way of Nourifhment.

Subftance, (Lat.) is whatever fubfifts by it felf independantly from any created Being; alfo Goods, Eftate, Wealth.

Subftantive, is a word that defcribes the abfolute Being of a thing.

Subftitute, to appoint or put in the place of another.

Subftylar

Substylar-Line, in Dyaling, is that Line on the Plane of of the Dial, over which the Stile stands at Right Angles with the Plane.

Subtense, in Mathematicks, is a Right Line connecting the two Extremities of an Ark, or other Curve-Line.

Subterfuge, (Lat.) a shift or evasion.

Subterraneous, is whatever is within the Surface, Bowels, or Caverns of the Earth.

Subtil, or *Subtle*, (Lat.) thin, shrewd, fine, witty, cunning.

Subtraction, (Lat.) a Term frequently made use of in Arithmetick and Algebra, and signifies the taking one Number or Quantity from another Number or Quantity, in order to find the remainder or difference.

Subtriple, one Number is said to be *Subtriple* of another when it is just one third part of it.

Subvert, (Lat.) to overturn, overthrow, or ruin.

Suburb, (Lat.) that part of the City or Town that lies without the Walls.

Succedaneous, (Lat.) succeeding or coming in the room of another, as a *Succedaneous Medicine*, i. e. a Medicine used instead of another.

Succession, (Lat.) a following one after another.

Successive, that follow one after another.

Successor, (Lat.) he that

succeeds or comes after another in a place.

Succinct, (Lat.) compendious, short, comprehended in a few words.

Succotrine Aloes, is the finest sort that comes from the Isle *Succotra*, on the Coast of *Arabia*.

Succubus, (Lat.) a Devil that sometimes in the shape of a Woman, lies with Men.

Succula, is a Term in Mechanicks for a bare *Axis* or Cylinder with Staves in it, to move it round without any *Tympanum*.

Succulent, (Lat.) sappy, moist, full of juice.

Sudamina, are little Pimples in the Skin, like Millet-Grains.

Sudorisicks, (Lat.) are Medicines causing Sweat; and they do it by heating and fermenting the Blood, and by that means driving out a watery sort of Humour.

Suffitus, a Powder made up of odoriferous Plants, Gums, &c. which thrown upon Coles smell pleasantly.

Sufflation, a blowing or puffing up.

Suffocation, (Lat.) stifling, a stopping of the Breath, a smothering.

Suffragan, a Bishop's Vicar, or a Bishop that is subordinate to an Arch-Bishop.

Suffrage, (Lat.) a Voice or Vote at an Election.

Suffusion, (Lat.) a Disease in the Eye, consisting in a Pin or Web in the Eye.

Suggestion,

Suggestion, (Lat.) a prompting, or putting into one's Mind, an Insinuation.

Suit, a Request, or a legal Process, or following another.

Sulphur, the second Hypostatical Principle of the Chymists, which we call Oil.

Sulphureous, of the nature of, or belonging to Sulphur.

Sultan, in the Persian Language, properly signifies an Earl, and also it denotes a Soveraign, and is a Title given to the Emperor of the *Turks*.

Summage, a Toll paid for Horse Carriage.

Summary, (Lat.) a brief gathering together of a matter in a few words; an Abridgment.

Summit, or *Summity*, (Lat.) the highest part or top of a thing.

Summoneas, is a Writ Judicial of great diversity, according to the diverse cases wherein it is used.

Summons, in Law, is a citing to a Court of Judicature.

Summons in terra petita, is that Summons which is made upon the Land, which the Party, sending the Summons, seeks to have.

Summons ad Warrantizandum, in Law, is the Summons whereby the Vouchee is called.

Sumpter-Horse, a Pack-Horse that carries necessaries for a Journey.

Sumptuary Laws, were Laws made to restrain excess in Apparel, of which sort we had several formerly in *England*, but now they are all repealed.

Sumptuous, (Lat.) costly, stately, or magnificent.

Sunday Letter. See *Dominical Letter*.

Sunday, the first Day of the Week so called ever since the Heathen *Saxons* dedicated it to the Idol of the Sun.

Superable, (Lat.) that may be overcome or surpassed.

Superabundance, very great Plenty, Excess, Superfluity.

Superadd, (Lat.) to add over and above.

Superaffusion, a pouring upon, or on the top.

Superannuated, worn out with Age, or past the best.

Supercargo, (Ital.) is one employ'd by the Owners of a Ship, to oversee the Cargo or Lading, and to dispose of it to their best advantage.

Superchery, (Fr.) a Cheat, Fraud, Deceit.

Supercilious, (Lat.) Proud, Arrogant, Haughty.

Supereminence, (Lat.) Singular Excellency, or Prerogative above others.

Supererogation; (Lat.) a giving or doing more than is required.

Superficies, or *Surface*, is an Extension which has length and breadth without depth.

Superficial,

Superficial, belonging to a Superficies; outward, light, or perfunctory.

Superficial Tournean, a Term in Fortification, the same with *Caisson*, which is a wooden Chest or Box, with 3, 4, 5, or 6 Bombs in it, and sometimes 'tis only filled with Powder, and is used in a close Siege to blow up any Lodgment that the Enemy shall advance to.

Superfluous, (Lat.) overmuch, or more than needs.

Superfœtation, (Lat.) a second Conception, or the breeding of young upon young.

Superinduce, (Lat.) to bring or draw any thing over another.

Super-institution, one Institution upon another, as when one Clerk is admitted and instituted to a Benefice upon one Title, and another is likewise instituted to it by the presentment of another.

Superintendent, (Lat.) a chief Overseer.

Superiour, (Lat.) higher, or above others in Dignity and Power.

Superlative, (Lat.) of the highest degree, very eminent or extraordinary.

Supernal, (Lat.) that comes from above.

Supernatation, a floating or swiming at top.

Supernatural, (Lat.) above the Course of Nature.

Super-numerary, (Lat.) above the usual number; al-

so an Officer in the Excise.

Superscription, (Lat.) a writing on the out-side of a Letter, &c.

Supersede, to omit the doing of a thing; to forbear or countermand.

Supersedeas, a Writ to stay the doing of that which otherwise ought to be done according to Law.

Superstition, (Lat.) a being over scrupulous, too much Ceremony in Divine Worship; mistaken Devotion.

Superstitious, addicted to Superstition.

Superstruct, (Lat.) to build upon, as to build one thing upon another.

Supervene, (Lat.) to come unlooked for, or on a sudden.

Supervisor, (Lat.) an Overseer or Surveyer.

Super statuto de York, a Writ against him that uses Victualling either in Gross or by Retail, during the time he is Major.

Supervacaneous, (Lat.) superfluous, unnecessary, needless.

Supine, (Lat.) idle, careless, negligent.

Supinator Radii Brevis, is a Muscle of the *Radius*, that, together with the *Supinator Longus* moves the *Radius* outward.

Supinator Radii Longus, is a Muscle of the *Radius*, that helps with the *Supinator Brevis*, to move the *Radius* outwards.

E e e e   *Supped-*

Suppeditate, (Lat.) to find, or furnish.

Supplant, (Lat.) to plant or set under; to undermine, circumvent, or deceive.

Supplement, (Lat.) any addition that is made to supply something deficient before.

A Suppliant, (Fr.) a Petitioner or humble Suiter; also humble.

Supplication, (Lat.) an urgent or submissive Prayer.

Supplicavit, a Writ out of the *Chancery* for taking the surety of the Peace against a Man.

Supporters, in Heraldry; are some kind of salvage Beasts, which, in an Atchievment, are drawn standing on each side of, and supporting the Shield or Escutcheon; no one under the degree of *Knight Banneret* can have *Supporters* to his Arms.

Supposition, (Lat.) a thing supposed, taken for granted, or imagined to be true, to be done, &c.

Supposititious, (Lat.) put in the place of another, forged or counterfeit.

Suppository, a Remedy applied outwardly to the Fundament to loosen the Belly.

Suppress, (Lat.) to keep under, to put a stop to.

Suppuration, (Lat.) a ripening of a Bile or Impostume, a gathering into Matter.

Supputation, (Lat.) a counting or reckoning.

Supremacy, Primacy, supreme or soveraign Power.

Sural-vein, a Vein which runs down on the Calf of the Leg.

Sur cui in vita, a Writ for the Heir of that Woman, whose Husband has alienated her Land in Fee, and she brings not the Writ *cui in vita*, for the recovery of her own Land: In this case her Heir may have this Writ against the Tenant after her Decease.

Surcease, (Fr.) to give over.

Surcharge, (Fr.) to overcharge or over-load.

Surcingle, a Girdle wherewith the Clergy tie their Cassocks.

Sur-coat, (Fr.) an upper Coat; also a Coat of Mail blazon'd with Arms.

Surd Roots, if a Number whose Root is proposed to be extracted, be not a true figurative Number of that kind; that is, if the square Root of a Number be required, which is not a true Square; or the Cubick Root of a Number that is not a true Cube, &c. such Roots either extracted nearly, or expressed by a mark of Radicality are called *Surd-Roots*.

Surdity, (Lat.) deafness, dulness.

Surety, a Bail or Security; also one that undertakes for a Child.

Surface, the same with *Superficies*; which see.

Surfeit, a surcharge of
Stomach

Stomach by immoderate eating or drinking.

Surge, the Sea-mens Term for a Wave or Billow of the See.

Surgery, an Art which teaches to cure the outward Diseases of the humane Body by the help of the Hands; in Latin 'tis called *Chirurgia,* from the Greek *cheir* a Hand, and *ergon* a Work.

Surkney, a kind of white Garment like a Rocket.

Surmise, (Fr.) to imagine or have a suspicion of.

Surmounted, the Term in Heraldry for bearing of one Ordinary upon another, as in the Figure, *A Pile surmounted of a Chevron;* also surpassed, or overcome.

Surplice, (q. *Super pellicium*) a linnen Vestment worn by Clergy-men that officiate at Divine Service.

Surplussage, (Fr.) in Common Law, is a superfluity or addition more than needeth, which is the cause sometimes that the Writ abateth.

Surprisal, (Fr.) a sudden assaulting or coming upon a Man unawares.

Surprizing, wonderful, strange.

Surquedry; (old word) Pride, Presumption.

Surrejoynder, is a second defence of the Plantiff's Action opposite to the Defendants Rejoynder.

Surrender, in Law, a Tenants yielding up his Lands to him that has the next Remainder or Reversion.

Surreptitious, (Lat.) stollen or done by stealth, falsly come by.

Surrogate, is one substituted to supply the room of another.

Sursolid, in Algebra, is the fifth Power from any given Root either in Species or Numbers.

Sursolid Problem, is that which cannot be resolved but by Curves of a higher Gender than the Conick Sections.

Surveying, (Fr.) is the Art of Measuring of all sorts of plain Figures, in order to know their superficial Content.

Surveyor, one that has the overseeing and care of some Lord's Lands or Works; also a Measurer of Land.

Survive, (Fr.) to outlive.

Survivor, in Law, signifies the longer liver of two Joint-Tenants.

Susceptible, (Lat.) capable of receiving any Impression or Form.

Suscitation, (Lat. a rising, quickning, or stirring up.

Suspence, Doubt, uncertainty of Mind.

Suspend, (Lat.) to stop for a time, as to *suspend* a Man's Judgment; also to deprive of an Office for a time. In Law, it signifies a temporal stop of a Man's Right.

Eeee2   *Sus-*

Suspensor Testiculi, the name of a Muscle, otherwise called *Cremaster*.

Suspensorium, a Ligament of the *Penis*; the use whereof is to assist the *Musculi Erigentes* in their Action.

Suspicable, liable to suspicion.

Suspicion, (Lat.) Jealousie, Fear, Conjecture.

Sustain, (Lat.) to bear, hold, or keep up; to nourish or strengthen; also to bear or endure.

Sutura ossium, (Lat.) a Suture in the juncture of the Bones of the Skull, like the Teeth of a Saw meeting together. *Sutura* also signifies the connexion of the Sides or Lips of a Wound.

Swabber, an inferiour Officer aboard a Man of War, whose Office is to take care that the Ship be kept neat and clean.

Swain, a Country-man, a Clown, or Rustick; also a Boy. *Spencer.*

Swainmote, a Court touching matters of Forest.

Swallow-tail, in Fortification is an out Work, differing only from a single Tenaille, in that its sides are not parallel like those of a Tenaille, but if prolong'd, would meet and form an Angle on the middle of the Curtin.

Swamp, or *Swomp*, a Bog or marshy place.

Swap, or *Swop*, to exchange one thing for another; to Barter or Truck.

Sweep, the *Sweep of the Ship*, is the Mould of her when she begins to compass at the Rung-heads.

Sweepage, a Crop of Hay in a Meadow.

Swerve, to depart, or go from.

Swifters, are Ropes in a Ship belonging to the Main-masts or Fore-masts.

Swifting of a Ship, is encompassing her Gun-wale round with a good Rope to strengthen her in stress of Weather; also a bringing her a Ground, or upon a Careen.

Swifting of the Capstan-Bars, is straining a Rope all round the outer end of the Capstan Bars, in order to strengthen them and make them bear all alike.

Swing Wheel, in a royal Pendulum-Clock, is that Wheel that drives the Pendulum; in a Watch it is called a *Crown Wheel*.

Swink, Labour, *Spencer.*

Swoop, to fly down hastily and catch up with the Claws, as a Bird of Prey.

Sybil, a name of all Women that had the Spirit of Prophecy; they are generally reckoned ten, who prophesied of Christ's Incarnation.

Sybilline, belonging to a Sybil or Prophetess.

Sycophant, (Gr.) properly an Informer among the antient *Athenians*, that gave notice of the Transportation of of Figs contrary to their Law; whence the word is used to denote any false Accuser, Tell-tale or Pick-thank.

Sycosis, (Gr.) an excrescence of Flesh about the Fundament; also an Ulcer so called from the resemblance of a Fig.

Syderation, (Lat.) blasting of Trees with great Heat and Drought; also a corruption, not of the solid Parts only, but Bones also.

Sydereal Year. S. *Sidereal Year.*

Syllabical, belonging to Syllables.

Syllepsis, in Grammer, is an agreement of a Verb or Adjective not with that word which is most near, but with that which is most worthy.

Syllogism, (Gr.) an Argument in Logick consisting of three Propositions, wherein some things being supposed or taken for granted, a conclusion is drawn different from the things supposed.

Syllogistical, belonging to a Syllogism.

Sylvatick, (Lat.) belonging to Woods or Forests.

Symbol, (Gr.) a Badge, Sign, Mark, a secret Note, or Mystical Sentence. 'Tis a Term frequently used in Algebra for a Letter by which any quantity is represented.

Symcolical, belonging to, or of the nature of a Symbol; Mystical.

Symmtral, (Gr.) the same as Commensurable.

Symmetry, (Gr.) a due proportion or uniformity of each part in respect of the whole.

Sympathetical, that pertakes of a Sympathy.

Sympathetick Inks, are such as can be made to appear or disappear by the application of something that seems to work by Sympathy.

Sympathetick Powder, a Powder prepared from green or blue Vitriol Chymically, or else only opened by the Sun-beams piercing into it, and imperfectly calcining it; which is said to cure Wounds at a distance, if some of it is spread on a linen Cloth dipt in the Blood of the Wound.

Sympathize, to agree or be affected with; to have a mutual Affection or Fellow-feeling.

Sympathy, (Gr.) the natural agreement of things; a conformity in Nature, Passions, Dispositions, or Affections. In a Medicinal sense, it denotes an Indisposition of one Part of the Body caused by the Disease of the other.

Symphony, (Gr.) a melodious Harmony, or musical Consort.

Symptom, (Gr.) a preternatural Disposition of the Body occasioned by some Disease; also a Sign or Token discovering what the Distemper is.

Symptomatical, belonging to, attended with, or caused by some Symptom.

Syna-

Synagogue, (Gr.) a Congregation or Religious Affembly among the Jews; or the place where they meet.

Synalæpha, (Gr.) a contraction of two Vowels into one in a Latin Verfe, which happens when any word ends with a Vowel, and the contiguous word begins with another Vowel.

Synarthrofis, (Gr.) an Articulation of the Bones; it is of two forts, *viz. Sutura* and *Gomphofis*; which fee.

Synchondrofis, that fort of Articulation of the Bones where their Extremities are joyned to one another by means of an intervening Cartilage.

Synchronical, (Gr.) Contemporary,

Synchronifm, (Gr.) the being or hapening of two things at the fame time; co-exiftence.

Synchryfm, a fort of liquid or fpreading Ointment.

Synchyfis, in Grammer, is a confufed and diforderly placing of Words in a Sentence; alfo a preternatural confufion of the Blood or Humours of the Eyes.

Syncopalis Febris, a kind of Fever, in which the Patient often fwoons and faints away.

Syncopation, (Gr.) a Term in Mufick, when a Note of one part ends and breaks off upon the middle of a Note of another part.

Syncope, a Figure in Gram-

mer, whereby one or more Letters are taken out of the middle of a word, as *amarunt* for *amaverunt*. In Phyfick, it is a fudden Proftration or Swooning.

Syncritica,)Gr.) are relaxing Medicines.

Syndefmus, (Gr.) in Anatomy, is a *Ligament*, which fee.

Syndrome, (Gr.) a concurrence, or meeting together, as of feveral Symptoms in the fame Difeafe, *&c.*

Synecdoche, (Gr.) a Trope in Rhetorick, whereby the whole is put for a part, or a part for the whole.

Synecphonefis, a Figure in Grammer, whereby two Vowels are contracted into one.

Synneurofis, (Gr.) is an Articulation of Bones by a Ligament.

Synocha, is a continued intermitting Fever; this lafts for many Days with a great heat, and fometimes putrefactions of Blood.

Synod, (Gr.) a Meeting or Affembly of Ecclefiaftical Perfons concerning Religion, and 'tis either 1. *General*, where Bifhops, *&c.* meet of all Nations. 2. *National*, where thofe of one Nation only come together. 3. *Provincial*, where they of one only Province meet. 4. *Diocefan*, where thofe of but one Diocefs meet.

Synodical Month, is that fpace of time contained between

tween the Moon's parting from the Sun at a Conjunction, and her rerurning to him again; and this Month consists of about 49 Days, 12 Hours, and something more.

Synonymous, (Gr.) of the same signification.

Syntenosis, the Union of two Bones which are joyned by a Tendon, as the Knee-pan to the Thigh-bone and *Tibia*.

Synteretick Medicines, are such as tend to the preservation of Health.

Synthesis, (Gr.) is the method of arguing or demonstrating Propositions from their first Principles, or pre-demonstrated Propositions, which afterwards are of equivalent Authority with Principles, till you come to the last or conclusion that was to be demonstrated.

Synuloticks, Medicines that bring Wounds or Sores to a scar.

Syphon, an incurvated Tube.

Syringotomia, (Gr.) is an Incision of the Fistula.

Syssarcosis, (Gr.) is the connexion of the Bones by Flesh.

System, (Gr.) properly is a regular orderly Collection, or Composition of many things together.

System of the World, is the Order wherein the Planets move round the Earth, or round the Sun.

Systematical, belonging to;

or reduced to Systems.

Systole, in Anatomy, is the contraction of the Ventricles of the Heart, whereby the Blood is forcibly driven into the great Artery.

Systyle, in Architecture, is a Building where the Pillars stand thick, but not altogether so thick as in the *Pycnostyle*, the Intercolumniation being only two Diameters of the Column.

Sysygia, Conjunctions or Oppositions of the Stars.

T.

Tabefaction, (Lat.) a rotting, consuming, or wasting away.

Taber, Tabor, or *Tabret*, a kind of Drum.

Tabernacle, (Lat.) a Pavilion or Tent for War; a Booth or little Shop.

The Feast of Tabernacles, kept by the Jews for seven Days together, in remembrance that their Fathers lived for a long time in Tents, after their departure out of *Egypt*.

Tabes, (Lat.) See *Atrophy*.

Tabes dorsalis, a Consumption in the Spinal Marrow; incident to those who are too much addicted to Venery.

Tabid, (Lat.) dry, lean, wasting away.

Tablature, a kind of Musick Book directing to play on the Lute, Viol, &c. by Letters of the Alphabet; also one of the Laminæ or Plates of the Skull).

Table, in Architecture, is a smooth and simple part of a different Figure, but most commonly in the form of a Rectangle or a Triangle.

Table Projecturing, is an ornamental smooth part beyond the naked Face of a Wall Pedestal, &c.

Tables of Sines, *Tangents and Secants*, are Numbers proportional, calculated from, and depending on the given quantity of the Radius, or whole Sine in a Circle; whence any other Sine may be found: They are chiefly used in Trigonometrical Calculations.

Tables Astronomical, are Tables of the motions of the Planets.

Tables Loxodromick, are Tables which serve for the easy and ready Solution of Problems in Navigation.

Tablets, in Physick, are solid Electuaries, much of the same nature with Lozenges; also little Tables.

Tabling of Fines, in Law, is making a Table with the Contents of every Fine, past in any one Term, for every County where the King's Writ runs.

Tabulation, (Lat.) a fastening together of Boards or Planks; a making of a Floor.

Tachygraphy, (Gr.) the Art of swift writing.

Tacit, (Lat.) silent, implied, or meant, tho' not expressed.

Taciturnity, a being silent, or of few words; a close or reserved Humour.

Tack, in a Ship, is a great Rope with a Wale-knot at one end, which is seized into the Clew of the Sail, and so reeved through the Chess-Trees, and then brought through a hole in the Ship's side. Its use is to carry forward the Clew of the Sail, to make it stand close by a Wind.

To tack about, at Sea, is to bring the Ship's Head about so as to lie the contrary way.

Tackles, are Ropes running in three parts, having a Pennant with a Block at one end, and a Block with a Hook at the other end to hang any Goods upon, which are to be heaved in or out of the Ship.

Tactical, belonging to martial Array.

Tacticks, (Gr.) Books treating of the Marshalling of Souldiers in an Army: The Art of making the Machines of the Ancienrs for the casting of Darts, Stones, &c.

Tactile Qualities, are such as have a primary relation to our Sense and Feeling.

Taction, (Lat.) a touching.

Tania, in Architecture, is a Member of the Dorick Capital, resembling the shape of a square Fillet, and serving instead of a *Cymetium*, being fastened, as it were to a Capital below the *Triglyph*, whereof

whereof it seems to be the Base.

Tafferel, is the uppermost Part, Frame or Rail of a Ship abaft over the Poop.

Tail, in Law, is a Fee opposite to Fee-simple, and which it is not in a Man's Power to dispose of.

Tail general, is that whereby Lands or Tenements are limited to a Man, and his Issue by his Wife.

Tail Special, is when Lands or Tenements are limited to a Man and his Wife, and the Heirs of their particular Bodies.

Tails, Kentish-Men are said to have had Tails for some Generations by way of Punishment, for the cutting off the Tail of St. *Thomas* of *Canterbury's* Horse, who being out of Favour with *Henry* II. rode towards *Canterbury* upon a poor Horse, and was served in the foregoing manner by the common People.

Taint, to corrupt; also in Law, a Conviction.

Talent, a Jewish Coin of Siver worth in our Money 342 *l*. 3 *s*. 9 *d*.

A Talent of Gold, in our Money, reckoning Gold at 4 Pound the Ounce, is worth 5475 *l*.

A Talent, among the Greeks, is worth about 193 *l*. 15 *s*. of our Money reckoning Silver at 5 *s*. an Ounce.

Talent, a Jewish Weight, which being reduced to English Troy Weights, contained 189 *l*. 8 Ounces, 15 P. wt. 17½ Gr.

Talentum Atticum Commune, is 56 Pound, 11 Ounces, and 17½ Grains of Troy Weight.

Talentum Ægyptiacum, being reduced to the English Troy Weights, is in value equal to 75 *l*. 10 Ounces, 14 P. wt. 6 Gr.

Talentum Cleop. is about 82 *l*. 2 Ounces, 12 P. wt. Troy.

Talentum Alexandria, contained 91 *l*. 15 P.wt. Troy.

Talentum Insulanum, coneained 113 *l*. 10 Ounces, 1 P. wt. 10 Gr. Troy.

Talentum Antiochia, contained 341 *l*. 6 Ounces, 4 P.wt. 6 Gr. Troy.

Tales, (Lat.) in Law, signifies a supply of Journeymen for them that appear not, or are challenged by either Party as not indifferent Persons.

Tailsman, a Magical Image or Figure made under certain Constellations, according to the keeping or wasting of which, the Person represented by it is preserved or wasts away.

Talk, a kind of transparent Mineral, of which a curious white Wash is usually made.

Tallage, Custom or Impost.

Tally the Sheets, is a word of command at Sea, when the Sheets of the Main-Sail or Fore-Sail are to be halled aft.

Tally,

Tally, a cleft piece of Wood to score up an Account upon by Notches.

Talmud, (Heb.) a superstitious Book, containing the Body of the Jewish Law, composed by their *Rabbins*, and of great Authority among them.

Talmudist, one that studies the Talmud.

Talus, or *Apatement*, in Fortification, is the slope given to the Rampart or Wall that it may stand the faster, and is more or less, according as the Earth is looser or more binding.

Talus Exterior, is the slope given to a work on the side towards the Countrey, and ought to be as small as possible, that the Enemy may find it difficult to mount either by Scalade or otherwise.

Talus Interior, is the slope of the inside of the Work next the Town, which is much larger than that of the outside.

Tampkin, at Sea, is a round piece of Wood fitted for the Mouth of any great Gun, to keep out the Water, &c.

Tamarinds, a sort of Indian Fruit, the Tree of which is like a Date-tree.

Tampoon, (Fr.) a Bung or Stopple for a Vessel.

Tangent, in Mathematicks, is a Line which touches a Curve in one Point only, and does not cut it.

Tangible, (Lat.) that may be touched, or that is sensible to the touch.

Tantalize, to deceive under specious shew, or to make one eager for a thing, and yet not suffer him to enjoy it.

Tantalus, the Son of *Jupiter*, who, as the Story goes, having killed, dressed and served up his Son *Pelops* at a Feast made for the Gods, was set in Water up to the Chin, and had delicious Apples bobbing him on the Lips, and yet had no power to stoop to the one to quench his Thirst, nor to reach up to the other to satisfie his hungry Appetite.

Tantamount, amounting to, or worth as much; of like value.

Tantivy, a full Gallop; also a Nick-name given to a worldly Churchman, that bestirs himself for Preferment.

Tapassant, (Fr.) a Term in Hunting, signifying lurking or squatting.

Taper, broad beneath, and sharp towards the top.

Tapestry, Manufacture in Worsted, Silk, Silver and Gold Thread worked into Figures to adorn a Room by covering its Walls.

Tarantula, a venemous Spider, Ash coloured, speckled with little white and black, or red and green Spots. 'Tis so called from *Taranto*, a City of *Naples* where they abound; and they say its bite is of such a Nature, that it is to be cured only with Musick.   *Tardity*,

Tardity, or *Tardiness*, (Lat.) slowness, slackness.

Tardy, (Lat.) dull, slow, lingring; also guilty, found in a fault.

Tare and *Tret*, the first word *Tare* is the weight of Box, Straw, Cloths, &c. wherein Goods are packed; and the latter *Tret* is an allowance for waste in emptying.

Target, a sort of great Shield used by the Romans, which was bended in the form of a half Moon.

Targum, the *Caldee* Paraphrase of the Old Testament.

Tarnish, to lose its Lustre or Brightness, as Plate does.

Tarpawling, in a Ship, is a piece of Canvas well Tarred over to keep off the Rain from any place; also a Person bred at Sea, and skill'd in Martim Affairs; a downright Seaman.

Tarrass, (Fr.) a Bank or heap of Earth; also an open Walk or Gallery rais'd higher than the main Plot of the Garden.

Tartan, a Ship of great Bulk and Burden, used in the *Mediterranean*, and the Eastern Parts.

Tartar, a sort of Salt arising from reaking Wines, that hardens into a Crust, and sticks to the sides of the Vessel.

Tartarean, (Lat.) hellish, terrible.

Tartuff, an Hypocrite, a mere pretender to Devotion.

Taught, at Sea, is the same as setting a Rope stiff or fast.

Taunt, when the Masts of a Ship are too tall for her, the Sea-men say she is *Taunt-Masted*.

Taunt, to rail, revile, or use reproachful Language.

Taurus, the second Sign of the *Zodiack*, thus marked. ♉.

Tautology, (Gr.) a saying or repeating of the same thing over again.

Taw, in Heraldry, is an Ordinary reckoned among the Crosses called by that Name, and of this Figure.

Tawdry, ridiculously gay.

Taxation, (Lat.) an imposing or laying of Taxes; a valuation.

Technical, (Gr.) Artificial, belonging to an Art.

Technology, (Gr.) a Description of Arts, chiefly Mechanical.

Tedious, (Lat.) over long, slow, wearisome.

Teen, Sorrow. *Spencer*.

Tegument, (Lat.) a Covering. 'Tis a general Name given by Anatomists to the Coverings of the Body.

Telephium, a great Ulcer, and of difficult Cure.

Telescope, (Gr.) an optical Instrument, consisting of two or more Glasses placed in a Tube of various lengths. for observing Objects at a distance

ſtance. Its chief uſe is for Aſtronomical Obſervations.

Teleſcopical Stars, are thoſe that are not viſible to the naked Eye, and can be diſcovered only by a Teleſcope.

Tellers of the Exchequer, four Officers, whoſe Buſineſs it is to receive and pay all the Moneys upon the King's account.

Temerity, (Lat.) raſhneſs, unadviſedneſs.

Temperament, (Lat.) a proportionable mixture of any thing, but more eſpecially of the Humours of the Body; the Habitude or natural Conſtitution of the Body.

Temperance, (Lat.) Moderation, Abſtinence, a reſtraining a Man's Affections or Paſſions.

Temperate, in good Temper, nor too hot, nor too cold; moderate, ſober.

Temperature, the ſame as *Temperament*: This word is frequently applied to the Air, and ſignifies the quality of it as to Heat and Cold, Moiſtneſs and Drineſs, its Gravity and Elaſticity, &c.

Templars. See *Knights Templars.*

Temporal, (Lat.) that continues for a certain time; or ſecular in oppoſition to Spiritual.

Temporalis, a Muſcle of the upper Jaw, which, together with its Partner, draws the lower Jaw upwards.

Temporalities of Biſhops, the Temporal Revenues, viz.

Lands, Tenements and Layfees, belonging to them as they are Lords and Barons of Parliament.

Temporary, that laſts but for a while.

Temporize, (Lat.) to obſerve or comply with the Times.

Temporum Offa, the Bones of the Temples ſeated in the lower and lateral parts of the *Cranium*, called alſo the parietal Bones.

Temptation, a proving, trying, enticing or ſeducing.

Tenable, that may be held or maintained.

Tenacious, (Lat.) that holds faſt; cloſe Fiſted, Covetous; alſo ſaid of Liquors whoſe parts ſtick together.

Tenacity, a ſtiffneſs in Opinion; alſo niggardlineſs.

Tenaille, in Fortification, is a kind of Out-work longer than broad, whoſe long ſides are parallel, and is either ſingle or double.

Tenaille ſingle, is a Work whoſe Front is advanced towards the Country, having two Faces forming a Re-entring-Angle; its two long ſides terminate on the Counterſcarpe, oppoſite to the Angle of the Shoulder.

Tenaille double, is a Work, the Front whereof having four Faces, forms two Re-entring and three Salient Angles; its long ſides are likewiſe parallel, and terminate on the Counterſcarp, oppoſite to the Angle of the Shoulder.   *Tenaille*

Tenaille in the Foss, is a low Work raised before the Curtin in the middle of the Foss.

Tenaille of a Place, or *Front of a Place*, is what is comprehended between the Points of two Neighbouring Bastions, as the Faces, the Flanks and the Curtin.

Tenant, is one that holds or possesses Lands or Tenements by any kind of Right, either in Fee for Life, Years, or at Will.

Tenar, is the name some Authors give to the Muscle, which draws the Thumb from the Fingers.

Tendon, in Anatomy, a similar nervous Part, annexed to Muscles and Bones, whereby the voluntary motion of the Members is chiefly performed.

Tenebrosity, (Lat.) Obscurity, Darkness.

Tenebrous, dark, gloomy.

Tenement, (Lat.) signifies the House or Land which a Man holdeth of another.

Tenementis legatis, a Writ for a Corporation to hear Controversies touching Tenements devised by Will.

Tenerity, Tenderness.

Tenny or *Tawny*, in Heraldry, is a bright Colour made of Red and Yellow mixed.

Tenor, in Musick, is that part which is next above the Base; also the Order, Form, Content or Substance of a Matter.

Tenses, the distinctions of Time in a Verb.

Tension, (Lat.) a bending, or stretching out.

Tensors, are those Muscles that serve to extend the Toes.

Tentation, (Lat.) an essaying or trying.

Tenths, that yearly Portion or Tribute, which all Ecclesiastical Livings pay to the King.

Tenuity, (Lat.) smallness, slenderness.

Tenure, the manner whereby Lands and Tentments are held of their respective Lords.

Tepefaction, (Lat.) a making warm or hot.

Tepid, (Lat.) Lukewarm, Indifferent.

Teraphim, (Heb.) Images or Idols.

Terce, a Measure of Wine or Oil, being the third part of a Pipe, or the fifth part of a Tun.

Terebration, (Lat.) a boring or piercing.

Tergifatous Plants, are such as bear their Seeds on the back sides of their Leaves.

Tergiversation, (Lat.) i.e. turning the Back; a boggling, shuffling, or flinching; a fetch or shift; in the *Roman* Law, it signifies a Nonsuit, when the Plantiff drops the matter.

Term, in Geometry, is the extremity of any Magnitude.

Term of an Equation, is any of the Members of an Equation in Algebra.

Term, a fixed and limited time when the Courts of Judicature are open for all Law-suits, and there is four of these in a Year. *Ter-*

Terminate, (Lat.) to limit, bound, decide, or end.

Termination, (Lat) most commonly signifies the ending of a word.

Terminer, as a Commission of *Oyer* and *Terminer*, i. e. of hearing and determining, for the Tryal of Malefactors.

Terminthus, a swelling in the Thighs, with a black Pimple at Top.

Terms, Conditions, or Women's monthly Courses.

Ternary, (Lat.) that contains three in number.

Terra firma, the Continent is sometimes called by this name.

Terra damnata. See *damnata Terra*.

Terra extendenda, a Writ for the Escheator to find the true yearly value of Land.

Terra Sigillata, Earth sent from *Lemnos*, sealed against Wounds, Fluxes, Poisons, &c.

Terraqueous Globe, in Geometry, is the Globe of Earth and Water, as they both together constitute one spherical Body.

Terras, (Fr.) See *Tarrass*.

Terrene, (Lat.) Earthy, in whose Composition is much of Earth. *Milton*.

Terrella, when a Loadstone is turned into an exact Spherical Figure, and so placed, that its Poles and Equator, &c. correspond to the Poles and Equator of the World.

Terre-Plain of a Rampart, is the Horizontal Superfice of the Rampart, between the Interior Talus and the Banquet; 'tis on this *Terre-Plain* that the Defendants go and come. It is likewise the passage of the Rounds.

Tertian, (Lat.) that comes every third Day; as *Tertian Ague*.

To Tertiate a Piece, is to examine it whether it has the due thickness of Metal in every place, and whether it be true bored.

Terrestrial, (Lat.) Earthy, or that belongs to the Earth.

Terris bonis & catellis, &c. a Writ for a Clerk to recover his Lands, &c. having cleared himself.

Terris & Catallis ultra debitum levatum, a Writ for the restoring of Lands or Goods to a Debtor that is distrained.

Tersion, (Lat.) a wiping or cleansing the out side of any Body.

Test, an Instrument used by Chymists and Refiners to purifie Gold or Silver.

Testaceous, (Lat.) shelly; as *Testaceous Fishes*, are such whose strong and thick Shells are entire and all of one piece.

Testament, (Lat.) is a solemn and authentick Act, whereby a Man at his death expresses his Will concerning the disposal of his Estate.

Testa'or, (Lat.) he that has made his Testament or last Will.

Testatrix,

Teſtatrix, (Lat.) a Female Teſtator.

Teſtatum, in Law, is a Writ (after *Capias*) when a Man is not found in the County where the Action is laid.

Teſte, is a word commonly uſed in the laſt part of every Writ, wherein the date is contained beginning *Teſte meipſo*.

Teſtes Cerebri, are the two lower and leſſer Protuberances of the Brain, ſo called from the likeneſs they have to Teſticles.

Teſticular, (Lat.) belonging to the Stones of a Man or a Beaſt.

Teſtimonial, a Certificate under the Hand of a Juſtice of Peace, the Maſter and Fellows of a College, &c.

Teſtimony, (Lat.) Evidence, Depoſition; alſo a Law or Ordinance.

Teſtudo, (Lat.) a ſoft, large ſwelling in the Head, in form of an Arch-dome, or the back of a Tortoiſe, from whence its name.

Tetrachord, in Muſick, is a Concord or interval of three Tones; alſo a Muſical Inſtrument conſiſting of four Chords.

Tetradiapaſon, (Gr.) a Quadruple Diapaſon, is muſical Chord, otherwiſe called a Muſical Eighth, or nine and Twentieth.

Tetragonias, (Gr.) a Comet, the Head whereof is of a Quadrangular Form, and its Tail long, thick and uniform.

Tetragoniſm, (Gr.) the quadrature or ſquaring of any Curve.

Tetrahedron, (Gr.) one of the five regular Bodies, comprehended under four equal and equilateral Triangles.

Tetrapetalous Flower, is that which conſiſts of but four *Petala* or Leaves ſet round the *Stylus* to compoſe the Flower.

Tetrapharmacum, a Medicine conſiſting of four Ingredients.

Tetrarch, (Gr.) a Governour of the fourth part of a Country.

Tetraſtick, (Gr.) a Sentence or Epigram comprized in four Verſes.

Tetraſtyle, in Architecture, is a Building which hath four Columns in the Faces before and behind.

Tetraſyllabical, (Gr.) conſiſting of four Syllables.

Text, the very words of an Author, Writing or Book, without any Comment or Note; alſo the Subject of a Sermon or Diſcourſe.

Texture, a word frequently uſed in Natural Philoſophy, and ſignifies that peculiar Diſpoſition of the Particles of any natural Body, which makes it to have ſuch a Form, Nature or Qualities.

Thalaſſiarch, (Gr.) an Admiral or chief Officer at Sea.

Thalami nervorum Opticorum, are two Prominences of

of the lateral Ventricles of the *Cerebrum*, out of which the Optick Nerves rife.

Thane, (Sax.) among the ancient *Saxons*, fignified either a Prieft or a Temporal Lord.

Thaughts, a Sea Term, fignifying the Benches on which the Rowers fit in a Boat to row.

Theme, (Gr.) an Argument or Subject propofed to be treated of.

Theater, a Play-houfe or Stage.

Theatins, Friers fo called from the Town *Teate* in the Kingdom of *Naples*; their proper Name, according to the firft inftitution, was Regulars, and their firft Founder was one *Gaetan* of *Thiene*, they were eftablifhed at *Rome* in 1524. *&c*.

Theft, an unlawful taking away another Man's Moveable and perfonal Goods againft the Owner's Will, with an intent never to return them again.

Theodolite, is an Inftrument ufed in Surveying, and taking of heights and diftances.

Theology, (Gr.) a Difcourfe concerning God, it being the bufinefs of this Science to treat of the Deity.

Theomancy, (Gr.) a kind of Divination, by calling upon the Names of the Gods.

Theorem, in Mathematicks, is a fpeculative Propofition, which examins the Properties of things, and wherein fomething is propofed to be demonftrated.

Theories of the Planets, are Hypothefes or Suppofitions, according to which Aftronomers explain the reafons of the Phænomena or Appearances of the Planets.

Theorical, belonging to Theory; Speculative.

Theorbo, a Mufical Inftrument.

Theory, (Gr.) the Contemplation or Study of any Art or Science without Practice.

Therapeutica, (Gr.) that part of Phyfick which delivers the method of Healing.

Therioma, a wild cruel Ulcer.

Thermometer, a Tube of Glafs filled with Spirit of Wine, or other proper Liquor, and defigned to fhew or eftimate the degrees of Heat and Cold.

Thefis, (Gr.) a Pofition, a Propofition advanced and offered to be made good.

Thilk, this. *Spencer*.

Thomifts, are thofe Divines who follow the Doctrine of *Thomas Aquinas*.

Thor, an Idol of great efteem among the old *Saxons* and *Teutonicks*, and the Day now called *Thurfday*, was dedicated to his peculiar Service, and thence took its Name.

Thoracick, (Lat.) belonging to, or proper in Diftempers of, the Breaft.

Thorp,

Thorp, (Sax.) a Village or country Town.

Thoughts. See *Thoughts*.

Thowles, are those Pins in the Gunnel of a Boat, against which the Rowers bear the Oars, or between which they put their Oars when they Row.

Thraso, a vain-glorious, boasting, cracking Fellow.

Thrasonical, insolently Boasting, full of Ostentation.

Threap, (North. Word) to affirm positively, obstinately to persist in.

Threnody, (Gr.) a mournful or funeral Song.

Thrilling, piercing. *Spen.*

Throb, Sigh. *Spencer.*

Throb, to beat, pant or ake.

Thrombus, is the coagulation of Blood or Milk into Clots or Clusters.

Throne, (Lat.) a Chair of State raised two or three steps from the Ground, richly adorned, and covered with a Canopy, for Kings and Princes to sit on at times of publick Ceremonies.

Thrones, the third rank of Angels in the Celestial Hierarchy.

Thwart, a cross. *Milton.*

Thuriferous, (Lat.) bearing or bringing forth Frankincense.

Thursday, the fifth Day of the Week, named from *Thor*; which see.

Thymus, a conglobate Glandule in the Throat.

Thyroides, a Cartilage of the *Larinx*, called also *Scutiformis*.

Thyrse, (Gr.) the Scepter which the Poets gave to *Bacchus*, being a Truncheon wrapped about with Ivy and Vine-leaves. In Botany, it denotes the tapering Stem or Stalk of any Herb.

Tibialis Anticus, a Muscle of the *Tarsus*, so called from its situation on the fore-part of the *Tibia*; its use is to pull the Foot upwards and forwards directly.

Tide, the ebbing and flowing of the Sea.

A Windward Tide, is when the Tide runs against the Wind.

Lee-ward Tide, is when the Wind and Tide go both the same way.

Spring-Tides, are the Tides at New and Full Moon.

Neap-Tides, are the Tides when the Moon is in the second and last Quarter; they are neither so high nor so swift as the Spring-Tides.

Tierce, or a *Third*, the difference of three Notes in Musick, which is either *Major* or *Minor*; the first in the division of a *Monochord*, being as 5 to 4, the last as 6 to 5.

Ties, aboard a Ship, are those Ropes by which the Yards do hang; and when the Halliards are strained to hoise the Yards, these Ties carry them up.

Tide-Gate, that is, where the Tide runs very strong.

Ffff   *Tller,*

Tiller, the same with the Helm of a Ship.

Timariots, an Order of Knighthood among the *Turks*, who out of conquered Lands have a certain Portion allowed them during Life, to serve on Horse-back as often and as long as they should be required, and to find Arms at their own proper Cost. Their Allowance is called *Timara*, and from thence they are called *Timariots*.

Timber of Skins, a Term among Furriers, that signifies forty Skins.

Timbre, the Heralds Term for the Crest, which in any Atchievement, stands a top of the Helmet.

Timburins, an old kind of Instrument, some think a Clarion. *Spencer.*

Time, a certain Measure, depending on the motion of the Luminaries, by which the distance and duration of things is measured. Time is distinguished into absolute Time and relative Time.

Time-absolute, flows equably in it self, without relation to any thing External; and 'tis the same with Duration.

Time Relative, is the sensible and external Measure of any Duration estimated by Motion.

Time, in Musick, is that quantity or length whereby is assigned to every particular Note its due measure, without making it either longer or shorter than it ought to be.

Timid, (Lat.) timorous, fearful.

Timidity, fearfulness, bashfulness.

Tinct, died or coloured. *Spencer.*

Tinctures, in Heraldry, signifie the Colours in an Escutcheon or Coat of Arms.

Tincture, (Lat.) a stain or dye: In Chymistry, it is a dissolution of the more fine and more volatile Parts of a mixt Body in Spirit of Wine, or some such proper *Menstruum.*

Tind, to light; as *to tind a Fire or Candle*.

Tinged, (Lat.) coloured; or died lightly.

Tinnitus aurium, a certain buzzing or tingling in the Ears, proceeding from an obstruction of the Ear; for the Air that is shut up is continually moved by the beating of the Arteries and the Drum of the Ear lightly verberated; whence arises a buzzing or noise.

Tire or *Tear of Guns*, at Sea, is a row of them placed along the Ship's side, either above upon Deck, or below.

Tite, said of a Ship that is so stanch as to let in but very little Water.

Titillation, (Lat.) a tickling.

Tithe, the tenth part of all Fruits, &c. due to the Parson of the Parish.

Tithing-men, in the Saxon times,

times, every Hundred was divided into ten Districts or Tithings, each Tithing made up of ten Friborgs, each Friborg of ten Families; and within every such Tithing, there were *Tithing-men* to examine and determine, all lesser Causes between Villages and Neighbours, but to refer all greater Matters to the superiour Courts.

Titular, that bears a Title only.

Tmesis, (Gr.) a Figure in Grammer whereby a Compound word hath its parts separated from one another by the interposition of some other word, as *Septem Subjecta Trioni* for *Subjecta Septemtrioni*.

Tobacco, a well known Plant, which probably takes its name from *Tobago*, one of the *Caribbee Islands* in *America*, from whence it was brought into *England* by Sir *Francis Drake*, Anno 1585.

Tierce, an English Measure of Capacity for Wine, containing 42 Gallons.

Todd, a Bush or Thicket. *Spencer*.

Toilet, a kind of Table-Cloth or Carpet of Silk, Velvet or Tissue, spread upon a Table in a Bed-Chamber, where Persons of Quality dress themselves.

Toise, a Measure containing six Foot in length, a Fathom.

Toison d'or, the Heralds Term for a Golden Fleece, which is sometimes born in a Coat of Arms.

Tolerate, (Lat.) to suffer, permit, or connive at.

Toleration, (Lat.) a suffering, permitting or allowing of.

Toll, in Common Law, signifies either a liberty to Buy and Sell within the precincts of such a Mannor, or a Tribute or Custom paid for Passage, *&c.*

Tolt, in Law, is a Writ for the removing of a Cause from a Court Baron to the County Court.

Tome, (Gr.) a division or particular Volume of a Book.

Tomentum, properly signifies Flocks, Shear-wool. In Botany, it is that soft downy Matter which grows on the tops of some Plants.

Tondino. See *Astragal*.

Tone, a Term in Musick, signifying a certain degree of elevation or depression of the Voice or some other sound.

Tonica, are those things, which being externally applied to the Limbs, strengthen the Nerves and Tendons.

Tonnage or *Tunnage*, a Duty paid to the King for Goods Imported or Exported in Ships, *&c.* at a certain rate for every Tun weight.

Tonsils, or the Almonds of the Ears, as they are commonly called, are two Glands at the Root of the Tongue, on each side the *Uvula*.

Tooteing, prying, peeping, searching narrowly. *Spencer*.

Top of a Ship, is a round Frame of Boards lying upon the cross Trees near the head of the Maſt.

Top-armings, are a sort of Cloths hung about the Round Tops of the Maſts for ſhow.

Topaz, a precious Stone of a Golden Colour. In Heraldry, a Golden Colour in the Coats of Nobles is called by this name.

Top-gallant-Maſts of a Ship, are two, *viz.* the Main-Top-Gallant-Maſt, and the Fore-Top-Gallant-Maſt; which are ſmall round pieces of Timber, ſet on their reſpective Top-Maſts; having on their top the Flag-ſtaffs ſet on with the Flags, Pendants, *&c.* hang.

Top-Maſts of a Ship, are theſe four, *viz.* the Main-Top-Maſt, the Fore-Top-Maſt, the Miſen-Top-Maſt, and the Sprit-ſail Top-Maſt, which are fixed to the Heads of the Main-maſt, Fore-maſt, Miſen-maſt, and Bow-ſprit, reſpectively.

Top of Feſole, a Hill in *Tuſcany*, called alſo *Fieſoli*. Milton.

Tophet, (Heb.) ſignifies a Drum: It was a Valley where the *Ammonites* ſacrificed their Children to *Moloch*, and cauſed Drums to be beat to hinder their Cries from being heard.

Tophus, a ſtony Concretion in any part of an Animal Body.

Topical, (Gr.) belonging to Place, or applied to a particular Place.

Topicks, common Places, or Heads of Diſcourſe; alſo the Art of Invention or finding out of Arguments.

Topography, (Gr.) a deſcription of a Place, or ſome ſmall quantity of Land, ſuch as that of a Mannor, or particular Eſtate, *&c.*

Top Ropes, are thoſe with which the Top-maſts are ſet and ſtruck.

Top the Yard Arms, that is, make the ends of the Yards hang higher or lower.

Top a Starboard, that is, hale up the Starboard Lift.

Torce, in Heraldry is a Wreath.

Tore or *Thore*, in Architecture, is that round Ring which encompaſſes in the Column between the Plinth and the Lift.

Torment, (Lat.) violent Pain of Body, or great Trouble of Mind.

Tornado, (Spa.) a ſudden or violent Storm at Sea.

Torniquet. See *Tourniquet*.

Torpid, (Lat.) benummed, ſlow, heavy.

Torrefaction, (Lat.) a ſcorching or parching.

Torrent, a ſtrong Stream.

Torricellian Inſtrument, or Experiment from *Torricellius* its Author, is when a glaſs Tube of about three Foot long, and ½ of an Inch Bore, being ſealed at one end, is at the other quite filled with Quick-ſilver, and then being

ing ſtopt with the Finger, hath its unſealed end thruſt down under the Surface of ſome Quickſilver contained in a Veſſel, and then the Finger being remov'd from the Orifice, and the Tube put into an erect Poſture, the *Mercury* will deſcend till it remain in the Tube, to the height of between 18 and 31 Inches, leaving in the top of the Tube an apparent empty ſpace.

Torrid, (Lat.) burning hot, ſcorched or parched.

Torrid Zone. See *Zone*.

Tort, (Fr.) in Common-Law, Injury or Wrong.

Torteauxes, a bearing in Heraldry, of round coloured Figures like Cakes.

Tortuous, (Lat.) winding, turning in and out.

Torture, (Lat.) Rack, exquiſite Torment or Pain.

Total, (Lat.) whole, entire, utter.

Totted, marked in the Exchequer, with the word Tot, as a good Debt to the King.

Tottie,, wavering, tottering. *Spencer.*

Tour, (Fr.) a Journey, or walking about a Place; as to make the *Tour* of *Italy*.

Tourniquet, a Turn-ſtile; alſo the Gripe-ſtick uſed by Surgeons for ſtopping the flux of Blood in Amputations.

Tow, a Sea Term, which ſignifies to hale a great Ship or Barge with another Veſſel, either with an Engine or with Ropes.

Trabeation, in Architecture, is the ſame as *Entablature*, viz. the Projecture on the top of the Walls of Edifices, which ſupports the Timber-work of the Roof.

Trachoma, is a Scab, or Aſperity of the inner part of the Eye-lid.

Track, the print of a Foot, Rut of a Coach-wheel, Run of a Ship, or any other mark remaining of a thing.

Tract, (Lat.) an extent of Ground, or ſpace of Time; a ſmall Treatiſe.

Tractable, that may be handled, ordered, or managed, flexible or gentle.

Trade-Wind, a Wind which at certain Seaſons blows regularly one way at Sea, very ſerviceable in Trading Voyages.

Tradition, (Lat.) the ſucceſſive delivering or tranſmitting of Doctrines or Opinions to Poſterity.

Traditional, of, or belonging to Traditions.

Traduce, to defame, ſpeak ill of, or diſparage.

Traffick, Trade or Commerce.

Tragedian, a Writer or Actor of Tragedies.

Tragedy, a ſort of lofty Play in which great Perſons are brought on the Stage, the Subject being full of trouble, and the end always doleful; ſo called from the Greek word τραγ۞ a Goat, and ᾠδὴ a Song, becauſe the Actors uſually had a Goat given

ven them for a reward.

Tragical, belonging to Tragedies; also sad, cruel or fatal.

Tragi-Comedy, a Play consisting of partly Tragedy, partly Comedy.

Tragus, that Protuberance of the *Auricula*, which is next the Temple, so called because it is sometimes hairy.

Frajectitious Money or Wares, such as are carried over Sea at the peril of the Creditor.

Trajectory of a Planet or Comet, is that Curve Line which by its motion it describes.

Train, the Attendance of a great Person.

Train of Artillery, the great Guns that belong to an Army in the Field.

Tramontane, (Ital.) the North Wind, so called in *Italy*, and on the *Mediterranean*, because it comes from beyond the Mountains.

Trance, a Rapture, Extacy or transport of the Mind.

Tranche, a word used by the *French* Armorists, to express a manner of counterchanging in an Escutcheon of this Form.

Transaction, (Lat.) Negotiation, dispatching of Business.

Transactions, the most remarkable Occurrences, Passages, and Observations of a State or Society.

Transalpine, that is on the other side of the *Alps*.

Transcend, (Lat.) to surpass or go beyond.

Transcendent, that which surpasseth or exceeds others.

Transcendental Curves, in Mathematicks, are such as when their Nature comes to be expressed by an Equation, one of the flowing Quantities is a Curve Line; and if it be a Geometrick Curve, then the Transcendental Curve is a Curve of the second Degree or Kind.

Transcribe, (Lat.) to write or copy out from another.

Transcript, (Lat.) a Copy.

Transfer, (Lat.) to remove or convey from one place to another.

Transfiguration, (Lat.) a change of Figure or Shape.

Transform, to change from one Form or Shape to another.

Transformation, (Lat.) a changing out of one Form into another.

Transfretation, (Lat.) crossing of Rivers or Seas.

Transfusion, (Lat.) a pouring out of one Vessel into another.

Transgression, (Lat.) a going beyond due Bounds, a violating or breaking a Law.

Transgressione, a Writ or Action of Trespass.

Transient, (Lat.) that soon passes away, momentany, fleeting.

Transfi

Transit, in Astronomy, denotes the passing of any Planet, just by or under any fixed Star; or the Moon's passing by, or covering any other Planet.

Transition, (Lat) a passing from one thing to another, or from one Subject or Point of Discourse to another.

Transitory, (Lat.) soon passing away, fading, perishing.

Translation, (Lat,) a removing from its place, or a rendring out of one Language into another.

Translucid, that shines through.

Transmarine, (Lat.) lying beyond Sea, foreign.

Transmeation, a passing through.

Transmigration, (Lat.) a departing from one place to dwell in another.

Transmission, (Lat.) a sending forward, or delivering over, a conveying.

Transmit, to convey or make over.

Transmutation, (Lat.) to change from one thing to another.

Transmutation of Metals, is a changing a Metal into another, a thing which the Chymists have long sought after to no purpose.

Transom, a piece of Timber in a Ship that lies athwart the Ship's Stern, between the two Fashion-pieces directly under the Gun-Room Port.

Transparent, (Lat,) that may be seen through.

Transpiration, (Lat.) the breathing of Vapours thro' the Pores of the Skin.

Transplantation, (Lat.) a planting in another place.

Transportation, (Lat.) a carrying over Sea.

Transpose, to put out of its proper place.

Transposition, an inverting or changing the Order of things.

Transvasate, to pour from one Vessel to another.

Transubstantiated, changed into another Substance,

Transubstantiation, (Lat.) the change of the Sacramental Bread and Wine (according to the Papists) into *Christ's* real Body and Blood.

Transversalis Colli, a Muscle of the Neck, which, when it acts, moves the Neck obliquely backwards, as when we look over one Shoulder.

Transversalis Musculus, one of the Muscles of the *Abdomen*, the use whereof is to press the *Abdomen* exactly inwards.

Transversalis Pedis, a Muscle of the Foot, which brings towards the great Toe, that Toe which is next to it.

Transversalis Sutura, a Suture that runs a cross the Face.

Transverse Diameters, are Lines belonging to an Ellipsis and Hyperbola.

Trape, to go idly up and down.

Trapezium, (Gr.) a Quadrilateral Figure in Geometry

try, whose opposite sides are parallel to one another.

Trapezius, a Muscle of the Shoulder-blade which serves to move it upwards, backwards and downwards.

Trappings, Furniture and Ornaments for Horses. *Shakespear.*

Traverse, at Sea, is the way of a Ship when she makes Angles in and out, and cannot keep directly to her true Course.

Traverse, there is also a Partition of an Escutcheon used in Heraldry of this Figure, which they call *Parted per Pale Traverse Argent* and *Gules.*

Traverse-Board, a Board on which all the Points of the Compass are set down with marks for the Hours the Ship has gone on every Point.

Traverse, in Gunnery, to turn or remove a piece of Ordnance this way and that way, in order to bring it to bear.

Traverse, in Fortification, is a Trench with a little Parapet, sometimes two on each side, to serve as a Cover from the Enemy that might come on their Flank; sometimes it is covered over head with Planks and loaded with Earth.

To Traverse, or go cross a Country.

To Traverse an Indictment, is to contradict or invalidate some point of it.

Traverses, Turning and Windings; also Crosses, Troubles, Vexations.

Travested, (Fr.) disguised, as the Poems of *Virgil* or *Ovid* travested, *i. e.* turned into Burlesque Verse.

Traumatick, belonging to, or good for the cure of Wounds.

Traumaticks, Vulneraries, that is, Herbs or Drugs inwardly exhibited for curing Wounds.

Traytor, a Person guilty of High Treason.

Treason, is of two sorts, either High Treason or Petty Treason; High Treason, is an Offence against the security of the Prince, whether it be by Imagination, Word or Deed, as to compass or imagine the death of the King, Queen or Prince; to levy War against them, to adhere to their Enemies, to Coin false Money, to counterfeit the King's Great Seal or Privy Seal. *Petty Treason.* See *Petty.*

Treasonable, belonging to, or full of Treason.

Treasure-trove, is Money, Gold, Silver, Plate or Bullion that is found, and none knows to whom it belongs; then by the Common Law, the property thereof belongs to the King; but the Civil Law gives it to the finder.

Treasury

Treasury, a place where Treasures are kept.

Treatise, a written Discourse on some particular Subject.

Treaty, a Covenant or Agreement between several Nations for Peace, Commerce, Navigation, &c.

Treble, the highest part in Musick, or the highest of the four Parts in Musical Proportion.

Trellis, (Fr.) a Lettice or Grate; Cross-bars; also Cloth called Buckram.

Trennels, the same as Tree-Nails, or Nails to fasten the Planks of a Ship to the Timbers.

Trental, (Ital.) an Office among the Romanists for the Dead, continuing thirty Days, or consisting of thirty Masses.

Tremendous, (Lat.) much to be feared, dreadful.

Trench, which is likewise called *Lines of Approach*, and *Lines of Attack*, is a way hollowed in the Earth in form of a Foss, having a Parapet towards the place besieged, when the Earth can be removed; or else it is an elevation of Fascines, Gabions, Wool-packs, and such other things, that can cover the Men and does not fly in Pieces or Splinters to hurt them; this latter is seldom used but in rocky Ground. The use of a Trench is that the Besiegers may approach the more securely to the place attacked.

Trepan, a Surgeon's Instrument for the curing of Fractures in the Skull.

Trepan, (Ital.) to bring one into a Premunire, to ensnare, circumvent, &c.

Trepidation, (Lat.) trembling.

Trespass, signifies any transgression of the Law, except Felony or Treason.

Tressed Locks, Curled. *Spen.*

Tressel-Trees, are those Timbers of the Cross-trees that stand along Ships, or fore and aft at the top of the Mast.

Tresses, (Fr.) Locks of Hair loosly hanging down, *Milton.*

Tressure, in Heraldry, is an *Orle* deflowered.

Trestle, a three-footed Stool; a wooden Frame for supporting Tables, Scaffolds, &c.

Tret, an allowance for wast in the weight of Goods. *See* Tare.

Trevet or *Trivet*, an Instrument of Iron with three or four Feet for setting Pots or Sauce-pans on, over the Fire.

Tria prima, (Lat.) the 3 Hypostatical Principles of Chymists, *viz. Salt, Sulpher,* and *Mercury,* of which, they say, all mixt Bodies are made up.

Trial, in Law, signifies the examination of a Cause Civil or Criminal, according to the Laws of the Land, before a proper Judge.

Triangle, (Lat.) a Figure cont-

comprehended within three Lines, and that has three Angles.

Triangle Rectilineal, a space comprehended within three Right-Lines.

Triangle Spherical. See *Spherical Triangle.*

Triangular, belonging to a Triangle.

Triarians, (Lat.) Souldiers who were always placed in the Rear-ward, and were the strongest Men.

Tribes or *Orders,* were the distinct Families of the *Israelites* descended from the Patriarch *Jacob's* twelve Sons.

Tribulation, (Lat.) great Trouble, Affliction, Adversity.

Tribunal, or Judgment Seat, properly the Seat of the Tribune an Officer among the old *Romans,* whose Office it was to maintain the Rights of the Commons.

Tributary, (Lat.) that pays Tribute, *i.e.* a Tax, Toll, Custom, *&c.*

Tricennial, of, or belonging to thirty Years.

Trident, the three pronged Mace of *Neptune,* the fabulous Deity of the Sea; also any Tool or Instrument with three Fangs or Prongs.

Tridentine, belonging to the City or Council of *Trent,*

Triduan, (Lat.) of three Days continuance.

Triennial, (Lat.) of three Years continuance.

Trifarious, (Lat.) three manner of ways.

Triform, (Lat.) having three Forms or Shapes.

Trigamy, a having three Husbands or Wives at once.

Triglyph, in Architecture, is a Member of the *Frize* of the *Dorick Order,* set directly over every Pillar, and in certain spaces in the Intercolumniations; also the end of Joysts which fasten in or fill their corresponding holes.

Trigon, (Gr.) in Mathematicks, a Figure or Instrument with three Angles.

Trigonometry, (Gr.) is the Art of Measuring Triangles, whether Right-lined or Spherical, or an Art that teaches how from three things given, *viz.* Angles and Sides, or Sides (but not Angles alone) to find the rest, *viz.* the other Sides or Angles.

Trilateral, having three Sides.

Trill, (Ital.) a quivering or shaking with Voice or Instrument.

Trimmer, one that Trims or carries it fair with both Parties.

Trine, (Lat.) belonging to the Number three.

Trine Aspect of two Planets, is when they are distant from one another 120 Degrees, or a third part of the Zodiack.

Tringle, (Fr.) a Curtin-Rod, a Lath that reaches from one Bed-post to another. In Architecture, 'tis a little Member fixed exactly upon every Triglyph under the Plat-band of the *Architrave,* from whence hang down the

the *Gutta* or Pendant drops in the *Dorick Order.*

Trinitarians, a Christian Order, who hold that all their Churches ought to be dedicated to the Holy Trinity; and among other Tenets this is one, that it is not lawful to ride on Horse-back, but on Asses only.

Trinket or *Trinket-Sail*, the Top-gallant, or highest Sail of any Mast.

Triones, seven Stars in the *Ursa Minor* are so called.

Trip; as *a Ship goes with her Top-Sails a trip;* that is, when she carries her Top-Sail hoisted up to the highest, and when it blows not too hard, but a gentle or Loom-gale.

Tripartition, (Lat.) a division into three parts.

Tripetalous, (Gr.) that has a Flower consisting of three Leaves.

Triphthongue, (Gr.) three Vowels joyn'd together and making one Sound.

Triple, (Lat.) threefold.

Triplicate Ratio; in four Terms Geometrically proportional the *Ratio* of the first to the last is said to be *Triplicate* of the *Ratio* of the first to the second.

Tripos, a three-footed-Stool.

Tripudiation, (Lat.) a tripping on the Toes in a Dance.

Trireme, (Lat.) a Gally with three ranks of Oars on a side.

Trise, is to hale up any thing by a dead Rope, that

is, one not running in a Pulley.

Trisdiapason, a Chord in Musick, otherwise called a Triple Eighth, or Fifteenth.

Trismus, is the grinding of the Teeth, or a Convulsion of the Muscles of the Temples, whereby the Teeth gnash whether one will or no.

Trispast, (Gr.) an Engine consisting of three Pullies.

Trissyllable, (Lat.) a word of three Syllables.

Tritæophyes, (Gr.) an Ague that comes every third Day.

Trite, (Lat.) thread-bare, common.

Tritheites, a sort of Hereticks that held there were three distinct God-heads in the Trinity of the Persons.

Triton, (Gr.) a fabulous Sea-Diety, *Neptune's* Trumpeter; a Fish shaped like a Man; also a Vane or Weather-Cock.

Tritone, a Musical Term, signifying a greater Fourth.

Trituration, (Lat.) a pounding in a Mortar, a reducing Medicines to Powder.

Trivial, (Lat.) common, ordinary.

Triumph, (Lat.) a solemn Pomp or Shew at the return of a victorious General from the Wars.

Triumphal, (Lat.) belonging to a Triumph, as a Triumphal Arch.

Triumvirate, the Office of a *Triumvir*, or of three in equal Authority.

Triune,

Triune, (*i. e.* three-one) a Term apply'd to God, to express the Unity of the Godhead in a Trinity of Persons.

Trochile, in Architecture, is that hollow Ring or Cavity which runs round a Column next to the *Tore*. It is the same with what is commonly called the *Casement*.

Trochings, the small Branches on the top of the Dear's Head.

Trochisks, are little round, or other figured Medicinal Balls made out of a soft Paft, and then dried.

Trochlea, is one of the Mechanick Powers, the same with what we call the *Pully*.

Trochoid, the same as *Cycloid*; which see.

Trocholicks, that part of Mechanicks that treats of Circular Motions.

Trode, Path. *Spencer.*

Troma, a Wound from some External Cause.

Trembosis, (Gr.) a trembling, or depravation of the voluntary motion of the Senses.

Tromperie, (Fr.) Fraud, Cozenage, Deceit.

Tronage, (Lat.) a Custom or Toll for weighing of Wool from *trona*, a Beam to weigh with.

Trope, (Gr.) a Term in Rhetorick, an elegant turning of a word from its proper and genuine signification to another.

Trophy, (Gr.) properly a Monument set up where the Enemies were vanquished with their Ensigns and other Spoils hanging on it; a Sign or Token of Victory.

Tropicks, (Gr.) are two Circles of the Sphere equally distant from the Equator; whither the Sun being arrived returns again towards the Equator; so that they are the Bounds of its motion towards the North and South.

Tropick of Cancer, is that towards the *Arctick* or North Pole, so called from *Cancer*, the Sign of the Ecliptick the Sun is in when is comes to this Circle.

Tropick of Capricorn, is that which is towards the South Pole, so called from the Sign the Sun is in when he comes to this Circle.

Tropological, (Gr.) belonging to Tropology; Moral.

Tropology, (Gr.) a figurative Speech; a moral Discourse.

Trover, in Law, is an Action which a Man hath against one, that having found any of his Goods refuses to deliver them upon demand.

Trough of the Sea, the hollow made between any two Waves in a Rowling Sea.

Trounce, to harrass or punish severely; to sharp, bubble, or cheat.

Troy-weight, contains 12 Ounces in the Pound for the weighing of Bread, Gold, Silver, Precious Stones, Drugs, &c.

Truant, (Fr.) a Vagabond, a lazy loitering Fellow, a common Beggar.

Truce, a Cessation of Arms for a time agreed upon by both Parties.

Truch-Man or *Truchman*, an Interpreter.

Truck, to exchange or barter one thing for another.

Truckle, a little running Wheel; *verbally*, to yield or buckle to.

Truculent, (Lat.) of a cruel, stern, or fierce Look, or Disposition.

Trumpery, old Baggage or paltry Stuff.

Trunckated, (Lat.) cut shorter; maimed, mangled.

Trundle, a sort of Carriage with low Wheels to carry heavy Burdens.

Trundle-Shot, an Iron Shot about seventeen Inches long, sharp pointed at both ends, with a round Bowl of Lead cast upon it about a hand breadth from each end.

Trunnions of a piece of Ordnance, are those Knobs or Bunches of the Gun's Metal which bear her up upon the Cheeks of the Carriage.

Trusses, are Ropes made fast to the Parrels of a Yard in a Ship.

Trustee, one that has Money or an Estate put into his Hands in trust for the use of another.

Truth, according to Mr. Lock, is the joyning or separating of Signs, as the things signified by them, do agree or disagree with one another.

Try, a Ship is said to *Try*, when she has no more Sails aboard but her Main-Sail, or the Missen Sail only.

Trutination, (Lat.) a weighing or ballancing; a considering a thing throughly.

Tuant, (Fr.) killing; as a *Tuant Jest*, i.e. a tart, biting Jest.

Tubæ Fallopianæ, are two slender Passages proceeding from the Womb; which receive the Eggs from the Testicles and carry them to the Womb.

Tube, (Lat.) a Pipe.

Tuberosity, a bunching out of some parts of the Body.

Tuberous Plant, in Botany, a Plant full of Bunches or Knots.

Tubuli vermiculares, are certain small winding Cavities, formed on the outsides of the Shells of Marine Shell-Fishes, in which some small Worms inhabit and breed.

Tuck of a Ship, is the trussing or gathering in of her Quarter under Water.

Tuel, a Term in Hunting, the Fundament of a Beast.

Tuesday, the third Day of the Week, so called from *Tuisco*, the most antient and peculiar Idol of the *Teutonicks*, or old *Germans* and *Saxons*, to which this Day *Tuesday* was more especially dedicated.

Tuition,

Tuition, Gardianship, Protection, Patronage.

Tulipant, a Sash, a Wreath worn by the *Indians* instead of a Hat.

Tumefaction, (Lat.) a swelling or making to swell.

Tumid, swelling, rising up. *Milton.*

Tumify, (Lat.) to cause a Tumor, or Swelling; to rise or swell.

Tumour, (Lat.) a preternatural Swelling in any part of the Body.

Tumult, (Lat.) a Bustle, Uproar, Sedition or Mutiny.

Tumultuary, (Lat.) done in haft, or on a sudden, without Confideration and Advice.

Tumultuous, full of Tumults.

Tun, an Englifh Meafure of Capacity for Wine and other Liquids, containing 252 Gallons, or 58212 folid Inches, allowing 231 folid Inches to each Gallon.

Tunable, harmonious or comformable to the Rules of Mufick.

Tunicle, in Anatomy, a Membranous Coat covering any part of the Body.

Tunnage, an Impoft paid for every Tun of Merchandize Exported or Imported in Ships.

Turbant, a Turkifh Hat or Ornament for the Head, made of fine Linnen, wreathed into a Rundle, broad at the bottom to enclofe the Head, and leffening for Ot-

tament towards the top.

Turbary, (Law Term) a right to dig Turves on the Ground of another; alfo the Ground where Turves are digged.

Turbith Mineral, in Chymiftry is a yellow Precipitate of Mercury.

Turbulent, (Lat.) troublefome, boifterous, feditious.

Turcifm, the Religion of the *Turks.*

Turcois, a Precious Stone of an Azure Colour.

Turgefcence, (Lat.) a swelling up, or growing big.

Turgid, (Lat.) swelling, rising, puffed up.

Turiones, in Botany, are the firft young tender Shoots which any Plants do annually put forth of the Ground.

Turmoil, Stir, Buftle; *verbally*, to toil, or make a heavy to do.

Turnament, jufting or tilting; a Martial Exercife of Gentlemen encountring one another on Horfe-back with Lances.

Turn-Pike, a Spar of Wood about fourteen Foot long, and about eight Inches Diameter, cut in form of a Hexagon, every fide being bored full of holes, through which fhort Pikes are run, about fix Foot long, pointed with Iron, fo that they ftand out every way. Their ufe is to ftop the Enemy, when fet in a Breach, at the entrance of a Camp, or in a Gap.

Turn

Turno vice comitum, a Writ that lies for those that are called out of their own hundred into the Sheriff's Turn or Court.

Turpitude, (Lat.) Filthiness, Dishonesty, Villany.

Tuscan Order of Architecture, so called because it was invented in *Tuscany*: Here the Columns, together with Base and Capital, are to be seven Moduls in length, and to have the upper part of the Pillar ⅓ less in diameter than the bottom.

Tutelage, (Lat.) Guardianship, Protection.

Tutelar, or *Tutelary*, (Lat.) that protects or performs the Office of a Gardian.

Tutor, one that is made choice of, to instruct another in some Art or Science.

Tutoress, a Female Tutor, a Governante or Governess.

Twang, a sharp sound, or harsh Pronunciation.

Tweag or *Tweak*, Perplexity, Trouble.

Tweezers, small Nippers or Pincers for pulling up Hairs by the Roots.

Twelfth-Day, the Festival of the Epiphany, or Manifestation of Christ to the Gentiles; so called, as being the twelfth Day exclusively from the Nativity or *Christmas-Day*.

Twilight, is that dubious Light which we perceive before the Sun rising, and after Sun setting.

Twinge, to gripe, or cause

a very sharp pain.

Twitten, blame. *Spencer*.

Tympan, (Gr.) the Drum of the Ear; also a Frame belonging to a Printing-Press, covered with Parchment, on which every Sheet is placed in order to be printed off. In Architecture, 'tis that part of the bottom of the Frontons, which is enclosed between the Cornices, and answers to the Naked of the Frize.

Tympany, a Disease consisting in a constant, equal, hard, resisting Tumour of the *Abdomen*, which being beat or struck yields a sound.

Type, (Gr.) the Figure or mystical Shadow of a thing.

Typhodes, (Gr.) a continual burning Fever.

Typhon, a violent Whirlwind, a Hurricane; also a fiery Meteor.

Typical, belonging to a Type.

Typographer, a Printer.

Typography, (Gr.) the Art of Printing.

Tyrannical, acting like a Tyrant.

Tyrannize, (Gr.) to play the Tyrant.

Tyrannicide, Murder of a Tyrant, or a Tyrant-killer.

Tyrant, a Soveraign Prince, that abuses the Royal Power in oppressing his Subjects; a cruel Governour or Usurper.

Tyro, (Lat.) a fresh Water Souldier; a young beginner in any Art or Science.

Tyrociny, the first exercise
of

of any Art or Faculty; an Apprentiſhip.

Tyroſis, a curdling of Milk in the Stomach into a ſubſtance like Cheeſe.

VI

Vacancy, (Lat.) the time during which a Benefice or Office is vacant; alſo a time of leiſure.

Vacant, that is at leiſure, or that is not filled up, as a vacant Living or Office.

Vacat, to empty, to annul or make void.

Vacation, (Lat.) a ceaſing from ordinary Buſineſs; alſo the time between the end of one Term and the beginning of another.

Vaccary or *Vacchary*, (Lat.) a place to keep Cows in; a Dairy.

Vacillation, (Lat.) a reeling or ſtaggering; a juggling; a wavering; uncertainty.

Vacuation, See *Evacuation*.

Vacuity, (Lat.) emptineſs, void ſpace.

Vacuum, ſpace devoid of all Body, and this Philoſophers diſtinguiſh into

Vacuum diſſeminatum or *interſperſum*, i. e. ſmall void Spaces interſperſed about between the Particles of Bodies.

Vacuum coacervatum, a larger void Space made by the meeting together of the ſeveral interſperſed or diſſe-

minate Vacuities.

Vade Mecum, (Lat.) a Title given to any little Epitome of a Treatiſe which a Man may carry in his Pocket.

In Vadio Exponere, in Law, is to pawn or leave any thing as a Pledge or Surety of returning Money borrowed or owing.

Vadium Mortuum, in Law, is a Mortgage, Lands, or immovable Goods ſo pawned or engaged to the Creditor, that he has a right to the mean Prophets for the uſe of his Loan or Debt.

Per Vadium ponere, to take Security for the appearance of a Delinquent.

Vafrous, (Lat.) ſubtil, crafty.

Vagabond, (Lat.) an idle Wanderer or Straggler.

Vagaries, Freaks and Pranks of wanton People. *Milton*.

Vagrancy, a diſorderly or ill Courſe of Life.

Vagrant, wandering or roving.

Vail, a piece of Stuff that hinders any thing from being ſeen.

Vail the Bonnet, to put off one's Hat, or give any ſign of Reſpect. In Sea-Affairs to ſtrike Sail, in token of ſubmiſſion.

Vails, Profits that ariſe to Officers or Servants beſides Salary or Wages.

Vain, (Lat.) empty, frivolous, unprofitable.

Vairy, See *Verry*.

Vairy

Vairy Coppy or *Potent Counter Potent*, is a bearing in Heraldry of the following form, and in *Blazon* the Colours must be express'd; as *Azure & Argent*, &c.

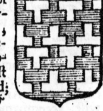

Valediction, a farewell, or a bidding farewell.

A Valedictory Speech., a farewell Speech.

Valentines, in the Church of *Rome*, Saints chosen for the Year ensuing, on the Festival of St. *Valentine* a Roman Bishop, *Feb.* 14. among us Men and Maids chosen for Sweet-hearts.

Valentinians, a sort of Christian Hereticks, so called from *Valentinus* the Author of this Sect, who spread his Errors in the Eleventh Age; he collected Dreams of certain Gods to the number of thirty, whom he called *E-ones*, that is, Ages, out of *Hesiod's* Fables, of whom he would have fifteen to be Male, and the rest Female, and said that our Saviour sprung like another *Pandora* out of their correspondence, and added that he passed with a Body brought out of Heaven, through the Virgin as a Conduit or Pipe, and that all Men would not rise to Life again. His Disciples followed also the Errors of the *Gnosticks*.

Valet, (Fr.) the Groom or Houshold Servant of the meaner sort.

Valet de Chambre, one that waits upon a Person of Quality in his Bed-Chamber.

Valetudinary, (Lat.) sickly, subject to sickness, or often indisposed.

Valiant, (Fr.) bold in Fight, courageous, stout, bold.

Valley or *Vale*, a low space of Ground surrounded with Hills.

Valid, (Lat.) strong; valiant, tho' more frequently it signifies done in due form, firm, and ratified.

Validity, (Lat.) Strength, Power, Force; the Authentickness, or binding force of a Deed or Instrument.

Valorous, Valiant, Courageous, Magnanimous.

Valore Maritagii, or *value of Marriage*, in Law, is a Writ that lies for the Lord, to recover the value of a Marriage proffered to an Infant and refused.

Valve, is a little thin Membranous Substance, found in several Vessels of the Body; which, like a Door, opens and gives free passage to the Fluids moving one way, but won't suffer them to return the same way, but shuts and hinders their passage.

Vambrace, (Fr.) Armour for the Arm.

Vamp, (Fr.) the upper Leather of a Shoe; *verbally*,

ly, to trim or trick up.

Vamplate, a Gauntlet, or Iron Glove.

Vane or *Fane*, a Device erected on the top of a Pole, or of a Building to shew the sitting of the Wind; a Weather-Cock.

Van-guard, (Fr.) a Military Term, signifying the first Line of an Army drawn up in Battalia.

Vanned, fanned or Winnowed.

Vantage, that which is given over and above just Weight and Measure.

Vant-Courier, (Fr.) a forerunner.

Vapid, (Lat.) ill tasted, musty, flat.

Vaporation, a sending forth of Vapours or Fumes.

Vaporous, full of Vapours, or that sends forth Vapours.

Vapours, in a Medical sense, is now a-days used for the Disease called otherwise *Hysterick* or *Hypochondriack Fits* or *Melancholy*. But the word commonly signifies watery Exhalations raised up either by the heat of the Sun or any other heat.

Variable, subject to variation, changeable, inconstant.

Variance, Enmity, Difference, Dispute.

Variation of the Needle, is the turning or deviation of the Needle in the Mariner's Compass, more or less in all places from the true North; or more properly it is the Angle which the Needle makes with the true Meridian-Line drawn through the Center of Motion of that Needle.

Variegated, (Lat.) streaked or deversified with several Colours.

Variola, the Small-Pox, consists in a contagious disorder of the Blood contracted from the Air, or otherwise, accompanied with a continued wandering Fever, with a pain in the Head and Loins, and with a breaking forth of Pimples and Wheals, which swell and suppurate.

Varlet, a sorry Wretch, a Rogue.

Vary, (Lat.) to alter or change.

Vasa, in Anatomy, the Vessels in an Animal, are the Cavities through which the Liquors of the Body pass, as a Vein, Artery, &c.

Vasculiferous Plants, are, according to the Botanists, such as have, besides the common Calix or Flower-Cup, a peculiar Vessel or Case to contain their Seed.

Vase, a kind of Flowerpot in a Garden. In Architecture, an Ornament above the Cornice.

Vassal, a Slave; or, in Common Law, he that holds his Land of another by Homage and Fealty.

Vassalage, Subjection, or the condition of a Vassal.

Vast, (Lat.) huge, large, spacious.

Vastation,

Vaſtation, (Lat.) a deſtroying, ſpoiling or laying waſte.

Vaſto, a Writ againſt a Tenant making waſte.

Vatican, the chief Library of *Rome*, founded by Pope *Sixtus* IV. who ſtor'd it with the choiceſt Books he could pick out of *Europe*, and alſo allowed a large Revenue for its perpetual Augmentation: It is ſo called from the Hill Vatican where it ſtands.

Vaticination, (Lat.) a prophecying or divining, a foretelling.

Vavaſory, Lands held by a Vavaſour.

Vavaſour or *Valvaſour*, a Noble-man in former time that was next in Dignity to a Baron.

Vault, an Arched Building; alſo to leap.

Vaunt, to brag or boaſt.

Vauntlay, (Fr.) a Term in Hunting, when Hounds are ſet in a readineſs where a Chace is like to paſs, and caſt off before the reſt of the Kennel come in.

Vayvode, a Prince or chief Ruler of *Tranſylvania*, *Valachia* and *Moldavia*, who is tributary to the Grand Signior.

Ubiquitarians, a Sect holding that Chriſt's Body is every where preſent as well as his Divinity; moſt of the *Lutherans* are called by this Name, becauſe they maintain this Point.

Ubiquity, (Lat.) a being in every place at the ſame time.

Vectis, (Lat.) a Lever, is the firſt of the Mechanick Powers, and, by writers of Mechanicks, is ſuppoſed to be a perfectly inflexible Right Line of no weight at all, to which are applied three Weights or Powers at different diſtances for the raiſing or ſuſtaining of heavy Bodies.

Vedette, a Military term, ſignifying a Centinel on Horſeback detached from the main Body of the Army, to diſcover and give notice of the Enemies Deſigns.

Veer, veering out a Rope, at Sea, is letting it go by hand, or letting it run out of it ſelf; *veer*, with regard to the Wind, is to change often and ſuddenly.

Vegetables, (Lat.) are ſuch natural Bodies as grow and encreaſe from Parts Organically formed, but have no proper Life nor Senſation.

Vegetation, (Lat.) is the way of Growth or Increaſe of Bulk, Parts, and dimenſions proper to all Trees, Shrubs, Plants and Herbs.

Vegetative, (Lat.) that quickens or cauſes to grow.

Vegete, (Lat.) lively, quick, ſound.

Vehement, (Lat.) fierce, violent, impetuous.

Vehicle, (Lat.) that which ſerves to carry or convey a thing; as the *Serum* is a proper vehicle for the Blood.

Vein, a ſanguiferous Veſſel, whoſe larger Branches

in the habit of the Body, e-
specially in the Limbs, run
next under the Skin, and
both there, and also in the
Venters serve to convey
back again towards the
Heart that Blood which was
sent from the Arteries into
the respective Parts.

Velitation, (Lat.) a skirmishing ; a quarreling in
words.

Vejours, are such as are
sent by the Court to take a
view of any Place in question for the better decision of
the Right, for the taking a
view of an Offence, as a
Man Murdered, &c.

Vellam, the finest sort of
Parchment made of Calves-
Skin.

Vellicate, (Lat.) to pluck,
twitch , or give a sudden
pull.

Vellications, in Physick, are
certain Convulsions that
happen to the Fibres of the
Muscles.

Velocity, (Lat.) a word
frequently used in natural
Philosophy and Mechanicks,
which denotes swiftness, or
that by which a Body passes
over a certain space in a certain time.

Venal, (Lat.) that is to
be sold, that does any thing
for gain ; mean, base ; also of or belonging to a Vein.

Venality, a being venal or
saleable.

Venatick , belonging to
Hunting or Chasing.

Vendible, (Lat.) saleable,

fit for sale.

Vendication, a challeng-
ing to one's self, a claiming.

Venditioni exponas, a Writ
commanding the Under-
Sheriff to sell Goods formerly taken for the satisfaction
of a Judgment.

Veneering, a kind of inlaid Work among Joyners,
Cabinet-Makers, &c.

Venefick, belonging to the
Art of making Poisons ; poi-
soning.

Venerable, (Lat.) worthy
of Reverence, Honour, Re-
spect.

Veneration, (Lat.) Honour,
Respect.

Venereal, (Lat.) belonging
to Venery, Lustful.

Venery, Carnal Copula-
tion, Lustfulness.

Venial, (Lat.) pardonable,
or which may be forgiven.

Venire facias, a Writ for
the Sheriff to cause twelve
Men of the same County to
say the truth upon an Issue
taken.

Vent, in Gunnery, signifies the difference between
the diameter of a Bullet, and
the diameter of the Bore of
the Piece.

Venters, in Anatomy, are
the three principal Cavities
or hollow parts of Animal
Bodies, the *Belly*, *Chest* and
Head, or the *Abdomen*, the
Thorax, and the *Caput*.

Venteth, snuffeth up the
Wind. *Spenser*.

Ventiduct , a conveying
Wind

Wind by Pipes, or othrewise.

Ventilation, (Lat.) a fanning or gathering of Wind; also winnowing of Corn.

Ventose, a Cupping-glass.

Ventosity, windiness, or Wind pent up in a humane Body.

Ventre inspiciendo, a Writ for the search of a Woman who saith she is with Child, and thereby with-holdeth Land from him that is next Heir at Law.

Ventricle, (Lat.) the Stomach; also any round Concavity in the Body.

Venue, in Law, the place next to that where the thing in Trial is supposed to have been done.

Venus, the Goddess of Love and Beauty; also the Evening Star; in Alchymy it signifies Copper.

Veracity, (Lat.) a speaking truth.

Verb, (Lat.) in Grammer, one of the Parts of Speech which signifies doing, suffering, or being, in that Thing or Person to which 'tis joined.

Verbal, (Lat.) belonging to a Verb; also delivered in Words; by word of Mouth.

Verbatim, (Lat.) in the same words, or word for word.

Verberation, (Lat.) a beating or striking.

Verbose, (Lat.) full of words, talkative.

Verdant, (Lat.) green.

Verdegrease, a green Substance made of the Rust of Brass or Copper, contracted by being stratify'd with the Husks of pressed Grapes.

Verderor, a judicial Officer of the King's Forest, sworn to keep the Assizes of it; to enroll the Attachments of all manner of Trespasses committed there, and to take care that the Vert be well maintained.

Verdict, (*quasi vere dictum*) a true Report, the Jury's Answer upon any Cause committed to their Examination by a Court of Judicature.

Verditure, a sort of green Colour used by Painters.

Verdoy, in Heraldry, a Bordure of a Coat of Arms, charged with any kinds or parts of Flowers, Fruits, Seeds, Plants, &c.

Verdure, the greeness of Fields, Meadows, &c.

Verge, (Fr.) a Rod, Switch or Wand; a Sergeant's Mace: Also the compass of the King's Court, formerly of twelve Miles extent, within the Jurisdiction of the Lord High Steward of the King's Household; also the compass of a Man's Power, Capacity, &c.

Veridical, (Lat.) speaking the Truth.

Verification, (Lat.) a verifying, a proving or making good.

Verisimility, the probability or likelihood of a thing.

Verity, (Lat.) Truth.

Vermiculated, inlaid, imbroidered, wrought with Checker-work, or small pieces of divers Colours.

Vermiculation, (Lat.) an Infection of Plants by Worms.

Vermilion, a kind of deep red Colour.

Vermin, any kind of hurtful Creatures or Insects, as Rats, Mice, Fleas, Lice, Bugs, &c.

Vermivorous Animals, are such Animals as feed upon Worms.

Vernacular, proper and peculiar to the House or Country one lives in; natural.

Vernal, (Lat.) belonging to the Spring.

Verrel or *Verril*, a little small Ring of Metal at the small end of a Cane or Handle of a Tool.

Verry, in Heraldry, is of two sorts; if the Colours (which is a sort of Chequerwork of the shape of little Bells) be *Argent* and *Azure*, you need say on more but *verry*, but if the Colours be any other, they must be named expresly; it is thus exprest.

Versatile, (Lat.) apt to be turned or wound any way.

Versicle, (Lat.) a little Verse.

Versification, (Lat.) a making Verses, or the Art of making Verses.

Versify, to make Verses.

Version, (Lat.) a translation out of one Language into another.

Vert, in Heraldry, a green Colour, that in Engraving is expressed by Lines drawn a-thwart, beginning at the sinister Corner of the Escutcheon: Thus. In Coats of Nobles this Colour is called *Emerauld*, and in those of Kings 'tis called *Venus*.

Vert, (a Forest-Law-word) every thing that grows or bears a green Leaf in a Forest, and is capable of covering a Deer.

Vertebra, the Joints of the Neck and Back-bone of an Animal.

Vertex, in Mathematicks, the top of any Line or Figure; also that Point in the Heavens directly over our Heads.

Vertex, a Term in Anatomy, signifying the Crown of the Head, or that part of the Head where the Hairs turn, as it were, round a Point.

Vertical, belonging to the *Vertex*.

Vertical Circles. See *Azimuths*.

Vertical Plain, a Plain perpendicular to the Horizon.

Verticillate Plants, in Botany, are such as have their Flowers

Flowers intermixed with small Leaves growing in manner of Whirls about the Joints of the Stalk.

Verticity, the Property of the Load-ftone, or a touched Needle to point North and South.

Vertiginous, (Lat.) giddy.

Vertigo, (Lat.) a giddineſs, dizzineſs, or ſwimming in the Head.

Veſica, in Chymiſtry, is a large Copper Body tinn'd withinſide, uſed in diſtilling ardent Spirits, ſo called becauſe in Figure it is ſomething like a blown Bladder.

Veſica Biliaria, or the *Gall-bladder*, is a hollow Bag placed in the under or hollow ſide of the Liver, and in Figure repreſenteth a Pear.

Veſicatoria, are bliſtering Medicines.

Veſicle, (Lat.) a little Bladder.

Veſpers, Evening Prayers in the Church of *Rome*.

Veſpertine, (Lat.) belonging to the Evening.

Veſſels, in Architecture, are certain Ornaments, uſually ſet over the Cornices, and ſo called, becauſe they repreſent divers ſorts of Veſſels, which were in uſe among the Antients.

Veſt, (Lat.) a kind of Waſtcoat; a Garment; *verbally*, to beſtow upon, to put in full Poſſeſſion of Lands.

Veſta, a Heathen Goddeſs of the Earth; conſidered

ſometimes as the Mother, and at other times as the Daughter of *Saturn*; *Numa Pompilius* ſecond King of *Rome* dedicated to her an everlaſting Fire, and to keep it eſtabliſhed the Prieſteſſes called *Veſtales*, who were moſt ſeverely puniſh'd when they let it go out, ſince it could not be lighted again but by Fire from Heaven, or with the Rays of the Sun; they were buried alive when they ſinned againſt Chaſtity.

Veſtiary, a place in a Monaſtry where the Monks Cloaths are laid up.

Veſtibulum, (Lat.) a Porch or Entry to a Houſe.

Veſtigation, (Lat.) a tracing, a ſeeking or ſearching diligently.

Veſtiges, Foot-ſteps, Traces.

Veſtment, Rayment, Clothing, Habit.

Veſtry, a Room adjoyning to a Church where the Prieſts Veſtments and ſacred Utenſils are kept; alſo an Aſſembly of the Heads of a Pariſh uſually held in that place.

Veſture, any Cloathing; alſo in Law, admittance to a Poſſeſſion or the Profits of it.

Veteran, (Lat.) ſerving long in any Place or Office; but moſt commonly it ſignifies an old Souldier.

Vetitum Navium, a diſtreſs which the Lord forbids his Bailiff to deliver to the Sheriff who would replevy it.

Vexation, diſquiet or trouble of Mind.

V. G. an Abbreviation for *Verbi Gratia*; i. e. namely, or for inſtance.

Vial, a thin glaſs Bottle.

Via-lactea. See *Milky-way.*

Vibration, (Lat.) is the Swing or Motion of a Pendulum, or of a Weight hung by a ſtring on a Pin.

Viands, (Fr.) Meat, Food, Victuals.

Viaticum, (Lat.) all manner of Proviſions for a Journey. The Sacrament given to dying Perſons is ſo term'd by Romaniſts.

Vicar, (Lat.) a Deputy; the Prieſt of a Pariſh where the Tithes are impropriated.

Vicarage or *Vicaridge*, the Cure or Benefice of a Vicar.

Vicario Deliberando, is a Writ that lies for a Spiritual Perſon in Priſon, upon forfeiture of a Recognizance without the King's Writ.

Vicarious, (Lat.) belonging to a Vicar; ſubordinate.

Vice, in compoſition of words ſignifies inſtead, and implies a ſubordination, or the ſupplying of another's Place, as Vice-Admiral, Vice-Chancellor, &c.

Vice-gerent, a Deputy, or one that acts in the place of another.

Vice-Roy, a Deputy King, or one that governs a Kingdom inſtead of the King.

Vice-verſa, (Lat.) on the contrary.

Vicinage or *Vicinity*, (Lat.) Neighbourhood, Nearneſs.

Viciſſitude, (Lat.) Change or Turn, ſucceeding of one Thing after another.

Viciis & venellis Mundandis, a Writ againſt a Mayor, &c. for not cleanſing their Streets.

Vicount or *Viſcount*, Originally a Sheriff, or the chief Governour of a Province; alſo a Noble Man next an Earl.

Vicountiel, in Law, ſignifies as much as belonging to the Sheriff.

Victim, a Sacrifice; properly a Beaſt killed in Sacrifice after a Victory.

Victor, (Lat.) a Conquerour.

Victorious, that has got a Victory or Conqueſt.

Vi & Armis, by main force. In a Charge or Indictment it denotes the violent Commiſſion of any Crime.

Viewers, in Law, are thoſe ſent by the Court to view any Place or Perſon.

View of Frank-Pledge, the Office of the Sheriff or Bailiff, looking to the King's Peace, and ſeeing that every Man be in ſome Pledge.

Vigilance, (Lat.) Watchfulneſs; Application of Mind.

Vigilant, watchful, diligent, circumſpect.

Vigils, (Lat.) are thoſe Faſts which the Church has thought fit to eſtabliſh before certain Feſtivals, in order to to prepare our Minds for a due obſervation of the enſuing Solemnity.

Vigorous, (Lat.) lively, luſty, full of Courage.

Vi laica removenda, a Writ to remove a forcible Poſſeſſion of a Benefice by Laymen.

Vile, (Lat.) of no account, deſpiſable, wicked, baſe.

Vilify, to ſet at nought, to deſpiſe, to abuſe.

Villain, from the Latin *villa*, a Country Farm, where theſe Men of low and ſervile Condition had ſome ſmall Portion of Cottages and Lands allotted to them for which they were depending on the Lord, and bound to certain Works, and other Corporal Service; but now 'tis moſt commonly uſed in a bad ſenſe, and denotes an arrant Rogue, or pitiful ſordid Fellow.

Villanage, the meaneſt ſort of Tenure belonging to Lands or Tenements, whereby the Tenant is bound to do all manner of ſervile Work for his Lord.

Vincible, (Lat.) that may be overcome.

Vindemial or *Vendemiatory*, (Lat.) belonging to the Vintage.

Vindicate, (Lat.) to defend, maintain or juſtifie.

Vindication, (Lat.) a defending, clearing or juſtifying.

Vindictive, (Lat.) revengful.

Vinew, Mouldineſs, Hoarineſs, Muſtineſs.

Viol, in a Ship, is a kind of Hawſer made uſe of to purchaſe in the Cable, when the main Capſtan cannot do it.

Violate, (Lat.) to break, infringe, or deflower.

Violent, (Lat.) forcible, vehement, boiſterous.

Violiſt, one well skilled in playing upon the Violin.

Viperine, (Lat.) of, or belonging to a Viper.

Virago, a ſtout or manly Woman.

Virelay, a light Song. *Spen.*

Virga, a Meteor repreſenting a bundle of Rods.

Virgin Parchment, made of the Skin of a young Lamb.

Virginal, (Lat.) belonging to a Virgin; Virgin-like, Maidenly.

Virginity, (Lat.) the State or Condition of a Virgin; Maiden-head.

Virgo, one of the Signs of the Zodiack, the ſixth in order.

Virgula Divinatoria, a Hazel Rod in the ſhape of the Letter Y, whereby they pretend to diſcover Mines.

Virile, (Lat.) Manly.

Virility, (Lat.) Manhood, or the ability to perform the part of a Man.

Virtual, (Lat.) equivalent, effectual.

Virtue, Efficacy, Power, Force, Quality, Property.

Virtuoso, (Ital.) a learned and ingenious Man; more eſpecially a Perſon who is curious in Collecting Raritities, as Medals, Stones, Plants, &c.

Virulency, a poisonous or venomous Quality.

Virulent, venomous, infectious, malicious.

Vis centripeta, that force by which all Bodies (from what cause soever) tend to the Center of the Earth.

Vis Centrifuga, (Lat.) is the force by which any Body revolving round another, endeavours to fly off from the *Axis* of the Motion, in a Tangent to that Curve.

Visage, (Fr.) Face, Countenance.

Viscera, (Lat.) the Entrails, or Bowels.

Viscosity, (Lat.) Clamminess, a sticking or a gluish Quality.

Viscous, clammy, slimy, glewy.

Viser, (Fr.) the sight of an Head-piece.

Visibility, (Lat.) a being visible.

Visible, (Lat.) that may be seen, clear or manifest.

Visier, a principal Officer and Statesman among the *Turks*. The *Grand* or *Prime Visier*, is an Officer who is next under the *Grand Signior* in the Turkish Empire.

Vision, an Apparition or Phantom ; also a Divine Revelation in a Dream ; also seeing.

Vision direct, is when the Rays of Light come from the Object directly to the Eye.

Vision refracted, is when the Rays pass through different mediums.

Vision Reflected, is when the Rays are reflected from any Body to the Eye.

Visionary, a fanatical Pretender to Visions.

Visitation, a visiting of a Diocess by the Bishop every three Years, or by the Arch-Deacon once a Year, to inspect, relating to several Churches and their Rectors, &c.

Visorium, in Printing, is an Instrument to which a Leaf of Copy is fixt, for the Compositor's more convenient seeing thereof.

Visu Franci plegii, a Writ to exempt him from the view of Frank-pledge who is not Resident in the Hundred.

Visual, belonging to the Sight.

Visual Rays, are those Rays by which any Object is seen.

Vital, (Lat.) of Life, that has Life in it ; that gives and preserves Life.

Vital Faculty, an action whereby a Man lives, which is performed whether we design it or no.

Vital Flame. See *Flamma Vitalis.*

Vital Indication, in the Art of Medicine, is such an one as requires the restoring and preserving of the natural Strength of the Body.

Vitals, the Parts of the Body that chiefly conduce to the preservation of Life.

Vitiate, to deprave or corrupt.

Vitreal or *Vitreous*, glassy, belonging to Glass.

Vitreous Humor, one of the Humours of the Eye, so called from the resemblance 'tis said to have to melted Glass.

Vitrification, (Lat.) the turning any Body into Glass by the force of Fire.

Vitrify, (Lat.) to turn into Glass.

Vitriol, a kind of mineral Salt somewhat like Rock Allum.

Vitriolick or *Vitriolous*, belonging to, or pertaking of the Nature of Vitriol.

Vituperation, (Lat.) a blaming or discommending.

Viva voce, (Lat.) by word of Mouth.

Vivacious, lively brisk.

Vivacity, (Lat.) liveliness, briskness, sprightliness.

Vivary, a Place whether of Land or Water, where living Creatures are kept. In a Law sense, a Park, Warren, or Fish-pond.

Vivification, the making alive, or enlivening.

Vivify, to quicken or enliven.

Viviparous Animals, are such as bring forth their Young living and perfect.

Vizard, a Mask, or false Face for Disguise.

Ulcer, a running Sore in the soft parts of the Body, accompanied with Putrefaction.

Ulcerate, (Lat.) to cause, or break out into an Ulcer.

Ule, Yule, Yeule, Yool, from the French *Nouel*, i. e. *Christmass*, which the *Normans* corrupt to *Nuel*, and from *Nuel* we had *Nule* or *Ule*: Others derive it from the Saxon word *Gehul*, which signified *Christmass*.

Ullage of a Cask, is what it wants of being full.

Ultimate, (Lat.) final, last or utmost.

Ultion, (Lat.) a Revenging.

Ultra-marine, (Lat.) from beyond Sea.

Ultramontanes, i. e. inhabiting beyond the Mountains; so the *Italians* call all who live on the hither side of the *Alps*.

Ultra-mundane, (Lat.) beyond the World, or that part of it which is visible to us.

Ululation, (Lat.) a howling like a Dog or Wolf.

Umbeliferous Plants, according to the Botanists, are such as have their tops branched and spread like a Ladies Umbrella.

Umbilical, (Lat.) belonging to the Navel.

Umbilical Region, that part of the Abdomen which lies round about the Navel.

Umbilical Vessels, are the Veins, Arteries, &c. that belong to the Navel.

Umbilicus, the *Ficus*, or one of the *Foci* of any of the Conick Sections; also the Navel

Umbrage

Umbrage, (Fr.) a Shadow, a Covert; alſo a Suſpicion.

Umbrella or *Umbrello*, a ſort of Skreen that is held over the Head for preſerving from the Sun or the Rain; alſo a wooden Frame covered with Cloth or Stuff to keep off the Sun from a Window.

Umpire, a third Perſon choſen to decide a Controverſie left to Arbitration, in caſe the Arbitrators ſhould not agree.

Un, is an Engliſh Privative, which may be added at pleaſure to ſimple Words, and deprives them of their natural Senſe.

Unanimous, (Lat.) of one Mind, conſenting or according together.

Uncia, in Algebra, ſignifie thoſe Numbers which are prefixed or imagined to be prefixed before the Letters of the Members of any Power produced, from a Binomial or Multinomial Root.

Uncore priſt, in Law, is the Defendant's Plea (being ſued for a Debt due at a day paſt) to ſave the forfeiture of his Bond, ſaying that he tendered the Debt at the Time and Place, and that there was none to receive it.

Uncouth, (Sax.) foreign, barbarous, harſh, not to be underſtood; alſo ſtrange, unuſual. *Milton.*

Unction, (Lat.) an anointing,

Unctuous, oily, greaſie, fatty.

Undee, in Heraldry, waved, reſembling Waves. *See* Wavey.

Underling, an inferiour; one that acts under another, or only by his Orders.

Undermine, to dig under or ſupplant.

Undulated, waved, or wrought in Waves, or like Waves in Water.

Undulation of the Air, the waving of the Air to and fro.

Unguent, (Lat.) Ointment or Liquid-ſalve.

Ungula, a ſort of hooked Inſtrument uſed by Surgeons, to draw a dead Fœtus out of the Womb.

Uniform, (Lat.) of one form, regular, having all parts alike.

Uniformity, (Lat.) one and the ſame Form, Shape, or Faſhion.

Union, (Lat.) a joining together, a growing into one; Peace, Concord, Agreement.

Union Pearls, the beſt ſort of Pearls that grow in couples.

Uniſon, (Fr.) a Term in Muſick, an agreement of two Notes in one tone.

Unitarian, a Socinian, or one that denies the Trinity.

Unity of Poſſeſſion, in the Civil Law, is a joint Poſſeſſion of two Rights by ſeveral Titles.

Univerſal, (Lat.) general, extending to all.

Univerſity, (Lat.) in the Civil Law, ſignifies a Body Politick

Politick or Corporation; also a Nursery where Youth is instructed in the Languages and Sciences.

Univocal Terms, in Logick, are such whose Name and Nature is the same.

Unlimited Problem. See *Problem.*

Unques prist, a Plea in Law, whereby a Man professeth himself always ready to do what is required of him.

Unreeve a Rope, among Sea-men, to pull a Rope out of a Block or Pully.

Unrig, to take away the Rigging or Cordage; also to undress.

Unscriptural, not prescribed in the Holy Scriptures.

Vocabulary, (Lat.) a Dictionary; an *Index* or Table of words.

Vocal, (Lat.) belonging to, or consisting in the Voice.

Vocation, (Lat.) a Calling, Employ, or Course of Life.

Vocative Case, is the fifth in Declension of Latin Nouns; so called, because 'tis used in calling or speaking to.

Vociferation, (Lat.) a bawling or crying out alond.

Vogue, (Fr.) popular Applause, Esteem, Reputation or Sway.

Voidance, a want of an Incumbent or Clerk in Possession of a Benefice.

Voided, in Heraldry, is when there are Lines drawn within; and parallel to the Out-lines of any Ordinary: This expresses an Exemption of something of the thing voidable, and makes the Field appear transparent through the Charge.

Voider, in Heraldry, is one of the *Ordinaries* whose Figure is made like that of the *Flanch,* only it does not bend or bow in so much; they are always born by Pairs thus; the Field is *Tenn,* two *Voiders, Or.*

Volant, Flying.

Volatil, (Lat.) (a Chymical Term) apt to evaporate or resolve it self into Air.

Volatility, (Lat.) the property of such Bodies whose Particles are apt to evaporate with Heat, and mix with Air.

Volery, a great Bird Cage where there is room for them to fly up and down in.

Volitation, (Lat.) a flying or fluttering about.

Volition, (Lat.) the Act of Willing.

Volley, a great Shout, or a general-discharge of Musket-shot.

Volubility, (Lat.) a round Delivery, or ready Utterance.

Voluble, that speaks with great fluentness.

Voluble Earth; the swiftly Moveable, Terrestrial Orb. *Milton.*

Volum-

Voluminous, of a large Volume ; bulky.

Volunt, in Law, is when the Tenant holds at the will of the Leſſor, or Lord.

Voluntary, (Lat.) free, withoutCompulſion orForce; that which a Muſician plays *Extempore*.

Volunteer, one that ſerves voluntarily in the Wars.

Voluptuary, (Lat.) a Perſon voluptuous, or given to ſenſual Pleaſures.

Voluptuous, (Lat.) ſenſual or given to Carnal Pleaſure.

Voluta, a Term in Architecture, ſignifying that part of the Capitals of the *Jonick*, *Corinthian* and *Compoſit* Orders , which repreſents the Barks of Trees twiſted and turned into Spiral Lines. *Volutas* are different in the three Orders ; thoſe that appear above the Stems in the Corinthian Order, are ſixteen in number in every Capital, whereas there are only four in the Ionick Order, and eight in the Compoſit.

Vomica , a Diſeaſe in the Lungs.

Volutation, (Lat.) a rolling, tumbling or wallowing.

Voracious , (Lat.) ravenous, gluttonous, immoderate in eating.

Voracity, Greedineſs, Gluttony.

Vortex; in the Carteſian Philoſophy, is a Syſtem of Particles of Matter moving round like a Whirl-pool ,

having no void Interſtices or Vacuities between the Particles.

Votary, one that has bound himſelf to the Performance of a Religious Vow.

Vouchſafe. to condeſcend, or be pleaſed to do a thing.

Voucher , (Fr.) a calling one into Court, to warrant or make good a thing ; alſo to avouch, avow, or affirm boldly.

Vowels, Letters of the Alphabet which are ſo named, becauſe of themſelves they expreſs a Sound, as *a, e, i, o, u, y,*

Voyage, (Fr.) a paſſing from one Country or place to another; but 'tis now almoſt only uſed for a Paſſage by Sea.

Upland, high Ground, as diſtinguiſhed from mooriſh, marſhy, or low Grounds.

Upſhot , Iſſue, End, or Succeſs of a Buſineſs.

Urachus, is one of the umbilical Veſſels, the uſe whereof is to convey the Urine from the Bladder of the *Fœtus* into the *Alantoides*, which is placed between the *Chorion* and the *Amnion.*

Uranoſcopia, (Gr.) a view of the Heavens.

Urbanity, (Lat.) Civility, Courteſie, good Manners or Breeding.

Ureter, in Anatomy is a Fiſtulous Membranaceous Veſſel , which conveys the Urine from the Reins to the Bladder.

Urethra,

Urethra, the Urinary Paſſage whereby the Urine is diſcharged.

Urgency, preſſing Importunity, haſte of Buſineſs.

Urim and *Thummim,* we know nothing certain concerning the *Urim* and *Thummim* of the Hebrews, but that they were certain Ornaments belonging to the High Prieſt's Habit, by which he gave Oracular Anſwers to the People. The High Prieſts of the Jews conſulted God in the moſt important Affairs of their Commonwealth who acquainted them with the *Urim,* which ſignifies Lights or Explanations, and which, according to *Spencer,* was nothing elſe but the antient *Teraphims,* or little humane Figures which the Prieſt carried hid in the fold of his Robe or Gown, and by which God anſwered their Queſtions. The word *Thummim* by the Septuagint, was tranſlated Truth, which agrees well enough with the like Ceremony much in uſe with the *Egyptians,* whoſe principal Miniſter of Juſtice, according to *Diodorus Siculus,* carried an Image of precious Stones about his Neck which was called Truth.

Urinal, a glaſs Veſſel for receiving the Urine, chiefly when 'tis to be carried to the Phyſician for his Judgment.

Urinous, (Lat.) of, belonging to, or of the nature of Urine.

Urinous Salts, are thoſe volatile Salts drawn from Animal or other Subſtances that are contrary to Acids.

Urna, a Roman Meaſure for things Liquid, containing 3 Gallons, 4½ Pints, 5 ſolid Inches, and 33 decimal Parts of our Wine Meaſure ; alſo a Veſſel made of different Matter, and made uſe of to draw out of it the Names of thoſe who were firſt to enage at the publick Plays, or to throw in their Notes and give their Votes in the Aſſemblies held at *Rome* and Courts of Judicature ; as alſo to keep the Aſhes of Mens Bodies after they had been buried according to ancient Cuſtom.

Uromancy, (Gr.) a divining or gueſſing at a Diſeaſe by the Urine.

Uroſcopy, (Gr.) an inſpection of Urines, called commonly caſting of Waters.

Urſa Major, the *great Bear,* a conſtellation in the Northern Hemiſphere, otherwiſe called *Charles's Wayn.*

Uſance, (i. e. a Months Uſe) the ſpace of Time between any one day of a Month, and the ſame day of the next following, which time is generally allow'd for Payment of a Bill of Exchange after Acceptance.

Double Uſance, is the ſpace of two ſuch Months allow'd on the ſame account.

Uſer de Action, the purſuing an Action in the proper County.

Uſher, properly the Doorkeeper of a Court; alſo an Under-Maſter in a School.

Uſher of the Black-Rod, is the Gentleman Uſher to the King, the Houſe of Lords, and the Knights of the Garter, and keeps the Chapterhouſe-Door, when a Chapter of the Order is ſitting.

Uſucaption, (Lat.) Preſcription or long Poſſeſſion.

Uſufructuary, one that has the Uſe and Profit of a thing, but not the Property and Right.

Uſurpation, (Lat.) a taking wrongfully to one's own uſe that which belongs to another.

Uſurper, one guilty of Uſurpation.

Uſury, is the gain of any thing above the Principal, or that which was lent; exacted only in conſideration of the Loan, whether it be in Money, Corn, Wares, or ſuch like.

Utenſil, (Lat.) a neceſſary Implement, any thing fit for uſe; Houſe-hold-ſtuff.

Uterine, (Lat.) belonging to the Womb.

Utlagato capiendo, &c. a Writ for taking an Out-Law.

Utlary or *Utlawry*, (Lat.) a Puniſhment for ſuch as being called into Law, do contemptuouſly refuſe to appear, whereby they forfeit their Goods or Lands to the King or State.

Utter Barriſter, a young Lawyer admitted to plead at the Bar.

Utterance, a delivery in ſpeaking.

Uvea Tunica, a coat of the Eye, reſembling the skin of a Grape, whence it hath its name.

Vulcan, a Pagan Deity, eſteemed to be the God of ſubterranean Fire, to preſide over Mettals, and to be the Son of *Jupiter* and *Juno*.

Vulcano or *Volcano*, a burning Mountain that throws out Flames, Smoak and Aſhes, ſo called from *Vulcan*.

Vulgar, (Lat.) common, trivial.

Vulnerable, (Lat.) that may be wounded.

Vulnerary, belonging to, or good to cure Wounds.

Vulpine, (Lat.) belonging to, or like a Fox; crafty, ſubtil.

Vulture, a Gripe, a large Bird of Prey.

Vulturine, (Lat.) pertaining to, or of the nature of a Vultur, rapacious.

Uvula, that little piece of red ſpungy Fleſh that hangs down from the Palate between the Tonſils.

Uxorious, (Lat.) that is over fond of, or dotes upon his Wife.

W.

W *Ad-hook* or *Worm*, is a small Iron turned Serpent-wise like a Screw, and put upon the end of a long Staff, to draw the Wad out of a Gun when she is to be unloaded, or that stopper of Paper, Hay, &c. which is forced into a Gun upon the Powder, to keep it close in the Chamber.

Wakes, Country Feasts that used to be kept for some Days after that of the Saint to whom the Parish-Church was dedicated, which are still observ'd in some parts of *England*.

Wae, Woe. *Spencer.*

Waft, to *Waft a Ship*, is to convey her safe; to *make a waft*, is to hang out some Coat, Sea-gown, or the like, as a sign for Men to come on Board, oftentimes signifying that the Ship is in danger by a Leak, &c. and wants help from Shore.

Waif or *Stray*, in Law, are lost Goods claimed by no Body, which belong to the King unless challeng'd by the Owner within a Year and a Day; also Goods that a Thief drops or leaves behind him when over-charg'd or close pursued, which also belong to the King or Lord of the Mannor.

Waive, is a Woman that is Out-law'd; she is so called as being forsaken of the

Law, and not an Out-law as a Man is.

Wake of a Ship, is the smooth Water a Stern, when she is under Sail.

Wale, a Sea Term, signifying those outward Timbers in a Ship's side, on which Men set their Feet when they clamber up a Ship's side.

Wale-knot, at Sea, is a round Knot, so made with the lays of a Rope, that it cannot slip.

Walfleet Oysters, are so called from a Wall on the Coast of *Essex*, which keeps the Sea from overflowing the Places where they lie.

Walt, a Ship is Walt when she has not her due Ballast, *i. e.* not enough to enable her to bear her Sails or keep her stiff.

Wap, in a Ship, is that Rope wherewith the Shrouds are set Taught with Wale-knots.

Wapentake, the same as Hundred, is a division of a County, so called because the Inhabitants were wont to give up their Weapons to the Lord in token of subjection.

Warble, to sing as a Bird; to sing in a quavering way; to purl like a Stream.

Ward, in *London*, is a portion of the City committed to the special charge of one of the Aldermen of the City; also one of the Divisions of a Forest; as also a Prison.

Hhhh *Warden*,

Warden, fignifieth the fame thing as Gardian, but is commonly ufed for one who has the keeping or charge of Perfons or Things, by vertue of his Office.

Wardmote or *WardmoteCourt*, a Court kept in every Ward in *London*, for choofing Officers, and managing the other Bufinefs of a Ward.

Wardrobe, (Ital.) a place where a Prince's or Nobleman's Robes are kept.

Wafrare, the State of War, a military Expedition.

Wark, Work, *Spencer*.

Warifon, (old word) Reward.

Warp, to warp up a Ship at Sea, is to hale her to a place, when the Wind is wanting, by means of a Hawfer or Cable, and an Anchor bent to it.

Warping, bending, tending the wrong way, crooking. *Milton*.

Warrant, an Order, authentick Permiffion, Power, &c.

Warrant of Attorney, is that whereby a Man appoints another to do fomething in his Name and warranteth his Action.

Warranty, a Covenant by Deed, to fecure a Bargain againft all Men.

Warre, worfe. *Spencer*.

Warren, a Franchife or priviledged Place by Prefcription or Grant to keep Beafts and Fowl of Warren, as Coneys, Hares, Partridges and Phefants.

Wafe, a Wreath of Cloth, or other Materials put under a Veffel born on the Head.

Wafte of a Ship, is that part of her which lies between the Main-maft and Fore-maft.

Wafte-Cloaths, a Sea Term, certain Cloaths hung about the Cage-work of a Ship's Hull, to fhadow the Men from the Enemy in a Fight.

Watch, at Sea, fignifies the fpace of four Hours.

Quarter-watch, is when but a quarter of the Ship's Company watch at a time.

Watchet, a kind of blue Colour.

Water-born, is faid of a Ship when fhe is where there is no more Water than will juft bear her from the Ground.

Dead-water, is the Eddy-water that follows the Stern of a Ship, not paffing away fo faft as that which flides by her fides.

Water-gage, a Sea-wall or Bank to keep off the Current or overflowing of the Water.

Water-line, is that which diftinguifhes that part of a Ship which is under Water, from that above when fhe is duly laden.

Water-fhot, is a fort of riding at Anchor, when a Ship is Moored, neither crofs the Tide, nor right up and down, but quartered betwixt both.

Waved, (in Heraldry) is when a Bordure, or any Ordinary or Charge in a Coat of of Arms that hath its out Lines refembling the rifing and falling of Waves; thus.

Way of a Ship, is fometimes the fame with the Rake or Run of a Ship forward or aftward on: But 'tis commonly ufed as to her Sailing, for when fhe goes a pace they fay, *She hath a good way.*

Way of the Rounds, in Fortification, is a fpace left for the paffage of the Rounds, between the Rampart and the Wall of a fortify'd Town.

Wayward, froward. *Shake-fpear.*

Way-wifer. See *Perambulator.*

Weald or *Weld*, (Sax.) the Woody part of a Country.

Wear or *Ware*, a Stank or great Dam in a River, fitted for taking Fifh, or conveying the Stream to a Mill.

Weather Coyle, is when a Ship has her Head brought about fo as to lie that way which her Stern did before without loofing any of the Sail, but only by bearing up the Helm.

Weather-gage, that Ship is faid to have the Weather-gage of another when fhe is to the Windward of her.

Weather-glafs, a fort of Inftrument to fhew the change of the Weather, with the degrees of Heat and Cold.

To Weather, (Sea Term) to double, or go to the Windward of a Place; to overcome a Difficulty.

Wednefday, (q. d. Wodenfday) the fourth Day of the Week, fo called from its being dedicated to *Woden* the God of War among the antient *Saxons.*

Welkin, (Sax.) a Cloud; 'tis now taken fometimes for the Firmament or Sky.

Welter, Wallow. *Spencer.*

Wend, goe. *Spencer.*

Wending, is bringing the Ship's Head about.

Were, (Sax.) a Man.

Wharf, a Yard near a River ot Creek, to hold Wares brought to or from the Water.

Wheel-Fire, is the fame with what the Chymifts call *Ignis Rota*, and is a Fire which covers the Crucible, Coppel, or Melting-Pot, entirely over; at top as well as round the fides.

Whelps of a Capftan, at Sea, are fhort pieces of Wood made faft to it, to keep the Cable from coming two nigh in turning it about.

Wherlicotes, open Chariots ufed in *England* by Perfons of Quality, before the invention of Coaches.

Whip or *Whip-ftaff*, in a Ship is a piece of Timber like a ftrong Staff, faftened into the Helm for him that fteers in fmall Ships to hold in his Hand, thereby to move the Helm and fteer the Ship.

Whitaker, the North-East part of a Flat or Shole, *the middle Ground*.

Whitfunday, that is, *White-Sunday*, so called from the admission of the *Catechumens*, cloathed in white Robes to the Sacrament of Baptism, on the Eve of this solemn Festival, which was instituted to commemorate the descent of the Holy Ghost upon the Apostles in the shape of fiery cloven Tongues.

Whoodings, in a Ship, are those Planks which are joined and fastened along the Ship-side into the Stern.

Whorlbat, a kind of Gauntle with Straps and leaden Plummets, used by the ancient Heroes in their solemn Games and Exercises. *&c.*

Wick, (Sax.) a Borough, or Village; 'tis now almost only us'd at the end of some Name of Towns; as *Berwick*, &c.

Wight, (old word) Man; also quick. *Spencer.*

Wightly, quickly. *Spencer.*

Wiles, fly cunning tricks. *Milton.*

Will with a wisp or *Jack in a Lanthorn*, a fiery Meteor, or Exhalation that appears in the Night, commonly haunting Church-yards, Marshy and Fenny Places, as being evaporated out of a fat Soil; it also flies about Rivers, Hedges, *&c.*

Wimple, the Muffler or plaited Linnen-Cloth, worn by Nuns about their Neck;

also a Flag or Streamer.

Wind, is defined to be the Stream or Current of the Air, which runs or blows from some one of the two and thirty Points of the Compass.

Wind-lass, is an Instrument in small Ships, placed upon the Deck just abaft the Fore-mast.

Wind-Taught, a Sea Term, signifying as much as stiff in the Wind, or stooping too much in a stiff gale of Wind.

Wings, in Fortification, are the large sides of Horn-works, Crown-works, Tenailles, and the like out-Works; that is to say, the Ramparts and Parapets with which they are bounded on the Right and Left from their Gorge to the Front.

Wire-draw, to draw out Gold or Silver; to spin out a Business; to decoy a Man.

Wisards, Learned Heads, or Conjurers. *Spencer.*

Wite, (Sax.) Penalty, Punishment, Fine.

Withernam, (Sax.) is the taking or driving away a Distress, so that the Sheriff cannot upon Replevin deliver it to the Party distrained.

Woden, a certain Idol worshipped by the ancient *Saxons*, and thought to be the same with *Mars*.

Wold, (Sax.) a Down or Champian Ground, hilly and void of Wood.

Wood

Wood and Wood, a Sea Term for two pieces of Timber; being so let into each other, that the Wood of the one joins close to the other.

Wood-ward, a Forrest Officer that walks with a Forrest-Bill, and takes cognizance of all Offences therein committed.

Worm, to work one out of a place.

Worming, at Sea, is laying a small Line or Rope all along betwixt the Shrouds of any Cable or Hawser in order to strengthen it.

Would, at Sea, signifies to bind.

Wrack, Ruin or Violence. *Spencer*.

Wrack or *Ship-wrack*, is a Sea Term, when a Ship either splits or sinks, and those that escape are said to suffer *Ship-wrack*.

Wreath, in Heraldry, signifies a roll of fine Linnen or Silk (like that of a Turkish Turbant) consisting of the Colours born in the Escutcheon, which in an Achievement, is placed between the Helmet and the Crest; *verbally*, to twist or twine about.

Wretch, an unfortunate, forlorn Creature.

Wriggle, to turn here and there as a Snake does; to insinuate or screw into one's Favour.

Wright's or *Mecator's Sailing*, is the method of finding on a Plain the place of a Ship upon any assigned Course true in Longitude, Latitude and Distance, the Meridians being supposed Parallel, and the Parallels of Latitude straight Lines.

Writ, in Common Law, is a written Order or Precept from the King or a Court of Judicature, whereby any thing is commanded to be done concerning a Suit or Action, as a Defendant to be summoned, a Distress to be taken, *&c.*

Writhed, twisted together. *Milton.*

Wydraught, a Water-course or Water-passage; a Sink, or Common-shore.

X.

XEranticks, Drugs, or other things of a drying Quality.

Xeriff, the Title of a Prince or chief Ruler in *Barbary.*

Xerophthalmy, (Gr.) a dry Ophthalmy or Blood-shot of the Eyes without Weeping.

Xestes, an Attick Measure of Capacity for things either Liquid or Dry; for things Liquid it contains 1 Pint, 5 solid Inches, and 636 decimal Parts of our Wine Measure; for things Dry, it contains 1 Pint, and 48 decimal Parts of a solid Inch of our Corn Measure.

Xiphias, a sort of Comet shaped like a Sword.

Xyphoides, (Gr.) the pointed Cartilage of the Breast, called *Cartilago Ensiformis.*

Xyster,

Xyſter, a Surgeon's Inſtrument to ſcrape Bones with.

Y.

Yards of a Ship, are thoſe long pieces of Timber, which are made a little tapering at each end, and are fitted each a-thwart its proper Maſt, with the Sails made faſt to them.

Yards-arm, is that half of the Yard that is on either ſide of the Maſt when they lie a-thwart the Ship.

Yare, at Sea, ſignifies quick, ready, expeditious.

Yatches, are one-Deck'd Veſſels, carrying four, eight, or twelve Guns, with thirty or forty Men, and from thirty to an hundred and ſixty Tuns.

Yaws, the Ship Yaws, that is, does not Steer ſteady but goes in and out when there is a ſtiff Gale.

Yblent, blinded. *Spencer*.

Ybrent, burned, burnt. *Spencer*.

Yclad, Clad, Cloathed. *Spencer*.

Yconne, to learn. *Spencer*.

Yean or *Ean*, to bring forth Lambs as a Sheep does.

Year, the time the Sun takes to go through the twelve Signs of the Zodiack, and is either Sydereal or Civil; *which ſee*.

Year, Day and Waſt, is a part of the Queen's Prerogative, whereby ſhe challenges the Profits of the Lands and Tenements of thoſe who are attainted of Petty Treaſon or Felony for a Year and a Day; and may at laſt waſte the Tenements, root up the Woods, Gardens and Paſtures, Plough up the Meadow, &c. unleſs the Lord of the Mannor compound for Redemption.

Yearn, to bark as Beagles or hunting Dogs; alſo to be moved with Compaſſion.

Yede, gone. *Spencer*.

Yelling, roaring. *Milton*.

Yeoman, a wealthy Country Man that has an Eſtate of his own; alſo an inferior Member of any Company or Corporation.

Yeven, given. *Spencer*.

Yfere, together. *Spencer*.

Ygoe, ſince I go. *Spencer*.

Ylike, a like. *Spencer*.

Ynca, a Name given to the ancient Kings of *Peru* in *America*, and Princes of their Family, ſignifying Lord, King, or Emperor, or one of the Blood-Royal.

Yode, went. *Spencer*.

Yoke. See *Sea-yoke*.

Yore, heretofore, antiently. *Spencer*.

Younkers, thoſe young Fellows on board a Ship, that take in the Top-ſails, furl the Sails, ſling the Yards, &c. they are called Foremaſt-men.

Yſhend, hurt, blamed. *Spencer*.

Yule, North Country word, the Feſtival of our Lord's Nativity, or *Chriſtmas*.

Ywis, I ſuppoſe. *Spencer*.

Zacovin,

Z.

Zacovin, Satin or Silk.

Zamorin, the Title of the Sovereign Prince among the *Malabars* in *East-India*, as much as King or Emperor.

Zany. (Ital.) one that professes to move Laughter by his Gestures, Actions and Speeches; a Buffon, Meery-Andrew, or Jack-Pudding.

Zeal, (Gr.) on earnest Passion for any thing, especially Religion, or the good of one's Country.

Zealot, a zealous Person, a great Stickler or Party Man, chiefly in Matters of Religion: Also a Separatist or Schismatick.

Zechin or **Zachin**, a gold Coin about 7 *s*. 6 *d*. in value. The *Turkish Zechin* is worth 9 *s*.

Zenith, (Arab.) in Astronomy, is the Point of the Heavens directly over one's Head, being 90° from the *Horizon*; 'tis also call'd the *Vertex*, and *The vertical Point*.

Zereth, an Hebrew Measure of nine Inches.

Zest, (Fr.) a Chip of Orange or Lemon Peel; also a short Afternoon's Sleep or Nap.

Zetetick Method, (in Mathematicks) the Analytick or Algebraical Way of resolving Problems or Questions, by which the Nature and Reason of the thing is chiefly sought after.

Zeugma, (Gr. *i.e.* a joining together) a Figure in Grammer, when a Verb agreeing with divers Nouns, or an Adjective with divers Substantives, is referred to one expresly, and to the other by Supplement, as *Hic illius Arma, hic Currus fuit*.

Zodiack, (Gr.) one of the greater imaginary Circles in the Heavens, passing obliquely between the two Poles of the World, so called from the twelve Constellations or Divisions named *Celestial Signs*, supposed to represent the Figures of living Creatures. 'Tis reckon'd 20°. in breadth, and in the middle is the Ecliptick Line, in which the Earth moves once a Year round the Sun.

Zone, (Lat.) a Girdle, a Belt, a Purse on a Girdle, particularly such a Girdle as Maids antiently wore about their Middle when they were espoused, and which the Bridegroom unty'd the first Night of their Marriage.

Zones (in Astronomy and Geography) are certain Spaces or Divisions of the Heavens and Earth, bounded by the lesser Circles of the Sphere, namely, the two Polar Circles and the two Tropicks: They are five in number, *viz.* one *Torrid*, which is bounded by the Tropicks of *Cancer* and *Capri*...

of forty seven Degrees in breadth, and is divided by the Equator into two equal Parts : Two *Temporate*, one of which being the Northern is bounded by the Tropick of *Cancer* and the *Arctick* Polar Circle; and the other, which is the Southern, by the *Antarctick* Polar Circle and the Tropick of *Capricorn*, each of then forty three Degrees in breadth: And two *Frigid Zones*, that are bounded by the two Polar Circles, and have each of them one Pole in the middle, betwixt which and the bounding Circle, the distance is 230°. 30'. The *Frigid* and *Torrid Zones* were, by the Antients, thought uninhabitable; but later Experience hath discover'd the contrary.

Zoography, (Gr.) a description of the Nature and Properties of living Creatures.

Zoophytes, or *Plant-Animals*, Substances that partake of the Nature of Plants and Animals.

Zootomy, (Gr.) an Artificial Dissection of the Bodies of any other living Creatures besides Man.

Zur, an Hebrew Coin, 7½ d. in value, four of which make a Shekle.

Zymosimeter, (Gr.) an Instrument whereby the Degree of Fermentation from the mixture of divers Liquors is measured, or the degree of Heat in the Blood of Animals.

F I N I S.

CPSIA information can be obtained
at www.ICGtesting.com
Printed in the USA
BVOW06s1915071217
502235BV00007B/114/P